Charles Seale-Hayne Library

University of Plymouth

(01752) 588 588

LibraryandITenquiries@plymouth.ac.uk

Behavioral Analysis and Measurement Methods

Behavioral Analysis and Measurement Methods

DAVID MEISTER

Navy Personnel Research and Development Center
Department of the Navy
San Diego

A Wiley-Interscience Publication

JOHN WILEY & SONS

New York Chichester Brisbane Toronto Singapore

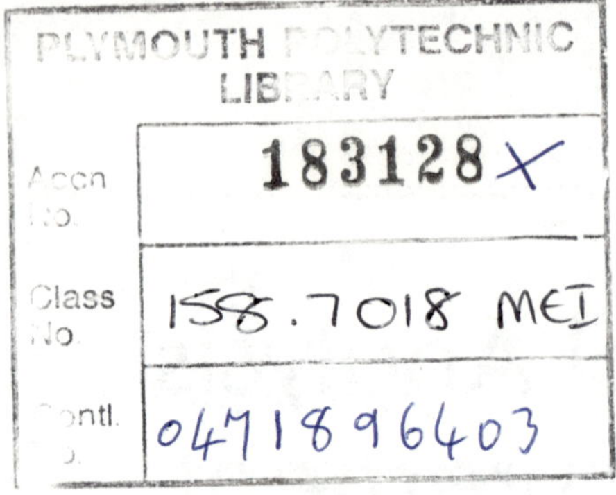
PLYMOUTH POLYTECHNIC LIBRARY
Accn No. 183128X
Class No. 158.7018 MEI
Contl. No. 0471896403

Copyright © 1985 by John Wiley & Sons, Inc.

All rights reserved. Published simultaneously in Canada.

Reproduction or translation of any part of this work beyond that permitted by Section 107 or 108 of the 1976 United States Copyright Act without the permission of the copyright owner is unlawful. Requests for permission or further information should be addressed to the Permissions Department, John Wiley & Sons, Inc.

ISBN 0-471-89640-3

Printed in the United States of America

10 9 8 7 6 5 4 3 2 1

In Memory of My Wife

Shirley Davis Meister

This Small Offering

Preface

This book had its inception in a workshop on applied methodologies held in December 1981 by the Human Factors Committee of the National Research Council. Although this book is not a product of that committee or workshop, the latter stimulated its writing. The eight-person group, of which I was a member, agreed that there was a lack of adequate and accessible documentation about these methods, despite the availability of some excellent textbooks on human factors/ergonomics. If this book is successful, it will help somewhat to fill the gap.

The purpose of this book is to describe the methods generally used by behavior specialists, particularly those working in industrial and applied psychology, ergonomics, and human factors. The description of each method will include:

1. Definition and purpose of the method. (What are the elements of the method? What is it designed to do?)

2. How the method was developed and how it has changed, if relevant.

3. Assumptions underlying the method. (Every method makes explicit or implicit assumptions, and the method cannot be fully understood without knowing what these are: Are these assumptions valid? Do they imply any difficulties in making use of the method?)

4. Input data needed to use the method. (All methods require some data upon which to operate. What are those data? Where can they be secured? How difficult is it to secure these data? What must be done with them?)

5. Procedure for utilizing the method (to include definition of terms and processes, stages in the use of the method; any subprocedures that are part of the primary method; terminal outputs).

6. Analysis of the data derived from method application. (How is it accomplished?)

7. How the method relates to other methods.

8. Advantages, disadvantages, problems. (What are the special features that make the method distinctive or present special difficulties to the user? What prob-

lems must the user look out for? Under what conditions would one wish to use, or not use, the method?)

9. Relevant research performed.
10. Additional research required.

I would briefly like to present a broader scope of my attitudes and biases than is revealed in the text, since these color much of what I have to say. Pragmatism (the confrontation with reality) has already been mentioned. Beyond that, the following concepts have undoubtedly influenced my writing over the years:

1. That the purpose of ergonomics/human factors is to describe, analyze, measure, predict, and control the real world of systems functioning operationally (i.e., not under experimental control).

2. That in consequence, the ideal environment in which to gather data is the operational environment. It may be necessary for various reasons to measure in some environment other than the real world, such as a laboratory or a simulator, but in such cases the conclusions derived from the data must be verified in the operational environment. I prefer predictive validation to other methods that are more statistically based.

3. That the human—a subsystem—works as part of a superordinate entity—the system—and while the person is working he subordinates his needs, goals, and interests to the accomplishment of the system goal. The study of the relationship between this personnel subsystem and the other system elements, including most importantly, the terminal system output, is the most important research goal for ergonomics/human factors.

4. That the research model behavioral science follows has been largely derived from the physical sciences and the field of experimental psychology and is oriented around objectivity and the controlled experiment. Since, however, the operational environment which is the reference environment for the data is uncontrolled, the preferred research model may not be entirely appropriate for behavioral science. Subjective data are often richer and more descriptive of events than are objective data; the controlled experiment is less than adequate because it cannot, as yet, reproduce the characteristics of the operational environment.

5. That part of the scholarly ethic which has been established by academia is a concentration on theory, sometimes to the exclusion of fact. Because human factors/ergonomics is action oriented, its preoccupation is not so much with theory as with control and quantitative prediction of system processes. Because methodology as a design or measurement *tool* is to a large extent *a*theoretical, readers may not find as much theory in this book as they might wish.

6. That the infrastructure of a discipline—and I firmly believe that human factors/ergonomics is a distinctive discipline apart from its beginnings in psychology—is its methodology, and that there must be constant awareness of, and concern for, the adequacy of that methodology. This book has been written in pursuit of that concern and as an effort to organize in one conceptual whole the many behavioral methods and their variations.

Chapter One presents the conceptual framework for future chapters. Chapters Two, Three, Four, Five, and Six present techniques for aiding system design. Chapters Seven and Eight describe ways of evaluating the effectiveness of the system as it is being and after it has been designed and developed. Chapters Nine, Ten, and Eleven present what I term "generic" measurement methods such as observations, interviews, questionnaires, and scaling. Chapter Twelve suggests some statistical techniques for studying complex systems, and Chapter Thirteen completes the work by reprising what has been learned and suggesting what research is needed to refine these means.

Although it would be presumptuous of me to suggest that this is an encyclopedic collection of procedures, it may do until one is written. For reasons of space alone it has been necessary to be somewhat selective in the choice of procedures and even more so in the amount of detail presented. The book is therefore primarily an introduction to behavioral methodology; it will, however, have accomplished its purpose if it encourages the reader to explore original sources. For that reason I have tended to be somewhat expansive in my reference list. Although there is a chapter on these topics, it is not a textbook on experimental design or statistical analysis.

It is my hope that the book will provide useful information for the behavioral researcher, the practitioner, the teacher, and student. Because of a naturally pragmatic trait in my makeup, I have endeavored to describe the methods not only as they are supposed theoretically to be implemented but as they are actually utilized under the constraints of real world system development and operation. In my opinion, the field of behavioral science has not paid enough attention to the failure to confront reality and the impact this failure has on what we do.

A number of colleagues have helped me in the writing of this book. Dr. Scott Newcomb and Mrs. Eleanor Robinson of the Navy Personnel Research and Development Center (NPRDC) and Mr. Richard A. Newman of the Martin-Denver Company reviewed a number of chapters and made many helpful suggestions, as did Dr. Arthur I. Siegel in Chapter Four. The staff of the NPRDC library was, as always, extremely helpful in providing books and reports. I am particularly indebted to the head librarian, Ms. Marie McDowell, and only slightly less so to her assistants, Maria Alves, Mary Pasquariello, Grace Cleary, Pachola Walden, and Sonia Popovich. Mrs. Joanne Newton, also of NPRDC, drew the figures with her usual exuberance; Mrs. Lou Davis and Mrs. Bea Neher typed the manuscript with their usual care.

Despite my affiliation with the Department of the Navy I am, of course, solely responsible for the opinions expressed.

DAVID MEISTER

San Diego, California
January 1985

Contents

Behavioral Analysis and Measurement Methods

CHAPTER ONE

The Structure of Analysis and Measurement

This chapter presents some of the conceptual background needed to understand the methods described in this book. The reader cannot truly understand these methods unless they are viewed in a larger framework, since they were developed to answer questions and solve problems arising out of that structure.

The two classes of behavioral methods are employed in two distinct but overlapping situations. The first class is what we have termed *analytic techniques*, for example, mission/function/task analysis, operational sequence diagramming, etc. (Chapters 2 through 6). These are employed in the development of *man–machine systems (MMS),* the functioning of which requires that people operate and maintain machines. The development of these systems and the application of these methods takes place in the engineering design and test facility.

The second methodologic class consists of *measurement methods* (Chapters 7 through 12) which are applied to some extent in the later stages of MMS development but which are more extensively employed with functioning systems. These methods include, among others, observation, interviews, questionnaires, ratings, objective measures, and judgments. The scope of these is much broader than that of the analytic techniques which are presently applied only in the development of MMS. The measurement methods are applied not only to MMSs but also to what have been termed *man–man* systems (those involving few if any machines) and to individuals functioning as part of no formal system. In the case of the latter, if one wishes to maintain the system concept, the individual can be considered as a subsystem within a higher order system of cultural, physical, social, and economic influences. In fact, measurement methods are relevant to all systems and all situations. The following are merely a few examples of measurement situations and methods: political polling (surveys); traffic and industrial accidents (accident investigation techniques, interviews); forecasts of economic activity by consumers (questionnaires, interviews); attitudes toward immigrants (questionnaires, rating scales); the performance of athletes (objective measures).

Additional factors relevant to behavior technology must be considered. Much of the development of MMS is performed under government sponsorship, primarily, but not exclusively, for the Department of Defense. Government system development is controlled by formal regulations that specify certain behavioral analyses and evaluation (1977a, b, c) although there is some question about how completely these regulations are implemented. It is uncertain to what extent the same behavioral methods are employed in the development of commercial MMS; less, one presumes, but little information is available about nongovernment system development practices. In describing the analytic techniques, most of our attention will be directed to military systems because, as we have indicated, these techniques are utilized more often for government systems. The literature about these techniques is illustrated primarily by military examples.

DEFINITIONS

Pervading this book is the notion of the *system* and particularly the MMS as an organization of personnel with the machines they operate and maintain to perform assigned tasks. As was indicated previously, the MMS is only one type of system; others are man–man, military, commercial, social, welfare, economic, and cultural. The purpose of the analytic techniques is to aid in the design of the human subsystem so that the performance of the superordinate system will be maximized. The purpose of the measurement methods is to gather information about personnel function in order to assess the adequacy of human subsystem performance with reference to the terminal outputs of the overall system; and/or to understand the relationship between the human subsystem and the overall system.

The importance of the system concept lies in the fact that without it the notion of task performance in relation to a higher-order goal has no meaning. A task is an arrangement of behaviors (perceptual, cognitive, motor) related to each other in time and organized to satisfy both an immediate and a longer-range purpose. Examples of types of tasks are: simple (throwing a switch); moderately complex (reading this book); highly complex (diagnosing a patient's illness).

One performs a task to accomplish a goal which is tied to the output of a superordinate entity which is a system. The purposive behavior of the individual cannot be understood outside of the system concept; without a task/system orientation human behavior cannot be interpreted meaningfully. This applies of course only to *work* performance; the performance of the individual in a nonwork context (e.g., recreation) need not be viewed as an activity within an overriding system, although one can hypothesize that the human in a nonwork situation functions as an element of interactive social, cultural, and economic systems. One critical consequence of viewing the individual (or group) as a system component is that it requires the behavior analyst to consider all system factors that could influence the performance of the individual (or group).

The methods described in this book were therefore designed to secure information about and to improve the adequacy of relatively molar (i.e., task) behaviors. However important they may be as building blocks for tasks, molecular behaviors such as simple reaction time or eye reflexes are not very relevant to a description of task performance, except under special circumstances.

The term *operator* is also used in this book. I prefer this to the equivalent *human* or *subject* found in many behavioral texts. Used here it means the one who performs or behaves in a work situation or who is acted upon by external forces. The term is intended to include both the operator or user of an equipment and the one who maintains it—anyone who functions within a system, whatever its type. Since the term is gender neutral, it refers to both men and women.

HOW BEHAVIORAL METHODS WERE DEVELOPED

The analytic techniques which have a narrower and more applied scope were derived from the measurement methods. The latter are generic in the sense that they depend upon innate human observational and judgmental responses. We hypothesize that the generic measurement methods developed from primitive observational processes. An event occurs, is perceived and examined, and one wonders what it is. This initial infantile scrutiny is quite passive, only later giving way to more active processes. Because of its passivity, its almost reflex nature, this initial perceptual examination response cannot be considered a behavioral method. A method does not exist until observation is accomplished *purposefully*. Observation and judgment about what is observed become methods when they are employed actively to achieve some goal: to answer a question, solve a problem, or secure something physically.

An example is when the observer selects some attribute of the phenomenon being observed and concentrates on that attribute while ignoring others. The examination process becomes a rating when the *observer* (henceforth, *O*) recognizes that the attribute being observed varies along one or more dimensions and that the dimension has quantity. When *O* recognizes that it is unnecessary to be physically present when an event occurs (i.e., someone else can observe and report the event), then *O* has invented the interview, the self-report, and the survey (although obviously not all at the same time).

Since the measurement methods are extrapolated from or patterned after basic human observational and judgmental processes they are limited by those processes. Because of this it seems unlikely that we will be able to develop significantly "new" measurement methods, regardless of technologic developments such as the computer. Because the applied techniques are derivations of the generic measurement methods, it is possible to develop new applied techniques, yet they reduce upon examination to generic measurement processes: data gathered by observation or self-

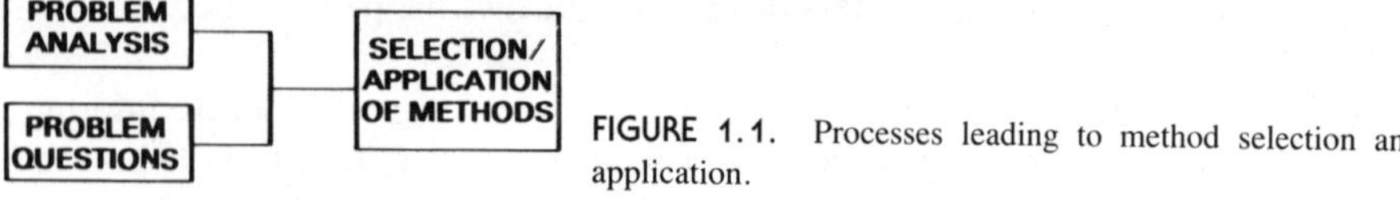

FIGURE 1.1. Processes leading to method selection and application.

report or formalized judgments (as in the case of human engineering checklists). Although genuinely "new" methods cannot be developed, the examination of present methods is valuable because it is possible to improve the efficiency with which we use them. The final chapter of the book will consider some potential ways of improving method effectiveness.

METHODOLOGY AS A TOOL

We have said that the behavioral methods are a response to a problem to be solved, a question to be answered, or a purpose to be achieved. The method selected is the means of answering that question, solving that problem, or achieving that purpose. This orientation describes even pure research, since research cannot be meaningful unless it is performed to answer a specific question.

The analytic techniques and the measurement methods both have their own set of initiating questions. Since the analytic techniques were developed to aid design, these questions center about the major problems arising during design. The questions are fairly specific and include, inter alia: Which is the best design alternative from a behavioral standpoint? Will personnel be able to perform effectively in a particular design configuration? Is the system properly human engineered? What characteristics should system personnel have to be effective? What training should be given them? A more detailed listing of these questions by stage of system development will be provided in Chapter 2.

Whereas the analytic techniques are design aids, the measurement methods are information-gathering tools. Measurement questions are, as is fitting, more general: What does a particular phenomenon, event, object, job, etc. consist of? What did the object or the individual do, see, think? What happened? How did the individual, group, team, subsystem, system perform? How did the individual or group feel about certain things, events, people?

Measurement methods overlap tremendously in terms of which questions they can answer. For example, to answer the question, *What happened?* one can use observation, questionnaires, interviews, diaries, activity analysis, accident investigation, automatic performance measurement, objective indices, and ratings. The same is roughly true of other measurement questions. However, one method is often more efficient than another to answer a particular question.

To determine what questions need answering, the specialist must first analyze (observe and evaluate) the problem aspects of the situation. *Problem analysis* proceeds in parallel and in interaction with the determination of problem questions—both eventually leading to the selection and application of one or more methods. Since various methods can be used to solve virtually any problem, problem analysis sharpens the process of selecting an appropriate method. Schematically the process can be depicted as in Figure 1.1.

The problem analysis also consists of questions, although these differ from the problem questions:

1. In performing the research, or solving the problem, what is our goal? In other words, what questions do we seek to answer and what problems do we seek to solve?
2. What is taking place in the system's operation, in the phenomenon, that is relevant to these questions?
3. What variables affect—or could affect—the phenomenon, operation, or the system performance we are observing?
4. What performance criteria describe the functioning of the system, phenomenon, etc.? In the case of the system, what are its outputs? In the case of a phenomenon or behavior, what are its consequences and how can these be described?
5. What assumptions must we—do we—make about the object of our investigation? What do we know about that object?
6. What constraints do we have on achieving the goal of the investigation? Can these be overcome?
7. What factors (e.g., the nature of the subject population, the time available to test) will have a negative effect on the method we select?
8. If we are at all concerned about the generalization of our conclusions to the "real world," how representative of that real world must our measurement situation be?
9. What method (or combination of methods) is most likely to answer the question or solve the problem? What are the advantages and disadvantages in terms of answering the preceding questions?

Later, having conducted the study and performed the data analysis, the specialist will ask, How effective has the study/measurement been and have the results of applying the method answered the question or solved the problem? The specialist will also want to know how unequivocal are the data? (Can alternative explanations, answers, and solutions be excluded statistically and logically?) If so, can the data and conclusions be applied to situations other than the measurement situation from which they came? And practically speaking, do the results mean anything?

All analysis and measurement—all research—is problem solving, in which one finds varying amounts of uncertainty. Analysis and measurement are attempts to eliminate as much of that uncertainty as possible, although some will always remain.

In selecting the methods to be utilized, the behavior specialist must consider: *Effectiveness*: the degree to which the method accomplishes its purpose; *Ease of use*: the simplicity of application; *Cost*: Not just monetary but cost in terms of data requirements, equipment needed, personnel, and time needed to apply the method;

Flexibility: the ability to use the method in many measurement contexts, with many system types, at several system levels; *Range*: the number of phenomena, behaviors, and events the method can analyze or measure; *Validity*: the extent to which method application produces data descriptive of specific behaviors or responses as they occur in real life; *Reliability*: the extent to which repeated applications of a method to the same situation by the same specialist produces identical (or at least very similar) data or the extent to which several specialists who apply the same method to the same situation produce identical or very similar data; and *Objectivity*: the extent of reliance on indices external to the one who applies the method.

No one method satisfies all these criteria nor any of the criteria to the degree one would wish. It is the specialist's task to select the one or more methods that reflect these criteria most completely.

REFERENCES

Department of Defense. *Major System Acquistions* (DOD Directive 5000.1). Washington, DC: Author, January 1977. (a)

Department of Defense. *Major System Acquisition Process* (DOD Directive 5000.2). Washington, DC: Author, January 1977. (b)

Department of Defense. *Test and Evaluation* (DOD Directive 5000.3). Washington, DC: Author, January, 1977. (c)

CHAPTER TWO

Function/Task Analysis

We begin with the *analytic techniques*. It might have been more logical to start with the measurement methods from which the analytic techniques are derived, but we follow a developmental sequence in which system design and test (which require analysis) precede evaluation of the operational system (which requires measurement).

This chapter describes a set of methods which, as a whole, are termed function and task analysis but which are composed of distinctive although interrelated procedures. These procedures are *mission analysis*, *determination of functions*, *function allocation*, *task description/identification*, and *task analysis (TA)*. A number of TA variations will be described and we will also consider the behavioral taxonomies that are at the heart of TA.

Before describing these analyses in detail, it is important to consider in greater detail the system development context in which they are employed.

ANALYTIC METHODS IN SYSTEM DEVELOPMENT

Man–machine systems development proceeds over a series of logical, sequential and overlapping phases: *planning*, *preliminary or conceptual design*, *detail* (engineering) *design*, *testing and evaluation*, *production*, and, once the system has been turned over to the user, *operation*. (Because of the perversity of those who strive constantly to invent new names, these phases are sometimes called by other names; but the ones used in this book have the advantage of being traditional and relatively self-explanatory.)

The Department of Defense (DOD), which is the major procurer of new government systems, formalizes these phases (Department of Defense, 1977a, b, c) by breaking them down into a series of milestones at which the system under development is critically reviewed before permission is given to continue development.

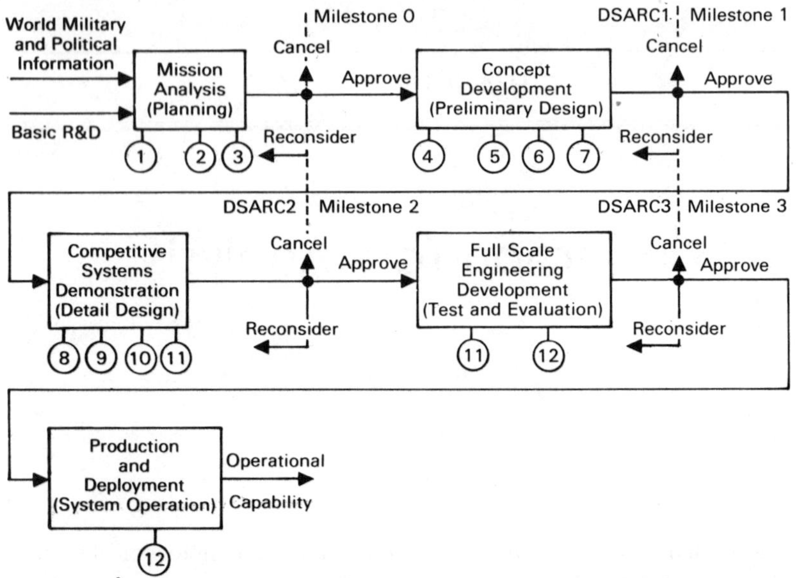

1. Mission Profile/Scenario Analysis
2. Function Analysis — Function Flow Diagrams
3. Decision/Action Diagrams
4. Function Allocation Trade Offs
5. Time Lines
6. Operational Sequence Diagrams
7. Task Descriptions
8. Workload Analysis
9. Task Analysis
10. Mockups
11. Evaluation of Man-Machine Interfaces
12. Operational Testing

FIGURE 2.1. Phases of the military's system acquisition model. (Modified from Sawyer, Fiorello, Kidd and Price, 1981.)

Among the elements to be reviewed are those dealing with personnel. [For descriptions of this cycle and the relationship of behavioral factors to the various milestones, see Price, 1980a, b]. The four DSARC (Defense System Acquisition Review Council) milestones are milestone O, program initiation; milestone I, demonstration and validation; milestone II, full-scale engineering development; and milestone III, production and deployment. Figure 2.1 suggests only approximately, of course, the sequence of phases, the methods that are applied, and the points at which DOD reviews are made. Although Figure 2.1 implies complete demarcation of phases, in reality there is considerable overlap.

The Department of Defense also mandates that certain behavioral activities be performed during the system development process. MIL-H-46855B (Department of Defense, 1979) requires that as *appropriate* for a particular project the following analyses and evaluations be performed: definition and allocation of system functions; information flow and processing analysis; estimates of potential operator/maintainer processing capabilities; identification of human roles; task analysis; analysis of critical tasks; workload analysis; studies, experiments, laboratory tests; development of mockups and models; dynamic simulation; application of human factors engineering to preliminary and detailed design; test and evaluation of design.

Each of the system development phases described previously raises behavioral questions that must be answered. These are listed in Table 2.1.

Note that some questions persist over several phases—for example, the application of human engineering, and the ability of personnel to do their jobs. Table 2.2

TABLE 2.1. Behavioral Questions Arising in System Development

System Planning

1. (Assuming a predecessor system) What changes in the new system require changes in numbers and types of personnel employed in the previous system?
2. What changes in tasks to be performed will require changes in personnel, selection, training, and system operation?

Preliminary Design

3. Of the various design alternatives available, which is the most effective from the standpoint of behavioral performance?
4. Given a system configuration, will system personnel be able to perform all required functions effectively?
5. Will personnel encounter excessive workload?
6. What factors are responsible for potential error and can these be eliminated?

Detail Design

7. Which is the better of two or more subsystem/component design alternatives?
8. What level of personnel performance can one achieve and does this level satisfy system requirements?
9. What training should be provided to personnel?
10. Are equipment design and job procedures properly human engineered?

Production

Since the questions raised in this phase are primarily the concern of industrial engineering, they will not be discussed in this book.

Test and Evaluation

11. Have all system dimensions affected by behavior variables been properly human engineered?
12. Will system personnel be able to do their jobs effectively?
13. Does the system satisfy its personnel requirements?
14. What design inadequacies exist that must be rectified?

System Operations

15. Do any behavioral problems still exist?
16. What is the specific cause of these problems and what solutions can be recommended?

Source. Meister, D. The role of human factors in system development. *Applied Ergonomics*, 1982, *13*; 119–124.

TABLE 2.2. The Availability of Behavioral Methods to Assist in Answering Development Questions

Behavioral Methods	Behavioral Questions															
	1	2	3	4	5	6	7	8	9	10	11	12	13	14	15	16
Mission/function analysis	X															
Function allocation			X	X			X									
Task description/analysis		X		X												
Operational sequence diagrams			X	X		X	X									
Workload analysis					X											
Information/decision analysis				X	X											
Time line/link analysis				X	X											
Computerized methods	X	X	X	X	X		X	X								
Error/failure mode analysis				X	X	X										
Human reliability prediction				X		X	X	X								
Instructional system development									X							
Design evaluation methods			X				X			X	X					
Developmental test procedures							X			X	X	X		X		
Operational test procedures											X	X	X	X		
System exercises															X	X

shows the relevance of the methods to the system development questions listed in Table 2.1.

Several points should be noted about Tables 2.1 and 2.2:

1. Some methods have a broader range than others (i.e., help to answer more questions). However, even those that have only a single use, like instructional system development, can be critical.

2. A number of different methods may be used to answer the same question.

3. Some methods are limited by the phase in which they can be implemented. For example, *mission/function analysis* is utilized early in development and then is superseded by other methods. Some, like those used in operational testing, would be ideal for answering questions that arise earlier in development but are not available since the conditions for their use do not exist except in a fully completed system.

It is most important to recognize that there are two kinds of methodology. There is the one that is described in instruction manuals, journal articles, government reports and in this book; this is the way the methods should be utilized. The other kind of methodology is the same as the first but modified by the way it is actually performed. The actual application of a technique is often different from the way its originators described it and intended it to be performed. This is particularly true of large-scale methods such as instructional system development (ISD) and operational system testing, which are processes that cannot be reduced easily to step-by-step procedures. An attempt has been made in this book to describe the factors influencing how methods are implemented and what the reader is likely to find when actually applying behavioral methods.

Certain characteristics of system development are germane to our consideration of methods used in this context. First, development is a highly interactive process: As one proceeds from system planning through preliminary and then detail design, the same behavioral requirements tend to occur—demanding, however, new answers because they apply to a different developmental level. So, for example, if one allocates functions at a very gross level in preliminary design, one must do so also at the detailed design level for smaller components. Hence some methods are used repeatedly throughout development.

Secondly, although one would prefer to think of system development as a very logical intellectual process, in actuality there are many irrational and nonintellective elements (see Meister, 1971). Design is characteristically "fuzzy and poorly articulated" (Malhotra, Thomas, Carroll and Miller, 1980). The efficiency with which one can apply the methods often depends on such fortuitous factors as opportunity, availability of money, time factors, and the cooperation of engineers. When behavioral methods are applied to functioning systems and individuals and groups in the operational environment, one may encounter resistance from the subject population and constraints such as the requirement not to interfere with ongoing activities. Hence, the methods are rarely as effective in actual application as they could be. In consequence, therefore, many weapon systems suffer from behavioral deficiencies (General Accounting Office, 1981).

In attempting to understand the role of behavior analysis and measurement in system development, it is important to note that development has certain critical characteristics:

1. *Molecularization.* The development process as a whole is one of working from broad, molar functions to progressively more molecular tasks and subtasks. When the behavior specialist first encounters system requirements, he deals with the total system and major subsystems; as development proceeds, he works his way down to subtasks at the level of switch activation and the placement of controls and displays. Actions taken at an earlier, more molar (system, subsystem) level have profound consequences for molecular (task, subtask, component) levels. For example, if the developer decides in Preliminary Design that information will be presented via a cathode ray tube (CRT), in Detail Design he must face all the problems involved in using a CRT, including display brightness, resolution, ambient lighting, etc. This is why the specialist is so insistent upon being part of the design team from the beginning of development.

2. *Requirements as forcing functions.* System requirements drive the design tasks that are performed during development. The criterion of design adequacy is always the system requirement; design options are developed to satisfy that requirement. That is why the absence of formal behavioral requirements in the design spec-

ifications or development contract makes it much more difficult for the specialist to secure adequate consideration of behavioral inputs.

3. *System development as discovery.* Initially there are many unknowns about the system. In some systems (fortunately only a few) development may begin even before system requirements have been thoroughly specified. Often system requirements are changed during development; the military has a habit of complicating original design by adding new requirements. In addition, system requirements can be implemented in at least several different ways; early on the designer may not know the best way or indeed the range of choices available. Similarly, the behavioral implications of system requirements are unknowns to the specialist. For example, what kind of workload will personnel be exposed to? Progressively, as choices among design options are made, these unknowns are clarified until—when the system is produced, installed, and operationally tested—almost everything about the system is known.

4. *System development as transformation.* For the designer, system development is the transformation of system requirements into physical mechanisms to perform system operations: hardware, software, procedures, and so forth. For the specialist, system development is also a transformation from the physical requirement to the behavioral implications of that requirement to the physical mechanisms for implementing these behavioral implications. Almost without exception the major system requirements are physical—for example, speed, range, endurance, power consumption, and reliability. Almost never is there an explicit behavioral requirement. Behavioral requirements are inferred from a concept of how the system should function ideally (e.g., the system should not impose too heavy a burden on its personnel, or the pilot of an aircraft should have adequate visibility outside his cockpit). The specialist examines the physical requirement, determines its behavioral implications, and suggests a physical mechanism for encompassing these implications. In an absurdly simplistic (and therefore more obviously illustrative) example, the specialist asks himself, what does it mean that the system must be operated outdoors in arctic conditions? Well, operators will probably have to wear gloves; in consequence it would be advisable to make controls larger to accommodate for gloved clumsiness. Operators will respond more slowly to stimuli; hence, system events requiring fast responses should be slowed if possible. This example is relatively obvious, but others are by no means so simple. For example, the operator may be required to correlate several channels of information presented in overlapping fashion. What is the significance of this for the operator? What physical implementing mechanisms should be recommended for reducing errors resulting from this requirement? This process of implication/transformation proceeds throughout system development.

5. *Time.* Because of all the unknowns that must be resolved, system development is time driven. There is never enough time for practitioners to perform the analyses, studies, and tests that they would do if they had their "druthers." In this respect, system development is a degraded process. The implication is that whatever is done must be timely, or it is wasted effort.

6. *Cost.* Cost is another forcing function. First of all, if support money is tight, there may not be a human factors (HF) program at all, or it may be severely curtailed (fewer analyses and evaluations than are desirable); or it may be aborted early on to reallocate the HF money to another (supposedly more important) development effort that is suffering financially. Second, a behavioral recommendation cannot be too costly or it will be rejected automatically. That is why recommending redesign after hardware has been "bent" (as developers say) is like spitting into the wind.

7. *Iteration.* System development is iterative, for two reasons:

(a) The same questions and activities arise and must be performed at different development phases.

(b) Where a required analysis has not been performed earlier, or because there is new information which was not available earlier, or even because the design team cannot make up its mind, design becomes a process of "cut and try" in which a design solution is proposed, rejected, revised, and, finally, accepted.

8. *Design competition.* Where the system is large, its design is performed by a team of specialists, such as those in electrical, hydraulic, controls, reliability, weights and even behavioral disciplines. One engineering group is prime and one designer in that group is the prime coordinator of the team. The dominant group/engineer exercises veto power over the others. The less influential groups (among whom one finds the HF group) must function under constraints established by the dominant one. Inputs from supporting team members are funneled to the prime designer and somehow integrated.

System development may be viewed as a process of choosing among competing design options. The inputs made to the designer by the various specialists describe various aspects of those options and competing interests. Competition here is a matter of how well each design option satisfies system requirements. Each specialist group has its own special interest: The reliability group is concerned for equipment reliability; the weights group is concerned about reducing system weight as much as possible, and so forth. Interests clash and may have to be reconciled. For example, to improve reliability in a fighter fire control system the reliability engineer desires redundancy, but the weights engineer fears the additional weight of that redundancy. The behavior specialist has his own constituency—the human, whose interests must be compromised with those of the others. This does not mean that the design team functions discordantly; it is merely that each point of view is pushed vigorously and must be reconciled.

9. *Relevance.* To be considered meaningful the design inputs the behavioral specialist makes must be relevant to performance capability, because that is what the designer is most concerned about. All other things being equal, a behavioral input directly relevant to a hardware, software, or even a procedural aspect of the system will be more gracefully received by the designer than one dealing with an input related solely to personnel, such as selection, training, or technical documentation. Design relevance as perceived by engineers is critical for the acceptance and judged value of behavioral inputs during development.

What has been said so far suggests that, much as one would prefer to believe that system development is a logical, rigorous, rational process of intellectual discovery and creation, that ideal is distorted by nonintellective influences such as unrealistic cost and schedule estimates, organizational confusion, lack of communication among designers, and (not least, for the behavioral specialist, anyway) ignorance of and prejudice against human factors.

Compounding this, there is considerable subjectivity in many of the analytic techniques, as in all behavioral methods. Hence the methods are heavily dependent on individual experience, skill, and judgment; judgment is required in skipping procedural steps, in utilizing intuition and insight, and in taking shortcuts. A major reason for the practitioner's use of intuition with these methods is the lack of human performance data to support them. It is commonly supposed that the relatively large outpouring of behavioral papers and reports supplies the needed data, but this literature fails to provide relevant guidelines for effective system design. Usually, this literature is excessively academic and only indirectly relevant to the practitioner's needs.

The mission/function/task analysis methods described in this chapter are major methods and all are required. One cannot consider a system properly developed unless these means are applied. There is room for some choice in the way in which they are applied (e.g., the different questions that may be asked in performing task analysis) but none for their application.

AN OVERVIEW OF FUNCTION/TASK ANALYSIS

The processes in function/task analysis are *logical and deductive*. That is because system design begins with requirements to which the system must be designed, and constraints that narrow the range of design options. These physical requirements (e.g., aircraft speed of 650 mph) and constraints (e.g., mean repair time of 2 hours) must be analyzed to determine what their behavioral implications are, for example, what number and type of personnel will be required to exercise the system and how the job should be designed to maximize human performance. Behavioral mission analysis is the process by which system requirements are analyzed to determine their behavioral implications. The logical-deductive process partitions gross requirements into finer detail by asking at each step of the process the following question: To accomplish this requirement or this function, to satisfy this constraint, what is needed in the way of inputs and outputs and implementing mechanisms? This permits the analyst to subdivide molar functions such as "to navigate the ship." These have limited usefulness because they include large behavior segments and must be subdivided into more manageable, detailed ones, such as "to take compass readings." This detailed analysis leads to the determination of the functions to be performed by the system.

These functions also have behavioral implications in terms of the *demands* (for capabilities and effort) they impose on both personnel and equipment. Thus, the function, "to monitor a display," raises the question of the possible perceptual difficulties the operator may experience in the monitoring process. All systems impose demands on personnel and equipment; in many if not most cases the demands (e.g., for strength, visual acuity, intelligence) are within the capabilities of personnel to satisfy. However the analyst must examine all demands to find those that do not match personnel capabilities—to these, special attention must be given. (The notion of system demands on personnel—we are not concerned with those demands on equipment—and the need to match demands and capabilities represents the beginning of a crude theory of personnel–system relationships.)

The listing of system functions does not determine how these functions are to be carried out. A function is initially neutral in the sense that it may be implemented by a human, by a machine, or by some combination of both. The process of determining which shall implement the function, and more particularly *how*, is known as *function allocation* (FA). There are usually many ways in which a function can be performed, and the choice can be ordered on a continuum from completely manual (no machine intervention) to completely automatic (no human intervention). In actual practice FA usually involves both human and machine interaction. The choice of the way in which the function is to be performed depends on the application of criteria such as cost, performance, reliability, maintainability, logistics, etc. and should also include human considerations—whether the operator will be able to perform effectively, for example. Since most design alternatives involve both advantages and disadvantages in terms of these criteria, FA also involves tradeoffs or compromises among these advantages and disadvantages. Tradeoffs often require what are called *trade studies* or analyses of the relative advantages and disadvantages of the design alternatives.

The determination through FA of how functions will be performed in turn determines the specific tasks to be performed. If, for example, navigating a ship by taking sun and star readings is the selected design alternative, then certain tasks are implied and must be identified. If navigation is accomplished using the more automatic LORAN (Long-Range Radio Aid to Navigation) equipment, then other tasks are implied. Each set of task implications will also impose a set of demands on the system as a whole and on the operator/technician in particular. For example, the task may require a certain number of personnel with a certain amount of skill level to perform the task, and then it is the responsibility of the system to produce these people. Or the task may make demands upon the operator/technician such as extremely acute hearing or pitch discrimination (e.g., sonar operators in World War II). These demands can only be ascertained by analysis of the task, since the function is too broad a behavioral unit to be useful in determining personnel requirements.

Like much of system development itself, these analyses are iterative; although mission analysis and function determination are usually performed only at the beginning of development, *function allocation* and *task description/analysis* occur at progressively more detailed stages. Moreover, what will be described as a relatively formal, step-by-step process is in actual development much more informal and much less ordered.

In describing the methods in this and subsequent chapters, various examples will be provided, but it may be helpful to have a single example that carries through the chapters and serves as a common thread. This example is the analysis and testing of a hypothetical system, but one which is not so far advanced beyond the present state of the engineering art as to be pure fantasy.

The Automated Interviewer is a computer-controlled device for collecting information from applicants to welfare agencies and social security branch offices. The force driving the development of this device is the desire to reduce demands upon the time of agency personnel by having applicants provide routine data directly to computer files. In its physical form the device is much like that of any office word processor or display terminal, consisting of a cathode ray tube terminal to communicate to the applicant, various controls with which the applicant enters data, and a chair for the applicant to sit in while inputting information. The feature that renders the device to be designed critical from a behavioral standpoint is that it must process inputs from those who may be weak, sick, or otherwise physically impaired; have poor eyesight or limb coordination; or who may be intellectually retarded or functionally illiterate.

MISSION/FUNCTION ANALYSIS

Mission analysis is also called system requirements analysis. The mission is what the system is supposed to do. Mission analysis has the following steps.

System Analysis

Mission analysis analyzes system requirements. Its purpose is:

1. To gather all available information about the system mission from such sources as planning documents, the system specification, the request for proposal and previous test results. The contractor for a government system is given a system requirements description which, when analyzed, generates further requirements.

2. To extract from this information: (a) Specific system missions or goals (e.g., to detect a submarine, to produce machine tools); (b) Any required outputs that are specified (e.g., 40 messages must be transmitted per unit time); (c) Any required inputs that are specified (e.g., receive electronic signals on 2250 Hz); (d) System capabilities and performance requirements demanded by the mission (e.g., store enough fuel for 30 days); (e) Environmental factors that may affect system performance (e.g., the anticipated temperature in which the system must function is 10° F); and (f) Constraints on system performance (e.g., repair of any equipment module must not take more than 1.5 hours).

Behavioral Implications

Mission analysis indicates the behavioral implications of these system requirements.

Not all the above categories are equally important for every system. In the case of the Automated Interviewer system, goals are to: collect information; verify data correctness; provide assistance to applicant when requested; display applicant status when requested; provide applicant in a tutorial mode with information about how the Interviewer functions; interrogate the applicant. Although the device does not have specific output requirements, it does have input requirements (e.g., name, date of birth, etc). As far as system capabilities are concerned, it must be able to respond to the applicant both visually and aurally (the latter for the seriously vision impaired). Since its environment is that of an office, environmental factors are not particularly important (except that display luminance must be adjustable to ambient illumination so that visual stimuli are highly visible). Constraint factors are user impairments.

System requirements are those characteristics which the system (both personnel and machines) must manifest to satisfy the goal (mission) of the system. Ideally, requirements are stated in terms of output tolerances which must be met (e.g., battery output of 24 ± 2 volts). There are two reasons for analyzing system requirements. First, analysis of system requirements is a prerequisite for determination of system functions, since these functions are inherent in and derived logically from requirements. For example, if an aircraft is to fly, it must take off from the ground; to take off, the engine must be started; to start the engine, the pilot must engage the throttle; to engage the throttle, there must be an appropriate control. The analysis of system requirements implies progressively more molecular implementing functions.

The second reason for analyzing system requirements is that they may have important behavioral implications. If, for example, the mission must be performed in an extreme environment, such as the Arctic or the Equator, special environmental demands may be levied on system personnel. If the system must be exercised in 10° F, operator movements are likely to be slowed down (thus possibly increasing system performance time), special cold weather gear will be required, and controls may have to be larger because personnel will operate them using gloves. Most requirements will have no discernible implications for personnel performance, but all must be examined to ask what potential effects, if any, could this have on personnel performance?

Each of the system inputs and outputs, performance requirements, constraints, etc. may impose its own behavior demands on personnel. One looks for the extremes of system characteristics, because only the extremes may impose unacceptable demands. Although it may not be possible at this very early stage of system planning to do more than alert the analyst to potential areas of concern, any warning is valuable.

The following steps related to system requirements analysis are optional. Some analysts proceed immediately to the determination of system functions. However, where the system has a natural sequence of activity over time which can be readily broken down into distinct segments, it may be valuable to profile the performance of the mission as described below. The mission profile is particularly useful for transportation systems like aircraft which have very distinctive sequential phases in their operations, such as takeoff and landing. A mission profile or scenario would be irrelevant for systems like the Automated Interviewer which do not change their functions in a specified, sequential manner.

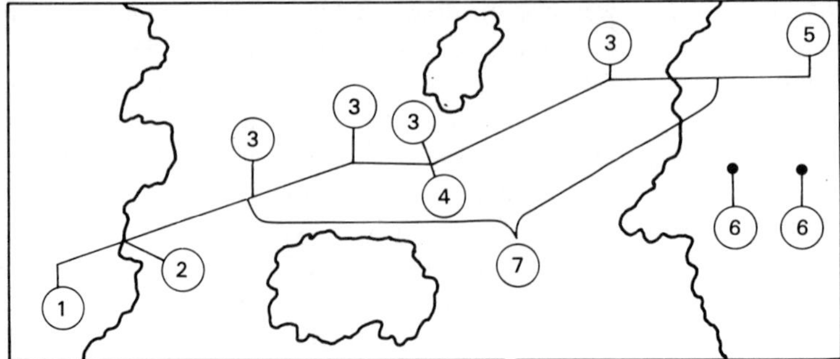

TIME AND/OR DISTANCE

1. Takeoff point
2. Rendezvous
3. Check points
4. Point of mission recall
5. Target
6. Alternate targets
7. Fighter cover (where to where)

FIGURE 2.2. Sample mission profile.

Profiling, Developing, and Segmenting

Mission analysis describes the system mission in greater detail. It profiles the system mission, develops a mission scenario, and divides the mission into segments.

Mission profiles and scenarios are two techniques used to assist in the mission analysis. A mission profile is a graphic and/or pictorial model of the mission a system is expected to perform. If a system has several missions, it is necessary to draw individual profiles for each.

The purpose of profiling the system mission is to indicate the effects on system performance of changes over time in system variables. It is then possible to examine the interaction of system elements as well as to suggest possible ways of segmenting the mission.

Most missions are conceived in terms of a terminal goal (e.g., to produce bottle caps, to reach Newfoundland, etc.) However, this terminal goal depends upon a sequence of preceding, supporting activities which the profile depicts.

For any system that moves from point *A* to *B* to . . . *n*, an outline map is drawn of the geographic area to be covered and the course to be followed. The major stages of the mission are indicated by name or number (e.g., takeoff, rendezvous, checkpoints, target, etc.) Other information, such as control stations, communication nets or weather fronts, can be tagged onto the profile. A time or distance base can be plotted against the flight path. A sample profile is shown in Figure 2.2.

The mission scenario verbally describes mission events and summarizes typical operations, assumptions, and environments. Mission scenarios are relatively simple to develop because they make no use of elaborate symbology or graphics. They are useful for gross rather than detailed analysis. Any system, however complex, can be described. Descriptions of new and unique systems may, however, require considerable time to prepare.

There are no precise rules for writing scenarios. The scenario should describe whatever factors could significantly influence system performance, for example, starting and ending times, locations if relevant, planned changes in own system status, expected performance of other systems (if relevant), and important geographic or climatic features. The scenario, like the other products of behavior analysis, should be verified by consultation with system engineers and in some cases with representatives of the eventual system user.

A mission segment is a time period in the system profile, selected on the basis of coherence of activities within the segment and natural start and stop points. The time period included is one of convenience to the analyst, although different segments may have different time spans. For example, the segments of a flight mission could be takeoff, climb, cruise, etc.

The objective of dividing the mission into segments—especially when the mission is long and complex—is to develop smaller and more convenient units of analysis. Segmenting also helps identify requirements, interfaces, and functions that differ in different mission phases.

Segmenting is often an iterative, "cut and try" process. The choice of segment is whatever appears to make most sense to the analyst, although that choice is guided by the criteria of coherence and recognized time points. Segments of a hypothetic missile mission might include: transport system to launch site, assemble missile and prepare pad, erect missile, etc.

DETERMINATION OF FUNCTIONS

System functions are identified and described by determining function inputs and outputs, establishing functional performance criteria, and preparing function flow diagrams (FFDs).

Determine Inputs and Outputs

The function is the purpose for which a behavioral activity or an equipment subsystem is included in the system. Functions may be implemented by machines alone, by personnel alone, or, as in most cases, by some combination of personnel and machines. Unless the new system has a predecessor system for which a FA has been performed, the analyst theoretically begins working with no preconception about how a particular function will be implemented and is not concerned with this question at this stage. Although some functions appear to belong exclusively to personnel or to machines, it is a mistake for the analyst to jump to conclusions.

The function translates inputs into outputs and contributes to the accomplishment of some part of the mission. This is a fancy way of saying that subordinate, more molecular functions are derived from more molar ones by imagining the processes required to implement the molar function. For example, one of the gross functions (actually system goals) of the Automated Interviewer is to collect information. How? First, it must present on its screen a set of questions to be answered. The respondent must reply (method of doing so as yet unspecified, see function allocations subsequently). The Interviewer must display the respondent's input on the screen and ask if it is correct. If the applicant has previously been interviewed (another question to be answered), the present input data must be cross-checked against past inputs. Each of these activities is a subordinate function.

Functions describe relatively molar behaviors, for example, to detect, to analyze, to repair; the individual tasks and behaviors needed to implement or carry out the function are much more detailed. There are unfortunately no clearcut rules that determine whether the analyst should call a set of behaviors a function or a task. Because the looseness of language enables the analyst to use different words—each with its own connotation—to describe the same function, the analyst is confronted with a problem, a taxonomic problem to be discussed later.

Functions can be instantaneous (start engines) or prolonged (monitor radar scope), apparently simple (detect blip), or complex (analyze battle strategy). At a certain level of detail—which is difficult to specify—the function shades almost imperceptibly into a task.

Often major system functions are quite obvious from the nature of the system. So, if one is dealing with an aircraft it is obvious that two major functions (essentially identical with two major time segments) are "takeoff" and "landing." By the time the analyst becomes involved in the system development process, such top-level functions may be specified; this is particularly the case if the system under development is an advanced model of an already existent system. It is in the identification of subordinate-level functions (particularly as they require human implementation) that the analyst may make a contribution because these may have been overlooked by system planners. Where a predecessor system exists, the procedure is to analyze that system and the new system to determine the differences between them and to concentrate attention on the functional differences between the systems. If major items of equipment have already been specified, for example, a radar, then certain functions are, by nature of the equipment, associated with that equipment. Such given functions should be examined further by the analyst because they may have behavioral implications unrecognized by the designers who specified the equipment.

If the system being developed is quite novel, one can assume a tabula rasa with regard to function identification; but this is almost never the case. In many systems the top level functions to be performed are immediately obvious from the nature of the system (remember takeoff and landing?) or they stem from a predecessor system of which the one under development is merely an advanced version, meaning that functions are carried over from the old to the new system. In reality, then, the effort the behavioral specialist expends on function identification is really analysis of functional implications (what does it mean that the system has such and such functions?).

Functional Performance Criteria

Functional performance criteria are the yardsticks against which the system or function will demonstrate its ability to meet performance requirements. These criteria may range from gross to detailed; it is again the analyst's judgment that determines the level of detail.

The purpose of establishing functional performance criteria is to enable the analyst to have a standard against which to predict or measure the accomplishment of performance requirements. This step also provides the basis for preparing a *functional flow diagram* (FFD) for the next stage of analysis.

Functional performance criteria are stated in terms of those test results that must be satisfied to indicate the performance will be met. For example, the function "activate gyro" is a response to the requirement to warm up and stabilize the circuit. At this point no decision has been made about how the warm-up will be implemented. Several alternatives might be developed to indicate that warm-up is complete: (1) Individually measure each of several points with a suitable instrument; (2) Meter each of the circuits through a bank of meters; (3) Use individual lamps to indicate that each point has been warmed; (4) Indicate by single panel lamp when all points are at proper voltage; and (5) Automatically program next function when system senses that it is properly warmed up.

The selection of one of the five methods will be performed during the FA phase. At this stage the performance criteria are simply the end result of the warm-up process, for example: 1. 28V D.C. Measured at points *N-1*, *N-3*, *N-6*, *N-9*; 2. 400 cycles A. C. Measured at points *a*, *b*, *x*, *y*, *z*. Until the FA process has been completed the method by means of which the performance criteria will be implemented should not be established. At this point any such decision limits the degrees of freedom of decisions that are properly made further along in development.

The fact that in any reasonably sized system there is a fairly complex hierarchy of functional relationships suggests that these relationships can be more readily understood if they are depicted graphically. The usual way of displaying these interrelationships is through a *functional flow diagram*.

Functional Flow Diagram

A FFD is a chart which displays the sequence and arrangement of functions—hence flow of activities—within the system. Some FFDs are organized on a time basis, others are not. The FFD enables the analyst to examine the sequence, timing, and time relationships of system functions to see how much flexibility he has in organizing functions to increase their use and efficiency. Those functions which must be accomplished in a certain sequence or at a particular time have different behavioral effects from those that vary in performance time or sequence.

The FFD's major value lies in preparing the ground work for the allocation of functions. More detailed information about it will be presented in Chapter 3.

FUNCTION ALLOCATION

The procedures involved in *function allocation* (FA) include:

1. *Determining* those functions that have already been allocated (i.e., the means by which the function will be performed has been determined). For those

functions that remain unallocated, determining those that must be performed primarily by equipment because of the nature of the function. Less attention need be paid to equipment functions, although they should not be completely ignored. Emphasizing those functions that appear likely to be performed either manually or by some combination of personnel and equipment.

2. *Describing*, preferably in written form and using function flow diagrams, the various ways (design alternatives) in which each unallocated function can be implemented.

3. *Establishing* and weighing criteria by which each alternative can be compared with the others.

4. *Comparing* the alternative configurations.

5. *Selecting* the most cost-effective design alternative to implement.

Several points should be noted about the preceding five steps in this procedure. Only in the very rare contingency that the behavior analyst has sole responsibility for the design of the system will these procedures be performed by the analyst alone. The far more common situation is one in which the engineer has primary responsibility for design; the analyst carries out FA by encouraging the designer to make his allocations systematically, or the analyst will make his own allocations and present them to the designer as suggestions; or (most commonly) he will review the designer's allocations from the standpoint of their behavioral suitability and make suggestions based on his reviews.

The 5-step procedure described in this section is a very formal one, involving quantitative comparisons. Less sophisticated methods are more common. For example, the analyst can resort to the so-called Fitts list (Fitts et al., 1951) which qualitatively describes the relative advantages of men and machines, for example, man excels in the ability to exercise judgment where events cannot be completely defined; machines excel in performing complex and rapid computations with high accuracy. Such qualitative comparisons provide only general guidelines; they mean very little even when related specifically to a proposed design alternative.

The method described in this section is the way in which FA should be performed. More often however FA is performed by designers quite informally and qualitatively, although the essence of the method is maintained. Designers do examine and compare alternative configurations but they often do so mentally rather than by writing out descriptions of the alternatives. They undoubtedly use certain criteria to compare their alternatives, but these criteria may be covert, poorly articulated and in any case rarely involve behavioral considerations.

If the system is an advanced model of a previous one, certain functions will have already been allocated; for these no further allocation is required although the behavioral implications of these functions should be examined. Other functions, such as the transmission of a sonar signal by transducer, can obviously be performed only by equipment and need not divert the analyst's attention further. It is only when there is genuine uncertainty as to how a function is to be performed that FA is necessary.

FA is performed iteratively at more and more molecular system/equipment levels; it is not a one-shot affair and the behavior analyst should be alert to opportunities to utilize the procedure. Moreover, even if a function has already been allocated, it is worthwhile examining the premises upon which the allocation has been made, because the allocation may not have been optimal and should therefore be reconsidered (but not if equipment has been built; under these circumstances reexamination of the design alternative is almost always useless).

Of greatest importance, the allocation, no matter how it has been decided, may have behavioral implications which should be examined. Although the analyst may not have had a role in selecting a design alternative, he has always the responsibility of reviewing and commenting on that selection. Assuming that the operator/technician has a part to play in this alternative, for example, controlling it, monitoring it, etc., will he be able to perform his role? Will the manner in which the function is to be performed cause excessive demands upon personnel or lead to an unacceptable error probability? Questions such as these will be asked in greater detail at the task analysis stage but they should be asked also during FA, because if something is badly wrong with the design alternative selected, it is easier to correct it at this stage than during task analysis.

Procedural Steps

The first step in the allocation process is to consider without bias all possible ways in implementing the function. This is the most creative aspect of design analysis; the process cannot be described in step-by-step fashion. There are almost always more than one or two ways of performing a function. For example, there are at least two different ways of activating the Automated Interviewer described previously. In one, which is completely automatic, a pressure-sensitive switch underneath the cushion of the chair in which the applicant sits is activated when he sits. This switch activation sends a signal to the Interviewer which initiates the visual/aural program. In the other alternative a placard on the Interviewer is read by the applicant when he sits which instructs him to press the switch on either arm of his chair, which sends a signal to the Interviewer. The more manual design mode requires the applicant to read the placard and press the switch button, a perfectly feasible alternative for most applicants except those who cannot see or read the placard or have difficulty exerting pressure on the switch.

Engineers rarely conceptualize all possible alternatives—they concentrate on a relatively few, usually those they have found successful in the past (Meister, 1971). The role of the behavioral specialist at this point may be to stimulate the designer by suggesting alternatives that involve an operator and by asking the designer why the latter's list of alternatives does not consider manual modes (if it does not).

The second step is to write in narrative form a description of each design alternative as shown in Table 2.3. This permits the analyst to make a qualitative first-cut comparison of the alternatives in what has been termed a "trade" (for tradeoff) study. Drawing a FFD of the functions in each alternative may be useful also. In complex systems the trade study may also be quantitative, making use of models and simulations.

Issues to be addressed in comparing design alternatives include: (1) How well

TABLE 2.3. Analysis of Alternative Man–Machine Configurations

Alternative 1 (Operator primarily)	Alternative 2 (Man–machine mix)	Alternative 3 (Machine primarily)
Sonarman detects target signal on scope, examines brightness, shape, recurrence, movement, etc., and reports "probable submarine" or "non-submarine target."	Sonarman detects target signal on scope. Associated computer also detects signal, records it, and searches library of standard signals. Computer displays to sonarman original signal and comparison signal on sonar gear, together with the probability of its being a submarine. Sonarman decides on basis of his own analysis and computer information whether target signal is submarine or non-submarine and reports accordingly.	When a signal having a strength above a specified threshold is received by the sonar array, a computer associated with the detection apparatus automatically records the signal, analyzes its strength, brightness, recurrence, etc. according to preprogrammed algorithms, compares it with a library of standard sonar signals, and displays an indicator reading "probable submarine."
Operator Functions	Operator Functions	Operator Functions
1. Detection of signal 2. Analysis of signal 3. Decision-making 4. Reporting of decision	1. Detection of signal 2. Analysis of signal 3. Decision-making 4. Reporting of decision	1. Take action on receipt of "probable submarine" signal.
Machine Functions	Machine Functions	Machine Functions
1. Display of signal	1. Detection of signal 2. Recording of signal 3. Searching of comparison signals 4. Analysis of signal 5. Display of information	1. Detection of signal 2. Analysis of signal 3. Decision-making 4. Display of conclusion
Advantages/Disadvantages	Advantages/Disadvantages	Advantages/Disadvantages
1. No machine backup for operator inadequacies	1. Operator/machine each back each other up.	1. No operator backup for machine inadequacies

Source. Meister, D. *Human Factors: Theory and Practice*. New York: Wiley, 1971.

will the operator perform in each alternative? Will he be able to satisfy system requirements? On what evidence is this judgment based? (2) Also topical is a comparison of the anticipated operator effectiveness (in terms of performance, reliability, fatigue, etc.) in each alternative against anticipated machine effectiveness. (3) What special provisions/facilities (e.g., special displays, increased working area, etc.) would one have to have for personnel in each alternative? Indicate impact on selection, training, number of personnel required, etc. (4) What potential problems might the operator encounter in each alternative? (5) What special advantages or disadvantages will the operator add in each alternative?

In examining the design alternatives the analyst must first determine whether any humans involved in an alternative can do the job. Certain physical limitations that may prevent the operator from performing the function cannot be ignored. These limitations include: strength (one could not expect the human to lift 500 pounds unaided), response speed (one cannot respond in less than 200–400 milliseconds), and aggregation (he cannot "handle" more than some maximum number of targets).

To verify that personnel can perform their functions involves two possible methods.

If the system requirements examined previously required personnel to perform at some specified level, the analyst should have determined whether that requirement was within the operator's capability. Unfortunately very few requirements documents are written to suggest the specific demands that will be placed upon personnel.

The other much more common verification method is to determine by examining the suggested design alternatives what actions will be required of the operator. One can then ask whether these actions are within the operator's performance repertoire. Data are available concerning the extreme upper limits of the operator's physical capability and speed of response. For cognitive and perceptual behaviors much less information is available, but sufficient qualitative or intuitive doubt of a requirement will probably lead to rejection of the alternative.

Where a design alternative imposes requirements on the personnel that obviously exceed their physical, cognitive or perceptual limitations, the alternative is not feasible and must be discarded or revised. Engineers are unlikely to make such gross design errors. It is much more likely that within some intermediate range of behavior one design alternative or the other creates a greater propensity to error or stress. It is this increased error or stress probability that the behavioral analyst can point out to the designer as his contribution to FA. Unfortunately as will be seen in Chapter Five our techniques for predicting error quantitatively are extremely crude.

Until now the analyst has merely been ensuring that the operator functions involved in the various alternatives have been described and that they can be performed satisfactorily. If the operator functions required by the various alternatives are all capable of being performed by personnel, it is then necessary to select the most effective alternative by comparing the alternatives in terms of appropriate *system criteria*. Even though the operator may be able to perform at least minimally in each design alternative, he can probably perform most effectively in only one.

At this point it is necessary to apply system criteria (e.g., cost-effectiveness) because the configuration involves equipment as well as personnel. Such a comparison can only be performed in conjunction with the designer or system engineer because it is his responsibility to establish or accept system criteria.

To apply system criteria requires whoever performs this comparison to determine the weight or importance each criterion should have. This is the third step. Cost may be a crucial factor for one system development, reliability for another. In general, the significant potential criteria to be applied in evaluating alternatives are cost, per-

TABLE 2.4. Assignment of Weights to Functional Design Criteria

Criteria	Choice Tally	Total	Weighting Coefficient
1. Performance requirements	1 1 1 1 1 1 1	7	.25
2. Cost	0 1 1 1 1 0 1	5	.178
3. Reliability	0 0 1 1 1 0 1	4	.143
4. Maintainability	0 0 0 1 0 0 1	2	.0715
5. Producibility	0 0 0 0 0 0 0	0	.0
6. Safety	0 0 0 1 1 0 0	2	.0
7. Number of personnel required	0 1 1 1 1 1 1	6	.214
8. Power requirements	0 0 0 0 1 1 0	2	.0715
		28	.9995

Source. Meister, D. *Human Factors: Theory and Practice*. New York: Wiley, 1971.

formance output, reliability, maintainability, producibility or ease of fabrication, the number of personnel required by a system, etc. In some cases one criterion—cost, for example—may be the overriding factor in dictating a design decision; in others, several criteria may each have some influence on that decision. The specialist will be particularly concerned about ensuring that behavioral requirements are part of those criteria and that the weighting given behavioral requrements is appropriate.

The determination of the weight or value each criterion should have for a particular system is an entirely subjective judgment because it is a matter of *value*. The following procedure for assigning quantitative weights to these criteria, taken from Hagen (1967), and illustrated in Table 2.4, merely formalizes and quantizes these value judgments. It forces the specialist—but more importantly the design engineer—to make his decision biases visible. In actual development few designers quantize their judgments, which makes these easy prey to irrational persuasions. However, when required to do so, design engineers can make formal criterion judgments.

Weights are assigned on the basis of paired comparisons. This means comparing each potential criterion with every other and assigning a value of 1 to whichever is judged to be the more important of any two criteria considered; 0 is assigned to the less important of the two criteria. For example, if performance requirements are more important than cost, it receives a value of 1; cost, 0. The performance requirements criterion is then compared with each of the remaining criteria and values assigned as above. The next criterion, cost, is compared with the remaining criteria, and this process is continued until all criteria have been compared with each other.

The 1's for each criterion are then summed across Table 2.4 and divided by the total number of 1's assigned (28). This gives the specialist a weighting coefficient for each criterion. The weighting coefficient is a relative value (indicating importance of one criterion relative to all others considered), not an absolute value. The sum of the weighting coefficients should approximate 1.00.

TABLE 2.5. Comparison of Alternative Configurations

Alternative Configurations	Criteria	Choice Tally			Total 1's	Choice Coefficient
A	Performance requirements	0	0		0	0
B		1		0	2	.67
C			1	0	1	.33
A		1	1		2	.67
B	Cost	0		1	1	.33
C			0	0	0	0
A		0	0		0	0
B	Reliability	1		0	1	.33
C			1	1	2	.67
A		1	1		2	.67
B	Maintainability	0		0	0	0
C			0	1	1	.33
A		1	0		1	.33
B	Producibility	0		0	0	0
C			1	1	2	.67
A		1	1		2	.67
B	Safety	0		0	0	0
C			0	1	1	.33
A	Number of personnel	0	0		0	0
B	required	1		0	1	.33
C			1	1	2	.67
A		1	1		2	.67
B	Power requirements	0		0	0	0
C			0	1	1	.33

Source. Meister, D. *Human Factors: Theory and Practice*. New York: Wiley, 1971.

It is now possible to compare each design alternative with every other on the basis of each criterion, giving the favored alternative a value of 1 and the less favored a value of 0. The procedure, which is the fourth step and is illustrated in Table 2.5, is essentially the same as that employed in weighting criteria. Alternatives A, B, and C are each compared with each other on the basis of the performance requirements—criterion first, then cost, reliability, and so forth. For example, when A is compared with B on the basis of functional performance, B is favored and given a value of 1 (see choice tally column); when A is compared with C, C is favored and given a value of 1. Since there are three alternatives, the total number of 1's in each tally row is divided by three. The resultant choice coefficient for each alternative can be either .00 (no 1 choices), .33 (one choice out of three), or .67 (two choices out of three).

The final step is to construct a matrix with the alternatives as columns and the criteria as rows (Table 2.6). The values in the columns under the alternatives represent the multiplication of the criterion weighting coefficients (Table 2.4) times the

TABLE 2.6. Matrix for Selecting Alternative Configurations

Criteria	Alternatives		
	A	B	C
1. Performance requirements × 0.25	0.0	0.168	0.0825
2. Cost × 0.178	0.119	0.0588	0.0
3. Reliability × 0.143	0.0	0.0472	0.0958
4. Maintainability × 0.0715	0.048	0.0	0.0836
5. Producibility × 0.0	0.0	0.0	0.0
6. Safety × 0.0715	0.048	0.0	0.0236
7. Number of personnel required × 0.214	0.0	0.0707	0.1430
8. Power requirement × 0.0715	0.048	0.0	0.0236
	0.263	0.3447	0.3921
	3rd Choice	2nd Choice	1st Choice

Source. Meister, D. *Human Factors: Theory and Practice*. New York: Wiley, 1971.

choice coefficients derived in Table 2.5. Alternative A, for example, had a choice coefficient of .00 (see Table 2.5); this, when multiplied by the weighting coefficient for performance requirements (.25) equals zero (0). The same multiplicative process is performed for every other alternative times the criterion weight. For example, alternative B = .67 (the choice coefficient for performance requirements) × .25 (criterion weight) = 0.168. The values achieved by each alternative when evaluated by all the criteria are summed. The first choice for design implementation is the alternative with the largest value, the second choice is the one with the next largest value, etc.

The application of such a formal FA procedure encounters a number of difficulties:

1. The engineer does not often construct and systematically compare alternative design configurations but settles on the preferred configuration without adequately considering other potential candidates.

2. The engineer may decide on the preferred configuration so rapidly that it is a *fait accompli* before the behavior specialist has a chance to analyze that configuration.

3. The essence of FA from a behavioral standpoint is the comparison of operator capability with a requirement for operator performance. Except in systems in which human functions are especially critical, most system specifications do not include quantitative operator performance requirements.

4. Even if an operator performance requirement can be inferred, the specialist may have some difficulty in securing from the behavioral literature appropriate operator performance data (expected average performance, plus standard deviations) to compare with the requirement. Much of this literature is quite general. One might

do what many behavior specialists refer to as a "quick and dirty" experiment to secure the data, but this is rarely possible.

Notwithstanding these difficulties, at a minimum the specialist can and should analyze, from a behavioral standpoint, whatever design configurations are under consideration or even those that have already been selected. The output of the FA process is a selected design configuration which is the basis for the next step of task description/identification.

TASK DESCRIPTION/IDENTIFICATION

Task description/identification (TD/I) includes the following steps:

1. To examine each selected design alternative.
2. To list in sequence all the actions that must be performed to accomplish that function for each function found in the design alternative.
3. To categorize actions in terms of whether they are operator or maintainer activities and by the hardware/software subsystem to which they belong.
4. To describe each action in terms of a behavioral verb that describes the action (e.g., to monitor, to turn on); the equipment acted upon (e.g., switch, motor, display); the consequence of the action (e.g., voltage display is stabilized); the stimulus that initiates the action (e.g., pilot's command); the feedback information resulting from task performance (e.g., heading 320°); and the criterion of task accomplishment.
5. To break tasks down into subordinate tasks by specifying the inputs and outputs from each task (as necessary; this step is performed only to the level of detail the analyst desires).

TD/I has several purposes. First, it is necessary to describe the task before one analyzes it. Second, the listing of tasks permits the specialist to organize and group them on the basis of criteria such as purpose or function, a common equipment and location, performance by the same operator, etc. This is a necessary first step in the organization of tasks into groupings of jobs and positions. Third, the TD can suggest required control and display hardware. And fourth, TD is a prerequisite for the determination of required numbers of personnel and the skills and knowledges they must have.

The identification of a task poses few problems as soon as one knows which system functions have been definitely assigned to the operator and with what equipment he performs the function. Task identification (TI) is basically quite logical. That very logic asks, "Given that the operator function must be performed, what are the things—the tasks—the person must do to implement the function?" No special behavioral training is required for this determination although obviously experience in performing the determination helps the process considerably. On the other hand, the behavioral specialist may have difficulty defining tasks if he is unfamiliar with the equipment configuration.

The specialist may encounter difficulty in deciding on the particular level of detail a task should describe. He must decide whether he wants to describe the action (task) at the level of the individual control or display manipulation with which that action is involved (e.g., reads meter) or at a somewhat more molar level (e.g., determines that temperature is within acceptable range). This is not merely a matter of semantics. In the first case the task has been reduced to its behavioral fundamentals. In the second case the task description subsumes, but does not make explicit, a number of more molecular subtasks inherent in the performance of the task, and it will probably be necessary eventually to break the task down into those subtasks. The particular level of task description (TD) is a matter of expert judgment; precise rules cannot be specified. However, recommendations for appropriate hardware and software to implement the man–machine interface demand detail. The consequences of describing the task at a more abstract level is that the analyst may overlook some hardware or software needed to implement the task and/or some behavioral implications of performing the task.

If the system being described is an advanced model of an already existent one, it is likely that the new system's tasks will closely resemble those of the predecessor system. The specialist would logically concentrate on any new tasks required (as a consequence of developing or purchasing new equipment) or significant modifications of previous ones.

There is no consensus about the amount of input data needed to develop TDs. Some researchers want more information than do others. Because TD is fundamentally a taxonomic method, based on categories of information considered important, TD/I formats are essentially only differences in taxonomy. A great deal has been written about the need for a generally accepted task taxonomy (Fleishman, 1982) and a great deal of effort has gone into the development of such a taxonomy (see later section). Controversies among specialists usually reduce to a matter of the level of detail to be provided in the task description. If one describes a task in highly molecular terms, such as what discriminates the difference between two radar blips, the resultant task descriptions will be different than if one uses a more molar term for the same task—scope monitoring, for example. Task description/identification methodology is, as was pointed out previously, one of partitioning the unitary task into at least three behavioral elements: stimulus for initiating the task (S), internal processes (O), and response (R), together with the equipment acted upon. The absence of a standard TD/I format does not represent disagreement about this methodology, but only about how many behavioral elements are important.

As a general rule the more TD information the better, but this depends on the availability of that information. The purpose for which the TD is created should be considered; there is no point in developing information unless it will be used. If the TD is to be used to examine alternative equipment configurations, maximum detail would be desirable, although in practice this use is infrequent.

The specialist should not confuse task description with task analysis. Some of the information desired, for example, probability of error in performing the task, may require complex analysis and should be postponed until the TA is initiated. TDs are therefore neither good or bad; the adequacy of a TD depends on the purpose for which it is being developed. If we wish to compare tasks performed over a variety of systems, then a molar descriptive level is preferable because otherwise we become confused by the system–peculiar details of each task. On the other hand, if we wish to explore task implications for system design, then the more detail the better.

From a pragmatic system development standpoint, controversies over which word to use to describe a task are largely irrelevant as long as the categories applied are reasonably descriptive of system operations. The important thing is not so much the word or phrase describing a task as the implications drawn from them.

TASK ANALYSIS

It is necessary to distinguish between TD/I, the output of which is a listing of tasks and their description, and task analysis (TA) which requires that some deduction be made from the TD. The dividing line between the two is unclear. Some authors, such as Baker et al. (1979) ignore task description as a distinct step and go directly to TA. This is incorrect. TD/I is necessary as a preliminary step to TA; and TA represents conclusions derived from the TD.

TA activities determine which tasks shall be analyzed. In this respect, as well as in others, TA differs from TD/I. All tasks are identified and described, at least listed. Because TA is a complex and time consuming process not all tasks are analyzed. Those tasks that have already been analyzed, are relatively simple and already well learned, or are not critical to system operations need not be analyzed. Factors important for selection of tasks in TA are, system complexity, task characteristics (criticality, difficulty, frequency, proficiency required), and the amount of money and time available to perform the TA.

Task Analysis analyzes the individual tasks in terms of:

1. *Design questions.* What tasks are to be performed? How critical is each task? In what sequence will tasks be performed? What information is required by the task performer? What control activations are required? What performance requirements are important? Is coordination with other tasks or personnel required? Are perceptual, cognitive, psychomotor or physical demands imposed by the task excessive? What errors are possible and how likely are they?

2. *Manning questions.* How many people are needed to perform a task or job? What skill level is required to perform the task/job?

3. *Training questions.* On what behavioral dimensions are the tasks based? How difficult or complex is the task or job? What information does the operator need to perform his task or job? What performance criteria indicate that the task has been correctly performed? What are the consequences if the task or job is not performed or performed incorrectly? How is the task related to other tasks? To the total job? How frequently is the task or job performed?

4. *Test and Evaluation questions.* What are the performance criteria for the task or job?

Task analysis develops operational sequence-type diagrams as considered necessary or desirable to support the questions presented above. (See Chapter Three for operational sequence diagram description.) The results of the TA can be applied to the determination of work station and job design, manning requirements, training, and test and evaluation requirements.

TA is an essential part of the behavioral analysis of systems during development. MIL-H-46855B (Department of Defense, 1979) requires TA for all systems developed for the Defense Department. There are four major reasons for performing a TA: To assist in (1) The design of the system, meaning the man–machine interface, the total job, construction of procedures, job aids, etc. (2) The manning of the system, meaning the development of the selection criteria and determination of the number and type of personnel needed. (3) The development of an instructional system, meaning the development of the curriculum, selection of critical tasks to be trained, etc. (4) The evaluation of the completed system, by establishing performance criteria against which system personnel performance can be measured.

TA as we know it today was first developed by Miller in 1953 (Miller, 1953), although the notion of TA can be found even earlier in the work of Taylor (Taylor, 1911) and of Gilbreth (Gilbreth, 1911). This chapter endeavors to summarize the significant TA formats, although it is impossible in a single chapter to present all those who have written on the subject and advocated minor variations of the basic methodology (for these, see White, 1971; Vallerie, 1978; and Fleishman and Quaintance, 1984).

Underlying the TA methodology, as it does TD/I, is the assumption that one can partition a unitary behavioral activity into its three constituent elements. What is distinctive about TA is the assignment of certain meanings (e.g., implications for design, manning, training) to those elements. Procedures for developing the deductions resulting from analysis of the information contained in the task description are indicated somewhat sketchily in reports describing TA methodology but for the most part are left to the analyst's "expertise."

Data for the TA can be secured from many sources: (1) *The task description* should be the sole source of input data but since many analysts do not differentiate between the task description and the TA process the task description is often the end product of the TA. (2) *System documentation* includes any previous task analyses of a predecessor system, planning documents, test reports and specifications, procedural documents, operator manuals, and so forth. (3) *Interviews* with predecessor system personnel or other subject matter experts are by far the most common method of securing TA information. (4) *Observation* of predecessor or related system operations is yet another means.

In general the guidelines for performing the TA are not explicit. It is easier, for example, to ask a *subject matter expert* (SME) whether a particular task is difficult or complex then to derive this conclusion from a written description of the task. It is assumed that the SME is a valid judge of the dimensions of that task. The author knows no empirical studies in which this assumption has been tested.

Before beginning his TA, there are certain questions the analyst needs to answer: (1) What is the purpose for which he is performing the TA? (2) What should be the scope of the TA, that is, does it encompass all tasks or only certain ones? All subsystems or only certain ones? (3) What level of detail should his TA include, down to the cues used to initiate the task? How many information categories? (4) What questions does the analyst wish the TA to answer? (5) How are these questions to be answered? This last question is the essence of the analytic methodology.

A review of the TA literature suggests that TA has been applied more for instructional system design than for any other purposes. TA is a necessary part of system design in terms of defining the tasks to be performed and their implications. However it plays little or no role in the selection of design alternatives (FA, trade studies) because much of the information needed for the TA is not available at very early design stages. TA does help in staffing determination and can play a significant role in test and evaluation if sufficiently precise quantitative information can be secured. It can indicate incompatabilities which may not be identifiable at less detailed levels of analysis.

Determination of TA scope is likely to be a heuristic matter. Project managers usually wish to apply a time demanding methodology like TA only to critical tasks, whose failure might make serious system difficulties, to those tasks of special importance and those most frequently performed. There is nothing inherent in the TA methodology that specifies the tasks to which it is applied.

Similarly the determination of how far down to go in the vertical hierarchy of tasks (molar tasks→detailed tasks→subtasks→cues) is a matter of the specialist's deciding how profitable it is to continue his analysis beyond a certain point. Most task analysts break down to the detailed task level but go no further if the subtasks are relatively simple and already well learned behaviors. If the tasks being examined are very critical, the analyst may include subtasks as well. Like the question of scope, the answer to the question of vertical level is not inherent in TA methodology.

The number of analytic categories is a function in part of how much one needs to know about the task. As we shall see later in reviewing TA variations, certain items of information are always required, but others are optional. Information about the latter should be gathered only if the analyst can make practical use of it.

Each of the purposes for which TA is performed has implicit in it a number of questions to be answered. These, which were listed at the start of this section, are the heart of the analytic methodology. The analytic process utilized to answer specific questions can only be suggested because the instruction manuals offer few rules. The following assumes that the answers can be supplied largely through task descriptive information; however, when TD information is not sufficient, the analyst may refer to SMEs or predecessor system personnel.

Job Design Questions

1. *What tasks are to be performed?* The answer to this question indicates the type of task being performed (e.g., operator, maintenance, communication) and describes how it should be performed. If the task description is sufficiently de-

tailed—down to the subtask level, for example—it can serve almost as a step-by-step procedure. Task descriptions are weak in their implication of maintenance requirements unless these deal with preventive maintenance which can be handled like any other operator task. Corrective maintenance—troubleshooting—is by its nature a response to an infrequently occurring, obscure and highly contingent event.

2. *How critical is this task?* The answer to this question is important to training, test, and evaluation. To answer this, one must examine the system consequences if the task is not performed or if it is performed incorrectly or inadequately (e.g., danger of malfunction, safety hazard). Consequence information can generally be secured from system engineers.

3. *In what sequence will tasks be performed?* The answer to this question aids development of procedures. Some tasks are ordered on the basis of logical dependency, for instance, one must start an automobile engine before starting to drive. If a logical sequence is not evident, functions can be arranged sequentially on the basis of their derivation from inputs to and outputs from higher order functions (see functional flow diagrams). Tasks are derived from functions. Referring the task to its higher order function will help suggest its sequence. However, this may not help too much where several tasks belonging to the same function must be arranged sequentially. In this case examination of the initiating cue or stimulus condition for task initiation will suggest the order in which the tasks should be performed.

4. *What information is required by the task performer?* The answer to this question aids in design of displays and in a larger sense in the design of the total task because information is often the single most important organizing principle in task design. The answer to this question may be indicated by the initiating stimulus for the task. To initiate a task, the stimulus must contain some information to which the operator responds by performing the task. The information required can therefore often be inferred from the initiating stimulus. For example, if the initiating stimulus is the condition "steam pressure too high," as a result of which the operator must "begin shutoff procedure," it is obvious that the operator must know what the steam pressure is and that requires either a meter, a warning light or an alarm. The output of the task, or the indication that the task has been completed, may also suggest displays for feedback information.

5. *What control activations are required?* The answer to this question suggests the need for a control but will not indicate the type of control (for this, see human factors engineering criteria in MIL-STD 1472C, Department of Defense, 1981). The information is implicit in the task description.

6. *What performance requirements are important?* These may be either accuracy or time or quality of performance or all three. The output of the task or the conditions under which the task must be performed may suggest performance criteria. These may also be reflected in displayed information.

7. *Is coordination with other tasks or personnel required?* The answer to this question will suggest communication requirements and aid workplace design. The task itself may be one of communicating information. The initiating stimulus for the task may also imply coordination.

8. *Are perceptual, cognitive, psychomotor or physical demands imposed by the task excessive?* The answer to this question serves as a minimum criterion for accepting or rejecting the task configuration as adequate on behavioral grounds. Demands may be found in the following areas: strength; intelligence; perceptual/discriminative acuity; response speed; required accuracy; and psychomotor capability. The questions noted in Table 2.7 should be asked.

Unfortunately there are few books or reports to which one can refer the reader for information about threshold values for these demands. Threshold values for physiologic variables are available, as in Poulton, 1970, but usually not for psychologic variables. The analyst must then use his own judgment or he may refer that judgment to a SME.

9. *What errors are possible and how likely are they?* This question can be answered by imagining all the things that could go wrong in performing the task. The number of possible errors for the individual task is not large. Assigning an error likelihood to each error is very difficult because of the absence of an error data base (see Chapter Five for further discussion of this point); however, the analyst may ask a SME and in any event the error probability need not be extremely precise because the specialist is attempting only to pick out the most likely possibilities. Knowing potential errors may suggest ways to guard against them by task or equipment modification or by training.

Manning Questions

The answer to the following two questions helps determine manning of the system.

1. *How many people are needed to perform a task or job?* By definition a task is an activity to be performed by one person. However, one personnel position, such as a radar operator, may be required to perform several tasks. When these tasks are plotted along a time dimension (see discussion of time line analysis in Chapter Three), more than one task may have to be performed concurrently, in which case more than one person may be required at that position.

2. *What skill level is required to perform the task/job?* This question has two parts. First, what skills underlie the performance of the task? The skill requirement must be defined in terms of a capability underlying task operations, not in terms of the operations themselves. For a skill analysis technique that may prove useful, see Chapter Three. And second, how much of each such skill or capability is needed?

Judgments of the amount of skill level required are based on an evaluation of the complexity of the task or job in terms of the following indices. More skill is required when: (a) Patterns of events or stimuli (rather than single stimuli) must be recognized or compared. Stimuli, whether single or multiple, have ambiguous meaning; cues to respond, as in many detection tasks, are weak. (b) The operator must respond after first integrating a number of stimuli occurring either concurrently or sequentially. (c) Very precise hand/eye coordination (as in tracking) is required. (d) The task involves problem solving of a troubleshooting nature or other

TABLE 2.7. Questions to Be Asked in Performing Design Task Analysis

1. Functions/Tasks
   A. Are functions/tasks to be performed within operator capability? Consider requirements in the following functions: (1) sensory/perceptual, (2) motor, (3) decision-making, (4) communication.
   B. Do task characteristics impose excessive demands on the operator?
      1. task duration (possible fatigue effects?)
      2. frequency of task performance (possible fatigue effects?)
      3. information feedback (insufficient operator guidance?)
      4. accuracy (too demanding?)
      5. error probability (supportable?)
      6. error criticality (effect on task performance?)
      7. concurrent multitask requirements (effect of one task on another?)
2. Environment
   A. Events requiring operator response
      1. speed of occurrence (too fast?)
      2. number (too many?)
      3. persistence (too short-lived?)
      4. movement (excessive?)
      5. intensity (too weak to perceive?)
      6. patterning (unpredictable?)
   B. Physical effects
      1. temperature, humidity, noise, vibration (excessive?)
      2. lighting (substandard or special effects?)
      3. safety (problems?)
   C. Mission conditions
      1. potential emergencies (can operator recognize and overcome rapidly?)
      2. mission response characteristics
         (a) accuracy requirements (excessive?)
         (b) speed requirements (excessive?)
      3. event criticality (effect on error probability?)
3. Equipment
   A. Display information requirements
      1. too much to assimilate?
      2. difficult to perceive/discriminate/track?
      3. require excessively fast operator response?
      4. too much memory required?
   B. Control requirements
      1. excessively fine manipulations required?
      2. too much force required?
      3. must be responded to too rapidly?
      4. too many to perform in sequence?

Source. Meister, D. *Human Factors: Theory and Practice*. New York: Wiley, 1971.

significant cognitive activity as in calculating, analyzing or decision making. (e) A high degree of visual and/or auditory acuity is demanded by the task. (f) Responses must be made rapidly in a precise order. (g) Accuracy requirements are high. (h) The steps in the task/job are very lengthy. (i) Short term and long term memory requirements are high. (j) Task criticality is high.

Any one of these task dimensions should be sufficient to require a higher than ordinary skill level (assuming that one can define "ordinary"). Two or more of these dimensions demand a very high degree of skill indeed. Within the context of a specific system and specific tasks, SMEs can be used to rate the degree of skill required, for example, an apprentice can do so much, someone with two years of experience can do this much more, etc. (See McCallum and Dick, 1982, for an example).

Training Questions

1. *On what behavioral dimensions are the tasks based?* The answer to this question has implications for the type of training to be provided and/or training methods used. For example, perceptual tasks are not trained in the same way as are psychomotor tasks (see Chapter Six for guidelines). The information desired must be inferred from the task description, for example, if the task requires one operator to communicate with another, then communication is involved; if a decision must be made, the task is obviously based on cognition. Where a task has several dimensions, it is a matter for the analyst's judgment to decide which is preeminent.

2. *How difficult/complex is the task or job?* The answer to this question will suggest the relative amount of training required. It is based on the same indices as those needed to estimate skill level, since skill level depends ultimately on task difficulty. See item (2) under Manning.

3. *What information does the operator need to perform the task/job?* The answer to this question has implications for the training content to be provided. The procedures described under item (4) of Job Design apply here also.

4. *What performance criteria indicate that the task has been correctly performed?* The answer to this question will suggest the standards to which the task should be trained. Each task description should contain an output which represents the system state the task was designed to accomplish. If the task is to operate ship boilers, then the output is fuel flow at a specified rate and/or a steam temperature to be achieved (1000° F). The analyst should ask how the operator will know that the task is being or has been correctly accomplished or what feedback information the operator must receive to tell him when to cease operating. This information should suggest criteria of correct performance, for example, the temperature of 1000° F. These criteria will also be used to determine in an actual performance situation (test/evaluation or operational) whether the task has been correctly performed.

5. *What are the consequences if the task or job is not performed or is performed incorrectly?* The answer to this question suggests the priority to be as-

signed the training of the task or job. This question is essentially the same as Job Design question (2) and the analysis suggested for that item would apply here also.

6. *How is the task related to other tasks, to the total job?* The answer to this question will suggest the part/whole task sequencing on which a training schedule is based. The procedure described under item (3) of Job Design can be applied here also.

7. *How frequently is the task or job performed?* The answer to this question has implications for training priorities. It can be determined by examining the mission description for the number of times the task is noted as being performed during the mission.

Test and Evaluation Questions:

1. *What are the performance criteria for the task or job?* The answer to this question is significant for the development of performance standards to be used to evaluate performance during system testing. See question (4) under Training.

TASK ANALYSIS VARIATIONS

One of the major problems in the application of TA is that there is no single generally accepted TA format. Variations of the original Miller (1953) methodology have been developed over the years, although few are significant.

One reason for the variations is a certain degree of dissatisfaction with the adequacy of the methodology (e.g., Miller, 1967). The judgments that the analyst wishes to make are extremely subtle and the information he has to base them on is often very tenuous.

Another reason for the lack of standardization is that as the purpose of the TA changes the need for categories of information also changes, to some extent. A TA performed to develop a training curriculum requires somewhat different information categories than one developed to aid in the evaluation of a completed system. There is an underlying assumption that the TA should be an all-purpose instrument, but in practice this is not possible.

The sheer ease with which changes can be made in TA format and taxonomy also encourages variation. Researchers tinker with TA formats to develop the "one best method," when in fact, as Montemerlo and Eddowes (1978) point out, no single best method is attainable.

The variations in TA involve formatting—the tabular or graphic arrangements of information; the particular information categories utilized (the taxonomy); and the underlying methodology by which the TA is performed. In terms of these distinctions the variation in TA methods is more apparent than real. The basic procedure of breaking a task down into its component parts has never been seriously challenged, but format and taxonomy have been varied many times.

Table 2.8 presents a listing of the categories that have been utilized in the most important (or at least well known) TA variations. Each variation could be examined

TABLE 2.8. TA Categories Applied by Various Authors

TA Category	Authors												
	1	2	3	4	5	6	7	8	9	10	11	12	13
Duty: general activity			X				X				X		
Task: action verb/purpose			X	X		X	X	X	X	X		X	
Subtask								X	X	X			
Function/Activity/Behavior			X			X		X			X	X	
Display: initiating cues			X						X	X			
Display: critical cues										X			
Control used			X							X	X		
Required decisions										X			
Characteristic errors			X			X		X		X			
Response required								X		X	X		X
Criterion, response adequacy										X			
Feedback: cues, delay, critical values			X					X		X	X		
Time to perform task			X			X	X	X			X		
Tools; equipment: job aids						X					X		
Skills: level, type, newness, critical			X					X			X		
Task location			X			X		X					
Work cycle segment						X							
Task: frequency, newness			X			X							
Error probability						X							
Task: error consequences			X			X							
Coordination/communication			X				X						
Task: difficulty, criticality		X		X					X				
Required accuracy		X											
Required speed		X											
Function complexity		X											
Adverse conditions, probability							X						
Percent attention required							X						

Table 2.8 (*Continued*)

TA Category	Authors												
	1	2	3	4	5	6	7	8	9	10	11	12	13
Sequence of activity				X									
Amount of training required				X									
Training functions					X								
Probability task will not be accomplished	X												
Initiating cues													X
Number of personnel required				X									

in detail, but the degree of overlap is so great that it would merely confuse the reader. Those interested in the details of these variations should consult the following authors: (1) Annett et al., 1971; (2) Armsby, 1962; (3) Baker et al., 1979; (4) Chenzoff and Folley, 1965; (5) Demaree, 1961; (6) Folley, 1960; (7) Folley, 1964a, b; (8) Kidd and Van Cott, 1972; (9) Meyer et al., 1975; (10) Miller, 1953; (11) Miller, 1956; (12) Miller, 1963; (13) Shriver, 1975. (The numbers in the preceding list of names refer to the author columns in Table 2.8.) A few variations are described in more detail subsequently.

The range of TA variations extends from the original Millerian formulation (1953) which is fairly molar to the extremely molecular formulations of Meyer et al., 1975 and Shriver, 1975. Miller (1953) supplied procedures for both procedural and continuous (tracking) tasks, but TA is rarely applied to the latter because of the difficulty of defining task boundaries. The original Millerian TA was primarily task descriptive, but later variations have emphasized the effort to extract inherent properties of the task. To categorize a task as being perceptual, cognitive or physical is simply a primitive way of attempting to find these underlying task dimensions. Having once discovered these dimensions, the role of TA is to translate these dimensions into principles that can be used for equipment design, development of training, etc. The task description has little value if such a translation cannot be made.

Armsby's Method

In Armsby's (1962) method called *task demands analysis* (TDA), tasks are defined in terms of the demands placed on the operator, a demand being defined as a condition that limits, allows, or prescribes certain operator activities.

In this method a task description is the statement of the demand dimensions applicable to that task. Armsby felt that standard task definitions could be developed on the basis of specific demand configurations; this would permit comparison of tasks on the basis of these configurations. However, the large number of variables makes this a very cumbersome and time consuming process. An alternative means of task comparison is based on four composite measures: *difficulty* (D), *accuracy required* (A), *speed required* (S), and *function complexity* (C).

The TDA method of task analysis might be valuable if it were supported by experimental or operational data. There is no evidence however that this approach has been further developed or applied since it was first described.

Folley's Method

Folley's method (1964a, b) deviates from Miller and Miller-type variations by reversing the sequence of first developing a task description and then analyzing the details of that description. He merges the two processes and thus minimizes the amount of detailed task information required. The details of a procedural task are not written out but merely identified as, for example, "procedure following" and by basing the TA on

1. The extent to which each of several defined kinds of "ongoing activities" are involved in the task;
2. The temporal, sequential, and causal relationships among these activities;
3. Characteristics of the detailed behaviors that constitute the activities;
4. Contingencies that might affect task performance;
5. Disruptive conditions under which the task might have to be performed.

In use, Folley's method of task analysis is implemented in four phases. The first step, the completion of a system block analysis, breaks the system into major phases or blocks arranged according to sequence and time (when possible). Each block is then analyzed and summarized in a task time chart to depict the relationships between tasks in terms of a time sequence and the proportion of total time occupied by the task.

Each task is then analyzed in greater detail to identify the activities within tasks and the relationships among these activities. The results are formatted in a functional task description sheet which partitions the gross task into categories of activity, for example, procedure following, monitoring, etc. These terms, which are relatively obvious in the abstract, may present difficulties when the percent of attention each requires must be determined, since Folley fails to provide guidelines for making this determination. The proportion of time occupied by each activity is also noted.

The functional task description requires some fairly complex judgments such as the frequency of individual malfunctions and the probability of occurrence of adverse conditions. These judgments are made by interviewing a single subject matter expert and the information supplied is simply his judgments based on past experience. Use of an SME is appropriate when there is considerable similarity between a predecessor task and the one being developed or—and this is where TA has had its greatest use—in the development of training requirements when training follows development of the primary equipment and knowledgeable personnel are available to answer pertinent questions.

The last stage of Folley's TA involves the completion of checklists (behavioral details description) describing task elements in terms of functional subcategories, for example, *procedure-following*, *monitoring*, etc. The equipment involved in each activity is noted, as well as relevant attributes, special knowledge requirements, and so forth, that define what is going on in the major heading.

Folley obviously takes into consideration some factors that Miller did not, such as the importance of timesharing between tasks, the relative proportion of each activity type, potential adverse conditions and error probability. One cannot say, however, that Folley's method is superior to that of Miller because there has been no empirical comparison of the two methods. In fact, almost no comparison of TA methods has been performed. However, if one relies as does Folley on SMEs to provide judgments of complex task dimensions, it is quite possible to build a complex TA structure, but whether that structure is valid and useful for its assigned purposes remains to be seen.

Demaree's Method

Demaree's (1961) form of TA is for use specifically in the planning and development of training equipment. His procedure involves the identification from task descriptions of "training functions" which are skills and knowledges inherent in the various types of tasks. The training functions are learning of knowledge, learning skills and task components, whole-task performances and learning integrated team performances, with task examples from which the training functions are inferred. Each of these functions is then categorized according to ten "training equipment effectiveness characteristics," further broken down into activities to be learned, each of which is scaled to define the tasks in terms of the type of training required.

Instructional System Development

There is no standard TA method but if there were one that could be called "officially approved" it would be the TA employed in *instructional system development* (ISD). ISD, which is described in detail in Chapter Six, is the formal methodology adopted by the Department of Defense to control the manner in which instructional programs for the military services are developed.

TA is an essential part of ISD (Block I.1, analyze jobs). Information gathered is divided into the following categories: (1) *Task*—job performance measure; (2) *job elements*—subtasks; (3) *conditions* of task performance (e.g., where, what tools); (4) *initiating cues*; (5) *standards* of task performance; and (6) *notes*: all other information.

These categories revert to the relatively simple descriptiveness of Miller's original method, although the categories are not identical. All the categories that represent inferences about skills and knowledges have been discarded (although they appear at a later stage of ISD development).

Input data are gathered by means of a jury of SMEs, group interviews, observations of job performance and questionnaire survey. Implicitly a predecessor system is assumed; if the system under development does not have a predecessor, one still has the SME to provide general guidance.

One suspects that some of the more elaborate and sophisticated techniques previously described were rejected because the TA technique in ISD must be utilized by those who are essentially lay persons, even though they have received some training in the TA methodology. Hence there is a premium on simplicity and the proceduralization of all TA steps.

Summary

Every TA must be tailored to a certain extent to the particular type of system one is analyzing. For example, if a task involves decision making, it is likely that categories dealing with cognition would be emphasized.

However, there is a nucleus of information that is required in every TA: (1) task title; (2) initiating stimulus; (3) equipment acted upon; (4) response to be made; (5) feedback; and (6) output characteristics, including performance criteria. One might call these the descriptive part of the TA; they correspond closely to what Miller (1953) originally developed.

Additional categories, which are optional, are more analytic since they require inferences from the preceding categories or inferences from information derived from other sources (e.g., SMEs). These include: task criticality; frequency of performance; accuracy, speed, information, coordination, communication requirements; aptitude, skills and knowledges required, decisions to be made; probability of task error; characteristic errors; task difficulty; and workload. Since the TA is a design tool, it can be anything the specialist finds useful for a specific project. Considerations of good or bad do not apply. There is little substantive difference among the various TA formats and the process is almost wholly subjective. Over the past 30 years there has been little progress in improving TA.

BEHAVIORAL TAXONOMIES

Since the heart of the analytic techniques (perhaps all the behavioral methods) is some scheme for categorizing activities, the problem of developing a standard human performance taxonomy has been avidly pursued by behavior researchers (see, for example, Companion and Corso, 1977).

Miller (1967) defines "a taxonomy [as] a means of classifying objects or phenomena in such a way that useful relationships among them are established. A taxonomy is therefore not a mere list of labels with semantic definition: it it also has inner syntactic structure."

A behavioral taxonomy is required:

1. To analyze or to partition an object, phenomenon or behavior into its constituent elements, as in TA.

2. To compare or relate two sets of objects, phenomena or activities in terms of their common underlying characteristics and behaviors.

3. To serve as the common basis for collecting, analyzing and reporting behavioral data.

Taxonomies have value not only in behavioral analysis but also in training, performance measurement and prediction (Berry, 1980) and the development of retrieval systems and data bases. Fleishman (1982) has pointed out a number of more general uses such as (1) finding literature relevant to one's research; (2) conducting and reporting research; (3) standardizing laboratory tasks; (4) generalizing research results to new tasks; (5) assisting in theory development; and (6) exposing gaps in our knowledge of human performance.

Other sciences, such as biology, have taxonomies; Theologus (1969) has published a review of the biological taxonomy and its application to the taxonomy of tasks. On a more pragmatic level, in the absence of a set of common task categories or dimensions, it is difficult if not impossible to compare tasks from one system to another or to extrapolate task data from a laboratory situation to an operations one. Design, training, and evaluation decisions can be hampered by the inability to apply historical data to new problems. A taxonomy is also the structure around which the human reliability databases described in Chapter Five are built. One must ask, then, why a consensus on a behavior taxonomy has not been developed. It is easier to ask this question than to answer it.

A basis of organization, a conceptual framework, is inherent in any taxonomy. Consequently the various task taxonomies (which in many cases describe functions and task dimensions as well) have often been driven by their creators' theoretical interests. Perhaps because of this researchers have been unable to agree upon a necessary and sufficient set of categories to describe behavior.

Fleishman (1982) conceptualized four approaches to task classification based on *behavior description*, *behavior requirements*, *ability requirements* and *task characteristics*. These approaches have been described in detail in his latest book (Fleishman and Quaintance, 1984).

Behavior description schemes classify tasks in terms of *overtly observed behaviors* such as reading meters, throwing switches and communicating. These are then grouped into broader categories. Examples of such taxonomies are Berliner et al., 1964, Willis, 1961, and Finley et al., 1970.

The *behavior requirements* approach emphasizes the inferred processes required to accomplish the task. The individual is assumed to possess a repertoire of processes or functions that intervene between the initiating stimuli and his responses. For example, it would be possible to build a taxonomic framework based on the need to process information by transforming inputs into outputs. Such taxonomies contain terms such as identification, scanning, short-term memory, troubleshooting (see Gagne, 1962, 1977, Miller, 1962, Folley, 1964(a), and Alluisi, 1967).

The *abilities requirements* framework is similar to the behavioral requirements concept. Abilities, such as intelligence, are inferred attributes of individuals that underlie task performance. It is assumed that tasks require certain combinations of abilities if they are to be accomplished correctly. Abilities differ from behavior requirements in terms of concept derivation (stemming from factor analysis) and levels of description (see the schemes of Guilford, 1967, and Fleishman, 1972).

The *task characteristics* approach assumes that the human activities representing performance are elicited by dimensions of the task such as the purpose or the performance criteria that must be met. These are apart from the operator and the behaviors he performs; they are in fact imposed on him. The difficulty lies in selecting the task dimensions that trigger performance. An example of this approach is Farina and Wheaton (1973).

Some taxonomies are *system-specific*, that is, they are based on tasks required by a type of system and system activity, such as aircraft and flying. In these, tasks performed might include preparing a cockpit checklist, advising the tower of readiness, starting the engine, taxiing to takeoff area, etc. This type of taxonomy has the advantage that it is highly descriptive of the activities performed in a particular class of system so that one can compare activities within that system (for example, multi-engine aircraft); but because of its specificity it cannot be applied outside that system class, hence it cannot be used to compare across systems (aircraft vs. tanks). There is no theoretical basis to such taxonomies and its categories are derived from the system terminology and its functions.

Man–machine interface taxonomies are organized around equipments, most often controls and displays, and their characteristics. Nonetheless, they are behavioral taxonomies because the attributes associated with the control/display components have behavioral properties or are designed to shed light on task performance. The most well-known example of this type of taxonomy is the Data Store (Munger et al., 1962) which describes the probability of correct performance for activations or reading of these controls and displays. For example, the Data Store is categorized in terms of inputs or stimuli (scales, lights, scopes, etc.), mediating processes (identification, recognition), outputs or responses (levers, switches, pushbuttons, etc.), and further categorized in terms of the outstanding attributes of a component (e.g., size, number, length, etc.).

Because controls and displays are found in all man–machine systems the applicability of the Data Store to various systems is quite broad. However, it is extremely molecular and cannot deal with complex cognitive activities.

System-nonspecific taxonomies are those general categories of functions and tasks that can be applied across the spectrum of systems. This type of taxonomy falls into Fleishman's (1982) behavior description category.

There are probably more examples of this type of taxonomy than any other but the one best known is that of Berliner, Angell and Shearer (1964). The taxonomy is tri-partite, with four major behavioral processes that break down into six functions, which in turn break down into a larger number of general tasks (see Table 2.9). Another such taxonomy, by Rouse and Rouse (1983), is most appropriate for tasks in which diagnosis of system events is a leading function. The six general categories are:

1. observation of system state
2. choice of hypothesis
3. testing of hypothesis
4. choice of goal
5. choice of procedure
6. execution of procedure

TABLE 2.9. Classification of Task Behaviors

Processes	Activities	Specific Behaviors
Perceptual processes	Searching for and receiving information	Detects Inspects Observes Reads Receives Scans Surveys
	Identifying objects, actions, events	Discriminates Identifies Locates
Mediational processes	Information processing	Categorizes Calculates Codes Computes Interpolates Itemizes Tabulates Translates
	Problem solving and decision-making	Analyzes Calculates Chooses Compares Computes Estimates Plans
Communication processes		Advises Answers Communicates Directs Indicates Informs Instructs Requests Transmits

Table 2.9. (*Continued*)

Processes	Activities	Specific Behaviors
Motor processes	Simple/Discrete	Activates Closes Connects Disconnects Joins Moves Presses Sets
	Complex/Continuous	Adjusts Aligns Regulates Synchronizes Tracks

Source: Berliner, C., Angell D. and Shearer, J. W. Behaviors, measures and instruments for performance evaluation in simulated environment. *Proceedings*, Symposium and Workshop on the Quantification of Human Performance. Albuquerque, N.M., 1964.

These are further broken down into 31 more specific categories. Other nonspecific functional taxonomies that have surfaced from time to time include those by Miller (1967) and Alluisi (1967). The categories they developed are actually functions rather than tasks and in the case of Miller are a mixture of task characteristics and inferred functions, such as purpose, scanning, identification and interpretation of cues, short-term and long-term memory, decision making and problem solving, and effector response. Alluisi's functions include those of watchkeeping, memory, communication, higher-order functions, etc. Since these behavior categories are not system-specific, they can be applied to all systems across the board. In actual practice only the task categories in Berliner et al. are much used because the more molar categories are too gross.

Error taxonomies classify types of errors and error mechanisms. Error may be classified in terms of several aspects, for example, the situation in which error occurs, the nature of the error, where the error occurs, its consequences, etc. The error taxonomy may be general (as is Altman's, 1967) or it may be tied to a particular situation like the nuclear power plant (as is Rasmussen's, 1981). There may be an elaborate theoretical structure underlying the taxonomy (Rausmussen) or the taxonomy may have been developed largely on logical and experiential grounds (Altman).

Learning taxonomies represent tasks in terms of the behaviors required to learn them or the types of learning to which they are related. Learning taxonomies are subsumed under Fleishman's behavioral requirements approach. One of the earliest attempts to develop a learning task taxonomy was a preliminary classification of task variables proposed by Cotterman (1959), who used categories such as serial learning, ranking, concept formation, successive discrimination, etc. Nothing has been done with this taxonomy.

A more useful example of a learning taxonomy which has had considerable influence on education specialists is that of Gagne (1962, 1977) who developed classes of what might be termed learning requirements, that is, signal learning, stimulus-response learning, chaining, verbal association, discrimination learning, and problem solving. Each of these classes is presumed to be related to different states of the human with different capabilities for performance.

Some taxonomies, like the system-specific and system nonspecific, attempt to describe functions, tasks and behaviors as they appear to an observer. Other taxonomies seek to describe some underlying (and hence not visible) dimensions of these behaviors. The TA approach developed by Armsby (1962) and the Farina and Wheaton (1973) taxonomy are examples. The latter breaks task components (goal, response, procedure, stimulus and stimulus-response) into a number of task characteristics for each (e.g., complexity of output units, response rate, dependency among procedures).

The underlying dimensions approach has the virtue of concentrating on enduring characteristics of the task—how—rather than on its content—what. The latter obviously changes from system to system. Such an approach can be considered diagnostic because it helps one to determine why a task presents difficulty to the operator and permits one to compare tasks from different systems in terms of underlying commonalities. Since this taxonomy does not enable one to identify tasks, it must always be used with another more descriptive taxonomy, for example, Berliner et al.

Another feature of the approach is that it can be used to stimulate hypothesis testing. Certain task characteristics should be positively, and others negatively, related to operator performance. Thus one can use a task characteristics taxonomy as a general outline for a program of task oriented research. Unfortunately neither the Armsby nor Farina/Wheaton taxonomies has led to any substantive empirical research.

It is also possible to develop a taxonomy based on the abilities required for task performance. The leading proponent of this point of view is Fleishman (1982). Over a period of several years Fleishman and his colleagues have investigated the organization of abilities in a wide range of psychomotor tasks. They were able by using factor analysis to account for their performance in terms of 52 abilities under two major categories: cognitive (e.g., oral expression, inductive reasoning, speed of closure) and physical (e.g., stamina, gross body coordination, reaction time).

The work of Fleishman and his colleagues on the abilities taxonomy has extended into studies of the effects of drugs on tasks developed to represent the various abilities (Elkin, Freedle, Van Cott and Fleishman, 1965; Baker, Geist and Fleishman, 1967); and noise stressors (Theologus, Wheaton and Fleishman, 1974). The abilities classification was also evaluated in terms of its capacity to integrate areas of the human performance literature (Levine, Romashko and Fleishman,

1973; Levine, Kramer and Levine, 1975) and related to the determination of the abilities and skills needed by fire fighters, clerks, telephone linemen, etc. (Fleishman, 1982). Fleishman and Quaintance (1984) provide the latest information about these studies. These studies suggest not only that task characteristics affect personnel performance (which has generally been accepted by behavioral scientists) but also that discrepant results in studies of functions like vigilance can be attributed to subtle differences in the tasks presented by researchers.

A *composite* may contain elements of two or more other taxonomies. For example, I once developed (in Finley et al., 1970) a taxonomy that contained elements of the system-specific, system nonspecific and the task characteristics type. This could be achieved because the taxonomy represented different levels of behavior. It included a taxonomy based on functions or gross tasks (e.g., steers aircraft, tracks target), a taxonomy based on tasks (e.g., perform control-display operations), a taxonomy based on behavioral elements at the subtask level (e.g., depresses single control, adjusts control to specified value, etc.), a task dimensional taxonomy (e.g., type of initiating stimulus, task duration, etc.). In composite taxonomies such as that of Smode, Gruber and Ely (1962) each higher-order task level is partitioned into more molecular tasks at the subordinate level.

The previous taxonomies were developed on the basis of some a priori organizing principles or theory. It is possible also to develop an empirical taxonomy on the basis of content-descriptive categories found in the behavioral literature (Meister and Mills, 1971). The value of such a taxonomy, which would have certain similarities to the conventional text index, would be in its ability to retrieve information from a data base developed from that literature.

With the exception of the categories developed for use in TA and the extremely systematic effort of Fleishman and his colleagues, nothing very much or very practical has resulted from the various taxonomic schemes. A classification category like skill level in TA raises a question in the mind of the analyst: what does one need to know about skill level? The answer is: *how much* skill level; but the category does not provide this answer. It is necessary to go at least one step beyond the definition of skill level to—initially—an ordinal scale of the amount of skill level. To their great credit, Farina and Wheaton (1973) have done this for their task characteristics approach.

Why are there so many behavioral taxonomies? Many of them illustrate the fuzzy speculative thinking which is unsatisfactory as the basis for a scientific discipline. There are in fact some who denigrate the very notion that a behavioral taxonomy is necessary or could be useful. Nevertheless, classification is at the heart of any science and is especially important to a young one; this is particularly true of behavioral science which is comparatively undeveloped.

COMMENTARY

Mission/function/task analysis has been portrayed in this chapter as a logical, deductive process. There is even some theory (S-O-R) behind its procedure of partitioning molar entities into more molecular ones. There are, however, practical difficulties with the methodology.

What has been described is what should be done but in actual system development the process is not quite so elegant. The fact that most new systems have predecessors means that many functions and tasks are carried over to the new system and therefore have already been determined. It is however important to apply the mission/function/task analysis process to the new functions in the new system and to examine the original system requirements, because often these have not been or at best have been inadequately analyzed.

Then, too, the behavior specialist often finds that the assumption that behavioral analysis should precede design choices does not hold true and he has to scramble to keep up with the designer's pace, perhaps abbreviating his analyses in an effort to do so.

Moreover, FA is not really a procedure performed by most behavior analysts. It is usually performed by the design engineer and, most often, in a highly informal manner. The analyst has, however, a role to play in FA by revising and criticizing the design alternatives being developed by the designer—from a behavioral standpoint only, of course. In the course of that review the analyst may perform a study comparing the engineer's design alternatives, and this can be quite valuable.

TA is at the heart of the behavioral design process. When properly performed, it is immensely valuable not only for training but for all the behavioral aspects of system design. Moreover, it is something the analyst can do, if not completely alone, then largely on his own—though consulting with the design engineer is still a part of the process.

The heyday of TA methodologic development was the period circa 1953 to about 1965. Few variations have been developed since then but behavior specialists continue to be concerned about TA.

The reason for this concern is the recognition that the methodology has the following serious weaknesses:

1. There is no standard form of the methodology; so which form should the analyst use? Perhaps, since each system is an individual one, any TA methodology should be tailored to the individual system. But if this is done, what happens to comparability of data and conclusions?

2. The methods proposed all lack concrete procedures to guide the analyst in making his deductions, some of which are extremely subtle, for example, the anticipated probability of error for the task or required skills and knowledges. Guidelines for making these judgments are quite unclear and in consequence the TA methods are highly intuitive. There is confusion between task description and task analysis. Geer (1981) suggests that the distinction between the two has disappeared, but what does the task analyst analyze if not the task description? But perhaps the analyst need not analyze if all he has to do is to find an SME and ask the latter questions. There is undue reliance on the SME whose judgments may or may not be valid.

The academic reader may be concerned about a topic that has only infrequently been referred to in this chapter—the validity and reliability of the analytic techniques. The author is unaware of efforts to thus measure these techniques, especially as utilized by practitioners. Beyond this one must ask whether it is possible to apply validity concepts to these analytic methods. (Reliability is easy to establish by determining agreement among analysts working individually on the same jobs, but again this has almost never been done.) The analytic techniques are simply design tools producing conclusions and judgments. These outputs are not data that can be validated empirically.

However one does it, we badly need empirical studies of how the analytic techniques are actually applied and their utility in that application. In fact, technique utility might be much more important than technique validity—especially if the latter is so difficult to determine—because validity does not automatically guarantee utility. Highly valid methods may be so complex and difficult to use that their utilization is near zero. Utility may be a second-best criterion but it is important. And critical examination of how the analytic techniques are actually applied in development may help to improve their efficiency.

REFERENCES

Alluisi, E. A. Methodology in the use of synthetic tasks to assess complex performance. *Human Factors*, *9* (4), 375–384 (1967).

Altman, J. W. Classification of human error. In W. B. Askren (ed.), *Symposium on Reliability of Human Performance in Work*. Report AMRL-TR-67-88, Aerospace Medical Research Laboratories, Wright-Patterson AFB, OH, May 1967.

Annett, J., Duncan, K. D., Stammers, R. B. and Gray, M. J. *Task Analysis*. Information Paper No. 6, Department of Employment Training, London: HMSO, 1971.

Armsby, D. H. Task demands analysis. *Human Factors*, *4*, 381–387 (1962).

Baker, C. C., Johnson, J. J., Malone, M. T., and Malone, T. B. *Human Factors Engineering for Navy Weapon System Acquisition*. Essex Corporation, Alexandria, VA, July 1979.

Berliner, C., Angell, D. and Shearer, J. W. Behaviors, measures and instruments for performance evaluation in simulated environment. *Proceedings*, Symposium and Workshop on the Quantification of Human Performance, Albuquerque, NM, 1964.

Berry, C. L. Task taxonomies and modeling for system performance prediction. *Proceedings*, Human Factors Society Annual Metting, 425–429 (1980).

Chenzoff, A. P. and Folley, J. D. *Guidelines for Training Situation Analysis (TSA)*. Report 1218-4, Naval Training Device Center, Orlando, FL, 1965.

Companion, M. A. and Corso, G. M. Task taxonomy: Two ignored issues. *Proceedings*, Human Factors Society Annual Meeting, 358–361 (1977).

Cooper, J. I., Rabideau, G. F. and Bates, C. *A Guide to the Use of Function and Task Analysis as a Weapon System Development Tool*. Report NB-60-161, Northrop Corporation, Hawthorne, CA, January 1961.

Cotterman, T. E. *Task Classification: An Approach to Partially Ordering Information on Human Learning*. Technical Note 58-374, Wright Air Development Center, Wright-Patterson AFB, OH, January 1959.

Demaree, R. C. *Development of Training Equipment Planning Information*. Report TR-61-533, Aeronautical Systems Division, Wright-Patterson AFB, OH, October 1961.

Department of Defense. *Major System Acquisitions* (DOD Directive 5000.1). Washington, DC: Author: January 1977. (a)

Department of Defense. *Major System Acquisition Process* (DOD Directive 5000.2). Washington, DC: Author: January 1977. (b)

Department of Defense. *Test and Evaluation* (DOD Directive 5000.3). Washington, DC: Author: January 1977. (c)

Department of Defense. *Human Engineering Requirements for Military Systems*, MIL-H-46855B. Washington, DC: Author: 31 January 1979.

Department of Defense. *Interservice Procedures for Instructional Systems Development*, NAVEDTRA 06A. Washington, DC, 1 August 1975.

Elkin, E. H., Freedle, R. O., Van Cott, H. P. and Fleishman, E. A. *Effects of Drugs on Human Performance—The Effects of Scopolomine on Representative Human Performance Tests*. Technical Report E-25, American Institutes for Research, Washington, DC, 1965.

Farina, A. J., Jr., and Wheaton, G. R. Development of a taxonomy of human performance: The task characteristics approach to performance prediction. *JSAS Catalog of Selected Documents in Psychology, 3*, 26–27 (Ms. No. 323) (1973).

Finley, D., Obermayer, R. W., Bertone, C. M., Meister, D. and Muckler, F. A. *Human Performance Prediction in Man–Machine Systems: A Technical Review, Vol. I*. Report CR-1614, National Aeronautics and Space Administration, Ames Research Center, Moffett Field, CA, 1970.

Fitts, P. M. et al. (Eds.) *Human Engineering for an Effective Air Transportation and Traffic Control System*. National Research Council, Washington, DC, 1951.

Fleishman, E. A. On the relation between abilities, learning, and human performance. *American Psychologist, 27*, 1017–1032 (1972).

Fleishman, E. A. Systems for describing human tasks, *American Psychologist, 37*, 821–834 (1982).

Fleishman, E. A., and Quaintance, M. K. *Taxonomies of Human Performance: The Description of Human Tasks*. New York: Academic Press, 1984.

Folley, J. D. *Development of an Improved Method of Task Analysis and Beginnings of a Theory of Training*. Technical Report NAVTRADEVCEN 1218-1, Naval Training Device Center, Orlando, FL, June 1964(a).

Folley, J. D. *Guidelines for Task Analysis*. Technical Report NAVTRADEVCEN 1218-2, Naval Training Device Center, Orlando, FL, June 1964(b).

Gagne, R. M. Human functions in systems. In R. M. Gagne (Ed.), *Psychological Principles in System Development*. New York: Holt, Rinehart and Winston, 1962.

Gagne, R. M. *The Conditions of Learning* (3rd ed.) New York: Holt, Rinehart and Winston, 1977.

Geer, C. W. *Human Engineering Procedures Guide*. Report AFAMRL-TR-81-35, Aerospace Medical Research Laboratories, Wright-Patterson AFB, OH, September 1981 (AD-A108-643).

General Accounting Office. *Effectiveness of U. S. Forces Can Be Increased Through Improved System Design* (Report PSAD-81-17). Washington, DC: Author, 29 January 1981.

Gilbreth, F. B. *Motion Study*. New York: D. Van Nostrand Company, 1911.

Guilford, J. P. *The Nature of Human Intelligence*. New York: McGraw-Hill, 1967.

Hagen, W. C. *Techniques for the Allocation and Evaluation of Human Resources*, Report OR 8735, Martin-Marietta Corporation, Orlando, FL, March 1967.

Jones, E. M. and Fairman, J. B. Identification and analysis of human performance requirements. In J. D. Folley (Ed.) *Human Factors Methods for System Design*. Report AIR-290-60-FR-225, American Institute for Research, Pittsburgh, PA, 1960.

Kidd, J. S. and Van Cott, H. P. System and human engineering analysis. In H. P. Van Cott and R. G. Kinkade (Eds.) *Human Engineering Guide to Equipment Design* (Revised Edition), Washington, DC: U. S. Government Printing Office, 1972, pp. 1–16.

Levine, J. M., Kramer, G. G. and Levine, E. N. Effects of alcohol on human performance: An integration of research findings based on an abilities classification. *Journal of Applied Psychology, 60*, 285–293 (1975).

Levine, J. M., Romashko, T. and Fleishman, E. A. Evaluation of an abilities classification system for integrating and generalizing human performance research findings: An application to vigilance tasks. *Journal of Applied Psychology*, *58*, 149–157 (1973).

Malhotra, A., Thomas, J. C., Carroll, J. M. and Miller, L. A. Cognitive processes in design. *International J. Man–Machine Studies*, *12*, 119–140 (1980).

Malone, T. B., Gloss, D. S. and Eberhard, J. W. *Human Factors Techniques Employed in Deriving Personnel Requirements in Weapon System Development*. Report PRR 68-3, Matrix Corporation, Alexandria, VA, October 1967.

McCallum, M. C. and Dick, R. A. Design Guide to Operator and Technician Requirements, Vol. I, Overview for Surface Ship Electronic Systems. Anacapa Sciences, Inc., Santa Barbara, CA, October 1982.

Meister, D. *Human Factors: Theory and Practice*. New York: Wiley, 1971.

Meister, D. *Behavioral Research and Government Policy*. New York: Pergamon Press, 1981.

Meister, D. The role of Human Factors in system development. *Applied Ergonomics*, *13*, 119–124 (1982).

Meister, D. and Mills, R. G. Development of a human performance reliability data system. In *Annals of Reliability and Maintainability*, New York: American Society of Mechanical Engineers, 1971, 425–439.

Meister, D., Sullivan, D. J. and Askren, W. B. *The Impact of Manpower Requirements and Personnel Resources Data on System Design*. Report AMRL-TR-68-44, Aerospace Medical Research Laboratories, Wright-Patterson AFB, OH, September 1968.

Meyer, R. P., Leveson, J. I., Pape, G. L. and Edwards, F. J. *Development and Application of a Task Taxonomy for Tactical Flying*. Report AFHRL-TR-78-42 (Vols, I, II, and III), Air Force Human Resources Laboratory, Brooks AFB, TX, September 1978.

Miller, R. B. *A Method for Man–Machine Task Analysis*. Report 53–137, Wright Air Development Center, Wright-Patterson AFB, OH, June 1953.

Miller, R. B. *Suggestions for Short Cuts in Task Analysis Procedures*, American Institute for Research, Pittsburgh, PA, January 1956.

Miller, R. B. Analysis and specification of behavior for training. In R. Glaser (Ed.) *Training Research and Education*, Pittsburgh, PA: University of Pittsburgh Press, 1962.

Miller, R. B. *A Classification of Learning Tasks in Conventional Language*, Report 63–74, Aerospace Medical Research Laboratory, Wright-Patterson AFB, OH, 1963.

Miller, R. B. Task taxonomy: science or technology? In W. T. Singleton, et al. (Eds.), *The Human Operator in Complex Systems*, London: Taylor & Francis, Ltd., 1967, pp. 67–76.

Munger, S. J., Smith, R. W. and Payne, D. *An Index of Electronic Equipment Operability: Data Store*. Report AIR-C-43-1/62-RP (1), American Institute for Research, Pittsburgh, PA, January 1962.

Montemerlo, M. D. and Eddowes, F. The judgmental nature of task analyses. *Proceedings*, Human Factors Society Annual Meeting, 247–250 (1978).

Poulton, E. C. *Environment and Human Efficiency*. Springfield, IL: C. C. Thomas, 1970.

Price, Harold, E. et al. *Department of Defense and Service Requirements for Human Factors R & D in the Military System Acquisition Process* (Research Note 80-23). DOD Human Factors Engineering (HFE) Technical Advisory Group (TAG), U. S. Army Research Institute, Alexandria, VA, July 1980(a).

Price, Harold E. et al. *The Contribution of Human Factors in Military System Development: Methodological Considerations*. (Technical Report 476). U. S. Army Research Institute, Alexandria, VA, July 1980(b).

Rasmussen, J. *Human Errors, A Taxonomy for Describing Human Malfunctions in Industrial Installations*. Report RISO-M-2304, RISO National Laboratory, Roskilde, Denmark, August 1981.

Rouse, W. B. and Rouse, S. H. Analysis and classification of human error. *IEEE Transactions on Systems, Man, and Cybernetics*, 1983, vol. SMC-13, 539–549.

Sawyer, C. R., Fiorello, M., Kidd, J. S. and Price, H. E. *Measuring and Enhancing the Contribution of Human Factors in Military System Development: Case Studies of the Application of Impact Assessment Methodollogies*. Technical Report 519, Army Research Institute, Alexander, VA, July 1981.

Shepherd, A. An improved tabular format for task analysis. *Journal of Occupational Psychology*, *47*, 93–104 (1976).

Shriver, E. L. *Fully Proceduralized Job Performance Aids: Guidance for Performing Behavioral Analysis of Tasks*. USR/Matrix Research Company, Falls Church, VA, 1975 (AD-AO15059).

Smode, A. F., Gruber, A., and Ely, J. H. *The Measurement of Advanced Flight Vehicle Crew Proficiency in Synthetic Ground Environments*. Report MRL-TDR-62-2, Aerospace Medical Research Laboratory, Wright-Patterson AFB, OH, February 1962.

Taylor, F. W. *The Principles of Scientific Management*. New York: Harper, 1911.

Theologus, G. C., Wheaton, G. R. and Fleishman, E. A. Effects of intermittent, moderate intensity noise-stress on human performance. *Journal of Applied Psychology*, *59*, 539–547 (1974).

Vallerie, L. L. *Survey of Task Analysis Methods*. Research Note RN-80-17, Army Research Institute, Alexandria, VA, February 1978 (AD AO 96868)

White, R. T. *Task Analysis Methods: Review and Development of Techniques for Analyzing Mental Workload in Multiple-Task Situations*. Report MDC 55291, Douglas Aircraft Company, Long Beach, CA, September 1971.

Willis, M. P. and Peterson, R. O. *Deriving Training Device Implications from Learning Theory Principles, Vol. I: Guidelines for Training Device Design, Development and Use*. Report NAVTRADEVCEN 784-1, U. S. Naval Training Device Center, Port Washington, NY, July 1961.

CHAPTER THREE

Design-Aiding Techniques

The behavior analyst has a variety of techniques to select from in aiding the design process: time and motion methods; function flow diagramming; decision/action diagrams; time line analysis; link analysis; the design option decision tree; operational sequence diagrams; skill analysis; workload prediction; and workload measurement methods.

Most of these techniques are highly graphic, a feature which enables them to illustrate and make more vivid relationships among task elements and personnel. Another critical feature of some of these techniques (time and motion methods, time line analysis, workload prediction) is that they center around time. Time may be a significant requirement—or constraint—when tasks must be completed at a precise time, or as quickly as possible. All but workload measurement are aids to design analysis.

Particular attention will be paid in this chapter to the topic of workload. There are two reasons for doing so: (1) This is a "hot" topic, as they say, among behavioral researchers. It generates a great deal of interest and empirical research. (2) More important, the problem of workload is assumed to be central to the efficient operation of the system and the understanding of human performance. If there are factors in system design that tend to "load" personnel, their performance will degrade and so will system output.

With the exception of workload, these techniques are not deeply rooted in theory. To understand workload prediction, however, it is necessary to go into theory to a certain extent and to be aware of the research performed in support of that theory.

Because most of these techniques are relatively simple from a conceptual standpoint, it is possible to present them fully, but this is not the case with time and motion methods or workload, both of which have required individual volumes when fully treated.

TIME AND MOTION METHODS

The earliest task analysis method was the analytic method developed by Gilbreth (1911). From this has stemmed a number of time and motion (T/M) methods that analyze any manual operation into its component body movements and assigns to each an appropriate time value. The variations are described in Bailey and Presgrave, 1958; Barnes, 1968; Geppinger, 1955; Holmes, 1938; Ireson and Grant, 1955; Maynard, Stegemerten and Schwab, 1948; Quick, Duncan and Malcolm, 1962; Schaefer, 1946; and Segur, 1956. Manifestly it is impossible to describe each system in detail and the interested reader is referred to Barnes, 1980, on which the following is largely based.

The T/M systems developed by industrial engineers are extremely elemental. They are based on variables such as the body member used, the distance moved in inches, the manual control required and the weight or resistance involved measured in pounds. The work factor system (Quick et al., 1962), for example, recognizes the following standard elements of work (behavior analysts would call these subtasks). They are transport (reach and move), grasp, pre-position, and assembly.

The *Methods-time measurement* (MTM) system (Maynard et al., 1948) will be described as representative of the various T/M methods. This system, which has proliferated to include a number of versions, analyzes any manual operation or method into the basic motions required to perform it, and assigns to each motion a predetermined time standard which is determined by the nature of the motion and the conditions under which it is made.

Various tables (Table 3.1 is representative) supply the motion time data for each basic element. The unit of time used in these tables is one hundred-thousandth of an hour (0.00001 hour), and is referred to as one *time-measurement unit* (TMU). One TMU equals 0.0006 minute.

Methods-Time Measurements

Reach. *Reach* (R) is the basic element used when the operator intends to move his hand or finger to a destination. The time for making a reach varies with the following factors: (1) condition (nature of destination), (2) length of the motion, and (3) type of reach.

There are five classes of reach (see Table 3.1). The time to perform a reach is affected by the nature of the object toward which the reach is made.

Move. *Move* (M) is the basic element when the goal is to transport an object to a destination. There are three classes of moves: Case A, object to other hand or against stop; Case B, object to approximate or indefinite location; Case C, object to exact location.

The time for move is affected by condition (nature of destination), length of the motion, type of move, and weight factor, static and dynamic.

TABLE 3.1. Extracts from a Representative MTM Table

Distance Moved Inches	Time TMU A	Time TMU B	Time TMU C or D	Time TMU E	Hand in Motion A	Hand in Motion B
3/4 or less	2.0	2.0	2.0	2.0	1.6	1.6
1	2.5	2.5	3.6	2.4	2.3	2.3
2	4.0	4.0	5.9	3.8	3.5	2.7
3	5.3	5.3	7.3	5.3	4.5	3.6
.	.	.	.	.	.	.
26	15.8	22.9	23.9	20.4	13.7	20.2
28	16.7	24.4	25.3	21.7	14.5	21.7
30	17.5	25.8	26.7	22.9	15.3	23.2
Additional	0.4	0.7	0.7	0.6		

A. Reach to object in fixed location, or to object in other hand or on which other hand rests.
B. Reach to single object in location which may vary slightly from cycle to cycle.
C. Reach to object jumbled with other objects in a group so that search and select occur.
D. Reach to a very small object or where accurate grasp is required.
E. Reach to indefinite location to get hand in position for body balance or next motion or out of way.

The time for move is affected by its length, in a manner similar to reach. The three types of moves are the same as those described for reach. Additional time is needed when an object is moved or a force is applied (above 2.5 pounds).

Turn. *Turn* (T) is the motion employed to turn the hand, either empty or loaded, by a movement that rotates the hand, wrist, and forearm about the long axis of the forearm. The time for a turn depends on two variables—the degrees turned, and the weight factor.

Grasp. *Grasp* (G) is the element employed when the purpose is to secure sufficient control of one or more objects with the fingers or hand to permit the performance of the next element.

Position. *Position* (P) is the element employed to align, orient, and engage one object with another object, where the motions used are so minor that they do not justify classification as other basic elements. The time for position is affected by class of fit, symmetry, and ease of handling.

Release. *Release* (RL) is the basic element to relinquish control of an object by the fingers or hand. The two classifications of release are *normal release*—simple opening of fingers; and *contact release*—the release begins and is completed at the instant the following reach begins (no time allowed).

Disengage. *Disengage* (D) is the element in breaking contact between one object and another. It includes an involuntary movement resulting from the sudden ending of resistance. The time for disengage is affected by the class of fit, the ease of handling, and the care of handling.

EYE TIMES. In most work, time for moving and focusing the eye is not a limiting factor and consequently does not affect the time for the operation. When the eyes do direct the hands or body movements, however, eye times must be considered. *Eye focus time* is the time required to focus the eyes on an object and look at it long enough to determine certain readily distinguishable characteristics within the area which may be seen without shifting the eyes. *Eye travel time* is affected by the distance between points from and to which the eye travels, and the perpendicular distance from the eye to the line of travel.

BODY, LEG AND FOOT MOTIONS. These include turning body, walking, rising or kneeling, and are described by TMU and distance.

Time and motion methods make extensive use of graphics and symbols, a tendency which behavior specialists have carried over into such techniques as link and time line analyses and operational sequence diagramming. Codes are used to clarify the motions described, for example, *R8C* for reach, *8 inches*, *class C*. Where these symbols are recorded, they are written to indicate the hand making the motions, the sequence and the time units, etc., as in the following example of a production worker disposing of one component and obtaining the next:

	LH	TMU	RH
Move part 8 inches from fixture to disposal chute		10.6	M8B
Release part		2.0	RL1
Reach 12 inches to bin for next part	R12C	14.2	
Grasp part	G4B	9.1	
Move part 10 inches to fixture	M10C	13.5	
Position part in fixture	P2SE	16.2	
Total time		65.6 or 0.039 minute	

Because the time and motion methods are extremely elemental the behavior analyst is likely to find a use for them only in a very special production situation.

Industrial engineers who make almost exclusive use of these methods are gradually becoming increasingly concerned about the factory task, rather than its elements. This may be due in part to the increasing tendency even in factories to think of work in terms of integral units, as tasks rather than as a composite of physical elements. If the goal is to predict assembly line performance, the analyst wishes to predict task success or failure rather than element success or failure. Indeed one cannot assign the notion of success or failure to elements; they merely exist. Although defined in this section in purposive terms, the goal ascribed to them stems from the task of which they are only a part.

The microanalysis of performance represented by these time and motion methods still has value in a diagnostic or a training situation. Such methods might be useful in, first, aiding in the design of and evaluation of proposed methods of operation and design of equipment and, second, establishing and auditing time standards and estimating labor costs.

FUNCTIONAL FLOW DIAGRAMS

Functional flow diagrams were referred to in Chapter Two as a common part of the mission/function analysis, although it is theoretically possible to perform this analysis without constructing FFDs.

The utility of the FFD is the vivid way in which it depicts functional interrelationships. Starting with data derived from mission profiles and scenarios (see Chapter Two), FFDs are developed iteratively for more detailed system requirements down to the level of specific tasks (at which point other techniques such as the OSD become more important).

The concept of the FFD is taken from engineering practice and is based on schematic block diagrams that depict relationships between equipments in a system. The major difference between the FFD and the schematic block diagram is that the block in the FFD represents a human function.

The major use of the FFD is to assist the analyst in the determination of required operator functions. It will be recalled from Chapter Two that functions become progressively more detailed by inferring inputs and outputs from higher order functions such as "monitor and check out on-board subsystems." These inputs and outputs then become second order functions, for example, "interrogate and monitor avionics subsystems."

Function flow diagrams aid in the derivation of these subordinate level functions, serve as a checklist or outline of system functions that must be performed, aid in function allocation when an FFD is drawn (and analyzed) for each design alternative to be compared, depict interrelationships among functions at the same level and hierarchically, and aid in determining the sequencing of functions.

The FFD is best suited to gross analysis at a very early stage in system analysis because the amount of information they contain is limited to function sequence and relationship.

Function flow diagrams are constructed by arranging in sequence all the functions that are believed to pertain to a particular subsystem or equipment. Each function is a verb-noun combination; occasionally nouns are assumed and adjectives added. Each function is depicted within a rectangular block which is numbered for reference according to its sequence on the page. The numbering system represents a progressive level of indenture: top level: *1.0*, *2.0*, etc.; first level: *1.1*, *1.2*, etc.; second level: *1.1.1*, *1.1.2*, etc. These numbers, which are important to ensure trace-

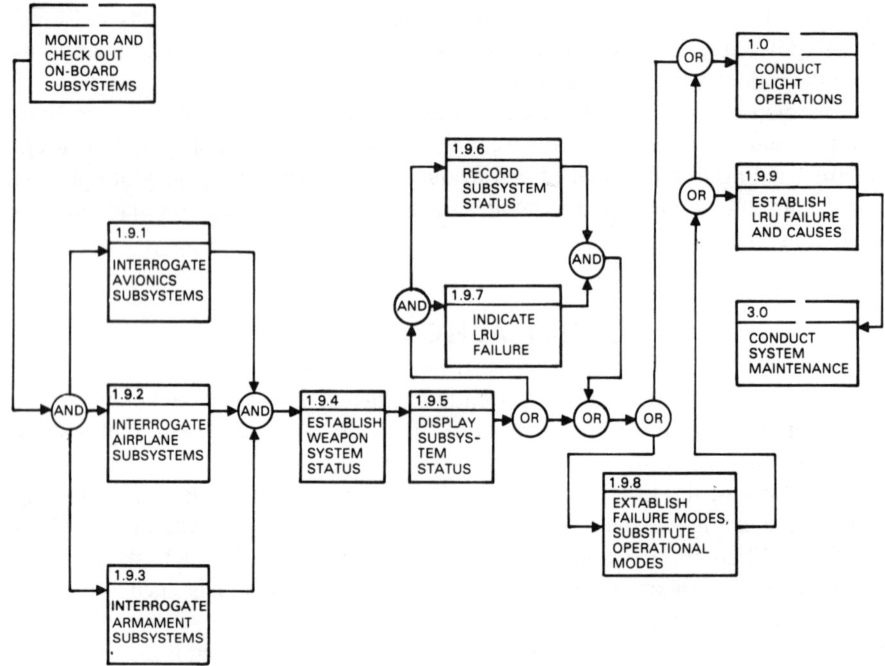

FIGURE 3.1. Sample functional flow diagram. (Modified from Geer, 1981.)

ability to higher level functions or between functions, remain with the function as long as that function is unique. If the function is repeated elsewhere the same number is used and the block is drawn as a reference block. Each FFD contains a reference to its next higher functional flow through the use of a reference block which in Figure 3.1 is broken in the middle. Reference blocks can also be used to indicate functions occurring at the same level on different pages.

Functions are drawn from left to right and usually from top to bottom. Arrows indicating directionality are drawn left to right. When arrows are joined or split out, they should be connected by an *and*, *or* or *and/or* gates or functions as seen in Figure 3.1. An *and* function indicates that all the following or preceding functions must be performed. The *or* function indicates a choice between two or more of the following or preceding functions as to which is to be performed.

For major development programs, such as a complete space vehicle, first-level functions represent gross system operations. Second-level functions tend to describe system operation or maintenance functions in various mission phases. The third-level may define specific functions. Function allocation between operators, equipment and software may occur at this level. Fourth-level functions may be the level at which gross operator task analysis may occur. The concept of functional level detail is based on the total size and scope of the system being analyzed. The smaller the system, the more detailed the corresponding level of functional analysis will be. Larger systems require more levels to get down to the same level of detail.

DECISION/ACTION DIAGRAMS

The *decision/action* (D/A) diagram (see Figure 3.2), also referred to as an information flow chart, decision/logic diagram or operation/decision diagram, is a technique similar to the FFD. It is used to show the flow of required system data in terms of decisions and actions performed. As an information flow chart it may have vertical orientation on the page rather than usual left-to-right horizontal orientation. Special symbology may also be used at a more detailed level to indicate allocation to man or machine (e.g., single-line symbols mean manual, double-line means automatic).

Like FFDs, D/A diagrams may be developed and used at various system development phases and levels of detail. The initial D/A diagrams describe gross functions without regard to whether these are performed by people, machine or software. The D/A diagrams prepared subsequent to function allocation will reflect this man– machine allocation in the decisions, operations and branching represented. Like the FFD, input data come from mission profiles and scenarios.

Decision/action diagrams are so similar to FFDs (and only slightly more complex) that one would not draw both for the same project. D/A diagrams are generally used when the program is software oriented. The most significant difference between the two techniques is the addition of the decision blocks (diamonds) to the FFDs.

In recording the sequence of operations and decisions, the D/A diagram is similar to the flow charts used by computer programmers. Both charts are based on binary choice decisions and intervening operations. There are two reasons for using binary decision logic in D/A diagramming. The first is to expedite communications through use of simple yet generally applicable conventions, the second to provide for easy translation of decision/action flow charts into logic flow charts for computerized sections of the system. A D/A diagram was developed for the Automated Interviewer (described in Chapter Two) primarily because the Interviewer is oriented around software.

The partitioning process, so characteristic of behavioral analysis, is found also in D/A diagrams. A decision at a general level may split into several decisions at a more detailed level. For example, at the general level the question may be asked: Do any targets need identification processing? At a more detailed level: Do any newly entered targets need identification processing? Do any target tracks need confirmation of tentative identification? Do any confirmed identifications need rechecking?

Each of these more molecular decisions may have associated with it one or more detailed operations.

The example in Figure 3.2 is a molar detection and tracking function, for which no allocation has yet been made to operator or machine. At this level the chart could describe any number of detection and tracking systems; their decisions and operations are essentially the same. Even here, however, the usefulness of the flow chart diagramming technique is apparent. It makes the analyst begin to consider such implementation alternatives as: (1) How any given signal can be compared with known

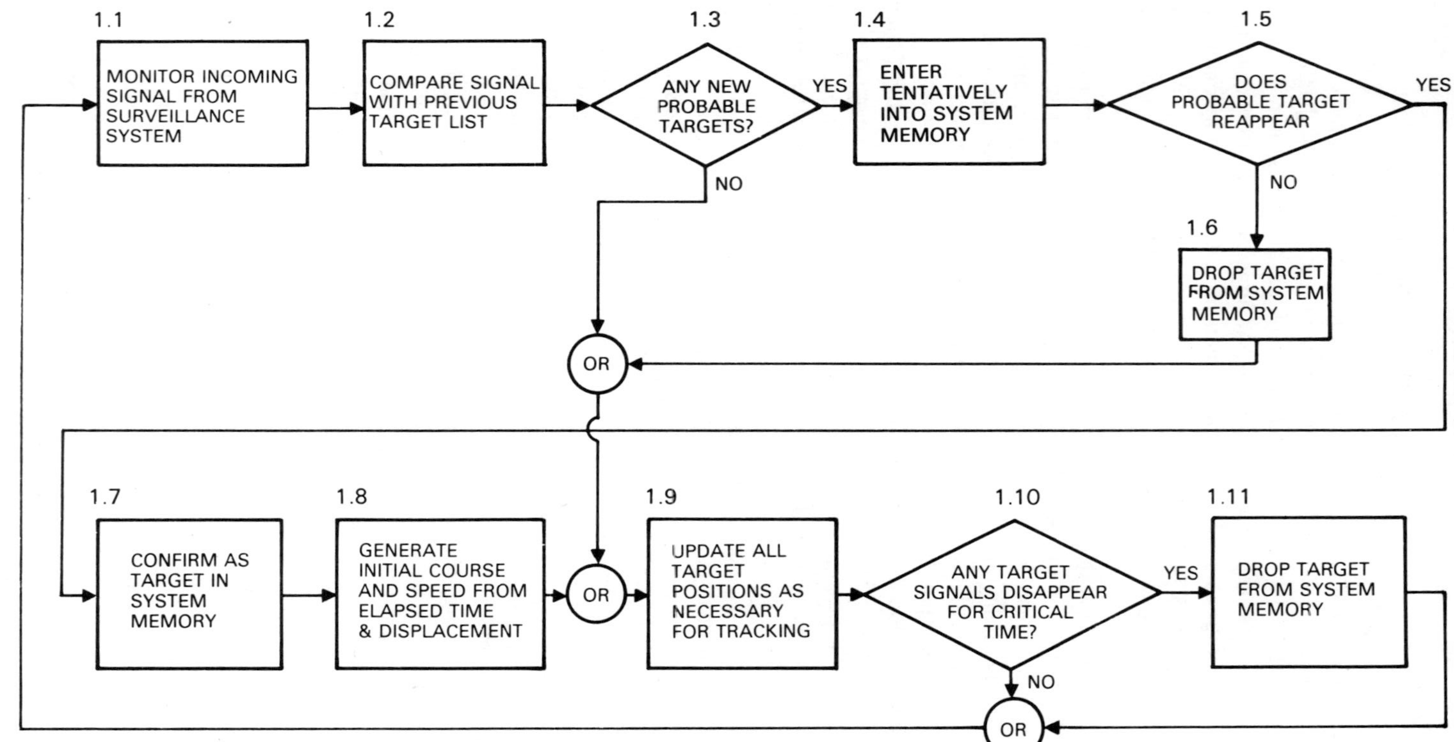

FIGURE 3.2. Sample decision/action diagram. (From Geer, 1981.)

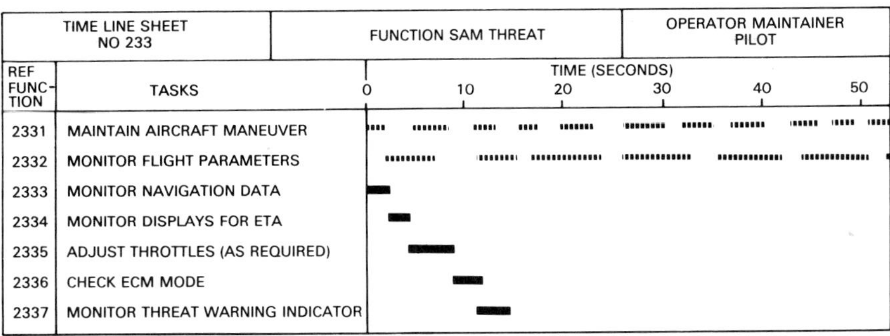

TIME LINE SHEET
NO 233
FUNCTION SAM THREAT
OPERATOR MAINTAINER
PILOT
REF
FUNC-
TION
TASKS
TIME (SECONDS)
0
10
20
30
40
50
2331 MAINTAIN AIRCRAFT MANEUVER
2332 MONITOR FLIGHT PARAMETERS
2333 MONITOR NAVIGATION DATA
2334 MONITOR DISPLAYS FOR ETA
2335 ADJUST THROTTLES (AS REQUIRED)
2336 CHECK ECM MODE
2337 MONITOR THREAT WARNING INDICATOR

FIGURE 3.3. Part of a timeline sheet. (From Geer, 1981.)

targets? (2) How probable targets can be marked so that they can be recognized upon reappearance?

The results of the D/A analysis can be used to develop more specific system requirements and to assist in the performance of trade studies. Time line analyses are almost always needed following these diagrams in order to investigate the effect of time on system performance. Computer simulations can be performed with the addition of time data to detailed D/A diagrams that have preliminary function allocations to operators. The technique can help in initial development of software programs in general, and display software in particular. All the actions and decisions required can be separated out to determine the information needed by the operator to take the action or make the decision. The errors possible for each action/decision can also be more easily isolated.

The procedure for constructing D/A diagrams is essentially the same as that for functional flows, except for the emphasis on decisions.

TIME LINE ANALYSIS

Time line analysis examines the temporal relationships among tasks and the duration of individual tasks. Time line sheets are usually constructed with the time on the horizontal axis and the listing of tasks on the vertical axis of a graph (Figure 3.3). The time estimates associated with a task are indicated by bar graphs beginning at the start of the task and ending when the tasks are completed.

Time line sheets permit an appraisal of time-critical sequences to verify that necessary events can be performed and that there are no time-incompatible tasks. Time line charts serve as one of the inputs for workload evaluation. They are also used for determination of required number of personnel.

Input data for time lines are the listing of tasks, the sequence in which tasks are performed, and the start and stop time for performance of each task.

Task listings can be secured from the FFD or task description. However, only a few of the task analysis formats described in Chapter Two provided for time estimates. Where the tasks to be analyzed are similar to those performed in a predecessor system, it is possible to secure reasonable estimates of when they begin and their duration by querying experienced personnel about how they do their jobs. It will not be as easy for new tasks (i.e., those created by new equipment and new operational requirements). Although the new task can be broken down into its subtasks (estimates made for those subtasks, and subtask estimates then combined), there is an error component in this combination.

The time reference in this analysis can be anything relevant to the task/mission: hours, minutes, seconds. Of course, once a time unit is adopted it must remain constant for all tasks in a particular analysis. It would obviously be impossible to use one time scale for one task in a sequence and another scale for a different task in the same sequence.

Making a Time Line

Some simple rules are to be followed in making up a time line. Each time line should be related to a higher-level functional requirement by indicating the function title and FFD reference on the time line. The nature of the task being analyzed, for example, control manipulation, cognitive functioning, etc. can be written out or indicated by symbols. Each task is numbered and listed on the left side of the sheet.

One can approach time line analysis in various ways. One could, for example, chart all tasks without considering who and how many personnel will perform these tasks. Such a time line would have value in determining required manning because where there are overlaps of control or monitoring actions, it is apparent that at least two operators will be needed. If the tasks are identified as to type, one could note

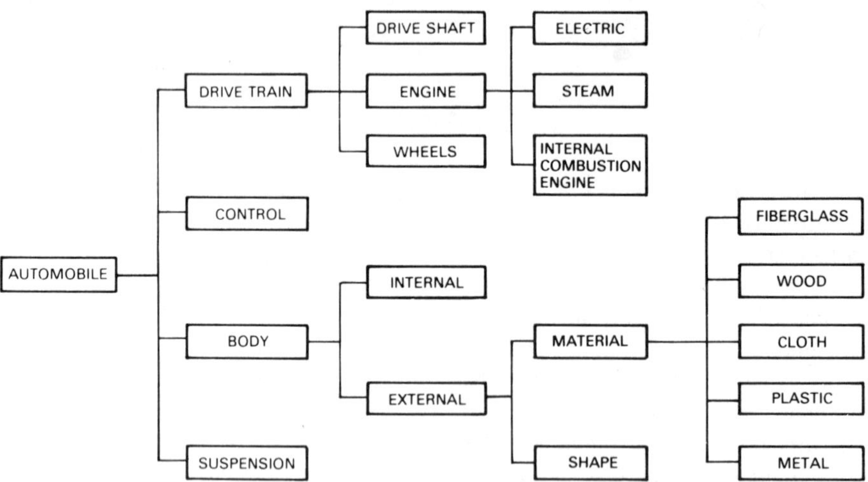

FIGURE 3.4. Illustration of the Design Option Decision Tree concept using automobile design information. (From *Proceedings of the Human Factors Society 18th Annual Meeting*, 1974, pp. 368–375. Copyright 1974 by the Human Factors Society, Inc., and reproduced by permission.)

whether the most frequent behavioral requirements are those of control activation, monitoring, cognitive functioning, etc. This helps to understand the overall job. One can determine whether personnel will be continuously loaded—where load is the absence of free time between tasks—and this might suggest the possible influence of fatigue.

A more advanced form of time line is one in which the tasks have been distributed among individual operators. In one example, the time line lists on a time basis all tasks performed by operator X. The question this analysis might answer is: Can operator X perform all assigned tasks without excessive strain? Where tasks are categorized by type, control movements for instance, it is possible to determine whether operator X is being asked to perform in incompatible ways. (e.g., operate three controls simultaneously).

The function of the time line is highly limited. It illustrates only task–time relationships; it hints at incompatibilities in terms of time. It is a natural adjunct to task analysis and because it is relatively easy to prepare, it is usually cost-effective to prepare time line sheets. They are particularly useful when tasks are highly time dependent.

DESIGN OPTION DECISION TREE

The *design option decision tree* (DODT) was developed as a response to the need for a means of anticipating and identifying the tradeoffs that would be made in the course of design (Askren and Korkan, 1971). It is a graphic means of showing the design options available at each decision point in the design process and of depicting the sequence of engineering decisions required for resolution of a design problem. Hence DODT can be useful both in the function allocation process and in performance of trade studies. Its similarity to the FFD is marked.

Figure 3.4 illustrates the DODT concept using automobile design information. The engineer concerns himself with four subsystems—the drive train, control, body, and suspension. Further, the drive train must include three features—the drive shaft, engine, and wheels. At this point, the engineer must make the decision of whether to incorporate an electric, steam, or internal combustion engine in the automobile. This leads to the tradeoff—or comparison of alternatives—and to the eventual selection of a design approach. It is at these decision points that the behavioral specialist presumably would input data on the impact of the design alternatives on the operators and maintainers of the automobile system.

The DODT concept was evolved primarily for the purpose of locating points in the design process for input of human factors data. However, subsequent work has evolved a number of other potential uses for the DODT. One application, which appears promising, is the use of the DODT to analyze the total design problem. This includes quantizing the design options in the tree, and tracing paths through the tree as dictated by specific design goals.

Developing a DODT

In general the following steps can be utilized.

1. *Perform a survey of the literature.* This suggests design options which are incorporated into a first generation DODT.

2. *Conduct "inhouse" interviews with engineers and update the original DODT.* The original DODT is verified and additional design options and suggested revisions are evaluated, all of which results in a second generation DODT.

3. *Interview outside experts* at major contractor facilities and update the previous DODT.

One difficulty with the DODT is the amount of time and effort required to develop one. Askren and Korkan (1974) report that one DODT, consisting of five sub-DODTs—parts of which were very detailed—required six months and a total of about 2000 worker-hours. This appears to be excessive and impractical in real world system development but the technique can undoubtedly be modified to some more pragmatic practice.

A numerical scheme can be adopted by assigning a scale rating of *1* to *10* for each of the following representative criteria: physical weight, dollar cost, performance, developmental risk, and human factors. A scale rating is given by the analyst on the basis of available data and interview conclusions to each downstream branch of a decision node in each subsystem DODT.

For example, if the goal is to minimize physical weight, the DODT is traversed for this criterion and the minimum numerical value and its associated path are found.

The DODT is primarily a graphic technique, relying largely on the collection of information from various studies and making use of expert opinion expressed in terms of a 10-point rating scale. It would seem to have some value in function allocation (specifying design alternatives and rating these on the basis of behavioral factors). However, it is a complex and tedious process and its utility remains to be determined. One user (Beevis, 1981) is, however, quite enthusiastic about the technique.

OPERATIONAL SEQUENCE DIAGRAMS

Chapter Two indicated that the *operational sequence diagram* (OSD) is a significant aid in the performance of task analysis. Baker et al. (1979) feel that the OSD can be used to develop operational procedures, evaluate man–machine interfaces and function allocations, identify critical mission areas, identify task under and overload situations, identify critical decision/action points, develop workspace design and evaluation criteria and identify points of high error likelihood. This is almost certainly an exaggeration but suggests the potential utility of the technique.

The OSD is a technique for plotting the sequential flow of information, decisions and actions through the performance of a subsystem or system mission. This flow is portrayed symbolically using a standardized symbology to represent the reception of information, decision making and control responses. The OSD can be drawn at a system or task level and it can be utilized at any time in the system development cycle provided the necessary information is available. It can aid the analyst in examining the behavioral implementation of design alternatives by permitting the comparison of the actions involved in these design alternatives. It is particularly useful in the integration of task analysis information because it emphasizes interfaces, interactions and interrelationships. The three significant OSD attributes are its sequential flow, its classification of activity type and its ability to describe interfaces. In these respects OSDs are similar to D/A diagrams, but more complex. Where D/A diagrams are used, often OSDs are not. The OSD simulates the system operation in graphic form, although obviously it is a static simulation. But this is also the reason why, in complex systems, development of the OSD becomes tremendously tedious and quite expensive in terms of analyst time.

Several authors (e.g., Baker et al., 1979, and Geer, 1981) suggest that the reason the OSD is so valuable is that in order to construct a "good" OSD a great deal of information must be gathered and analyzed before the diagram can be developed. This suggests that the OSD is not so much useful in itself as that it forces the analyst to work.

As illustrated in Figure 3.5, the flow of events in the OSD is always from the top of the sheet to the bottom. The operators and the equipment they control are entered into column headings. It is helpful to place the operators and the machines they deal with in adjacent columns. Any number of operators may be depicted on the OSD (although beyond a certain point the complexity of the diagram reduces its effectiveness) and it helps to group together all the operators and equipment of a specific subsystem or functional division of the system. The functions performed by the operator are shown by symbology which is more or less standardized (Figure 3.6). The OSD is initiated by the first event in the set of operations. The event and event times are written in the two left hand columns. The machines or men who will receive inputs are shown and the transmission/reception mode is noted by using an appropriate letter code. Subsequent actions taken by the crew and its equipment as they react to the input are shown. External outputs are plotted in the far right column.

Variations

There are a number of OSD variations. In the *spatial* OSD the flow of events (observations and control manipulations) and symbols are overlaid on a sketch of the control panel. The spatial OSD thus may provide a graphic description of the perceptual-motor load a particular panel imposes on the performance of the operator. The spatial OSD is much like a link analysis and represents the sequence of operator actions in exercising the panel. It seems unlikely however that the spatial OSD would supplant the link analysis.

The *task analysis* OSD (TA-OSD) combines the TA and OSD. The TA-OSD is drawn vertically down the left side of the page and the remainder of the form con-

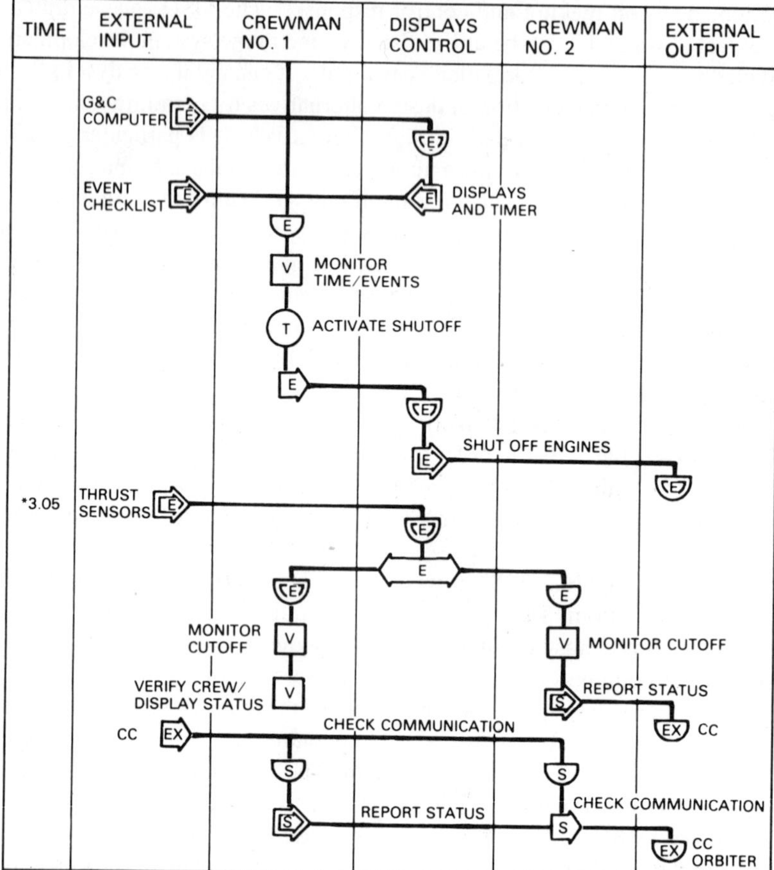

FIGURE 3.5. Sample Operational Sequence Diagram. (From Geer, 1981.)

tains the information usually provided by a TA in a series of columns. In point of fact one can add any type or amount of information one wishes to the OSD as a set of annotations.

Beyond the necessity of securing a great deal of input data, the task of drawing a complex OSD is extremely cumbersome and expensive. The computer can be used to reduce the effort needed to draw the OSD manually (Lahey, 1970, Larson and Willis, 1970). A character printer can draw lines as strings of dots and rather than using symbols alphabet characters can indicate the types and modes of action performed.

Despite glowing claims made for it, it must be emphasized that the OSD does not have within itself the answers to questions such as points of excessive workload or high error likelihood. The analyst must make these judgments himself but undoubt-

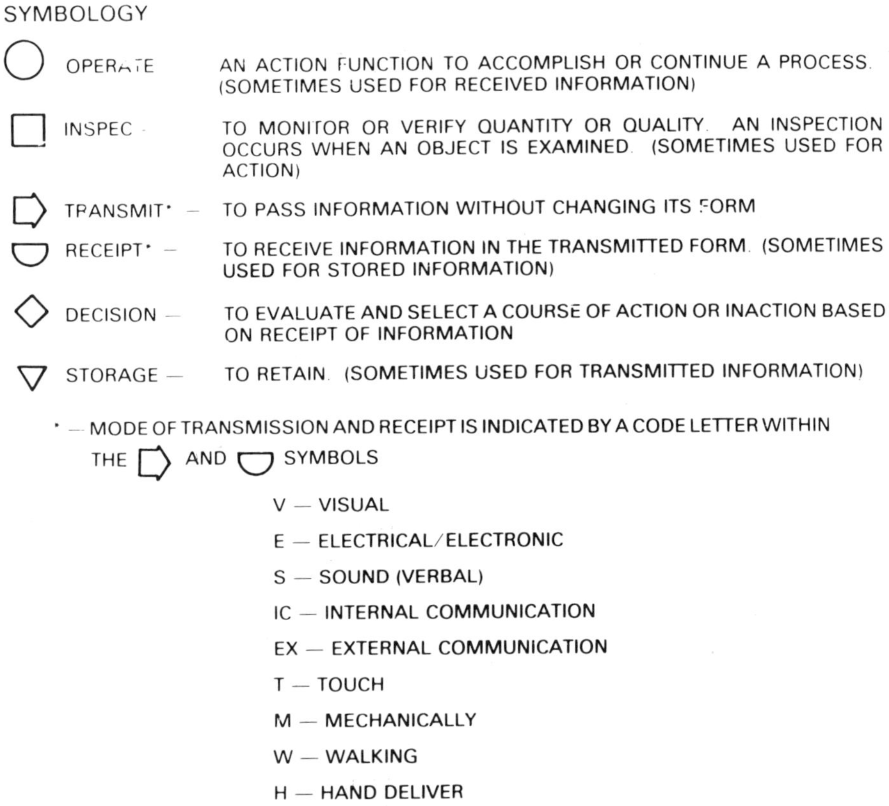

SYMBOLOGY

OPERATE — AN ACTION FUNCTION TO ACCOMPLISH OR CONTINUE A PROCESS. (SOMETIMES USED FOR RECEIVED INFORMATION)

INSPECT — TO MONITOR OR VERIFY QUANTITY OR QUALITY. AN INSPECTION OCCURS WHEN AN OBJECT IS EXAMINED. (SOMETIMES USED FOR ACTION)

TRANSMIT* — TO PASS INFORMATION WITHOUT CHANGING ITS FORM

RECEIPT* — TO RECEIVE INFORMATION IN THE TRANSMITTED FORM. (SOMETIMES USED FOR STORED INFORMATION)

DECISION — TO EVALUATE AND SELECT A COURSE OF ACTION OR INACTION BASED ON RECEIPT OF INFORMATION

STORAGE — TO RETAIN. (SOMETIMES USED FOR TRANSMITTED INFORMATION)

* — MODE OF TRANSMISSION AND RECEIPT IS INDICATED BY A CODE LETTER WITHIN THE AND SYMBOLS

V — VISUAL

E — ELECTRICAL/ELECTRONIC

S — SOUND (VERBAL)

IC — INTERNAL COMMUNICATION

EX — EXTERNAL COMMUNICATION

T — TOUCH

M — MECHANICALLY

W — WALKING

H — HAND DELIVER

FIGURE 3.6. OSD symbols.

edly his familiarity with the data he has collected to construct the OSD assists in that process.

LINK ANALYSIS

Link analysis (L/A) is a very simple diagrammatic technique which represents the interactions among system components. The interactions include the communications channels between personnel, the sensory or motor relationships among personnel, between personnel and machines, and connections among machines. Link analysis is most often used to plot the manipulations required in operating a control panel or on a larger scale the physical interactions among personnel and their machines in a working area. In the former case the link diagram is an aid to the arrangement of controls and displays on a console; in the latter case the diagram aids the arrangement of machines in a facility or what is more commonly termed workspace layout. It aids in minimizing traffic flow and observational and information flow distances and is frequently used to verify the adequacy of design layouts.

Topics in studies that have applied link analysis include pilot eye movements that resulted in more effective arrangement of aircraft control panels (Fitts, Jones and Milton, 1950), the interaction of operators with computer hardware (Galitz and Laska, 1969, 1970), the travel patterns of nurses in a hospital ward (Lippert, 1971), and police intelligence work (Harper and Harris, 1975).

Input data requirements for the analysis are: information flow requirements, information flow medium (auditory, visual, electronic and ambulatory), station requirements (number of work stations, number of operators, functional allocations), and any special constraints.

L/A is performed using paper and pencil in the following steps:

1. Identify each required operation and operator by drawing a circle.
2. Identify the equipment with which the operation is performed by drawing a square.
3. Indicate the links between operators and between personnel and the machines they operate by drawing a line between them. Indicate the form of these interactions, usually verbal (communication) or electronic (displays), by appropriate symbols.
4. Evaluate each link for importance and frequency of use by applying scales on dimensions such as importance or frequency of use.
5. Redraw the diagram, reducing wherever possible link length and number of crossing lines.

The procedure, illustrated by Figure 3.7, is a general one that can be applied at a variety of levels, for example, a control panel, a work area, or at a total system level such as a ship or aircraft, although in this last case the drawing could be quite complex.

The reader will recognize the similarity between the link diagram and the spatial OSD. There is relatively little difference between them. The utility of L/A is that it displays various design alternatives thought of by the analyst. Numerous and crossing lines suggest busyness and confusion; hence the reduction and simplification of these lines produces a cleaner design. Elaborate analytic deductions need not be made using this technique.

SKILL ANALYSIS FLOW DIAGRAMS

A variation of the D/A diagram described previously is a graphic format developed by Mallamed, Levine and Fleishman (1980) to determine the skills required of new jobs. The skills are the 52 human abilities developed by Fleishman and his colleagues over a number of years (see Chapter Two). Their approach describes a task in terms of the human abilities required to perform it. An entire task can be described in terms of a profile of basic abilities.

One way of estimating skill requirements is through ability rating scales. Unfortunately the rating scale technique is tedious, and Fleishman and his colleagues have developed this alternative method, which is somewhat simpler than rating scales.

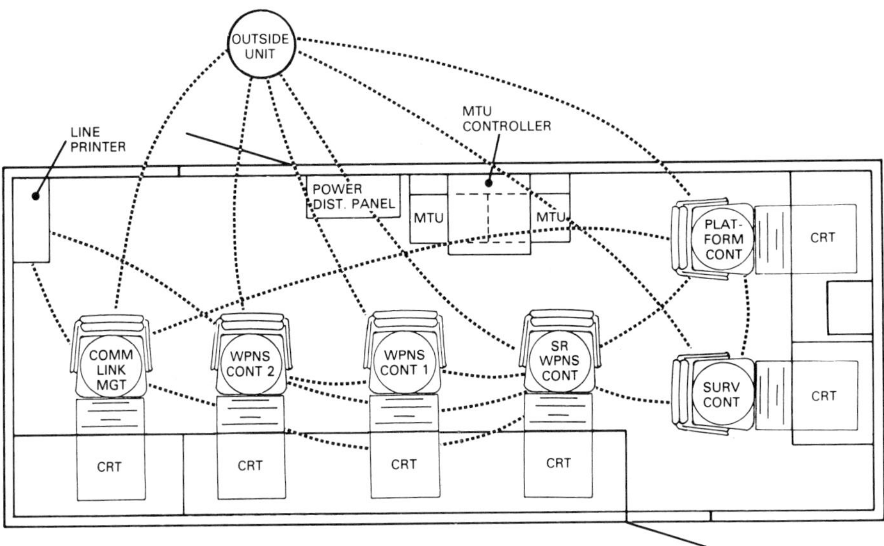

FIGURE 3.7. Sample link analysis for workspace layout. (From Geer, 1981.)

This approach involves the use of binary decision flow diagrams which serve as a decision aid to the analyst (see Figure 3.8). The analyst is led, step by step, through a series of yes or no decisions which result in the specification of the abilities required for the job or task. However, these diagrams do not permit an estimate of the amount of ability required for job performance, only whether or not an ability is required. Hence they merely identify abilities; it is necessary to use the scales or some other means to quantify them.

The diagrams consist of yes or no questions pertaining to features of an ability that are essential in determining its presence or absence in the job. Each question deals with only one dimension of an ability, thereby minimizing the difficulty of the decision. Exemplary activities previously scaled on the ability dimensions (Theologus and Fleishman, 1973; Fleishman, 1975) are included as classification aids.

A series of studies (Mallamed et al., 1980) indicates that the diagrams can be used more rapidly and resulted in increased interrater reliability over the rating scale procedure. The one undesirable aspect is that since the technique can be used only with the Fleishman taxonomy of abilities, one must accept that taxonomy. The concept of a decision flow diagram to facilitate manpower determination is a clever one. One wishes that others besides Fleishman would exploit the technique for skill identification purposes.

WORKLOAD ANALYSIS

In this section we discuss two aspects of *Workload analysis* (W/L). The first is the methods to predict the amount of W/L a system will impose on personnel; the second involves the methods to assess or measure how much W/L exists.

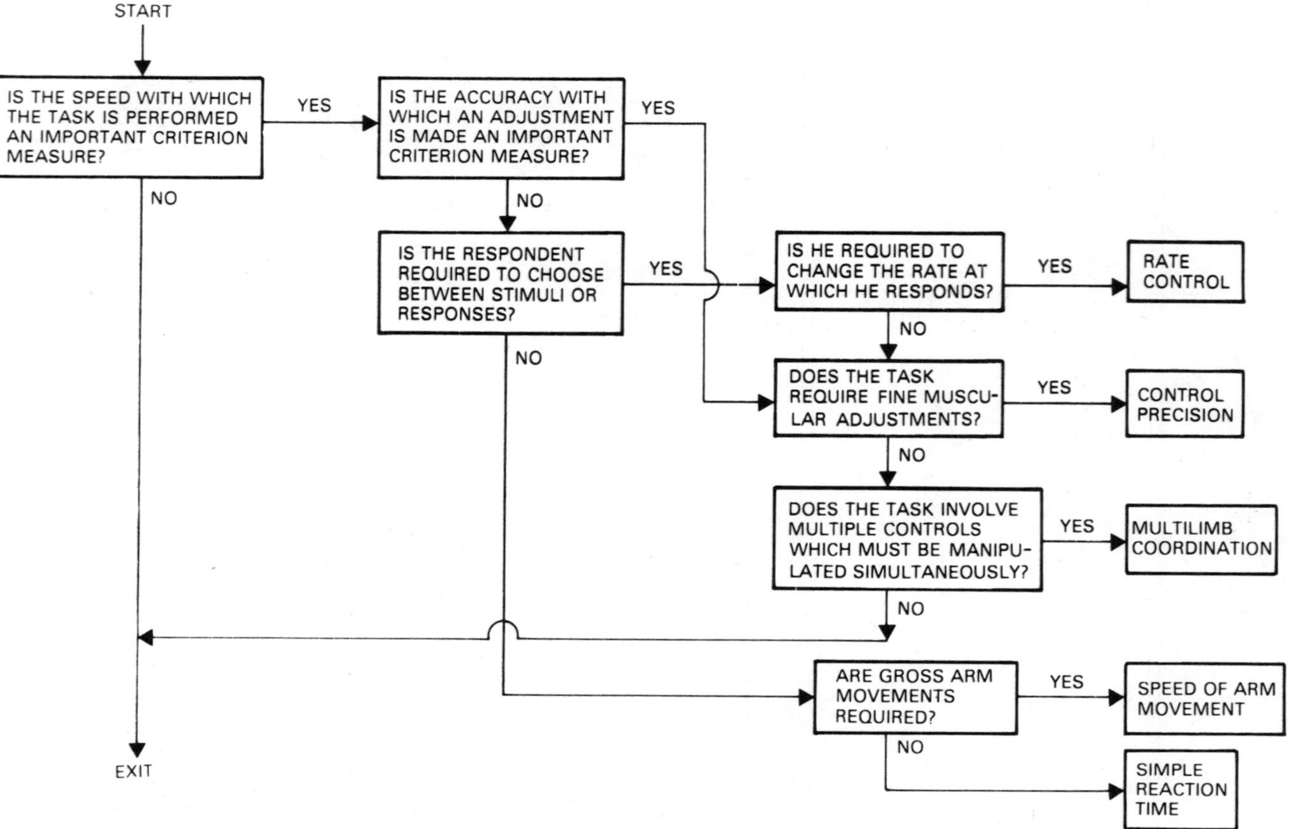

FIGURE 3.8. Sample binary decision skill analysis diagram.

In contrast to the techniques described previously there is much theory associated with W/L methods and to understand them one must be conversant (however superficially) with that theory. Our review of theory does not pretend to be completely comprehensive because volumes have been written on these topics (e.g., AGARD, 1978a, b; Moray, 1979; Weiner, 1982). Our discussion is at best introductory.

To deal with this topic adequately is, however, difficult. Not only is there no single, commonly accepted definition of W/L, there are many conflicting concepts of what W/L is and often the term is used without any definition at all. There is also the maddening difficulty of differentiating W/L from stress which has many features in common with W/L. Often the term W/L and stress are used interchangeably.

There are two problems of definition: W/L is multidimensional and it is also an intervening variable. W/L is multidimensional because it can be viewed (see Johannsen, 1979 and Rolfe and Lindsey, 1973) in many ways. As an input, W/L is represented by stimuli that load the operator in the sense of causing him to bear a burden. W/L is also the operator's internal experience of difficulty and discomfort, his recognition that he is experiencing a load, and his strategy to overcome it. Also, as an output, W/L affects not only his performance (and can be measured) but, when the operator is part of a larger system, impacts (usually negatively) on the system itself. One can view W/L, then, as some feature of the system (even when it is his own incapacity) that forces the operator to work harder, as the operator's feeling of being stressed and having to work harder, and as the effect of all the preceding that cause him to make errors.

Others indices of multidimensionality are that the stimuli initiating the W/L process can be either outside the operator or within him. They can be physical or mental, can be expressed overtly or internally, and can be modified by the operator's intelligence, attitudes, experiences and knowledge of consequences. They can, additionally, result in performance modifications, such as a change in problem solution strategy. Any stimulus can be a load-producing stimulus, almost any response can be the operator's response to the recognition of load.

OTHER VARIABLES

Overt Consequences. The overt consequences of failing to perform adequately in the situation may range from grave to minimal. The consequences of failure to a student in a spelling test are objectively different from those of a pilot in an aircraft on fire, although subjective evaluation of consequences is obviously idiosyncratic. The operator's knowledge of the consequences of his performance has an important effect on that performance.

Operator's Recognition. The operator's recognition of the performance situation as being stressful or highly loaded, a dimension ranging from none to highly acute, makes the operator's situation one of loading. If the operator does not know the situation is loaded, it is per se not loaded *for that operator*.

Internal Criteria. The operator's internal criteria or standards as to what constitutes adequate performance in the situation, a dimension ranging from no standards at all to extremely high standards, determine how he evaluates his performance.

External Criteria. External criteria such as time, accuracy or quality may dictate the operator's performance and also serve as standards by which his performance can be evaluated.

Wide Range of Indices

The range of W/L indices, some overt, such as sweating or errors, others covert, such as "tunnel vision" for critical stimuli, makes it irrational to talk of W/L as a unitary phenomenon. It is more probable that there are different types of W/L, each type being described by a profile (high on some dimensions and low on others). Some W/L types may be indistinguishable from what we commonly think of as stress. The diversity of W/L dimensions creates difficulties not only in definition but also in measurement.

As an intervening variable, the definition of W/L becomes almost impossibly diffuse. For example, Pew (1979) considers W/L as "a function of a collection or assortment of tasks and of detailed task components and features as well as personalized variables that, together, define and contrast task demands vs. ability to perform and in turn contribute to overall system performance." What this says is that whatever W/L is, it is affected by tasks and individuals, involves comparison between demand and ability to satisfy that demand, and produces an effect on the human and the total system.

Underlying the notion of W/L is the concept of *demand* which we encountered in Chapter Two and the discrepancy between demand and the capability to respond to that demand. The system in which the individual functions (the term system being defined in its broadest sense as any situation or context in which the human performs) imposes a demand on him. This demand is like a cost of performance. Simply to be alive, even though one is in a coma, imposes a minimal physiological cost in terms of blood flow, heart beat, etc. To read displays means to discriminate artificial, learned patterns of symbols or alphanumerics; to correct a system malfunction requires extensive cognitive activity, etc.

W/L can also be conceptualized in physiological terms as *effort* that must be expended to achieve a goal. That effort can be either physical (as in lifting a weight) or mental (as in concentrating to solve a difficult problem).

W/L is variable depending on the characteristics of the system and what one is required to do to exercise the system. Some demands are relatively light but others are excessive. Some systems, some jobs, some situations make us work harder than we wish—we experience them as uncomfortable; in addition they affect our performance by causing us to make errors, by slowing our responses, etc.

When errors occur, responses are slowed and performance quality reduced, the system is less efficient than it could be and less effective than we would wish it to be. It is logical that if system characteristics are in part responsible for excessive W/L and hence for reduced efficiency, we should attempt to reduce W/L by modifying these characteristics in some way.

If we assume that equipment/system characteristics are the primary cause of W/L (defined in the broadest sense, as we said before, as demand imposed on the operator), then a primary rationale for human factors as a design discipline is to reduce that W/L, preferably to something more than zero (lest the operator become bored) but fairly low. The essential questions from the standpoint of system development are therefore: What is the relationship of W/L to system design? What are the design characteristics that increase or decrease W/L?

Workload Measurement

Workload can be measured in various ways, which only serves to compound the confusion. These ways are associated with the three aspects of W/L mentioned previously—input, internal functioning, and output. Johannsen (1979) classifies techniques usable for measurement of operator effort into four groups: 1. time line analyses; 2. information processing studies; 3. operator activation level studies; and 4. subjective effort rating.

In time line analyses the W/L factor is the relationship between maximum time allowance and actual time for performance. If it appears there is too little time to complete the task, the operator experiences stress because he anticipates failure. In information processing studies the operator is regarded as an information processing element with a fixed, limited channel capacity. If a large number of concurrent information channels stimulate the operator, so that he has difficulty attending to all of them, he will feel stressed.

Workload can also be represented by control-theoretic measures of operator effort based on time history and frequency domain measures or on human controller models. Operator activation level studies are based on the hypothesis that the level of physiological activity of the operator depends on his effort.

To some researchers subjective rating of effort is only an additional useful assessment technique. To Johannsen (1979), however, failure of the operator to experience and to express W/L means that the phenomenon is not truly one of W/L.

The wealth of W/L theory that has grown up like mushrooms around trees makes the subject quite confusing. Moray (1979), for example, refers to random walk theory, accumulator theory, discrete and continuous information theory, supervisor theory, queuing theory, the Theory of Signal Detection, linear control theory, optimal control theory, and adaptive control theory. And this list does not include the physiologically oriented theories such as those of Selye (arousal theory, 1936). Wickens (1981) distinguishes between what he calls structural and capacity theories. The former can also be referred to as "bottleneck" theories because it is hypothesized that a parallel system capable of processing separate and concurrent information channels "narrows" to a serial system that can handle only one input at a time. Where this bottleneck occurs (at initial perception, at a central processing stage, or at response) becomes a matter for much argumentation and experimentation. Capacity theories model the operator as possessing a pool of limited resources. As a primary task demands more of these resources and therefore becomes more difficult, fewer resources are available for a concurrent secondary task and performance of the latter degrades. Unfortunately W/L theory is not sufficiently developed

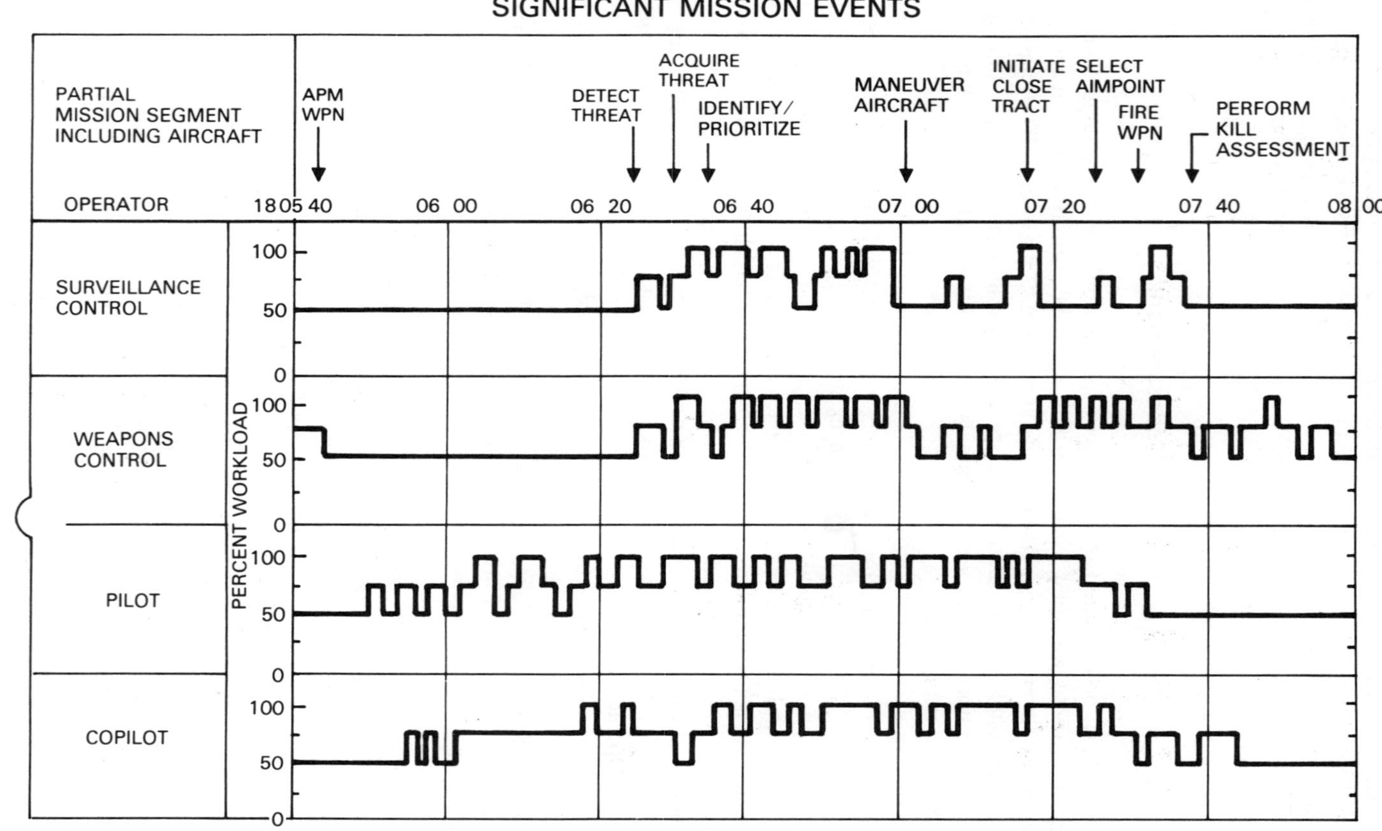

FIGURE 3.9. Sample attentional workload analysis profile. (From Geer, 1981.)

to guide the construction of predictive and measurement metrics or to solve system design problems.

WORKLOAD PREDICTION

The section that follows describes a manual W/L prediction method. Computerized mathematic models that attempt to predict W/L, such as those of Siegel and Wolf, 1969, and Strieb and Wherry, 1979, are discussed in Chapter Four. In system development the analyst wishes to determine those aspects of the developing system that will impose an unacceptable load on the operator. These can then be altered or ameliorated.

Prediction of W/L is based on two concepts:

1. Tasks must be performed in a certain length of time; the degree of W/L is the percent of that time which the operator actually has to perform those tasks.

2. The operator has only a limited capacity, usually conceptualized in terms of attention. When the operator must perform multiple tasks in the same time period, there is competition among the tasks for his attention. That competition "loads" the operator. Intuitively one feels that both concepts are somewhat simplistic.

The W/L predictive method described below (taken from Parks, 1979; and Geer, 1976, 1981) applies both concepts. In concept (1) the operator's W/L is based on estimates of time required to perform a task in relation to the time allowed or available to perform that task. If, for example, the operator has 15 minutes to perform the task but it will take him only 10 minutes, he has a W/L of 66 percent. (One might say of course that if the operator knows he has enough time to accomplish a task within his capability, why should he feel "loaded" at all?) This is *average* W/L per task over the time of its performance and is psychologically very different from the *instantaneous* W/L developed following concept (2). In this concept, W/L is the degree of loading in terms of attention-per-task per operator, during the time the task is performed. This W/L can fluctuate during the time of performance as attention requirements rise or fall. A degree of loading scale used to provide this rating is calibrated in terms of percent—*0* to *100*—of operator attention required by the task during its performance. Figure 3.9 is a graphic depiction of the W/L profile described by degree of loading. It is my impression that W/L analysis is performed more often in terms of attentional requirements than in terms of time availability, although manifestly W/L in terms of time is a more objective and easily secured measure. This is true only of the manual mode of W/L analysis. The mathematical models described in Chapter Four utilize time as a W/L measure.

Loading in terms of attentional demands has some relationship with task difficulty. At the same time one can think of many individual tasks which are inherently difficult, even when performed apart from any other task. W/L is therefore not task difficulty, but task difficulty is one of the factors that can cause W/L. However, W/L theory and method do not attempt to account for task difficulty.

The analysis of W/L in terms of attention is performed as follows. Where multiple operators are involved in performing integrated tasks as in Figure 3.9, list the individual operators down the left-hand side of the page and give each operator a percent of the W/L scale. Next, on the left/right axis of the page (top or bottom), indicate the time scale in which the various tasks must be performed. Above the time scale describe the major task events. Estimate the degree of loading-per-operator per task during the time the task must be performed (as stated previously, in terms of percent—*0* to *100*—of operator attention required by the task). At each interval of interest (e.g., each 5 minutes) graph the degree of loading values.

Special Problems

Special problems arise in summating W/L for more than one task performed concurrently or on the basis of individual perceptual–motor channels. Because of the interaction between tasks and between perceptual–motor channels, it is not particularly clear how one should summate: simple addition is likely to be incorrect but there is no other obvious way of weighting task or channel loadings. If the analyst evaluates W/L in terms of the individual perceptual–motor channels, he cannot equate a 75 percent loading on each channel to an overall 75 percent loading. When the effects of loading on individual channels are summated, the result cannot be accurately predicted but one would expect that the total W/L would be greater than that of each individual channel.

Geer (1981) suggests that workloads over 100 percent are unacceptable, those between 75 percent and 100 percent are undesirable and those under 75 percent are acceptable provided the operator has sufficient work to remain reasonably busy. Operator loading in excess of 75 percent should receive special consideration. However, the empirical data underlying these criteria appear to be lacking. The same author (Geer, 1981) suggests that because of the many unknowns in the W/L estimation process, such as the subjectivity of expert judgments and the summation of individual channel effects, the accuracy of most W/L assessments has a range of ± 20 percent.

Average W/L based on time availability results in a simpler chart than that of Figure 3.9. In this chart the left-hand axis of the form lists the individual tasks, followed by 2 bars for each task. One broken line indicates the time needed to perform (e.g., 5 minutes), the second unbroken line, the time actually available, as shown in Figure 3.10.

Task Loading Estimates. Task loading estimates may come from several sources. For example, the task may be the same as—or similar to—another task in a predecessor system. Objectively gathered task time data from a predecessor system is most reliable since it presumably has been or can be verified empirically. Such task time data are often not available, however. The next most desirable data are from operators who have performed similar tasks. In this case one must secure estimates from several operators because their judgments will almost invariably differ, even though slightly. Enough detail about the tasks must be provided these "ex-

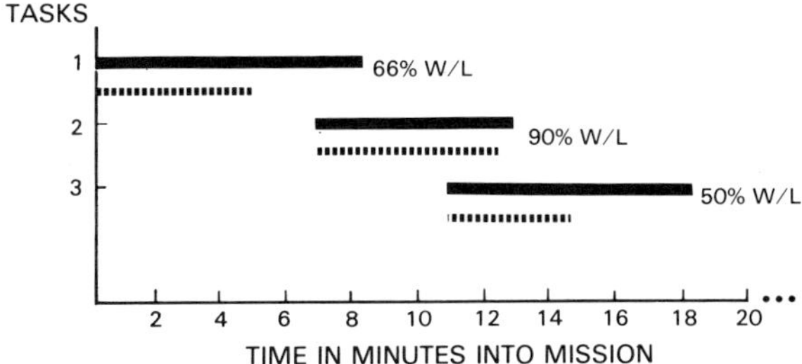

FIGURE 3.10. Sample time-availability workload analysis profile.

perts" to enable them to make valid estimates. When these sources are not available the analyst, together with knowledgeable project designers, must make an educated guess. One way of making this guess is to partition the task into subtasks, apply a data base of subtask data (e.g., from the Data Store, Munger et al., 1962) and then recombine the subtask times to form an estimate of total task time. This last is not however likely to be very satisfying to the analyst because the basis of combination is simple addition.

In some W/L analyses task performance is broken out by the individual sensory and motor channels involved, i.e., visual and auditory monitoring, the operation separately of the right and left hands and the right and left foot. Estimates of percent loading for the sensory and motor channels can be secured on the basis of the amount of time each channel is involved during any particular time interval. A problem arises in the cognitive area. One would think that the individual was 100 percent cognitively occupied during the task but that is not apparently what happens. Geer (1981) suggests that partitioning the W/L into sensory and motor channels is not necessary to secure a successful analysis. Still he feels that the more detail, the better the analysis.

In some situations operators can effectively perform more than one task at one time. However it is obvious that an operator cannot accomplish two tasks simultaneously if both tasks require the use of a single perceptual–motor channel about 100 percent of the time. When properly developed, the W/L analysis chart exposes such contradictions.

Workload estimations can be either gross or detailed in terms of time and number of perceptual–motor channels considered. As W/L situations become more critical, shorter time intervals are important.

The W/L chart may be a single continuous chart from the beginning to end of a mission or the analyst may construct a number of charts, each of which expands a particularly critical segment of the mission. Time scale should be commensurate with task complexity, for example, 15-minute intervals may be all that is required for simple tasks, 5-second intervals for more complex tasks. Whatever intervals are used should, of course, be common for all similar tasks.

Most W/L analyses have been performed with aircraft pilot tasks in which there is considerable monitoring of instruments and motor movement (of pedals, throttles, and throwing of switches). But the question arises how to predict W/L for tasks that are more cognitively oriented, such as troubleshooting or control operations in the process control industry. Since much of their activity is covert, estimation of their loading may prove more difficult (although see the later discussion of W/L rating scales). In addition, Wickens (1984) points out that the W/L prediction methods assume that observable activity demands full attention, whereas non-observable activities like decision making are assigned zero W/L values because they are not associated with overt motor acts. If the cognitive activity presumably going on throughout the task is considered, this may produce 200% W/L, which is obvious nonsense.

Results

The results of the W/L analysis serve multiple purposes. They provide a basis for identifying and resolving potential W/L problems and can be used to compare the relative merits of design alternatives. They also may be useful in examining operating procedures and training requirements.

Design Aid. As a design aid, to help the analyst pinpoint potential problem areas, the W/L prediction method may be reasonably satisfactory. Stacked up however against the highly sophisticated theory that has been built up about W/L (see, for example, Senders, 1979) it appears somewhat simplistic. The technique assumes that time constraints and attentional competition are the primary causal factors for W/L, an assumption which is as yet unverified. The method is one of simple estimation based in most cases on expert judgment, although there may be some empirical data. If so, these data have not been published in the open literature.

Theoretical Basis. The theoretical basis for W/L prediction in terms of attention is the assumption of a limited channel, sampling model of the operator. An example is Broadbent's (1958) single channel, limited capacity model for the human in which incoming stimuli compete for resources by competing for access to the one channel. This approach assumes that an upper bound exists in the operator's ability to gather and process information. Spare mental capacity is the difference between the total W/L capacity of the operator and the capacity needed to perform the task. As spare mental capacity decreases, W/L increases until overload ensues. Since Broadbent (1958), other models have been developed (see Lane, 1982) which suggest that the operator is more flexible than the single channel theory would posit.

The use of the W/L prediction method by behavior analysts illustrates a phenomenon we have already experienced, particularly in the task analysis methodology. This is the phenomenon of not dealing with system characteristics directly but of utilizing "expert" judgments (estimates) about the effect of these characteristics on performance. Instead of asking, what is the effect of system dimension *X* on operator performance of task *Y*? analysts ask someone who has performed task *Y* on a predecessor system with similar equipment, what is the W/L associated with that task? Presumably one then regresses from the task W/L to the equipment/system characteristics involved in the task. The problem with estimating W/L in this way is in part the subjectivity involved. More important, however, task performance is affected not only by system dimension *X* but other system dimensions and factors as well. Thus, the W/L associated with task *Y* cannot be equated with the W/L resulting from system dimension *X*. Ideally one would wish to have experimental data to the effect that the major system dimensions each have an individual—and combined—effect on task performance which one can attribute to W/L. The tendency however, to use subjective judgments about the task rather than analyzing system or task characteristics directly is a reflection of the difficulty researchers have in conceptualizing the significant dimensions of these tasks and systems and the consequent lack of data about them.

One might ask whether it is not possible to develop a method of W/L prediction derived directly from an examination of task and equipment characteristics. If one could assign a W/L scale value—albeit only on a relative basis—directly to task/equipment characteristics, then it should be possible to determine very early in development where points and features of markedly excessive W/L may arise (which is all the present W/L prediction method attempts to do). Efforts have in fact been made to develop such a scale (Kitchin and Graham, 1974).

Instead of assigning the source of W/L to the discrepancy between available and required time, W/L might be conceptualized as arising from certain features of the equipment and the task that make unreasonable demands upon the operator and hence increase task difficulty. W/L might be measured on a 10 point scale where *1* is low and *10* is extremely high. To develop such a scale would require first the establishment of a taxonomy of W/L inducing characteristics; then a review of the experimental literature to indicate which characteristics appear to be correlated with overload performance. Finally, the ratings of a number of "expert" judges applying perhaps a psychometric technique to develop the scale would be required. Given a W/L inducing characteristic such as information presented via displays, the following W/L values which are purely hypothetical might be established:

Workload Inducing Characteristic	Predicted Workload Value
Information is	
1) Simple (e.g., warning light)	1
2) Complex but unambiguous	4
3) Ambiguous	6
4) Simple but must be interpreted under time constraints	4
5) Complex and must be interpreted under time constraints, etc.	10

One might develop similar scales for other W/L inducing factors such as the number of controls and displays, the length of procedure, highly precise hand movements, memory requirements, and interaction with team members. Since any task or equipment feature which is complex or requires operator performance under severe constraints or handicaps may serve as a W/L inducing characteristic, the number of potential W/L characteristics is very large—although in practice their number would be limited because only a few characteristics would apply in most cases to the individual equipment/task.

Each design would be evaluated in terms of factors appropriate to its characteristics. Each factor would receive a W/L prediction value, after which all the W/L values would be combined (how, remains to be determined). The scale values to be assigned to each W/L characteristic would be developed only after extensive analytic and empirical scaling efforts such as those made by Fleishman and Stephenson (1970) in their taxonomic studies.

What has been suggested here is of course quite crude and subjective but not much more so than the W/L prediction methods themselves; and it would have the virtue that it directly addresses system design. It has the disadvantage that the measure reflects equipment characteristics only and does not take into account operator capability (but then, present W/L predictive methods do not account for capability, either). Moreover, equipment characteristics are in variant over the course of the mission; it might therefore be difficult to tie the W/L prediction to varying mission phases. On the other hand, there is no reason why one could not make use of present W/L predictive methods in addition to addressing system characteristics directly.

Predictions could be validated experimentally by developing functional mockups and experimental tasks representing varying equipment characteristics with varying W/L (as Mirabella and Wheaton, 1974, did for task complexity) and then requiring subjects to perform with these. But this brings us to W/L assessment.

WORKLOAD ASSESSMENT

The distinction between W/L as a prediction of the future effect of the system upon operator performance and W/L assessment as a measurement of the operator's ongoing state is obvious. If, after a system becomes operational, the W/L of its personnel is measured, it is possible to validate the prediction method, though the author is unaware that this has ever been done. The results of W/L assessment research should assist W/L prediction by suggesting aspects of operator/system performance which the analyst should look for in making his predictions. However, the utility of W/L assessment results for assisting W/L prediction is not clear, because the former is heavily theoretical, and academic, whereas the latter is system oriented and pragmatic.

There are only a few W/L predictive methods (even if one includes the computerized versions to be discussed in Chapter Four) but Wierwille and Williges (1979) report 28 assessment measures which fall into three categories: a. physiologic, b. objective (primary and secondary task performance), and c. subjective.

Physiologic Workload Measurement Methods

These methods are used to measure the physical effort required to perform a job. Most of the experimental research has been performed on aircraft pilots, although a little has been done on air traffic controllers, foresters, steel workers, etc. (see Wierwille, 1979, for a review of relevant research).

The rationale of using physiologic measures to measure mental load is based on the concept of *activation* or *arousal*, a bodily state associated with increased activity in the nervous system when stimulated. It has been suggested (Welford, 1973) that any task requiring effort raises the level of arousal.

Critical to the concept of arousal is what has been termed the *inverted U* hypothesis, or the *Yerkes-Dodson curve* (1908) which depicts a relationship between arousal (expressed perhaps as motivation) and learning. The relationship has also been associated with Selye's (1936) stress theory. In general the relationship suggests that performance is optimal when the level of activation is moderate, being low when activation is either very low or very high. Many studies have been done to verify the relationship, but the evidence is ambiguous. McGrath (1976), for example, has data to indicate that performance continues to improve indefinitely as arousal increases.

The concept of arousal is a convenient way of relating physiological activity to W/L. If the task being performed, the effort (arousal) being exerted by the operator and the resulting performance are all related, then levels of physiologic activity should provide useful estimates of W/L levels.

The major physiologic variables in the assessment of W/L are shown in Table 3.2. Restrictions imposed by the job—safety, noninterference, ease of data gathering and acceptability to subjects—severely limit the number of physiologic variables that can be used in practice. A much larger number of physiologic indices have been used during laboratory and simulator studies.

TABLE 3.2. Physiologic Measures of Workload

System	Measure
Cardiovascular system	* Heart rate
	* Heart rate variability (sinus arrhythmia)
	* Blood pressure
	Peripheral blood flow
	* Electrical changes in skin
Respiratory system	* Respiration rate
	Ventilation
	Oxygen consumption
	Carbon dioxide estimation
Nervous system	* Brain activity
	* Muscle tension
	* Pupil size
	Finger tremor
	Voice changes
	Blink rate
Biochemistry	* Catecholamines

Note: Those measures most commonly utilized have been indicated by an asterisk.

Cardiovascular System

HEART RATE. Heart rate is one of the easiest of all physiologic measures to record and by far the most popular. It can be obtained directly by measuring the heart action or indirectly by counting the arterial pulse which in the healthy individual is synchronous with heart rate. Direct measurement involves the use of the electrocardiogram (EKG) to sense the electrical potentials associated with heart beat.

A partial listing of studies that have attempted to correlate heart rate with W/L include Auffret, Seris, Berthez and Fatras (1967), Barnard and Duncan (1975), Ettema (1969), Jex and Allen (1970), Mobbs, David and Thomas (1971), Spyker, Stackhouse, Khalafalla and McLane, (1971) and Schane and Slinde (1968). The evidence for such a relationship is conflicting. Some authors have reported good agreement between heart rate values and flight task difficulty (e.g., Hasbrook and Rasmussen, 1970). There is however some evidence (Lacey and Lacey, 1974) to indicate that simple attention to the environment produces cardiac deceleration which accompanies improved performance of varied tasks. Wierwille (1979) concludes from his review of the literature that heart rate generally does not change with mental load, although in some cases stress may change heart rate.

HEART RATE VARIABILITY. The heart rate of the normal healthy individual at rest varies over periods of seconds by up to 15 or more beats per minute. Sinus arrhythmia, as it is called, is caused by complex feedback mechanisms associated with respiration, blood pressure and regulation of skin temperature. The relationship between heart rate variability and W/L is unclear. Heart rate variability has been found to decrease with mental load (Kalsbeek, 1973a), but others (e.g., Luczak and Laing, 1973; Sayers, 1973; Kalsbeek, 1973b) have found that the relationship is highly variable and occurs only with certain measures of sinus arrhythmia. Schick and Radke, 1980, were unable to demonstrate a consistent relationship.

BLOOD PRESSURE. Laboratory studies have demonstrated the value of blood pressure measurements to indicate levels of arousal and mental activity and several investigators have measured blood pressure on the ground before and after aircraft flight as an indicator of stress and fatigue (Melton et al., 1975, and Blix et al., 1974).

Inflight blood pressure measurement has been carried out in a number of studies (Holden et al., 1962, Roman et al., 1962, 1963). Roman et al. found that blood pressure correlated reasonably well with pilots' estimates of task difficulty. However, Wierwille (1979) concludes that blood pressure is not a reliable index of W/L.

PERIPHERAL BLOOD FLOW. Variations in peripheral blood flow have been associated with changes in levels of arousal, with mental activity and various emotional states, but blood flow is not a very useful measure of such phenomena. Because peripheral blood flow is influenced by temperature, carefully controlled ambient conditions are necessary, restricting the measurement.

ELECTRICAL PROPERTIES OF THE SKIN. Variations in electrical properties of the skin are known to occur in response to changes in emotional states and arousal levels and have been studied for many years. In response to a stimulus, skin resistance, measured by passing a small direct current between two electrodes, shows a characteristic decrease known as the *galvanic skin response* (GSR). These responses are associated in some fashion with an increase in the activity of sweat glands. GSR is usually measured with electrodes applied to the ventral wrist. Amplified signals from skin electrodes form an important part of the well known "lie detector" test.

GSR has been used to perceive changes in arousal, to measure stress as an indicator of mental activity, and to assess car drivers in light and heavy traffic (Preston, 1969; Helander, 1975). Skin resistance has been used to detect changes during a compensatory tracking task (Benson et al., 1965) and to measure pilot stress during landing (Corkindale, 1969).

Unfortunately, the results of GSR tests are very susceptible to misinterpretation. There are large individual differences and only through wholesale averaging of data can consistent changes in GSR be demonstrated. Wilkins (1982) feels that "electrodermal activity as a correlate or predictor of work has proved to be rather disappointing" (p. 62).

Respiratory System. The few respiratory indices of interest from the standpoint of W/L include respiratory rate, airflow and volume, and estimating oxygen and carbon dioxide.

RESPIRATORY RATE. Measurement of breathing rate is probably the most useful and most common of the respiratory variables. Certainly it is the easiest to record and has been used extensively in studies involving emotion, stress, arousal and mental load. Commonly used instruments for continuous monitoring are the impedence strain gauge or thermistor. Unfortunately respiratory patterns are interrupted and modified by speed, thereby reducing the value of this index in flight situations.

RESPIRATORY AIRFLOW AND VOLUME. Airflow is measured by a pneumotachograph. One device measures the pressure across an orifice, another measures the change in capacitance.

ANALYSIS OF RESPIRATORY GASES. Estimation of carbon dioxide and oxygen using some form of gas analysis is normally a laboratory procedure but small and semiportable instruments have been modified for use in flight simulators and aircraft.

The results of research (e.g., Jex and Allen, 1970; Spyker et al., 1971; Stackhouse, 1973) suggest that breathing patterns vary with stress and therefore with W/L, since W/L is related to stress. However, the equipment required to measure respiration may be obtrusive.

The Nervous System

THE ELECTROENCEPHALOGRAM. Electroencephalogram (EEG) potentials represent the combined effect of nerve cell potentials over a large area of the cerebral cortex. They are detected by two or more surface electrodes placed in contact with the scalp or from needle electrodes inserted into the skin.

Although the normal EEG consists of many different frequencies, one usually predominates. For example, a common type is the alpha rhythm of about 9 to 13 Hz which is most noticeably affected by visual inputs, predominating when the eyes are closed. Under anaesthesia the alpha rhythm is replaced by the beta rhythm of 14 to 30 Hz.

Experiments have shown that mental activity affects the frequency of the EEG but its meaning is confused by large inter- and intraindividual variations. Results are frequently ambiguous and difficult to interpret.

EVOKED CORTICAL POTENTIALS. External stimuli such as intermittent noises or flashing lights evoke a measurable response in the electroencephalogram. Many of these evoked potentials are of low amplitude but with suitable summation techniques the signal–to–noise ratio can be amplified. Evoked potentials have been measured in studies of vigilance, attention or expectation (Groves and Eason, 1969), and learning (Lewis, 1982). Spyker and his colleagues (1971) decided that the potentials were unsuitable as a measure of W/L but Lewis is using them to investigate stress, and Israel, Wickens, Chesney and Donchin (1980) found that they predicted display monitoring W/L quite well. The large amount of averaging required to secure consistent results in the evoked potential and the fact that evoked cortical potentials (ECPs) may be dependent on the subject's attitudes, understanding and expectations tend to make the meaning of this measure ambiguous.

MUSCLE TENSION AND ELECTROMYOGRAPHY. Body movement and the use of force are accompanied by increased tension in the active muscle groups and a decrease in the passive groups. These changes are reflected by changes in the electrical activity which accompanies muscle fiber contraction. Measurement of this activity is called electromyography (EMG) which can be recorded by surface electrodes placed on the skin over the muscle or by inserting needle electrodes directly into the muscle itself. However, recordings are difficult to interpret. EMGs have been used to indicate levels of anxiety and fatigue, to measure reaction times and to detect and measure tremor. Schnore (1959) showed good correlation between arousal levels and physiologic measures which included EMGs from neck muscles. However Spyker et al. (1971) found that EMG was not highly correlated with subjectively estimated W/L. Wierwille (1979) considers this measure to be unreliable.

FINGER TREMOR. Most normal subjects exhibit a fine tremor of the outstretched fingers which during emotional states becomes much more obvious. It is possible to measure this by attaching a strain gauge accelerometer to a finger of the outstretched hand (Nicholson et al., 1973).

SPEECH ANALYSIS. The characteristics of a person's voice vary when he is subjected to emotional stress. A few researchers (Simenov et al., 1975; Older and Jenney, 1975) have studied the voice frequencies of pilots, cosmonauts, and actors and attempted to identify stress and fatigue, but the results are ambiguous.

PUPILOGRAPHY. The pupil of the eye contracts in bright light and dilates in dim light. Methods of measuring pupil size are mostly based either on photoelectric or photographic techniques. The latter tend to be somewhat tedious, although infrared photography has made it possible to record pupil size in very poor light. Workload and task difficulty appear to be related to pupil diameter (Hess, 1972; Kahneman, Beatty and Pollack, 1967; Noel, 1974; Westbrook, Anderson and Pietrzak, 1966). However, many factors, such as fatigue and ambient light level affect pupil diameter and must be carefully controlled. Because of this, pupilography may be a practicable measure of W/L in carefully controlled conditions but cannot be seriously considered for use operationally.

BLINK RATE. Blinking is a normal everyday action of the eyelids which can be recorded by photographic and photoelectric methods. It has been shown that blink rate varies with the difficulty of a task, irrespective of whether it is a visual task or not. However blink rate is of doubtful value in assessing W/L.

Biochemistry. Catecholamines and a host of other chemical substances such as parotid fluid and urine associated with endocrine and metabolic functions have often been used as indices of stress, W/L, and fatigue. For obvious reasons it is difficult to collect blood or urine at frequent intervals during operational activities and in most studies, specimens have been collected before and after the activity.

Street, Singh and Hale (1970) found a definite relationship between mental stress in graduate students and the level of 17-hydroxycorticosteroid (17-OCHS) in parotid fluid. Storm, Hartman, Intano and Peters (1976) found changes in the level of 17-OCHS and other chemicals for three different flight conditions and stress. Wierwille (1979) considers that, beyond the difficulty in collecting samples in operational situations, biochemicals measure stress, anxiety, and fatigue more directly than they do W/L.

Summary Evaluation of Physiologic Measures

Only a few of the indices described can be considered of practical value in assessing W/L. Kak (1981) has attempted to describe the available physiologic methods in terms of the criteria listed in Table 3.3. The application is to occupational stress but the value judgments apply as well to W/L. Minus—" – "—indicates that a measure is especially poor, plus —" + "—that it has a special advantage, and zero—"0"—is neutral.

All of these measures have serious disadvantages. The evidence for the relationship between physiologic and performance indices is ambiguous at best. Often the meaning of the relationship, even when it exists, is unclear. The sensitivity of these

TABLE 3.3. Features of Physiological Measures

	Criteria							
Measures	Concept validity	Empirical validity	Freedom from artefacts	Standard-ization	Reliab-ility	Represen-tativeness	Invasiv-eness	Practi-cality and cost
GSR	–	0	–	–	–	0	+	+
EKG	+	+	0	0	+	+	+	0
Heart rate	+	+	0	+	+	+	+	+
Sinus arrhythmia	0	0	0	–	–	0	+	+
Blood pressure	+	+	0	+	+	+	0	+
Pupilary dilation	0	0	–	–	0	–	0	–
Breathing pattern	+	0	–	–	0	0	0	0
Body fluids	+	+	0	+	+	+	+	0
Muscle tension	0	0	0	–	0	0	0	0
EEG	+	0	0	+	0	0	0	0
EP	+	0	0	–	0	0	–	–

Source. Kak, A. V. Stress: an analysis of physiological assessment devices. In G. Salvendy and M. J. Smith (Eds.) *Machine Pacing and Occupational Stress*. London: Taylor and Francis, Ltd., 1981.

measures to possible contaminating conditions, for example, ambient temperature, is very high. Wierwille (1979) suggests that none of these measures is well proven; the most promising are pupil dilation, ECP, and body fluid analysis. Often the instrumentation, although small, is quite obtrusive, interfering with the operator's primary operational task.

Objective Workload Measurement Methods

Objective methods are performance oriented, that is, they do not rely on the operator's opinion or on his physiology. Since these methods emphasize input stimuli or responses to these input stimuli, objective measures describe the outputs or consequences of task performance. Viewed in this sense, any task output can be used under certain experimental circumstances to reflect W/L.

Measures can be taken of primary task performance (in which no comparison is made of the task performance with the performance of any other task) and of tasks in a comparative situation. Primary task performance is not experimentally controlled; comparative task performance is—more or less—controlled.

PRIMARY TASK PERFORMANCE. If a single task is being performed, it is possible to assume that variation in performance of that task reflects changes in W/L. Any task can therefore be used to measure W/L. If W/L is made sufficiently high, degradation in performance over time will inevitably occur. Unfortunately, primary task performance does not seem to be sensitive to moderate or low levels of W/L, largely because the operator adapts his performance strategy to changes in W/L. Workload can only be measured on a comparative basis because there is no absolute measure of it. Hence, primary task performance as a measure of W/L is inadequate when no other task condition exists with which it can be compared. Moreover, because there are no controls over the performance of the primary task, it is impossible to estimate the influence of possible contaminating factors such as fatigue or motivation or any other intrusive factor.

COMPARATIVE TASK PERFORMANCE. A general paradigm for measuring W/L experimentally is to present two or more conditions to a single subject group. The conditions differ in terms of some set of inputs which are assumed on the basis of theoretical concept or empirical data to differ in terms of input loading, for example, five signals (condition 1) vs 10 (condition 2), four meters to read vs eight, etc. Assuming a linear relationship between number of meters and load imposed on the subject, condition 1 is less load inducing than condition 2. One cannot assume an absolute level of loading because there is no baseline.

This comparative task loading procedure is useful primarily under controlled laboratory conditions because it is difficult to create such conditions in the operational environment. Moreover, unless the experimental conditions being tested describe dimensions of the loading stimuli, the procedure tells the experimenter nothing about the mechanisms operative in the situation. It is of course possible to have the subject report to the experimenter about the degree of loading he feels but the objectivity and precision we would wish to have in this situation does not exist. There is no particular theoretical basis for this methodology.

Special cases of the comparative performance situation are the information processing, secondary task, and synthetic work situations described below.

1. *Information Processing*. Early efforts in an information processing context were directed at breaking complex reaction time into its constituent components. In a typical situation the subject might be presented with two indicators—one red, the other green—and two response buttons; the right one to be depressed if the light presented were red, the left button if the light were green. After measuring response times in this situation the subject was exposed to a situation in which there was one light and one button. The assumption was that the difference in average response times between the two-light/two-button condition and the one-light/one-button condition represents the mental processing time required to recognize whether the red or green light was illuminated.

An example of research using this paradigm is the work of Conrad (1955, 1956) who treated load as being a function of the number of signal sources presented and considered load stress to be produced by increasing that number beyond some value. Knowles, Garvey and Newlin (1953) compared performance on a 10 × 10 matrix of lights and response buttons against a 5 × 5 matrix of lights and buttons.

The rate of information presentation (not signals) was equalized across the two conditions: rates were 1.75, 2.25, 2.7, and 3.0 bits per second. They found that increased display size had a greater effect on error rate than signal presentation rate.

Measurement of reaction time to simultaneous or immediate successive signals has become a popular method of testing hypotheses relative to channel theory (see Sanders, 1979). In fact, one such task, the Sternberg memory-search task (Sternberg, 1969) has become so popular it is being marketed commercially. In this task reaction time to an unexpected stimulus is measured by a yes/no decision whether the stimulus is or is not a member of a previously memorized set of characters. When the number of such characters is increased, reaction time is prolonged as more items must be searched in the working memory.

2. *Secondary Loading Tasks.* The most general direct approach to the study of W/L in the laboratory has been through the use of secondary loading tasks. Knowles (1963) summarizes early work and provides the general rationale for the application of this technique to W/L measurement in a part–task simulation context. The operator is required to perform two simultaneous tasks, assigning one (the primary task) a higher priority than the secondary or auxiliary task. The primary task's W/L is defined in terms of the degradation in secondary task performance occurring under the dual task condition relative to single task performance. The comparison is between the auxiliary task when performed alone and the auxiliary task when paired with another primary task. The methodology assumes that primary task performance is maintained at a stable level, whereas secondary task performance fluctuates as a direct function of reserve capacity.

Many tasks have been used as the secondary task. Ogden, Levine and Eisner (1979) provide an extensive list based on their review of 600 citations. The most common tasks are mental mathematics, memory, tracking, reaction time, auditory detection, problem solving, monitoring, time estimation, random sequence generation, and classification. They are unable to recommend the best task or class of tasks to use. Williges and Wierwille (1979) describe these tasks under six categories: time estimation, adaptive and nonadaptive tracking, and adaptive and nonadaptive arithmetic/logic tasks. They point out certain difficulties in applying secondary tasks: intrusion (performance on the primary task may be degraded on introduction of the secondary task), the possibility that the secondary task approach actually estimates *average* W/L over a time period rather than peak W/L. Knowles (1963) suggested the following criteria for selection of a secondary task: noninterference with the primary task, ease of learning, self-pacing (to allow the secondary task to be neglected, if necessary), continuous scoring, compatibility with the primary task, sensitivity, and representativeness. Tasks meeting these criteria include choice reaction time, mental arithmetic, self-adaptive tracking and monitoring, all of which are in fact frequently used in W/L studies.

The secondary task approach depends upon the validity of certain assumptions, the most important of which is that human processing capacity is limited, so that there is competition for attention among multiple tasks being performed concurrently. Other important assumptions are that (1) human processing capacity is unitary or undifferentiated; (2) the human information processing system contains no significant task-specific capacities; and (3) overall capacity remains invariant across changes in processing demand. To the extent that these assumptions and models are incorrect, the secondary task measurements of W/L lose some of their metric qualities and their capability of interpreting W/L. Pew (1979) and Fisk, Derrick and Schneider (1983) have criticized secondary task methodology; Hawkins and Ketchum (1980) have analyzed the models and cast doubt on their validity. Moray (1984) has pointed out that many studies making use of the secondary task methodology are deficient in safeguarding against changes in operator criteria. The relationship of the secondary task to the primary one is usually unknown. The evidence for and against secondary task theory is equivocal, but the approach has considerable intuitive appeal which accounts for its continued popularity.

3. *Synthetic Multiple Tasks.* Synthetic multiple-task situations are a special case of the secondary task approach. The important difference is that in the multiple task situation the subject is presented simultaneously with a number of tasks rather than only two. He is asked to perform these tasks individually and then in combination. His performance in combination (as a battery of tasks) is compared with his performing the individual tasks. The most detailed description of this approach has been provided by Chiles, Alluisi and Adams (1968).

The specific tasks employed by Chiles et al. involved monitoring of lights and meters (thus providing measures of reaction time), mental arithmetic, pattern discrimination, elementary problem solving, and two-dimensional compensatory tracking. The difference in performance between single- and multiple-task performance is shown in Figure 3.11, which presents the response latencies on a normalized scale for the responses to the offset of any one of five green lights located one at each corner and one in the middle of the equipment. The figure contains two curves, one for the monitoring task only, the other for monitoring performance as part of the full battery of tasks.

It is not immediately apparent that W/L research centered around secondary task theory has had any great or direct effect on methods of W/L prediction. To the extent that such research bolsters the limited capacity concept, it presumably increases confidence in those methods, but the connection is not very close.

Subjective Measures

The performer's opinion has traditionally played an important role in W/L assessment. If the operator feels loaded or stressed, if he feels that he is performing in an effortful manner, he *is* loaded, regardless of what physiologic and objective measures show. If he does not feel loaded these other indices of W/L, whatever they imply, are difficult to interpret. Whatever other measures are applied, operator opinion is essential.

It has been common practice to use subjective assessment as a backup for other measures. Physiologic and objective measures are compared with the subjective, and the latter are used—hopefully—as a sort of confirmation of the former. There

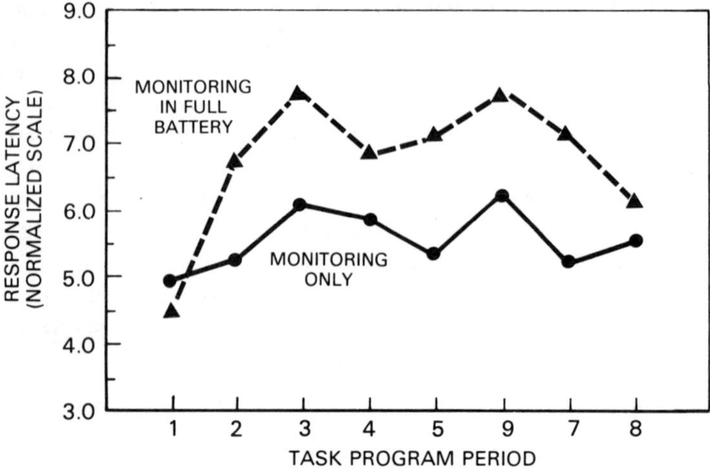

FIGURE 3.11. Mean response latency in detecting warning signals during each 15-minute period of a 2-hour test. (From Hall, Passey, and Meighan, 1965.)

is a directness to the phenomenologic experience that one does not find in the other indices.

The subjective experience of W/L helps to validate other W/L indices because performance and physiologic measures are subject to contamination, can be interpreted as being caused by other factors, or are uninterpretable. Objective performance differences in an apparent W/L situation may, for example, result from the presence or absence of learning or fatigue, but this is less likely to be the case if the subject can report that he feels loaded. Of course, subjective expressions are not necessarily "clean," either; there is possible contamination by the effects of motivation, internal and external criteria of what is appropriate behavior, etc.

A variety of techniques (e.g., magnitude estimation, paired comparisons) have been applied in W/L judgments, but the rating scale is the most frequently used. Other less structured subjective methods that have been used are questionnaires (dichotomous or multiple-choice items) and structured and unstructured interviews. None of these less structured methods provide quantitative data and hence will not be considered here.

The most common way of getting a linear opinion measure is to ask the subject to state a numerical rating on a Likert-type scale, typically with seven or nine intervals. The respondent is guided to his rating by the addition of verbal adjective anchors at certain sections of the scale. Rating scales are discussed in some detail in Chapter Ten.

Another rating scale used by Nicholson, Hill, Borland and Ferres, 1970, is the 10-cm line method. The pilot is asked to indicate his opinion by making a mark on a line the ends of which are labelled with the opposite extremes of opinion (e.g., *extremely difficult* and *no difficulty*). The rating is then taken from the position of the subject's mark. The 10-cm line technique has several disadvantages which are shared by many other rating scales. (1) It is, for instance, uncertain that one subject's mental scale will be linear as compared with another's. (2) Not all researchers are capable of making the extremes of their scale reflect true opposites. (3) There is, with this technique, a natural tendency for subjects to start rating in the middle of the scale to allow room for movement either way. (4) The linear aspect of the scale encourages the researcher to ascribe unwarranted fineness to the resulting measurement.

A major problem in developing a W/L rating scale is deciding which dimension or dimensions should be built into it. One the author developed (Meister, 1978) combined effort and task difficulty, but should one put these two into the same stew pot? If W/L is multidimensional, presumably one should either include several dimensions in the same scale—in which case one hardly knows how the dimensions interact in the respondent's mind—or create several individual scales—in which case there is the problem of combining their individual values.

The most serious restriction on the rating scale methodology is that although such scales have often been used in W/L research (e.g., Helm, 1975, 1976; Stackhouse, 1973) none of these applications has been based on a rigorously developed rating scale based on psychometric theory.

More sophisticated efforts are now being made to develop a standardized, validated subjective rating scale for W/L. Wierwille and Casali (1983) claim that they have validated a rating scale for systems other than those in which the operator performs motor tasks. Theirs (shown in Figure 3.12) is a modified Cooper-Harper scale (1969) which replaces references to handling qualities with terms more appropriate to other activities. The scale apparently differentiated between experimentally determined levels of W/L, although in a flight simulator context.

Another rating scale currently under development is something called SWAT—*subjective workload assessment technique* (Reid, Shingledecker and Eggemeir, 1981a, b). In this scale W/L is composed of time load, mental effort load and stress load dimensions. Each dimension is represented by an individual 3-point rating scale with descriptions for each load level. SWAT is based on conjoint measurement scaling (Krantz and Tversky, 1971) in which ratings on the three dimensions are combined into one overall interval scale of W/L. The three ordinal levels of the three dimensions yield a 27-cell matrix for each of which a W/L description is provided. Subjects rank order the cells (each on an index card) based on the amount of overall mental W/L they predict they would experience under the conditions described. Boyd (1983) reports that the three dimensions are not orthogonal which presents some difficulty for the technique.

Any W/L scale must satisfy certain criteria. It must apply to a variety of task situations, must represent the various ways in which W/L can be expressed by the operator, should correlate with other W/L indices, its dimensions should be orthogonal, and it should be validated—if at all possible in an operational (not a laboratory) situation. No scale or subjective measure exists that will satisfy all these criteria.

Williges and Wierwille (1979) point out some inherent deficiencies in the use of subjective W/L estimates. The estimator may be unaware of the extent to which he is loaded, he may confuse physical and mental W/L, and his estimates may change

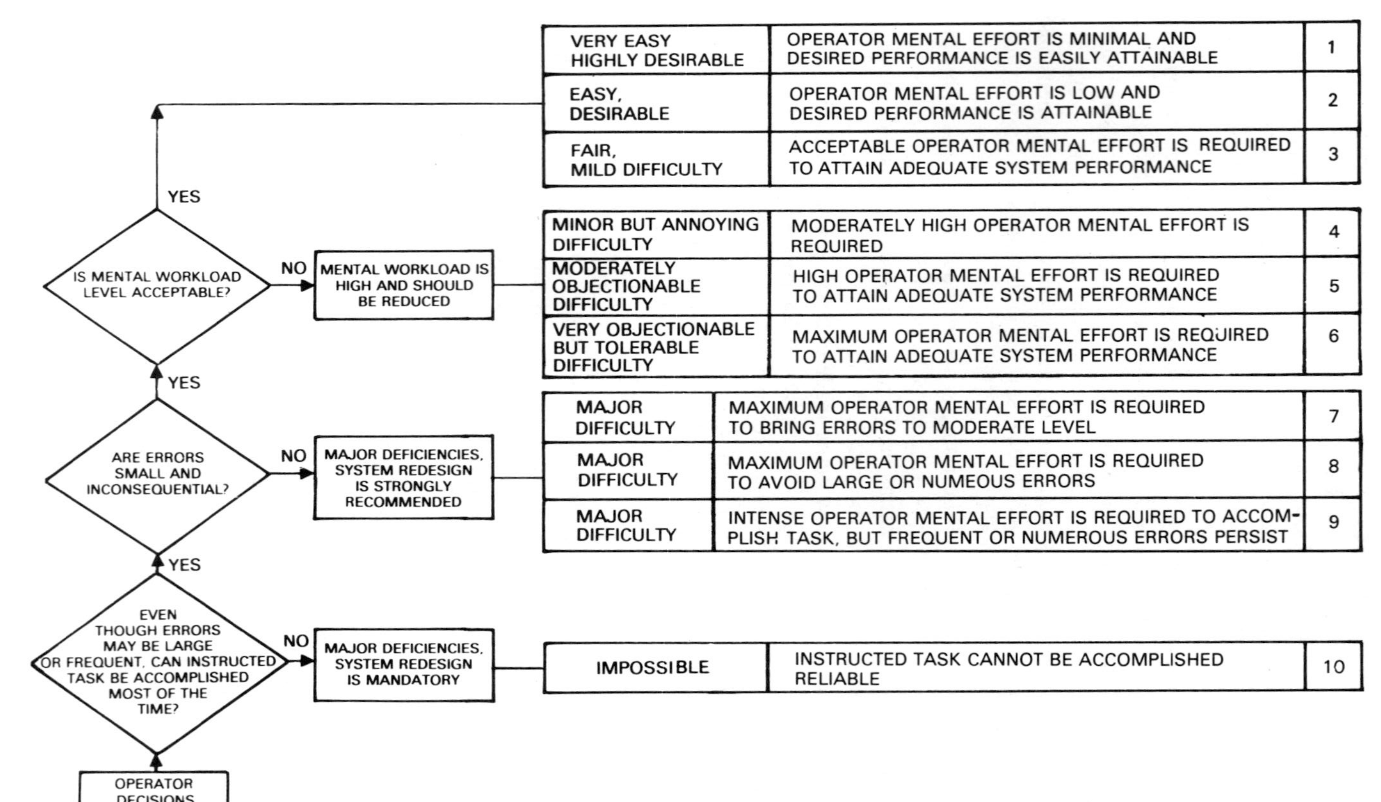

FIGURE 3.12. Modified Cooper-Harper workload rating scale. (From *Proceedings of the Human Factors Society 27th Annual Meeting*, 1983, p. 133. Copyright 1983 by the Human Factors Society, Inc., and reproduced by permission.)

over time. Just how valid rating estimates of W/L are is still an unknown, although in their study Childress, Hart and Bortolussi (1982) found that overall W/L ratings appear to be predicted by different scales depending on the situation. There are apparently complex W/L components or moderators whose effects require further research.

COMMENTARY

In the best of all scientific worlds, it would be possible, using the criteria of Chapter One, to make clear-cut comparisons among the methods described in this chapter. Because some readers of an early draft asked for it, I have attempted to do so in Table 3.4, but I have done so with great trepidation. These comparisons are highly subjective and for many of the criteria objective evidence is lacking. Only three judgments are possible—low, moderate, high; any attempt at being more precise would be fraudulent. No quantitative values can be linked to the three judgments. Where no judgment could be made because of lack of data, a question mark was noted. It is not possible to derive an overall judgment, to say for example, that this method is excellent and this one poor, since all the techniques have advantages and disadvantages.

Time and Motion Methods

For what these methods purport to do—to measure molecular actions—they are highly effective. These actions are relatively easy to measure but undoubtedly tedious. They have a low frequency of use by behavior specialists, but industrial engineers working in a factory environment may use them quite frequently. Cost is moderate: No input data are required to initiate the method (the data are gathered by applying the method), but the time cost may be relatively high. Flexibility is high: Any kind of motion may be timed but range is quite low, being confined to physical

TABLE 3.4 Comparison of Design Aiding Techniques

	Methods								
Criteria	T/M	FFD	D/A	T/L	L/A	DODT	OSD	SK	W/L
Effectiveness	H	M	M	H	H	M	H	M	M
Ease of Use	M	M	M	H	H	L	L	M	L
Frequency of Use	L	H	M	H	M	L	H	L	M
Cost	M	L	L	L	L	H	H	L	H
Flexibility	L	H	H	H	M	H	H	H	M
Range	L	H	M	L	L	H	H	M	M
Validity	H	H	H	H	H	?	H	M	?
Reliability	H	?	?	H	H	?	?	?	?
Objectivity	H	M	M	H	H	L	H	L	L

actions. Validity and objectivity should be high, since the method measures the actions that occur using simple measurement methods, for example, a stopwatch, and because of this measurement reliability also should be high.

Function Flow Diagrams

Technique effectiveness is moderate. Although the technique is graphic, it depends on analysis of input and output relationships and deductions from these; this analysis is sometimes defective. The graphics are relatively easy to draw except when functional relationships are complex. The FFD is very frequently applied and it has low cost because it requires little input data (although considerable analysis). Flexibility and range are high because the technique can be applied to any system, and to any set of functions. If validity is defined as identity between hypothesized and actual system functions, the validity is high because the FFD will be redrawn until that identity is achieved. Objectivity is only moderate because much of the technique depends on subjective analysis. There is no evidence about the reliability with which different analysts construct the same FFDs.

Decision/Action Diagrams

Since FFDs and D/A diagrams are very similar, only the points of difference will be noted. The D/A diagram is less frequently employed than the FFD. It has less range than the FFD because it emphasizes decision making whereas the FFD handles all functions. Moreover, the D/A diagram is less flexible than the FFD, since the former can be applied only at the individual level, whereas the FFD can be applied at all system and subsystem levels.

Time Line Analysis

For what it attempts to do T/L, which is restricted to analysis of activity durations, does very well. The drawing of the T/L is relatively simple and the technique is ordinarily applied when time relationships are important. It is a relatively low-cost technique in terms of required input data and time to draw the T/L chart. It is flexible because it can be applied to any time dependent system but its range is low because it deals only with time dependent functions. Because this technique is largely descriptive, validity and reliability can be assumed to be high, although empirical evidence is lacking. Because it deals only with an objective dimension—time—its objectivity is relatively high.

Link Analysis

This technique concentrates on relationships between personnel and personnel and machines. It has a low range because it concentrates on physical relationships and does not consider underlying functional or behavioral relationships. For what it attempts to do, which is fairly limited, it does it quite well. But it is a minor technique because of its restricted application.

Design Option Decision Tree

This newly developed technique is somewhat cumbersome and relatively little used. It attempts to display graphically design alternatives and it is effective only to the extent that behavioral specialists stimulate systems engineers to analyze systems imaginatively. It is a high cost technique requiring extensive input data and many worker-hours to complete. Its flexibility and range are high because it can describe any system. Objectivity is low because it depends on the creativity of the system engineer. Data on validity and reliability are not available.

Operational Sequence Diagrams

This technique is applied with great frequency during development, in large part because it is required by MIL-H-46855B (Department of Defense, 1979). As a graphic display of task-person-machine interrelationships, it is undoubtedly effective, if only because it requires the analyst to understand personnel and system operations in great detail. However, the amount of work required to draw OSDs for any complex activity renders its cost high. Its flexibility and range are both high because it can be applied to any system, for any set of functions, at various system levels. As a purely descriptive device its validity is inherently high; no information is available concerning the reliability with which different analysts diagramming the same operations will do so in a similar manner. As a purely descriptive device its objectivity is high.

Skill Analysis

This technique is moderately effective in the sense that it will identify the skills needed to perform the job—at least those skills in Fleishman's taxonomy—but it does not identify the *amount* of skill required: for that one must use Fleishman's rating scales. Since the skill analysis (SK) makes use of decision making flow diagrams, it is relatively easy to perform the analysis, although one must conceptualize the task and its elements to use the diagrams. This technique is new and so far infrequently employed. It has low cost in terms of effort and input data and high flexibility because it can be applied to a variety of systems. On the other hand, it has only moderate range because it does not—at least in the author's opinion—identify molar cognitive skills very well. Because of this one can assign only moderate validity to the technique. Reliability of use is unknown and because it is heavily dependent on the user's judgment its objectivity is low.

Workload Prediction

The W/L prediction methods described in this chapter are considered to be only moderately effective because they rest on somewhat simplistic assumptions. These assumptions also have somewhat negative implications for validity but we consider this in Table 3.4 to be somewhat of an unknown. The author has encountered no studies in which a W/L prediction made during system development was verified by subsequent personnel testing when the system was functional. The technique is considered to have low ease-of-application because when performed for each sensory channel and with short time intervals it is quite tedious. The technique is used only moderately, primarily by aircraft developers. It is a high-cost item in terms of the amount of input data required; most of these data are secured from SMEs, which means intensive interviewing. It is moderately flexible which means only that it can be applied to a variety of systems like aircraft that emphasize psychomotor activity. Its range of application to other behavioral functions is somewhat limited because it has difficulties dealing with covert behaviors like monitoring or cognition. Reliability is an unknown, since studies of interanalyst consistency have not been reported in the literature. Objectivity is low because at bottom the technique depends largely on the subjective W/L estimates of SMEs.

The methods described in this chapter have a number of characteristics. Most obviously, they use graphics prominently and this in fact may be their greatest value. For many people, graphics aid analysis. Guidelines for performing these analyses are not inherent in the techniques themselves, nor are they adequately described in instructions for applying the techniques. This is a difficulty we have had occasion to note previously with task analysis. In some of these methods there is excessive reliance on expert opinion.

Outside of W/L analysis, none of the methods described in this chapter has been influenced very much by behavioral theory. In fact, the utility of theory for applied behavioral methods appears to be minimal. W/L prediction has been influenced by the concept of the human as a single channel, limited capacity system (Broadbent, 1958). Still, the emergence of other information processing models has not changed the existing W/L prediction method. Lane (1982) has indicated that "existing theoretical accounts of the limits of human information-processing capacity do not appear to be well enough developed to provide much guidance to a psychologist or engineer working in the applied setting." (p. 135).

It must be emphasized again that it is difficult to compare these techniques, since they possess different strong and weak points. Moreover, these techniques are not alternative versions of the same methodology; each technique has a distinctive function. For example, if one has to predict W/L one has to use the W/L prediction technique. None of the other techniques will satisfy the need. Some of the methods are more closely related than others, for example, FFD, D/A and DODT or T/L and W/L analysis, but the similarities between the techniques conceal important differences.

Although these methods have serious weaknesses, the reader should not disdain them; they are useful in the hands of a skilled analyst. The weaknesses merely imply a need for improvement.

REFERENCES

AGARD (NATO Advisory Group for Aerospace Research and Development), *Assessing Pilot Workload*, AGARD-AG-233, Neuilly sur Seine, France, February 1978 (a).

AGARD (NATO Advisory Group for Aerospace Research and Development), *Methods to Assess Workload*. AGARD-CP-216, Neuilly sur Seine, France, June 1978 (b).

Askren, W. B. and Korkan, K. D. Design Option Decision Tree: a method for schematic analysis of a design problem and integration of human factors data. *Proceedings*, Annual Meeting, Human Factors Society, 1974, 368–375.

Askren, W. B. and Korkan, K. D. *Design Option Decision Tree: A Method for Relating Human Resources Data to Design Alternatives*. Report AFHRL-TR-71-52, Air Force Human Resources Laboratory, Wright-Patterson AFB, OH, December 1971 (AD 741 768).

Askren, W. B., Korkan, K. D. and Watts, G. W. *Human Resources Sensitivity to System Design Tradeoff Alternatives: Feasibility Test with Jet Engine Data*. Report AFHRL-TR-73-21, Air Forces Human Resources Laboratory, Wright-Patterson AFB, OH, November 1973 (AD 776 775).

Auffret, R., Seris, H., Berthoz, A. and Fatras, B. Estimate of the perceptive load by variability of rate of heartbeat: application to a piloting task. *Le Travail Humain*, 1967, *80*, 309–310.

Bailey, G. B. and Presgrave, R. *Basic Motion Timestudy*, New York, McGraw-Hill Book Co., 1958.

Baker, C. C., Johnson, J. H., Malone, M. T. and Malone, T. B. *Human Factors Engineering for Navy Weapon System Acquisition*, Essex Corporation, Alexandria, VA, July 1979.

Barnard, R. J. and Duncan, H. W. Heart rate and ECG responses of fire fighters. *J. Occupational Medicine*, 1975, *17*, 247–250.

Barnes, R. M. *Motion and Time Study, Design and Measurement of Work* (7th ed.). New York: Wiley, 1980.

Beevis, D. Bridge design - a human engineering approach in Canada. *Proceedings*, Sixth Ship Control Systems Symposium, National Defense Headquarters, Ottawa, Canada, volume 2, pp. E1/2-1 through E1/2-16, October 1981.

Benson, A. J., Huddleston, J. H. F., and Rolfe, J. M. A psychophysiological study of compensatory tracking on a digital display. *Human Factors*, 1965, *7*, 457–472.

Blix, A. S. et al. Additional heart rate, an indication of psychologocal activity. *Aerospace Medicine*, 1974, *45*, 1219–1222.

Boyd, S. P. Assessing the validity of SWAT as a workload measurement instrument. *Proceedings*, Human Factors Society Annual Meeting, 1983, 124–128.

Broadbent, D. E. *Perception and Communication*. London: Pergamon, 1958.

Childress, M. E., Hart, S. G. and Bortolussi, M. R. The reliability and validity of flight task workload ratings. *Proceedings*, Human Factors Society Annual Meeting, 1982, 319–323.

Chiles, W. D., Alluisi, E. A. and Adams, O. S. Work schedules and performance during confinement. *Human Factors*, 1968, *10*, 143–196.

Conrad, R. Adaptation to time in a sensori-motor skill. *J. Experimental Psychology*, 1955, *49*, 115–121.

Conrad, R. The timing of signals in skill. *J. Experimental Psychology*, 1956, *51*, 365–370.

Cooper, E. and Harper, P., Jr. *The Use of Pilot Rating in the Evaluation of Aircraft Handling Qualities*. Report TN-D-5153, Ames Research Center, Moffett Field, CA, April 1969.

Corkindale, K. G. et al. Physiological Assessment of Pilot's Stress During Landing. *Conference Proceedings* No. 56, Measurement of Aircrew Performance, AGARD, Paris, 1969.

Department of Defense. *Human Engineering Requirements for Military Systems* (MIL-H-46855B), Washington, DC: Author, 31 January 1979.

Ettema, J. H. Blood pressure changes during mental load experiments in man. *Psychotherapy and Psychosomatics*, 1969, *17*, 191–195.

Ettema, J. H. and Zielhuis, R. L. Physiological parameters of mental load. *Ergonomics*, 1971, *14*, 137–144.

Fisk, A. D., Derrick, W. L., and Schneider, W. The assessment of workload: dual task methodology. *Proceedings*, Human Factors Society Annual Meeting, 1983, 229–233.

Fitts, P. M., Jones, R. E. and Milton, J. L. Eye movements of aircraft pilots during instrument landing approaches, *Aeronautical Engineering Review*, 1950, *9*, 24–29.

Fleishman, E. A. *Development of Ability Requirement Scales for the Analysis of Bell System Jobs*, Management Research Institute, Bethesda, MD, 1975.

Fleishman, E. A. and Stephenson, R. W. *Development of a Taxonomy of Human Performance*: a review of the third year's progress. JSAS Catalog of Selected Documents in Psychology, 1970, *48*, 1–68 (MS. 113).

Galitz, W. O. and Laska, T. J. Computer system peripherals and the operator. *Computer Design*, 1969, *8*, 52.

Galitz, W. O. and Laska, T. J. The computer operator and his environment. *Human Factors*, 1970, *12*, 563–573.

Geer, C. W. *Analyst's Guide for the Analysis Sections of MIL-H-46855*. Report D180-19476-1, Boeing Aerospace Corp., Seattle, WA, June 30, 1976.

Geer, C. W. *Human Engineering Procedures Guide*. Report AFAMRL-TR-81-35, Aerospace Medical Division, Wright-Patterson AFB, OH, September 1981 (AD A108 643).

Geppinger, H. C. *Dimensional Motion Times*. New York: John Wiley & Sons, 1955.

Gilbreth, F. B. *Motion Study*, New York: D. Van Nostrand Company, 1911.

Groves, M. and Eason, R. G. Effects of attention and activation on the visual evoked cortical potential and reaction time. *Psychophysiology*, 1969, *5*, 394–398.

Hall, T. J., Passey, G. E. and Meighan, T. W. *Performance of Vigilance and Monitoring Tasks as a Function of Workload*. Report AMRL-TR-65-22, Aerospace Medical Research Laboratories, Wright-Patterson AFB, OH, 1965.

Harper, W. R. and Harris, D. H. The application of link analysis to police intelligence. *Human Factors*, 1975, *17*, 157–164.

Hasbrook, A. H. and Rasmussen, P. G. Pilot heart rate during in-flight simulated instrument approaches in a general aviation aircraft. *Aerospace Medicine*, 1970, *41*, 1148–1152.

Hawkins, H. L. and Ketchum, R. D. *The Case Against Secondary Task Analyses of Mental Workload*. Technical Report No 6, Department of Psychology, University of Oregon, Eugene, OR, ONR Contract NOO14-77-C-0643, 10 January 1980.

Helander, M. G. Physiological reactions of drivers as indicators of road traffic demand. In *Driver performance studies*, Technical Report TRB/TRR-530, U. S. Transportation Research Board, Washington, DC, 1975, 1–17.

Hess, E. H. Pupillometrics: a method of studying mental, emotional and sensory processes. In N. S. Greenfield and R. A. Sternback (Eds.), *Handbook of Psychophysiology*, New York: Holt, Rinehart and Winston, 1972.

Holden, G. R. et al. Physiological instrumentation system for monitoring pilot response to stress at zero and high G. *Aerospace Medicine*, 1962, *33*, 420–427.

Holmes, W. G. *Applied Time and Motion Study*. New York: Ronald Press, 1938.

Ireson, W. G. and Grant, E. L. (Eds.) *Handbook of Industrial Engineering and Management*. Englewood Cliffs, NJ: Prentice-Hall, 1955.

Israel, J. B., Wickens, C. D., Chesney, G. L. and Donchin, E. The event-related brain potential as an index of display-monitoring workload. *Human Factors*, 1980, *22*, 211–224.

Jex, H. R. and Allen, R. W. Research on a new human dynamic response test battery. Part II: Psychophysiological correlates. *Proceedings*, 6th Annual NASA-University Conference on Manual Control, Wright-Patterson AFB, OH, April 1970.

Johannsen, G. Workload and workload measurement. In N.Moray (Ed.) *Mental Workload. Its Theory and Measurement*. New York: Plenum Press, 1979, 3–11.

Kahneman, D., Beatty, J. and Pollack, I. Perceptual deficit during a mental task. *Science*, 1967, *157*, 218–219.

Kak, A. V. Stress: an analysis of physiological assessment devices. In G. Salvendy and M. J. Smith (Eds.) *Machine Pacing and Occupational Stress*. London: Taylor and Francis, Ltd., 1981.

Kalsbeek, J. W. H. Sinus arrhythmia and the dual-task method in measuring workload. In W. T. Singleton, J. G. Fox and D. Whitfield (Eds.), *Measurement of Man at Work*. London: Taylor and Francis, Ltd., 1971.

Kalsbeek, J. W. H. Do you believe in sinus arrhythmia? *Ergonomics*, 1973, *16*, 99–104.

Kitchin, J. B. and Graham, A. Mental loading of process operators: an attempt to devise a method of analysis and assessment. In E. Edwards and F. P. Lees (Eds.), *The Human Operator in Process Control*, London: Taylor and Francis, Ltd. and Halsted Press, 1974.

Knowles, W. B. Operator loading tasks. *Human Factors*, 1963, *5*, 155–161.

Knowles, W. B., Garvey, W. D., and Newlin, E. P. The effect of speed and load on display-control relationships. *Journal of Experimental Psychology*, 1953, *46*, 65–75.

Krantz, D. H. and Tversky, A. Conjoint measurement analysis of composition rules in psychology. *Psychological Review*, 1971, *78*, 151–169.

Lacey, J. E. and Lacey, B. C. On heart rate responses and behavior: a reply to Elliott. *Journal of Personality and Social Psychology*, 1974, *30*, 1–18.

Lahey, G. F. *Automating the Operational Sequence Diagram (OSD)*, Report SRM 71–8, Navy Personnel and Training Research Laboratory, San Diego, CA, December 1970, AD 718 842.

Lane, D. M. Limited capacity, attention allocation, and productivity. In W. C. Howell and E. A. Fleishman (Eds.), *Human Performance and Productivity, Vol. 2, Information Processing and Decision Making*, Hillsdale, NJ: Lawrence Erlbaum Associates, 1982.

Larson, O. A. and Willis, J. E. *Human Factors Methods Development and Test: II. Evaluation of the Automated Operational Sequence Diagram (OSD)*. Report SRM 70-17, Navy Personnel and Training Research Laboratory, San Diego, CA, May 1970, AD 707 719.

Lewis, G. W. Event related brain electrical and magnetic activity: toward predicting on-job performance. *International J. Neuroscience*, 1983, *18*, 159–182.

Lippert, S. Travel in nursing units. *Human Factors*, 1971, *13*, 269–282.

Luczak, H. and Laurig, W. An analysis of heart rate variability. *Ergonomics*, 1973, *16*, 85–97.

Mallamad, S. M., Levine, J. M. and Fleishman, E. A. Identifying ability requirements by decision flow diagrams. *Human Factors*, 1980, *22*, 57–68.

Maynard, H. B., Stegemerten, G. J. and Schwab, J. L. *Methods-Time Measurement*, New York: McGraw-Hill, 1948.

McGrath, J. E. Stress and behavior in organizations. In M. D. Dunnette (Ed.), *Handbook of Industrial and Organizational Psychology*, Chicago: Rand McNally, 1976, 1351–1395.

Meister, D. *Human Factors in Operational System Testing: A Manual of Procedures*. Report SR 78-8, Navy Personnel Research and Development Center, San Diego, CA. April 1978.

Melton, C. E. et al. Effect of a general aviation trainer on the stress of flight training. *Aviation, Space and Environmental Medicine*, 1975, 46, 1–5.

Mirabella, A. and Wheaton, G. R. *Effect of task index variations in transfer of training criteria*. Report NAVTRAEQUIPCEN 72-C-0126-1, Naval Training Equipment Center, Orlando, FL, January, 1974 (AD 773-947/7GA).

Mobbs, R. F., David, G. C. and Thomas, J. M. *An evaluation of the use of heart rate irregularity as a measure of mental workload in the steel industry*. Report BISRA, OR/HF25/71, British Steel Corporation, London, England, August, 1971.

Moray, N. Mental workload. *Proceedings*; 1984 International Conference on Occupational Ergonomics. Vol. 2, Reviews. Human Factors Society of Canada, Ontario, Canada, 1984, 41–46.

Moray, N. Subjective mental workload, *Human Factors*, 1982, *24*, 25–40.

Moray, N. (Ed.) *Mental Workload, Its Theory and Measurement*. New York: Plenum Press, 1979.

Moray, N. Models and measures of mental workload. In N. Moray (Ed.) *Mental Workload, Its Theory and Measurement*. New York: Plenum Press, 1979, 13–21.

Munger, S. J., Smith, R. W. and Payne, D. *An Index of Electronic Equipment Operability: Data Store*. Report AIR-C43-1/62-RP (1), American Institute for Research, Pittsburgh, PA, January 1962.

Nicholson, A. N., Hill, L. E., Borland, R. G., Ferres, H. M. Activity of the nervous system during the let down, approach and landing, a study of short duration high workload. *Aerospace Medicine*, 1970, *41*, 436–446.

Nicholson, A. N. et al. Influence of workload on the neurological state of a pilot during the approach and landing. *Aerospace Medicine*. 1973, *44*, 146–152.

Noel, C. E. *Pupil diameter versus task layout*. Master's Thesis, Naval Postgraduate School, Monterey, CA, September 1974.

Ogden, G. D., Levine, J. M. and Eisner, E. J. Measurement of workload by secondary tasks. *Human Factors*, 1979, *21*, 529–548.

Older, H. J. and Jenney, L. L. *Psychological stress measurement through voice output analysis*. Planar Corporation, Alexandria, VA, Contract NAS 9-14146, March 1975.

Parks, D. L. Current workload methods and emerging challenges. In N. Moray (Ed.), *Mental Workload, Its Theory and Measurement*. New York: Plenum Press, 1979, 387–416.

Pew, R. W. Secondary tasks and workload measurement. In N. Moray (Ed.), *Mental Workload, Its Theory and Measurement*. New York: Plenum Press, 1979, 23–28.

Preston, B. Insurance classification and driver's galvanic skin response. *Ergonomics*, 1969, *12*, 437–446.

Quick, J. H., Duncan, J. H. and Malcolm, Jr., J. A. *Work-Factor Time Standards*. New York: McGraw-Hill, 1962.

Reid, G. B., Shingledecker, C. A., and Eggemeier, F. T. Application of conjoint measurement to workload scale development. *Proceedings*, Human Factors Society Annual Meeting, October 1981(a), 522–526.

Reid, G. B., Shingledecker, C. A., Nygren, T. E. and Eggemeier, F. T. Development of multidimensional subjective measures of workload. *Proceedings*, 1981 IEEE International Conference on Cybernetics and Society, 1981(b), 403–406.

Rohmert, W. An international symposium on objective assessment of workload in air traffic control tasks—introduction. *Ergonomics*, 1971, *14*, 545–547.

Rolfe, J. M. and Lindsay, S. J. E. Flight deck environment and pilot workload: biological measures of workload. *Applied Ergonomics*, 1973, *4*, 199–206.

Roman, J. A. et al. School of Aerospace Medicine physiological studies in high performance aircraft. *Aerospace Medicine*, 1962, *33*, 412–419.

Roman, J. A. Cardio-respiratory functioning in flight. *Aerospace Medicine*, 1963, *34*, 322–337.

Sanders, A. F. Some remarks on mental load. In N. Moray (Ed.), *Mental Load: Its Theory and Measurement*. New York: Plenum Press, 1979, 41–77.

Sayers, B. M. Analysis of heart rate varaibility. *Ergonomice*, 1973, *16*, 17–32.

Schaefer, M. G. Establishing time values by elementary motions. *Proceedings*, 10th Time and Motion Study Clinic, IMS, Chicago, IL, November, 1946.

Schane, W. P. and Slinde, K. E. Continuous EEG recording during free fall parachuting. *Aerospace Medicine*, 1968, *39*, 597–603.

Schick, E. V. and Radke, H. *Analysis of Heart Rate Variability as an Estimate of Pilot Workload*. Report ESA-TT-653, European Space Agency Technical Translation, October 1980.

Schnore, M. M. Individual patterns of physiological activity as a function of task differences and degree of arousal. *J. Experimental Psychology*, 1959, *58*, 117–128.

Segur, A. B. Motion-time analysis. In H. B. Maynard (Ed.), *Industrial Engineering Handbook*. New York: McGraw-Hill, 4–101 to 4–118, 1956.

Selye, H. Stress in aerospace medicine. *Aerospace Medicine*, 1973, *44*, 190–193.

Senders, J. W. Axiomatic models of workload. In N. Moray (Ed.), *Mental Workload, Its Theory and Measurement*, New York: Plenum Press, 1979, 263–267.

Siegel, A. I. and Wolf, J. J. *Man–Machine Simulation Models*, New York: Wiley. 1969.

Simonov, P. V. et al. Use of the invariant method of speech analysis to discern the emotional state of announcers. *Aviation and Space Environmental Medicine*, 1975, 46, 1014–1016.

Spyker, D. A., Stackhouse, S. P., Khalafalla, A. S. and McLane, R. C. *Development of techniques for measuring pilot workload*. Report NASA CR-1888, National Aeronautics and Space Administration, Washington, DC November, 1971.

Stackhouse, S. P. *Workload evaluation of LLNO display*. Report 7201-3408, Honeywell, Minneapolis, MN, October, 1973.

Sternberg, S. The discovery of processing stages: Extensions of Donders' method. *Acta Psychologica*, 1969, *30*, 276–315.

Storm, W. G., Hartman, B. O., Intano, G. P. and Peters, G. L. *Endocrine-metabolic effects in short-duration high-workload missions: feasibility study*. Report SAM-TR-76-30, USAF School of Aerospace Medicine, Brooks AFB, TX, August, 1976.

Street, R. L., Singh, H. and Hale, P. N. Jr. The evaluation of mental stress through the analysis of parotid fluid. *Human Factors*, 1970, *12*, 453–455.

Strieb, M. K. and Wherry, R. J., Jr. *An Introduction to the Human Operator Simulator*, Technical Report 1400.02-D. Analytics, Willow Grove, PA, December 1979.

Theologus, G. C. and Fleishman, E. A. Development of a taxonomy of human performance: validation study of ability scales for classifying human tasks. *JSAS Catalog of Selected Documents in Psychology*, MS. No. 326, 1973, 3, 29.

Welford, A. T. Stress and performance. *Ergonomics*, 1973, *16*, 567–580.

Westbrook, C. B., Anderson, R. O. and Pietrzak, P. E. *Handling qualities and pilot workload*. Report AFFDL-FDCC-TM-66-5, Air Force Flight Dynamics Laboratory, Wright-Patterson AFB, OH, September, 1966.

Wickens, C. D. *Engineering Psychology and Human Performance*. Columbus, OH: Charles E. Merrill Publishing Co., 1984.

Wickens, C. D. *Processing resources in attention, dual task performance, and workload assessment*. Technical Report EPL-81-3/ONR-81-3, University of Illinois, Champaign, IL, July 1981. (AD A102 719)

Wiener, J. S. The measurement of human workload. *Ergonomics*, 1982, *25*, 953–965.

Wierwille, W. W. Physiological measures of aircrew mental workload. *Human Factors*, 1979, *21*, 575–593.

Wierwille, W. W. and Williges, R. C. Behavioral measures of aircrew mental workload. *Human Factors*, 1979, *21*, 549–574.

Wierwille, W. W. and Casali, J. G. A validated rating scale for global mental workload measurement applications. *Proceedings*, Human Factors Society Annual Meeting, 1983, 129–133.

Wilkins, W. L. Psychophysiological correlates of stress and human performance. In W. C. Howell and E. A. Fleishman (Eds.), *Human Performance and Productivity, Vol. 3, Stress and Performance Effectiveness*, Hillsdale, NJ: Lawrence Erlbaum Associates, 1982, 57–90.

Yerkes, R. M. and Dodson, J. D. The relation of strength of stimulus to rapidity of habit formation. *J. Comparative and Neurological Psychology*, 1908, *18*, 459–482.

CHAPTER FOUR

Computerized Methods

This chapter focuses on computerized aids to system development and mathematic models of human performance that can be used in system development. Its two sections describe: (1) *automated methods* of performing some of the design analyses described in Chapters Two and Three, for example, function allocation and task analysis; and (2) computerized *mathematical models* for evaluating and predicting operator performance. This chapter is not, however, a guide to mathematic modeling or computer simulation in general. Although the computer is a primary mechanism for implementing these procedures, we do not describe in detail specific computer algorithms or languages. Nor is it possible to describe all the individual mathematic model applications—rather we discuss the types of models and provide exemplary illustrations.

The major difference between automated methods and mathematical models is that models attempt to simulate or represent personnel behaviors (tasks and subtasks) as these are performed. Automated design methods sometimes simulate, but more often merely represent, procedures for handling these behaviors. Since automated methods are most often merely the original manual methods in computerized form, their computerization does not necessarily improve their validity and utility. Models make much more extensive use of psychological theory than do automated methods. One advantage of the automated methods is the reduction of processing time. Some of the analyses described in Chapters Two and Three, such as OSD or W/L, are very tedious and automation eliminates much of the "hack" work involved in data processing, even if it does not reduce the necessity for collecting those data. Because only the processing time is reduced, the overall gain in time and efficiency is not as great as it might be. The automated methods would work more efficiently if they had available to them a computerized data bank of task data, for example, task descriptions, performance times, error probabilities, etc. Although attempts have been made (see, for example, Tulley, Meyer, Oller, Mitchell, Reardon and Reed,

TABLE 4.1 CAFES Capabilities

Module	Purpose/Capability
Data management system (DMS)	Data storage/retrieval processing system for the other modules.
Function allocation model (FAM)	Analyzes function allocation schemes.
Workload assessment model (WAM)	Identifies areas of operator overload.
Computer-aided crewstation design model (CAD)	Aids development of cockpit configurations.
Crewstation geometry evaluation model (CGE)	Analyzes cockpit reach characteristics.
Human operator simulator (HOS)	Evaluates feasibility of operator requirements and measures operator performance (mathematical model).

1968) to develop these, they have not been overly successful. Most data must still be manually and laboriously collected. On the other hand, because of their operating speed, greater memory storage and enhanced graphics capability (very useful, for example, in the automation of control-panel design), the automated methods can present for the analyst's decision more alternatives than he might be able to assess on his own.

AUTOMATED METHODS

CAFES

The most comprehensive and sophisticated of the computerized design aids is CAFES—the *computer aided function-allocation evaluation system*. CAFES is actually a family of modules as defined in Table 4.1.

According to its developers, CAFES can assist in many critical MMS development functions such as function allocation, task analysis, workload estimation, timeline assessment, tradeoffs, design of the crewstation (cockpit), development and evaluation of procedures, and operator performance evaluation.

Each of the CAFES modules will be discussed in this section in turn, with the exception of the *Human Operator Simulator* (HOS), which is given more extended treatment in the following section with other mathematic models. The discussion is based in large part on Parks and Springer, 1975, and Geer, 1981.

The developers suggest that CAFES can be applied at various levels of detail, and would normally be applied iteratively throughout the system development cycle. This iteration involves multiple module runs and examination of the effect of one module upon another. For example, the *Crewstation geometry evaluation model* CGE results may suggest a change in basic configuration layout, which would then be examined with the *computer aided design* CAD.

Data Management System. *Date Management System* (DMS) provides storage for data, the instructions and routines to manipulate the data for each module; and interfaces between the modules.

The analyst interfaces with DMS when he inputs new data, modifies or deletes data, instructs a module to perform its function, requests a report and receives data outputs.

Function Allocation Model. The purpose of the *function allocation model* (FAM), which is probably the most complicated of the CAFES modules, is to identify and allocate functions and tasks, to identify required equipment, and to analyze and rank order alternative man–machine configurations in terms of performance effectiveness.

A great deal of input data is required to enable FAM to perform, such as mission and task start and stop times, task attributes—criticality and load—and activation channels, for example, visual and tactile. Equipment events occurring during the mission, functional block diagrams, mission timelines, and weighting criteria, e.g., cost, weight, etc. are also required. The analyst rates tasks on accuracy requirements, as well as performance and time criticality, channel dedication and task continuity in order to scale task execution times or to prioritize tasks.

The analyst interacts with FAM by inputting system functions, performance data and candidate allocations. After FAM processes these, the FAM output is checked by the analyst against system requirements. If the allocations are inappropriate, the analyst modifies the FAM input data and reruns FAM.

FAM is composed of two major data processing routines: the *mission evaluator* and the *procedure generator*. The mission evaluator computes task reliabilities, mission success probabilities for various task allocation candidates and a gross W/L measurement of each crew member. It rank orders the variation in task allocations under consideration.

The heart of the mission evaluator procedure appears to be the determination of human and machine reliabilities (inputted previously by task) for each alternative configuration. The source of the human reliability input data is not indicated but presumably it is on the basis of already established data banks like Munger, Payne and Smith (1962), historical performance data on predecessor systems, or analyst expertise. The human reliability computation is modified by task execution time which in turn is affected by task load and W/L computations. System and task reliabilities are computed for both operator and equipment on the basis of their parallel-redundant-sequential relationships in accordance with standard equipment reliability practice.

The procedure generator applies a list of tasks against a mission scenario and determine who is doing what and at what time (task sequence per operation). The output data can be used to construct an OSD.

Major FAM outputs are task, objective and mission reliability, operator workload, and percent of tasks completed, interrupted and being performed simultaneously.

If FAM is effective—no data on this are supplied—it would be a tremendous aid to the designer because it would supply the systematization which is often lacking in consideration of design alternatives.

Workload Assessment Model. After functions are allocated, candidate equipment concepts and task details identified, and time constraints known, WAM can be initiated. The *workload assessment model*'s (WAM) objective is to estimate the effects on operator W/L of alternative function allocations. Where W/L problems are revealed, they can be mitigated by functional reallocations, increased automation, procedural changes, etc. Obviously there is an interaction between WAM and FAM.

In a manner identical with the way he does it manually, the analyst prepares a mission profile and scenario in which time, events, distances, altitudes and speeds—applicable, of course, primarily to aircraft—are sequenced over the mission. Missions are divided into 6-second or whatever interval is desired. Estimates of the time required to perform each task are made. A mission phase timeline chart is then prepared, showing which tasks are employed in each segment. The sensory/motor channels used for each task are identified and channel utilization time indicated. The data in this task timeline chart which is the basic tool for WAM are keypunched for insertion into the model.

WAM compares time required to perform a task sequence with time available for performance to establish a ratio reflecting excess or negative time to perform. This comparison is made for eyes, each hand, each foot, and auditory, verbal and cognition channels. When WAM receives the channel W/L data for each time segment, it computes channel utilization in percentage, for example, if the time segment is 6 seconds, the equation is:

$$\text{utilization} = \frac{\text{channel utilization (seconds)}}{\text{6 seconds}} \times 100 \qquad (4.1)$$

It then computes averages, standard deviations, etc., for channel W/L over all time segments. Given a specified W/L threshold value for example, 70 percent, WAM identifies those time segments and tasks in which average W/L exceeds the threshold.

Statistical workload assessment model (SWAM) functions like WAM with the additional feature that where the W/L threshold is exceeded it will determine if any tasks can be shifted without overloading other time intervals.

Computer Aided Design. *Computer aided design* (CAD) is a set of computer routines that can be used individually or collectively to assist in various aspects of cockpit design. Inputs include a defined workspace, control panels, controls, physical boundaries, reach envelopes, scale factors, eye reference point, etc.

The CAD functions available are as follows:

1. *Crewstation geometry description.* The analyst assigns a name and then defines a set of coordinate points or conic parameters to establish the shape and location of the objects in the cockpit and control/ display panels.

2. *Conversion of coordinates.* CAD can transform coordinate values between coordinate systems. Individual controls and displays can be located by two-dimensional panel coordinates rather than by an overall three-dimensional coordinate system.

3. *Crewstation scaling.* Geometric objects can be automatically expanded or contracted.

4. *Crewstation tailoring.* The analyst can make selective changes in cockpit geometry, by deleting a control or display and by writing a new description of the item.

5. *Panel space allocation: control/display arrangement.* As in 1.

6. *Reach analysis.* When the analyst specifies a reach envelope from available anthropometric data the computer will plot an instrument panel and designate points that can be reached. It will also report in tabular form a distance comparision between actual reach and specific panel locations. A different reach envelope for each so called percentile size can be developed.

7. *Vision analysis.* External vision analysis requires the analyst to specify which objects are opaque, which are transparent and the location of the eye reference point. Internal vision analysis is accomplished via the same elements in the reach analysis program.

8. *Crewmember escape analysis.* CAD checks for instances where a crewmember would contact an object as he ejects. The analyst supplies an escape envelope—the volume of space through which the crewmember must travel—and a list of cockpit objects to be checked. Inputs include a defined workspace, control panels, controls, physical boundaries, reach envelopes, scale factors, eye reference point, etc.

Crewstation Geometry Evaluation. Crewstation geometry evaluation is a computerized anthropometric evaluation tool. The heart of CGE is a three-dimensional man-model (BOEMAN) that synthesizes joint locations and orientations as it simulates human movement to perform required tasks (see Figure 4.1). CGE inputs include the tasks to be performed (e.g., set altimeter), cockpit geometric data, controls and eye reference data, and the shape of controls. CAD serves as a partial input to CGE.

CGE calculates body joint locations of BOEMAN as it simulates task performance, determines whether tasks are within reach capabilities, detects visual or physical interference in performing tasks and checks crewstation compliance with military standards. CGE outputs interferences, unfeasible tasks from a reach standpoint, crewstation compliance with military standards, and the tasks that are feasible.

A variation of CGE called CAR—*crewstation assessment of reach*—has been developed and validated against empirical data (Harris, Bennett and Stokes, 1982). CAR allows the user to define the crew station geometry and operator sample to determine the population percentage that can be accomodated by the design.

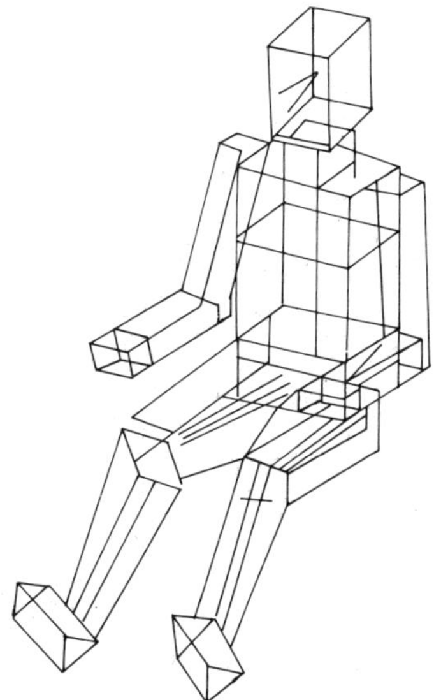

Figure 4.1. BOEMAN with links and body segments in standard position. (From Parks and Springer, 1975.)

Other Design-aiding Programs

CHESS. A further development of CAFES is *CHESS* (Crew Human Engineering Software System). CHESS includes five modules (Jones, Jonsen and Van, 1982). These are flightdeck configuration control, somewhat related to CGE, instrument readability analysis, which calculates the size of markings and legends; CAR which has been mentioned previously; SWAT, Subsystem Workload Assessment Tool, which is a variation of SWAM and analyzes workload for individual procedures; and *Time Line Evaluation* (TLE) which applies time line methodology (available versus required time) to assess physical workload.

CRAFT. Coburn and Lowe (1976) describe a computer program known as *CRAFT* (Computerized Relative Allocation of Facilities Technique). CRAFT helps to identify optimum control and display layouts on a panel based on 1. movement requirements; 2. frequency of control/display use; 3. control/display distance (grouping of associated controls and displays); 4. an initial panel layout (together with data such as initial distances, control/display relationships); 5. frequency of control/display usage; 6. eye–hand motion rate data; and 7. eye–hand W/L data.

The program makes layout changes and computes cost factors—such tradeoffs as extent of hand movement requirements vs. visual W/L. The program outputs cost (figure of merit) values for all combinations of panel layout.

CRAFT has predecessors. Freud and Sadosky (1967) reported a manual linear programming technique for control panel design. Subsequently Bartlett and Smith (1973) described the application of facilities allocation algorithms to control panel arrangement, one of which was CRAFT.

WOLAP. Rabideau and Luk (1974) describe a program—*WOLAP*—similar to CRAFT. The technique according to its developers has two advantages over CRAFT: the method yields more quantitatively optimized solutions and functional and sequential links are given proper consideration. The heart of the routine is a computerized link analysis, with criteria of frequency of usage, distances moved, criticality of components, etc. Inputs include relative positions of panel components in an *X-Y* plane, data on panel component links with hands and eyes, total number of instrument components, number of required iterations, and relative weighting of controls.

WOLAP establishes a cost figure—as a function of visual and manual transition distances, weighting of components that are accessed and probability of transitions—for the initial panel layout input by the analyst. It then rearranges panel components randomly and computes cost for each arrangement. The program outputs the three layouts with the lowest cost together with the initial layout.

HECAD. Another interactive computer graphic design technique called *Human Engineering Computer Aided Design* (HECAD) with strong similarity to CGE and other design aids is being developed at the Aerospace Medical Research Laboratory at Wright-Patterson Air Force Base, Ohio (Topmiller and Aume, 1978).

There are two major segments to the software package. First, the computer graphic geometry segment allows the designer to lay out the panel space and to selectively locate the candidate controls and displays either in the panel planes or anywhere in three-dimensional space. Second, in the analytic segment, link analyses of eye scan and hand movements are performed on these layouts. Algorithms from the Human Reliability Data Store (Munger et al., 1962) for computing probability of operator performance in terms of success or error and transfer or action times are provided. The reaching motion and eye scan time algorithms were derived from methods-time measurement data (see Chapter Three for a discussion of MTM).

The HECAD program requires three inputs: data describing the components (names, size, type, time to activate and probability of correctly activating the component, the last two from the Data Store, Munger et al., 1962), one or more panels described by their corner coordinates, and one or more task sequences. In its simplest form, the task sequence is a listing of the components in the order in which they are activated or scanned. There are also provisions for incorporating communication time and machine time periods.

The program presents on CRT a perspective projection of the workstation with panels represented by outlines and components outlined by dots. The designer can select the point from which the projection is taken and change it at will.

Having selected the geometrical routine the designer indicates, either by light-penning the component or entering its number, which component he wishes to be mounted on which panel. Then he positions the cross-hairs on the CRT until he finds a satisfactory location for the component. During this positioning process the designer receives numerical information concerning the location of the component, as well as an outline of the component projected where it has been positioned. An asterisk is superimposed on those components for which overlap or interference is computed.

Several analyses are available in a second routine. A reach analysis determines the distance between a component and a shoulder reference point. A second analysis presents fingertip paths during a task sequence. This analysis can be used to identify unnecessarily long excursions or frequent reaches back and forth. A third program is a task analysis which takes a task sequence and examines its list of components. It determines whether the component is a control or display and assigns either hands or eyes to the action as appropriate.

These choices can be overridden, if desired. The computer calculates transfer, that is movement, time for hands or eyes based on MTM data. The component activation time is added to the transfer time. This procedure is repeated until a task sequence is completed. HECAD sorts the 20 longest transfer times and presents them. Task reliability computations are performed by multiplying all the individual component reliabilities together used in a task sequence. This estimate of human reliability is unsatisfactory and work is currently being performed to improve it.

HECAD has certain limitations—at least as of 1978. The first is the difficulty of handling the very large number of controls and displays which could be candidates for inclusion in the workstation. The most important, however, is HECAD's inability to handle more than a one-person workstation, particularly if two or more operators are performing nonindependent, coordinated tasks. These problems are currently under study.

TX-105. *TX-105* (Geer, 1976) is a computerized technique similar to HECAD. It was developed to help evaluate W/L of aircraft crews and to evaluate cockpit design.

Three subroutines make up TX-105. The first two calculate the angle between the eyes and points in the cockpit. The third subroutine calculates the angular and linear distance changes for the eyes and hands as they move to perform flight tasks, the control/display nomenclature and location, the crewmember eye and shoulder reference points, the task name, sequence of points for each task, and the sequence of tasks. Outputs are similar to HECAD: implications for W/L as measured by the angular changes and changes in linear distance for both eyes and hands.

Like other cockpit design aids TX-105 is essentially a computerized link analysis because it aims to shorten the frequently used links between displays and controls. The not unreasonable assumption is made that the configuration with the shortest linear distances and smallest angular eye movement is the most efficient.

TLA-1. *TLA-1* (timeline analysis program—model 1) is a further development of the link analysis methodology created at Boeing. TLA-1 is a computer program which, like WAM, estimates operator W/L for task sequences within the cockpit. This description is based on Geer, 1981.

TLA-1 is initiated by the input of scenarios and crew task data from sources such as flight plans and aircraft performance data. If the analysis is for a completely new aircraft, the data are taken from existing similar aircraft. Operator tasks, categorized by aircraft subsystem, must be identified for every control, display, and communication link. As many as over 2000 tasks have been cataloged for a single TLA-1 analysis. The task description contains a task code number, a task description/name, task duration time and the channel activity (left hand, right hand, etc.). After the scenarios and tasks have been defined, the analyst develops the detailed task sequence required to execute the scenario. These data are then keypunched for input.

A variety of W/L analysis data reports can be requested, although data generally consist of mean W/L, W/L variance, tasks exceeding a specified threshold, and task performance over mission time. By specifying different variables for each of these outputs, literally thousands of data records can be selected for output. Obviously most will not be requested at any one time.

COMBIMAN. Other three-dimensional man-models similar to BOEMAN have been created.

The Aerospace Medical Research Laboratory has developed *COMBIMAN*, Computerized Biomechanical Man-Model, an on-line interactive computer model conceived as a three-dimensional manikin for workplace design and evaluation. COMBIMAN evaluates existing workplaces, selects criteria for personnel to fit workplaces and maps visibility plots (Evans, 1978; Geer, 1981).

Because an operator functions in three dimensions, it is difficult to evaluate a workplace from a two-dimensional drawing. Of course, mockups provide a three-dimensional representation but their construction is time consuming and expensive. Mockup evaluations are also somewhat limited because it is difficult to find subjects who display the anthropometric variability of the user population.

COMBIMAN may be moved about and viewed from any angle. Since the man-model and the workplace design exist only in computer memory and on a CRT display, there is no significant investment of time or materials in modifying these designs. Alternative designs can be evaluated and then recorded by means of a pictorial plot or tabular printout. In addition COMBIMAN's variable geometry permits one to define quickly a series of man-models which represent the entire anthropometric range of the system personnel population.

A man-model for a specific problem is constructed in three stages. The first is the generation of the link system consisting of 33 segments which correspond functionally to the human skeletal system. Link length can be specified either by the analyst or automatically by reference to an anthropometric data base in memory. The second stage is the definition of the enfleshment ellipsoids (a three-dimensional ellipse) about the link system joints. The third stage is connection of the ellipsoid silhouettes by tangent lines.

Starting with a list of workplace requirements, the analyst can call up the man-model to which he has assigned dimensions representative of the population of intended operators. He then defines the control/display panels around the man-model by indicating the corner points with a lightpen. These points are then connected by lines to indicate the panels.

Data representing design constraints such as maximum dimensions or already available control panels can be entered by various input devices, lightpen, keyboard, punched cards, magnetic tape storage or disc storage. To eliminate a feature the analyst simply points his lightpen at the panel and depresses a button.

Once a workplace has been entered into the program, it exists in three dimensions and can be made to interact with the man-model. Although the CRT is a two-dimensional display, two orthogonal views are simultaneously projected and can be rotated for viewing at any angle.

In addition to workspace dimensions, the analyst can input direct anthropometric measures of subjects, data base percentages, combinations of measures and data base values, required population dimensions to fit a workspace, required or established maximum rotational angles and body restrictions such as clothing.

COMBIMAN also incorporates visibility plots. These define the three-dimensional coordinates of the workplace with respect to the viewing angle. The printout shows the three-dimensional coordinates of the canopy (cockpit) frame at each five-degree increment of horizontal angle.

SAMMIE. A technique similar in design and function to both BOEMAN and COMBIMAN, *SAMMIE*—System for Aiding Man–Machine Interaction Evaluation—has been under development in England since 1967 (Bonney and Case, 1977).

Miscellaneous Man-Models. A computer model has also been developed to evaluate job performance aids. This approach described by Ayoub, Smillie, Edsall and Miller (1977) makes use of predetermined time and motion data and a simulation modeling allgorithm, GERT. Siegel, Wolf and Pilitsis (1982) describe a computerized technique involving multidimensional scaling for workspace layout of offices and plants. A computer program has also been applied to the performance of link analysis (Cullinance, 1977).

Summary

The automated design aids reviewed are still highly experimental, even though some of them like CAFES and SAMMIE have been under development for many years. Validation data are still scarce and comparisons of the various techniques even when they perform similar functions are lacking. The major systems like CAFES and CHESS are pretty much tied to aircraft design, but those who are interested in nonaircraft control panels or consoles may find HECAD and similar programs more useful. At the same time one must ask how frequently these design aids are utilized in actual system development. My impression, verified to some extent by a study reported in Chapter Thirteen, is that these automated aids are used much less frequently than their manual counterparts. The reasons for this must be explored later in greater detail.

MATHEMATICAL MODELS OF HUMAN PERFORMANCE

Mathematic modeling of behavioral processes has become extremely popular in the last 20 years. *Siegel and Wolf* (1981), from which much of this section is drawn, report that the Department of Defense catalog of logistics models includes more than 174 models. Models have been developed for a wide variety of topics, including cognitive processes in foreign policy decision making, travel simulation, student performance, urban decision making, family planning and organized crime (see Siegel/Wolf, 1981, for the complete list). There are in addition many models of military systems.

The models discussed in this section center on human or job-oriented performance, that is, they model the total task or job and not merely an individual function as do the control-theoretic tracking models. Our discussion has two parts. The first deals with a series of questions that are important in the development and use of behavioral models. The topics to be discussed are: 1. why models are useful and the uses made of them; 2. the different types of behavioral models and how to select from among them; 3. the questions behavioral models answer; 4. how model variables are selected and treated; 5. data requirements and level of data detail; 6. model validation; 7. their cost/effectiveness.

The second part of this section will describe the Siegel/Wolf and SAINT (*system analysis of integrated networks of tasks*) models, the *human operator simulator* (HOS), and a number of cognitive models. These models were selected for two reasons: the frequency with which they have been applied (at least the Siegel/Wolf and SAINT models), and their representativeness as types.

Why Models and Their Uses

Models are developed for any of the following reasons:

1. Because the phenomena to be studied are so complex that they cannot be measured (or measured only with great difficulty) in the operational environment. It is of course necessary to collect data from various sources, including the operational environment, as inputs to the model, and ultimately the model itself must be validated by gathering operational data, since construct validity strategies are not very satisfactory. Nonetheless, the model considerably reduces the need for operational data collection.

2. Because the systems we wish to study have not been developed to a sufficient state that they can be studied directly. For example, assume that a system is in development and one wishes to know what would be the effect of including or rejecting certain parameters; if one had a general model which could be modified to represent the new system by inputting data specific to that system, one could *predict* the performance of the new system, one would be able to examine various system alternatives and select the best.

3. Because the conditions one wishes to study cannot be created except at excessive expense, over long periods of time and, more important, at the risk of life.

For example, if one wished to assess system effectiveness of helicopters against a mixed armor and air defense threat (DARCOM, 1980) it is obvious that the only reasonable solution is to model this activity.

4. Modeling also becomes necessary when an already developed system is so fully occupied in performing its operational mission that experimentation with any element of the system is impractical.

5. Modeling reduces the complexities of the real world to simpler form because only those variables anticipated to have the most significant effect on personnel performance need be included in the model. This may however make the model somewhat artificial.

It is also is possible to experiment with the system, to vary inputs and task conditions and note the effect on dependent variables (outputs). Most behavioral models have been used for this purpose which we can term the *experimental* use of models.

Models (e.g., HOS and the Siegel/Wolf models) can also be used as a design aid; they can be used to predict the performance one would achieve with various design alternatives and different system components. This is the *design* use of a behavioral model.

In both the experimental and design cases the methodology is the same. A system configuration consisting of equipment, operator characteristics, task requirements, etc. is established and the model is exercised. Then certain parameters/and variables are varied. Finally, the model is run for a number of trials; and the performance outputs under each of the varied conditions are recorded and compared.

TYPES OF MODELS

Strieb and Wherry (1979) refer to task analytic, control theory, and microprocess models. Baron, Feehrer, Muralidharan, Pew and Horwitz (1982) refer to reliability analysis, network, information processing, knowledge-based, and control theoretic models. The *Siegel/Wolf* and SAINT models are task analytic or network models; the Human Operator Simulator is a microprocess or information processing model; the cognitive models are knowledge based models. THERP (*Technique for Human Error Rate Prediction*), which is a reliability analytic model is described in Chapter Five. The control theoretic models will not be discussed to any great extent because their scope is usually limited to tracking behaviors.

Task-Analytic Models

Task-analytic models, also called *network models*, are those in which the tasks assigned to the operator(s) are described, either implicitly or explicitly, as a network in which the timing and sequencing through each mission stage or network "node" are structured by the modeler. The modeler predetermines all node characteristics, including times or conditions under which the node will be executed, nominal execution times, probabilities of successful completion, and transition probabilities to other nodes.

Task-analytic models are of various types. For example, the task analysis described in Chapter Two can be considered as a static model. Other types (e.g., the Siegel/Wolf and SAINT models to be described in greater detail later), are stochastic (Monte-Carlo) models in which the network is exercised repeatedly with input conditions and nodal characteristics that vary according to distributions supplied by the modeler. Other models (e.g., CAFES) perform primarily bookkeeping functions or have built-in decision algorithms that modify the task network to optimize performance. The Siegel/Wolf technique which was the first to systematically exploit computer simulation of human performance as a systems analysis tool, drew on PERT (Program Evaluation Review Technique) concepts, in which a project is conceived to be made up of a network of tasks and subtasks, each of which has estimated completion times—or time distributions—and probabilities of successful completion. *Siegel and Wolf* created PERT-type networks for tasks and subtasks and obtained Monte Carlo simulation results from which they could estimate overall job completion times and workload. To this they added more sophisticated, psychologically-oriented concepts to examine the impact of such things as task-induced stress. This technology proved sufficiently attractive that the Air Force sponsored the development of a special purpose simulation language, SAINT, specifically for the purpose of implementing network based human performance models. SAINT technology has been widely employed.

Network techniques, particularly those that exploit the flexibility of decision branching structures, symbol manipulation capabilities, sampling distributions, and human performance submodels offer a promising approach to system modelling. However, Pew, Feehrer, Baron and Miller (1977) suggest that network techniques have a number of limitations:

1. The possibility of constructing a network may be severely limited where covert tasks, for example, diagnosis, situation assessment, and goal selection play a significant role.
2. The network as a tool for simulating performance is limited to reasonably well understood scenarios.
3. Human performance submodels used in network models, although based on laboratory or field experience, are often unverifiable in the special context being modeled.

Control-Theoretic Models

Not much need be said about control-theoretic models because they are used relatively little, other than for manual control behaviors. In control theory, the interactions between the operator and the system are represented by servo-control models. Unlike the task analytic models, control theory models do have an explicit but limited concept of human performance—an operator behaves in such a way that errors are minimized within fixed performance constraints. In this concept the operator is an information processing and control/decision element who relates to the system he is controlling in closed-loop fashion. Feedback is central, involving the comparison of actual system response with predicted or desired response. The role of information processing to filter noise and to predict future responses is emphasized.

Certain strengths and weaknesses characterize the control-theoretic approach. These models are more quantitative than other model types. Because of the explicit nature of their assumptions, inputs and outputs, they have been more thoroughly and carefully validated. Because human limitations are specified at the processing level rather than directly at the performance level, the models are typically general enough to predict performance in other control situations. They include explicit information processing algorithms, the validity of which can be independently verified. The models do not, however, attempt to deal with discrete operator inputs, with monitoring or decision making, nor with the procedural aspects of tasks which must be performed by the operator (communications, checklists). All of this makes it difficult to use this model–type to describe total job performance.

Microprocess Models

Microprocess models are very *detailed* representations of the operator in terms of the physical, psychological and physiological processes that are involved in carrying out a task. Microprocessor models such as the Human Operator Simulator are "bottom-up" models, which is to say, they synthesize human performance from a sequence of molecular fundamental activities such as bodily movements, reaction times, recall of events, etc. Consequently, they encounter the difficulty that the molecular phenomena they model must be combined in some manner to represent the higher-order task. There is some evidence that the amount of detail required in such models may be unnecessary (Baron et al., 1977) as a design aid; the effort involved in developing a system level, validated model may be greater than the resulting utility of the model.

The fundamental difference between the way in which microprocess models and both task-analytic and control theory models view human performance is that microprocess models assume an operator's behavior is explainable and not random, that an operator's actions and the times that those actions will take are determined fully by the state-of-the-system and the operator's goals at any particular point of time. Thus, microprocess models are basically deterministic models (although individual microprocesses may contain random components), rather than stochastic, as the network models are. However, because of the way in which various micromodels interact, the output from a microprocess model will exhibit variability, making it seem, in some cases, indistinguishable from stochastic output.

Cognitive Models

These are, properly speaking, problem-solving or diagnostic models in which the behaviors being modeled are those involved in determining the cause of an equipment malfunction or diagnosing the cause of an illness. What is modeled is:

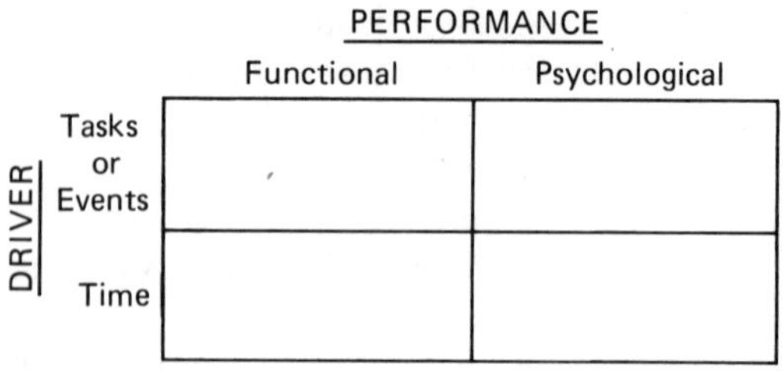

		PERFORMANCE	
		Functional	Psychological
DRIVER	Tasks or Events		
	Time		

FIGURE 4.2. Model dimensions. (From Siegel and Wolf, 1981.)

1. the task environment—that is, the objective problem to be solved—the rules to be applied in the solution, the information representing the status of the system, and
2. the program developed to solve the problem. Material for development of the models is often derived from verbal protocols of subjects performing ditagnostic tasks.

In terms of structure, the cognitive models are a variation of the task-analytic or network approach, although some cognitive modelers make occasional use of control- theoretic processes.

Selection of Model Type. The first question with which the model developer or user must concern himself involves the type of model he requires. This question is basic to subsequent model design decisions.

Siegel and Wolf (1981) describe behavioral models in terms of four dimensions represented by the 2 × 2 diagram below (Figure 4.2).

Models may be driven (controlled) on the basis of events (tasks) or on the basis of time increments. Performance may be functionally represented or it may be constrained on the basis of psychological constructs.

DRIVERS. Task or event driven simulations (e.g., Siegel/Wolf, 1969) sequentially simulate the performance of subtasks or events to be performed. Such simulations are most appropriate when the subtask or event sequence is to some extent known and fixed.

Time driven simulations are based on the passage of time, advancing on the basis of an internal clock. When a specified time is reached, the system state is simulated and the results recorded. There need be no list of events to be followed or processing associated with an event. The time advance approach is undesirable if there are many periods when no events occur. Event advance procedures are preferable if events occur on a fairly regular basis.

PERFORMANCE. Functional models simulate performance directly. Activities are simulated as events without the superimposition of higher order constructs or intervening variables; the model is event driven. Most engineering models probably fall into this category. Psychological models on the other hand, often rely on constructs such as stress, aspiration, etc. which function interactively as the basis for the simulation.

The functional model probably represent the easiest and quickest type of model to develop. It answers the question, "Does the system work?" but may not help in understanding why or determining how to make the system work more effectively. Psychological models which attempt to explain why and how are more difficult to develop. However, constructs are probably necessary in any simulation of a system in which personnel exert significant effects. Because psychological models depend on the availability of behavioral theory, it is necessary to determine how adequate that theory is, to choose among competing theories, and to ensure that the theory can be represented through computer simulation. In addition, the necessary input data must be available or obtainable at a sufficient level of reliability and validity.

The Relationship between Models and Theories

A behavioral model is not a theory of behavior. The purpose of a theory is to describe functional relationships (Feigl, 1949), and its value rests on its validity (Chapanis, 1961). Although a model must include functional relationships within its structure, its goal is pragmatic: to predict behavior and to determine the effects of variables on some system output. Hence, the model is judged on the basis of utility, or the extent to which model outputs assist one to reach a reasonable decision. The extent to which the model represents a nonmodel reality is its validity.

Theories may postulate intervening variables with tenuous dimensions, such as motivation. On the other hand, each variable in a model which simulates a real world system must ideally be defined, its relationship to other variables must be clear and it must be quantifiable to some degree.

Questions Models Can Answer

Behavioral models can help system developers answer questions which cannot be easily answered through other methods.

Behavioral computer simulations help provide the developer with answers to many of the questions asked in Chapter 2, for example,

1. Will personnel be able to complete all their required tasks within the time allotted?
2. Where in the task sequence are operators likely to fail most or least often?
3. Where during system utilization will operators be most over- or underloaded?
4. In which system functions and tasks are personnel least reliable and why?
5. How will task restructuring or reallocation affect system effectiveness?
6. How much will performance degrade when system operators are fatigued or stressed?

7. How will various environmental factors (e.g., heat, light) affect total man–machine system performance?

Once the system has been modified in response to the answers to these questions, computer simulations can be performed to predict the improvement produced by these changes.

Computer simulation can also be used to compare the effectiveness of alternative system concepts. The greatest advantage of computer models may be their ability to provide the basis for tradeoffs at an early stage of system development.

Selection of Variables

Since the simulation models a real world system, the modeler must understand the real world behavioral process before the model can be developed. Modeling development usually begins with two roughly concurrent analyses: of the real world system and situation which is to be modeled—a form of task analysis, as it were—and of the behavioral literature. These concurrent efforts are performed to select the variables to be represented. Since there are usually more variables than is feasible to include in the model, a choice must be made.

Criteria of variable selection (modified from Siegel and Wolf, 1981) suggest that a preferred variable is one:

1. which is backed by substantial empirical data (*data availability*);
2. for which the range of error is minimal (*data reliability*);
3. which is obviously relevant to the performance of the system and personnel being modeled (*relevance*);
4. which is sensitive to changes in system dynamics (*sensitivity*);
5. which can be empirically measured (*objectivity*);
6. which does not require unwarranted assumptions, excessive processing time or memory storage, and which can systematically vary along a continuum requiring no undue transformation (*suitability for simulation*);
7. which is applicable to a range of modeled situations (*generality*);
8. which is easily understood by model users (*comprehensibility*); and
9. which is most useful for answering the questions the user of the model wishes to ask (*utility*).

These criteria are an ideal, of course. Few variables ever satisfy all of them to the extent desired.

Some types of parameters can be selected without concern for data availability, for example, the parameter ("number of men in the crew"). Other parameters (e.g., feedback effect) may be selected if review of the literature indicates that experimental data or data banks are available for these parameters. If no data are available, the cost of developing the data via special experimentation or calculation should be considered.

The interaction of human performance with situational, performance shaping variables is important when these variables differentially affect that performance. Examples of situational variables are, failure rate and repair time, environmental conditions, rate of supply usage, number of personnel in an opposing force, work day length—the list could go on and on.

The use of situational variables lends significant realism to a model. However, the attempt to be completely realistic may make the model unwieldy. The true test of a model is its ability to assist in solving problems, and not necessarily to describe the world in all its details.

Data Requirements

The ultimate success of a model depends on the availability and validity of its input data. A model may be acceptable in terms of its constructs but may be unusable because the input data required for implementing these constructs are not available or fail to reach some necessary level of accuracy. While a number of behavioral data banks (e.g., Munger et al., 1962) are available, such data banks are quite deficient with regard to cognitive processes. Moreover, normative data based on general populations often do not take account of individual differences.

Model Validation and Generalizability

Model validation is one of the least understood and least accomplished aspects of model development. In part this results from the application of psychometric validation constructs to model validation. Models are not psychometric tests and the principal test of any behavioral model is its utility. However it is difficult for the user to have confidence in an unvalidated model.

Friedman (1953) contended that the validity of a model rests not on its assumptions and constructs but on its ability to predict how variables will perform empirically. It is possible that with a new simulation model about all that can be hoped for is a test of reasonableness and an act of faith. In the event few models are validated in a predictive sense.

Should the model apply only to a single system, task, situation or should it generalize to a class of systems? This question needs answering early in model development because the answer affects the cost of model development, development time, and the model's predictive validity.

Models representing a specific situation are easier, less costly and require less time to develop. However, their applicability to even similar situations will be limited. Although more general models are most costly to develop, they may be used regularly by a greater number of users. An example is the SiegelWolf (1969) model, initially developed by 1960, which according to Siegel and Wolf (1981) still remains in use. The cost of developing, maintaining and supporting such models can be amortized over a number of users. There may however be a tradeoff between generality and validity. As generality increases, validity probably decreases because the model represents no single specific situation very precisely. However, no one really knows because the number of models that have been validated is very few.

Simulation Outputs

The model output and its interpretation present another problem. One has, of course, to provide the user with information he needs at the level of detail he wants and in a form he can use. Unfortunately it is often not possible to make these decisions far in advance. Pragmatically it is best to let the user select those output tabulations he wants. The options are specified at run time and the user can select from these. A minimum of three output detail levels or levels of data reduction should be provided:

1. *Full detail.* The results for each event, time segment, operator, etc. simulated. This is particularly useful in checking out new input data sequences or for studying specific situations in detail.
2. *Intermediate detail.* Events or time segments are consolidated by hour, day, or other scaling. Useful for archives, for summaries, and for review of general results.
3. *Summary detail.* Major outputs are summarized across events, time segments, days, operators, etc.

Cost-Effectiveness

The cost of model development and application represents a significant consideration. Cost depends in large part on the extent to which the developer requires his model to satisfy criteria such as internal consistency, construct validity, and ease of use. The more criteria and the greater the extent to which they are satisfied, the higher model cost will be.

Both deterministic and stochastic models have high resolution—defined in terms of amount of detail they present. But the realism of the stochastic models is higher than that of the deterministic model because the former incorporates greater variability. Because of this stochastic models are generally preferable, though their use of computer time is greater and the model is usually more costly (*4* to *7* on a cost scale of *1* to *10*) than the deterministic model (*3* to *5* on the cost scale) (Siegel and Wolf, 1981). In most model development the cost of personnel resources is much greater than computer running costs.

The decision as to which type of model to develop on a cost/effectiveness basis must still be made on a case-by-case basis. Often test site availability, types of modeler skills, and computer equipment availability as well as schedule requirements may determine the type of model selected for a given application.

DIGITAL SIMULATION MODELS

In this section we consider the digital simulation models developed by Siegel and his co-workers. These models were selected not only because they are representative of a type, for instance, stochastic or network, but more importantly because they have been outstandingly successful—if success is defined as the variety of situations to which they have been applied.

There are three such models: the 1- to 2-man model; the 4- to 20-man model; and the 20- to 99-man model. We shall concentrate only on the first, which exemplifies the basic concepts and methodology. Moreover, the two larger models are so elaborate that it would require a separate book to describe them adequately. At the same time, our own description of the 1- to 2-man model, while comprehensive, cannot do justice to the richness of detail it includes. For this, the reader is referred to Siegel and Wolf (1969).

Goals

The purpose of the 1- to 2-man model is to serve as a tool for system designers during development, and to indicate where the system may over- or underload its operators.

The model simulates maintenance or operator tasks simply by identifying personnel as operators or technicians and the tasks as operator or maintenance tasks. It predicts task completion time and the probability of successful task completion. It also seeks to determine whether or not an average operator will successfully complete required tasks, how success probability changes for various performance shaping factors, and the operator proficiency required by the system. A complete list of questions answered can be found in Department of Navy (1977).

The model is both a design aid and an experimental tool. When the model is exercised with constant parameters, it is used as a design aid; when system parameters are varied on succeeding runs, the model is used in an experimental problem-solving mode.

Assumptions

The basic assumption in the Siegel models is that operator loading is the basic element in effective man–machine system performance. Although there may be a variety of reasons why the operator is loaded or unloaded, these reasons are compressed into a variable called "stress." Stress may be caused by 1. falling behind in time on an assigned task sequence; 2. a realization that the operator's partner is not performing adequately; 3. inability to complete successfully a subtask on the first attempt and the need to repeat the subtask; 4. the need to wait for equipment reactions. The model accounts for nonstress situations by utilizing the average probability of completing the subtask, which cancels out the stress effects.

In their most recent work in developing a model of nuclear power plant maintainer performance, Siegel and his collaborators have incorporated a probability of task success factor which depends on a comparison between the abilities required for successful subtask accomplishment and the maintainer's actual abilities (Knee, Krois, Haas, Siegel and Ryan, 1983). The inclusion of what is essentially a task difficulty factor significantly expands the model's capability of representing the mechanisms responsible for task accomplishment or failure.

Methodologic Scope

The methodology underlying the model can be applied to any type of system or task. The model's features (e.g., stress or urgency and the psychosocial formulation Siegel employs) apply regardless of the specific nature of the system.

The application of the general model to represent a specific system does, however, require the collection of new data descriptive of that system. For example, subtask execution times will vary depending on the specific nature of the task, such as landing an aircraft, or firing a missile.

Parameters

The following are the basic parameters of the model.

The parameter T_j, the mission time limit, specifies the total time allotted to each operator for performance of the task.

The parameter F_j accounts for variance among individuals operating the system. This parameter enables the model to simulate an operator who usually performs faster or slower than the average operator. The effects of faster, or more highly motivated operators ($F_j > 1$), and slower operators ($F_j < 1$) are examined by performing several computer runs with different F_j values.

A third parameter which is central to the model is the stress threshold M_j, operationally defined as the ratio of how much is left to do to the amount of time available in which to do it.

The critical importance of stress is indicated by its relationship to probability of successful performance of the subtask $\bar{p}_{ij}$. Thus the probability of success increases linearly with stress until it becomes unity at the stress threshold, after which the probability decreases linearly until, when stress has a value equal to $M_j + 1$, it levels off at a value which is decreased from $\bar{p}_{ij}$ by an amount equal to $\bar{p}_{ij}/2$.

Similarly, execution time for the subtask varies as a function of stress. If the average operator requires $\bar{t}_i$ seconds to perform subtask i when stress is unity, $\bar{t}_i$ decreases with increasing stress until M_j is reached after which $\bar{t}_i$ increases linearly with increasing stress.

In his later work, Siegel has added a fourth parameter, the waiting time period P_j, which is applicable only to cyclic subtasks, those in which the equipment imposes a time before which the operator cannot initiate the subtask. When such a subtask ocurs in the task sequence, the operator must wait until the start of the next period before beginning that subtask.

In the larger models one also finds such psychosocial parameters as leadership, group and crew size, and equipment data, for example, failure rate and repair time, etc. Parameters also extend to include personnel data, such as areas of specialization, morale threshold, number of working hours per day, and probability of emergency situation occurrence. The model can be applied with or without any of these more complex variables, depending on the kind of question to be asked of the model and the availability of relevant data.

Data Inputs

To exercise the model, 11 items of task analytic input data are needed for each subtask and operator/technician. These identify: 1. decision subtasks; 2. non-essential subtasks—which can be ignored in urgent conditions; 3. subtasks which must be completed by a second operator before it can be attempted by another operator; 4. time before which a subtask cannot be started; 5. the number of the subtask that must be performed next, assuming the current subtask is completed successfully; 6. the number of the subtask which must be performed next assuming the current subtask is failed; 7. average time in seconds required by the operator performing a subtask; 8. average standard deviation around $\bar{t}_{ij}$ for the average operator; 9. the probability that a task will be performed successfully; 10. time required to perform all remaining essential subtasks; and 11. the time required to perform all remaining nonessential subtasks, (10) and (11) both at average execution times, assuming no failures.

Data Sources

The level of data input is fairly molecular, describing individual discrete perceptual and motor actions. Sources of input data are varied. Data are secured from task analysis, formal experiments, informal measurements, simulator measurements, literature search or personal interviews.

Much of the input data is gathered by direct questioning of expert operators; the data gathering process is relatively informal. Although the model makes use of data banks, such as they are, it is likely that some new input data must be gathered for each new application of the model. Siegel notes that "on the other hand, experience with the model has indicated that it is relatively insensitive to input data vagaries" (Meister, 1971).

The probability estimates applied to the subtasks are *1* minus the percentage of error over a block of trials. Because subtask probabilities are generally very high (0.97 and higher) and because the multiplicative limitations of probability statistics are minimized in simulation models, the effect of these probabilities in reducing the estimate of overall system success is minimized. This is sometimes a problem in human reliability prediction—see Chapter 5. The type of data input does not differentiate significantly between equipment characteristics (e.g., two different types of meters), although it does differentiate between types of equipment components (e.g., indicator lights and meters). This has negative implications for use of the model results to suggest design modifications, but it makes the model capable of using almost any kind of data source.

Model Outputs

The model outputs a considerable amount of data for each operator. A run summary might contain total number of runs, number and percent of successful runs, average time used over N runs, average time over run, average waiting time, average peak and final stress, the number of times a subtask was failed or ignored, the time spent in repeating failed subtasks, and the average time—from the beginning of a malfunction correction—that the subtask was completed.

Procedures for Model Application

Task Analysis. The digital simulation methodology is, as was pointed out previously, a task analytic one. The subtasks that form the behavioral elements of the model are determined by a detailed task analysis. This molecular level of operation is required because the simulation must reproduce individual operator actions.

Output Methodology. The simulation operates through its Monte Carlo sampling process to arrive directly at the end result. Success or failure of the entire task or mission is not dependent on the probability of accomplishment of any single subtask, but whether or not the operator completes all essential subtasks in the required time. Each individual subtask p_i has an effect on ultimate system success but not necessarily a primary one.

As a consequence, all the computer does at the end of a series of computer runs is to divide the number of successful runs by the total number of runs performed to arrive at an estimate of effectiveness.

Because the simulation of any individual task is based in part on a random process, it is necessary to repeat the simulation a number of times to obtain sufficiently representative performance data for each set of conditions. A value of N, usually 100 to 200 iterations, is selected prior to the simulation.

Once the program, parameters, and initial conditions have been stored by the computer, it begins to process subtask data sequentially. (See Figure 4.3.) The sequence of subtasks to be performed is determined by the operator's success or failure on a prior task and the total time expended by the operator on all previous subtasks. If the model involves two operators, the operator who has expended less total time is selected and the next subtask is simulated. If the selected operator must wait for his partner, the sequence continues using data for the other operator.

One of three stages of urgency is next determined, based on the remaining time available to the operator for completing the task. The situation is nonurgent if there is sufficient time to complete all remaining subtasks. It is urgent if time is available only for completing essential subtasks; it is highly urgent if there is insufficient time for completing even essential tasks. Under urgent and highly urgent conditions the computer ignores nonessential subtasks.

The stress condition is calculated next. During nonurgent and urgent conditions stress is defined as equal to unity. When the situation is highly urgent, stress is defined as the ratio of the sum of average execution or completion times for remaining essential subtasks to the total time remaining.

Subtask execution time is next computed. For each subtask it is assumed that the actual subtask execution time is normally distributed. Specific time values are se-

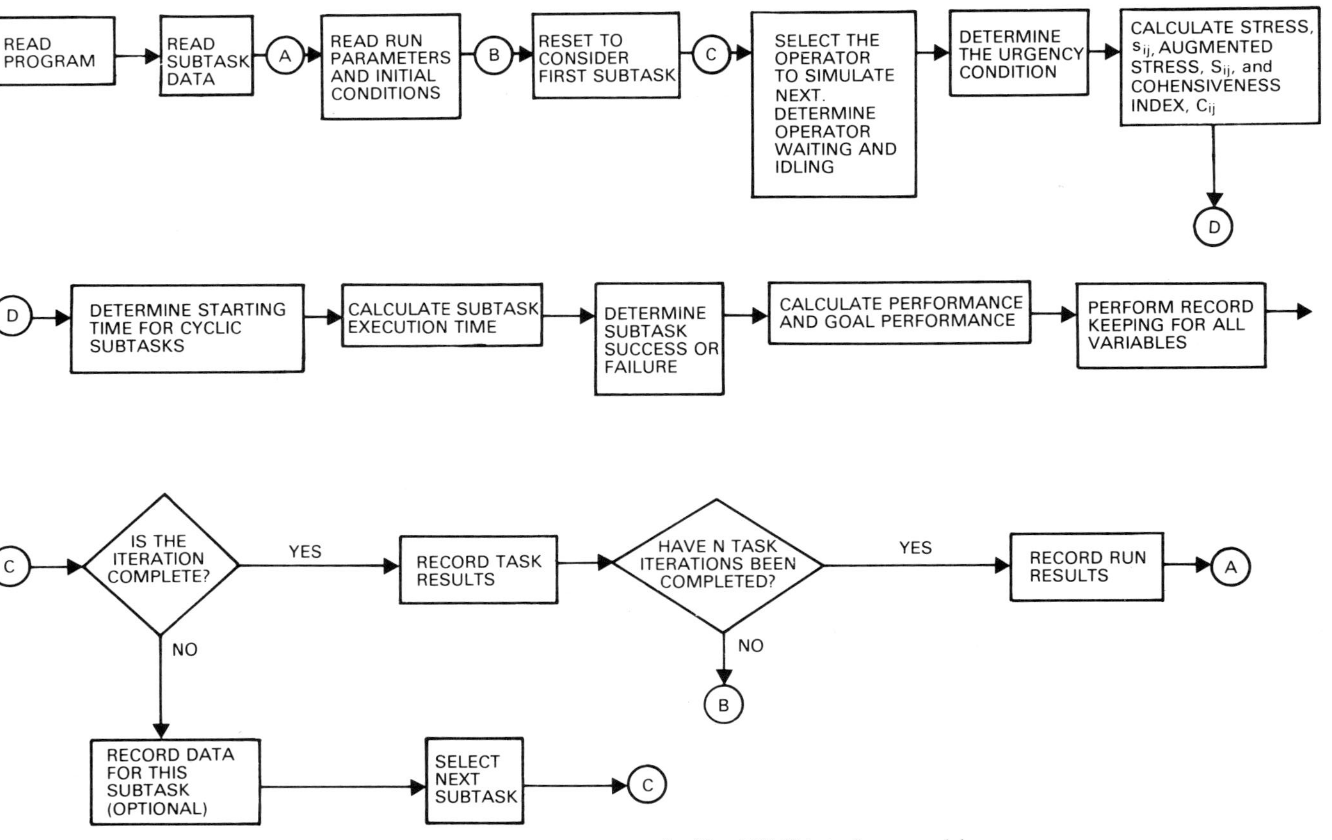

FIGURE 4.3. Processing sequence for Siegel/Wolf 1- to 2-man model.

lected by the Monte Carlo technique from a normal distribution limited by a fixed minimum, 0.75 second. As indicated previously, time varies with stress.

The probability of subtask success and failure is then generated in much the same way as are the subtask execution times, with essentially the same time–stress relationships.

Anticipated Model Uses

1. *Prediction of System Effectiveness.* The model can supply an absolute estimate of the system reliability to be anticipated when the system becomes operational (e.g., the system will eventually perform with a reliability of .99) and a comparison of estimated system reliability with that required to achieve mission success (e.g., estimated system reliability is .98 but mission requirements call for a performance of .99, or the mission must be accomplished in 32 minutes whereas estimated actual system performance is 34 minutes).

2. *Design Analysis.* The model compares alternative system configurations to determine which should be selected for implementation and determines redesign requirements for a system which cannot satisfy system requirements.

If the simulation model can predict the system effectiveness of one configuration, it can also predict the effectiveness of another, and compare the two estimates. Differences in system configuration will reveal differences in performance only if the nature and organization of the tasks involved in the two configurations differ. If the two configurations differ only in terms of molecular equipment characteristics, it is unlikely that significant differences in performance will result because the input data are responsive more to task factors than to equipment factors.

Validation Studies

Siegel (personal communication) lists at least 10 validation studies, the results of which are apparently highly promising.

SAINT

SAINT is an extension of the Siegel/Wolf (1969) model. It is a network technique that contains a variety of types of process branching, a set of alternative distributions to be used in modeling individual task elements and a Monte Carlo procedure for sampling these distributions.

SAINT is not itself a model but rather a special language baed on GASP (Pritsker, 1974) and GERT (Pritsker and Happ, 1967, and Whitehouse, 1973) for modeling systems. Although most models represent the human either as a discrete or continuous process, SAINT can do both.

It is this flexibility and the variety of applications possible that make SAINT so interesting to researchers. According to Chubb (1980), there are three levels of SAINT concepts ranging from the elementary, requiring no programming experience, to intermediate concepts, in which programming experience would be useful, to the advanced level which requires programming experience. With increased levels the sophistication of SAINT and what it can do increases. Chubb (1980) provides examples of the use of each of these levels.

SAINT has been employed in a wide range of model contexts, such as choice reaction time (Hann and Kuperman, 1975), remotely piloted vehicle control facility (Wortman, Duket and Seifert, 1975), Digital Avionics Information System (DAIS) design (Kuperman and Seifert, 1975), airborne warning and control system (Mills, 1976), the performance of industrial inspectors (Adams and Reddy, 1978), and the evaluation of job performance aids (Smillie and Ayoub, 1977).

We shall highlight the major characteristics of SAINT without attempting to describe its simulation language characteristics, for which the reader should refer to Pritsker et al., 1974 and Wortman et al., 1977a, b.

Like Siegel/Wolf, tasks are related to each other in SAINT by precedence relationships which specify the flow of operations through the network and indicate which tasks can be initiated following the completion of previous tasks. The completion of individual tasks in a network can modify later precedence relationships, altering network flow.

A SAINT task has associated with it input, task and output parameters that specify the nature of the predecessor tasks, task characteristics and branching to other tasks. Time to perform a task is specified in terms of a variety of sampling distributions, for example, constant, normal, lognormal, Poisson, Beta, etc. If none of these is suitable, the SAINT user can write his own and use it in the simulation.

Tasks are graded in terms of their importance to the system mission which means that during a mission when time grows short, less important tasks can be skipped.

SAINT can simulate six types of tasks: single operator, joint operator, one of several operators, hardware (machine only), cyclic tasks and gap filled tasks (to be performed only if time is available).

After a task has been completed, SAINT decides which of the remaining tasks shall be initiated. The decision is based on five decision rules: *Deterministic* (all *n* branches selected); *Probabilistic* (selection on a random basis); *Conditional, Take-first* (first branch satisfying specified conditions is selected); *Conditional, Take-all* (all *n* branches satisfying specified conditions are selected); and *Modified probabilistic* (same as probabilistic except branch probabilities are modified by number of previous completions of the task from which the branches stem).

Like Siegel/Wolf, individual differences and their effects are represented by differences in operator speed and accuracy (based on differences in operator proficiency and training). Stress is defined as in Siegel/Wolf as the ratio between time available to complete tasks and time required. Goal gradient effects, an increase in performance accuracy as one nears task completion, are simulated by adding to the probability of success a value whose size is a direct function of the extent of prescribed completion.

SAINT collects statistics on the temporal aspects of task performance: time of first completion of a particular task, time of all completions of that task, time between completions of a given task, time required to complete the task, time from completion of first predecessor task to start of a given task.

Pew et al., (1977) give very high marks to SAINT, considering it "without peer at this time" (p. 40) but it seems to this author that there is very little to choose between Siegel/Wolf and SAINT, except perhaps that the latter is a general purpose computer language rather than a model.

THE HUMAN OPERATOR SIMULATOR

The Human Operator Simulator is a digital computer program designed to be used in the evaluation of complex crewstations. It dynamically simulates the activities of an operator and the performance of the hardware in response to the operator's actions.

Unlike Siegel/Wolf and many other computer models, HOS does not sample distributions of performance data. Rather, it is deterministic, relying on equations describing relationships between parameters and performance outputs. The equations are of course based on experimental data, but the use of functional relationships in equation form rather than sampling from distributions reduces the need for data banks.

The Human Operator Simulator is extremely molecular, operating at a very fine level of task element detail. It is one of the few examples of the microprocess models defined previously. For example, it makes use of inputs such as the state of displays (e.g., 5000 feet altitude), their locations within the cockpit, reach distance, and time to reach controls.

Oddly enough, for such a molecular model it places great emphasis on cognitive processes, particularly recall, memory decay, strength of recall, etc. which are basic elements in the decision-making process. Less molecular models include the decision-making process but deal with it as a total entity rather than in terms of the elements making up the decision. Currently the HOS developers are attempting to upgrade its cognitive capabilities (Glenn, Zaklad and Wherry, Jr., 1982).

Goals

The Human Operator Simulator is not simply a design tool for its developers (Strieb and Wherry, 1979). They see HOS as an effort to substitute computer control for the performance of experimental studies. They think of HOS as being sufficiently valid and precise so that its output may be analyzed and used in exactly the same manner as that obtained from an experiment with actual subjects.

Definition and Assumptions

The Human Operator Simulator consists of four major components:

1. The simulated human operator;
2. The procedures governing system operation;
3. The physical layout of the operator's workspace;
4. The mission to be run.

The HOS operator is assumed to be a highly motivated, well-trained, average operator. Other characteristics of the HOS operator are:

1. His position relative to the displays and controls in the crewstation is fixed—that is, he is stationary.

2. The operator can process only one task statement at a time. However, once a statement has been processed, the operator can begin work on the next statement. Thus, the HOS operator can perform several actions concurrently.

3. The HOS operator carries out instructions without omitting a step. He makes no incorrect decisions nor does he incorrectly carry out an instruction.

This last point refers to one of the most controversial issues associated with HOS—its model of operator error. By definition, a well-trained operator is one who carries out instructions "by the book," without omitting a step, making an incorrect decision or incorrectly carrying out an instruction. Given, for example, that an operator recalls an instruction he will perform it correctly. The only element of uncertainty is how long it will take him to recall the proper procedure.

However, this does not preclude all sources of operator error. For HOS, the significant sources of operator error are:

1. Requiring the operator to perform more activities in a given period of time than possible, because of human and/or equipment limitations, thereby causing the operator to fall behind in the mission.

2. Giving the operator an incorrect set of decision rules and/or operating instructions, thereby causing tactical and/or operational errors.

3. Giving the operator poor displays and/or controls that do not permit proper operation of the system.

These errors result in operator errors but they are really *failures in system design*. They are not errors such as an operator inadvertently pushing the wrong button. True operator errors are either random or of low frequency (in which case, argue the developers, it is unfair to use them to evaluate the nominal performance of the system).

The inclusion of the physical layout of the workspace as one of the main components of HOS means that, if the layout is properly taken into account, HOS will be highly sensitive to the design configuration of the system.

Another important assumption is that all operator actions are composed of relatively few basic activities. For example, if an action is to *manipulate throttle*, the manipulate instruction itself breaks down to reach and twist actions. The consequences of this assumption is the micro-level of detail noted previously; the simulator takes more molar behaviors and partitions them into their molecular constituents.

In order to provide flexibility in the model, instructions or tasks—for example, alter desired position of throttle to 50 percent—are defined as goals for the operator rather than as rigid actions for him to take. In adjusting a throttle, the concept of the task as a goal causes the operator to adjust the throttle setting if the throttle is not at

50 percent, but to do nothing if the throttle is already at 50 percent and the operator knows it.

Methodologic Scope

The Human Operator Simulator in its present formulation is strictly pilot-task oriented. However, HOS developers insist that HOS is not a model of a pilot but a general model for any seated operator whose primary task is to observe displays, compute, make decisions, and manipulate controls. If so, the logic of the model could be applied to other types of systems and tasks, although a very substantial rewriting of program specifics would probably be required.

The simulated operator is conceptualized as performing a general monitoring function interspersed with specific mission-directing and corrective actions. Having once been given a task, the pilot sets his instruments for the specified parameters and merely corrects any deviations that occur. Thus, continuous activities are formulated in a discrete manner, as points at which the operator is required to take a discrete action because a deviation from the requirement has appeared. This considerably simplifies the model because it is not required to simulate continuing actions.

Model Parameters

In order to understand the logic of the model it is necessary to start with the inputs to HOS. These require a specific programming language (Human Operator Procedures or HOPROC) to enable users of HOS to input both operating procedures for the system and mission instructions in English language statements. The output of HOPROC is then input to HOS.

HOPROC

HOPROC is an English/FORTRAN-like language. HOPROC statements are not converted into numeric entries—HOS interprets HOPROC statements directly, just as an actual system operator can interpret English language instructions.

The HOPROC language is divided into three major sections—the *title declarations* section, the *hardware* section, and the *operator* section. In the title declarations section the model identifies the displays and controls in the crewstation and their generic characteristics. The operator section is divided into *operator procedures* and *operator functions*. The operator procedures describe the operator's tasks. The operator functions describe the mental calculations that the operator has to perform to carry out those tasks.

Similarly, the hardware section is divided into hardware procedures and hardware functions. The hardware procedures describe the hardware changes that occur as the result of operator actions, as well as independent events, such as the movement of external targets or changes in the environment. The hardware functions describe the mathematical calculations required to support the hardware procedures.

The Human Operator Simulator interprets each HOPROC statement and converts it into a series of operator actions, each of which is a combination of one or more of seven fundamental functions: 1. Obtaining information; 2. Remembering information; 3. Performing a mental computation; 4. Making a decision; 5. Moving a body part; 6. Performing a control manipulation; and 7. Relaxing. HOS itself determines the functions required to accomplish a particular task.

These functions are often either imbedded in, or contain within themselves, human performance models. For example, when the operator attempts to recall some item of information, there is a *recall model* that is automatically elicited by the program that simulates the operator's short-term memory processes.

The other micromodels may be accessed as a consequence of other types of procedural statements or on an as needed basis. For example, the decision making micromodel is accessed whenever a task statement requires a decision or whenever the operator must make a decision about what procedure to work on next. The statement decisions are expressed as IF . . . THEN . . . constructs. The information required to make the decisions is gathered by calls to the recall, anatomy movement, information absorption, and mental computation micromodels. Procedural decisions (what procedure to work on next) are based on how long it has been since each procedure was last worked on and how important each procedure is.

HOS Outputs

The primary output from HOS is a time history of operator activities. In addition to the raw timeline data produced by HOS, statistical analysis routines developed specifically for use with HOS can produce a variety of composite statistics, for example, link analysis, timeline and channel loading analysis and device usage statistics.

Data Inputs

Those inputted by the analyst include: 1. initial states of controls, displays and mediated functions; 2. the physical location of controls and displays; 3. information absorption times, and 4. output specifications.

Data sources are largely the experimental literature. Because of the molecularity of the relationships involved, the data required can only be secured from a highly controlled laboratory situation.

Anticipated Model Uses

Like most model developers Strieb and Wherry (1979) feel that HOS can be used to help define the functional requirements of the system—including function allocation—,can help evaluate proposed designs, and define operator training requirements.

Validation

The developers refer to a number of tests of HOS validity which have involved simulations of specific experiments drawn from the human factors and experimental psychological literature (Strieb, et al., 1975; Glenn, Strieb and Wherry, 1977; Lane, Strieb and Wherry, 1977). User model validations have included simulations of specific Navy crewstations (Strieb, et al., 1975; Strieb, et al, 1976; Strieb, et al., 1978; Strieb and Harris, 1978; Lane, Strieb, and Leyland, 1979). These documents are not generally available so they cannot be examined.

COGNITIVE MODELS

Cognitive models are models of how humans solve problems, particularly those of a diagnostic nature, which one finds in troubleshooting failed equipment, assessing system dynamics in process control and diagnosing medical problems. In contrast to Siegel/Wolf and HOS, cognitive models emphasize a single function, although obviously these models also imply perceptual and psychomotor functions as well, since actions are taken on the basis of hypothesis testing. Like the other models described, the situation modeled is a full mission one (a problem solution).

Cognitive models exhibit other differences from the models described previously. They have not generally been computerized, although computers are used in performing experiments to test model hypotheses. They have not been used very much in aid of system design (certainly not in any routine manner), although some researchers (e.g., Card, Moran and Newell, 1980) have modeled the way people use computer programs and have attempted to apply their conclusions to the improved design of computer software. Cognitive models have been used primarily, if not exclusively, in a research mode, although certain aspects such as Rasmussen's taxonomy and search strategies (1981) have influenced the development of data collection methods in nuclear power plants. The cognitive models represent the work of investigators in various disciplines, that is, psychology, mathematics and engineering, who have not formally published a single, unitary model as such. However, there is substantial overlap among the individual models.

In the process control situation which is the one most researchers have used explicitly or implicitly as a model for the cognitive situation, the team proceeds through the following stages:

1. The operator—either individually or as part of a team—is monitoring information displaying system dynamics (e.g., meters that record liquid flow or pressure).

2. During the monitoring process the operator/team recognizes that there is a discrepancy between expected system dynamics (i.e., the values the system should present when the system performs as it should) and present readings of that system. The operator/team recognizes that there is a failure or an incipient failure that may occur if the system is not stabilized. In troubleshooting the similar stage is recognition that the equipment has failed. In medicine the comparable situation is the physician's recognition that the patient has an illness.

3. At this stage, in all three situations, the operator/team analyzes the system situation which may have several subprocesses such as establishing a search (test)

strategy, and developing hypotheses to direct that strategy and mapping symptoms into the operator/team's internal (conceptual) model of how the system functions. It may also include what could have caused the difficulty.

4. As time progresses the (process control) system continues to degrade; the operator/technician/physician updates his information about the system (equipment or human) and he does this in various ways: by monitoring system changes, by performing tests on the basis of hypotheses, and noting the results of these tests.

5. The operator/technician/physician takes some action as a consequence of the system information he has gained. If his tests give him confidence that he knows the cause of the difficulty of the action needed to restabilize the system, he performs that action and looks for feedback to tell him whether his action was correct. Some action will ultimately be successful and the situation will be resolved; but if no action is successful, the plant will break down, the malfunction will remain unresolved or the patient will die.

The scenario above is recursive and iterative and most certainly is far more complex in terms of the hypotheses and tests made and information evaluated than can be described here. Moray (1981) describes the kind of situation we are dealing with in the cognitive models: there are multiple sources of information and feedback loops; dynamic state variables are richly interconnected and functioning in relation to time; and values of state variables in different parts of the system are often highly correlated so that knowledge of one provides information about the value of others. Cognitive models are of two types, mathematic/engineering and psychological models.

Mathematic/Engineering Models

[This subsection is based on the following references: Rouse, 1977, 1979, 1980, 1981, 1982, and 1982b.]

Fault diagnosis involves two processes. Ideally, given a set of symptoms, the problem must be partitioned into two sets; a feasible set—those components that could cause the symptoms—and an infeasible set—components that could not possibly cause the symptoms. Once the partition has been accomplished, the diagnostician chooses a member of the feasible set for testing and then repartitions on the basis of the test results. This is in essence the well-known half-split method (Miller, Folley and Smith, 1953) which is logically the most efficient method of troubleshooting.

Alternatively one can start with the assumption that diagnosis begins with use of rules-of-thumb from which the operator selects one or more, using some set of priorities. There are two types of rules, one for context-specific, the other for context-free situations. In a context-specific situation the operator attempts to use rules that map directly from the symptoms to a solution. However, the rules may be irrelevant to a particular set of symptoms.

Performance in state estimation tasks (which is what the operator does when he checks system dynamics against his model of how the system should function ideally) is dependent on his ability to develop an adequate internal or conceptual model of system dynamics. Rouse's theory incorporates a short-term model tor the immediate problem, and a long term model for the system as it works generally. In decision making the operator trades off estimates based on each of these models. Decision making is partitioned into a memory process and actual decision making. Experiences are encoded into an internal model of the system.

The rule based model referred to previously comprises a series of rules which the operator invokes to determine whether or not the rule is satisfied. The first rule checks to see whether or not sufficient information is available to designate the failed component. If not, more information must be gathered by testing. Subsequent rules look for patterns that satisfy the requirements for particular types of test. After a test is made, the operator's state of knowledge of the network or system is updated on the basis of test results.

Certain rules are preferred over others on the basis of success experiences; these are used first or more often. When one starts a diagnostic task he has some knowledge (an internal model) of the equipment he is working on, as well as several system performance outputs, mostly in the form of meter readings or annunciator alarms, some of which correspond to correct system functioning while others do not.

In his latest writings Rouse (1982a, b) points out the pattern recognition nature of behavior in problem solving. However, not all problems can be solved by direct mapping from observation to solutions.

Rouse emphasizes the distinction between context-specific and context-free patterns of responding to observations. Humans prefer context-specific pattern recognition because it is easier than context-free (i.e., more abstract) processes. In the latter one must make use of a cognitive model of the system—which is not easy. However if the diagnostician does not recognize a pattern, he must go beyond the context-specific process—beyond system state information which is immediate and direct—and consider system structure information which is less direct and immediate. Humans prefer to operate on state or symptomatic information rather than on structural information such as internalized model of the system referred to previously.

Problem solving occurs on three levels: 1. Recognition and classification (of state information, of symptoms); 2. Planning; and 3. Execution and monitoring. At the recognition/classification level the operator attempts to identify the problem context and category by examining the state information and to match that information with a familiar pattern or template which is in the subject's memory. If the pattern does not match the one he has memorized, he must go to structural information or employ something like the deductive method of science.

In the planning phase or level the operator decides how to attack the problem. Again he goes through the pattern recognition process in which he matches state information to a mental template (or if he has a job performance aid such as a symptom-matrix, he would use that); in other words, he repeats the level 1 process. If this does not work, again he reverts to structural information and plans alternatives, imagines consequences of tests, etc.

Familiar patterns of state information allow use of context-specific symptomatic rules (S-rules) that may map directly from observation to hypothesis or action. If the pattern is unfamiliar he will use structural information to apply topographic rules (T-rules) for searching problem structure.

Sheridan's point of view is expressed in Sheridan, 1979, 1981, 1982 and Sheridan and Tulga (1980). He maintains that the operator is becoming a supervisor of a set of autonomous systems with independent tasks. That is, instead of being "in the loop" of the system, he stands somewhat outside it. He is a monitor and decision maker who shifts attention among many tasks.

Sheridan's model contains elements of queuing theory. When a task appears it queues for the action of the decision maker in its particular ensemble. Each queue is characterized by a different mean interarrival time between tasks, also by loss of transition time in transferring from one queue to another.

Each task to be supervised and monitored is characterised by a number of variables to indicate first, how far away the task is from the deadline for successful action on the task, second, the speed with which the task is moving to this deadline, third, the duration of the task, that is, number of units to be processed, fourth, the productivity of the decision maker for that task or group of tasks, such as the time rate at which task durations are completed, and fifth, the *value density* of the task to indicate the benefits accrued per unit time if the decision maker acts on it. The first two factors together specify the amount of available time the decision maker has to act on the task. The third and fourth variables above combine to give the amount of time the decision maker has to spend to sucessfully complete the task.

Loading in Sheridan's concept is therefore defined as

$$L = \frac{\text{time required to perform average task}}{\text{time available to perform average task}} \tag{4.2}$$

which is identical to the classic W/L prediction model.

Sheridan includes four cognitive steps in his problem-solving model: attending to stimuli, recognizing patterns, assessing the situation, and deciding on the response. These stages are similar to Rouse's assumptions and to Curry (1981) and are equally obvious. The operator's cognitive model consists of knowledge of the hardware configuration, dynamic behavior of plant variables, operating procedures, criteria or objectives, abstract event relations, and administrative procedures and management policies. Sheridan's procedures might include Rouse's S- and T-rules but he is not specific. He does, however, include mediating processes and hypotheses in his model. Emphasis is placed on the operator's internal model and matching between that model and external reality.

For Wickens (1979, 1981) the operator establishes criteria of what is right or wrong, acceptable or not, normal or abnormal. This in part determines the false alarm rate in monitoring warning stimuli. The operator has an internal model of how the system works normally. This consists of a set of expected system outputs to known system inputs, given that the system is working normally. The internal model also consists of expectations of outputs from the system.

Effective monitoring of the system is accomplished by constantly comparing observed outputs (e.g., meter readings) with expected outputs to observed inputs. If a discrepancy beyond some error margin occurs between observed and expected outputs, it is stored—presumably in central memory—and discrepancies are accumulated over time. If the number of discrepancies exceed the internal criterion of what is acceptable over time, a failure is presumed to be detected. The number of channels of input available from the observed system versus the internal estimate of current system state is one determinant of observed discrepancy.

For Moray (1981), a plausible model for data acquisition is sequential decision theory. The operator sets criteria in terms of a priori probabilities and utilities for each observation and continues to sample until acquiring enough evidence to satisfy the criterion for making a decision as to whether the system is normal or not. One must have extensive practice in order to incorporate payoffs and probabilities into the internal model.

Moray makes a great deal out of the speed–accuracy tradeoff for the observation of dynamic functions. If the emphasis is on accuracy then the data acquisition algorithm will take precedence, while if the emphasis is on speed of observation, the sampling algorithm will take precedence, fixation duration will be decreased and accuracy will suffer.

When the system appears normal, successive samples of information are monitored from weakly correlated variables. However if an abnormal state arises under these conditions it may be a long time before it is recognized. A strong internal model will help an overloaded operator by allowing that person to predict future states of the system, providing it stays normal. But if the operator relies on predicting the future on the basis of recent past experience, and fails to make observations on the current values of state variables, abnormal readings will not be noticed. Thus the paradox: the better the system is known to the operator, the less likely the operator will be to discover it is in abnormal state (but only within limits, surely).

Psychological Models

Probably the most recent important figure in psychological modeling of cognitive processes is Rasmussen (1981a, b, 1982) whose work represents a European tradition. Rasmussen attempts to understand the diagnostic processes of a nuclear power plant control operator who must be alert to guard against or to restore a deteriorating nuclear situation (e.g., core meltdown) of the Three-Mile Island type.

The operator's actions in a plant must always be based on identification of the operational state of the system. The boundary between routine identification and identification of abnormal states depends on his prior experience.

Diagnosis may have different goals which presumably affect the strategy adopted. Depending upon the situational context, the object of the diagnostic search may be to protect the plant, to compensate for the effect of a change, or to restore a normal state. Diagnosis implies a complex mental process which is very situation and person dependent.

Human data processes can be described in terms of data, models and strategies.

Data are the mental representations of information describing the system state which function on several levels of abstraction and which in turn specify the appropriate information coding for data presentation. *Models* are the mental representation of the system's anatomical or functional structure which can be related directly to displays. *Strategies* are higher level structures of the mental processes and they relate goals to sets of models, data, etc. The operator's actual performance can be analyzed using *tactical rules* to describe the control of the processes within a formal strategy.

Diagnostic search can be performed either as a *symptomatic* search or as a *topographic* search. In symptomatic search, symptoms or observations can be used as a search template in accessing a library of symptoms related to different abnormal system conditions (the library residing in memory). In topographic search the individual has a template of normal operation and matches this against actual system operations. The difference between the two is a mismatch and is identified by its location in the template. The difference between the two searches is in the use of observed information.

In topographic search the system is mapped as good/bad and the extent of the potentially bad field is gradually narrowed until the location of the change is determined with sufficient resolution to allow selection of an appropriate action. In most cases, says Rasmussen, the search is an abstract operation.

The rule behind the strategies adopted by the diagnostician is the line of least resistance. Instead of making overall plans for the search, he tends to make rapid and impulsive decisions all along the search based only upon the information received at the moment. As long as simple, familiar routines appear to be progressing, there is little tendency to try more complex functional or causal arguments. This agrees with observations of the way in which maintenance personnel attack the problem of troubleshooting a failed equipment (see Bond and Towne, 1979).

In Rasmussen's model *values, goals* and *performance criteria* play important roles. The search for information is mediated by these. He draws a distinction between three levels of behavior: skill, rule, and knowledge-based performance, a distinction related to the reference used for error judgment, since different concepts are used to control behavior. Skill-based performance is controlled by stored patterns of behavior. The rule-based domain includes performance in familiar situations controlled by stored rules for coordination of subroutines; errors are related to mechanisms like wrong classification or recognition of situations, erroneous associations to tasks, or to memory slips. Knowledge-based behavior is called upon in unique, unfamiliar situations for which actions must be planned from knowledge of the functional and physical properties of the system (i.e., rules and skills are not sufficient).

Computer Models of Cognitive Processes

Rouse, Rasmussen, Sheridan et al. did not develop computer simulations of the diagnostic process, but Baron, Feehrer, Muralidharan, Pew and Horwitz (1982) have developed a computerized model based on their work.

The Baron et al. model builds on a series of operator functions and processes:

1. Monitoring displays,
2. Situation assessment,
3. Decision to act—or not to act—based on that assessment, and
4. Action to implement the decision.

These functions are implemented by various processors:

1. *A display processor* selects an appropriate displayed quantity and accounts for sensory/processing limitations in observation.

2. *An information processor* includes a mental model of the plant from which is derived a predict/correct logic for state estimation and prediction.

3. *A situation assessor* provides a template matching scheme which checks symptoms against a template which is part of a procedure residing either in a manual or in memory. The range of algorithms permits symptomatic and topographic search strategies.

4. *A response selector/formulator* includes major decision making at several levels. Choices are made on the basis of utility theory.

5. *A response effector* permits three types of actions: control, observation and communication. Time is associated with each action.

Cognitive Science Models

The *cognitive science* researchers (e.g., Norman and Bobrow, 1975) have as yet provided no very useful *design-aiding* models, although they have influenced those researching human-computer interaction (e.g., Card, Moran and Newell, 1983).

COMMENTARY

It would be highly desirable to compare the various computerized design aids and mathematic models, but the best basis of comparison—an empirical test—is not available. One can compare, therefore, only on the basis of internal criteria such as the structure of the techniques, the adequacy of the theory on which the techniques rely and the amount of input data they require. On this basis, CAFES and CHESS are obviously much more sophisticated than the other design aids; for example, they are the only computerized techniques that incorporate workload assessment modules—whatever one may think of the theoretical basis for those modules.

With regard to the mathematic models, no empirical or test comparisons have been made. Leaving aside the cognitive models which so far are primarily research instruments, the stochastic network models (Siegel/Wolf and SAINT) and the deterministic model (HOS) take diametrically opposed approaches to model development. The latter relies on equations describing molecular relationships between parameters and performance outputs, the former rely on data distributions for relatively molar parameters.

The author tends to prefer stochastic models because they are probabilistic and we live in a probabilistic world. A fixed equation may demand more precision in our data than we can presently satisfy. In addition, HOS is at present strictly pilot-oriented, whereas the Siegel/Wolf and SAINT techniques can model anything. HOS has a more serious disadvantage: the manner in which it deals—or does not deal—with error. Nevertheless, the manner in which HOS is built up of behavioral elements is fascinating. However, as Siegel and Wolf (1981) suggest, extraneous influences, such as whether one has a computer compatible with the software of a particular technique, often determine the particular technique selected.

The most important question to ask is: How do these design aids and mathematical models perform on the system development job? It is our impression that they are used much *less* frequently than manual methods. Why?

Unfortunately there are no extensive data on use of these methods which renders any hypotheses highly speculative (although see Chapter 13). The author has the impression however that the market for these computerized techniques and models is rather restricted. One wonders, for example, whether many developers other than Boeing, or the Naval Air Development Center (which paid for its development), make use of CAFES. The published descriptions of models represent in large part demonstrations of the applicability of the model to this or the other behavioral phenomenon, but one hears very little about routine use of these methods afterwards in system development or indeed in any other nonresearch context. Either these uses are not reported or methods are developed, demonstrated, and described and then put on a shelf. If the latter is the case, perhaps we should ask: Why are they not used? Is it because these techniques and models require too much time and too many data inputs, are too costly or too effort demanding? Is it perhaps reluctance of analysts to make use of innovations? Are potential users inadequately aware of advances in behavioral technology?

Where utility is a factor, data on method usage should be routinely gathered so that if techniques and methods possess some flaw that makes them ineffective, they can be modified.

The great weakness of models is the lack of appropriate data with which to exercise them. It is a cliché to say that a model is only as good as its data. The proliferation of behavioral models in recent years does not seem to have led to any marked increase in efforts to perform research directly supporting those models. The model-maker seems not to be a researcher, except in terms of developing models, and experimental researchers do not develop models. In any event, no one performs research solely to secure data for model purposes. Modelmakers may gather data to demonstrate model validity but they appear not to make efforts to create data by performing relevant studies—though they are avid in collecting whatever inadequate data are already available.

Such qualifications aside, true models, which are those containing explicit assumptions, definitions of parameters and variables, specified data inputs and outputs, and quantitative relationships among variables, probably offer the best hope behavioral science has for developing a discipline with firm quantitative underpinnings.

REFERENCES

Adams, S. K. and Reddy, M. R. Potential use and applications of SAINT to the analysis of quality control systems. *Proceedings*, Human Factors Society Annual Meeting, 1978, 184–190.

Baron, S., Feehrer, C., Muralidharan, R., Pew, R. and Horwitz, P. *An Approach to Modelling Supervisory Control of a Nuclear Power Plant*. (Draft) Bolt, Beranek and Newman, Inc., Cambridge, MD, July 1982.

Bartlett, M. W. and Smith, L. A. Design of control and display panels using computer algorithms, *Human Factors*, 1973, *15*, 1–7.

Bond, N. A. and Towne, D. M. *Troubleshooting Complex Equipment in the Military Services: Research and Prospects*. Technical Report No. 92, Behavioral Technology Laboratories, University of Southern California, Los Angeles, CA, December 1979.

Bonney, M. C. and Case, K. The development of SAMMIE for computer aided work place and work task design. *Proceedings*, 6th Congress of the International Ergonomics Association, 1976, 340–348.

Broadbent, D. E. *Perception and Communication*. London: Pergamon Press, 1958.

Card, S. K., Moran, T. P. and Newell, A. Computer text-editing: an information processing analysis of routine cognitive skill. *Cognitive Psychology*, 1980, *12*, 32–74.

Card, S. K., Moran, T. P., and Newell, A. *The Psychology of Human-Computer Interaction*. Hillsdale, NJ: L. Erlbaum Associates, 1983.

Chapanis, A. Men, machines and models. *American Psychologist*, 1961, *16*, 113–131.

Chubb, G. P. SAINT, A digital simulation language for the study of manned systems. *Proceedings*, Conference on Manned Systems Design, New Methods and Equipment, Freiburg, West Germany, September 1980, 300–329.

Coburn, R. and Lowe, T. D. *Human Factors Engineering Integration for Ship Systems: FY76 Report on Methodology for Command, Control and Communictions*. Naval Electronics Laboratory Center, San Diego, CA, 1976.

Cullinane, T. P. Minimizing cost and effort in performing a link analysis. *Human Factors*, 1977, *19*, 151–156.

Curry, R. E. A model of human fault detection for complex dynamic processes. In J. Rasmussen and W. B. Rouse (Eds.) *Human Detection of System Failures*. New York: Plenum Press, 1981, 171–183.

DARCOM Material Systems Analysis Activity. Hellmates: a helicopter engagement computer simulation. In *Department of Defense Catalog of Logistics Models*, U.S. Army Logistics Management Center, Ft. Lee, VA, 1980 (No. 193).

Department of the Navy, Sea Systems Command, *Human Reliability Prediction System User's Manual*. Author: Washington, DC, December 1977.

Evans, S. M. *Updated User's Guide for the COMBIMAN*. Report AMRL-TR-78-31, Aerospace Medical Research Laboratory, Wright-Patterson AFB, OH, 1978 (AD-A-057968).

Feigl, H. *Readings in Philosophical Analysis*. New York: Appleton-Century-Crofts, 1949.

Freund, L. E. and Sadosky, T. L. Linear programming applied to optimization of instrument panel and workspace layout. *Human Factors*, 1967, *9*, 295–300.

Friedman, M. *Essays in Predictive Economics*. Chicago: University of Chicago Press, 1953.

Geer, C. W. *Analyst's Guide for the Analysis Section of MIL-H-46855*. Report D180-19476-1, Boeing Aerospace Company, June 1976.

Geer, C. W. *Human Engineering Procedures Guide*, Report AFAMRL-TR-81-35, Aerospace Medical Research Laboratories, Wright-Patterson AFB, OH, September 1981 (AD A108643).

Glenn, F. A., Strieb, M. I. and Wherry, R. J. *Applications to Assessment of Operator Loading. The Human Operator Simulator, Vol. 8.* Technical Report 1233-A, Analytics, Willow Grove, PA, 1977.

Glenn, F. A., Zaklad, A. L. and Wherry, R. J., Jr. Human operator simulation in the cognitive domain. *Proceedings*, Human Factors Society Annual Meeting, 1982, 964–968.

Hann, R. and Kuperman, G. SAINT model of a choice reaction time paradigm. *Proceedings*, Annual Meeting of the Human Factors Society, 1975, 336–341.

Harris, R., Bennett, J. and Stokes, J. Validating CAR: a comparison study of experimentally-derived and computer-generated reach envelopes. *Proceedings*, Human Factors Society Annual Meeting, 1982, 969–973.

Knee, H. E., Krois, P. A., Haas, P. M., Siegel, A. I. and Ryan, T. G. *Maintenance Personnel Performance Simulation—(MAPPS)—A Model for Predicting Maintenance Performance Reliability in Nuclear Power Plants.* Paper presented at the 11th Water Reactor Safety Information Meeting, National Bureau of Standards, Washington, DC, October 24–28, 1983.

Kuperman, G. and Seifert, D. J. Development of a computer simulation model for evaluating DAIS display concepts. *Proceedings*, Annual Meeting of the Human Factors Society, 1975, 347–353.

Lane, N. E., Strieb, M. I., and Leyland, W. *Modeling the Human Operator. Applications to System Cost Effectiveness. Proceedings*, NATO/AGARD Conference No. 268, Modeling and Simulation of Avionics Systems and Command, Control and Communications, Paris, France, 1979.

Lane, N. E., Strieb, M. I. and Wherry, R. G. The Human Operator Simulator: workload estimation using a simulated secondary task. *Proceedings*, NATO/AGARD Conference No. 216, Methods to Assess Workload, Cologne, West Germany, 1977.

Miller, R. B., Folley, J. D. and Smith, P. R. *Systematic Troubleshooting and the Half-Split Technique.* Report TR 53-21, Human Resources Research Center, Chanute AFB, IL, 1953.

Mills, R. G. *System Modeling and Simulation: Application of a Research Methodology and Test.* Unpublished Ph.D. Dissertation, Ohio State University, Columbus, OH, 1976.

Moray, N. The role of attention in the detection of errors and the diagnosis of failures in man–machine systems. In J. Rasmussen and W. B. Rouse (Eds.), *Human Detection of System Failures*, New York: Plenum Press, 1981, 185–198.

Munger, S. J., Payne, D., and Smith, R. *An Index of Electronic Equipment Operability: Data Store.* Report AIR-C43-1/62-RPI, American Institute for Research, Pittsburgh, PA, January 1962.

Norman, D. A. and Bobrow, D. G. On data-limited and resource-limited processes. *Cognitive Psychology*, 1975, *7*, 44–64.

Parks, D. L. and Springer, W. E. *Human Factors Engineering Analytic Process Definition and Criterion Development for CAFES.* Report D180-18750-1, Boeing Aerospace Company, Seattle, WA, 1 June 1975 (AD-A040478).

Pew, R. W., Feehrer, C. E., Baron, S. and Miller, D. C. *Critical Review and Analysis of Performance Models Applicable to ManMachine Systems Evaluation.* Report AFOSR-TR-77-0520, Bolt, Beranek and Newman, Inc., Cambridge MA, 1977 (AD AO38597).

Pritsker, A. A. B. *The GASP IV Simulation Language.* New York: Wiley, 1974.

Pritsker, A. A. B. and Happ, W. W. GERT: Graphical evaluation and review technique. *Journal of Industrial Engineering*, 1967, *17*, 267–274.

Pritsker, A. A. B., Wortman, D. B., Seum, C. S., Chubb, G. P. and Seifert, D. J. *SAINT: Volume I, Systems Analysis of Integrated Networks of Tasks*, Report AMRL-TR-78-126, Aerospace Medical Research Laboratory, Wright-Patterson AFB, OH, 1974.

Rabideau, G. F. and Luk, R. H. *A Monte Carlo Algorithm for Workplace Optimization and Layout Planning (WOLAP),* University of Waterloo, Waterloo, Ontario, Canada, 1974.

Rasmussen, J. Models of mental strategies in process plant diagnosis. In J. Rasmussen and W. B. Rouse (Eds.), *Human Detection of System Failures.* New York: Plenum Press, 1981, 241–258 (a).

Rasmussen, J. *Human errors. A Taxonomy for Describing Human Malfunctions in Industrial Installations.* Report Riso-M-2304, Riso National Laboratory, Roskilde, Denmark, August 1981 (b).

Rasmussen, J. *The Role of Cognitive Models in the Design, Operation and Licensing of Nuclear Power Plants*. Workshop on Cognitive Modeling of Nuclear Plant Control Room Operators, Dedham, MA, August 15–18, 1982.

Rouse, W. B. A theory of human decision making in stochastic estimation tasks. *IEEE Transactions on Systems, Man, and Cybernetics*, 1977, vol. SMC-7, No. 4, 274–282.

Rouse, W. B. A model of human decision making in fault diagnosis tasks that include feedback and redundancy. *IEEE Transactions on Systems, Man, and Cybernetics*, 1979, vol. SMC-9, No. 4, 237–241.

Rouse, W. B. A rule-based model of human problem solving performance in fault diagnosis tasks. *IEEE Transactions on Systems, Man, and Cybernetics*, 1980, vol. SMC-10, No. 7, 366–375.

Rouse, W. B. Experimental studies and mathematical models of human problem solving performance in fault diagnosis tasks. In J. Rasmussen and W. B. Rouse (Eds.), *Human Detection and Diagnosis of System Failures*. New York: Plenum Press, 1981, 199–216.

Rouse, W. B. *Outline of a Model of Human Problem Solving in Failure Situations*. Workshop on Cognitive Models of Nuclear Plant Control Room Operators, Dedham, MA, August 15–18, 1982 (a).

Rouse, W. B. Models of human problem solving: detection, diagnosis and compensation for system failures. *Proceedings*, IFAC Conference on Analysis, Design, and Evaluation of Man–Machine Systems. Baden-Baden, West Germany, September 1982 (b).

Sheridan, T. B. Criteria for selecting measures of plant information with application to nuclear reactors. *IEEE Transactions on Systems, Man, and Cybernetics*, 1979, vol. SMC-9, No. 4, 165–175.

Sheridan, T. B. Understanding human error and aiding human diagnostic behavior in nuclear power plants. In J. Rasmussen and W. B. Rouse (Eds.), *Human Detection of System Failures*. New York: Plenum Press, 1981, 19–35.

Sheridan, T. B. *Cognitive Models and Computer Aids for Nuclear Plant Control Room Operators*, Workshop on Cognitive Models of Nuclear Plant Control Room Operators, Dedham, MA, August 15–18, 1982.

Sheridan, T. B. and Tulga, M. K. Dynamic decisions and workload in multitask supervisory control. *IEEE Transactions on Systems, Man, and Cybernetics*, 1980, vol. SMC-10, No. 5, 217–224.

Siegel, A. I. and Wolf, J. J. A model for digital simulation of two-operator man–machine systems. *Ergonomics*, 1962, *5*, 557–572.

Siegel, A. I. and Wolf, J. J. *Man–Machine Simulation Models: Psychosocial and Performance Interaction*. New York: Wiley, 1969.

Siegel, A. I. and Wolf, J. J. *Digital Behavioral Simulation—State-of-the-Art and Implications*. Applied Psychological Services, Wayne, PA, for the Army Research Institute, Alexandria, VA, June 1981.

Siegel, A. I., Wolf, J. J. and Pilitsis, J. A new method for the scientific layout of workspace. *Applied Ergonomics*, 1982, *13.2*, 87–90.

Smillie, R.J. and Ayoub, M.A. The assessment and evaluation of job performance and formats using SAINT. *Proceedings*, Human Factors Annual Meeting, 1977, 311–315.

Strieb, M. I. and Harris, R. *Sensitivity Analysis for Cost Effectiveness of P-3C SS-3 Operator Station. The Human Operator Simulator, Volume 10, Part 2*, Technical Report 1330, Analytics, Willow Grove, PA, 1978.

Strieb, M. I. and Wherry, R. J. *An Introduction to the Human Operator Simulator*. Technical Report 1400.02-D, Analytics, Willow Grove, PA, December 1979.

Strieb, M. I. et al. *HOS Simulation Descriptions. The Human Operator Simulator, Volume 6*. Technical Report 1181-B, Analytics, Willow Grove, PA, 1975.

Strieb, M. I. et al. *LAMPS Air Tactical Officer Simulator. The Human Operator Simulator, Volume 7*. Technical Report 1200, Analytics, Willow Grove, PA, 1976.

Strieb, M. I. et al. *P-3C SS-3 Operator Station Cost Effectiveness Evaluation. The Human Operator Simulator, Vol. 10*. Technical Report 1289, Analytics, Willow Grove, PA, 1978.

Topmiller, D. A. and Aume, N. M. Computer graphic design for human performance. *Proceedings*, 1978 Annual Reliability and Maintainability Symposium, Los Angeles, CA, January 1978, 385–388.

Tulley, A. A., Meyer, G. R., Oller, R. G., Mitchell, P. J., Reardon, S. E., and Reed, L. E. *Development and Application of Computer Software Techniques to Human Factors Task Data Handling Problems*. Report AFHRL-TR-68-13, Air Force Human Resources Laboratory, Wright-Patterson AFB, OH, November 1968.

Whitehouse, G. *Systems Analysis and Design Using Network Techniques*. Englewood Cliffs, NJ: Prentice-Hall, 1973.

Wickens, C. D. The effects of participatory mode and task workload on the detection of dynamic system failures. *IEEE Transactions on Systems, Man, and Cybernetics*, 1979, vol. SMC-9, No. 1, 24–34.

Wickens, C. D. and Kessel, F. Failure detection in dynamic systems. In J. Rasmussen and W. B. Rouse (Eds.), *Human Detection of System Failures*, New York: Plenum Press, 1981, 155–169.

Wortman, D. B., Duket, S. and Seifert, D. SAINT simulation of a remotely controlled piloted vehicle/drone control facility. *Proceedings*, Annual Meeting of the Human Factors Society, 1975, 342–346.

Wortman, D. B., Duket, S. D., Seifert, D. J., Hann, R. L., and Chubb, G. P. *Simulation Using SAINT: A User-Oriented Instrauction Manual*. Report AMRL-TR-77-61, Aerospace Medical Research Laboratory, Wright-Patterson AFB, OH, 1977 (a).

Wortman, D. G., Duket, S. D., Seifert, D. J., Hann, R. L., and Chubb, G. P. *The SAINT User's Manual*, Report AMRL-TR-77-62, Aerospace Medical Research Laboratory, Wright-Patterson AFB, OH, 1977 (b).

CHAPTER FIVE

Human Reliability Analysis and Prediction

In this chapter we discuss methods of quantitatively predicting and evaluating the performance of personnel in man–machine systems (MMS). This process is known as *human reliability* (HR). We are talking about systems. Models and methods for quantitative assessment of discrete functions like tracking or monitoring are not included.

Major emphasis in this chapter has been given to *THERP*-Technique for human error rate prediction—and to the Siegel/Wolf models; to THERP because it is the one HR technique most often employed, as well as representing a reliability model, and to Siegel/Wolf because it illustrates how it is possible to derive HR indices from behavioral models that are not primarily reliability oriented.

The material in this chapter is organized around the following topics: definitions, the importance of HR, historical review, HR methodologies, procedures for applying THERP, assumptions, HR studies, error analysis, error data collection, databanks, and HR critiques.

DEFINITIONS

Human reliability as an activity is the analysis, prediction and evaluation of work-oriented (MMS) human performance in quantitative terms using, for example, such indices as error likelihood, probability of task accomplishment, and response time. HR can be applied to any activity which has a goal, a set of procedures—more or less fixed—which personnel perform to accomplish that goal, and some output or consequence of the performance which can be used to determine success or task accomplishment. This is accomplished by comparing it with a standard of correct or adequate performance. For example, batting records are an HR for baseball because baseball involves work with fixed procedures. On the other hand it is impossible to determine the HR of an activity, like a party, that lacks a specific goal, fixed procedures, and a measurable output.

There is a difference between HR and what psychology attempts to do in predicting human performance. Because psychology is concerned primarily with the determination of general principles and hypothesis-testing—the performance of experiments to determine which of two concepts is correct—it tends to phrase its conclusions in qualitative generalities, rather than specific numerical terms; although of course psychological measurement leads to numerical data (Meister, 1982). The HR procedure on the other hand has nothing to do with hypothesis-testing and always leads to a quantitative evaluation or prediction as an output of the process.

The term *reliability* in HR should not be confused with its traditional psychometric usage as consistency in performance or judgment. HR describes performance accuracy, or its converse, error.

Human reliability can be any of three things: a methodology, a theoretical concept, and a measure. Only the first and last are important. As a methodology HR is a formal procedure for performing a quantitative analysis, evaluation and prediction of job oriented personnel performance. There are alternative ways of deriving HR measures as this chapter illustrates, but if the analyst once decides to use a particular HR technique, that technique must be followed without significant deviation. As a theoretical concept HR implies an explanation of how error is produced and how it affects personal performance. Although a few error theories have been advanced (these will be discussed later), theory plays little part in HR, which is very pragmatic.

Human reliability as a measure is associated with methodology, because the output of the HR methodology is a measure describing the present and future performance of the individual, team and/or system. As a measure HR is the probability of successful performance of the human activities necessary for task accomplishment and effective system performance. In THERP this probability is associated with the errors that occur in performing the task. HR expressed in probabalistic form is 1.0—meaning invariably correct performance—minus the error rate, where error rate is equivalent to task failure. Error rate is simply error frequency. For example, the probability of correctly reading a particular display may be .9983, meaning that during 10,000 opportunities to read that display there were 17 incorrect readings $(1.0 - 17 = .9983)$.

THE IMPORTANCE OF HUMAN RELIABILITY

Human reliability analysis (HRA) can be of value in the following ways:

1. In early design HR can be used to compare alternative design configurations in terms of the personnel and system performance that can be expected of each alternative. Each alternative is analyzed to determine its probability of successful task accomplishment and the one with the highest probability should (all other things being equal) be selected for implementation.

2. Human reliability can also be used to predict the absolute human performance that can be expected of a system, although one must be careful with absolute measurement when databases are inadequate. Comparative analyses are far less risky. Thus if there is some quantitative human performance requirement the system must satisfy, one can determine in advance of operationally testing the system whether it is likely to satisfy that requirement. This analysis is rarely performed beacuse few systems have quantitative human performance requirements.

3. Human reliability can be useful in diagnosing those factors in the system that lead to less than desired human performance. It is possible to isolate the error rate anticipated for individual tasks and to determine where errors are likely to be most frequent—hence where overloading may occur. Once these sources of inadequacy have been identified, steps can be taken to correct them by making a design or procedural change.

4. Human reliability can be used to determine the increase in performance that can be achieved by incorporating a proposed design change or to evaluate the relative value of some proposed tradeoff. One analyzes the system with and without the change to determine the predicted difference in performance probability.

Since one goal of behavioral science is to design more efficient MMS, imagine the increased system effectiveness the system developer could command if he were able to predict accurately the performance of the personnel elements in his new system.

Beyond such a pragmatic use of HR, behavioral science has goals of prediction and explanation which cannot be accomplished without quantitative assessment. Eventually the researcher must go beyond the general predictions inherent in the conclusions derived from most experimental behavioral studies to be able to say that in certain types of situations a class of individuals or teams will perform with a certain accuracy (probability of correct response of 0.98, for example) or will make a choice of *A* over *B* 98 times in 100 (with a certain standard deviation, of course, to account for individual variability).

HISTORICAL REVIEW

To understand the genesis of HR it is necessary to place it in its chronological and conceptual context. Interest in HR grew in the middle 1950's along with or perhaps as one aspect of the interest in "system theory" and formal procedures for analyzing the behavioral aspects of systems. Equipment reliability engineers already possessed well-established techniques for quantifying the effect of equipment performance on system output, but ignored the personnel element because they had no means of dealing with it. Why was it not possible to quantify the personnel element in much the same way that reliability engineers quantified the hardware element?

In industries such as *aerospace* and *missiles human factors* groups were often organizationally part of the reliability or quality assurance division. In this context many behavior specialists felt it necessary to align their thinking with that of the host discipline. They pointed out that reliability numbers assigned to systems were incorrect because they ignored the effect of personnel on the system, thus usually making reliability estimates overly optimistic. Moreover, in working with design engineers they were often challenged—or felt that they were challenged—to quantify their recommendations and the rationale for these recommendations. If a metric describing the performance of the personnel element in the system was to be developed, it was desirable that, conceptually at least, it be the same as that for equipment elements. This would permit the combination of separate estimates for equipment and personnel into a single system prediction. This consideration had the effect of disposing researchers interested in quantifying job related human performance to think in terms of adopting traditional reliability methodology, to the extent that this was feasible.

The work of Williams (1958) and of Shapero, Cooper, Rappaport, Schaeffer and Bates (1960) was influential in pointing out the effect of human errors on system performance. In 1962 a prototype demonstrational database containing data that could be applied to individual systems to predict their performance (Munger, et al., 1962) was published. Around the same time the pioneering work of Rook (1962, 1965) and particularly of Swain (1963) and his colleagues at the Sandia National Laboratories began—work which still continues. Although this work has resulted in methodologic refinements, much of it has been frankly propagandistic and tutorial, an attempt to "spread the gospel" and to convince equipment and human engineers of the need for HR. To a certain extent it still is.

Efforts were also made, unfortunately with only indifferent success, to elicit funds from the military services to stimulate HR research, particularly the gathering of data to expand the available data base. There has been no instant, uncritical acceptance of HR concepts, either by equipment reliability engineers or psychologists (although in connection with equipment reliability, see Dhillon, 1980). That situation has changed slightly since the Three-Mile Island nuclear incident which has prompted some research on HR as applied to nuclear power plants (for a description of this, see Hall, Fragola and Luckas, Jr., 1981, and U. S. Nuclear Regulatory Commission, 1983).

HUMAN RELIABILITY METHODOLOGIES

This section describes the major HR methodologies. The most important of these are:

1. THERP—Technique for Human Error Rate Prediction;
2. the stochastic mathematic models, that is, Siegel/Wolf and SAINT (Pritsker, Wortman, Seum, Chubb and Seifert, 1974);
3. the American Institute for Research (AIR) Data Store. Not presently used, but potentially important if anyone picks up on this technique is TEPPS, (The Establishment of Personnel Performance Standards, Smith, Westland and Blanchard, 1966a).

More recently Pew, Baron, Feehrer and Miller (1977) reviewed a very large number of human performance models, including the Data Store, THERP and Siegel's models; but although a few of the others, most significantly SAINT, which was reviewed in Chapter 4, appear to be compatible with HR goals, they have not been used in this context and therefore will not be discussed here. Major emphasis will be given to THERP. The Siegel/Wolf methodology has been described in some detail in Chapter 4, so it will be necessary only to amplify that discussion in terms of the model's HR implications. The Data Store is now active only as a data base. For more information about THERP, the Data Store and the HR aspects of the Siegel/Wolf models, see Meister (1971c, 1973).

The descriptions presented in this section will be amplified by discussion of particular methodologic issues in later sections.

THERP

THERP is well known, having been described extensively by its primary developer (Swain) and his co-workers in a long list of 63 reports, handbooks and lectures (Swain, 1982). It is a method for predicting human error rates and of evaluating the degradation to the MMS likely to be caused by human error—(in association with equipment reliability, of course). The following description is quite abbreviated but the example in the next section will amplify it.

The method involves a series of steps (called by Swain a "man–machine systems analysis"). This method requires that the analyst:

1. Describe system goals and functions, situational and personnel characteristics.
2. Describe the jobs and tasks performed by personnel and analyze them to identify error-likely situations. In other words, perform a function/task analysis oriented around error identification.
3. Estimate the likelihood of each potential error in each task and the likelihood that the error will be undetected.
4. Estimate the consequences of the undetected or uncorrected error. Steps (3) and (4) are performed by referring to one or more databanks and making use of expert judgment.
5. Suggest changes to the system and evaluate these.

The method depends heavily on task analysis to determine the error-likely situations. Potential system or subsystem failures are defined, after which all the human operations involved in the failure and their relationship to system tasks are described by drawing them in the form of a human event probability tree. Error rates for both correct and incorrect performance of each branch of the event tree are predicted by drawing upon a variety of data sources for inputs (e.g., the Data Store, and data in the behavioral literature, test reports, expert opinion). Where an error rate is excessively large the system is analyzed to determine the factors causing that error rate and changes are recommended.

With regard to mathematics, THERP employs two primary measures. First the probability that an operation will lead to an error of class i – (P_i), and second, the probability of an error or class of errors that will result in system failure (F_i).

P_i is based on what is termed an error rate, which is the frequency of error occurring during a block of time. $1 - P_i$ is the probability that an operation will be performed without error. F_iP_i is the joint probability that an error will occur in an operation and that that error will lead to system failure. $1 - F_iP_i$ is the probability that an operation that does not lead to error and system failure will be performed.

$$Q_i = 1 - (1 - F_iP_i)^{n_i} \tag{5.1}$$

is the probability of a failure condition existing as a result of class i errors occurring in n_i (independent) operations. Total system or subsystem failure rate resulting from human error is expressed as

$$Q_t = 1 - [\Pi_{k=1}^{n} (1 - Q_k)] \tag{5.2}$$

where Q_t is the probability that one or more failure conditions will result from errors in at least one of n classes and the quantity in brackets is

$$(1 - Q_i)(1 - Q_2)\ldots(1 - Q_n). \tag{5.3}$$

A number of factors complicate this apparently straightforward procedure. In order to implement the procedure it is necessary to determine all possible errors, select error rates appropriate to the anticipated errors that have been identified, determine the degree of dependence/independence among tasks and errors, and determine the factors that affect error likelihood (*performance shaping factors* or PSFs) and therefore influence the precise error value drawn from the data sources.

Each of the above requires much judgment. For example, the criteria for selecting the appropriate error rates from the data sources are not precisely specified. The data sources THERP uses generally provide a range of error values with a normative or nominal value. Depending on the PSF operative in the error situation—stress, for example—and the degree of dependence among tasks, the correct error value will shift up or down in the range of values provided. To select the correct error value from the data source requires expert judgment and considerable practice.

Stochastic Simulation Models

The significance of the Siegel/Wolf and SAINT simulation models to HR is that one of the measures they output is HR. The summary of runs performed with the model lists the total number of iterations ("runs") and the number of those that were successfully completed. The percentage of successful runs is an indication of the task/job HR. Siegel, Leahy and Wiesen (1977) and Siegel, Wolf and Lautman (1975) provide a complete listing of the HR studies performed with the Siegel/Wolf models. We are unaware of HR studies using SAINT, but since SAINT is a derivation of Siegel/Wolf, it can undoubtedly be used for this purpose.

It is one of the advantages of the simulation technique of determining HR that one can experimentally vary parameter values and determine their effect on HR. For example, in a study of the SQS-26 sonar system, Siegel et al. (1977) were able to compare the percent success achieved as a function of the various conditions. Percent of success for the simulated operators varied from 55 percent to 94 percent as time permitted the operators rose from 23 to 25 minutes. Success percentage also varied from 76 percent to 85 percent as a function of increasing team proficiency. THERP can attempt the same procedure by selecting varying values for a given parameter from the distribution or error probability values available and modifying these by PSF "fudge" factors, but this procedure is somewhat clumsier than the task simulation method.

A somewhat different technique developed by Siegel which is called the *hand calculation model* (Department of the Navy, 1977) outputs a measure which, while not identical with HR based on error probabilities or task success, is perhaps related to them. This model is derived from multidimensional scaling analysis of maintainer performance and can be used to determine the probability that a particular maintenance technician or group will successfully accomplish corrective maintenance on an equipment or system. The predictions are based on the estimate of the ratio of the number of unusually effective (UE) to the number of unusually *in*effective (UI) performances in a sample of required tasks.

To determine the structure of the electronic maintenance job Siegel and Schultz (1963) first performed a multidimensional scaling analysis of the job as performed by naval technicians. Nine factors emerged: a. electrocognition, b. electrorepair, c. instruction, d. electrosafety, e. personnel relationships, f. electronic circuit analysis, g. equipment operation, h. the use of reference materials, and i. equipment inspection. It is impossible in this brief review to define these (they are described in some detail in Department of the Navy, 1977), but they appear reasonably descriptive of the electronic technician's job. The maintenance job is analyzed in terms of all the factors although any single task may require only one or two of them.

To apply the prediction system to a particular maintenance organization, each technician must be rated on each of the 9 factors. Ratings are obtained by having supervisors observe and evaluate a sufficient number of maintainer performances involving each job factor to provide a valid sample of the technician's capability. For each job factor the technician's unusually effective and unusually ineffective performances are recalled and identified. (Based on Flanagan's (1954) critical incident technique.) The technician's performance index or probability of successful job performance for each job factor is then computed by the formula,

$$\frac{\Sigma \text{UE}}{\Sigma \text{UE} + \Sigma \text{UI}} \tag{5.4}$$

For example, in 25 performances on a particular job factor technician D was rated unusually effective in six and unusually ineffective in one. Hence his HR for that factor would be $6/6 + 1 = .86$

The technician's overall HR would be a compound of individual HRs for the individual job factors. Obviously this HR is not the same as that derived from THERP or the stochastic models which are based on error rate and simulated task accomplishment, respectively. The hand calculated HR is much more subjective and is not necessarily based on error, although the definition of effectiveness probably includes consideration of error.

The actual method of computing the hand calculation HR depends upon several variables such as the interdependence among the job factors involved in the correction of the malfunction and the number of technicians assigned to the problem.

Siegel and Miehle (1967a) developed methods of calculating the overall probability of successful task completion when the probability of accomplishing each of the task elements is known. These methods require that one know which technicians are making use of which job factors involved in the task. Given this knowledge, compounding logic is applied, making use of *and*, *or* and negation logic. The compounding methodology permits prediction of electronic maintenance success with series or parallel tasks and by a single technician or group of technicians. The assumption is made that technician actions on each job factor are independent of other job actions. This assumption, which is doubtful, is made because no data are available for the conditional case.

The AIR Data Store

The Data Store (Munger, et al., 1962) is a databank. Any such bank presupposes a methodology for its use and until THERP became better known the Data Store was used to evaluate and predict equipment, subsystem and system HR. The Data Store was originally intended to illustrate only what a HR databank could look like. Because for some time nothing better was available, its use as a prediction/evaluation methodology began to grow.

The Data Store is organized around common controls and displays (e.g., knobs, meters). It consists of a compilation of performance data taken from 164 psychological studies (out of at least 2,000 examined) describing various characteristics of these controls and displays (e.g., joystick length, number of indicators). The data indicate:

1. the probability of successfully operating these instruments as a function of their characteristics,
2. the minimum time needed to operate instruments with these characteristics (this aspect is of minimal importance to HR developers),
3. increments of time (see Item 2 above) which must be added together when a component has multiple characteristics.

The equipment or system whose personnel performance is to be predicted or evaluated is analyzed to determine which controls and displays are utilized by the equipment and which control/display characteristics are relevant (e.g., switch angle). Probability and time information appropriate to these characteristics is then extracted from the Data Store. A measure of equipment operability is developed by multiplying the probabilities serially (the so-called "product rule") for the individual component characteristics involved in the task—and adding the times needed for their operation—to determine the performance reliability of the task. The reliability of a control or display (R_{c_n}) is a function of the parameters (p) that describe that control or display ($R_{c_n} = r_{P_1} \times r_{P_2} \times r_{P_3} \; ....r_{P_n}$). The reliability of any task (R_{t_n}) is a function of the reliabilities of the individual controls and displays (c_n) used in that task ($R_{t_n} = r_{c_1} \times r_{c_2} \times r_{c_3} \; ....r_{c_n}$). The reliability of any equipment, subsystem or system operation (R_{op_n}) consisting of n tasks is a function of the individual reliabilities of the tasks (t) comprising that operation ($R_{op_n} = r_{t_1} \times r_{t_2} \times r_{t_3} \cdot\cdot r_{t_n}$). The following examples taken from Meister, 1966, illustrate the use of the technique.

Example 1.

Component: Joystick

Relevant component dimensions	Value	Probability
Stick length	6–9 in.	0.9963 ×
Extent of stick movement	30–40°	0.9975 ×
Control resistance	5–10 lb.	0.9999 =
Product		0.9937

The designer can determine whether this particular combination of control dimensions gives him sufficient reliability or whether some other set of dimensions will be more satisfactory.

It is also possible to analyze written procedures to predict the probability of error occurrence in performing the procedure. For this analysis each procedural step is analyzed individually and broken into its stimulus-input, internal-process, and response-output elements as shown in the following very abbreviated example:

Example 2.

A light becomes green. In consequence the operator activates a push button. Predict the HR of this subtask. The light has the following characteristics:

Component: Light

Relevant component dimensions	Value	Probability
Diameter	¼–½ in.	0.9997 ×
Number of lights on	3 or 4	0.9975 ×
Presentation	Continuous	0.9996 =
Product		0.9968

The recognition of the light by the operator is assumed to have an HR of 0.9990. The response object is the push button, which has the following characteristics:

Component: Pushbutton

Relevant component dimensions	Value	Probability
Size	Miniature	0.9995 ×
Single column	1–5	0.9997 ×
Distance between edges	⅜–½ in.	0.9993 ×
Detent	Absent	0.9998 =
Product		0.9983

Overall values for the input, recognition and output are then multiplied together serially *as previously illustrated* to derive the HR estimate for the step.

HR = Light (0.9968) × recognition (0.9990) × pushbutton (0.9983) = 0.9941.

A similar process is performed for all the steps in the procedure. Thus, by progressively multiplying individual procedural elements together, one finally arrives at a total human reliability for a given procedure. This HR does not imply any equipment reliability. To determine the reliability of the entire system while performing a particular operation, it would be necessary to multiply reliability figures for human performance against estimated reliability figures for equipment performance.

The use of the Data Store in this way is limited to discrete tasks only and assumes complete independence of component operations and tasks, an assumption which is manifestly incorrect and which has led in practice to gross underestimation of HR for actual equipment operation. Nevertheless the Data Store has been widely used because it provides a formal data base.

TEPPS

One need only mention TEPPS (technique for establishing personnel performance standards) because this method has not been used since an experimental test—badly flawed in execution—failed to verify the HR predictions it made (Smith, Westland and Blanchard, 1969b). The method is similar to THERP except for the peculiarity that its developers rejected empirical data sources for TEPPS and preferred to rely on quantized expert judgments (Blanchard, Mitchell and Smith, 1966). TEPPS as a data bank will be discussed later.

PROCEDURES FOR APPLYING THERP

The following, taken from Bell and Swain (1981), is a relatively detailed description of human reliability analysis (HRA) based on THERP. The example involves the probabilistic risk assessment of a nuclear power plant.

The analysis is preceded by a visit to the plant. A review of information from system analysts and a walk through the plant are designed to familiarize the analyst with the equipment, procedures, and tasks involved in the analysis. The actual HRA procedure picks up from that point with task analysis.

Task Analysis

The plant operating procedure must be partitioned. For each step in the procedure its component tasks must be identified, along with other information relative to these performances. These tasks are the behavioral elements for which potential errors are identified. This information is entered on a task analysis table, the precise format of which Bell and Swain consider relatively unimportant. It should include, however, information about the equipment on which an action is performed, the action required of the operator, the limits of his performance, the locations of the controls and displays, and potential errors. The level of detail necessary in the task analysis and the amount of information recorded are determined judgmentally. The guiding rule is that one should be able later to recapitulate the rationale for the *human error probability* (HEP) estimates that were used in the analysis.

Once the individual tasks are identified, the errors likely to be made must be identified for each step. The determination of the specific errors—omission and commission—must be based on the relevant PSFs and on the task analysis itself. The steps should be listed sequentially.

The determination of potential errors is obviously highly judgmental. For example, if an operator is directed by a set of written procedures to manipulate a valve and that valve is fairly well isolated on the panel; if it is of a different shape than other valves on the same panel, and has been very well labeled, the analyst may decide that an error in selecting the valve is unlikely, in which case that error would not be considered further. He might consider, however, that an error of omission might be made in the following the written procedures. The authors (Bell and Swain, 1981) suggest that "extreme care should be exercised in deciding which errors, if any, are to be completely discounted for an analysis."

Once potential errors have been identified, the analyst considers other factors that may influence performance, including elements outside task procedures that could influence the operator's performance. For example, if something is to be done at the discretion of the shift supervisor, whether the supervisor remembers to order the task will have a significant effect on whether the operator performs the task.

Develop Human Reliability Analysis Event Trees

Each error defined in the task analysis as likely is entered sequentially as the right limb in a binary branch of the HRA event tree. A schematic example of an event tree is shown in Figure 5.1. The first potential error starts from the highest point on the tree at the top of the page. Solid lines represent success; dashed lines, error.

Any given task appears as a two-limb branch, with each left limb representing

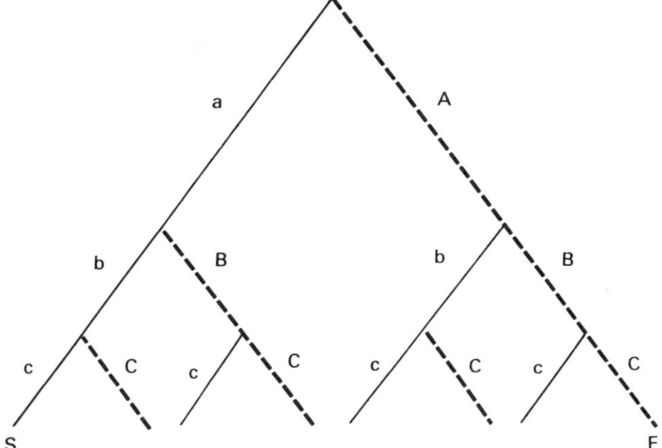

FIGURE 5.1. An example of HRA event tree diagramming.

the probability of success and each right limb representing the probability of failure. Each limb is described or labeled, usually in a shorthand. Capital letters (A) represent the probability of failure of that task. Lower case letters (a) represent the probability of success. The same convention applies to Greek letters, which represent non-human events such as equipment failures. The letters S and F are exceptions to this rule, in that they represent system success and failure, respectively. In actual practice the limbs of an event tree are sometimes labeled with a short description of the error itself.

When the analyst wants to know the probability of all tasks being performed without error, a complete success path through the event tree is followed. Once an error has been made on any task, the system may be presumed to have failed. However, in actuality errors are recovered (e.g., a display wrongly read is then reread correctly) and probabilities of event success do follow a failure and end in system success.

Development of the event tree is the most critical (and tedious) part of the process for quantifying error probabilities. If the task analysis has listed the potential errors in order of their anticipated occurrence, the transfer of this information on to the event tree is made much easier.

Assign Nominal Human Error Probabilities

Now that the errors have been identified, defined, and diagrammed, estimates of the probability of occurrence for each must be assigned. The nuclear power plant analyst will use Chapter 20 of Swain and Guttmann (1983) to make most of these estimates because this handbook contains most of the estimated HEPs that THERP uses. Application of THERP as a general procedure to some other types of systems is entirely possible, but will require an appropriate HEP data base.

First the task itself must be categorized. The analyst determines whether an operator is manipulating valves, performing a check of another's work, using a written procedure, etc. Errors are then categorized as being either errors of omission or commission. The tables in Chapter 20 of Swain and Guttmann (1983) are organized to contain groups of HEPs describing a particular type of error that may occur in the performance of a specified type of task. The description in Chapter 20 that most closely approximates the error being estimated should be identified. In some cases the error description will depict a scenario differing slightly from the one being analyzed. If the differences are not great, the analyst may use the Swain and Guttmann (1983) HEP as is. Where the differences are sufficiently great, the HEP must be modified to reflect the conditions of actual task performance. Uusually this is done during the assessment of the PSFs acting on the task. An example of the derivation of an HEP follows.

The error is that the operator omits monitoring RCS pressure and temperature. Failure to maintain RCS temperature and pressure was designated as a failure by system analysts. Since this involves the operator's following written procedures, the analyst uses an estimate of this error from Table 20-7, pages 20 to 23 in Swain and Guttmann (1983). These estimates reflect the probability of an operator omitting any one item from a set of written procedures. Since the preocedures in the example are emergency procedures that do not require a check-off of steps by the operator, the section of Table 20-7 that deals with procedures having no check-off provision is used. Given that this error occurs when using a long list of written procedures but which does not require a checkoff, the estimated HEP for such an error is given in item 4 of Table 20-7, 0.1 (midpoint of the range .005 to .05). This is entered on the event tree.

Estimate the Relative Effects of Performance Shaping Factors

A primary consideration in conducting an HRA is the variability of human performance. This variability occurs within any given individual and also results from the performances of different personnel. Variability is caused by PSFs acting within the individual or on the environment in which the task is performed. Because of this variability, the reliability of human performance usually is not predicted solely as a point estimate but is considered to lie within a range of uncertainty. However, a point value HEP can be estimated by considering the effects of relevant PSFs for the task.

Nominal HEPs are to be used when the scenario outlined in Swain and Guttmann (1983) reflects the error being analyzed. If the analyst judges that the situation under study is more likely to result in error than the one outlined in the Handbook, an HEP closer to the upper bound than the nominal value should be used. If a plant's situation is judged to be less likely to result in a human error than the one described in Swain and Guttmann (1983), an HEP closer to the lower bound than the nominal should be used.

Next, the analyst should consider the influence of PSFs that have a global effect, those that affect the probability of error on all or most of the events in the analysis.

The most commonly encountered ones deal with stress and the level of operator experience.

The original assumption was that the operators in this example were experienced. Since they are following an emergency procedure, they are considered to be under a moderately high level of stress. Table 20-16, page 20 to 32 of Swain and Guttmann (1983) indicates that HEPs for experienced personnel operating under a moderately high level of stress should be doubled for discrete tasks and multiplied by 5 for dynamic tasks. Discrete tasks are defined as those tasks requiring essentially one well-defined action (such as throwing a switch). Dynamic tasks are those requiring a series of connected, continuous subtasks (such as monitoring an indicator over a period of time).

The only dynamic tasks in the example are those calling for monitoring of the RCS temperature and pressure indicators, the interpolation of these values onto the cool-down curve and the monitoring of the borated water storage tank level. The nominal HEPs for these tasks should be multiplied by 5; those for the other events should be doubled.

Assess Dependence

Except for the first branch of an event tree, all branches represent conditional probabilities of success and failure. Dependence between events directly affects these conditional probabilities. Dependence can occur between any two performances with respect to error of omission, commission, or both. Guidelines for determining the level of dependence assigned to a situation are found in Swain and Guttmann (1983). There are no cut and dried rules but every task must be analyzed to determine dependency.

Determination of complete dependence or complete independence is relatively easy, because it should be obvious if one action is the causal factor for another or if two actions are totally unrelated. Distinctions between the three intermediate levels of dependence—low, medium, and high—are more difficult. If the analyst decides that the dependence demonstrated by the situation is much closer to zero than to complete dependence, he should assign a low level of dependence. If, on the other hand, he decides that the situation exhibits a degree of dependence that is very close to but not equal to complete dependence, he assigns a high level of dependence. If he cannot make a definitive statement that either of the above is true, he should assign a moderate level of dependence. All of this says only that the analyst uses best judgment.

Another method of assigning an intermediate level of dependence is to estimate the percentage of time during task performance that the effects of zero or complete dependence will be manifested. From that estimate, assign the intermediate dependence level that most closely approximates it. For example, if the analyst makes a judgment, perhaps based on a frequency count from actual data or from knowledge of the work situation, that task *B* will be performed correctly half the time, given that task *A* has already been performed correctly, the analyst assigns a conditional probability of $a|b = .5$.

Determine Success/Failure Probabilities

Once errors have been identified and individually quantified, their contribution to the probabilities of system success and failure must be determined. All paths in an event tree should be defined as resulting in system success or failure in terms of their possible *system consequences*, not in terms of the specific errors leading to these consequences. That is because all errors may not lead to significant consequences. The HR analyst must quantify potential errors for tasks but he does not decide whether a given sequence through the event tree will contribute to system success or failure. This is the responsibility of the system analyst.

The latter considers the implications of each path through the event tree and labels each end point of the tree as a system success or failure. These end points should be quantified as probabilistic statements; the statements will be combined to formulate total system success and failure probabilities. All terminal success probabilities (i.e., for each task tree) are then summed to secure the total system success probability. The failure probabilities are obtained by subtracting total system success probability from 1.0.

Determine the Effects of Recovery Factors

This term describes the operator's recognition that the error has been made and his repetition of the task once more—this time correctly. Such a recovery can be accomplished in a number of ways. The operator himself may note that he has made an error or a team member/supervisor may do this for him. The system may provide information to the operator that indicates an error was been made. In performing the HRA the analyst must factor into the analysis the probability that an error will be recovered. Otherwise the probability of system failure resulting from error may be unrealistically high.

An example of the use of recovery factors is the operator's failure to respond to the borated water storage tank (BWST) falling to the 6-foot level. His response is cued from two sources. If he follows the written procedures correctly, he will monitor the meter indicating BWST level. If he does not use written procedures, there is still a possibility that the annunciator alarm will remind him that he needs to perform the follow-up actions. Bell and Swain (1981) treat the alarm as an additional alerting cue and analyze its effect as a recovery factor. From Chapter 20 of Swain and Guttmann (1983)* they find the HEP for responding to an annunciator. Table 20-23, pages 20 to 39, of Swain and Guttmann lists HEPs for failing to respond to one of any number of annunciating indicators. Assuming that at this time into the problem there are 10 annunciators alarming, the probability of the operator's failing to respond to any one of the 10 is .05 (.005 to .5). The inclusion of this factor in the analysis increases the probability of total system success from .918 to .927. If this increase in probability is considered sufficient to accept the system as human reliable, no more recovery factors need be analyzed.

*Swain and Guttmann (1980) was updated in 1983; the figures provided are from the updated version.

Perform a Sensitivity Analysis, if Warranted

During the HRA the analyst may wish to determine the effects of manipulating the values of one or more of the elements analyzed. He may do this because of some uncertainty he has about the assumptions he has made, because the data he used are very uncertain, or because he has not been able to obtain detailed information about some set of PSFs he judges to be important determiners of his task HR. Changing the assumptions of the analysis or the values of certain parameters may affect system success/failure probabilities. Or he may wish to manipulate these values to determine the effects of a design or procedure change before such changes are incorporated.

If the probabilities of some errors in an analysis are significantly higher than others, or if the system consequences of that error are especially undesirable, the analyst may wish to see what effect lower error probabilities would have. HEPs can be decreased by the action of recovery factors or by changing the characteristics of the task to reflect a less error likely situation. These changes can be accomplished by redesigning man–machine interfaces, by increasing feedback adequacy, or by upgrading the quality of associated procedural steps. The new, lower HEPs can be entered into the event tree, and the resulting differences in total system success and failure probabilities evaluated. Sensitivity analyses are extremely useful in tradeoff analyses of proposed design changes and in pinpointing areas of potential system improvement.

Obviously a good deal of judgmental fine-tuning is involved in the selection of THERP probability estimates. A similar fine-tuning, based on algorithms, enters into the selection of probabilities in the simulation models. Which procedure is preferable can be determined only by empirical test.

THEORETICAL ASSUMPTIONS

Because HR is in part a concept about human performance, it contains certain assumptions that stem from what we know about human performance in general. In addition, it makes other assumptions that are peculiar to HR itself and the individual methodologies.

General Assumptions

1. A major assumption is that the human can be treated analytically like other MMS components. Swain and Guttmann (1983) point out that "this assumption has led some researchers to the conclusion that the human functions like any other system component, which in view of human variability is incorrect. Still, human failures can be studied objectively, just as can any other component failure."

2. Task performance is modified/influenced by PSFs. The list of such modifiers is very long and varies from environmental conditions to idiosyncratic characteristics of the human to attitudes and social/organizational conditions. The Data

Store, for example, assumes that operator performance is influenced by molecular equipment features such as joystick length. Siegel includes a variety of PSF in his computer algorithms, for example, stress, proficiency, environmental factors, and motivation. The assumption that PSFs influence HR predictions requires the analyst to attempt to factor these into the predictions, but how adequately this can be done is not clear. Of the multitude of PSFs presumably influencing human performance, researchers attempt to account for only a few, such as stress or overload, proficiency, and experience. Our relative inability to account for other PSFs, such as motivation, reflects a lack of data about how PSFs affect job performance.

3. All the methods explicitly or implicitly accept the notion that behavior can be described in terms of the stimulus-organism-response paradigm which separates behavior into input-internal processing-response segments. This is the conceptual basis on which the methods utilize task analysis to break down behavior at a molar level into their individual elements and to resynthesize them. During this partitioning process it is necessary to decide which behavioral parameters are relevant to system operation. HR researchers have created few novel theoretical concepts but have preferred to rely on the current thinking in behavioral science.

4. All the methods except the Data Store assume the interdependence of task parameters and tasks. A great deal of experimental and anecdotal evidence (which need not be cited here because the evidence is so generally known) reinforces this assumption. Of course this complicates the HR predictive task because one must take this dependency into account. THERP (Swain and Guttmann, 1983) distinguishes among three types of probability: the probability inherent in the task when it is considered as an isolated entity, conditional human error probability which is the error probability of a task given success or failure on other tasks, and the combination of these two probabilities.

5. A common assumption of most HR methods is that there are different kinds of error, for example, visible, invisible, recoverable/nonrecoverable, with different kinds of consequences. The types of error one would find in process control systems such as the nuclear power facility are errors of analysis, problem solving and hypothesis testing. Piloting errors are more likely to be procedural and psychomotor.

6. A major assumption of the AIR Data Store and Swain's THERP (although not with stochastic network models) is that human error, unless recovered or trivial, is equivalent to failure to accomplish a task or some system required activity. As Swain puts it, the basic measure of human performance is the HEP, which is the probability that when a task is performed an error will occur. "The probability of successful performance of a *task* (author's italics) is generally expressed as 1-HEP" (Swain and Guttmann, 1983). Thus if the HEP for a particular task is 0.09, the probability of successfully accomplishing that task is 1-0.09 = 0.91. However, many errors do not result in task failure; they are too insignificant or they are recovered.

7. The use of probability mathematics is common to all the HR methodologies and represents the recognition of the probabilistic nature of human performance.

8. The variability of performance among individuals which we observe normally suggests that the analyst must take account of the distribution of errors. For

the simulation models the nature of the distribution is important because on each run the model selects from that distribution. For Swain the particular distribution selected is relatively unimportant. In this he follows Knowles, Burger, Mitchell, Hanifan, and Wulfeck (1969).

Specific Assumptions

Certain assumptions are specific to individual HR models. For example, the basic assumption in Siegel's simulation models is that operator loading is the basic element in effective MMS performance. Stress is the key to operator performance in terms of both speed and quality of performance. Time is critical for Siegel/Wolf.

On the other hand, although time does not play much of a role in THERP (since THERP does not simulate performance over time), stress is also a major PSF for Swain; it is assumed to reduce HR substantially. Swain follows arousal theory (Hebb, 1955) as does Siegel/Wolf in supposing that very low and very high stress levels are both damaging to performance. He points out that most of the HEPs in his handbook presume an optimal level of stress. Using a number of sources (e.g., Ronan, 1953; Berkun, 1964; and Berkun, Bialek, Kern, and Yagi, 1962), he estimates 0.25 for average error probability for nuclear power personnel in a high stress situation (Swain and Guttmann, 1983). Another assumption is that under very high stress, "Performance would be about a factor of 10 higher HEP than it would be under optimum stress" (Swain and Guttmann, 1983).

Skill level requires another set of assumptions. Swain suggests that novices under optimum stress performing nonroutine tasks are twice as error likely as experienced personnel (Swain and Guttmann, 1983). Siegel also sees proficiency as a critical factor. The concept that less experienced personnel would perform less well than more experienced personnel is entirely reasonable. However, there are few experimental data that support this premise.

HUMAN RELIABILITY STUDIES

A few empirical studies have been conducted by HR researchers, but by and large the greatest amount of "research" effort—particularly in the case of THERP—has gone into applying and expanding on methodology and providing material that would persuade potential users to apply the methodology.

The HR literature has been dominated by the papers and reports of Swain and his co-workers (e.g., Swain, 1963, 1964a, 1964b, 1967a, 1967b, 1969a, 1969b, 1971, 1974), and to a lesser extent by Siegel and his co-workers (e.g., Siegel and Federman, 1971; Siegel and Wolf, 1969). The research pursued by Swain has focused on application of THERP to real world problems and not on experimentation.

Many of the methodologic expansions of THERP resulted from the application of the methodology to new problems, in the course of which something new was tried out which, if it worked, was incorporated as part of the methodology in the next report to be published. Unfortunately the classified nature of his work with atomic systems has made it difficult for Swain to describe these applications and so the observer is often left with the feeling that part of the action about which he would like to know is behind a curtain that cannot be raised.

This is particularly true with regard to validations of the HEP and the model's predictions. Two kinds of validation are possible: formal and informal. In the first, which is preferable, a study is performed which replicates the tasks whose HR has been predicted and a comparison is made between predicted and empirically derived HR; in the second, the methodology is applied to a real world system problem and one notes the success of that application. The first has been more characteristic of the mathematic models; the second, more characteristic of THERP. In either case the number of validations has not been great. Validation in the application situation is often a matter of judgment or fortuitous opportunity. For example, a weapon component was found to have been incorrectly assembled. Swain and his co-workers were asked to predict the rate at which this error would occur in the component population. His estimated error rate and that actually found were very close.

Swain has performed a number of individual studies or methodologic critiques and has advanced proposals. For example, he proposed (Swain, 1967a) the concept of "field calibrated simulation" in which both field and simulator studies are run and then the simulator is calibrated by developing a ratio scale based on the field data and applying the scale to the simulator data. In 1967(b) he used a Monte Carlo simulation technique to generate artificial tasks of varying complexity using the Data Store parameters. The number of parameters selected from the Data Store varied from 10 to 40. Computer runs using Monte Carlo technique were made for each of several levels of task complexity (number of parameters). The output of each computer run was an estimated system failure probability. When the distributions of failure probabilities for each task were plotted, the distributions approached a normal curve for parameters greater than 15. The upshot of the analysis was that with the simple multiplicative model used in the Data Store the failure probability of any task could be determined by multiplying the number of relevant parameters in the task by 0.0001. In 1971 Swain suggested development of a human error rate data bank which however was never implemented (Swain, 1971).

Siegel has performed a number of HR experiments by modifying the variables in his models, exercising the models and seeing what has resulted. For example, in Department of the Navy, 1977, he presents graphs indicating event success and failure percentage, fatigue and physical load as a function of workday length and proficiency (pp. 4–34, 4–35), success and failure as a function of crew pace, sea state and crew size (pp. 4–36 to 4–39), and hours slept as a function of crew size (p. 4–41), etc. In Siegel et al., 1977, he presents percentages of mission success as a function of three levels of time allowed and four team proficiency levels.

One of the very few true experimental attempts to model HR is represented by the work of Askren and Regulinski (1969, 1971). Classical engineering reliability analysis uses statistical deduction to translate time of equipment failure observations to a relevant model. The reliability prediction is obtained from the model via probability theory. In the time-continuous domain this procedure requires knowledge of an analytic stochastic function, such as, the probability density function of equipment failures with respect to the time of the operations involved. Askren and Regulinski attempted to determine the feasibility of applying this classical reliability formulation to the analysis of human performance and to determine the effect of different amounts of training on HR.

HR for such time-continuous tasks as vigilance, monitoring, and tracking was modeled in the form of the equation

$$R_h\ (t) = \exp\ \{ - \int_0^t\ e(t)\ dt\ \} \tag{5.5}$$

where: $R_h(t)$ = the reliability of human performance for any point in time of task operation, and

e(t) = the error rate for the specific task.

A series of measures based on classical reliability were developed. Examples of these are: mean time to failure (MTTF) was translated into mean time to human-initiated failure (MTTHIF), mean time to first failure was translated into mean time to first human error (MTTFHE) and the term MTBF to mean time between human errors (MTBHE).

Two experimental tasks—a vigilance and a tracking task—were developed to generate error data for testing the model. In the first experiment the Weibull distribution of errors over time yielded the best fit. The probability density functions for the second study were more complex and did not yield a single best distribution. Askren and Regulinski conclude that equation 5.5 is a useful general model of human reliability in the time-space continuous domain. Unfortunately the interesting and provocative work these investigators began has never been carried further. This failing is characteristic of much of the empirical work reported in the behavioral literature and makes one wonder why the work was begun if there was no intent to carry it to completion.

Interesting work was also performed by Mills and Hatfield (1974). Their research tested the assumption of normality of distribution of task performance times and combinatorial rules. Five university students performed six tasks (reading of meters and digital readouts and looking up of data in reference tables) that generated empirical data about HR and task time. The results indicated that

1. the normality assumption for distribution of task times was inappropriate,
2. rules for combining task times are satisfactory if the underlying distribution of task times is known, and
3. HR is strongly affected by combining tasks. The researchers considered that within very wide limits, assumptions as to distribution of times and errors are not very meaningful.

Another series of experimental studies was performed by Goldbeck and Charlet (1974, 1975) which help to verify the AIR Data Store values. As one of the outputs of these studies, it was possible to compare HR values for subjects operating various controls and displays with those predicted by Data Store estimates. In the first study there was low agreement between Data Store and empirical performance reliabilities (rho = 0.29 and 0.33 for the two tasks involved). In a second study the highest correlation between the actual and predicted HR of any single component was 0.42 which is statistically respectable even if not awe inspiring.

Some empirical data have been collected on what the author has termed *human-initiated failures* (HIF, equipment failures resulting from operator and technician error, Meister, et al., 1970). The purpose of the studies was to investigate the frequency and impact on system reliability of HIF. Over a 5-month period personnel stationed at two Air Force bases investigated, by means of interviews and review of records, equipment failures reported on four airborne avionics subsystems. Failures were categorized as Human-initiated failures, false reports, failures that could not be duplicated, and equipment caused failures. Human-initiated failures amounted to 13 percent, false reports 5 percent, nonduplicatable failures, 18 percent. System reliability calculated without HIF being counted in was significantly higher than when HIF were included. Which proves that human error is important—an assumption which must be demonstrated time and again to convince doubters. Although a subsequent study (Barneby, Finley and Meister, 1972) found similar results, like the other empirical studies in this area the effort was not continued.

The recent intenstification of human factors efforts at nuclear power plants has produced a number of empirical studies. There is, for example, the effort of Luckas and Hall (1981) to quantify human errors associated with reactor safety system components. Nuclear plants are required to report all events (*licensee event reports* - LER) including human error induced events that could have affected the safety of the plant. One of the problems one runs into with routinely reported data such as that is that only the error is reported, not the number of opportunities to make the error; and this last is necessary for determination of the error rate. The authors indicate that they have developed a method of inferring number of error opportunities based on experience with operation and testing of the safety components.

One cannot say that the scattered empirical studies have led very far in a particular direction. Certainly they appear to have had little impact on HR as a whole. One reason may be that they were not sustained over time; another, that they did not work within a distinctive methodology or frame of reference (although this cannot be said of the Askren/Regulinski studies).

ERROR ANALYSIS

In reliability engineering one sometimes performs what is termed a *failure modes and effects analysis*. This systematically examines the various ways in which components can fail and the system consequences of each failure. The goal is to anticipate potential design weaknesses and to guard against them.

Similarly, if one were to examine the system in terms of all the errors its personnel might make, one could perhaps design or redesign equipment to reduce the likelihood of these errors. A distinction is ordinarily made between situation- or system-caused errors (SCE) such as an error resulting from a design inadequacy, and those that are human-caused (HCE), resulting from some factor within the individual, such as lack of skill. Even the latter can be considered SCE, since system developers should have trained the operator more effectively or should not have selected him for the job to begin with. Lees (1976) suggests that the ratio of SCE to HCE is 80:20; Kragt (1978), after analyzing the data from several studies, suggests that SCE and HCE range between 70 percent and 40 percent. Whatever the precise values for SCE and HCE, they indicate something that is important to point out to the developer: that his design can actually produce operator error. Whether he will listen is another matter.

Error analysis can be performed independently of an HRA, although obviously an HRA must include an error analysis. Such an analysis would probably include the following categories of information:

1. *Step or task description*: description of the individual task step in which an error may be made.
2. *Behavioral function* performed by the operator, such as, application of rule, use of memory, development of hypothesis, and data evaluation.
3. *Description of the potential error* in terms specific to the equipment/system and task being performed. There are gross categories of error—for example, errors of omission, commission or out-of-sequence—and there are more general categories of errors such as those developed by Altman (1967),—failure to note a change in signal (monitoring) or failure to apply an applicable rule (decision making). These categories, however, have limited value. In connection with error analysis in computerized systems the reader should refer to Nawrocki, Strub and Cecil (1973). The analyst must describe the error as specifically as possible so that it may suggest possible design or task revisions.
4. *Estimated frequency of error*: either qualitatively—very frequent, occasional, or rare—or in terms of a probability estimate—the latter would of course be automatic in an HRA. The point of estimating error frequencies is to eliminate very unlikely ones.
5. *Location and equipment*: where the error will occur and in the operation or maintenance of what equipment.
6. *Performance shaping factors*: any significant condition or circumstance that would seem to be influencing error occurrence.
7. *Error consequences*: again in specifics so that one can evaluate criticality.
8. *Recommendations* for preventing the error.

The error analysis is a design tool to indicate where changes may be necessary and there is no suggestion that a precise prediction of error with a particular equipment has been made.

Often the most difficult part of an error analysis is to get a precise definition of what the tasks are in which the errors will be made. Sometimes no previous task analysis information is available and the engineering information on which to base the error analysis (at the function level) is vague from a behavioral standpoint, for example, *verify that system safety has been assured*. Does this mean that meters are read, and if so, which meters, etc.?

It is necessary to consider all the potential errors that might be made in each subtask and then to eliminate those of a nonconsequential nature. This demands the analyst possess a more than minimal knowledge of the system.

A form of error analysis may be performed during operational testing and problem investigation (see Chapter 10). After determining the types of possible errors, the analyst may ask personnel whether they have seen a specific type of error occur in system operations, how often it has occurred and what its consequences were.

Error analysis is a descriptive procedure. Theories of error are vague and so far have little to offer the error analysis procedure. Rouse and Rouse (1983) provide a good summary of error theories and, in addition, present an interesting taxonomy of error based on their own error theory which owes much to the work of Rasmussen (see Chapter 4).

The preceding error analysis procedure deals only with discrete (procedural) tasks. McRuer, Clement and Allan (1980) and Clement, Heffley, Jewell and McRuer (1980) have proposed a conceptual framework for treating error in continuous (tracking) tasks such as are found in piloting. It is not clear whether this work has been applied.

ERROR DATA COLLECTION

It has been pointed out that the problem of securing data to serve as an HR data base is central to HRA. The few databases are fragmentary and inadequate. THERP makes use of the Data Store categories but has substantially expanded its taxonomy because it has expanded its data sources. The error probabilities of Swain and Guttmann (1983) were derived from actual errors in nuclear power plants, training simulators used in these plants, job situations in other process control industries and military situations that were psychologically similar to nuclear power plant tasks; also experiments and field studies with real world tasks; data from the psychological literature using artificial tasks; and expert judges. Every researcher and modeler makes use of whatever data he can find..

Behavior researchers do not ordinarily perform studies to collect data but rather to test hypotheses, so that the data provided by such studies are somewhat limited, containing only those data peculiar to the hypothesis test. Moreover, although millions of people perform tasks daily, resulting in millions of performances and errors, no system exists to collect data on these, even in a quasiauthoritarian controlled situation such as the military. The ideal data source is an operational real world, on-the-job one but data from this source are almost never available to the researcher in useful form. The inability to combine experimental data from various sources, each of which uses its own methodology, severely hampers development of databases (Meister and Mills, 1971).

The first step in the development of an HR database is the determination of the uses to which the data should be put, because that use in large part determines its database characteristics. These uses are in turn determined by the questions the users of the database wish to be able to answer. Blanchard (1972, 1975) did a survey of Navy user desires for human performance data and developed a database specification based on those desires. Although a number of data sources such as operational test and training simulator data were identified, almost nothing is available except traditional laboratory studies which are sadly lacking.

Methods of Collecting Data

There are a number of ways in which error and task success/failure data can be collected. The major ones are manual collection in the real world, automatic data collection in the real world, self report, experimental studies, and expert opinion. Each method has been utilized at some time or other.

Manual Collection in the Real World. This method presumes a human data recorder physically present in a facility who observes task performance and records specified events (e.g., errors). Usually the observer has a standardized data recording format. He may or may not make judgments about error causation as he collects the data.

This method is expensive because it requires that at least one person must be physically present at all times and to cover the range of situations that makes data appear representative a large number of data collectors may be required. The method is fallible because the observer may fail to recognize errors. He may not be sufficiently alert, the event may occur too rapidly, the error may be covert or else, since the observer's presence may create doubts in the minds of workers concerning the reason for his being here, the workers will deliberately set out to conceal the event and the error. This method is often used in operational system testing of MMS (Meister, 1971b). It is used by supervisors in Siegel's hand calculation HR method (critical incidents) although in that the data are mostly collected on an ad hoc basis. Manual data collection may be conducted either by periodic sampling of time and events, continuously, or by incidental observation of the critical incident type.

Automatic Data Collection. It is tempting to develop instrumentation that automatically records events so that the defects of the manual method are avoided. One such system was *OPREDS*, the Navy's operational recording data system (Osga, 1981) which was designed to record all control actions in the Navy Tactical Data System; another is the *performance measurement system* (Kozinsky and Pack, 1982) designed by the General Physics Corporation to record actions in nuclear power plant simulators.

Such systems are expensive to develop (few have been constructed), subject to malfunction and most serious of all, limited to control actions so that the operator's perceptual and cognitive functions must be ignored unless they can be inferred from the control data. The OPREDS system was tried out on an experimental basis but never collected any publishable data because inadequacies in its instrumentation made it too slow for the actions that it was supposed to record. Nevertheless, the increasing proliferation of computerized systems presents the possibility of including software programs in these systems specifically to record operator actions.

Self-Report. In this situation the one who made the error reports the error. Self-report can occur in various ways. For example, the operator may fill out a report form at the time the error is made, or he can report verbally to a supervisor who completes the form. The operator can be interviewed following the shift. Alternatively he can submit a written error report anonymously.

A variation of the self-report method is the questionnaire survey. Stewart (1981) mailed questionnaires to seven nuclear power facilities where supervisors distributed them to specified types of maintenance technicians. The purpose of the survey was to relate the number of times a task was performed to the number of errors made in the performance. Respondents were asked the number of times they performed certain jobs and worked with equipment, the difficulty of performing maintenance, and how often maintenance was not performed well.

There are tremendous difficulties with the self-report methodology because workers are reluctant to confess making an error. Negative consequences are anticipated. Moreover, the individual may genuinely forget to report or, if he does report, he may not have noted all the circumstances about the error that are desired. Systems such as the Navy's 3M system that require personnel to routinely complete forms describing time to perform a task or provide information about corrective maintenance provide data that are known to be grossly incorrect (Williams and Malone, 1978) and of doubtful usefulness for behavioral research purposes (String and Orlansky, 1981).

Experimental Studies. There are two types of such data sources: those performed specifically by the researcher to study HR, for example, Askren and Regulinski (1969, 1971) and Mills and Hatfield (1974), and the general behavioral literature (the source of the AIR Data Store). The ideal method would of course be the experiment performed specifically to secure data for use in the data base. This method is tremendously expensive, however, both in time and money because the amount of data gathered in any single study is quite small. Moreover, if the experimental study is performed in the laboratory, as is usually the case, laboratory conditions may be grossly at variance with real world conditions.

To my knowledge no systematic analysis of the experimental literature for expansion of the HR data base has been performed since the Data Store was originally published (Munger et al., 1962), but an updated Data Store, with all its inadequacies, would seem to be an obvious path to pursue. However, behavioral scientists seem reluctant to compile data, preferring to perform individual experiments.

The disadvantage of the experimental literature as a data source is that one is at the mercy of the original study—the conditions which were manipulated, the manner in which data were collected, etc. As the developers of the Data Store found (Payne and Altman, 1962), unless criteria for data selection are reasonable, the percentage of return on investment (that is, amount of data extracted per hundreds or thousands of studies reviewed) is quite small.

Expert Judgment. When all else fails, researchers resort to expert judgment. This data source is commonly used by all HR methodologists and was the only data source admitted by TEPPS (Blanchard, Mitchell and Smith, 1966; Smith, Westland and Blanchard, 1969a; and Smith, Blanchard and Westland, 1971). Such judgments can be formal or informal. The formal ones employ psychometric techniques. The informal ones, such as those described in connection with the THERP application, are purely judgmental and make no use of psychometrics. It is probably not feasible to ask even admitted experts to make direct judgments of error probability, such as, an error of type X in performing task Y has a probability of 0.9876, but one can ask judges to make paired comparisons or to rank tasks in terms of error probability.

There are number of advantages to formal judgments (Meister, 1978). Experts are usually available when all other data sources are unavailing. The cost in terms of time and money is, on a relative basis, rather small. This allows one to build a fairly large database in not too long a time. Stillwell, Seaver and Schwartz (1982) have reviewed available techniques of psychological scaling as these apply to the problem of probabilistic risk assessment (see Chapter Eleven).

The disadvantages are obvious. Often experts are not as expert as one would wish them to be. Data based on expert judgments are likely to be less reliable than data gathered by other means and their validity is suspect until verified by empirical data.

Nevertheless, all HR analysts have used expert opinion at one time or another. Expert judgments can be secured formally and systematically from judges but the most common use of expert opinion is when the HR researcher extrapolates data or quantifies his hunches. The informal use of judgment is much more common than the formal.

DATABASES

In this section we review the formal or published databases. The term formal is used because HR analysts have many informal sources of data that are not clearly identified in the reports they write. For some systems there may be a little error data extracted from industry reports. These are too fragmentary to be called a database but when they are added together they probably form a substantial part of what the HR developer utilizes as his data base.

The formal databases are quite few and very limited. The primary one is of course the AIR Data Store (Munger et al., 1962, also reprinted in Meister, 1966, and Topmiller, Eckel and Kozinsky, 1982). Over the years there have been a few attempts to add to the Data Store in an attempt to apply it to particular systems. For example, Irwin, Levitz and Freed (1964) built on the Data Store to predict personnel effectiveness during scheduled checkout and maintenance activities on the Titan II propulsion system. They identified the tasks and task elements to be performed, obtained expert ratings of error likelihood for these, obtained a small amount of actual HR data from Titan tests and applied regression analyses to task elements for which both ratings and empirical data were available. Because it can be applied to another maintenance situation only if the latter were sufficiently like the Titan II, the Irwin et al. databank is only an historical curiosity. The same methodology was also used by Pontecorvo (1965) with similar results.

The author (in Hornyak, 1967) also attempted to expand the Data Store by providing estimates that would fill in certain gaps such as the effect of number of controls and displays on a control panel. The probability estimates in the Data Store for the variables the author dealt with were extrapolated from data found in 37 experimental studies. This is a data source which the reader may feel, as the author does, is somewhat restricted.

To supplement these data subjective judgment was employed. A number of typical control/display situations was presented in written form to 10 human factors specialists who were asked to estimate the percentage contribution of the parameters described to the error that would arise in these situations. These percentages were then used to assist in deriving probability values. This databank has never been used and like the Irwin, etal. data bank is merely an historical curiosity.

In his handbook (Swain and Guttmann, 1983), Swain has reported a significant number of HEP which are useful in applying THERP. To a limited extent one can consider these HEP as a special THERP nuclear data base. The HEP in the tables Swain provides are function and task oriented and at a more molar level than those of the Data Store. At the same time they are more specific to the operation and maintenance situations found in nuclear power plants. For example: "Operator restores wrong manual valve when the one he should restore is one of two or more adjacent, similar-appearing valves, and at least two are tagged out for maintenance." The HEP is 0.005 with a range from 0.002 to 0.02. The specificity that makes this HEP useful for estimating nuclear power plant operations makes it less useful for other applications. The THERP data base is the only one that has been expanded and modified over the years; all the others have been frozen as they were published.

Occasionally efforts have been made to gather performance data specifically for prediction purposes. For example, the Army Research Institute supported a study of truck mechanics use of job site information sources and quality of task performance (Schurman and Porsche, 1980). But such studies are rare and are not performed to develop general data bases; their uses are quite limited. Nevertheless, the fact that they are performed demonstrates what can be done if the will exists.

TEPPS made use of a fairly rigorous paired comparison technique to derive expert estimates of performance probabilities and time (Blanchard, et al., 1966). The technique provided judges with individual task descriptions and asked them to compare each description with all others to determine which had the higher probability of correct accomplishment. The paired comparison process is extremely time consuming. It took the judges a week or more to complete the required comparisons. The resultant data formed a scale with meaningful distances or intervals between scale values. These scale values, which varied from around 3.0 to zero, were then transformed into the more conventional probability scale (0.000 to 1.0). If the transformation is accurate the resultant probabilities can be used as estimates of the probability of task accomplishment. The TEPPS database assumed performance under optimum conditions—no PSF and no time constraints—which is, of course, somewhat unrealistic.

Transformation of the scale values into probabilities requires that one have *empirically determined* task accomplishment probabilities for the two activities with the highest and lowest scale values. With these two empirical values it is possible to solve two simultaneous equations which, in turn, permits the transformation of scale values into probabilities.

Where judgments are involved, consistency among judges is important. Within judge consistency for the TEPPS data base was high (0.909), but between judge consistency was only 0.683 and decreased in a subsequent user test to 0.416.

The TEPPS database has never been used for other than its original TEPPS purpose.

The interest in expert opinion as a source of data has not died. Embrey (1981) has suggested a methodology similar in some respects to that used in developing the TEPPS scale. The essence of the Embrey approach is something called *simple multi-attribute rating technique* (SMART, Edwards, 1977) which in Embrey's application he calls the *success likelihood index method* (SLIM).

SLIM is a systematic method for positioning the likelihood of success of a task on a scale as a function of the various conditions affecting successful task completion. The rationale is that the likelihood of an error occurring in a particular situation depends on the combined effects of a relatively small set of PSFs such as operator competence, motivation and work conditions. The absolute probability of success for tasks placed on this scale can be determined by calibrating the scale with reference tasks for which success probability is known.

Although it is not possible in a restricted space to describe SLIM fully, the following are the highlights of the method. Determine the relative importance of various PSF to the tasks under consideration. Weight the various PSF by judging the importance of each factor in terms of its likely effects on HR. Describe and analyze the specific tasks. Then rate each PSF to reflect its quality in enhancing or degrading reliability of the specific task. The product of the weightings and ratings for each factor represents the relative effect of each dimension. The sum of the products is the index of the overall effect of the PSF on HR. The formula is shown below:

For task phase i: $SLI_i = \Sigma W_j \times R_{ij} \ldots.$ (5.6)

where SLI_i = the combined utility of the various PSF in enhancing likelihood of success for task i.

W_j = the normalized importance weight for the jth PSF ($\Sigma W_j = 1$).

R_{ij} = the scaled position of the ith task phase on the jth PSF.

Initial results of a pilot evaluation of SLIM (Embrey, 1983) appear to be encouraging, although as one would expect there are difficulties (e.g., inconsistency among judges) that must be overcome. Further studies are proceeding (Embrey, Humphreys, Rosa, Kirwan and Rea, 1984), making use of a computer-based system to aid judges in rating and weighting the information used with SLIM.

With the increased interest in HR prompted by the Three-Mile Island nuclear failure incident, several attempts are being made to compile and analyze all available databanks.

One study supported by the *Nuclear Regulatory Commission* (NRC) was to summarize and publish all available databases (Topmiller et al., 1983), to find any additional data sources and to develop a methodology for human error data collection at nuclear power stations. The effort to find additional data sources has been somewhat disappointing. The Institute of Electrical and Electronic Engineers made a survey of models and data bases from aerospace, military, fossil fuel and nuclear power sources—including some of those described in this chapter—and concluded that "although it may seem . . . that a significant amount of data exists, this is far from the case" (IEEE, 1981, p. 13). The HR research effort sponsored by NRC has been described in Comer and Miller (1983).

A second study supported by the NRC has attempted to validate the HEP values in Swain and Guttmann (1980). Beare and Dorris (1983) collected error data from trainees in nuclear control room simulators and compared those data with the Swain/Guttmann HEP. Observed error rates for errors of commission were in close agreement, but errors of omission were not. The latter discrepancy may have resulted from the artificial nature of the training exercises.

HR CRITIQUES

The HR concept has been criticized on a number of points (Regulinski, 1977; Adams, 1982)

Conceptual Criticisms

Conceptual criticisms center around the nature of error and its relationship to equipment reliability. Adams (1982) has also raised, somewhat simplistically, questions with regard to the behavioral unit of analysis (how to define it), the synthesis of response units (the problem of inter-task dependencies), and the difficulty of combining human with equipment reliability values. The human error rate concept assumes that a nontrivial, nonrecoverable error is equivalent to an equipment failure. Consequently, 1.0 minus the frequency of error is defined as the probability of task accomplishment. This definition stems from classic reliability theory. Regulinski (1971) points out, however, that the human performance tasks most analogous to hardware system performance and therefore most amenable to equipment reliability methodology are continuous tasks such as vigilance, monitoring, controlling, and tracking. The two tasks used by Askren and Regulinski (1969, 1971) in their studies involved vigilance and tracking. Consequently the point estimates used by HR workers would seem to be inapplicable to continuous tasks. On the other hand, tasks of a discrete nature may not be amenable to classical reliability modeling. Hence the mathematic functions applied may not be relevant to the behaviors being modeled and in consequence error estimates may be inaccurate.

The response made to this objection is typically pragmatic: that in the absence of data on time-continuous performance, HR developers categorize these tasks in a discrete manner and use point estimates. Although there may be a substantial discrepancy in any HR prediction made, for the purpose of discovering needed improvements in system design the amount of error in that discrepancy is considered not to be as important as it would be otherwise. Even if we cannot precisely predict them, we need some idea of where errors can be expected. To reject the methodology because of its deficiencies would be to become essentially impotent to predict performance.

Pragmatic Criticisms

The pragmatic criticisms of HR methodology are that first an adequate database does not exist with which to make assessments and predictions and that second, an unacceptably large subjective element is present in all HR methods, making their predictions invalid. Some behavioral scientists object to the tendency to extrapolate predictions from the rather scanty number of trials on which the data are based to the level of precision represented by four "9's" (e.g., 0.9999). The latter is of course an attempt to model the HR metric on equipment reliability, usually based on thousands of operations, in order to combine HR with equipment reliability predictions.

Another objection is that lacking empirical data, the analyst who attempts to apply THERP must be highly skilled in performing the necessary analyses before his quantitative estimates can be accepted. For example, in assigning HEP to the events depicted in the fault tree, "If there is no exact match between the descriptions of the task found in the handbook (Swain and Guttmann, 1980) and that defined by the task analysis, the estimated HEP for a similar task may be used as is or may be used for *extrapolation for that situation* (italics those of this author), depending on the degree of similarity between the descriptions . . . a person skilled in human performance technology is required for these kinds of judgments" (Bell and Swain, 1981, p. 9).

It is impossible to counter the objection that the data are too scanty and subjectivity too rampant. How much data would be enough? and should one wait until there are enough data? HR researchers assert that because the HR methodology is designed to respond to problems of the here and now, it cannot hibernate until some hypothetical time when there will be enough data.

COMMENTARY

There are certain similarities between THERP and the mathematical model (Siegel/Wolf and SAINT) methods. I ignore the Data Store because as a methodology it is primitive. Both THERP and the mathematical models make use of task analysis to partition higher-order, more molar, operations into tasks and subtasks. Both apply probability estimates and use a graphic mode of describing task interrelationships.

TABLE 5.1 Comparison of THERP and SAINT in Application to Human Reliability

THERP	SAINT
Fixed probability ranges from which single values are chosen	Selection from statistical distribution
One type only of probabilistic branching	Five types of probabilistic branching
Static analysis but comparisons can be made with varied parametric values	Dynamic analysis; comparisons can be made with varied parametric values
One level only of conditional probability (P = A|B)	Conditional probabilities can occur on the basis of five branching mechanisms
Shows human reliability as a function of time only with difficulty	Events can be represented in real time
Can show crew reliability relationships but with some difficulty	Greater ease in showing crew reliability relationships
Event dependencies shown with some difficulty	Greater ease in showing event dependencies

There are, however, significant differences between the network simulation methods of calculating HR and that of THERP (Table 5.1). Metwally, Sabri, Adams and Husseiny (1981) have compared THERP with SAINT (and therefore, by implication, THERP with Siegel/Wolf, since SAINT and Siegel/Wolf are almost identical) in terms of seven criteria (for details about SAINT see Chapter 4).

THERP is an analytic technique whereas the mathematical models involve simulation. The mathematical models produce an estimate of HR not by recourse to a database (the database is used only to construct data distributions from which the model selects values while running) but by reproducing in its simulation the operations whose HR it is predicting. In THERP, selection of a point estimate HEP from the estimate range requires a good deal of judgment. In the mathematical models that estimate is based on Monte Carlo (random) selection from a specified distribution and the correctness of the algorithms that make up the model architecture. Use of the simulation method requires a computer and some computer expertise, but these are becoming commonplace.

The comparisons made by Metwally et al. (1981) are, however, oriented around internal structure and thus purely conceptual. Moreover, the differences between the two techniques seem to be those of degree rather than of absolutes. Consequently, in order to decide which method is more efficient, it would be necessary to present both with the same problem and to determine which derived a more acceptable answer—ideally followed up by validation. It seems unlikely, however, that such an empirical comparison will be made, perhaps because researchers dislike exposing their methods to test.

What can one say about the theoretical formulations developed by the two major methods of determining HR? Neither exhibits any extremely unusual concept, one that goes significantly beyond what most behavioral scientists would think reasonable, although S/W is a bit more daring in the parameters it attempts to include in its models. THERP is even atheoretical about error, which is the centerpiece of its methodology. There is little attempt to explain how error occurs. HR, and THERP in particular, is pragmatic. It is concerned about the genesis of error but only as this helps the analyst diagnose the error source and eliminate it.

There are two ways of looking at HR prediction and evaluation. The first is scientific: A behavioral science ought to be able to predict and control. From that standpoint the primary question in HR is validation: How closely do the HR techniques predict to operational performance? There are difficulties with this approach for several reasons: lack of predictive databases, difficulty in defining what is "close," and even greater difficulty in empirically validating predictions.

The second way of looking at HR is as a design tool. If the techniques lead to more effective design choices, they are worth applying even if predictions are somewhat inaccurate, and even if there is considerable subjectivity in the predictive process. From that standpoint it is unnecessary to be unduly concerned about high precision in predictions. Indeed, the diagnostic factor in HR becomes most important and the only point is whether an HR technique allows the designer to make a more informed choice about the design. The requirement to consider errors, the criticality of those errors and event relationships makes the designer produce more considered choices. If the designer fails to apply an HR technique, he simply allows his prejudices about operator behavior to control the design. It is possible to justify HR on the second, pragmatic ground alone, although it would be unfortunate if we forgot its first, scientific and ultimately more important purpose.

One can also ask about the influence of HR on behavioral science as a whole. Here it has had relatively little impact. HR is still the purview of, literally, a handful of people, although the number is increasing since the Three-Mile Island nuclear incident.

If the majority of human factors specialists and industrial psychologists appear quite uninterested in the subject, the question is: Why? One would think that if prediction is the goal of behavioral science, and if a database is defined as a formal organization of quantitative data for predictive purposes, the development of such databases and their use in prediction should be viewed favorably.

There may be a number of reasons for the failure of HR to attain acceptability. The association of HR with engineering may have turned some behavioral scientists off. Others who are academically oriented may be distressed by the fact that the HR concept is not particularly oriented toward theory. There may also be a feeling that the amount of data available is so small that attempts at prediction are useless. It is possible that when behavioral scientists talk about the prediction of human performance they mean it only in a general qualitative sense that does not require quantitative prediction.

Another possible explanation is that the central research interest in Human Factors and Psychology is in experimentation whereas HR focuses on application and on the gathering of data by methods that are not necessarily experimental.

Some psychologists may feel that behavior is so variable from day to day that it cannot be assigned a single number—a point estimate—without distorting the meaning of that number.

All of these reservations and doubts are quite understandable. Eventually, however, behavioral science must become a predictive discipline in quantitative terms. Then HR or a technique like HR will become the norm.

REFERENCES

Adams, J. A. Issues in Human Reliability. *Human Factors*, 1982, *24*, 1–10.

Altman, J. W. Classification of human error. In W. B. Askren (Ed.), *Symposium on Reliability of Human Performance in Work*. Report AMRL-TR-67-88, Aerospace Medical Research Laboratories, Wright-Patterson AFB, OH, May 1967, 5–16.

Askren, W.B. and Regulinski, T.L. *Mathematical Modeling of Human Performance Errors for Reliability Analysis of Systems*. Report AMRL-TR-68-93, Aerospace Medical Research Laboratories, Wright-Patterson AFB, OH, January 1969.

Askren, W.B. and Regulinski, T. L. *Quantifying Human Performance Reliability*. Report AFHRL-TR-71-22, Air Force Human Resources Laboratory, Brooks AFB, TX, June 1971.

Barnebey, S., Finley, D., and Meister, D. *Prediction of Human Related Field Failures in Electronic Equipment*. Report RADC-TR-72-245, Rome Air Development Center, Griffiss AFB, New York, October 1972.

Beare, A.N. and Dorris, R.E. A simulator-based study of human errors in nuclear power plant control room tasks. *Proceedings*, Human Factors Society Annual Meeting, 1983, 170–174.

Bell, B.J. and Swain, A.D. *A Procedure for conducting a Human Reliability Analysis for Nuclear Power Plants*. Report NUREG/CR-2254, U.S. Nuclear Regulatory Commission, Washington, DC, December 1981.

Berkun, M. M. Performance decrement under psychological stress. *Human Factors*, 1964, *6*, 21–30.

Berkun, M. M., Bialek, H. M., Kern, R. P., and Yagi, K. Experimental studies of psychological stress in man. *Psychological Monographs: General and Applied*, 1962, *76*, Whole No.

Blanchard. R.E. *Survey of Navy User Needs for Human Reliability Models and Data*. Report 102-1, Behaviormetrics, Santa Monica, CA, December 1972.

Blanchard, R.E. Human performance and personnel resources data store design guidelines. *Human Factors*, 1975, *17*, 25–34.

Blanchard, R.E., Mitchell, M.B., and Smith, R.L. *Likelihood of Accomplishment Scale for a Sample of Man–Machine Activities*. Dunlap and Associates, Inc., Santa Monica, CA, June 1966.

Clement, W.F., Heffley, R.K., Jewell, W.F., and McRuer, D.T. *Technical Approaches for Measurement of Human Errors*. Report NASA-CR-166314, National Aeronautics and Space Administration, Washington, DC, May 1980.

Comer, K. and Miller, D. P. Human reliability databank: Pilot implementation, *Proceedings*, Human Factors Society Annual Meeting, 1983, 175–179.

Dhillon, B. S. On human reliability—bibliography. *Microelectronics and Reliability*, 1980, *20*, 371–383.

Edwards, W. How to use multiattribute utility measurement for social decision making. *IEEE Transactions on Systems, Man, and Cybernetics*, 1977, SMC-7, 326–340.

Embrey, D. E. A new approach to the evaluation and qualification of human reliability in systems assessment. *Proceedings*, Third National Reliability Conference - Reliability 81, Birmingham, England, 1981, pp. 5B/1/1-5B/1/12.

Embrey, D.E. *The Use of Performance Shaping Factors and Quantified Expert Judgment in the Evaluation of Human Reliability*. Report NUREG/CR-2986, BNL-NUREG-51591, Brookhaven National Laboratory, Upton, New York, May 1983.

Embrey, D.E., Humphreys, P., Rosa, E.A., Kirwan, B., and Rea, K. *SLIM-MAUD: An Approach to*

Assessing Human Error Probabilities Using Structured Expert Judgment. Report NUREG/CR-3518, BNL-NUREG-51716, Vols. I and II, Brookhaven National Laboratory, Long Island, New York, March 1984.

Flanagan, J.C. The critical incident technique. *Psychological Bulletin*, 1954, *51*, 327–358.

Goldbeck, R.A. and Charlet, J.D. *Task Parameters for Predicting Panel Layout Design and Operator Performance.* Report WDL-TR-5480, Philco-Ford Corporation, Palo Alto, CA, June 1974.

Goldbeck, R.A. and Charlet, J.D. *Prediction of Operator Work Station Performance.* Report WDL-TR-7071, Aeroneutronic Ford Corporation, Palo Alto, CA, November 1975.

Hall, R.E., Fragola, J.R., and Luckas, Jr., W.J. (Eds.) *Proceedings*, 1981 NRC/BNL/IEEE Standards Workshop on Human Factors and Nuclear Safety, the Man-Machine Interface and Human Reliability: An Assessment and Projection. Report NUREG/CP-0035, BNL-NUREG-51579, Institute of Electrical and Electronics Engineers, New York, NY, September 1981.

Hebb, D. Drives and the C.N.S. (Conceptual Nervous System). *Psychological Review*, 1955, *62*, 243–254.

Hornyak, S.J. *Effectiveness of Display Subsystem Measurement and Prediction Techniques.* Report TR-67-292, Rome Air Development Center, Griffiss AFB, New York, October 1967.

IEEE (Institute of Electrical and Electronic Engineers). *Report of a Survey for Models and Databases Relating to Human Performance in Nuclear Power Generating Stations (working draft, revision 1).* Task Group on Human Performance Evaluation of IEEE Human Factors Working Group, SC5.5, Washington, DC, July 1981.

Irwin, I.A., Levitz, J.J., and Freed, A.M. *Human Reliability in the Performance of Maintenance.* Report LRP 317/TDR-63-218, Aerojet General Corporation, Sacramento, CA, May 1964.

Jenkins, J.P. (Ed.), *Proceedings of the U.S. Navy Human Reliability Workshop 22–23 July, 1970, Washington, DC.* Report NAVSHIPS 0967-412-4010, Naval Ship Systems Command, Washington, DC, February 1971.

Kozinsky, E. J. and Pack, R. W. *Performance Measurement System for Training Simulators.* Report EPRI-NP-2719, Electric Power Research Institute, Palo Alto, CA, November, 1982.

Knowles, W. B., Burger, W. J., Mitchell, M. B., Hanifan, D. T., and Wulfeck, J. W. Models, measures, and judgments in system design. *Human Factors*, 1969, *11*, 557–590.

Kragt, H. Human reliability engineering. *IEEE Transactions on Reliability*, 1978, *27*, 195–201.

Lees, F.P. Design for Man-Machine System Reliability in Process Control. In G. Henley and R.T. Lynn (Eds.), *Generic Techniques in Systems Reliability Assessment.* Leyden, Netherlands: Noordhoff, 1976, 233–253.

Luckas, W.J. and Hall, R.E. *Initial Quantification of Human Errors Associated With Reactor Safety System Components in Licensed Nuclear Power Plants.* Report NUREG/CR-1880, BNL-NUREG-51323, Brookhaven National Laboratory, Upton, New York, January 1981.

McRuer, D.T., Clement, W.F., and Allen, R.W. *A Theory of Human Error.* Report NASA-CR-166313, Systems Technology, Ltd., Hawthorne, CA, May 1980.

Meister, D. What and where are the data in Human Factors? *Proceedings*, Annual Meeting, Human Factors Society, Seattle, WA, October 1982.

Meister, D. Methods of predicting human reliability in man–machine systems. *Human Factors*, 1964, *6*, 621–646.

Meister, D. Human factors in reliability. In W. G. Ireson (Ed.), *Reliability Handbook*, Section 12. New York: McGraw-Hill, 1966.

Meister, D. Criteria for development of a human reliability methodology. In J.P. Jenkins (Ed.), *Proceedings of the U.S. Navy Human Reliability Workshop 22–23 July, 1970, Washington, DC.* Report NAVSHIPS 0967-412-4010, Naval Ship Systems Command, Washington, DC, February 1971. (a)

Meister, D. *Human Factors: Theory and Practice.* New York: Wiley, 1971. (b)

Meister, D. *Comparative Analysis of Human Reliability Models.* Report L0074-1U7, Bunker-Ramo Corporation, Westlake Village, CA, November 1971. (AD 734 432) (c)

Meister, D. A critical review of human performance reliability predictive methods. *IEEE Transactions on Reliability*, 1973, vol. R-22(3), 116–123.

Meister, D. and Mills, R. G. Development of a human performance reliability data system. *Annals of Reliability and Maintainability-1971*, 1971, 425–439.

Meister, D., Finley, D.L., Thompson, E.A., and Hornyak, S.J. *The effect of operator performance variables on airborne electronic equipment reliability*. Report RADC-TR-70-140, Rome Air Development Center, Griffiss AFB, New York, July 1970.

Metwally, A. M. M., Sabri, Z. A., Adams, S. K., and Husseiny, A. A. Application of the SAINT code in modelling and analyzing some human tasks in nuclear power plants. *Proceedings*, Human Factors Society Annual Meeting, 1981, 105–109.

Mills, R. B. and Hatfield, S. A. Sequential task performance: Task module relationships, reliabilities, and times. *Human Factors*, 1974, *16*, 117–128.

Munger, S.J., Smith, R.W., and Payne, D. *An index of electronic equipment operability: Data Store*. Report AIR-C43-1/62-RP(1), American Institute for Research, Pittsburgh, PA, January 1962. (AD 607 161)

Nawrocki, L.H., Strub, M.H., and Cecil, R.M. Error categorization and analysis in man-computer communication systems. *IEEE Transactions on Reliability*, 1973, *22*, 135–140.

Osga, G. *Guidelines for Development, Use and Validation of a Human Performance Databank for NTDS Combat Operations*. Systems Exploration, Inc., San Diego, CA, March 1981.

Payne, D. and Altman, J.W. *An Index of Electronic Equipment Operability: Report of Development*. Report AIR-C-43-1/62-FR, American Institute for Research, Pittsburgh, PA, January 1962.

Pew, R.W., Baron, S., Feehrer, C.E., and Miller, D.C. *Critical Review and Analysis of Performance Models Applicable to Man–Machine Systems Evaluation*. Report AFOSR-TR-77-0520, Bolt, Beranek & Newman, Cambridge, MA, March 1977. (AD A038 597)

Pontecorvo, A.B. A method of predicting human reliability. *Annals of Reliability and Maintainability*, 1965, *4*, 337–342.

Pritsker, A.A.B., Wortman, D.B., Seum, C.S., Chubb, G.P., and Siefert, D.J. *SAINT: Vol. I. Systems Analysis of an Integrated Network of Tasks*. Report AMRL-TR-73-126, Aerospace Medical Research Laboratories, Wright-Patterson AFB, OH, April 1974. (AD A014 843/7)

Rasmussen, J. *Human Errors. A Taxonomy for Describing Human Malfunctions in Industrial Installations*. Report RISO-M-2304, RISO National Laboratory, Roskilde, Denmark, August 1981.

Regulinski, T. L. Quantification of Human Performance Reliability Research Method Rationale. In J.P. Jenkins (Ed.), *Proceedings of U.S. Navy Human Reliability Workshop 22–23 July 1970, Washington, DC*. Report NAVSHIPS 0967-412-4010, Naval Ship Systems Command, Washington, DC, February 1971.(AD 722 689)

Ronan, W.W. *Training for Emergency Procedures for Multi-Engine Aircraft*. Report AIR-153-53-FR-44, American Institute for Research, Pittsburgh, PA, March 1953.

Rook, L.W. *Reduction of Human Error in Industrial Production*. Report SCTM, 93-62(14), Sandia National Laboratories, Albuquerque, NM, June 1962.

Rook, L.W. *Motivation and Human Error*. Report SCIM-65-135, Sandia National Laboratories, Albuquerque, NM, September 1965.

Rouse, W.B. and Rouse, S.H. Analysis and classification of human error. *IEEE Transactions on Systems, Man, and Cybernetics*, 1983, vol. SMC-13, 539–549.

Schurman, D.L. and Porsche, A.J. *Baseline Data. Vol. I: Likelihood of Occurrence (One or More Times) of Information-Seeking or Error Events Under Different Task Conditions*. Research Note 82-9, Army Research Institute, Alexandria, VA, September 1980. (AD A126 916)

Shapero, A., Cooper, J.I., Rappaport, M., Schaeffer, K.H., and Bates, C.J. *Human Engineering Testing and Malfunction Data Collection in Weapon System Programs*. Report WADD Technical Report 60-36, Wright Air Development Division, Wright-Patterson AFB, OH, February 1960.

Siegel, A.I. and Federman, P.J. *Prediction of Human Reliability. Part I: Development and Test of a Human Reliability Predictive Technique for Application in Electronic Maintainability*. Final Report, Contract N63369-71-C-0014, Naval Air Development Center, Warminster, PA, 1971. (AD 738 572)

Siegel, A.I. and Miehle, W. *Extension of a Prior Personnel Subsystem Reliability Determination Technique*. Applied Psychological Services, Wayne, PA, 1967.

Siegel, A.I. and Schultz, D.G. *Post-Training Performance Criterion Development and Application: A Comparative Multidimensional Scaling Analysis of the Tasks Performed by Naval Electronic Technicians at Two Job Levels*. Applied Psychological Services, Wayne, PA, 1963.

Siegel, A. I. and Wolf, J.J. *Man–Machine Simulation Models: Performance and Psychological Intereactions*. New York: Wiley, 1969.

Siegel, A.I., Wolf, J.J., and Lautman, M.R. *A Model for Predicting Integrated Man–Machine System Reliability*. Applied Psychological Services, Wayne, PA, 1974. (AD A009 814/5).

Siegel, A. I., Wolf, J. J., and Lautman, M. R. A family of models for measuring human reliability. *Proceedings*, 1975 Reliability and Maintainability Symposium, Washington, DC, January, 1975, 110–115.

Siegel, A. I., Leahy, W. R. and Wiesen, J. P. Applications of Human Performance Reliability - Evaluation Concepts and Demonstration Guidelines. Contract N00024-76-C-6126 (Naval Sea Systems Command), Applied Psychological Sciences, Wayne, PA, 15 March 1977. (AD A037 632/7)

Smith, R.L., Westland, R.A., and Blanchard, R.E. *Technique for Establishing Personnel Performance Standards (TEPPS), Technical Manual*. Report PTB-70-5,Vols. I and II, Personnel Research Division, Bureau of Naval Personnel, Washington, DC, December 1969. (a)

Smith, R.L., Westland, R.A., and Blanchard, R.E. *Technique for Establishing Personnel Performance Standards (TEPPS), Results of Navy User Test*. Report PTB-70-5, Vol. III, Personnel Research Division, Bureau of Navy Personnel, Washington, DC, December 1969. (b)

Stewart, C. *The Probability of Human Error in Selected Nuclear Maintenance Tasks*. Report EGG-SSDC-5580, EG&G, Idaho, Idaho Falls, ID, November 1981.

Stillwell, W.G., Seaver, D.A., and Schwartz, J.P. *Expert estimation of human error probabilities in nuclear power plant operations: a review of probability assessment and scaling*. Report NUREG/CR-2255, SAND81-7140, Nuclear Regulatory Commission, Washington, DC, May 1982.

Swain, A.D. *A method for performing a human factors reliability analysis*. Report SCR-685, Sandia National Laboratories, Albuquerque, NM, August 1963.

Swain, A. D. Human factors in design of reliable systems. *Proceedings*, 10th National Symposium on Reliability and Quality Control, Institute of Electrical and Electronic Engineers, January, 1964, 250–259. (a)

Swain, A. D. Some problems in the measurement of human performance in man–machine systems. *Human Factors*, 1964, *6*, 687-700. (b)

Swain, A. D. Field calibrated simulation. *Proceedings*, Symposium on Human Performance Quantification in Systems Effectiveness. Washington, D. C.: Naval Material Command and National Academy of Engineering, January, 1967, IV-A-1 to IV-A-21. (a)

Swain, A. D. Some limitations in using the simple multiplicative model in behavior quantification. In W. B. Askren (Ed.), *Symposium on Reliability of Human Performance in Work*. Report AMRL-TR-67-88, Aerospace Medical Research Laboratories, Wright-Patterson AFB, OH, May 1967, 17–31. (b)

Swain, A.D. *Human Reliability Assessment in Nuclear Reactor Plants*. Report SCR-69-1236, Sandia National Laboratories, Albuquerque, NM, April 1969. (a)

Swain, A. D. Overview and status of human factors reliability analysis. *Proceedings*, 8th Annual Reliability and Maintainability Conference, American Institute of Aeronautics and Astronautics, July, 1969, 251–254. (b)

Swain, A.D. Development of a human error rate data bank. In J.P. Jenkins (Ed.), *Proceedings of U.S. Navy Human Reliability Workshop 22–23 July 1970, Washington, DC*. Report NAVSHIPS 0967-412-4010, Naval Ship Systems Command, Washington, DC, February 1971, 113–148.

Swain, A.D. *Human Factors Associated With Prescribed Action Links*. Report SAND74-0051, Sandia National Laboratories, Albuquerque, NM, July 1974.

Swain, A.D. *Description of Human Factors Reports by Sandia National Laboratories*. Sandia National Laboratories, Albuquerque, NM, January 1982.

Swain, A.D., Altman, J.W., and Rook, L.W. *Human Error Quantification: A Symposium*. Report SCR-610, Sandia National Laboratories, Albuquerque, NM, April 1963.

Swain, A.D. and Guttmann, H.E. *Handbook of Human Reliability Analysis With Emphasis on Nuclear Power Plant Applications*. Report NUREG/CR-1278, SAND80-0200, RX, AN, Nuclear Regulatory Commission, Washington, DC, August 1983. (Earlier draft version, October 1980)

Topmiller, D. A., Eckel, J. S. and Kozinsky, E. D. *Human Reliability Databank for Nuclear Power Plant Operations. Vol. I: Review of Existing Human Error Reliability Databanks*. Report NUREG/CR-2744/1 of 2, SAND82-7057/1 of 2, General Physics Corporation, Dayton, OH, December, 1982. (NUREG 2744-V1)

U.S. Air Force. Military standard 803A-1. *Human Engineering Design Criteria for Aerospace Systems and Equipment. Part I. Aerospace System Ground Equipment*. Washington, DC, January 1964. (a)

U.S. Air Force. *Handbook of Instructions for Aerospace Personnel Subsystem Design*. Report AFSCM 80-3, Air Force Systems Command, Washington, DC, 15 July 1964. (b)

U.S. Department of Defense. Military standard 1472C. *Human Engineering Design Criteria for Military Systems, Equipment and Facilities*. Washington, DC, 1981.

U.S. Department of the Navy. *Human Reliability Prediction System User's Manual*. Sea Systems Command, Washington, DC, December 1977.

U.S. Nuclear Regulatory Commission. *Reactor Safety Study—An Assessment of Accident Risks*. Report WASH 1400 (NUREG/75/014), October 1975.

U.S. Nuclear Regulatory Commission. *Tenth Water Reactor Safety Research Information Meeting*. Report NUREG/CP-0041, Vol. 3, RH, RS, RV, RX. January 1983.

Williams, H.L. Reliability evaluation of the human component in man–machine systems. *Electrical Engineering*, April 1958, 78–82.

CHAPTER SIX

Training Analysis

This chapter describes the analyses to be performed in designing, developing, conducting and validating a training course or curriculum. Training program development is a significant part of system development because no system can function without trained personnel.

The special focus of attention is a set of procedures called Interservice Procedures for *Instructional System Development* (ISD) which was first published in 1975 and mandated for use in the development of training systems for the American military. The Navy version (NAVEDTRA 106A, 1975), updated in 1981 (NAVDEDTRA 110A), which differs hardly at all in essentials from the versions used by the other services, is the basis of this description. It is essentially a formalization of methods developed by learning theorists such as Skinner and education specialists over a long period of time but rarely applied to actual training course development. The novel aspect of ISD is that it was made obligatory in the military, is utilized in actual training course development and is designed to permit a nonspecialist to perform the analyses. The latter is of special note because it requires that the methodology be stripped down to its concrete essentials, thus reducing the semantic vagueness and theoretical obscuration which one finds in many educational texts.

The reason ISD was selected for examination is because it is pragmatic and therefore permits one to do something with it, whereas most educational "methods" are abstract and tenuous. Moreover, ISD represents in one highly integrated model many of the disparate facets of other models and practices and it is used in the system development context. Although ISD is used by many civilian companies the procedures they follow were first developed by the military. It is important from our standpoint to say that almost all descriptions of ISD come from military applications. ISD has been described in educational textbooks (e.g., Wong and Raulerson, 1974) but not with the same degree of formalization. Some of the theoretic concepts underlying ISD have influenced civilian schooling but not in the structured prescriptive manner of ISD.

If ISD is atheoretical, there are two reasons for this. First, the nonspecialists for whom ISD was specifically written have no need of theory and in fact lack the psychological background needed to understand theory. That is also why the ISD manuals are written in such a prescriptive style. Second, and moreover, as Goldstein (1974) has pointed out, "there is a wide gulf separating learning theories and principles from what is actually needed to improve performance" (p. 92). He also talks about "the basic gulf between learning theory and its application to instructional technology." (p. 94), a gulf also pointed out by Mackie and Christensen (1967).

Nevertheless both psychology and education have influenced the development of ISD. The work of Gagne on learning hierarchies (Gagne, 1977; Gagne and Briggs, 1979) and of Skinner on reinforcement have had an influence; in educational theory the work of Bloom on learning taxonomies (Bloom, 1956), and of course the work of Popham (1971) leading to behavioral objectives which are all important in ISD.

Instructional system development is neither a theory nor a method, although it has elements of both. It is an extremely complex and lengthy *process*, depending on the complexity of the system under development. Any one system's ISD may take months, if not years, before full development. Like other design tools, ISD can really be evaluated only on the basis of *utility*: Does it work and how well? Here, because one is dealing with very complex training programs and systems, no controlled experimental comparisons are possible, although the documentation which supposedly plays so important a part in ISD should help. Only the major technical sequences of ISD will be described. Purely administrative and managerial aspects of little interest to the general reader have been ignored.

Instructional system development is not really new. Montemerlo and Tennyson (1976) point out that there have been previous avatars of ISD, and ISD is merely the latest manifestation of something called the *system approach to training* (SAT). They report that between 1960 and 1975 over 100 SAT manuals had been published under various names.

The system approach to training evolved from system analysis, a methodology developed during World War II to solve problems created by rapidly advancing weapon system technology. After the war, the methodology was found useful in the solution of problems in a variety of fields. In the late 1950s the first attempt to apply system analysis to the design of training programs was undertaken (Kershaw and McKean, 1958; Hoehn, 1960). The system approach to training provided an alternative to the traditional approach which relied solely on subject matter experts (SMEs) although ISD also relies on them heavily.

The new training technology was based on the hypothesis that if training experts could formalize models of the methods they used, laymen could follow these models and produce the same results at lower cost. The main thrust of SAT developmental efforts has been the production of manuals which reduce training design to a linear sequence of procedures which can be carried out by inexperienced personnel.

Andrews and Goodson (1980) compared 40 different SAT models of instructional design. Rather than attempting to describe each of the 40 models or even their common characteristics, it was considered simpler to focus on a model that is widely utilized: ISD.

The ISD process is characterized by a number of features common to system analysis in general:

1. A system is comprised of subsystems and their interfaces. In ISD, training is a subsystem of the total operational system and interfaces with other subsystems (e.g., job requirements, personnel classification policies). Training design decisions during ISD are made in consideration of the total system.

2. Subsystem development is based on an analysis of system requirements and subsystem relationships. The ISD process begins with a detailed analysis of job requirements and a determination of which requirements are to be met through training. Decisions about the functions of the training are to be made on the basis of costs and constraints of time, resources, and feasibility.

3. System analysis involves the empirical and iterative evaluation of alternatives. The impact of alternative training configurations on the system often cannot be clearly anticipated. Training development involves a series of approximations involving test and modification.

4. Considerable emphasis is placed on evaluation. Instructional development is evaluated in terms of the degree to which behavioral objectives are met and the extent to which costs have been minimized. Evaluation of the effectiveness of the ISD process itself is therefore at least partially accomplished in terms of criteria external to training.

Although ISD interfaces with other system components, its focus is subordinate to the demands of the operational system. ISD does not determine the role of the operator in the system or how the system mission will be implemented. That is the responsibility of the designers of the primary or operational system.

The formalization of ISD had coincided with the appearance of a variety of techniques popular in contemporary training technology (e.g., criterion-referenced testing, self-pacing of instruction, audiovisual media, computer assisted and computer managed instruction) and in consequence there is sometimes a tendency for such techniques to be considered synonymous with ISD. ISD is, however, essentially a process by which training alternatives are selected rather than the application of a specific training strategy.

Whitmore (1981) has summarized the outstanding characteristics of modern instructional technology. It focuses on 1. developing effective performance in future situations rather than on presenting subject matter; 2. learning required skills rather than on presenting subject matter knowledges; and 3. what the learner must do in order to learn each skill.

Furthermore, modern instructional technology 1. separates judgments about what is to be learned and how it is to be learned into a number of distinct stages arranged in a theoretical rational order; 2. uses more precise language than one is accustomed to find in educational writing; and 3. allows the designer to choose from a number of technologies and procedures for accomplishing each stage in the design process.

The remainder of this chapter follows the organization of the ISD process as

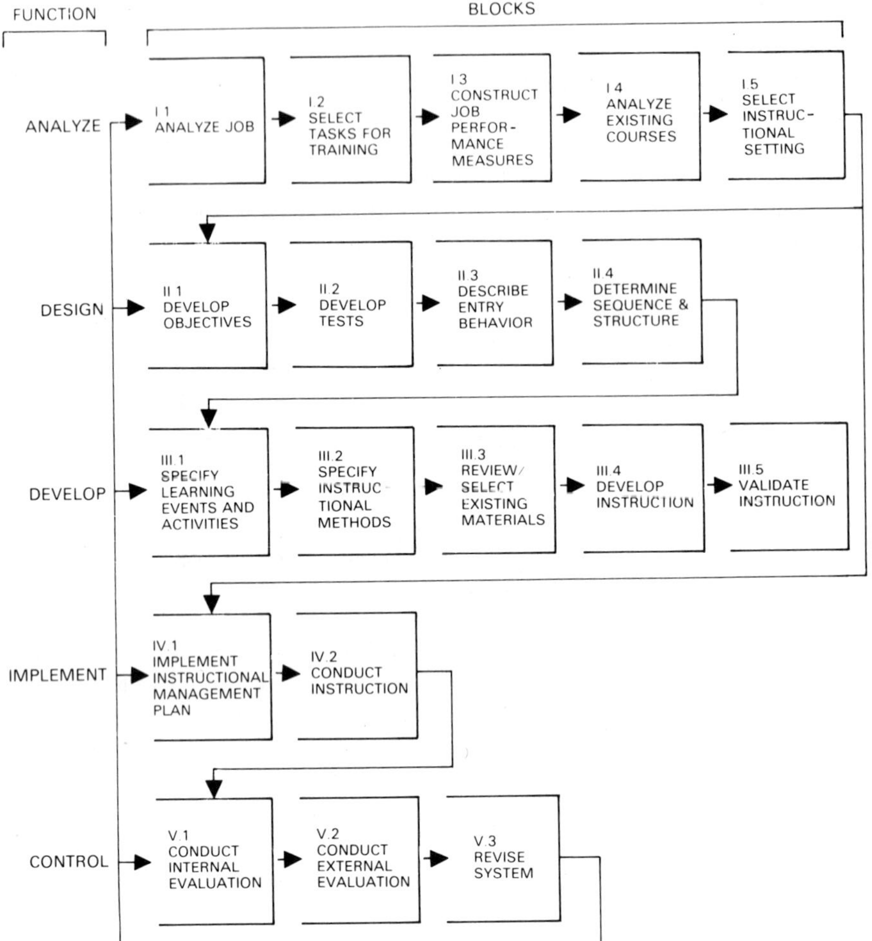

FIGURE 6.1. Stages in ISD development. (Modified from NAVEDTRA 106A, 1975.)

shown in Figure 6.1. ISD is divided into five major functions, each of which consists of a number of blocks; the outputs of each block serve as the input for the next block.

BLOCK I.1: ANALYZE JOB

ISD begins with the identification of a need to develop new or revise existing instruction. Either a new man–machine system is being developed and therefore system personnel must be trained, or inadequacies in an existing training program, such as changing job requirements or inadequate personnel performance, require that training be changed. The analysis of training needs is specifically part of ISD or is an antecedent condition. No decisions about training can be made until an accurate picture of the requirements of the job is obtained. Job and task analysis are the first steps in developing training and represent probably the greatest investment of time and money of any of the initial ISD steps. Job analysis as a generic technique will be discussed in detail in Chapter Eleven. For purposes of this discussion it is enough to say that job analysis determines what tasks are performed on the job and provides information useful for establishing instructional priorities. Because job analysis and task analysis involve different activities, they are ordinarily performed as separate steps of ISD. Task analysis generally requires a lengthy detailed specification of the task's behavioral elements. It is probably more efficient to undertake it only after eliminating some tasks in Block I.2.

Procedure

Job analysis is ordinarily conducted by (1) observing the job incumbent do his job and making detailed notes; (2) interviewing incumbents about what they do on the job; and (3) occupational survey methods. The extent to which one uses which method depends on the nature of the job being analyzed, the job data already available and the availability of analysis resources. However, in the military at any rate, a predecessor system to the one being developed is usually available, which simplifies the job analysis requirement.

Job analysis consists of three parts: 1. compiling a provisional list of tasks believed to comprise the job; 2. verifying the accuracy of the list and adjusting it as necessary, and 3. gathering task priority information. Task lists are developed in two phases: development of the task list and its verification. After the list is developed, it is exposed to operational personnel for verification, which may take different forms, ranging from use of SMEs who are convened to review the task list, to a phone survey or much broader mail survey. The primary purpose of the verification process is to make sure that all tasks performed by all levels of personnel who do the job are incuded in the task list, and the task statements are worded so that individuals surveyed for additional information will understand what is meant by them.

Task priority information describes such factors as where the task is performed, percent of persons performing, frequency of performance, difficulty in learning and performing, probability of deficient performance, consequences of deficient performance, and average time between training and performance. Since these are subjective estimates, to increase their reliability, the information should be gathered from a fairly large sample of job incumbents.

A final part of the process is to determine the *conditions* under which the tasks are performed, *cues* that initiate and guide performance of the task, and the *standards* which represent adequate task performance. Conditions are those on-the-job factors that significantly influence task performance: tools/equipment used, special job aids and manuals, supervision required, special physical and mental demands of the tasks, special physical environmental conditions, and performance location. Cues determine when the task is performed, for example, perception of a flat tire initiates tire removal. Standards refer to the acceptable quality of performance of that task, that is, how well the task must be performed. Standards are the basis for job performance measures.

BLOCK I.2: SELECT TASKS FOR TRAINING

The second step in the ISD procedure is the selection of tasks which are important enough to warrant training. This block represents a critical step in the ISD process because those tasks selected for training will obligate resources throughout the ISD process. There are rarely enough time or resources to train everything that might be desirable to train. Hence decisions must be made in terms of priorities. In addition, some tasks must be trained before others because of the serial nature of the job and intertask dependencies.

Procedure

Criteria for selection of tasks for training include:

1. *Percentage performing.* The percentage of respondents or interviewees who said they actually performed the task.

2. *Percent of time spent performing.* Of those who performed a particular task, the percent of their total work time spent on that task. All other things being equal, which they rarely are, tasks performed by more personnel and consuming most time will have a higher training priority.

3. *Consequences of inadequate performance.* Some tasks are of such a nature that if they are performed improperly the consequences to mission success, equipment or personnel safety are extremely hazardous. This increases the need for their training.

4. *Task delay tolerance.* Task delay tolerance refers to the amount of time that can be tolerated between the initiating cue and the actual performance. For example, taking time to refer to a manual or instruction on how to do the task. If there is sufficient time to refer to a *job performance aid*, the JPA may take the place of training.

5. *Frequency of performance.* All other things being equal, tasks performed more frequently should have higher training priority. Of course, this criterion is less important than task criticality.

6. *Task difficulty*, which refers to the amount of time required to learn the task to an acceptable level of performance. An extremely simple task might not be trained or would be given a lower priority for training.

7. *Probability of deficient performance.* This is the same as lowered human reliability as defined in Chapter 5, the likelihood that job incumbents will fail to perform a task adequately. This is a more satisfactory criterion than task difficulty, with which it is correlated, because it is phrased in performance terms.

8. *Immediacy of performance.* This refers to the time lapse between an individual's assignment to a job and the time when he is expected to perform that job. If a lengthy delay is expected (which often happens in the military, for example, spending the first six months of a first assignment on kitchen police duty), then presumably learning will decay and more training will have to be given in advance to counter that decay. However, this criterion would not apply in a properly managed situation.

To specify more fully how to select and weigh the various criteria it is necessary to know how the criteria are related to job performance. Unfortunately this job performance information is not usually available.

The next part of the process is to categorize tasks, based on these criteria, into those for which training is not required, those for which training must be provided, and those whose training is optional depending on availability of training resources.

Finally, based on the available resources, selection criteria, and the composition of the task list, recommendations are made about which tasks should be trained and which tasks should be learned by individuals on their own.

Although cost factors are not included in the criteria for task selection, it is highly likely that the initial list of tasks to be trained will have to be pared further after a cost analysis of the task list. This will require further prioritization of the tasks until available resources can handle them.

BLOCK I.3: CONSTRUCT PERFORMANCE MEASURES

A third critical function in the ISD process is the construction of *job performance measures* (JPMs) for each task selected for training. JPMs are used to determine personnel proficiency in the job, to design and evaluate training, and to maintain training quality control. Individual JPMs will be combined to make up the tests which tell whether, or how well a person can perform a job.

The JPM is the criterion of the correct accomplishment of the task after the task has been performed. When the task is overt, concrete and has a demonstrable product—for example, turning a lathe to construct the leg of a chair—the JPM of that task most closely resembles the actual task itself, such as, a chair leg with certain characteristics of size, shape, and smoothness. When the task is abstract, covert, cognitive, does not have a well defined output, or can be performed only under very special circumstances, (e.g., under combat conditions) the JPM may deviate markedly from the task as defined.

The emphasis is on performance. The ISD designer is told that to be effective JPMs must be developed before training objectives and tests are developed, that is, they must be independent of training because they describe task performance rather than task training.

The development of JPMs may be a difficult assignment primarily because of problems with

1. *Validity*, the degree to which a JPM measures what it is intended to measure. Obviously predictive or criterion referenced validity is most preferable, but this, particularly in combat or other hazardous tasks, is almost impossible to determine. One may have to rely on content validity, sometimes termed "face" validity, or on concurrent validity, such as, the capability of a test to distinguish performers acknowledged by supervisors to be effective, or highly experienced, from those who are ineffective or novices.

2. *Fidelity*. This refers to the extent that the actions, conditions, cues and standards of the JPM approximate those of the task. If the JPM is identical to the actual performance of the task in the real world, fidelity is maximum. One may have to retreat from this ideal because the administration of performance tests in many systems and jobs is extremely difficult. Again, this problem is found most often in hazardous tasks which even in a simulator may present difficulties of adequate measurement.

3. *Administration*. The administration of JPMs in some situations can present complex problems of logistics, for example, problems involving the use of heavy, complicated, or delicate equipment which may or may not be continuously available.

4. *Costs*. Obtaining high validity and fidelity may be more expensive than the probable benefits.

5. *Time*. It may take more time to administer some tests than is practical under normal circumstances.

The degree to which these constraints can be overcome will determine in part the relative success of the JPMs.

Procedure

A variety of processes must be performed to insure that the output of Block I.3 is adequate. The following procedure is performed with each task in turn:

1. *Determine task product, process and accomplishment indices*. The first step in development of JPMs is to examine the task in terms of the following questions:

   a. Is there a product produced when the task is completed?

   b. Are there indices that permit one to know when the task has been completed properly? For example, the task satisfies a requirement of some sort, for example, to go from *A* to *B* in two hours or to lift a certain weight to a specified height.

c. Is the process by which the task is performed observable? For example, driving a car is observable, a player's thoughts in considering a move in chess is not.

If there is a product the JPM can be phrased in terms of the characteristics of the product. If there is a quantitative requirement, a measure of the degree to which the requirement is satisfied can be used as a JPM. If the process is observable and the process of performing the task is important, one can use the process as a JPM. However, practical constraints may force a change from a higher to a lower fidelity JPM. These contraints, time, manpower and equipment availability, and cost are all interrelated and often manifest different aspects of the same problem. Fortunately, many tasks have no constraints.

2. *Determine if product, process or both should be measured.* The end product is the most obvious task output. It can be observed and inspected. A tactical operation plan, a computer program, are examples of task products.

The other output which signals the accomplishment of the task is the completion of the task process. Although the process itself may be evanescent, it is measurable. For example, the process of a truck driving from point *A* to point *B* will disappear (unless it is observed or photographed) but it can be measured in terms of the time required to complete the task.

In some cases, product and process should both be examined as task output. The processes in a task may be critical when they insure personnel safety or prevent equipment damage. For example, a bus driver may arrive at point *B* from *A* as required, but in the process violate laws and safety regulations. In such cases product evaluation alone is not adequate.

It is desirable that the JPM measure the same factors, product and process as described in the task statement, but this is not essential. If considerable simulation is required, it may be more practical to measure another factor.

3. *Determine whether a simulator is required for JPM measurement.* ISD defines simulation merely as "any change from, or imitation of, reality" (NAVEDTRA 106A, 1975, p. 172).

Three logistical factors will have a direct bearing on a decision to use a simulator to measure job performance.

a. *Downtime.* If operational personnel or equipment must be used for measuring performance, what is the effect on system readiness and efficiency?
b. *Cost.* What is the cost of using operational personnel, equipment, and materials for measuring performance?
c. *Damage or danger.* What are the potential damages or dangers to operational personnel or equipment if the operational system must be used for measurement?

If downtime, cost and damage/danger are potentially high or serious, serious consideration should be given to use of a simulator. However, if it will take years to produce the simulator and it is extremely expensive, it may not be feasible for ISD purposes.

4. *Specify the conditions under which the JPM will be measured.* These are the settings in which the job is performed, for example, maintenance at an airfield, at a dirt strip, or an off-shore oil rig. Some conditions seriously impact job performance, others do not. Conditions may be constant or they may vary, including factors that cannot be controlled such as weather, lighting, etc. It is necessary to determine which conditions will be used for measurement purposes.

Where conditions are fairly constant and controllable, one would choose to measure under all of them. For other jobs the conditions must be sampled for any one JPM. For example, it is difficult to combine blizzards and desert in one measure.

5. *Determine the cues that initiate task measurement.* When the task is one that involves an emergency or hazardous situation, it may not be practicable to use the task-initiating cues to initiate the JPM, even though this reduces the fidelity of the JPM. For example, the cue for a paramedic to perform mouth-to-mouth resuscitation is that a patient is not breathing. However, this would not be a realistic cue for a training situation. Probably the best that could be done would be to have the test administrator say, "At this station the patient (a dummy) next to you is unconscious with a weak pulse and has stopped breathing. Take immediate action."

Insofar as constraints permit, the critical JPM cues should be realistic. A critical cue is one for which the proper response determines success or failure in performing the task.

6. *Determine JPM standards.* Performance measures must have specific standards which are applied to all persons taking the test. The standard will include the following: the characteristics of the task product (where a product is produced); time limits within which the task must be performed (if required); the order in which all required procedures must be performed; criteria for judging the product; error tolerances. Standards must be realistic, neither excessively high or loose, and inherent in the task itself rather than being imposed by the analyst.

7. *Determine if all or part of the task will be tested.* The decision to test all or part of the task depends on whether it is a unitary task or a multiple task. For unitary tasks, that is, tasks that have only one correct procedure, the entire task is tested (unless some of the constraints noted previously, e.g., time to test, apply). If the task can be performed in a number of different ways, for example, troubleshooting a variety of failures, it may be possible to test only a sample of these ways. However, this introduces the problem of having a part measurement predict the performance of the whole. It is necessary also to consider the appropriate sample, a problem which properly belongs in a discussion of sampling statistics.

8. *Develop a sampling plan.* When there are multiple possible actions, conditions or cues, the analyst must decide if they are all equally likely to occur and if

all are equally critical. If so, he would sample equally from them until each is included in one alternative form of the JPM. These alternative forms are equal but different versions of the JPM. Constructing alternate forms makes it possible to include all of the important variables without making any single test too long to administer. Occasionally however it is not practical to construct alternate forms because of the large number of variables involved.

9. *Develop scoring procedures.* From a scoring point of view, the best performance measure is one which permits the job performer himself to produce the record of his tested performance. Examples include holes in a rifle-shooting target, the correct assembly of a piece of equipment, and the elimination of a known fault in a system. All these performances leave evidence or records that can be scored in a relatively objective manner and have high physical fidelity with the job.

When task performance does not provide a record of performance, supervisors or SMEs will be required either to observe the trainee's performance or to inspect a product of his work.

10. *Validate and revise JPMs.* The ISD procedure for JPM validation is fairly simplistic as befits its designed use by nonspecialists. "A validated JPM is one that has been tested and found to have high predictive validity or, where constraints preclude testing, has been verified as having high fidelity (by SMEs) . . . The validator observes the performer and thereby checks his checklist or measure . . ." (NAVEDTRA 106A, 1975, p. 205). The validation here is observation that the trainee performs the task but says nothing about how well he performed it. This procedure confuses validation and verification. Validation always involves measurement of on-the-job performance that leads to successful task accomplishment. Verification substitutes other methods for on-the-job measurement and task accomplishment.

Jobs that are performed rarely or only in situations where validation may be hazardous both to the job performer and the validator (e.g., combat) or completely new tasks, such as, ones that have never been performed, like a space mission, are "verified" by SMEs rather than validated. Such JPMs should be considered tentative and subject to revision when the job is actually performed. Haas, Selby, Hanley and Mercer (1983) have developed a JPM checklist which can be used during JPM development to ensure their adequacy. The following items are rated on a 5-point scale from 5 (completely) to 3 (generally) to 1 (not at all):

Is the JPM written at task level?

Are JPM standards adequate for performance measurement without being too stringent?

Were JPMs validated on a representative sample of the target population?

Is each JPM as good as it can be considering cost, time, and measurement constraints?

Is each JPM capable of discriminating satisfactory from unsatisfactory performance?

Are JPMs observable?

This checklist is not a validation tool but is rather a cue-sheet for the JPM developer.

BLOCK I.4: ANALYZE EXISTING COURSES

The primary purpose of this activity is to determine whether an existing course teaches the same tasks that the new curriculum needs to teach.

Procedure

This involves locating the existing courses and obtaining sufficient information via published documentation to make a careful analysis.

BLOCK I.5: SELECT INSTRUCTIONAL SETTINGS

ISD considers five instructional settings

1. Noninstructional, that is, replace instruction with job performance aids (JPAs) such as technical manuals which presumably eliminate the need for instruction.
2. Self-teaching exportable packages, i.e., self-instruction.
3. Formal on-the-job training.
4. Installation support schools, for instance, a local school developed by a local agency to satisfy its individual needs.
5. Resident schools, such as the kind of school situation we are most familiar with.

The process of selecting a training setting is a tradeoff between cost and the training efficiency of that setting. Cost includes not only equipment, instructors, facilities and supplies but also the effects of training in operational units. To make such a tradeoff requires information about the cost of each setting and the relative training efficiency we might expect from that setting. The first is barely possible to secure, the second does not exist.

Procedure

After tasks have been clustered according to the skill level requirements of personnel who will be taught (because skill requirement is one determinant of the setting in which the skill is to be acquired), they are then clustered according to constraints such as required resources, equipment and facilities. After the initial categorization, the tasks are examined first to see whether they are suitable for treatment by JPA (noninstruction). Tasks can be assigned directly to a JPA when performance can be totally accomplished using the JPA. However, even then, some training must often be given on the use of the JPA.

If the JPA alternative is not acceptable, the second setting considered is the self-teaching exportable package which is any form of instruction which does not require the presence of an instructor at the training setting, for example, a programmed text, an audiovisual cassette, or a kit to be assembled. However, feedback must be provided either in the form of correct answers, school solutions or responses from correspondence course instructors.

A third training setting is formal on-the-job training. This type of training has the advantage of providing continuous training on tasks which are of immediate need to the trainee. Further, it can continue for whatever length of time in necessary for the trainee to achieve mastery of the test. On-the-job training is, however, limited to those situations where it is administratively possible to conduct the training, and where the facilities are adequate. In the military such situations are comparatively rare.

If a task is not assigned to any of the above settings, it might be assigned to an installation support school. These are operated by local service organizations, principally to meet local needs either where shortage of personnel exists, where new equipment or procedures are required in the field, or where there is only a temporary need for the training.

If none of the other settings prove to be satisfactory, the tasks must be assigned to resident, or traditional, school instruction. Since this is the most expensive of the settings, this option is adopted only when the other forms of training will not suffice.

BLOCK II.1: DEVELOP OBJECTIVES

The preceding steps, generally referred to as *front-end analysis*, have focused on job requirements. The development of training objectives is the first step in designing training to meet these requirements. It is a critical step because objectives provide the bridge between performing a task and learning to perform that task. Objectives are descriptions of what a trainee will be able to do following training. They thereby establish what trainee behavior will be accepted as evidence that instruction was successful. Thus, they become the goals for training. Training design from this point forward will be carried out with respect to the objectives rather than to the jobs/tasks themselves.

Each objective describes some trainee behavior to be observed, the conditions under which it will occur and the standard of proficiency that will be considered satisfactory. All objectives are based directly on JPMs. They describe either task performance itself, behavior which demonstrates knowledge, or basic skill required for task performance.

NAVEDTRA 110A (1981) categorizes training objectives into knowledge and performance objectives. Knowledge objectives require students to recall or recognize items of information but not necessarily to apply them directly in task performance. Performance objectives require students to use what they have learned to operate equipment, solve problems, etc.

Objectives which describe task performance are *terminal* objectives because this is what is ultimately desired. Objectives which correspond to the performance of subtasks are *enabling* objectives because subtask performance enables terminal objectives to be accomplished. Objectives for prerequisite knowledges or skills are *prerequisite* objectives.

The process of developing objectives from tasks selected for training involves several steps:

1. *Decide how closely capabilities for task performance, once trained, match the requirements of the job.* Capabilities may be identical to those identified in the original analysis of job requirements, or they may differ either because of constraints in the training situation or because it is not efficient to attempt to bring trainees completely up to job standards through formal training (see below).

2. *Identify objectives in hierarchic analysis.* Here a task is broken down in its coomponent parts and the skills and knowledges that are necessary to learn or perform each part. The analysis is taken down to the point at which it is estimated that entering trainees already have the capability—if not the skill—to perform. The product of this analysis is a hierarchy of dependent and coordinate relationships within tasks and subtasks. (See also Gibbons and Hughes, 1978.)

3. *Based on estimates of the abilities of entering trainees, decide what capabilities must actually be developed during training.* Selecting a task for training implies that the task is important enough that trainees must develop proficiency in it. Because trainees may already possess the ability to perform all or part of a task as it has been defined for training, it is necessary to determine which capabilities will actually require instruction.

Since JPMs are supposed to describe the actual task, the *terminal learning objectives* (TLOs) written for them should also closely resemble the actual task statement, although practical constraints may reduce their fidelity. Other JPMs only approximate the actual task, but the learned behavior should be virtually identical to the behavior on the job. Clerical, administrative and some technical tasks, such as, answering telephone inquiries and reporting weather warnings, can be duplicated wholly in the school environment. For other tasks, only portions of the actual required behavior can be represented in the school setting, for example, splinting a fractured leg or disposing of radioactive waste.

NAVEDTRA 106A estimates that only 15 percent of tasks fall into the category of those which cannot be completely represented in the school environment. However, these may be critical tasks with severe negative consequences for error. Adequate training of these tasks is, therefore, necessary but difficult.

In some cases, the TLOs will describe the behavior to be learned accurately, but will not require the ultimate level of proficiency that is required on the job. In many troubleshooting and repair tasks, job conditions require speed and proficiency which can only be achieved by practice on the job.

To translate the tasks into TLOs each task must be analyzed to determine what a person needs to be able to do in order to perform the task successfully. During this analysis, TLOs are broken down into their component parts which are documented as *learning objectives* (LOs) which may be further divided into *learning steps* (LSs). *LSs→LOs→TLOs*. Learning objectives identify the mental skills, information, attitudes, or physical skills that are required to perform the TLOs.

In actual practice of course the process is not as simple as the preceding statement would suggest. ISD describes the process as a single-thread, sequential one, but there are multiple, concurrent threads in any training situation.

Procedure

1. *Prepare TLO for Each Task.* Traditionally, words used to describe course content and objectives have been vague and susceptible to misinterpretation. The TLO avoids such terms as "develop capability to use the *XYZ* equipment," and stresses the actions the individual performs to be satisfactory in the operational environment. An example might be to use the *XYZ* equipment to establish communication with a specified station.

All objectives must contain a statement of behavior (action), such as a product or an overt act, which can be accepted as evidence that the intended outcome has occurred. The behavior called for must be observable and measurable against a standard. The conditions under which the student will perform must also be specified.

The objective has three parts:

a. *In the action part of the training objective* the verb reflects the type of learning the trainee is undergoing. If the student is to learn information, he must state, name, recite, write, etc. something. For mental skills he must demonstrate (discriminate, solve, etc.) his ability. To perform a physical skill, the student must execute the skill, such as operating, repairing, or adjusting.

b. *In the conditions part of the objective* the conditions under which the student will perform are specified. For example, "field-strip and assemble an M-16A1 rifle under conditions of total darkness" or, "using available library resources, write an essay on the inability of government to develop and acquire systems effectively and economically."

c. *In the standards part of the objective* the student has to satisfy one or more of the following standards: perform according to a required operating procedure without significant error, perform to some minimum acceptable level of performance ("to the nearest tenth"), perform to time requirements (type 40 words per minute) or rate of production (assemble 10 components per hour), or perform to some qualitative requirement (adjust carburetor to idle at its smoothest point).

2. *Determine the appropriate learning category for each TLO.* The appropriate learning category for each TLO must be determined because each learning category is analyzed differently. All objectives at every level fall into one of four learning categories—mental skills, information, physical skills, and attitudes. To determine the proper category for a particular TLO requires consideration of what must be learned to master the TLO.

a. *Mental Skills.* For tasks in the mental skills category it is necessary to identify those skills that must be learned *before* the student will be able to learn the task. For example, if the skill is that of decision making, the analysis should reveal the rules and concepts that a student must possess in order to be able to solve the problem. Mental skills include rule using and learning (selecting the correct fire extinguisher for different types of fires), identifying symbols (recognizing road signs), classifying (identifying different ship classes), detecting (inspecting parts for flaws), and making decisions (developing diagnostic procedures). The breaking down of the skill into its component parts results in a set of subskills. These form a hierarchy (Gagne, 1977) which is helpful later in sequencing objectives. To identify the learning subskills one must ask: What thought processes must a person be able to perform in order to achieve this learning objective?

b. *Information.* To identify learning objectives for information, one must ask: What information must a person know (be able to recall or state) in order to achieve this learning objective?

Given the ISD orientation to performance, information tasks should be comparatively rare. However, there are always some tasks that depend primarily upon knowledge or where it is more convenient to measure knowledge of desired performance than the performance itself. The latter may be the case in some emergency or hazardous tasks. For example, the TLO might be: describe the best procedures for escaping from a burning building.

c. *Physical Skills.* To identify the learning objectives for physical skills one must ask: What motor activities must a person be able to perform in order to achieve this learning objective? There are four subcategories of physical skills: (1) gross motor skills (load the truck); (2) steering and guiding continuous movement (track visual target); (3) positioning movement and recalling procedures (assemble and disassemble an hydraulic pump); (4) voice communicating (e.g., send and receive messages).

d. *Attitudes.* The learning of attitudes is part of the ISD process, but I have little confidence that *formal* attitudinal training is possible.

The rationale for attitude training is somewhat unclear, especially since each attitude must be translated into an objective behavior that should be found in one of the other learning categories. In consequence, our treatment of this topic has been abbreviated.

BLOCK II.2. DEVELOP TESTS

When learning objectives have been specified, it becomes possible to develop objective (criterion) referenced achievement tests. Such tests can be used for many purposes, such as determining the capabilities of the entry population, assessing the effectiveness of training, and diagnosing student performance. The tests may take a variety of forms: performance tests to assess performance, paper and pencil tests to assess knowledge, etc. A special requirement of the ISD model is that tests be developed directly from objectives, rather than from the content of lessons.

The procedures used resemble those of Block I.3. The principal difference is that tests required to measure LOs and LSs may have to be prepared in much greater detail than those required to test job performance, because the former are more molecular and are used for diagnostic purposes as well as measurement.

Procedure

1. *Determine how detailed the test should be.* This depends on the purpose of the test. If it is to be diagnostic, it must be more detailed than if the test is intended simply to discriminate between those who can and those who cannot perform.

2. *Translate TLOs and LOs into test items.* Because of practical constraints *mental skills* must often be tested with paper and pencil tests even when the task is not a paper and pencil task. For example, if the LO is to select the proper fire extinguisher for various classes of fires, the test item might be to match the fire extinguisher in a list of extinguisher types with the appropriate fire type.

The use of paper and pencil test items to measure performance results in some loss of fidelity because they utilize artificial initiation and termination cues. For instance, the real cue to select a fire extinguisher is the existence of a fire.

Information test items are relatively easy to develop from informational LOs because the two are almost identical. For example, if the learning objective is to describe the principles upon which bankruptcy law is based, the test item would be to describe the principles upon which bankruptcy law is based.

Two problems with testing information are (1) setting standards when there is no job criterion and (2) sampling when there is too much information to be tested. In both cases the test developer must make arbitrary decisions.

When the JPMs for physical skills have high job fidelity, tests should follow as closely as possible. For example, if the learning objective is, fire rifle at 300-yard-distant target, the test item would be the same.

3. *Set training standards.* When the trainee is on the job, his standard of performance should equal the job standard. Learning standards will differ from the job standard until the student has achieved proficiency. The end-of-training standard should approximate the JPM standard. During training standards should be based on reasonable expectations after given amounts of time in training, low enough to be attainable and high enough to be an interesting challenge.

4. *Set cutoff scores.* When a cutoff score is set, such as 70 percent or 7 out of 10 questions correct, *how many* items were correct must be related to *which* items were correct. Often, getting LOs correct does not guarantee getting the TLO correct, and the TLO is what counts.

BLOCK II.3: DESCRIBE ENTRY BEHAVIOR

Adequate design of ISD training requires a careful analysis of the trainee's behavior. Beginning students will already have certain skills and knowledges, and it is highly desirable to base new learning on what the students already have.

Since the entry behaviors of individuals may vary greatly, it is not always practical to start instruction at the point that matches the entry capability of all students. Some individuals should either be rejected or given remedial training. Usually the entry level is set at a point where *most* prospective students have the prerequisite skills, knowledge, and attributes.

The entry test can be used not only to determine the beginning of a course, but also to what extent students have already mastered certain skills which will enable them to bypass certain blocks of instruction.

Procedure

In Block II.1 each LO was analyzed to the point at which it was assumed that intended learners had already mastered the objective. In Block II.2 test items were prepared for each of these objectives. The first step in Block II.3 is the selection of items from those developed in II.2 to test a representative sample (e.g., 25–30) of individuals from the entry population. If students pass all the test items for learning objectives which the Block II.1 analysis considered had already been mastered, and if they fail test items for learning objectives requiring training, the analysis was correct.

BLOCK II.4: DETERMINE SEQUENCE AND STRUCTURE

The specific purpose of this block is to identify those TLOs, LOs, and LSs which are *independent* of each other, those which are *dependent*, and those which may have *supportive* relationships. Dependency here translates into the sequence in which material is taught. The learning of one independent objective has no effect on the learning of another and can be sequenced as convenient. It is necessary to learn a dependent task prior to learning the one on which it depends. When the learning of one LO supports or facilitates the learning of another, the order in which they are learned is not important. Learning in one will transfer to the other no matter which one is learned first. Consequently they are presented around the same time but not necessarily in sequential order.

Procedure

Learning objectives can be placed close together if the conditions under which they are carrried out are similar, and if these conditions occur at random times, and are difficult or expensive to produce. For example, if several learning objectives have conditions such as "at night," or "on muddy terrain," one would place the "at night," learning objectives and the "on muddy terrain" objectives together. This would also be the case if a particular piece of equipment must be available in order to accomplish a group of learning objectives, and if one is not likely to have continuous access to that equipment.

While common element LOs generally should be listed early in the training sequence because they represent information or skills basic to other LOs, the delay between introducing such objectives and their actual application should be minimized. This is so that material learned at the beginning of training will not be forgotten by the time it is practiced as a part of other LOs.

The instructional designer will probably be dealing with so many items that he has difficulty in maintaining a clear picture of the relationships anmong them. This difficulty can be overcome in part by dividing the LOs into more manageable groups. The basis for the grouping should be commonalities among the objectives. Learning objectives should also be combined so that the grouping has a natural beginning and ending point.

BLOCK III.1: SPECIFY LEARNING EVENTS AND ACTIVITIES

Before any instructional material is written or a presentation medium is selected the general manner in which training (learning guidelines) will be given must be identified. Some activities are appropriate to all types of instruction (e.g., inform the learner of the training objective, elicit his performance, provide feedback). However instructional activities also differ according to the nature of the capability (information, cognitive or motor skill) to be acquired. For example, visual discriminations are learned more readily when critical stimuli are presented with different backgrounds, acquisition of a motor skill requires extensive practice, etc.

Before the instructional activities are designed, objectives should be classified according to type of capability each represents. Information about appropriate activities to promote learning for each type of capability is also necessary. When objectives have been classified and the corresponding types of instructional activities identified, the activities themselves are specified. An example of this might be "show the engine both intact and also in disassembled form." These specifications will later be used to determine appropriate media and instructional content.

This block provides guidance for separating learning objectives into subcategories that may require different instructional treatment. Instructional guidelines are matched with varying subcategories of objectives.

Procedure

1. *Identify general learning guidelines.* Four general learning guidelines apply to most if not all learning categories. These are: (1) Inform the students of the objectives of their training; they should be told exactly what is expected of them. (2) Provide for active practice of the task to be learned. (3) Provide guidance and prompting for the student, particularly in the early stages of learning. (4) Provide feedback to the student.

2. *Classify each learning objective according to its category of learning and identify specific learning guidelines for each category.* The learning guidelines below are simply very gross training strategies which must be supplemented by detailed analysis of the individual training requirement. These guidelines may appear to be ludicrously simplistic to the training specialist, but not so to the layman trying to develop an instructional program.

a. *Mental Skills*

Rule learning and using as in solving mathematical equations. (1) Have student (S) state rule verbally. (2) Provide examples of when rule applies and when it does not. (3) Provide opportunities to apply rule. (4) Relate rules to operational tasks. (5) Use graphics and mnemonics to assist retention.

Classifying–recognizing patterns as in identifying ship types from screw sounds. (1) Emphasize distinctive features of pattern, in terms of mental pictures instead of abstract words. (2) Use graphics and mnemonics. (3) Use examples and nonexamples of patterns. (4) Progressively narrow differences between patterns presented. (5) Overlearn.

Identifying symbols such as those in a circuit drawing. (1) Present symbol to be followed by its meaning. (2) Vary order of presentation. (3) Emphasize graphics and mnenomics. (4) Allow self-paced practice.

Detecting as in inspection of hardware. (1) Train S to use systematic search procedures. (2) Sample from full range of signals. (3) Train S to establish mental set to search, to respond to internal cues when vigilance fades and to use peripheral vision. (4) Progressively reduce signal-noise ratio, knowledge of results, and signal density. (5) Where appropriate, train S to use binary schemes for detection.

Making decisions as in troubleshooting equipment. (1) Train S to avoid favorite solutions and generalization of problems. (2) Teach systematic decision process, that is, define problem, collect relevant information, develop and compare alternative solutions, evaluate solutions and decide on best. (3) Provide variety of decision situations. (4) Overlearn. (5) Make decision situations simulate operational environment.

b. *Information*

Recalling bodies of knowledge as in learning equipment nomenclature. (1) Organize learning around key words, phrases, or formulae. (2) Closely simulate operational tasks in which knowledge is required. (3) Train S to differentiate similar bodies of knowledge or similar features of tasks in which knowledge is required. (4) Vary order of presentation.

c. *Physical Skill*

Performing gross motor skills as in using hand tools. (1) Train S to differentiate between similar external and internal cues. (2) Progressively reduce emphasis on external and increase emphasis on internal cues. (3) Provide penalty for bad habits. (4) Practice simple tasks in entirety, complex tasks in parts, followed by whole. (5) Practice under varied conditions. (6) Progressively reduce reward frequency. (7) Overlearn and increase distractions to level of operational tasks.

Steering and guiding—continuous movement as in driving an automobile along a winding road. (1) Break complex tasks into parts. (2) Ensure critical cues are available. (3) Train S to scan continuously. (4) High fidelity to operational task is required. (5) Demonstrate correct performance. (6) Overlearn. (7) Progressively reduce reinforcement. (8) Practice on component skills under a wide variety of conditions.

Positioning movement and recalling procedures as in following a cockpit checklist. (1) Break skills into part-units. (2) Demonstrate skill. (3) Train S to differentiate similar checklist items. (4) Provide graphics and mnemonics. (5) Train S to practice running through checklist mentally. (6) Progressively reduce knowledge of results, rewards, and prompts; increase distractions and amount of material to be learned. (7) Emphasize postfeedback delay. (8) Overlearn. (9) For procedural and physical skill practice, equipment realism can be low, checklist items and responses must be high.

Voice communicating as in ground control vectoring a pilot. (1) Break material into types of voice communication. (2) Train S to differentiate similar cues (sounds, words) that are often confused. (3) Point out critical cues which differ from habitual communication. (4) Train S to listen for particular words/phrases. (5) Progressively increase stress/distractions to operational level. (6) Overlearn and cross-train where appropriate.

BLOCK III.2: SPECIFY INSTRUCTION METHODS

After the instruction strategy has been specified, instruction methods must be selected. These decisions involve group size and location (large group, seminar, individual study); individualization of curriculum (fixed curriculum, remedial loops, branching programs); pacing (group or individual), course management (instructor-managed, computer-managed, self-managed, media-controlled): and who will provide one-to-one tutoring if required (instructor, assistant, another student). Obviously, some methods are interdependent.

The choice of methods is influenced by the training strategies specified in Block III.1. For example, if trainees are to observe a live fire demonstration, it will be convenient to bring them together in a group. If they are to practice the procedure for preparing an accident report, individual study or peer instruction might be more appropriate. The choice of methods, in turn, influences the selection of media. If self-paced or individualized instruction is specified, for example, a live lecture will probably be precluded, but a videotaped one might be acceptable.

After training strategies and methods have been specified, it is necessary to identify the media to be used. For example, if trainees must understand how the working parts of an engine operate, the ISD analyst must now decide whether an operational engine, simulator, television or motion picture, still picture, diagram, computer generated image, or other device is appropriate for this objective and, of those which are appropriate, which is most economical.

A prerequisite to selecting media is information about the suitability and cost of different media for various instructional strategies and methods. Unfortunately, little information is available about the effectiveness of the individual presentation medium.

Procedure

1. *Select pool of media mixes.* Media alternatives are identified by selecting those media within the appropriate learning category that have required stimulus criteria. Selection is assisted by a media selection matrix for each of the learning categories (Figure 6.2).

The matrix has three parts. The first, on the lefthand side of the sheet, lists alternative characteristics or dimensions the training situation may have. The training specialist checks off in the blank vertical column (center) those characteristics or dimensions that apply to her particular training situation. In other words, is she dealing with alphanumerics or pictorial stimuli, an individual trainee or a group? The check marks already present on the right hand side of the matrix are those characteristics possessed by different media, such as CAI or microfilm. The training specialist compares her pattern of desired check marks against the ones describing the various media and selects the medium with the best match.

One point should be emphasized. The matrix is simply a cueing device, a mnemonic, to permit the sppecialist to order her training requirements more readily. There is nothing magical about the matrix.

Haas et al. (1983) recommend a slightly different approach: a binary decision-making flow chart (something like the skill analysis method described in Chapter 3) to assist in media selection. Media choices depend on prior determination of instructional settings and learning strategies: whether the training will be system oriented

SUB-CATEGORY 2
CLASSIFYING

DIRECTIONS:

To choose a delivery system:

1. Place a "√" (light pencil) in boxes representing criteria (rows) that must be met.

2. Select the delivery systems (columns) that have an "X" in each row designated by a "√". These are the Candidate Delivery Systems

A Criteria for Selecting Instructional Delivery Systems	√	F Alternative Instructional Delivery Systems									
		G Delivery Approaches Permitting the Application of All Learning Guidelines and Algorithm					H Delivery Approaches Not Permitting Complete Application of Learning Guidelines and Algorithm				
		I CAI w/Adjunct Equipment and Materials	Study Card Sets	Microfiche	Teaching Machine - Branching	Simulator with Adjunct Displays or Instructor	Slide Sets with Instructor	Traditional Classroom with AV Materials	Audio Recorders - Disc or Tape	Specimen Set	Sound Slide/Film Strip Program
C Stimulus Criteria											
• Visual Form											
Alphanumeric		X	X	X	X	X	X	X			X
Pictorial, Plane		X	X	X	X		X	X			X
Line Construction, Plane		X	X	X	X		X	X			X
Object, Solid						X				X	
Environment						X					
• Visual Movement											
Still		X	X	X	X		X	X		X	X
Limited		X			X			X			X
Full						X		X			
• Scale											
Exact Scale						X				X	
• Audio											
Voice Sound Range		X			X	X	X	X	X		X
Full Sound Range						X					
Ambient Sounds						X					
Other Tactile Cues						X				X	
Internal Stimulus Motion Cues						X					
External Stimulus Motion Cues						X					
D Training Setting Criteria											
• Individual Trainee at a Fixed Location		X	X	X	X	X	X		X	X	X
• Individual Trainee With Independent Instruction at Any Location			X	X					X		X
• Small Group							X	X	X		X
• Large Group at Single Location							X	X	X		X
E Administrative Criteria											
• Site of Courseware and Special Hardware Development											
Local			X	X	X		X	X	X	X	X
Cei		X	X	X	X	X	X	X	X	X	X
• Magnitude of Acquisition Cost											
Low			X	X			X	X	X	X	X
High		X			X	X					

FIGURE 6.2. Sample media selection matrix. (From NAVEDTRA 106A, 1975.)

(actual equipment) or academic (laboratory or classroom); self or group instruction; whether memorization and motor skills are required, etc.

2. *Make media selection.* Those media that are impractical should be rejected. Media types may be rejected because they cannot be easily implemented. Sometimes the medium is still under development and may not be available for practical application by the time it is required. Some media are useful within large training programs, others for small programs. A new course may be designed to fit into existing programs, which places constraints on media selection for the new course—equipment on hand, available classrooms, scheduling practices, etc. Some media, such as closed circuit television, may result in low costs per student graduate, but the initial investment is substantial. Unless these resources are available, the medium is not feasible.

In certain circumstances media selection may require the development of training devices or simulators. The considerations involved require however a more extended treatment than can be provided here. The interested reader is referred to Cream, Eggemeier and Klein (1978).

BLOCK III.3: REVIEW/SELECT EXISTING MATERIALS

See Block I.4 which should provide necessary inputs for this block.

BLOCK III.4.: DEVELOP INSTRUCTION

The product of the preceding is the development of instruction to accomplish LOs. Since already available instruction has been selected and included, what remains is to complete the remaining materials. This is essentially a production task—writing outlines, developing graphics, and the like. These first draft materials are tried on students and then sent to the appropriate production specialists for development.

Procedure

The initial step is the preparation of a script or storyboard which serves as an outline of production requirements. For formal on-the-job training and for job performance aids, the script or storyboard may be replaced with a fully descriptive outline of the steps to be followed.

BLOCK III.5: VALIDATE INSTRUCTION

The heart of ISD development is validation of instruction. ISD assumes that if students meet the training objectives with the materials prepared, those materials are validated. This is validation only from the limited perspective of the training environment. True validation is determination that personnel who have been trained can perform their jobs satisfactorily. This aspect is taken up later in the ISD process.

Procedure

Training validation in ISD is conducted by administering the course to a subsample of the trainee population (subjects) under conditions that closely approximate its final intended administration. Achievement tests developed previously are administered; indices of accomplishment are obtained. Measures of instructional adequacy such as time to complete lessons and acceptability to trainees are gathered.

Subjects go through the materials individually at first and revisions are made on the basis of subject understanding of the materials, questions asked and difficulties in comprehension. Following the initial revision, the number of students is increased and the process is repeated. When the materials are thought to be complete, they are tested on enough students so that their effectiveness can be demonstrated at an acceptable level of confidence.

In the ISD process, all test items are directly related to LOs. Because of this, the results of this testing can be used diagnostically to determine not only if the student has passed, but also which of the instruction areas seem to be causing the most problems.

BLOCK IV.1: IMPLEMENT INSTRUCTION MANAGEMENT PLAN

Instruction on a routine basis is now ready to begin. From a managerial standpoint instructors must check to insure that everything necessaary for the implementation of the training course is available. More need not be said about this.

BLOCK IV.2: CONDUCT INSTRUCTION

At this point instruction is given, presumably in accordance with the materials developed so far. This step in the ISD process need not be further elaborated.

BLOCK V.1: CONDUCT INTERNAL EVALUATION

After the instruction has been implemented, its actual effectiveness must be determined. Evaluation plays a significant part in ISD because cost-effectiveness, which is a major ISD motivation, can only be determined by evaluation.

Internal evaluation should be a more or less continuous process, since the capabilities of trainees and the manner in which instruction is conducted may change over time. The principal measure of instruction effectiveness is the trainees' performances on the objective-referenced achievement tests, although of course trainee's and instructors' opinions concerning the instruction are solicited.

As deficiencies in the instruction are discovered, an attempt is made to identify their causes and recommend remedies. In locating the source of a problem, the emphasis on documentation becomes important. It is important to know what ISD steps had been performed, what decisions were made, the rationale for these decisions, and the way in which they affected training. It is pointless to revise instruction without first considering how it had been developed.

Procedure

The first step is the development of an internal evaluation plan. Instruction progress is monitored to be sure it is consistent with required procedures and is on schedule. Evaluators check the actual procedures and outputs of each of the blocks to be sure the processes are consistent. Checklists are provided so that the internal evaluator can compare the required ISD process and outputs with the actual processes and outputs of each block. (Haas et al., 1983, provide several checklists which, although oriented toward nuclear power plant operator instruction, are illustrative of the type.) Each of the areas of student evaluation is spelled out in detail. Course requirements are compared with student entry behaviors. Evaluators determine whether the students are being given instruction on topics they have already mastered, or whether they are being given instruction for which they did not have the entry skills. Extensive student and instructor questionnaire data are collected to pinpoint the effective and ineffective aspects of the instruction.

BLOCK V.2: CONDUCT EXTERNAL EVALUATION

In addition to determining whether trainees are attaining course objectives (internal evaluation), the adequacy of the ISD process must be evaluated by the performance of the graduate on the job ("true" validation). If graduates are unable to perform certain tasks when they reach the job, and these deficiences are unacceptable, the course will have to be revised. The purpose of external evaluation is to discover any such deficiencies, identify their causes and recommend remedies.

Probably the most accurate methods of external evaluation are direct observation and testing of graduates on the job. Such approaches are costly, however, so a great deal of reliance is placed on supervisors' performance ratings. Graduates' evaluation of their own and their peers' performances may be included. Information also may be obtained on such factors as what tasks are performed, what aspects of training are perceived as insufficient, and what training is not used.

The evaluation information should be obtained at a task level of specificity. More general evaluations are of little use in isolating the causes of inadequate performance. The external evaluation should take place 2 to 3 months after the graduate has reached the field. Otherwise, it is difficult to discriminate between skills and knowledge acquired in training and those acquired on the job.

Chapter Eight discusses the evaluation of training systems in greater detail.

Procedure

Develop an evaluation plan. The plan should discuss (1) what data are required; (2) who will provide the data; (3) when will the evaluation take place; (4) how the data will be gathered. It is necessary to secure answers to questions such as, do a greater percentage of graduates of the current instruction show satisfactory performance than do graduates of previous courses or training methods? Current graduates working on the job are asked how well they are able to perform the job? How much and what kind of training have they received since they arrived on the job? How well did the instruction prepare them for the job? Were any parts of the instruction irrelevant to the job? What tasks are most difficult? What parts of the instruction should be changed?

Data are secured from all possible sources—graduates, supervisors, an evaluation team composed of operational and school personnel and from records of student performance during training. Supervisors are asked to rate the ability of graduates to perform the job and to indicate what training, if any, they have received on-the-job. Evaluators determine how well graduates scored on JPMs, the relationship between JPMs and the actual job requirements, the adequacy of the job supervisor and whether the job is actually performed as required.

BLOCK V.3: REVISE SYSTEM

After data from the internal and external evaluations are received, the training course is reviewed to determine whether revisions are required on the basis of those data. Since the procedures to be followed are fairly obvious, it is unnecessary to go into a more detailed discussion.

COMMENTARY

In line with the system orientation that led to its development, ISD is a *total* process, starting with the need to establish a training program, and ending—if it ends at all—with the evaluation and revision of that program. Its similarity to the overall man–machine system development process should be noted.

Fortunately ISD is a formal procedure or process which is sufficiently concrete that it can be critiqued, whereas most training/educational methodologic literature is fragmentary and can be evaluated only on a theoretic basis. ISD is a logical, problem-oriented process, which means that it is an attempt to answer questions derived from the need to create a training program, questions such as, Who should be trained and how should they be trained?

ISD has the flavor of empirical common sense (which may of course be only a reflection of the very simple and simplistic way it has been described in military manuals). This simplicity conceals a great deal of complexity and uncertainty. Because of this, some educational theorists are uneasy about ISD. Take the matter of media selection, for example. The procedure described ignores the fact that there is very little empirical data on the basis of which to compare the media in terms of their capability to train. Leaving aside the questions of cost, is the audiovisual cassette/learning carrel as effective as or more effective in teaching equipment operation than, for example, a programmed text or computer assisted instruction? Are cutaways as useful as mockups? Another example of complexity simplified by the way in which it is described is evaluation of the training program in terms of on-the-job performance. There are almost insuperable difficulties in measuring transfer of training to on-the-job performance, but these are only hinted at in the ISD manuals. One wonders to what extent external evaluation, as it is called, is actually practiced considering its difficulty, but we have no data on this. Formalization and standardization of a method tends to gloss over the difficulties which training specialists have never eliminated.

It is refreshing to deal with a system created to be used by nonspecialists but one wonders whether the simplification required to make a complex process usable by laymen has not concealed certain problems that need to be attacked.

One of the most desirable aspects of ISD is that it is document oriented, since revisions to the training program cannot be made meaningfully without documentation. Documentation gives us the opportunity to evaluate the efficiency of the ISD process. In behavioral technology as a whole few attempts are ever made to document how analyses and evaluations are actually (instead of ideally) conducted, how they are utilized or the value they have when they are completed. It is our impression that although considerable documentation is required in ISD, the use of that documentation is quite fragmentary.

We have not yet seen objective, disinterested evaluations of the effectiveness of the ISD process as practitioners make use of it. This is a very clear need.

ISD is an "ideal" system in the sense that it describes the way in which training programs *should* be developed. Are they in fact fully developed in this mode? Since practitioners always fall short of an ideal, the probability is that there are deviations from the ISD model. One wonders whether these deviations stem from inadequacies in the ISD concept/process or from constraints of the environment in which ISD is appplied (e.g., financial and personnel constraints, organizational resistance, etc.). Probably both. The irrationality of a highly bureaucratic environment (any governmental agency) tends to exacerbate any weaknesses in a technological process.

At the start of this chapter the author said in justifying the selection of ISD to represent training system development that there was nothing comparable in the non-governmental sector. However, the system appproach to training has had certain effects on general education (Diamond, Eickmann, Kelly, Holloway, Vickery and Pascarella, 1974, see also Riegeluth, 1983). Their training program development procedures (along with those of Wong and Raulerson, 1974) also emphasize behavioral objectives (although they point out that "behavioral objectives can be overdone and can be used inappropriately", p. 63). Following the determination of objectives is the development of procedures and instruments to measure an instructional approach (learning guidelines) and selection of media. As in ISD a great deal of emphasis in Diamond et al. (1974) is also given evaluation. Obviously, ISD, having been influenced to some extent by educational theorists, is returning the favor.

Although ISD is a definite advance in educational technology, it still retains certain weaknesses and those weaknesses demand research. Since Schumacher and Wiltman (1974) have compiled "a compendium of research and development needs" based on over 2500 relevant articles, our listing of research areas would be somewhat superfluous. Fifty-one pages of research suggestions (Schumacher and Wiltman, 1974) indicate that if one examines closely almost any aspect of the ISD process, the need for further explanation and data becomes very obvious.

Nonetheless, as a general model of how one should develop a training system, ISD has considerable merit.

REFERENCES

Andrews, D. H. and Goodson, L.A. A comparative analysis of models of instructional design. *Journal of Instructional Development*, 1980 (Summer), *3*(4), 2–16.

Bloom, B. S. (Ed.) *Taxonomy of Educational Objectives*. New York: David McKay, 1956.

Briggs, L. J. (Ed.) *Instructional Design: Principles and Applications*. Englewood Cliffs, NJ: Educational Technology Publications, 1977.

Butler, F. C. *Instructional Systems Development for Vocational and Technical Training*. Englewood Cliffs, NJ: Educational Technology Publications, Inc., 1972.

Cream, B. W., Eggemeier, F. T. and Klein, G. A. A strategy for the development of training devices. *Human Factors*, 1978, *20*, 145–158.

Diamond, R. M., Eickmann, P. E., Kelly, E. F., Holloway, R. E., Vickery, T. R. and Pascarella, E. T. *Instructional Development for Individualized Learning in Higher Education*. Englewood Cliffs, NJ: Educational Technology Publications, 1975.

Folley, J. D., Jr. Joyce, R. P., Mallory, W. J., and Thomas, D. L. *Fully proceduralized job performance aids*. Vols. I and II. Report AFHRL-TR-71-53, Air Force Human Resources Laboratory, Wright-Patterson AFB, OH, December 1971.

Gagne, R. M. *The Conditions of Learning* (3rd edition). New York: Holt, Rinehart and Winston, 1977.

Gagne, R. M. and Briggs, L. J. *Principles of Instructional Design* (2nd ed.). New York: Holt, Rinehart and Winston, 1979.

Gibbons, A. S. and Hughes, J. A. A method of deriving hierarchies of instructional objectives. *Proceedings*, Human Factors Society Annual Meeting, 1978, 256–259.

Goldstein, I. I. *Training Program Development and Evaluation*. Monterey, CA: Brooks/Cole Publishing Company, 1974.

Haas, P. M., Selby, D. L., Hanley, M. J. and Mercer, R. T. *Evaluation of Training Programs and Entry Level Qualification for Nuclear Power Plant Control Room Personnel Based on the Systems Approach to Training*. Report NUREG/CR-3414 , ORNL/TM-8848, Oak Ridge National Laboratory, Oak Ridge, TN, September, 1983.

Hoehn, A. J. *The Development of Training Programs for First Enlistment Personnel in Electronic Maintenance MOSs: III. How to Design the Handbook Material*. HumRRO Research Memorandum, Human Resources Research Office, George Washington University, Alexandria, VA, February 1960.

Kershaw, J. A. and McKean, R. M. *Systems Analysis and Education*. Report RM-2190-RC, Rand Corporation, Santa Monica, CA, June 1958.

Mackie, R. R. and Christensen, P. R. *Translation aand Application of Psychological Research*. Report 716-1, Human Factors Research, Goleta, CA, January 1967.

Montemerlo, M. D. and Tennyson, M. E. *Instructional System Development: Conceptual Analysis and Comprehensive Bibliography*. Report NAVTRAEQUIPCEN IH-257, Naval Training Equipment Center, Orlando, FL, February 1976.

NAVEDTRA 106A. *Interservice Procedures for Instructional Systems Development*. Anonymous, 1 August 1975.

NAVEDTRA 110A. *Procedures for Instructional System Developmment.* Report 0502-LP-000-5510. Department of the Navy, Chief of Naval Education and Training, Pensacola, FL, 18 September 1981.

Popham, W. J. (Ed.) *Criterion-Referenced Measurement. (An Introduction).* Englewood Cliffs, NJ: Educational Technology Publications, 1971.

Riegeluth, C. M. (Ed.) *Instructional Design Theories and Models, An Overview of their Current Status.* Hillsdale, NJ: Lawrence Erlbaum Associates, 1983.

Schumacher, S. P. and Wiltman, S. *A Compendium of Research and Development Needs on Instructional System Development.* Report AFHRL-TR-74-15, Air Force Human Resources Laboratory, Brooks AFB, TX, February 1974.

Whitmore, P. G. The "Whys" and "Hows" of Modern Instructional Technology. *NSPI Journal*, 9–13 June, 1981.

Wong, M. R. and Raulerson, J. D. *A Guide to Systematic Instructional Design.* Englewood Cliffs, NJ: Educational Technology Publications, 1974.

CHAPTER SEVEN

Evaluation of the Man–Machine Interface

This chapter describes methods of evaluating the individual products of system design, primarily equipment and procedures, including those aspects of design that affect the maintainability of the equipment. These evaluative techniques focus on the *man–machine interface* (MMI), which for the operator consists of individual controls and displays, arranged in the form of control panels, consoles, and aircraft cockpits; the *MMI* also consists of the procedures used to operate and maintain them. The interface for the maintenance technician consists of modules and components within the equipment, test points, maintenance controls and displays, connectors, etc. These products are evaluated individually and as subsystems, often in a nonfunctional (nonperforming) state. The next chapter will deal with evaluations in which the MMI is evaluated as part of the total functioning system. These methods, like those of the preceding chapters, are used during system development because the products to which they apply arise from that development.

Evaluation methods can be categorized in a number of ways—as experimental or nonexperimental, as formal or informal, as dealing with two-dimensional (drawings and written procedures) and three-dimensional products (mockups, prototype equipment), and as being applied in a static (nonperformance) or performance context. The most significant dichotomy is the last one.

The evaluation methods described in this chapter are nonexperimental. Experimental evaluation methods measure subject performance in contrasting conditions in a highly controlled situation such as that of a laboratory. The use of statistical designs to control testing is a hallmark of experimental evaluation. The conditions under which most system development is pursued usually forbid experimental evaluation unless the evaluation is performed in a laboratory as part of advanced design which is different from routine system development. The reasons why experimental evaluations are not often performed as part of ongoing system development are the hectic pace of development which in most cases overtakes and makes obsolete the results of a study before it is completed and insufficient funds to construct alternative functioning equipment configurations.

Once the function allocation phase of development (see Chapter 2) has passed, it is rare that functioning mockups of *alternative* designs are constructed in system development. More often the task is to evaluate the adequacy of a single design and determine its weak points. For this type of situation experimental design, which is essentially a comparative technique, is not very appropriate. However, operational system testing to be described in the next chapter does make use to some extent of experimental design evaluation methods.

Formal evaluation methods have certain characteristics. They were specifically developed by researchers to accomplish certain functions and they usually have well defined, step-by-step procedures for their accomplishment. Informal procedures in large part grew out of informal practices by behavioral specialists working in system development. They do not have very clearly specified step by step procedures. The informal evaluation methods when applied to two-dimensional products usually consists of questions the evaluator asks himself about the *attributes* of these products. When applied to performance with three-dimensional products, they usually consist of simple timing of operations, counting of errors, interviews of operators, etc. Most commonly utilized evaluation techniques in system development are informal. Only a few, like the *display evaluative index* (DEI) and *analytic profile system* (APS), to be described later, are formal. Both formal and informal methods are valuable, although it is my impression that the informal ones being as it were native to system development are more often utilized in that development. Informal evaluation procedures may become formalized, as, for example, when the questions an evaluator asks about a control panel drawing are written down and published as a checklist. Curiously, almost all analytic techniques such as those described in preceding chapters, are formal ones, while most of the evaluation techniques are informal.

Two-dimensional methods emphasize examination of the product in terms of the attributes it should have; hence the need for attribute standards. Checklists are a common aid to that examination. Three-dimensional techniques make special use of mockups as a tool and performance measurement as a methodology. Two-dimensional evaluations are usually static and three-dimensional ones can be either static or performance oriented, although the special characteristics of the three-dimensional product make it more advantageous to conduct performance tests.

Like analytical techniques, the evaluation methods were developed to answer behavioral questions arising out of system development. The primary ones are: Which of two or more design alternatives is better from a behavioral standpoint? (This question arose also in function allocation); Does the design product contain the attributes of an effective product? (Again, from a behavioral standpoint); Will system personnel be able to utilize the product or system without excessive difficulty? Will the overall system be able to accomplish its mission when it contains this product? How can the design product be improved?

Some of the analyses described in the preceding chapters can also be used for evaluative purposes because they are based upon implicit evaluation standards. For example, in link analysis, an effective control panel or workplace is one which has the fewest links requiring physical movement. Or a system which has low error probability (as determined by a human reliability technique) is a more effective system than one with a higher error probability. If one applies workload analysis to a product and derives a W/L figure of merit for that product, it has obviously been evaluated in terms of its W/L potential. Other analyses can assist or prepare the ground for an evaluation. For example, if one is evaluating a control panel drawing and no step-by-step operating procedure is available, task analysis documentation may be helpful. Similarly, OSDs are useful for familiarizing the evaluator with procedural details before he begins his evaluation. Analysis and evaluation are therefore somewhat artificial distinctions.

To many researchers, an important criterion of methodologic adequacy is that the technique have some foundation in theory. In general, developmental evaluation techniques are not based on theory, unless one can say that the experimental designs occasionally employed in mockup and operational system testing originate in theory. More important in the very uncertain context in which system development proceeds is whether or not the logic of the evaluation method used, and its results, can convince the engineering designer of the validity of the conclusions reached. Evaluation techniques that produce only qualitative conclusions are not very effective in convincing the designer. Even when quantitative results are achieved, as in measuring subject performance in terms of time and errors, the meaning of those data may not be very evident unless the data can be compared with some accepted standard of effective performance.

Static evaluation is fundamentally a comparison between the attributes of the design product (drawings, written procedures) and some standard of desired characteristics. Performance evaluation is a comparison between measured performance and some performance standard. Behavioral evaluation cannot therefore be performed without standards of comparison which describe those characteristics and performances the MMI should have if it is to be effective.

One point must be made. We should not wish the reader to have the impression that every MMI must be evaluated with all the methods described in this chapter. When the MMI is commercially available, it is necessary only to ensure that the equipment satisfies accepted standards and that it is adequate for the intended application. For example, the Automated Interviewer described in Chapter Two utilized a purchased CRT television display. The evaluator would check merely to determine that whatever was purchased satisfied CRT display standards, such as those described in Banks, Gertman and Petersen (1982) and the special needs of the clients in terms of alphanumeric size, display brightness, etc.

STANDARDS

Because there are two types of evaluation, there are two types of standards: attribute standards (those describing how the design product should appear or should function) and performance standards (those describing how the design product should perform). Attribute standards are general, applying, for example, to all control panels or all displays, e.g., *cathode ray tube* (CRT) displays should have a frame rate of 50 to 60 Hz; performance standards are peculiar to the individual system being developed (system X must have a detection slant range of two miles). Attribute standards apply mostly at the component/equipment level; performance standards, at the subsystem/system level. Behavioral attribute standards are mandated by industry groups, government authority, and by behavior specialists—all working together (e.g., MIL-STD 1472C, Department of Defense, 1981). Performance standards for the system being developed are mandated by its customer. In this chapter we deal almost exclusively with attribute standards at the component/equipment level, because the MMI design products being evaluated do not ordinarily have individual performance standards. In Chapter Eight we shall deal with performance standards at the subsystem/system level.

Attribute standards should posses certain characteristics. They should be:

1 *Individualized and specific* to a particular characteristic or dimension of the equipment or procedure. For example, one item within the standard should deal with control panel layout principles, another with the amount of information transmitted by a type of display, a third with the accessibility of internal components, etc. Standards which are general and hence non-specific are of dubious value (e.g., design should be as simple as possible).

2 *Quantitative* in terms of the performance to be expected when using an equipment (ideally, in terms of probability of accomplishing a task if the standard is followed or error rate if it is violated). Ideally the standard would be presented in terms of tables or graphs and should specify any limits which the designer must not violate, such as noise levels that are dangerous to health, maximum height of standup consoles, and minimum space for access. The standard should describe the variables it deals with in a continuous manner, rather than describing one or only a few values of that continuum.

3 *Linked* to a preferred design practice. The means of putting the standard into design practice should be clearly described to the extent that is possible. For example, a standard describing desired control panel layout should specify the principles on which the layout should be made. Although the standard serves primarily as an evaluation criterion, the designer often attempts to use it as a design guide. It, in turn, loses much of its value if it cannot be related directly or indirectly to design.

Few attribute standards satisfy these criteria particularly (2) and (3) above and the probability of standards being written in this way is very low. This is because of the large amount of experimental data that would be needed to support these criteria and government directives that govern how standards are written. See Rogers and Armstrong, 1977, and Rogers and Pegden, 1977. In general, attribute standards for the concrete, physical aspects of the MMI, such as controls, displays, environment and anthropometry are relatively specific and somewhat quantitative. These describe, or are related to, the psychomotor aspects of design. Standards that describe cognitive aspects related to design—such as the manner in which information should be transmitted from a display—are largely nonexistent, although eventually it will be necessary for behavior specialists to deal with this aspect because of the increasing automatization and computerization of systems. (This last makes the operator less a manipulator/controller and more a supervisor of system processes, with consequent emphasis on cognition.)

STATIC EVALUATION TECHNIQUES

Evaluation of Equipment Drawings

The most frequently performed behavioral evaluation during system development is that of equipment drawings. These describe the equipment's internal and external configuration in full or partial scale, usually in blueprint form. Blueprints are drawn in layers, so to speak, with the top drawing describing the external packaging of the equipment and succeeding drawings becoming progressively more detailed as the drawings break down internal components into the assembly and part level.

The behavioral specialist will find top drawings the most useful for evaluating operability characteristics, since the MMI is at the surface of design and top drawings depict external packaging details. He may have to examine more detailed drawings of internal components if he attempts to evaluate maintainability. In either case he compares equipment characteristics as displayed in the drawing with certain desirable attributes (good human engineering characteristics) usually described in the form of a military standard like MIL-STD 1472C (Department of Defense, 1981).

Top level drawings present the following information: a. general equipment configuration, b. detailed spatial and dimensional relationships among control/display components, c. shapes and sizes of components, d. packaging details such as position of handles, fasteners, etc., and e. component nomenclature. Because the drawing deals only with gross physical dimensions, the evaluation of the MMI by means of drawings cannot encompass information transmission dimensions (although see the DEI methodology described later).

Much of the information the evaluator wishes to derive from the drawing must be inferred. For example, the fact that meters are shown on a drawing suggests a requirement for a monitoring function, but may not describe the nature of what is being monitored. Further information must be supplemented by other sources such as task analyses and operating procedures.

The development of equipment drawings begins very early in design and continues through various informal and formal design revisions until the drawing is released to production. Revisions are made as alternative design configurations are considered, revised, and refined. If the evaluator wishes to affect the design he is evaluating he cannot wait to evaluate until the final, agreed upon drawing, since by that time design details have hardened into concrete and his evaluation is largely irrelevant. When evaluation begins early in development, it becomes a part of the design-analytic process and thus more acceptable to the designer.

In evaluating the MMI drawing the evaluator begins with either a formal written procedure describing how the MMI will be utilized (although this may not be available—at least in detail—until after the drawing is completed and accepted), and/or a rough mental model of its operation. That is because behavioral design criteria are based on inferred relationships between the design, and the operator's future performance with that design. For example, in reviewing a control panel layout, the evaluator will ask questions such as: Are controls and displays laid out in accordance with sequence of operation? If this is not possible, because the operating sequence is nonsequential, are they laid out in accordance with the frequency with which controls must be operated or displays monitored? or the relative importance of controls and displays? or in terms of similar functions? (all controls mediating the same function located together). The evaluator thinks of the arrangement in terms of its possible effect on the ease with which the operating procedure will be learned and retained and the likelihood of error resulting from the arrangement. Some of the analytic products described previously (task analyses, OSDs, link analyses) can be of use here if they are available.

The evaluator can make use of a formal checklist containing the specific questions he should ask, but experienced specialists often memorize the most important questions. A later section will deal specifically with checklists as a class of evaluation tool.

The major aspects and factors to be concerned with in the evaluation of the MMI are: 1. characteristics of the individual controls and displays (size, shape); 2. input/output (control/display) relationships (are controls and displays that must be operated together located together?); 3. input/output characteristics such as stimulus brightness, duration, frequency of occurrence; 4. maintenance requirements (the existence of preventive maintenance inputs and outputs, such as calibration controls, test points and malfunction indicators); 5. the availability of feedback information concerning system status; 6. criticality of the equipment operation; 7. operator requirements (what the operator is supposed to do with the MMI); 8. environmental factors (where and under what conditions the equipment is to be operated); and 9. design constraints (the space in which the MMI is to be located). In consoles the evaluator will also be concerned with the height and width of the console in relation to the operator's seated or standing position; in cockpits where space is at a premium the evaluation will be concerned also with reach distance (distance between the seated pilot and each control he has to operate) and viewing envelope (what he can see beyond his windscreen).

A complete listing of all the questions that can be asked about a MMI would be lengthy and tedious at best. Some MMI checklists run to hundreds of questions, because for each relevant equipment characteristic an evaluation question can be generated. For practical reasons, however, most specialists do not evaluate to that degree of detail. Instead they scan the drawings to focus on their critical aspects, as suggested by the function of the equipment being designed.

The following are prerequisites for an effective evaluation of MMI drawings. The evaluator must have:

TABLE 7.1 Control/Display Characteristics That May Lead to Operator Error

Input Characteristics

1. Displays to be discriminated have many common characteristics.
2. Displays to be discriminated must be compared rapidly.
3. Events presented in displays change rapidly.
4. Inadequate visual feedback provided.
5. Low signal–to–noise ratio in detection displays.
6. Displays must be monitored over long periods.
7. Nature and/or timing of inputs cannot easily be anticipated.

Output Characteristics

1. Many controls must be operated in sequence or rapidly.
2. High degree of coordination required with other operators and panels.
3. Decisions are based on inputs from multiple sources.
4. Decision-making time is short.
5. Controls must be operated with excessive precision.

Physical Panel Characteristics

1. Controls and displays crowded together.
2. Controls and displays with differing functions not correctly distinguished.
3. Where there are many controls and displays, these are not organized in modules.
4. Controls not associated or associated only indirectly with corresponding displays.
5. Emergency, maintenance, and malfunction controls/displays mixed with operating controls/displays.
6. Nomenclature of different controls/displays too similar to each other.
7. Controls/displays located outside of optimal operating and viewing areas.
8. Critical controls not safeguarded.

1. A mental model, conceptualized as an operating procedure, of how the MMI is to be utilized.

2. Knowledge of the most important equipment characteristics that could negatively affect operator utilization of the equipment. A list of these, from Meister and Farr (1966b), is presented in Table 7.1.

3. Knowledge of the standards (primarily those in MIL-STD 1472C, Department of Defense, 1981) that apply to equipment dimensions.

4. Hypotheses about the potential effect of MMI dimensions/factors on the operator's performance.

In performing the evaluation the behavior specialist will mentally review the operating procedure in terms of the characteristics listed in Table 7.1 and will ask certain questions about that operation. Does the MMI possess any of these characteristics? Do any MMI characteristics conflict with applicable standards? Will any MMI characteristics lead the operator to make significant errors? (Note that quantitative HR analyses are not usually made as part of MMI evaluation.) Is an alternative design configuration possible and, if so, will it tend to reduce the potential for operator error?

It is necessary to determine that not only does a design inadequacy exist, but that its probable effect on operator performance will be seriously negative. The evaluator is not concerned with trivialities.

The product of the evaluation is a series of qualitative judgments indicating that such and such dimension or characteristic of the equipment is unsatisfactory. It is much easier to determine the negative attributes of the MMI than its positive ones. If a formal checklist is applied, it is possible to derive a quantitative figure of merit for the equipment represented by the drawing. This will be discussed later, but informal evaluations of drawings usually do not make use of checklists.

The evaluation of an MMI design based on a two-dimensional drawing is extremely crude. A more sophisticated examination of the MMI can be made when the latter is represented by a mockup, a prototype, or actual operational equipment, as in Seminara and Parsons (1979). However, by that time it may be too late to affect design.

Ideally, the evaluator would have access to a table of error probabilities associated with each equipment characteristic. But only the Data Store (Munger et al., 1962, Chapter Five), the closest to this ideal, exists and it is unsatisfactory for the purpose. Hence drawing evaluation places a premium on the imagination and creativity of the evaluator, especially when the MMI is complex. Data on the consistency with which MMI evaluation judgments are made during system development are almost nonexistent; and there is no way of assessing the validity of the evaluations made unless the MMI at each stage of its development is fabricated and personnel tested in its operation, which is never done. In a study by Meister and Farr (1966a) five "experts" were presented with nine control panel drawings and evaluated them using specified checklist items. Consistency among the evaluators was less than satisfactory. Nevertheless, given that one must evaluate the MMI from blueprints, it is hard to see how the process could be improved except by measurement of evaluator reliability and systematic training of specialists on the evaluation process. Most specialists simply fall into this type of evaluation without having been explicitly trained for it.

The evaluator's recommendations for MMI revisions should indicate the undesirable characteristic, the reason it is undesirable, the particular military standard provision it violates, nature of potential errors resulting from the characteristic and the criticality of those errors and suggested design modifications.

Evaluation of Procedures

The importance of the procedure is that it determines how the equipment and system will be operated. Inadequate procedures reduce the efficiency of system functioning, in severe cases effectively immobilizing the system.

Procedures are of various types. There are those for operation and maintenance, for individuals and crews, for individual equipments, subsystems, and the system as

TABLE 7.2 Standard for Evaluating Procedure Adequacy

An Effective Procedure Should Contain:

1. Identification information–number, title, date, revision number, page numbers, and final page number.
2. Statement of purpose; procedures to be completed previously; system conditions existing prior to use; precautions; equipment to which procedure is applicable; tools/test equipment required; other documents required; personnel qualifications needed to use procedure; and number of personnel needed.
3. All instructional information needed to perform procedure. If reference is made to other documents, the citation of these documents is precise, employing, for example, the page number.
4. Adequate quality control hold points; provision for verification/signoff of actions if required.
5. Information that is not overly complex (written in individual steps; single action per step; no more than three related actions per step).
6. Information that is specific (all actions specifically identified; equipment and equipment operating limits expressed quantitatively; equations up to date; in team procedure, primary performer with responsibility identified; graphics, charts and tables readible; no interpolation, extrapolation or extraction of values required).
7. All follow-up activities (post-procedure performance) clearly specified.
8. Contingency information (steps to take if equipment is performing out of tolerance).
9. Information that has been tested and verified as adequate for intended use and comprehensible by operators, using document review (by subject matter experts) and mock-up, simulator or walkthrough tests.

(Modified from Brune & Weinstein, 1980)

a whole. Some are highly detailed, step-by-step; others, general and gross. Because of the large number of procedures developed for systems of any size, the behavior specialist must select only those of greatest importance for evaluation.

A procedure can be evaluated in two ways. First the procedure is considered the surrogate of the job and the focus of the evaluation is the job design described by the procedure, rather than the procedure itself. In this evaluation the question asked is, Is this means of operating (or maintaining) the equipment adequate for the operator? Second, one can evaluate the procedure simply as a means of presenting information to the user, for example, the completeness and clarity of information presented, the amount of detail, etc. In the first case the evaluation criteria are those that have been described in Chapters 2 and 3; in the second one evaluates the procedure in terms of how well it communicates. The most effective evaluator will consider both aspects. Our disscussion, however, emphasizes communication of information because previous chapters have dealt with the job design.

It is of course necessary to establish in advance the attributes of a satisfactory procedure such as clarity, specificity, and detail. Once this has been done, one can evaluate that procedure by noting whether or not it possesses those characteristics (Table 7.2).

In shorthand form a procedure should contain the following:

1. A description of the equipment on which the task is to be performed;
2. All required setting up and securing operations;
3. A step-by-step, timed, if possible, sequence of instructions;
4. A listing of personnel required to perform the task;
5. Required safety precautions;
6. All critical operations emphasized;
7. Information about how to respond to contingency (e.g., emergency) events; and
8. Any additional reference procedures or technical data. (However, it is desirable, where feasible, to write all procedures out in full.)

Instructions should, if at all possible, be written in tabular checklist form similar to task analysis format (see Chapter Two):

1. Time at which the step is to be performed.
2. If the task as a whole requires more than one operator, the particular operator (by job title) who will perform the step.
3. The stimulus for the operator to initiate a procedural step.
4. The operator response required in terms of monitoring, deciding, manipulating.
5. Required communications.
6. Feedback display or communication.

Every procedural step should be capable of being analyzed into its component stimulus, response, and feedback elements, and each of these elements should be expressed clearly. If any element is missing or cannot be readily discerned by the user, there will be difficulty utilizing the procedure.

Procedures pass through various development stages in the same way as do equipment drawings. Procedures interact with equipment design. A procedural difficulty may require a design change, or a design revision may require a procedural change. The latter is more likely. Engineering test procedures in early development are often less detailed than procedures to be used by the customer, because the former assume a certain experiential background on the part of the user. The lack of detail found in early engineering procedures may present a problem to the evaluator. If one is evaluating a procedure as a communications/informational tool, later operational procedures—the ones to be placed in the hands of the user—are more significant for the evaluator.

The two major methods of procedural evaluation are by *inspection* of the written procedure and by *exercise* of the procedure in a walkthrough or by observation of actual operations. The exercise method requires a mockup or prototype equipment, which suggests later development. The exercise method inevitably intermingles evaluation of the job described by the procedure with evaluation of the characteristics of the procedure per se, but this may be useful because it helps to verify the adequacy of the job design. As with equipment drawings, if the evaluator wishes to have a substantial effect on the operation described by the procedure, his opportunities are maximized the earlier he begins. However, many procedures lag equipment design by substantial lengths of time. This may create difficulty if in examining the procedure the evaluator finds something wrong with a job design which has already been "cast in concrete."

The inspection method of procedure evaluation enables one to predict operator difficulty in using the procedure but qualitatively only, whereas the exercise method actually records that difficulty. It is possible to combine procedure evaluation with an error analysis (see Chapter 5) but this is almost never done when the focus of the evaluation is the procedure.

Procedure evaluation should be performed at different stages in system development: first, in initial design, using the inspection method as a means of examining the adequacy of design; later, in performance testing, to verify that the procedure is workable and is an adequate means of communicating information. Recommendations for procedure revision should state the step(s) that present problems, the nature of potential errors resulting, their criticality, and suggested modifications.

The Checklist as an Evaluation Tool

One tool used frequently by the behavioral specialist to evaluate design is the checklist—in written or mental form). The checklist is a series of statements that describe the individual attributes which an equipment or procedure ought to have to be properly human engineered. It is therefore only a short step from the creation of a standard to the development of a checklist in which that standard is incorporated.

The design checklist is usually broken up for convenience into sections corresponding to major equipment characteristics such as scales, counters, etc. Some checklists have spaces (*yes/no/not applicable/acceptable/nonacceptable*, etc.) to enable the evaluator to check off the response to the individual item.

Checklists describing product characteristics and designed by behavior specialists for human engineering evaluation purposes must be differentiated from procedural checklists, those used to tell operators what to do next in operating equipment—preflight checklists, for example. We are concerned only with the first.

Three aspects of checklist development are important.

1. *Determination of which MMI dimensions are important to personnel performance.* The MMI has many dimensions, such as size, shape, weight, color, number of controls, and displays; some of these are important, others less so. The checklist developer must select those that are most important in terms of affecting operator performance. Unfortunately, available standards do not help much because they do not differentiate equipment characteristics in terms of importance.

2. *Whichever dimensions are selected for incorporation in the checklist must be expressed in such a way that the checklist user is quite definite about what it*

describes. The level of detail with which the checklist item is described is probably important. However, lacking empirical test data, the best one can do is to be more rather than less detailed. The number of checklist items may also be important. There is probably some maximum number beyond which the evaluator tires of the task and/or the comparisons become less obvious and overly complex, but again we have no data on this.

3. Of lesser importance, *the checklist must be formatted*. Checklist items may be expressed as a positive statement demanding agreement or disagreement. They also may be phrased as questions. For example, Does the MMI manifest the following characteristics? Items may be verbal only or may include quantitative values and/or may be accompanied by an illustration of the dimension to be checked assuming, of course, that the dimension is capable of being illustrated.

How much these variations affect evaluation efficiency is not known. Obviously there is need for research but the checklist (unlike the rating scale—see Chapter 9) may appear to researchers as so mundane an instrument that there is little impetus to study its characteristics.

Since the items incorporated in the checklist represent selections from the total population of equipment characteristics that might affect performance, their selection represents a judgment (deliberate or unconscious) of relative importance and that judgment may be in error. Even if the item is important, it may be difficult to describe in verbal form or illustrate graphically. The items are selected on the basis of their presumed effect on operator performance. However, if data are lacking to support that presumed effect, checklist development is based largely on intuition.

The first few, most important, items in every checklist are likely to be the same, despite minor variations in wording. Variations are likely to be greater if less important equipment characteristics are included in the checklist.

It is in the level of specificity of the design characteristics to serve as an evaluation standard that we are most likely to encounter difficulty. One reason is in the hierarchy of abstraction that standard and checklist can represent.

Take the attribute, operability. At this level of abstraction (e.g., is this equipment operable?), it is impossible to make a meaningful evaluation since operability is a function of a number of specific characteristics such as the arrangement of controls and displays by function or procedure, color coding, and labeling. Obviously the use of an evaluative criterion, which merely asks if the control panel is operable, does not permit us to zero in on the factors responsible for operability.

One order of abstraction lower is the use of an evaluative criterion which asks a question phrased in terms of a standard (e.g., are functionally related controls and displays located in proximity to each other? as section 5.1.2.1 MIL-STD 1472C requires). This is more effective but still difficult to apply. Although one can determine which displays and controls are interrelated, the definition of what proximity means precisely is troublesome. What is the maximum distance that should separate interrelated controls and displays? Ideally the standard should specify some empirical value to represent the maximum separation permitted between interrelated controls and displays.

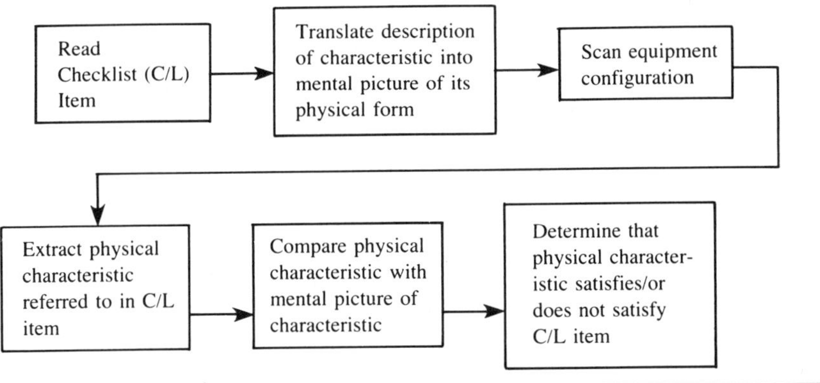

FIGURE 7.1. The checklist comparison process.

Checklists are *compilations* of items describing the individual characteristics of the equipment or procedure. That is because it is extremely difficult to evaluate design as a total package — as a single quality — because every equipment or procedure is itself a composite of many individual attributes, some of which are admirable, others less so. A global evaluation — even if one could make such a summary evaluation — would confuse these disparate elements. The checklist like the task analysis is based on the assumption that one can partition a total entity into individual elements.

The evaluator uses a checklist item in two ways: as a *mnemonic*, to remind him that an evaluation of a particular characteristic is required (this is easy), and *as a means of making a comparison* between the product and the standard reflected in the checklist item (this is not so easy).

The difficulty of this superficially simple comparison is indicated if one flow diagrams the process, as in Figure 7.1. If the checklist item is ambiguously written, the checklist user may have difficulty in construcing a mental picture of the characteristic. If the checklist item is not specific, he may have difficulty extracting from the drawing or procedure the characteristic referred to in that item. The greatest difficulty occurs in judging whether the attribute being evaluated does or does not satisfy the standard implicit in the checklist item, because the item is usually phrased in dichotomous terms (yes or no) and the characteristic as one sees it actually represents only one point on a continuum. Almost all checklist items are verbal and are compared with a pictorial representation or three-dimensional mockup or prototype equipment, a fact that increases the difficulty of using the checklist.

Checklists may be long or short, depending on the evaluator's concept of what is more or less important. If all possible equipment dimensions are used as checklist items, the checklist becomes impossibly long. For example, some developers have formatted the individual statements in MIL-STD 1472C (Department of Defense, 1981) as individual checklist items, making the checklist almost as long as the standard.

At the heart of the checklist is observation, a deceptively simple process. It is implicitly assumed that the evaluator can observe all the attributes included in the checklist but no tests to verify this point have been reported. Some complex equipment characteristics are very difficult to discern, even when the product being evaluated is an actual functioning equipment. For example, the dynamic characteristics of a display, such as the frequency of stimulus presentation and the amount of information transmitted are not readily observable because they are behavioral inferences from physical qualities. As systems become increasingly computerized, major equipment characteristics will become increasingly resistant to traditional human engineering criteria.

Another deficiency of the checklist is that it is binary. An attribute exists or it does not, but almost all attributes are continuous. A further deficiency is the lack of a method of deriving a quantitative figure of merit from the checklist. The checklist is used in system development mostly as a diagnostic tool to determine specific inadequacies that must be remedied. Very crude methods exist of quantizing a checklist evaluation, but with only dubious authority. For example, if the checklist consists of 100 relevant items representing supposedly the totality of significant characteristics for an equipment, one that checked-off as being satisfactory on 85 of these items would have an 85% adequacy score. What that really means is not clear. A score of 100% would presume that the characteristics in the checklist do, in fact, represent the totality of essential equipment dimensions and that they are all equally important, a very tenuous assumption at best.

One could combine the checklist with a rating scale. For each checklist item the evaluator would supply a rating of the extent to which the attribute was present or the degree of acceptability of the characteristic. Almost no checklists incorporate this feature and one wonders whether the evaluator could make a valid judgment of degree.

The checklist is a psychometric instrument but it has almost never been treated as such by its various developers. If it had, it would follow the conventional psychometric development process in which a. a pool of potential dimensions or standards is developed by soliciting suggestions from a number of behavioral experts; b. all redundant items are eliminated by some kind of paired comparison testing process; c. having winnowed the pool down to a smaller number of items, these are presented to personnel to be used in a standard stimulus situation, as with an equipment drawing; d. the results of the judgments made are statistically analyzed to determine, for example, inter- and intrajudge consistency; and e. inconsistent items are eliminated, etc.

We do not know whether the failure to produce a standard checklist using the psychometric process described above makes the checklists that are used invalid or less useful because there have been no empirical investigations of checklist development. A number of ergonomics checklists have been published for general use, for example, Malone, Shenk and Moroney, 1976; McAbee, 1961; Munger and Willis, 1959; Nuclear Regulatory Commission, 1981; U.S. Army Test and Evaluation Command, 1970; and Winter and Fremer, 1977. It is not clear whether these were developed using psychometric procedures. The author guesses not. Nor is it known whether those checklists developed informally by specialists for their individual use with a particular equipment or system do as well as the published versions.

Evaluation by means of a checklist is therefore less than completely satisfactory to the methodologic purist because of its serious conceptual and technical inadequacies. Yet it has one overwhelming advantage: apparent simplicity. In the hurly burly of system development, evaluators tend to reject more cumbersome if more accurate and sophisticated techniques—like those we shall describe next—in favor of easier ones.

The Display Evaluative Index and the Analytic Profile System

The two evaluative methods described in this section (Siegel, Miehle and Federman, 1964; Fischl and Siegel, 1970) are considerably more formal and sophisticated than those described previously. Although they have been used comparatively little, they are presented here to suggest how methods can be developed on the basis of theoretical principles. The *display evaluative index* (DEI) applies principles of information transfer. The *analytic profile system* (APS) applies multidimensional scaling and factor analysis methodology.

The Display Evaluative Index. The purpose of the DEI is to compare two or more design variations of the same equipment without constructing models or mockups. The technique evaluates the ability of system displays to transfer information to the operator and of the operator to process the information and perform required control actions.

The display evaluative index reflects the following information transfer principles. All else being equal, that system is best which

1. requires the least operator information processing per subtask unit;
2. has the greatest directness between the information transmitters (displays) and the receivers (controls);
3. has the least difference between the amount of information presented by an indicator and that required for a control action;
4. provides for redundancy of information;
5. requires the least intermediate data processing by the operator before he can perform the required control action;
6. has the least number of information sources and sinks (indicators and controls);
7. imposes the least amount of time stress on the operator as he performs the information processing;
8. has the least number of transfers which cannot be accomplished within a prescribed time;
9. possesses the least number of critical transfers; and
10. has displays and controls which are optimally encoded.

Each of these aspects is represented by a factor which varies from zero to one, the latter when the system is perfect with respect to the aspect. The DEI is the product of all factors involved, each suitably weighted by means of an exponent. Thus DEI varies between zero and one. Wisely the developers make no claim that a single numerical value of the DEI will indicate the absolute merit of a particular equipment. Rather, the DEI values for alternative designs of the same equipment rank the designs along a continuum representing information transfer effectiveness.

In applying DEI a chart representing the information transfers involved in task performance is drawn (see Figure 7.2). Transfer of information between an indicator and control is indicated by a link (line) between the two elements. If intermediate data processing is required, this is represented by a box inserted in the link, creating a total of two links. If information from two or more indicators is required for setting a control, a gate symbol, ▷ , is used to connect the indicators and the control. If a control is actuated on the basis of one out of several indicators, a mixer symbol ▷ is used in the link between the indicators and control.

The factors in the DEI are represented by the following.

1. *Complexity factor* (previous principles 1, 4): Each link is assigned a weight according to the amount and complexity of the information transfer involved. A box has a "link" weight of four while other link weights vary from zero to two. The rationale for the derivation of the link weights in accordance with the probability of successful information transfer is found in Siegel, Miehle and Federman (1962). Since the sum of the link weights (Σw) may equal zero, this factor is represented as $1/1 + \Sigma w$. Its greatest value is then one and it approaches zero as Σw *increases indefinitely*.

2. *Directness factor* (principle 2): The ideal system has one and only one link between each indicator and control. Although redundancy (indicated by the presence of an ▷ symbol in the transfer diagram) reduces the probability of operator error, a multiplicity of links to or from an element is, nevertheless, an undesirable feature. The factor which has a value of 1 under these conditions is

$$\frac{(n+m)_u^2}{2N(n+m)_t} \qquad (7.1)$$

where $(n+m)_u$ is the number of used indicators and controls, $(n+m)_t$ is the total number of indicators and controls, and N is the total number of information and instruction links. The lower limit of this factor is zero.

3. *Data transfer factor* (principles 5, 6): The minimum size system possesses one indicator, one control, and no logical operator functions. This suggests the form $2/Q + n_0$, which yields a value of unity when these conditions apply. Q is the number of gate, mixer, or box symbols on the tranfer chart.

4. *Encoding factor* (principle 10): This factor applies only when an equipment contains one or more indicators or controls which possess twelve or more independent states which are presented or controlled through on/off lights or pushbuttons. Optimal coding is a minimal decimal representation. For example, the ideal arrangement for representing fifty-six states in terms of on/off components would involve a units representation of ten parts (0–9) and a tens representation of

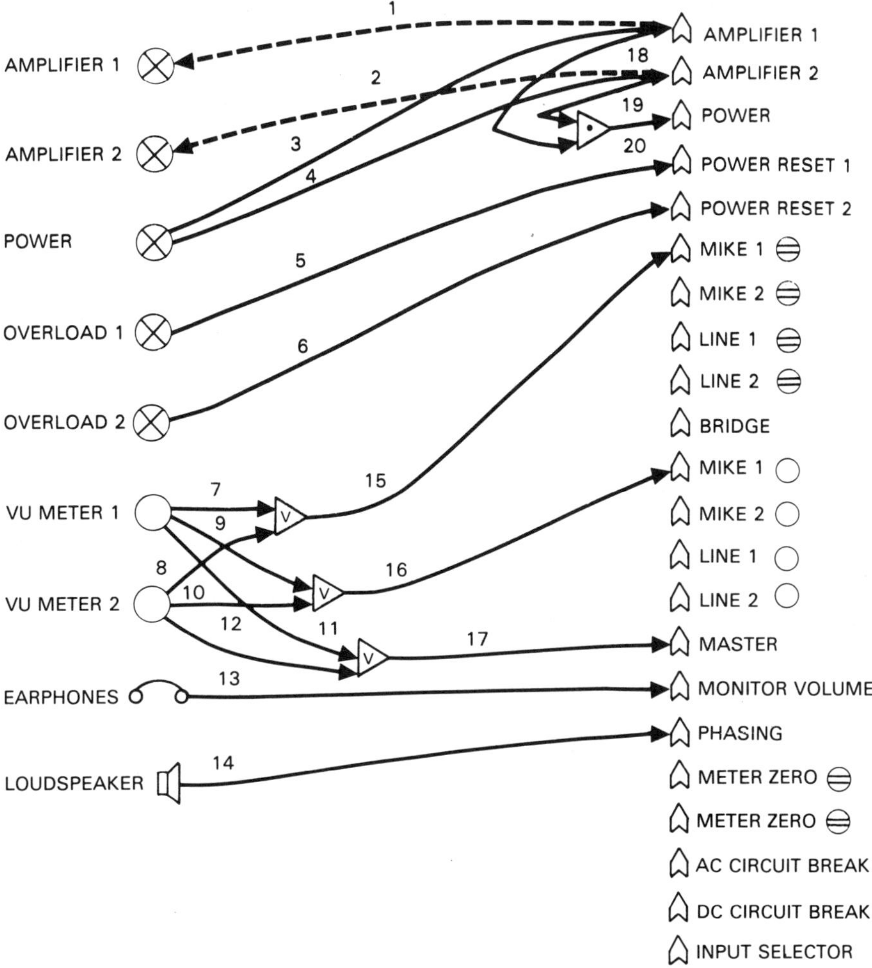

FIGURE 7.2. Transfer chart for public address set (numbers refer to sequential actions).

six parts (0–5)—a total of sixteen parts. The value of the factor (R) for each indicator or control is given by the lesser of either $r|q$ or $q|r$, where q is the actual number of parts and r is the ideal number in an indicator or control. When these values are equal, R is equal to 1. The overall factor ($\bar{R}$) is the product of all the (R) factors. The value of R for various values of Q is given in Siegel et al., 1964.

5. *Time factor* (principles 7, 8): For each subtask which has a prescribed time for execution, the quantity.

$$\left[\frac{1}{16}\ I \left(\frac{T'}{T}\right)^{3}\right], \tag{7.2}$$

is calculated, where I is the total information (in digits), T is the total time required for subtask completion, and T' is the prescribed time for subtask completion. T may be calculated from the formula, $T = 0.15 + 0.49I_d$, where I_d is the number of digits.

For subtasks in which the required time T is greater than the prescribed time T', the quantity,

$$\left[I\left(\frac{T}{T'} - 1\right)\right], \tag{7.3}$$

is also calculated. The critical time factor is given by:

$$\exp \frac{1}{16}\left[\Sigma I \left(\frac{T}{T'}\right)^3 + \Sigma I \left(\frac{T}{T'} - 1\right)\right] \tag{7.4}$$

When there are no time critical subtasks, exp(0) = 1, that is, the factor is not applied.

6. *Match factor* (principle 3): This factor enters when there is more or less information supplied than is needed for the required act. The mismatch is this difference. The match factor uses the sum of the absolute information differences in logarithmic units and is given by

$$\exp(\Sigma|M) \tag{7.5}$$

For a perfect match $\Sigma|M = 0$, therefore exp (0) = 1 and there is no effect on the DEI.

7. *Critical link factor* (principle 9): This factor takes the form, $\exp(N_c)/10$, where N_c is the number of critical links and a critical link represents a transfer which is not accomplished correctly, cannot be repeated, and causes task failure.

The final formula for the DEI is:

$$\frac{(n+m)_u \sqrt[4]{(R)}\exp\left(-\frac{1}{4}\left[\Sigma I\left(\frac{T}{T'} - 1\right) + \frac{1}{16}\Sigma I \left(\frac{T}{T'}\right)^3 + \frac{N_c}{10} + \Sigma|M|\right]\right)}{(1 + \Sigma w)\sqrt{N(n+m)_t(Q + n_0)}} \tag{7.6}$$

According to Siegel et al. (1964) this can be calculated by hand or on a digital computer from data obtained directly from the transfer chart and the task application.

To test user reliability two or three subjects applied DEI to several variations of each of six different equipments. For four tasks the ranking agreement was perfect and for two tasks the rank–order correlation coefficient was .93. DEI empirical validity was determined by exponentially weighting the factors according to criteria of maximum agreement between the mean opinion of a group of four engineers and psychologists and the results of the DEI applied to several design variations of each of six different equipments. This preliminary weighting was later cross validated by applying DEI with the derived weights to variations of six other equipments and comparing the obtained DEI values with the composite ranking of the individual equipments of a different pool of four human factors experts.

The correlations between the mean opinion of the experts on the relative adequacy of the displays and their DEI values ranged from 0.60 to 0.82 which is quite good for an instrument of this type. The technique was capable of differentiating among even minor design variations, for example, changing a display face.

If the DEI has not been used extensively for evaluation of MMI alternatives, it may be because the information needed is not easily available in early design and in any case requires fairly complex judgments of the evaluator. Although the developers feel that anyone with some grasp of basic algebra can handle the technique (Siegel et al., 1964), the two days required to complete the analysis and the computations are probably excessive for most development specialists. Moreover, this methodology is not designed for evaluation of a single design product and in this respect cannot substitute for a checklist.

Analytic Profile System

The APS was developed in part as an effort to overcome the complexity of DEI. It is a paper and pencil display evaluation instrument for use in evaluating a display relative to seven dimensions. It utilizes a forced choice judgmental format, but is not a checklist. It does not provide the same kind of information as the usual checklist of desired characteristics and should not be used by those who are seeking the type of information checklists provide.

The Analytic Profile System can evaluate almost any type of visual display, but it must be used by individuals with some background in behavioral technology or display design. The developers (Fischl and Siegel, 1970) maintain that "inasmuch as the use of the APS involves making judgments about the display(s) being evaluated, individuals without this background may lack the conceptual basis for performing a maximally valid evaluation. . . ." The same might be said of the DEI.

The Analytic Profile System was developed on the basis of a multidimensional scaling and factor analysis resulting from tests involving 12 displays, two display formats and three subject groups (Siegel and Fischl, 1971). There are seven factors isolated.

1. *Stimulus numerosity* (SN). Volume of material displayed. The more material, the higher SN.
2. *Primary coding* (PC). Refers to general format of the entire display and its appropriateness for conveying information.
3. *Contextual discrimination* (CD). Ease of differentiating relevant from irrelevant information.

4. *Structure scanning* (SS). Ease with which an observer would be able to organize the stimuli presented to him into meaningful structure.
5. *Critical relationships* (CR). Ease with which an observer would be able to order relationships described in the display.
6. *Cue integration* (CI). Ease with which an observer would be able to integrate cues and pertinent information.
7. *Cognitive processing activity* (CA). Extent to which the display facilitates or inhibits decision making.

The seven dimensions or factors are presented in a 35-item forced-choice format. Each item has 4 alternatives, two equally favorable to the display, and two equally unfavorable. The equating of favorable and unfavorable items was determined by previous analysis. Each alternative is a brief prose statement about some aspect of visual displays. In using the APS to evaluate a display the evaluator checks one of the four alternatives which is most descriptive of the display and one which is least descriptive. Each item is keyed to a different display dimension.

Space does not permit presentation of the full APS but Figure 7.3 shows an example of a representative item.

APS scoring is easily accomplished through use of a separate stencil sheet (template) for each of the 12 pages of the APS booklet.

Reliability and validity of the instrument have been examined (Fischl and Siegel, 1970) using two human factors specialists who independently applied the APS to eight visual displays. The product moment correlation between the total APS scores yielded by the evaluators was .98, which is encouraging even though only two subjects were involved. The between rater product moment correlation for each of the seven subscales varied from .91 for SS to .97 for PC and CR, with the other subscales between these two values.

The predictive validity of the APS was also investigated. Two specialists applied the APS to 24 stimulus variations of two basic display types. Ten college students were then trained to proficiency in the operation of these displays and were given a performance test requiring use of the displays in solving operational (command/control) problems. Point biserial correlations were computed between APS scores on each of the seven dimensions and performance scores dichotomized by the two display types. The total APS score validity coefficient was .87, with each of the dimensions correlating between .79 and .88 except for cognitive processing activity which was only .52.

The Analytic Profile System provides two types of scores—one, a descriptive profile of the display being evaluated, the other, a quantitative reflection of the evaluator's overall opinion of the display.

The profile describes graphically the score a display attains on each of the seven dimensions and indicates best and worst aspects of the display. Another way of using the profile is to compare two displays on the same dimensions.

Since neither DEI nor APS is much used in system development one must ask, Why? Here are techniques that are sophisticated, solidly grounded in theoretical and

	Most Descriptive	Least Descriptive
a. Materials of the same type are generally similar appearing and differentiable from materials of different types.	a.	
b. Major relationships, which are important for interpretation of the situations displayed, do not seem readily perceptible.	b.	
c. Because of the format and the coding scheme, interpretation is fairly straightforward.	c.	
d. There may be a problem of maintaining attention because of the large number of stimuli appearing in the visual field.	d.	

FIGURE 7.3. A representative item from The Analytic Profile System.

statistical methodology and they are not used. Granted DEI is cumbersome, but APS is apparently quite simple for the user.

Beyond the obvious problems of technology transfer from researchers to practitioners and the resistance that practitioners manifest, there are two difficulties. First, users must be able to make the judgments required by these instruments. We have had occasion previously to question whether all the judgments required by checklists can be made easily and reliably and the question reappears here. Discriminations derived from factor analysis may be somewhat artificial to an unpracticed user and hence difficult to make. Second, the logic behind a method must be clearly understandable by the user or he will tend to reject the method. The logic in DEI is very sophisticated and in APS is not immediately obvious to the user. Many human factors engineers working in development consider what they do as art rather than science (Meister, 1979), meaning presumably that their practices derive from an inner logic. They may tend therefore to prefer a methodology closely linked to the realities in which they work, which derives naturally, from that work.

PERFORMANCE EVALUATION METHODS

Mockups

In this section we describe the development and use of three-dimensional models and mockups to conduct performance tests on the MMI and the facility (e.g., cockpit, workplace) in which the MMI is located. The term mockup will be used henceforth to describe both models and mockups.

Mockups are full-scale simulations of the physical characteristics of equipment and systems. A model is a reduced scale representation. Both can be developed only after equipment drawings are produced, although these drawings may be only preliminary ones. The model is less useful than a mockup because it can deal with fewer MMI dimensions.

The reduced scale model can however be quite useful for some applications such as workplace layout. The author was once part of a human factors team which was assigned responsibility to arrange the layout of facilities and equipment within a maintenance area aboard a ship (Pope, Williams and Meister, 1978). A 1/12 scale model was built. Internal components were arranged in various configurations and measured to determine accessibility and travel distance required for each configuration. The best arrangement was selected for implementation.

The mockup, unlike other system products, is not automatically derived from routine system development processes. It is essentially a tool to assist system development by enhancing conceptualization of the MMI and permitting limited equipment testing. The behavior specialist does not evaluate the mockup as a product of system development. He evaluates the MMI represented by the mockup and he uses the mockup as a device with which to conduct evaluations. Even when not contractually required, mockups are so useful that all major system development efforts and many minor ones construct them.

The types of models and mockups are:

1. two-dimensional reduced scale model used for preliminary room layout and equipment location studies, in presentations, design reviews, and documentation. It is simple, inexpensive, lightweight and portable;
2. two-dimensional full scale mockup used for initial control panel layout studies. Reveals potential error likelihood, visibility, and reach problems,
3. three-dimensional reduced scale mockup, used as in (1). See Meister and Farr, 1966b, pages 105 to 115 for methods of developing control panel mockups.
4. three-dimensional static, full scale mockup. The uses are in Table 7.3; and
5. functional full scale mockup. The uses are as in Table 7.3.

Table 7.3 indicates the applications that can be made of mockups in system development phases. The two most important types of mockup are the *static* and the *functioning* mockup.

A static mockup is usually a three-dimensional full scale replica of an equipment or an assembly which will be, or has been designed, in prototype form. A complete system in very precise detail is rarely mocked up because unless the system is a small one, it is expensive to develop a full scale system mockup, although mockups of new aircraft are quite common. Generally the most critical equipment items, or ones which present potentially severe developmental problems, are selected for mockup.

The static mockup can neither be programmed to demonstrate the functions of the operating equipment nor can it be operated by personnel to perform operational routines, except on a simulated, "walk-through" basis. Also, some indicators may be illuminated but will not change functions. The static mockup may be inexpensively fabricated of materials such as plywood or cardboard and, depending on how sophisticated its makers wish it to be, may or may not contain actual controls, displays, or other hardware components.

TABLE 7.3 Mockup Applications in the System Development Cycle

Design/Development Phase	Mockup Application
Exploratory Development (concept formulation)	To develop and portray concepts of equipment configurations and room layouts. To document concepts with photographs of the mockups. To identify potential problem areas and additional study requirements.
Advanced Development (preliminary design)	To aid in the preliminary design of equipment operating and maintenance control panels. To aid in the identification of design requirements for ease of maintenance of equipment, for example, accessibility features, access covers, mounting hardware, test point locations, etc. To develop preliminary specifications for equipment operability and maintainability. To aid in design reviews. To document developed design for test and experimentation.
Engineering Development (detailed design)	To aid in detailed design of equipment panels, packaging and mounting characteristics, room arrangement, cable and duct routing, and accessibility features. Design review and presentation vehicle. To aid in developing preliminary installation, operating, and maintenance procedures.
Operational Systems Development (production/operation)	To refine installation procedures and to familiarize installation personnel with procedures. As a tool for reconfiguration management and control. To familiarize operational and maintenance personnel with the system. As a training aid.

Source: Modified from Buchaca, N.J. *Models and Mockups as Design Aids*. Technical Document 266, Revision A, Naval Ocean Systems Center, San Diego, CA, 1 July 1979 (AD A109511).

Its internal dimensions are usually those of the anticipated prototype or production equipment—(assuming these dimensions have been determined). Models of the major internal components should be included in the mockup to check their accessibility in a given workspace arrangement. If necessary they can be constructed of cardboard. If no single internal layout has been decided on, the human engineer can try these models in the various positions under consideration, thereby helping to establish the most desirable alternative positions. From an external packaging standpoint, the mockup will be an essentially exact replica of the outside envelope of the proposed equipment, but greater attention should be paid those internal dimensions which are relevant to the work place and the component panels, modules, controls, and displays included in that workplace. Unless it is expected that the mockup will be used to proof out ducting, tubing, or other equipment interfaces prior to production, tolerances need be only approximate.

The purpose of the static mockup is to permit the designer to make certain evaluational studies requiring a three-dimensional projection. For example, a static mockup can be used to: 1. evaluate and decide among alternative equipment arrangements, 2. determine workspace difficulties in simulated operational tasks, 3. discover accessibility problems in simulated maintenance operations, 4. plan the optimal location and routing of wiring harnesses, cabling, and piping, the location of junction and terminal boxes, connectors, etc., and 5. demonstrate a proposed or accepted configuration to the customer.

From a behavioral standpoint the mockup's three-dimensional characteristics can be used to check on the accuracy of previous equipment drawing evaluations and to answer operability questions which could not be resolved with previous two-dimensional drawings. For the first time a real study can be made of the accessibility and workspace arrangement characteristics of maintainability design.

One of the attractive features of simple static mockups is that they can be readily changed to agree with design changes. Indeed, if these changes are sufficiently great, as in proceeding from one prototype to another, another mockup may be built quite easily.

The decision to build a mockup will depend on whether the questions it is designed to answer can be answered with this technique faster, more adequately, and more cheaply than by other methods. The development of mockups after hardware is available is pointless expense, unless the mockup can do something that the hardware cannot—which is unlikely—, or unless the actual hardware is not available to the specialist for testing. Therefore, from the standpoint of utility, the simplest static mockups developed as early as possible have the greatest value. The advantage of sophistication in static mockups is lost if the sophistication takes excessive time to provide.

A functional mockup is a three-dimensional full-scale simulation which can function in a quasioperational manner by automatic programming or by manual operation. The most sophisticated of such mockups may utilize microcomputers and be indistinguishable from a simulator. Along with somewhat less sophisticated mockups which do not utilize a computer, they can be operated by personnel to perform all routine and emergency operating and minor maintenance sequences. The next less sophisticated mockup can be operated by personnel to perform all routine operating and maintenance sequences, but not emergency operations. Still less complex mockups can be operated by personnel to perform routine operating sequences. Normal maintenance or emergency sequences cannot be simulated. The least sophisticated mockup cannot be operated by personnel but can be activated to demonstrate a preprogrammed sample of normal and/or emergency operating routines.

Within these rough categories mockups may vary in terms of how much operational hardware is included and the degree to which a computer is used—and how. Almost every functional mockup has some static elements, since a complete working model of the equipment would be equivalent to the actual hardware. No functional mockup completely reproduces the performance of the actual equipment. To do so would require expensive simulation of minor and perhaps irrelevant environmental stimuli. For example, in building a mockup of electronic equipment to be used aboard a ship, there would be little point in incorporating the ship's motion (pitching, rolling) in the device, unless an interaction between the operation of the device and the ship's motion were anticipated.

Functional mockups are most often built in the later stages of system design because they require a great deal of time to develop and very detailed hardware information, neither of which is usually available early in development. Hardware information, in particular, is subject to major changes in early design.

Detailed discussion of the physical construction of mockups would take us a bit away from the major topic of this chapter, but Buchaca (1982) is an excellent source. A great variety of possibilities exist. Materials can be cardboard, foamboard, wood, plexiglass, metal or moldings/castings; panel faces of equipment can be fixed or removable and utilize tape, adhesive or magnetic backing; elements of equipment panel faces can be fixed or removable, have two or three-dimensional attachments and be either representative in general of or the actual controls and displays to be used in the equipment.

The evaluations performed in static mockups can be either *observational* (using a human engineering checklist to record judgments) or *demonstrational*. In the former, equipment components can be placed in various positions within a mockup and estimates made of the adequacy of their placement. In the demonstrational mode subjects simulate the performance of tasks by pointing to controls they would activate and displays they would read. Reach envelope and component accessibility can be determined on a performance basis. The distance the subject must move from a fixed position to grasp a control can be measured exactly by photographing a light attached to the moving limb, but such a level of sophistication is not often required. Simple observation will often indicate, although roughly, whether controls are located in reasonable positions.

If the mockup contains actual equipment which maintenance personnel would ordinarily check, the evaluator can have a subject perform the check while he observes for difficulties. Listed are certain of the tasks that can be performed.

1. Finding various components of the equipment in response to instructions.
2. Connecting and disconnecting cables or tracing harnesses.
3. Climbing or descending to reach a component that must be checked or removed.
4. Reaching for and manipulating controls.
5. Removing and replacing cover plates.
6. Finding test points.
7. Removing/replacing circuit boards or other internal components.
8. Reading labels within the equipment, with or without special lighting.
9. Performing visual inspection of components as in looking for cracks, holes, cuts, leaks, etc.

The functional mockup can of course be used in a static mode for checklist evaluations, but this negates its primary value which is to study the performance of operators—not maintenance personnel—in a simulated operational situation. With the functional mockup the specialist is now able, for the first time, to evaluate the adequacy of the equipment's operating characteristics and procedures in relation to operator performance in a simulated operational situation.

The advantages of a dynamic mockup, at least with regard to changing displays, can be achieved with only modest cost by using 35 mm. slide presentations of new displays (Gravely and Hitchcock, 1980). The slide can be either a photograph of an actual display or an artist's rendition. The projector mechanism can be a random access slide projector or video tape system linked to a timer. With such a mockup it is possible to study perceptual and decision-making aspects of systems.

If the functional mockup is sophisticated enough so that operational procedures can be performed in their entirety, the evaluator can approximate a true system test by determining whether the operator can perform the functions assigned to him, how long it takes him to do these, the types of errors he makes and his error rate, and the problems he encounters. These data are of course only an approximation because the functional mockup is not being exercised *in* the operational environment. Where that environment has a significant effect on the operator and system performance, such as buffeting from wind and waves, only an operational system test (described in Chapter 8) or a very realistic simulator will permit a completely valid evaluation. To the extent that the evaluator can vary equipment configurations, operating situations or environments (e.g., terrain), it is now possible to apply experimental design procedures to the mockup test. Certain limitations of the mockup test will almost always be encountered, however. Corrective maintenance cannot be studied outside the actual operational environment. Unless the mockup is also a sophisticated simulator it will not be possible to study personnel responses to emergencies.

Unless the mockup approximates a sophisticated simulator, it is a small stage upon which to perform an evaluation. But it is tremendously important until development produces prototype equipment.

Further examples of mockup use can be secured from Hawkins (1974), McLane, Weingartner and Townsend (1966), Janousek (1970) and Seminara and Gerrie (1966).

Walkthroughs

The *walkthrough* is a simulation of, rather than an actual, equipment operation. It can be performed with a static mockup or with prototype equipment which is as yet not functioning. The purpose of the walkthrough is to check the adequacy of design and to discover problems requiring rectification. Like the other techniques described in this chapter, the walkthrough is only partially an evaluation methodology. Its diagnostic aspect is equally or—in the minds of developers even more—important.

The walkthrough can be performed in several ways. It can be performed mentally, so that the evaluator imagines or pretends that he is carrying through the procedural steps involved in operating the equipment. Or the simulation can be partly realistic, so that the evaluator or a test operator points to or touches the mockup or actual control to be activated or display to be read.

I once participated in a nuclear power control room design assessment in which the control room was mocked up with full scale two-dimensional cardboard/paper representations of the control panels arranged in accordance with initial design. Test personnel were two highly experienced operators who followed standard procedures. The following description is only slightly modified from Starkey, Lutz and Donohoo (1982, pp. 2–40 through 2–43).

During the walkthroughs at the start of each procedure, the operator was stationed in front of the plant control console—the normal operating station—and the initial plant conditions were defined. The operator indicated where these conditions could be monitored, that is which control room displays provided the information. The first step of the procedure was then read aloud. The operator proceeded to whatever locations were necessary, explaining what controls and displays were required to implement the task, what positions or readings were expected, what the operator expected the system response time to be, and any other pertinent data. The actual controls and displays were explicitly touched or tapped with a pointer, to preclude the operator's body blocking the videotape camera, and each item was identified by its panel item identification number. The engineers observing interpreted the accuracy or intent of a step, if doubt existed, and simulated parameter readings where necessary. Once the evaluators had gathered all the data they needed, the next step was read. The initial walkthroughs frequently took as long as five hours each, slowly stepping through the first time and answering all the questions. With increased experience on the task, this time naturally decreased to an hour for some of the later procedures, especially since several evolutions were part of earlier procedures.

In addition, for those procedures that were time critical, a second walkthrough was conducted with no interruptions for questions. The operator performed actions as close to real time as possible, from the locations where actions were taken, and with a minimum of verbalization. A separate data sheet was prepared for every step of the procedure. Notes were also made directly on the mockup panels with a nonpermanent marker. The information gathered for each step included where the operator had to go (the particular control panel to be operated), which controls and displays were used identified by panel item numbers, the cues used to identify when to start and stop the action, the feedback provided, required communications, possible backup modes of operation or other redundant sources of information, and any obvious potential errors and likely consequences.

At the conclusion of the walkthroughs, the participants reviewed all data sheets and marks made on the panels during the walkthroughs. They also generated the list of comments, deficiencies, and recommendations defining the nature of the problem, its possible adverse effect on operations, and suggested improvements or recommendations.

The walkthrough in which a procedure is simulated with the use of highly expert personnel contains elements of analysis, since the personnel are asked to introspect, analyze those cues they respond to, and review data gathered for completeness. This is possible only when highly trained personnel act as evaluation subjects. They are also interviewed and may be asked to complete a questionnaire concerning their interpretation of the operating situation and its adequacy.

In a walkthrough of a nonfunctioning prototype equipment, the static mockup evaluation is replicated, except that now the realism of the situation is improved.

Developmental Tests

The Department of Defense (see Holshauser, 1977) specifies that certain tests will be conducted during development and denotes them as *developmental tests* (DT). Developmental tests are required for all acquisition programs and are conducted in each major system development phase.

Developmental tests are engineering equipment tests designed, in almost all cases, to study equipment design characteristics. They include tests of breadboards and prototypes, first production articles, qualification tests, and engineering mockup inspections. Since developmental tests are specifically oriented to equipment purposes, their objectives often fail to encompass human factors. Nevertheless, it is sometimes possible for the evaluator to gather information of behavioral value from these tests. Many developmental tests will have too narrow a focus, for example, tests of materials, nondestructive reliability tests, but the specialist ought to be on the lookout for those that have some value for him. Those include any test that involves the MMI, a test in which personnel take part by playing the role of operators and any conducted in the operational environment. Any tests which, in addition, reproduce some of the conditions under which the operational system will perform may be particularly useful.

The methods used to secure behavioral data from developmental tests do not differ substantially from those used with mockups, such as the recording of performance time and errors made, use of checklists, observations, and interviews. If there is an advantage of the developmental test over the mockup, it is that the equipment used is more realistic, although actual test operations may not be. It is also desirable to review official test records but it is unlikely that much of behavioral interest will be found there.

If the tests are suitable for behavioral evaluation, it may be possible to secure information to answer the following questions.

1. *Performance times.* How long did the operator take to perform his job? Was this time excessively long? Very short? Did any of the tasks performed require a particularly long time? Why? Lacking control over the tests, the evaluator may be reduced to time personnel performance with a stop watch and to record data on a clipboard. Because of the nonoperational character of these tests, time data will be at best only suggestive. If any tasks require an excessively long time (assuming no equipment breakdown contributes to that time), it may suggest the inadequacy of some aspect associated with the task such as improper job design or inadequate procedures. Ask the designer about what constitutes acceptable performance time.

2. *Errors.* If a formal procedure exists to which personnel are supposed to adhere, the number and type of errors made by test personnel may be significant and indicate some inadequacy in the task in which the error was made.

3. *Malfunctions.* If, as often happens early in development, malfunctions occur, the evaluator may be able to observe some troubleshooting. However, unless design is stable by the time of the test, design changes may make the troubleshooting information obsolete. Moreover, one cannot say that an isolated troubleshooting exercise validly represents the majority of corrective maintenance actions that will be taken when the system becomes operational.

4. *Interviews.* Information of behavioral value can often be secured from interviewing test personnel concerning their reactions to the equipment and procedures and any special difficulties they experienced.

The great disadvantage of gathering data from developmental tests is that they *are* developmental. This means that unless design is more or less stable at the time of the test, a changing system configuration may render the collected information useless for other than design improvement purposes. If a developmental test indicates a system inadequacy, the system is likely to be changed, which is exactly the reason for the test. The evaluator may wish to consider just how stable design is before he endeavors to collect his data.

COMMENTARY

In comparison with the more sophisticated analytic techniques described previously, evaluation methods used in system development are few in number and appear somewhat primitive. Why this should be is unclear.

In fact, these evaluation methods are more effective as diagnostic tools than as instruments to derive a summary quantification of effectiveness, something like a figure of merit. This is perhaps because for diagnosis one does not need great precision. There are tremendous conceptual difficulties in evaluating a product in terms of a single point value or even a profile of values. Does one think of effectiveness in terms of anticipated performance with the product or are there other criteria? What does it mean to say that a product will be 85 percent or 95 percent effective?

It may be that the evaluation methods appear more primitive than the analytic ones because they derive more directly from the developmental situation. It is, for example, natural to check-off certain attributes that equipment or procedures ought to have. This leads to the development of a checklist. The evaluator is not, as in the case of analytic methods, attempting to measure unobservable intervening variables or mechanisms. Of the methods described in this chapter only DEI and APS depend much on theory. Since both emphasize unobserved mechanisms and variables derived from factor analysis, they contain a considerable element of sophisticated analysis.

If there is considerable informality about developmental evaluation methods, it may be because they are linked to the opportunity to measure performance, such as the availability of drawings and of developmental tests. This is in contrast to the somewhat greater independence the behavior specialist has in initiating analyses. Because of this informality, the documentation describing evaluation is comparatively small, as the reader may determine by comparing the list of references for this chapter with that for most of the preceding chapters.

Another possible reason for the apparent lack of sophistication in developmental evaluation is that, in many if not most cases, one is evaluating a single product (a drawing, say) against a written or mental attribute standard. This as opposed to comparing two products. Comparative performance evaluations have available to them fairly sophisticated experimental designs. Moreover, in making a comparison one need select only the most overt and concrete measures of effectiveness to conduct the comparison. This is in contrast to the evaluation of the single product in terms of attributes because by the nature of attribute evaluation one must use all the attributes of importance if one wishes to secure a valid estimate of the product's effectiveness.

To evaluate a single product requires 1. that one conceptualize a set of desired attributes, 2. determine that these are meaningful for personnel performance, 3. characterize these attributes in such a way that they can be recognized and extracted from the product, 4. place the attribute being evaluated on a scale, and 5. assign the attribute for the individual product a particular scale value. A scale based on a continuum of what? Anticipated operator performance? This is the key problem. Attribute evaluation, which seems very appropriate for multidimensional scaling and factor analysis, is extremely complex and, to date, no one has satisfactorily developed a set of design product attributes that can be scaled. Very few researchers have tried to do so.

Because we lack quantitative "figures of merit" for individual design attributes, the evaluator adopts a back door approach in which he attempts to evaluate the total MMI (rather than individual attributes) in terms of the operator performance anticipated with that equipment. Given an operating procedure or detailed task analysis describing how the MMI will be utilized, it should be possible to apply the Human Reliability procedures described in Chapter Five to equipment drawings and procedures. Ideally,the specialist would have "look up" tables in which to pick out different classes of MMI based on combinations of design characteristics and could extract a single MMI human reliability figure of merit for that MMI. However, we lack this capability, because there is no completely satisfactory database. And although the methods described in Chapter 5 for quantitative evaluation are quite sophisticated, particularly the mathematical models, they may be too sophisticated for the rough and ready development environment in which one is handed on MMI drawing or procedure and asked to evaluate it on the spot.

Even actual measurements of performance time and the counting of errors in mockup tests which in theory should allow us to establish a performance oriented figure of merit do not suffice because our test samples are usually quite small and — more important — we lack standards with which to compare our empirical data. For example, if in a mockup test of a new command/control equipment each of six subjects operating the simulated controls makes on the average 2.3 errors, is this good, bad, or indifferent performance? If the errors are highly critical ones, one can perhaps say that performance is poor yet it is difficult to say from this that the new equipment is poorly designed. Even performance data will not avail if the meaning of those data, a meaning derived from some standard of comparison, cannot be discovered.

Not only are the measures we can apply to performance weak but the MMI aspects they describe are constrained in mockups and prototypes. Some answers can be supplied if the MMI is described in static mockup form. More answers are available if an operator can functionally exercise the MMI. Still more answers can be derived if operational conditions can be reproduced.

Another weakness in our evaluation methodology is that it is largely confined to operability (control-display arrangement) or those aspects of maintainability which are highly visible, for example, test points, accessibility, and maintenance displays. Evaluation of equipment architecture (i.e., the number, type and arrangement of internal components and circuitry and their associated symptomology) in maintainability is almost never performed because we lack a feasible methodology. Here there is a pressing need to conceptualize or develop by multidimensional scaling the design concepts that determine equipment maintainability.

Because in large part these MMI evaluation methods grew out of development and were not consciously created, they remain to a large extent unvalidated. Indeed it may not be possible to validate them in any formal sense. We lack even anecdotal documentation on how these methods are applied, under what constraints, what their effects are, their apparent usefulness, etc. Chapter 13 suggests that behavior specialists working in system development report on their experiences in the use of these methods. Such documentation might set the stage for possible method refinement.

REFERENCES

Banks, W. W., Gertman, D. I., and Petersen, R. J. *Human Engineering Design Considerations for Cathode Ray Tube-Generated Displays*. Report NUREG/CR-2496, EGG-2161, EG&G Idaho, Idaho Falls, ID, April 1982.

Brune, R. L., and Weinstein, M. *Procedures Evaluation Checklist for Maintenance, Test and Calibration Procedures*. Report NUREG/CR-1369 and SAND80-7064, Nuclear Regulatory Commission, Washington, DC, May 1980.

Buchaca, N. J. *Models and Mockups as Design Aids*. Technical Document 266, Revision A, Naval Ocean Systems Center, San Diego, CA, 1 July 1979 (AD A109511).

Department of Defense, MIL-STD-1472C. *Human Engineering Design Criteria for Military Systems, Equipment and Facilities*. Author: Washington, DC, 2 May 1981.

Fischl, M. A., and Siegel, A. I. *Further Research Into and Validation of the Analytic Profile System for Visual Display Evaluation*. Report 7071-3, Applied Psychological Services, Wayne, PA, December 1970.

Gravely, M. L., and Hitchcock, L. The use of dynamic mock-ups in the design of advanced systems. *Proceedings*, Human Factors Society Annual Meeting, October 1980, 5–8.

Hawkins, E. D. *Application of Helicopter Mockups to Maintainability and other Related Engineering Disciplines*. Report AD 786500, Red River Army Depot, Texarkana, TX, March 1974.

Holshouser, E. L. *Guide to Human Factors Engineering General Purpose Test Planning (GPTP) (Airtask A3400000/054C/7W0542-001)*. Technical Publication TP-77-14, Pacific Missile Test Center, Point Mugur, CA, 30 June 1977.

Janousek, J. A. The use of mockups in the design of a deep submergence rescue vehicle. *Human Factors*, 1970, *12*, 63–68,

Malone, T. B., Shenk, S. W., and Moroney, W. F. *Human Factors Test and Evaluation Manual, Vol. I—Data Guide*. Report TP-76-11A, Pacific Missile Test Center, Point Mugu, CA, 1 October 1976.

McAbee, W. H. *A Human Engineering Checklist*. Report APGC-TN-61-25, Air Proving Ground Center, Eglin AFB, FL, June 1961. (AD 260445)

McLane, J. T., Weingartner, W. J., and Townsend, J. C. *Evaluation of Functional Performance of an Integrated Ship Control Conning Console by Operator Personnel*. MEL R&D Report 333/65, Marine Engineering Laboratory, Annapolis, MD, May 1966 (AD 482 211).

Meister, D. The influence of government on human factors research and development. *Proceedings*, Human Factors Society Annual Meeting, October 1979, 5–13.

Meister, D., and Farr, D. E. *The Methodology of Control Panel Design*. Report AMRL-TR-66-28, Aerospace Medical Research Laboratories, Wright-Patterson AFB, OH, March 1966 (a).

Meister, D., and Farr, D.E. *Designer's guide for effective development of aerospace ground equipment control panels*. Report AMRL-TR-66-29, Aerospace Medical Research Laboratories, Wright-Patterson AFB, OH, September 1966 (b).

Munger, M. R., and Willis, M. P. *Development of an index of electronic maintainability*. Report AIR-275-59-FR-207, American Institute for Research, Pittsburgh, PA, 1959.

Munger, S. J., Smith, R. W., and Payne, D. *An Index of Electronic Equipment Operability: Data Store*. Report AIR-C43-1/62-RP(1), American Institute for Research, Pittsburgh, PA, January 1962.

Nuclear Regulatory Commission. *Guidelines for Control Room Design Reviews*. NUREG-0700, Author: Washington, DC, September 1981.

Pope, L. T., Williams. H. L., and Meister, D. *Analysis of Concepts for Maintenance of MCM Ship Vehicle Systems*. Special Report 79-7, Navy Personnel Research and Development Center, San Diego, CA, December 1978 (Confidential).

Rogers, J. G. and Armstron, R. Use of human engineering standards in design. *Human Factors*, 1977, *19*, 15–23.

Rogers, J. G. and Pegden, C. D. Formatting and organization of a human engineering standard. *Human Factors*, 1977, *19*, 55–61.

Seminara, J. L. and Gerrie, J. K. Effective mockup utilization by the industrial design-human factors team. *Human Factors*, 1966, *4*, 347–359.

Seminara, J. L. and Parsons, S. *Human Factors Methods for Nuclear Control Room Design. Vol. 2: Human Factors Survey of Control Room Practices*. Report EPRI NP-118, Electric Power Research Institute, November 1979.

Siegel, A. I., Miehle, W., and Federman, P. The DEI technique for evaluating equipment systems from the information transfer point of view. *Human Factors*, 1964, *6*, 279–286.

Siegel, A. I., and Fischl, M. A. Dimensions of visual information displays. *J. Applied Psychology*, 1971, *55*, 470–476.

Starkey, R. L., Lutz, R. I., and Donohoo, D. T. *Preliminary Control Room Design Assessment for the Washington Public Power Supply System's WPPSS Nuclear Projects 1 and 4*. Report BAW-1704, Babcock and Wilcox Company, Lynchburg, VA, April 1982.

Winter, A. N., and Fremer, A. J. *Checklist for the Qualitative Assessment of Maintainability Design Features*. Technical Note, Publication W77-1706-TN01, Air Force Test and Evaluation Center, Kirtland AFB, NM, 30 November 1977 (AD A052243).

CHAPTER EIGHT

Evaluation of the Man–Machine System

Figure 8.1 presents various ways of assessing human performance. Evaluation can be subdivided into *attribute* testing in which product characateristics are matched against standards. In Chapter Seven attribute checklists were used to evaluate equipment drawings and mockup characteristics. Attribute testing is sometimes employed as part of performance testing, especially in mockups and in operational and effectiveness tests, when the MMI is evaluated as an individual subentity.

Performance testing is applied to both the MMI and the total man–machine system. As was seen in the previous chapter, personnel performance can be tested in mockups, walkthroughs and sometimes in developmental tests. Full-bore system testing, which is described in this chapter, is determined in part by the stage of development. During development it is possible to test the system *analytically* by means of mathematical models and sometimes in a performance mode in developmental tests. It is also partially determined by the stage of development at system acceptance, during which the first prototype(s) of the complete system are exposed to *operational testing*. Following acceptance and extending throughout the life of the system (system operations) the system can be tested for *effectiveness*.

Chapter Seven described the evaluation of the MMI, largely in terms of control panel/console equipment drawings, mockups, and procedures. This chapter assumes that the entire system has been designed and now can be tested as a total entity composed of all its equipment interconnected and functioning as it will operationally. Assessment of individual performance in a nonsystem context will be discussed in a later chapter.

System evaluations are performed to determine system adequacy for mission accomplishment. The information gained in such evaluations has several uses. First, it verifies that the system can, in fact, do what is was designed to do. Second, it unearths any serious deficiencies that need remedy. Third, it can be used to design im-

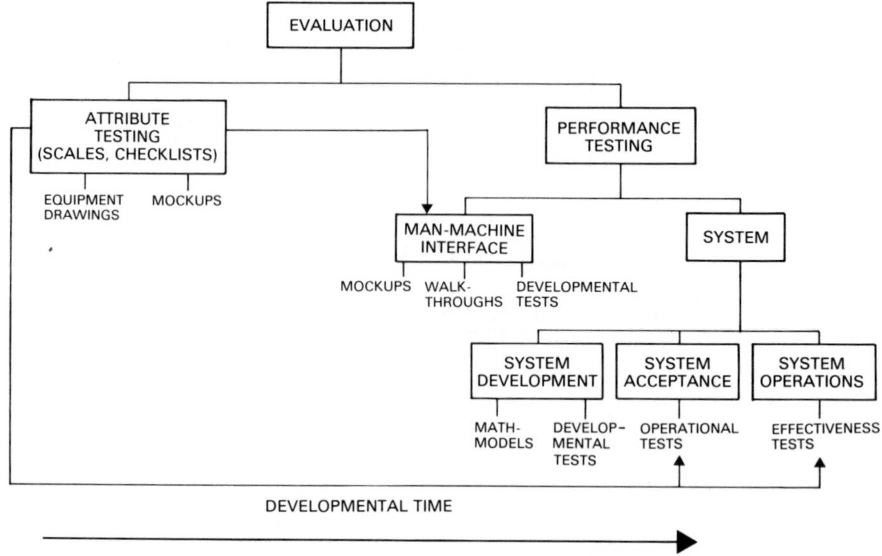

FIGURE 8.1. Types of evaluation.

provements in future systems or to modify training and selection programs. Fourth, it can serve as a source of quantitative predictive data, but this last is rarely the reason given for the evaluation.

System evaluation can be performed in a number of ways. The ideal, in terms of almost complete simulation fidelity, is the operational system performing routinely in the operational environment—for example, a ship steaming at sea. However, one can also evaluate systems at a special test facility or in a simulator (where the simulator realistically represents the operational system). Or a prototype system (not yet fully debugged) can be tested while performing in the operational environment (evaluation at sea of the first of a new ship class). All of these situations, even the first, are simulations to one extent or the other of the operational system. The question of simulation fidelity—how much is actually necessary, and what the consequences are of lack of fidelity to the performance evaluation—are questions that preoccupy the evaluator (see Meister and Rabideau, 1965). This, even when he measures in the operational system, because *it is always possible for the operational system to perform nonoperationally*.

If empirical evaluation of the operational system is most desirable, why are there alternative techniques? That is because there may be occasions when one cannot measure the system in its operating environment. For example, if for some reason it were impossible to provide a field test but skilled operators were available, one might utilize a subjective scaling techniques such as *MOAT* (mission operability assessment technique, Helm and Donnell, 1979).

The evaluations we discuss are those of the MMS or, these days, person–machine system. The proliferation of governmentally sponsored socially oriented projects (welfare, training of the disadvantaged, etc.) in this country over the past 25 years or so has led to an entire cottage industry devoted to the evaluation of these projects. A whole series of excellent texts has been written about the evaluation of social projects (e.g., Rossi, 1979: Struening and Guttentag, 1974), and it is no business of ours to add to them.

Nor is this a chapter describing laboratory research methodology or experimental design. *Operational testing* (OT) has certain characteristics (Johnson and Baker, 1974) that show little relationship to traditional controlled laboratory experiment research. Operational testing addresses real but messy problems, is time and resource limited, measures in macro units (minutes) rather than micro units (seconds), evaluates both men and equipment, employs a system approach, has high face validity, has somewhat less control over the conduct of the test, has multiple objects and multiple criteria (intermediate as well as ultimate), and includes many levels of entry into the test and/or into the system.

There is a rather extensive literature on OT which the interested reader may wish to consult. For some history (at least till 1969) see Snyder (1969). Askren and Newton (1969) reviewed and analyzed 95 documents related to personnel subsystem test and evaluation. Their abstracts of these reports supply the unique flavor of OT. Keenan, Parker and Lenzycki (1965) created an inventory of assessment practices in the Air Force. Kinkaid and Potempa (1969) edited the proceedings of a human factors testing conference which contains some excellent papers on varied aspects of test and evaluation. My own book (Meister and Rabideau, 1965) is a good primary source. The special issue on field testing in the *Human Factors* journal (1974) is also worth referring to.

PLANNING AND CONDUCTING THE OPERATIONAL TEST

A series of Department of Defense directives (see Holshouser, 1977) requires that before a system is accepted by the military, it must go through one or more operational tests.

The military divides *operational test and evaluation* (OT&E) into two major categories. The first is initial OT&E, which is all testing accomplished prior to the first major production decision, and the second, follow-on T&E which is all testing thereafter. Operational test and evaluation is further divided into five major phases but for our purposes such detail is unimportant. Depending on the characteristics of the individual system, its financing and scheduling, the sequence of testing may be compressed and combined into one or two more complex tests. Do nonmilitary systems proceed through such detailed tests? The answer is probably no, although data are lacking. However, we describe a model or process that runs through the various tests as a single, common thread, and the logic of that model applies as much to testing of civilian as to military systems.

Certain requirements exist if a prototype system is to be tested in a truly operational mode. The system has been fabricated as a complete entity. Personnel to operate the test system must be representative of or similar to those who will eventually operate the system, and must have been trained to do so. Procedures to operate the system as it is designed to function operationally have been written. An environment representative of the one(s) in which the system will routinely function (e.g., Alaska in winter for cold weather operations) has been prepared for testing.

The requirements specified in the preceding paragraph represent the optimal preconditions for OT and what we describe in this chapter is how such testing should be accomplished. In reality, there are often deviations from the optimum. The equipment may not be complete or totally integrated when prototype OT begins, operational procedures may not be completely developed, the test subjects may resemble the ultimate users only partially and their training may be less refined than that which the ultimate users will receive, and the test environment may include only certain aspects of the operational environment. Accepting that for financial, political and schedule reasons the ideal may not be achieved, this section at least establishes a baseline from which to deviate, if necessary.

One should not assume a complete dichotomy between the developmental tests (DT) described in Chapter Seven and OT. Indeed these tests overlap, with later DT and earlier OT shading into each other.

At the foundation of our thinking about OT is a continuing theoretical problem in behavioral science. This is the problem of how to determine the relationship between a particular *subsystem output*, which is personnel performance, and *total system output*. What behavior specialists (not necessarily system developers) want to know in OT is how the personnel subsystem through the performance of its personnel affects system output (which is the product of the interaction of equipment and personnel), and how the nonpersonnel elements of the system affect personnel performance.

In the course of conducting an OT the evaluator makes use of many techniques that have been referred to in previous chapters and will be described later in greater detail (see Table 8.1). There is no single methodology that one can point to as being distinctively OT. What makes OT distinctive is that it provides a formal framework in which these techniques can be applied; it organizes and systematizes them. In this respect OT is like ISD (Chapter Six). Both adapt more general methods to a specific system and problem. What further distinguishes OT are the conditions under which evaluation is performed, that is, the attempt to measure under conditions of *maximum fidelity* to the operational environment. In this OT differs fundamentally from laboratory oriented psychological studies which are only minimally concerned, if at all, with fidelity to a particular setting.

The description of OT that follows is organized in accordance with the topic headings in Table 8.2 used in developing the personnel performance part of the OT plan.

The development of the OT plan, called by the Department of Defense a *TEMP*, Test and Evaluation Master Plan, is a major planning task for evaluators in the military services because of the many facets that are examined in large, complex systems (only one of which, the behavioral aspect, we are concerned with in this chapter). Depending on the size of the system, the planning task may require the

TABLE 8.1. Summary of Elements in the Empirical Measurement of Human Performance

Data Collection Methods	Data Collection Contexts	Data Reduction Methods	Data Recording Methods
Automated data collection	Attribute evaluation (checklist type)	*Descriptive Statistics*	Automated instrumentation
Checklists	Case studies	Frequency distributions	Communication devices
Document review	Controlled experimental studies	Histograms	Closed circuit television
Interviews (Standardized/nonstandardized; single/group)	Operational system testing of the prototype system	Mean, median, range, standard deviations, etc.	Computerized measurement
Narrative recording	Problem investigation	*Comparative Statistics*	Environmental instruments, e.g., light meter
Observation (participant-observer, overt/covert; nonparticipant-observer, overt/covert)	Simulator measurement	(Parametric/nonparametric)	Paper and pencil forms
Performance testing (standardized)	Surveys	Measures of correlation (e.g., product-moment)	Physiological instruments
Questionnaire		Significance tests (e.g., analysis of variance)	Tape recorder
Ranking		*Test Documentation*	Timer
Rating scales		Test planning documents	Videotape/film
Self-report (diary)		Test reports published/unpublished	
Semi-automated data collection (time/event recorders)			
Survey techniques			
Walkthrough			

TABLE 8.2. Outline of the Personnel Performance Test Plan

1.0 Purpose of the Test
  1.1 *General.* Example: Verify that system personnel can perform required tasks.
  1.2 *Specific.* Example: Determine the type and magnitude of errors made by personnel; determine the effect of low temperature (Arctic) conditions on personnel ability to maintain a tank.
2.0 Description of System Being Evaluated
  2.1 *List of equipments* to be operated/maintained by personnel and for which personnel performance data are to be collected.
  2.2 *List of equipment tests* during which personnel performance data are to be collected.
    Example: Installation and checkout of the *XYZ* fire direction console.
  2.3 *List of tasks* for which personnel performance data will be collected.
    Example: Alignment of the M-113 theodolite.
  2.4 *Applicable technical manuals* or other procedures.
3.0 Experimental Comparisons (as required)
  Example: Comparison of accuracy of low-level navigation during daytime and nighttime reconnaissance flights
4.0 Standards, Criteria, and Measures
  4.1 *Personnel performance standards.*
    Example: Receive, code and transmit between 12 and 15 messages per hour.
  4.2 *Personnel performance criteria.*
    Example: Detection range; number of messages sent.
  4.3 *Personnel performance measures.*
    Example: Time taken to load handheld missile; officer evaluation of squad reconnaissance performance.
5.0 Data Collection Methods
  5.1 *Data Collectors*
    5.5.1 *Number.* Example: 4
    5.1.2 *Tasks to be performed.*
      Example: Record start/stop time in operation of laser tracking set.
    5.1.3 *Training* (if required).
      Example: All data collectors will receive 3 hours instruction in gathering data on the F42 machine gun (see training schedule appended).
  5.2 *Data collection forms.*
    Example: Data sheet for retractable machine gun (appended); post mission debriefing questionnaire for truck driver (appended).
  5.3 *Data collection procedures.* Example: See Appendix A to test plan.
  5.4 *Instrumentation* (only if required). Example: 2 tape recorders with 3 rolls of tape per data collector.
6.0 Subject Characteristics
  6.1 *Number.* Example: 3 squads
  6.2 *Required characteristics.*
    Example: All subjects will have 20/20 vision (corrected) and will have been qualified in operation of the retractable machine gun.
7.0 Constraints

TABLE 8.2. (*Continued*)

8.0 Data Analysis
Example: Determine mean number (and standard deviation) of messages transmitted between forward observers and batteries; develop equation relating gun loading speed and operator errors.

9.0 Testing Schedule
Example: Concurrent with other tests.

Source: Modified from Meister, D. Human Factors in Operational System Testing: A Manual of Procedures. Report SR 78-81 Navy Personnel Research and Development Center, San Diego, CA, April, 1978.

continuing services of half a dozen personnel for the better part of a year or more because of the many reviews and revisions the TEMP undergoes.

The utility of developing a test plan is obvious. It requires the evaluator to specify precisely what must be done in the test; the mere effort expended in writing a planning statement encourages clarity of thought. It also communicates information to others who are concerned both in test planning and test implementation.

The categories in Table 8.2 are similar to those that would be required of any research. Indeed, with the exception of the description of the system being evaluated (section 2.0), these categories can, and should, be used in the planning of all controlled experimental studies.

The full scale TEMP deals with many nonbehavioral elements (e.g., reliability, logistics). The categories in Table 8.2 apply to the behavioral aspects only. The behavior specialist is usually only one among a number of specialists developing the test plan and his requirements must be compromised with those of others. The test plan may have a separate section dealing with personnel performance (human factors), but human factors requirements do not take precedence over those of the engineering specialties. Rather the reverse is true.

Before OT can be effectively planned certain questions must be answered. These are the preconditions or prerequisites for testing.

1. What type of OT are we planning for? Operational testing as a generic category is simply a test involving a prototype as an operational system functioning in an actual or simulated operational environment and may have varying purposes.

   a. Acceptance testing of a new (as yet not fully operational) system.

   b. Testing of design modifications (change in or addition of hardware; new procedures) to an operational system to determine that the modified system performs as well as or better than the preceding version.

   c. Testing to determine how well an already operational system performs (effectiveness testing to provide feedback to management).

   d. Testing to develop a data base for improving research and development of new systems. Type a is performed immediately prior to a system becoming operational; types b, c, and d may be performed at any time during the operational life of the system. The type of OT will influence the particular strategy employed. For example, types a and c require some sort of acceptance or effectiveness standards. Type b requires no standards, merely a comparison.

2. Is the system to be tested a total system? By that I mean, have all the equipment subsystems been developed and interconnected in the manner in which the system will be arranged operationally? Presumably the system is no longer subject to any significant design change. If it is, one should not perform OT but rather DT. Are all operational procedures accepted and available? Are the major characteristics of the ultimate system users and the way they will be organized on the job known? Have test personnel been trained to operate the system and is that training adequate to exercise the system fully?

3. What does the *operational environment* (OE) consist of? This is what we are attempting to simulate in the OT, and OE characteristics may well determine the conditions to be contrasted experimentally such as performance under normal and hot/cold temperatures, day and night, flight at high and low altitudes, etc. The effort to achieve maximum operational fidelity drives much test planning. How much of the OE must be simulated? To answer this question requires the evaluator to anticipate the effect of the OE on personnel performance. If the OE is not expected to influence personnel performance significantly, it need not be simulated faithfully. For example, if one is testing an equipment that will never be used in other than an office environment, it is unnecessary to test it under diminished lighting, extreme cold, etc. If that equipment must be operated in the Arctic, an Arctic OE (at least in terms of temperature) must be provided. The evaluator should have empirical evidence or at least considerable logic to support a decision to ignore some aspect of the OE.

4. How much control will the behavioral evaluator have over the test situation and what constraints must he face? This may determine the kinds of measures he can apply and his data collection methodology. If, for example, he cannot interview system personnel because the system occupies them fully, or if the workplace is so cramped that he cannot use a video camera, he must take this factor into account in his planning. The objective is to avoid surprises.

Section 1.0 Purpose of the Test

This section describes the purpose of the personnel performance test. The general purpose of a system effectiveness test may be any or all of the following: (1) to verify that personnel can perform their assigned tasks and that this can be accomplished without excessive error or workload; (2) to verify that operating procedures and other equipment and system characteristics present no insuperable obstacles to effective personnel performance; (3) to verify that these characteristics satisfy desired human engineering attributes; (4) to determine the effect of any contrasting variables inherent in the equipment and system mission (e.g., day and night operations) on personnel performance; (5) to determine the adequacy from a behavioral standpoint of any modification in the job, equipment or system or its mission and of the adequacy of any design solution to a problem; (6) to determine by measuring the performance of personnel in operational systems that their performance is adequate; and, if not, what factors are causing performance deficiencies.

Although the purpose of personnel performance measurement may seem obvious at first glance, it is usually not. The requirement for evaluating a system is usually phrased initially in terms of the need to verify certain gross constructs, such as operability, maintainability and reliability, but these must be broken down into specifics because in the abstract they offer no guidelines for methodology.

The general behavioral purpose in acceptance testing is to verify that personnel can perform their assigned tasks within the new system to meet system requirements and to ensure that personnel functions are effectively integrated with other system elements. The general purpose points to the necessity for specifying, preferably in quantitative form, the standards that the system and the personnel must meet. It emphasizes the necessity of comparing actual and desired personnel performance.

Unfortunately, a general purpose, lacking specificity, does not indicate what and how one should measure. This can be determined only by breaking down the general purpose into specifics. For example, to verify that personnel can perform certain tasks satisfactorily and that training and technical documentation are adequate. A specific purpose of personnel performance measurement is simply a question about that performance which the test planner wishes to answer. The planner should list every question he wishes the personnel performance data to answer. Each such question becomes a test purpose. Consequently, personnel performance measurement usually has more than one specific purpose. The evaluator must tailor his test methodology to secure data relevant to those goals.

If there is a possibility that personnel performance will be affected by other system elements (the equipment configuration, its procedures, environment, or logistics), then a question must be answered. For example, if it is possible that heat/humidity within a tank may degrade tank personnel performance, then the planner wants to accept or reject this hypothesis. He must, therefore, arrange to measure personnel performance in relation to heat and humidity. A specific purpose of the test plan might be phrased as follows: Example: to determine the capability of tank personnel to operate tank controls while "buttoned up" under high heat/humidity conditions.

This specific purpose tells the evaluator that he must arrange to collect data on operation of tank controls under high heat/humidity conditions. This means that he may have to take the following actions.

1. Install a thermometer and hygrometer inside the tank to determine internal temperature/humidity.
2. Require operators to perform and measure that performance as a function of temperature/humidity conditions.
3. Compare that performance with heat/humidity standards specified in MIL-STD 1472C (Department of Defense, 1981). None of this would have been suggested by the general purpose.

These test purposes which are fairly discrete do not deal with more general questions of the relationship between personnel subsystem performance and system output, or the extent to which personnel performance contributes, either positively or negatively, to the efficiency of the system. As was pointed out previously, this question underlies the total test but it is essentially a research question, one which the evaluator cannot attack directly.

Section 2.0 Description of the System Being Evaluated

Since performance data will be collected with specific and equipments, conducted on specific tasks, and using specific procedures, it is necessary to list these. If those system operations for which personnel performance data will be collected are not described, data collectors may not have a clear idea of how to accomplish the measurement. The larger the system, the more necessary this section is.

Describing the system to be evaluated may appear unnecessary to those who are familiar with it. However, in most systems of any size, only *some* of the system equipment and only *some* of the tasks involved in operating that equipment will be of interest for personnel performance measurement. If the system under development has had a predecessor system and certain of its equipment and tasks have been tested and carried over to the new system, one would not repeat those tests. If the system is large and complex, if testing time is short, or data collectors are few, it may not be possible to record data on all tasks performed in all situations. For routine tasks and equipments it may not be considered cost-effective to do so. Under these circumstances it will be necessary to select those tasks/equipments with which personnel performance will be measured. The bases for selection of tasks will be those that were applied in function/task analysis and development of the ISD, for example: task criticality, task complexity, and likelihood of significant error.

Altman (1969) has addressed the considerations involved in the selection of tasks for measurement. To make the selection, the evaluator should identify: 1. tasks with critical time limits. These are likely to be tasks with higher error potential, 2. tasks in which personnel interact significantly, 3. tasks involving ambiguous stimuli and/or which require decision making; 4. tasks whose failure or inadequate performance could have significant negative effects on system output, 5. mission scenarios which impose heavy demands on system personnel, and 6. tasks with high error potential which possess critical system design features.

The function/task analyses performed previously, together with workload and error analyses, should help supply the information desired.

Where systems have changing functions and missions as a consequence of contingent occurrences, one must decide which functions/missions will be exercised during the test. The Navy (COMOPTEVFOR, 1979) makes a distinction between scenario oriented and operation oriented testing. Scenario oriented testing is commonly used for systems whose mode of operation or functions change according to a changing operational situation. For example, a shipboard *antiair war* (AAW) fire control system that is mostly in the search mode until an attack occurs is a prime candidate for scenario oriented testing. In such testing the system being evaluated is introduced into a realistic simulation of a developing operational situation, that is, a scenario. For the AAW system a raid consisting of strike aircraft could be programmed at a designated but unannounced time. Multipurpose systems may require several scenarios to exercise all their capabilities. The significance of scenario testing is that the test planning group will have to develop the scenarios and the behavioral specialist must know what the effect will be on his analysis and measurement activities, for example, a requirement for more observers, special checklist or measures of effectiveness.

Operation oriented testing is used for equipment whose mode of operation remains constant throughout an exercise. The tasks associated with such equipment will require less intensive behavioral measurement.

It is unnecessary for this section of the test plan to provide highly detailed task descriptions. These are probably already described in procedures and technical documentation. However, the names of the procedures should be listed, as also the equipments associated with these procedures.

Section 3.0 Experimental Comparisons

If the system is to be exercised in varying operational modes (e.g., reconnaissance and attack, preventive and corrective maintenance, day or night) or if there are factors inherent in system operations which may influence or reflect differences in personnel performance, these factors must be studied. Each such factor involving a contrasting condition establishes the requirement for an experimental comparison. Most systems of any complexity have a number of modes and factors that should be compared. A failure to do so is to lose valuable information.

Since such conditions are usually inherent in system operations, they do not require the setting up of special tests as conditions, other than the development of required scenarios. Moreover, test managers prefer minimal disruption of routine system operations. It is, however, necessary that personnel function under each contrasting condition and that data collected under each condition be so identified.

Each of the factors to be studied should be listed. Sometimes the factors represent different system missions (as in the scenarios); at other times they represent variations in normal functioning of the system (e.g., the individual shifts which a crew works). Or they may be differences in training and experience. Factors derived from different system missions and personnel differences must always be examined. Those inherent in routine system operations may be, if it is considered that they make a difference to performance.

After such conditions are identified, all that is needed is to assign personnel to collect data under these conditions.

Whenever differences between system conditions or factors are to be compared, it is possible to apply experimental designs of the type ordinarily used in more highly controlled research studies (e.g., analysis of variance). In a few cases it may be possible to modify the actual test arrangement in advance of performance to satisfy experimental design considerations, but this happens infrequently, sometimes because of the contingent nature of system tests, sometimes because test management is not particularly interested in behavioral test conditions. Where system operations are dependent on uncontrolled contingencies, such as weather or the action of a simulated enemy, it is difficult to utilize a highly controlled design. One study (Stinson, 1979) involved testing a prototype vehicle for transporting marines from amphibious ships to shore at high speed under various sea states. In the event, certain sea state conditions could not be realized because the ocean was uncooperative. This effectively eliminated the possibility of analyzing the data according to the original analysis of variance design.

Within limits, therefore, it is possible to apply standard experimental designs to system tests. However, the experimental design comparisons described in the data analysis section (8.0) may be post facto and contingent on the kind of data ultimately gathered.

Section 4.0 Standards, Criteria, and Measures

MIL-H-46855B (Department of Defense, 1979) requires that human factors tests be based on criteria that describe adequate performance of tasks. A criterion is however relatively abstract, e.g., speed, response time. What MIL-H-46855B means is that measures must be developed from these criteria and that *standards* of acceptable task performance should be available so that actual personnel performance can be compared with that standard.

Overview

A measure is simply a personnel performance or a system output. A standard is much more important; it is some performance output which personnel are expected to achieve. The three are closely related and may be confusing in the actual measurement situation. The three are means of organizing the ways in which performance (personnel and system) can be described. We wish to develop measures and standards, but we must begin with the criterion because it is the most molar. The logical process is 1. to identify the criterion, 2. to identify the measure which makes the criterion specific and precise, and 3. to establish the standard, which is coordinate with the measure.

In our discussion of the three, we reverse the process, starting with the standard, because it is what we ultimately hope to derive. Without standards true evaluation is impossible. We go next to criteria, because measures are developed out of criteria, and finish with a discussion of measures.

Standards. The goal of OT as it applies to personnel is to verify that personnel can perform to standards imposed by the system and its mission. The key word is *standards*. To determine whether personnel are performing adequately one must compare their performance with some standard. The need for standards is peculiar to evaluation. One does not have this problem in general behavioral research because verification of a particular condition or status is not the objective of that research.

Standards set by system requirements in formal documents are almost always physical. In evaluating a new fighter, for example, the aircraft must meet altitude, range, fuel consumption, etc. requirements; it is assumed that whoever flies it is qualified. The reason why system requirements involve physical parameters is that these requirements describe the terminal outputs of the system (what the system is supposed to accomplish); these outputs are almost always physical.

Behavioral requirements are almost always inferred, e.g., the pilot of an aircraft should have sufficient external visibility to maneuver safely. Because behavioral requirements are only inferred, they usually do not have quantitative standards associated with them. Such standards may only be implicit in the system operation. It is possible to derive these quantitative standards in two ways: by asking subject matter experts such as pilots to describe these implicit standards; or by empirical data describing what personnel typically do in a system like the one under development (normative data).

Theoretically the human performance standard should be inherent in the task description, but many task descriptions lack explicit, quantitative standards. One reason is that for discrete tasks (like throwing a switch or performing a sequence of switch-like actions) the performance standard is essentially univalued. The operator is simply supposed to perform the action. When the operator does not throw the switch, we simply record an error. No question of quality of performance enters in nor could it, because the switch can be thrown in only one way.

When the performance standard is binary, it is easy to determine whether or not the operator has satisfied the standard. On the other hand, with highly proceduralized tasks the amount of error is usually very small, since, unless the operator is unskilled or under great pressure, he rarely makes a mistake. Consequently, unless one can measure the operator's performance many times (e.g., 100-200 trials), no errors at all may be observed in the relatively few trials performed in the usual test program.

When a task can be performed in more than one way, we deal with the question of performance quality which can be expressed quantitatively or qualitatively. Performance quality implies a range of possible performances, some of which are acceptable whereas others are not. This suggests a limiting value beyond which performance is not acceptable. All performances up to that limiting value, while perhaps not optimal, are yet acceptable. In tracking performance, for example, allowable root mean square error (X) is acceptable but $X + .01$ is not. The limiting value is a judgmental standard.

If performance quality is measured qualitatively, it may be impossible to describe the standard in terms that everyone, except a very specialized few, can recognize. An example of this might be the judgment of the quality of a singer's voice.

Theoretically the standard for any task can be derived by the deductive logic of function/task analysis from initial system/mission requirements. That is because a task is meaningful only when it is related to its role in the system. However, the thread relating an individual task to an initial system requirement may be so long and convoluted that often the analyst producing a task description cannot and does not develop a standard for that task.

Lacking human performance standards, it is impossible for OT to verify human performance except in a very limited way. If the system performs its missions adequately and no outstanding operator performance deficiencies are noted, this *suggests* that personnel can do their jobs (a system engineering, not a personnel performance judgment, because it deals with terminal outputs).

Geer (1977) recommends the experienced evaluator's judgment as the basis for "making such determinations as test precision, personnel skill, degree of personnel training, etc." . . He notes that it would be "difficult to measure these qualities in any other way during a test" (p. 24).

From the standpoint of the behavioral evaluator this is very unsatisfactory even though it will satisfy most test managers. Such a situation makes the OT *merely* a context in which to discover human performance inadequacies, although from a purely developmental standpoint the uncovering of such deficiencies and their subsequent remediation is important.

The specification of precise quantitative standards presents a number of difficulties which the evaluator may be able to overcome by persistence and good humor.

For example, it is often extremely difficult to persuade even skilled system personnel to provide precise standards of their performance. A frequent response is, "It all depends." This may reflect the feeling that the performance depends on so many interactive and contingent factors that it cannot be specified although presumably it can be recognized by experts. Or personnel may fear that if they specify precise standards, their performance will be judged too stringently.

In systems under development one often finds that although hardware performance criteria are specified in explicit terms, there are few or no references to personnel criteria. In part this reflects a widespread impression among system developers who lack behavioral background that personnel performance either does not matter to system outputs, or is too variable to be described. Of course, some systems may require so many contingent responses of personnel that it is difficult to supply standards for every contingency. However, even in such systems it is possible to supply precise criteria for the major outputs required of workers.

The absence of performance standards does not mean that one cannot utilize test data to determine how well personnel are performing. One does so, however, through substitute secondary methods not involving the comparison of empirical data with an objective standard. For example, supervisor and peer ratings of personnel performance can be substituted. One examines errors and critical incidents, tries to infer the causes of errors, and attempts to develop a solution for those causes. One interviews personnel and inquires whether they have experienced any excessive difficulties. Even if the human performance is ambiguous with regard to its meaning, it is possible to do useful things with the description of that performance. However, description is all it is. It does not permit prediction, in the human reliability sense, because prediction is necessarily quantitative and comparative.

Since a standard is ultimately a value judgment, it is reasonable to utilize subject matter experts to attempt to derive a specific quantitative standard for a task. If the task is one that has been performed previously in other system contexts, it is possible to cross-examine the SME to extract a limiting value. This is usually done informally, by interview.

Moreover, even if the meaning of human performance data is ambiguous, it is possible to do useful things with it. For example, performance vastly different from that which the evaluator would anticipate on the basis of previous tests will suggest that something is wrong and must be investigated. The particular kinds of difficulties experienced by test subjects will suggest areas for further examination.

Criteria. Before one can develop standards one must have criteria which are system attributes or characteristics in the abstract. The difference between the two is a matter of specificity: a criterion in radar detection, for example, is detection range; the standard is 3.5 miles. Obviously, the more molar criterion—detection range—precedes the standard which specifies the criterion. One works from the molar criterion to the more molecular standard, via the measure.

The starting point of performance measurement is the criterion. Without it no meaningful measurement is possible. Without it, one can collect descriptive performance data (to answer the question, what are personnel doing?), but the meaning of those data—whether personnel are performing adequately or not—cannot be determined.

There are three distinct types of performance criteria: those describing the functioning of the system, those describing how missions are performed, and those describing how personnel respond. Only the last is of interest to us, but the fact that different criteria are available means that it is necessary to differentiate them. System-descriptive criteria include such aspects as reliability, maintainability, vulnerability, and cost of operation. Mission-descriptive criteria include effectiveness in mission accomplishment, output quality and accuracy, reaction time, performance duration, queues, and delays.

Each of the preceding includes personnel elements that must be differentiated from nonpersonnel elements. On the other hand, personnel performance criteria describing operator and crew responses (reaction time, accuracy, number of responses, response consistency, speed, etc.) lack meaning unless they are considered in relation to system and mission criteria.

Performance criteria may act as independent or dependent variables. As independent variables (e.g., the requirement to produce N units) they impose on the operator a requirement that serves as a forcing function for his performance. As dependent variables they describe his performance (i.e., the operator has provided N units) and can be used to measure that performance. The latter is what we are concerned with.

In evaluative performance measurement, the criterion requires a standard of performance acceptable to the system mission. In measurement research in general, criteria are also necessary (as dependent variables which describe the effects of independent variables) but they do not imply or require standards. In evaluative measurement a criterion (efficiency) is meaningless without a standard because it does not provide a means of determining whether personnel are performing well or poorly. Thus, for example, the number of requests for information handled is a criterion which can be used in research on telephone operator performance, but the evaluation of that performance makes it necessary to specify in advance of measurement the number of requests that must be handled in a given time period.

It is not enough to have general criterion like efficiency or number of information requests. The criterion must be precise or it cannot serve its evaluation purpose. To be precise it must be quantitative as well. A criterion such as one which is occasionally found in system procurement descriptions, "the system shall be so designed that personnel perform their duties with minimum difficulty," is meaningless because it is undefined in quantitative terms. Or rather it can be defined only in terms peculiar to the evaluator. With undefined criteria one must rely on the evaluator's ability to translate the criterion into concrete terms and unless those terms are specified in writing it is almost impossible to communicate their meaning to others.

Not all criteria are equally relevant and valuable for performance measurement. The level of adrenalin in the blood of subjects performing a visual vigilance task may be related to target detection but adrenalin level is not the most desirable criterion one can find to measure sonar detection because it is only indirectly output related. The evaluator should examine the criteria he has available and select those that seem most directly related to the performance at issue. The relevance and importance of a potential criterion can be determined by asking how seriously the achievement of or failure to achieve this criterion would affect system performance.

For example, if one were to contrast false alarm rate and adrenalin level in sonar performance, which would describe target detection more adequately? If the relationship of the criterion to system output is weak, the potential criterion is not a very satisfactory candidate. The criterion falls out of what is required of system personnel and whatever affects them strongly represents a potentially usable criterion.

What the evaluator is looking for are objective criteria, because the performance described by such criteria can be observed and recorded simply and directly without much interpretation. Unfortunately, many criteria fail this test. Some performances, primarily perceptual and cognitive, are inherently subjective. For example, it is not presently possible to measure the quality of decision making in a combat situation with instrumentation. The cues needed to describe quality may be so tenuous that only an expert can perceive them. Criterion objectivity and specificity will determine how adequately one can measure and by what methods. For qualitative criteria we must call upon the expert because only he has the requisite experience to recognize the performance involved. We can accept conclusions based on his judgments but with a somewhat lesser level of confidence, because, not being experts ourselves, we can never be quite sure just how expert he is. It is not acceptable, however, to rely on subjective, qualitative criteria when more precise, objective criteria are available—a problem that may arise with inexperienced managers.

Complex systems may also have multiple criteria because personnel must perform a variety of functions. If so, one must measure them all—assuming they are all substantially related to system output. The investigator should not pick and choose (especially not post facto) even though it may be embarrassing if he secures one set of results with one criterion and another set with another criterion.

Criteria interact with other variables, such as the organizational structure of the system. As the focus of performance shifts from individual operator to team or from subsystem to system, criteria may change. In measuring team performance, for example, one must consider member interactions, a factor which is obviously irrelevant to single operator performance.

Measures. Lacking criteria, in a system of any reasonable size, the number of performance outputs that could be measured might bewilder the evaluator because he literally has an embarrassment of riches with no basis for selection. The criterion allows the evaluator to select a subset of all possible performance outputs (measures). The situation is not so bad at the individual equipment level, but if one is dealing with a subsystem or the system as a whole, the number of operations that can be measured may be excessive. Table 8.3 lists classes of performance measures. For example, Vreuls, Obermayer, Goldstein and Lauber (1973) generated over 800 measures for a simple captive helicopter performing common maneuvers.

Because it is a general category, any single criterion may have a number of measures. For example, suppose the criterion is effectiveness of corrective maintenance. One obvious measure is downtime: the time it takes the technician to restore a malfunctioning equipment to operating condition. However, other measures are possible. For example, the number of malfunctions correctly diagnosed or the speed of malfunction diagnosis (not the same as remedying the fault).

All measures are not equally useful in describing performance because some of them may be only indirectly related to performance. The neatness of a lathe operator's workstation is not as good a measure of his performance as a lathe operator as the amount of scrap he discards. Nonetheless, within the limits of the evaluator's resources he should record all indirectly, as well as directly, relevant measures.

In translating the criterion into the measure one examines the operations performed by the operator. For example, if one of the major tasks of a forklift operator in a warehouse is to move boxes from the loading dock to an assigned storage area, the number of boxes moved per hour is an excellent measure of his effectiveness.

Measures may describe terminal performance (the output of the operator action) or intermediate performance (an operator behavior leading to an output). Intermediate measures are more likely to be more detailed than terminal ones. To measure rifle-firing proficiency, for example, one could record the tremor of the finger in squeezing the trigger (an intermediate measure) or one could record the number of hits on target (a terminal measure). Terminal measures are more valuable than intermediate ones, because the evaluator is interested in outputs, although intermediate measures are useful for diagnosing performance inadequacies. If, for example, the system output one is concerned with is the accuracy of rifle fire one is placing on a target, then highly molecular measures like trigger pressure would be largely irrelevant, since squeeze pressure is less directly related to firing accuracy than number of hits.

The level at which one measures may determine in part how the data are collected. For example, instrumentation would probably be required if one wished to measure trigger pressure but not if one measured error in hitting the target.

The difficulty in developing meaningful performance measures increases when the system has complex task interrelationships. Measures of secondary or dependent tasks may appear less relevant to the terminal system output. It is necessary to work

TABLE 8.3 Classification of Generic Performance Measures

Time

1. Reaction time, i.e., time to
   a. perceive event;
   b. initiate movement;
   c. initiate correction;
   d. initiate activity following completion of prior activity;
   e. detect trend of multiple related events.
2. Time to complete an activity already in process; i.e., time to
   a. identify stimulus (discrimination time);
   b. complete message, decision, control adjustment;
   c. reach criterion value.
3. Overall (duration) time
   a. time spent in activity;
   b. per cent time on target.
4. Time sharing among events

Accuracy

1. Correctness of observation; i.e., accuracy in
   a. identifying stimuli internal to system;
   b. identifying stimuli external to system;
   c. estimating distance, direction, speed, time;
   d. detection of stimulus change over time;
   e. detection of trend based on multiple related events;
   f. recognition: signal in noise;
   g. recognition: out-of-tolerance condition.
2. Response-output correctness; i.e., accuracy in
   a. control positioning or tool usage;
   b. reading displays;
   c. symbol usage, decisionmaking and computing;
   d. response selection among alternatives;
   e. serial response;
   f. tracking;
   g. communicating.
3. Error characteristics.
   a. amplitude measures;
   b. frequency measures;
   c. content analysis;
   d. change over time.

Frequency of Occurrence

1. Number of responses per unit, activity, or interval.
   a. control and manipulation responses;
   b. communications;
   c. personnel interactions;
   d. diagnostic checks.
2. Number of performance consequences per activity, unit, or interval.
   a. number of errors;
   b. number of out-of-tolerance conditions.
3. Number of observing or data gathering responses.
   a. observations;
   b. verbal or written reports;
   c. requests for information.

Amount Achieved or Accomplished

1. Response magnitude or quantity achieved.
   a. degree of success;
   b. percentage of activities accomplished;
   c. measures of achieved reliability (numerical reliability estimates);
   d. measures of achieved maintainability;
   e. equipment failure rate (mean time between failure);
   f. cumulative response output;
   g. proficiency test scores (written).
2. Magnitude achieved.
   a. terminal or steady-state value (e.g., temperature high point);
   b. changing value or rate (e.g., degrees change per hour).

Consumption or Quantity Used

1. Resources consumed per activity.
   a. fuel/energy conservation;
   b. units consumed in activity accomplishment.
2. Resources consumed by time.
   a. rate of consumption.

Physiological and Behavioral State

1. Operator/crew condition
   a. physiological;
   b. behavioral.

TABLE 8.3 (*Continued*)

Behavior Categorization by Observers

1. Judgment of performance.
   a. rating of operator/crew performance adequacy;
   b. rating of task or mission segment performance adequacy;
   c. estimation of amount (degree) of behavior displayed;
   d. analysis of operator/crew behavior characteristics;
   e. determination of behavior relevancy;
      (1) omission of relevant behavior;
      (2) occurrence of nonrelevant behavior.
   f. causal description of out-of-tolerance condition.
2. Subjective reports.
   a. interview content analysis;
   b. self-report of experiences ("debriefing");
   c. peer, self or supervisor ratings.

(Modified from Smode, Gruber, and Ely, 1962)

through the dependency relationships among tasks before deciding to accept or reject a measure.

Another difficulty is that in many cases the only objective, observable measures in performance are time and errors. It is not as hard to measure these as to make sense of them. Unless response/reaction time is critical for a task, time will mean very little. Only if time is unduly prolonged will it affect system output. Average performance time does not reveal very much. Errors may be indicative of performance quality but only if the errors have a significant effect on system performance. In well trained personnel significant errors may be so few that data collectors have difficulty observing them.

If the tasks being measured are cognitive (more and more likely these days) or if significant performance dimensions are so tenuous that only a specialist can pick them up, the evaluator is in measurement trouble, even if he can define these dimensions, since they may be observable only to a specialist. It is not uncommon for the evaluator to have to rely on the SME's judgment. For example, inspecting a product for deficient workmanship, the evaluator has to assume the specialist is correct in his judgments; he has no way of knowing for himself.

The fact that the usual response measures (time and errors) do not make much difference to many tasks makes it necessary to select critical tasks (in which time and errors do make a difference) for measurement.

If it is necessary to select among measures, the evaluator should select those that are 1. highly related to the output or product of the performance being measured, 2. objective, 3. quantitative, 4. unobtrusive, 5. easy to collect, 6. require no specialized data collection techniques, 7. are not excessively molecular and therefore require no specialized instrumentation, and 8. cost as little as possible monetarily and in terms of evaluator effort. Unfortunately, few measures satisfy all these criteria.

The process of selecting criteria, measures, and standards is more complex than many evaluators realize. Often they accept the obvious ones without working through their relationships to system outputs and consequently their real meaning. The selection criteria specified in the previous paragraph are easy to state but quite difficult to apply in real world evaluation.

Section 5.0 Data Collection Methods

This section deals with who will collect data and, more importantly, how they will collect it.

To ensure any possibility of success the evaluator must develop for the OT plan a scenario describing in as much detail as possible the data he is going to collect, and how he intends to collect it. He must do this even though it is almost inevitable that last minute changes will be required because of changes in overall test circumstances.

The specification of data collection methodology is necessary for a number of reasons: to communicate information to other test planners and to the data collection team, to enable the evaluator to have firmly in mind what he intends his data collectors to do, to expose to examination any difficulties or inadequacies that may exist in the evaluator's plans.

Note as a matter of record the number of personnel who are serving as data collectors (section 5.1.1). Where more than one data collector is required, how they are to be scheduled becomes important.

Indicate the tasks which the data collectors will perform (section 5.1.2). These tasks are not the same as system operating tasks for which personnel performance data are to be collected. Rather, they are the activities involved in gathering information about the task performance being measured. For example: At the conclusion of each truck driving cycle, data collectors will administer a questionnaire concerning ride quality.

Unless data collection tasks are complex, they need be described only as general functions, e.g., administer questionnaires. On the other hand, if data collection may pose special problems, the tasks involved should be described in step-by-step fashion. If there is much to say about them, section 5.1.2 can be an appendix to the test plan.

If data collectors must receive special training to enable them to perform their duties effectively, that training should be described (section 5.1.3). In general, all data collectors should receive training and practice in methods of recording data, even if technically they are specialists in the system being tested. If data collectors are not familiar with the system under test, they will require special training to give them this familiarity, since a data collector cannot function effectively without that knowledge. Data collection training should be oriented toward enabling collectors to recognize the events they have to record and how these should be recorded (as well as any instrumentation to be used). At the very least, several data collection dry runs should be held to habituate data collectors to their tasks.

All data recording forms should be noted in section 5.2. The actual forms themselves should be appended to the test plan. The reason for listing the forms is to remind the test director that these forms must be developed if they are not already available. Appending the forms to the test plan permits the test director or anyone else to examine them to determine if they are satisfactory for their purposes.

The rationale for the data collection methods that will be employed should be described, as also should be any demands upon the time of test personnel acting as subjects (e.g., interview time, the completion of questionnaires, etc.). Instrumentation used to record data is described in a separate section (5.4).

The specific data collection methods to be used will depend, in part, on the criteria/measures that have been developed previously and in part on convenience, where several methods can provide roughly the same information. It would however be a capital mistake to select one's data collection methods before determining criteria and measures.

Military test managers prefer manual methods, in large part because of their lesser cost, to some degree also because non-specialists understand interviews, questionnaires and rating scales more than they do instrumentation.

Where testing is performed in the field as at a test site or aboard a ship it is fair to say that behavioral data collection methods cannot be overly sophisticated because of the constraints which affect testing efficiency in a field environment (see section 7.0 of the test plan). OT provides a relatively crude measurement environment. Greater sophistication is possible in the simulator because the simulator is a more controlled environment.

OT measurement methods may not be inherently crude but evaluators often apply them crudely. If, for example, one uses observation as a means of determining whether teams are highly integrated in their performance, observation of those teams is not crude. What is crude is our conceptualization of the dimensions inherent in team integration (Goldin and Thorndike, 1980). In the use of attribute oriented measurement devices, such as rating scales, the devices themselves are not necessarily inadequate. It is our concept of the attributes they are asked to measure that is lacking.

Since OT data collection tools will probably not be standardized or developed using psychometric methods, they should be tried out before the test under conditions that approximate the ones in which they will be used (evaluators tend to make up their own tools). They can then be modified where deficiencies are found.

Unless the data collection procedure is very simple, it should be described, (section 5.3), including 1. The hours data collectors will work, or the sequence of operations (their beginning/completion) that will determine the data collection period. 2. How data collectors should process their data, for example, do they pass the data on to the evaluation personnel immediately or hold on to it? Do they partially analyze data while it is being recorded? 3. What data collectors should do if an emergency occurs (e.g., if an exercise is suddenly stopped before it is completed), or if something not covered by operating procedures occurs. 4. The level of detail to which they should record data (principally relevant when reporting qualitative observations). 5. The extent to which the data collector is permitted to interact with the personnel whose performance is being evaluated (e.g., the distance they must remain away from participants in the operation). 6. Any equipment data collectors will be required to operate.

Data collection instrumentation sometimes used in field operations includes small magnetic tape recorders for recording observer notes and communications, and hand held video tape recorders or motion picture cameras for recording events visually. To assess the environmental conditions under which performance occurs, if these are relevant, light meters and accelerometers (for vibration effects) may be employed or sound level meters may be used to record noise levels. If evaluations are held in fixed locations, either on the ground or aboard ship (i.e., where greater control can be exercised over environmental conditions), more elaborate automatic data recording apparatus may be used, again only if required.

It should be noted that automated data collection becomes increasingly feasible as the system becomes more computerized. When system control is exercised by means of commands to a computer, it is a relatively simple matter to arrange for subroutines to record all operator inputs and their timing in relation to equipment processes (see as an example Cohill and Ehrich, 1983). Even so, the automated data collection mechanisms pick up only overt responses, meaning that perceptual and cognitive activities will be ignored.

Section 6.0 Subject Characteristics

This section describes test personnel; that is, those personnel who are selected to operate and maintain the system during its testing and whose performance is used to evaluate personnel subsystem effectiveness.

If the operational test is to be valid, it must be performed with personnel who are representative of those who will eventually operate and maintain the system. This requires that one know as much as possible about the characteristics of the ultimate system operators as well as of those personnel who are intended to represent them. Geddie (1976) has pointed out that test personnel may be the major source of variance in test data. If test personnel are much more or less trained or experienced than eventual users of the system, evaluation results will fail to describe correctly the performance of these eventual users.

Characteristics to be considered in system users and test personnel include (as relevant to the task):

1. physical—vision, hearing, height, weight, and strength.
2. aptitude—general intelligence, special aptitudes (e.g., mechanical).
3. training.
4. experience—number of years in a given specialty.

Attitudinal and motivational factors are important also but cannot be precisely specified. Personnel used as subjects should be willing volunteers or at least not resistant to the notion of serving as test personnel. In any case it is important to explain to them why they are being asked to participate in the test, the importance of their participation, and the fact that there will be no negative consequences for them. It would be incorrect to think of test personnel simply as bodies to be manipulated.

Most frequently, subject requirements will involve training and experience. For example, it is obvious that to evaluate a prototype bus the subjects must be qualified bus drivers and, if driving the new bus requires new skills, driver subjects must have received special training.

Section 6.1 notes the number of subjects or the organizational units in which they function (e.g., the squad, the platoon). This item is for information only.

Section 6.2 describes required subject characteristics. These are characteristics that, in the evaluator's judgment, will significantly affect the accuracy of the data if not possessed by personnel acting as subjects.

A special case exists where both the ultimate users and the test personnel must be highly skilled, such as pilots, navigators, electronic technicians. These personnel possess a continuum of capability ranging from mediocre, through average, to highly qualified. The question is whether one selects test personnel who are at about the 50th percentile in skill or those who are exceptionally well qualified? The Navy and the Air Force have always selected specially trained and qualified personnel to test their aircraft; and this selection is justified because new aircraft are always very dangerous and require the greatest skill to test. Where the new system is not dangerous, although it may be complex and demanding, the question persists: Do we need average or exceptional personnel? The use of more skilled personnel will undoubtedly make the new system look better in the eyes of customers, because these personnel will be able to compensate for any deficiencies the new system may have. This solution has a political value. On the other hand, the new system will ultimately be operated by average personnel (by definition) and system managers will not discover the problems that are likely to disturb average personnel if exceptional people have managed to overcome them. In this respect the use of the most highly skilled personnel makes the OT somewhat less operational. (It is of course possible to sensitize test subjects to recognize factors that would present problems to less skilled personnel.) The answer to the question is a value judgment, but if one of the OT goals is a discover areas of weakness in the system, personnel of average skill are more likely to do so.

One undesirable aspect of military OT is that in some tests operators are military, but to ensure that undesirable consequences do not occur because an equipment may fail or an operator make an error they are backed up by contractors (engineers) who step in and take over control of the tasks being performed whenever a difficulty arises. From the standpoint of operational fidelity such a procedure completely invalidates the test, even if it makes the new system appear more effective, because the system in routine operations may not have access to engineers.

Section 7.0 Constraints

A major goal in system evaluation is to simulate the operational system and its operating environment as closely as possible. When an evaluation is performed on an actual operational system performing its assigned missions, in its assigned manner, the simulation is complete. The simulation cannot be complete where the system is only a prototype, probably incompletely debugged and often functioning in a special test facility (e.g., a test station like Vandenberg AFB).

In his effort to simulate the operational system, the evaluator may find that there is an inverse tradeoff between the amount of control he can exercise and the system's fidelity to the operational situation: the more the fidelity, the less control.

That is because the system when performing operationally is subject to many extra-system effects over which the evaluator lacks control.

If the system under test is to be operated with maximum fidelity, once operations have been initiated, it must function without interference (except for safety reasons) until its mission or goal is naturally accomplished or aborted. In consequence, the system must not be stopped or influenced in its operation in any way to allow the evaluator special time or facilities to interrogate system personnel or to gather special data (or for any other reasons). Also data collectors cannot interfere with the normal exercise of the system to gather data and data collection activities cannot be too obtrusive.

The physical configuration of the system may constrain desired data collection activities. For example, the lack of a necessary power source in the system may prevent the use of certain instrumentation. The space in which system personnel work may be so small that it precludes the use of an observer (see Clarkin, 1977, for further discussion of this point).

The evaluator must always consider the motivation and cooperation of the users. System personnel may resent the presence of outsiders, feeling that they are being asked to exert themselves unduly without receiving any particular reward or compensation for playing the role of guinea pigs. To ensure cooperation the evaluator may have to offer them an inducement. For example, to install and evaluate the effectiveness of nontactical computers aboard warships to perform certain administrative functions, it was necessary to provide the ship personnel with a special computer program that presented recreational video game programs.

Lacking an inducement, system personnel may become indifferent to the test or noncommunicative or may act out latent hostility by deliberately providing incorrect or partial information when asked or by concealing their task activities from an observer. It is good practice to enlist system personnel as integral participants and planners of the test, if this is possible.

Apart from all that, if the evaluation is performed on an operational system which has contingent demands placed upon it, as many military systems do, the system may change its mission abruptly, for example, a warship going almost immediately from a training mission to one of search for an unknown intruder. This may disrupt carefully laid test plans.

Where constraints are anticipated that may affect the efficiency of data collection and the resultant data, such as a small size of personnel sample, the evaluator should describe these in the test plan so that possible remedies can be sought.

Section 8.0 Data Analysis

The test plan must include a procedure for statistical analysis of the data. If the evaluator waits until after data are collected before developing his statistical plans, the chances are excellent that too much or too little data will be collected and—much more serious—much of his data may be unusable because it will not fit statistical requirements. On the other hand, the evaluator must recognize that because of uncontrollable events, his data analysis methods may have to be changed somewhat at the last moment to accomodate those events.

One can anticipate the kind of data that will be available for analysis (the following is only a sample, see Smode, Gruber and Ely, 1962, for a complete listing):

1. Error data: nature of error; by whom performed; part of which procedure; effect of the error, etc.
2. Start/stop times for task performance; reaction time (where appropriate); duration of runs, excessive delays in performance.
3. Tasks completed and aborted; effects of task noncompletion; equipment indications following performance of procedures (boiler values, course headings).
4. Communications recordings.
5. Logistics data in printout form (fuel or ammunition expended, sorties flown, number of shells or boxes loaded, trucks dispatched).
6. Self-report data (interviews, questionnaires, ratings): difficulties encountered and reasons for these; attitudes toward system/job design characteristics; ratings of fatigue or workload; checklist evaluations of equipment design.

The evaluator can perform three types of data analysis:

1. *Verification analysis.* This is comparison of personnel performance with a system requirement or performance standard; this verifies that personnel can perform required tasks effectively (general purpose of the test, section 1.1). Comparatively little of the data analysis will involve this type of comparison because few if any performance requirements are specified in advance of the test. Evaluators must make a deliberate effort to develop these requirements and performance standards and few do.

As was pointed out in section 4.0 of the test plan, many personnel requirements are only inferred; for example, although no document may explicitly say so, the operator should be able to perform without excessive workload. For such inferred requirements the basis for evaluation is likely to be the evaluator's own expert opinion, since objective standards are not available.

Where all tasks are necessary for mission accomplishment, where an error will fail the task and the failure of the task will fail the mission, it is possible to infer another performance requirement, that of error-less performance or at least performance with no *uncorrected* errors.

However, not all tasks may be necessary to mission accomplishment and here the performance analysis will be of two types: determination of the operators' error probability (see Chapter Five) and analysis of those errors that are particularly critical to system success.

Without a substantial number of trials, however, it is impossible to secure enough data to determine error-likelihood and probability of task accomplishment.

Few operational tests involving a prototype system run for hundreds of trials. This is where stochastic mathematical models (Siegel and Wolf, 1969) are useful because the usual operating sequence in this type of model involves 100 to 200 trials.

There may also be an inferred reaction time/duration requirement. If the system is exercised over a number of trials a subject matter expert can, for example, determine whether the duration of any trial is grossly disproportionate and might constitute a mission failure. Assuming that the system has been exercised a sufficient number of times, it is possible to develop a measure of duration adequacy. If one out of 10 system trials was grossly overextended, one would say then that the probability of accomplishing the mission *in sufficient time* was .90.

The reader will not have failed to notice the importance of the subject matter expert in determining the criticality of behavioral data in relation to system outputs and mission success. In contrast to controlled experiments in which the meaning and significance of data have been preestablished by the experimental design, much of the data in OT may have equivocal meanings that can only be resolved by expert judgment.

2. *Special conditions analysis.* The second type of analysis is a comparison of any special conditions that were tested, e.g., operator performance under daytime versus nightime conditions (section 3.0 of the test plan). Standard statistical techniques can be applied here if the number of trials per subject are large enough. This must be determined on a case by case basis. If, for example, the system being tested is exercised 30 times under each of three mission phases and the mean frequency of error for 12 subjects is 2.8, 3.6, and 1.2 for each phase, respectively, conventional analysis of variance techniques make it possible to determine whether the error frequency differences are statistically significant.

3. *Descriptive analysis.* The third data analysis method, which may include the bulk of the data, is descriptive only. Qualitative data are descriptive because they cannot be compared either with a requirement or with contrasting system conditions. Data gathered from interviews and questionnaires such as explanations of why errors were made or courses of action taken would be of this nature. Subjective data that can be quantified, e.g., rating scale values, can be statistically compared but the opportunity to do so does not often arise.

However, much of the most meaningful behavioral test data is of this type. It has been pointed out that often objective measures of time, task accomplishment or error frequency are difficult to understand unless they are related to a system requirement or an effect on the system. To make such data comprehensible it may be necessary to gather subjective qualitative data. These may include (a) test subject explanations of why behaviors and performance occurred; (b) analysis of error or failure causes and effects; (c) descriptions of human engineering inadequacies; (d) attitudes of test personnel toward system characteristics, the test situation, job design or their training.

The data analysis section of the test plan should therefore not confine itself solely to quantitative comparisons but should also describe the descriptive analyses to be performed and the rationale for them.

Section 9.0 Testing Schedule

This section of the test plan describes the data collection schedule. If the system test is very complex, and only some of the system operations will be used as occasions for the gathering of personnel performance data, then a daily, weekly, or monthly schedule of data collection activities should be appended to the test plan. In one flight navigation testing program for helicopter pilots, for example, pilots of varying levels of experience were to be tested over a year's time. Since pilot navigation performance was hypothesized to depend in part on the appearance of the terrain, it was necessary to arrange the subject schedule so that pilots with different experience levels could be tested during both summer (heavy foliage) and winter (bare trees, snow) conditions.

If the personnel performance data are to be collected during all test events, a detailed subject schedule is unnecessary because the overall test schedule will determine when data will be collected.

SPECIAL PROBLEMS IN PERFORMANCE MEASUREMENT: MAINTENANCE

Far greater attention in performance measurement is paid to evaluation of operator tasks than to maintenance tasks, although the latter are in general more complex, more difficult to accomplish well, and have a somewhat greater negative impact on system effectiveness. The reasons for this disparity in attention is simply that it is easier to measure operator behavior. *Corrective maintenance* (CM) activity—troubleshooting—is largely cognitive and hence not directly observable. The troubleshooter's activities often seem meaningless to an observer.

Preventive maintenance like routine programmed activities such as oiling, or cleaning, or inspecting can be treated for measurement purposes in the way of any other operator task. Its activities are programmed in step-by-step fashion and do not exhibit the variability found in troubleshooting.

In contrast to many operator tasks, CM has what might be loosely considered a standard: an estimated *mean-time-to-repair* (MTTR) for the individual equipment. This value is supposed to be developed prior to OT on the basis of past history with similar equipments (a CM data base). Often the estimated MTTRs will be wildly off base but at least they serve as an initial basis of comparison, though they may have to be revised following further experience with maintenance of the individual equipments.

For operational systems the military services (and one supposes the larger industries also) have well established maintenance reporting systems (e.g., 3M for the Navy, 66-1 for the Air Force) in which forms are completed for each malfunction by maintenance personnel reporting CM time for the individual equipment. Of course this information is suspect because the reporter often has reasons for making his troubleshooting indices appear in a favorable light.

The gathering of human performance data in OT is based on the assumption that those data represent how the system will function at a later time when the system becomes operational. This assumption is generally justified in the case of operator tasks because there are presumably no irrelevant operator tasks. A properly conducted OT exercises them all at least once, so that some data—even if less than adequate—are gathered on all programmed (operator) aspects of the system. This is not true of CM, however, because equipment failures are only samples of all the failures that will ever occur, and no OT lasts long enough to expose maintenance technicians to all possible failures. Hence any picture one draws of CM in OT is bound to be somewhat inaccurate.

Since reporting of troubleshooting time is required throughout the operational life of the system, it is possible to check estimated MTTRs and to revise them on a continuing basis. Estimated MTTRs can then be verified although not in OT nor by the behavior specialist. This is more probably done by maintenance or logistics specialists.

This is not the place to discuss behavioral studies of CM performance (see Bond and Towne, 1979, for a review of these) but it is important to note that the operational field environment is the only proper place to study equipment troubleshooting. All the substitutes for that environment (simulators, controlled situations in which malfunctions are inserted into functioning equipments, symbolic tests like the Tab Test, see Glaser, Damrin and Gardner, 1952) are seriously deficient because they do not offer an opportunity for the technician to manifest the richness of his cognitive activity nor to suffer the influence of environmental variables. Observation of the technician's troubleshooting activities has some descriptive value, but only in a research, not in an evaluational sense. It is impossible merely by looking at what the technician does to determine whether or not the CM function is being performed adequately. Lacking a true CM requirement and a reasonable sample of CM data, it is impossible to determine from performance testing whether or not the CM technician is performing effectively or not. It is even questionable whether because of the many unknowns in CM the expert judgment of the CM supervisor can supply a valid performance rating.

What the evaluator in OT can learn about the CM function can be expressed in a series of questions.

1. Are the technical manuals and other documentation understandable and do they provide complete, detailed information?
2. Are there any human engineering characteristics of the equipment that seriously hamper the technician (accessibility, labeling, color coding, etc.)?
3. Are there any special difficulties that he encounters?
4. Has what he was taught in school been useful in helping him troubleshoot?
5. Does he have any problem with spares? The preceding are diagnostic, not evaluation questions.

Because most of the activity engaged in by the technician is cognitive, the evaluator must use some form of self-report technique, such as an interview or questionnaire, to secure the answers to the questions in the preceding paragraph. To a much greater extent than in the operator area, because of the greater cognitive functioning, we are dependent for information on self-report techniques. These give us largely qualitative information.

SYSTEM EFFECTIVENESS MEASUREMENT

Since OT methodology is a developmental tool and developmental managers are more interested in fielding the system than assessing its characteristics, it generally leads to no quantitative assessment of personnel subsystem effectiveness unless human reliability techniques (Chapter 5) are included in OT and tasks are performed a sufficient number of times to derive a meaningful error rate.

When we talk about system effectiveness measurement, we refer to empirically oriented techniques that attempt to summarize the performance of the personnel subsystem. A number of ways to derive such an effectiveness measure exist, some of which are objective, others subjective. Most of the techniques are applied to a system which is already operational rather than, as in OT, just completing its development. War games, simulated combat in the form of fleet exercises or extended maneuvers, can provide such a behavioral effectiveness measurement for military units (industry almost never engages in such activities). But these tests are rarely used for this purpose, except for that rare situation in which the exercise is set up specifically to study a matter of personnel concern (e.g., Operation REFWAC, Johnson, Cory, Day and Oliver, 1978).

To measure behavioral effectiveness validly the war game or the exercise must be organized and conducted in the same way that OT is organized: with specific objectives, criteria, measures, formal methods of measurement, and sophisticated data analysis. This is seldom done because the military does not understand the requirements involved in securing valid measures, even when these are of a nonbehavioral nature. There is a lack of interest by the military in personnel performance and its measurement (so that in fact very little data relevant to personnel performance are gathered in the course of a war game); and the cost involved to set up procedures for collecting necessary data is high. Other factors are the lack of control over variables in the operational environment, the subjectivity which pervades all such measurements, and the political factor which is the need for presenting the appearance of adequacy, regardless of what the truth actually is. This is an overriding concern to officers.

In the Johnson et al. (1978) study troops were moved in accordance with the requirements of the evaluation, specially trained observers were attached to the troops, specifically defined data were collected—a near ideal situation for the behavioral evaluator, but one unlikely to be repeated very often. Nonetheless, even when behavior specialists do not control the war game or fleet exercise, it is possible to secure some data leading to a summary figure of merit. Special arrangements must be made, though, to collect error rate or task accomplishment data from individuals and teams. To determine the contribution of the personnel subsystem to overall system effectiveness it is necessary to collect data on the performance of the total system. These data are often missing, however, invented, heavily biased, or contaminated by extraneous circumstances. The military possesses a number of data reporting systems, such as the Navy's 3M or the Air Force's 66-1 system. These are oriented almost completely to logistics and very little information of a personnel nature can be extracted from them (see String and Orlansky, 1981).

If objective performance oriented measurement methods are unavailing, there are a number of subjective methods for quantitatively estimating the efficiency of system personnel aspects. One of the more sophisticated of them, MOAT—referred to early in this chapter—(Helm and Donnell, 1979) can be used as the system becomes operational or later (along with OT). The Department of Defense's operational readiness reporting scheme, and others like it, is designed for use with already operational systems.

MOAT

MOAT is an evaluation methodology that measures system/subsystem operability in terms of operator tasks performed during a mission. The technique is anchored in task analysis, scaling methodology, and *multiattribute utility* (MAU) theory (a Bayesian oriented decision-making paradigm, Edwards, 1976).

In MOAT the system is partitioned into a task hierarchy in much the same way as in function/task analysis (Chapter 2). Each of the tasks resulting is rated for operability where operability is a function of task criticality, task difficulty, and subsystem effectiveness. An interval scale combines these three functions making use of conjoint measurement (Krantz and Tversky, 1971). Personnel rate each task on scales for workload and effectiveness, the goal being to formulate a single interval scale for these ratings. To do this requires the formulation of a rating matrix which satisfies the axioms of additive conjoint measurement and which can be scaled to produce a unidimensional interval rating scale. This requires the separation of the scale into two subscales which form a rating matrix. Personnel then rank–order the cells of the matrix. The cell receiving the highest ranking, 1, receives the highest interval scale value of 100. This cell reflects the least amount of effort to accomplish a task along with a subsystem that accomplishes multiple tasks for the operator. The cell receiving the lowest ranking and lowest interval scale value of 0 is the cell that reflects the highest workload with the poorest performing subsystem. After having obtained the necessary rank order, a special scaling procedure (the Delta method, Coombes, 1964) yields interval scale values for all possible rating categories. Rank orders are then converted to interval scales.

The methodology therefore is a rating scheme whose sophistication stems from MAU and scaling theory. Operationally what one does is get subject matter experts —in the study by Helm and Donnell, A7-E pilots—to rate all the tasks required to perform specific missions. The output of their work is a rank order of tasks by cumulative weight.

Like most evaluations, MOAT does not produce a summary figure of merit value. Rather there is a listing of tasks with rank values and each task can be considered in terms of whether it should be improved. It is possible to derive an overall operability score which, since a perfect system would be rated 100, indicates the effective operability deficit. The methodology is computerized and provides a number of graphic outputs. Because of the hierarchical decomposition of the system into flight requirements, flight phase, mission phase, duty and task levels, it is possible to derive an operability score for each.

MOAT is in the process of development and there is no information about its extended use, nor about any validation, though validation of a summary figure of merit would present a very substantial problem in itself because it would mean essentially conducting a prolonged OT for the system. At the moment MOAT is aircraft oriented, but its developers aim at the generalization of the technique.

Operational Readiness

The Operational Readiness measurement system utilized by all military services is also a rating scheme (Department of the Army, 1979). Readiness is measured by the ability of a service to man, equip, and train its forces and to mobilize, deploy, and sustain them as required to accomplish assigned mission. Readiness consists of four components (personnel readiness, equipment on hand, equipment readiness and training readiness) which are evaluated to produce five readiness ratings:

C-1 = combat ready, no deficiencies,
C-2 = combat ready, minor deficiencies
C-3 = combat ready, major deficiencies,
C-4 = not combat ready, major deficiencies, and
C-5 = not combat ready, service programmed.

The personnel readiness rating is based on data describing required strength, available strength percentage, MOS qualified strength percentage, senior grade fill percentage, and personnel turnover percentage. The training readiness rating is based on data describing weeks to be fully trained and various constraints such as funds, equipment, and material, training areas, fuel, time, etc. The system receives the rating of its lowest component. For example, if three components are C-1 but one is C-4, the system is rated C-4.

This rating scheme is very crude, highly subjective, and quite global. It is popularly assumed to have been developed to satisfy congressional demands. Continuing efforts are being made to study the operational readiness problem and to refine the system without apparent appreciable success (though there may be political obstacles to this). Although two of the four components refer to personnel, the behavioral evaluator will find little of value in this scheme.

Another example of a subjective system effectiveness evaluation scheme is the *commander's unit analysis profile* under development by the Fort Hood unit of the Army Research Institute (Department of the Army, 1981). This is an attempt to develop a measurement tool with which the unit commander can assess the personnel readiness of his unit, which in turn should provide some estimate of mission readiness and operational effectiveness.

A simple 88-item questionnaire collects enlisted personnel attitudes toward factors related to mission readiness and operational effectiveness such as leadership and job satisfaction. These are of course only indirectly related to performance. They may influence performance, but they do not determine it. Currently the questionnaire has been administered to about 10,000 Army soldiers and from these data 21 dimensions have been generated factorially. Examples of these are leadership, promotion policy, and job satisfaction.

The profile provides two scores. The first indicates how positive or negative the unit's standing is on each factor (− 100 [worst] to + 100 [best]). and the average score of all other units in the Army that have recently utilized the profile. This permits the commander to compare his unit with the combined average score (standard) of all other units. A second score is a unit percentile rank for each factor which is the percentage of all units that have received lower or equal scores on the factor.

One cannot help feeling that the subjective ratings are mere excuses to avoid the expense and trouble of developing really effective field exercises or simulations.

PROBLEM INVESTIGATION

Problem investigation is closely tied to effectiveness evaluation. One evaluates a system, a subsystem, or a workplace in the expectation—too often fulfilled—that there will be deficiencies requiring problem investigation.

For example, following the Three-Mile Island nuclear incident a whole series of evaluations of nuclear power plant control rooms was implemented which revealed a number of serious problems (Seminara, Gonzalez and Parsons, 1977).

The methods employed in problem investigation are also much the same as those used in effectiveness evaluation (at least as far as nuclear power plant control room reviews are concerned: see NUREG-0700, 1981). These include review of documentation, interviews with operating personnel, function and task analysis, and human engineering analysis of equipment. The difference between effectiveness evaluation and problem investigation is that although the former may lead to the latter, problem investigation is always initiated by recognition of a problem situation (a significant discrepancy between desired and actual performance). Manifestly, some implicit or explicit standard is involved in that discrepancy.

The basic question the problem investigator seeks to answer is, What are the underlying causes of the problem? What is reported as the problem is often only the end result of a number of factors. For example, in one problem investigation (Harris and Williams, 1980) the problem reported was the relative inability of the detector/tracker in an air warfare surveillance system to detect "enemy" targets. The actual causal factors involved among other things lack of relevant training, poor job design and organizational inefficiencies. These factors were not immediately apparent and had to be unearthed by the investigation.

Once causal factors are discovered, potential solutions can be developed. Consequently, the catalyst in the investigation is the need to diagnose. This is, in part, because the behavioral aspects of the problem are often concealed by the more obvious hardware manifestations. If a problem is phrased in terms of electronic blips on a CRT display, it is more difficult to see the problem in terms of training or job design. Because of the propensity of system managers to view problems first in their hardware guise, it is not until solutions attuned to the hardware concept have failed that the behavioral specialist will be called in.

The problem investigation tends to recapitulate the analytical processes of system development that ultimately produced the system/subsystem under investigation. This is because the areas of investigation are much the same as those emphasized in development.

1. *Function/task analysis.* The investigator attempts to determine what the system is supposed to do. Only then can he determine how badly personnel are performing. Functional performance criteria in quantitative terms are especially important. There is a necessary initial familiarization phase during which system documentation is examined, system personnel are observed, and interviewed to secure detailed information about how their tasks are actually carried out—a sort of job analysis, possibly different from the way the task is described in technical manuals.

2. *Job design.* The investigator seeks to determine if the job as it is structured helps or hinders personnel performance. For example, in the detector/tracker situation it was found that the two functions performed—detection and tracking—were being performed by one operator and thus were competing for his attention.

3. *Human engineering.* The investigator will seek to determine if the design of the man–machine interface (e.g., a console) is adequate to permit personnel to perform their jobs efficiently. This can be done by examining and operating the equipment and by utilizing a human engineering checklist. In an investigation of boiler problems in the 1200 psi propulsion system used aboard many Navy ships (Williams, Pope, Pulu and Sass, 1982) the layout of the piping and valves that had to be opened and closed to run the boilers was such that it actually inhibited correct performance and led to safety problems.

4. *Training.* The investigator determines whether personnel have been adequately trained to perform their jobs. This means examining school curricula and on-the-job (OJT) training and interviewing instructors and supervisors to determine if the training satisfies actual operational requirements, as often it does not. In the detector/tracker situation it was found that these personnel received a bare minimum of training on shore, under the presumption that systematic shipboard OJT would be provided; but there was in fact no systematic shipboard training.

5. *Organizational context.* The investigator seeks also to determine whether the organizational context in which personnel perform contributes to the problem. In the detector/tracker study it was found that during fleet exercises key personnel were retained on duty for eight hours or more without a significant break (although evidence is very convincing that vigilance deteriorates markedly after 30 minutes to 1 hour on watch, Davies and Tune, 1969). Air warfare personnel also slept in quarters where they were constantly being disturbed by others who worked irregular hours, which meant that they began their work already impaired from lack of sleep.

The methods utilized in problem investigation were interviews, questionnaires, demonstrations of how equipment works, observations of personnel at their tasks, review of relevant documents and records, performance measurement (where feasible). Such methods may appear primitive and unsophisticated, but the fact that they are utilized in many contexts suggests that they are what might be termed fundamental or generic. Sophistication derives not from the methods themselves but from what the specialist can do with them. For example, the interview conducted by a novice supplies crude, imprecise answers. In the words of a highly skilled specialist, the interview supplies much more.

The setting for problem investigation is the system under full operation and consequently the question of simulation fidelity, which is a serious problem for OT, does not arise. Like detective work elsewhere, the interview is particularly important in problem investigation; performance measurement less so (because the opportunity for controlled performance measurement rarely arises). There are some constraints however. For example, system personnel are not test subjects and time has not been set aside to interview them (although investigators usually manage to "get their man") or to utilize their equipment for experimental purposes. The noninterference barrier is very strong.

The investigation is not complete until a solution is recommended. There may also be a phase in which the proposed solution is tried out and implemented. The range of solutions possible is quite restricted because the system has already been fabricated. Hence any redesign that involves hardware modifications is practically speaking impossible unless the problem is sufficiently critical and can be eliminated in no other way. Consequently easier, softer solutions are encouraged: retraining or the institution of new training, job performance aids, job redesign to the extent that again, this does not involve hardware.

It should not be thought that problem investigation is a slapdash procedure. On the contrary it may be prolonged and may require extensive effort (the detector/tracker study required two people full time for the better part of one year). Because the questions raised are difficult and the answers not obvious, problem investigation may demand more of the behavior specialist than more programmed evaluations.

EVALUATION OF TRAINING SYSTEMS AND DEVICES

Training Systems

There is a body of educational theory that deals with training evaluation (e.g., Berk, 1982; Gropper, 1975; and Bloom, Hastings and Madaus, 1971) but we can do no more than refer to it because this is not a text on education nor has that theory much influenced the evaluation of training systems, at least in the military (Mackie and Christenson, 1967). Nor, one suspects, in industry either. Most of that theory is speculative and not formalized or systematized sufficiently to enable one to derive a step-by-step procedure (and any methodology had better be in step-by-step form or it cannot be utilized except by the specialists who created it, and perhaps not even by them). Educational evaluation has focused on the evaluation of internal components of the training system (i.e., individual tasks) and not on the training system as a whole. It is the evaluation of the latter with which we are concerned. The methodology of educational evaluation was developed primarily for general education and not for job oriented training. The criteria of accomplishment are not the same, hence the methods which derive from those criteria are different. This is not to say that the techniques described in this section have not been influenced at all by educational theory but at least in the performance oriented evaluation methods the influence of experimental design for setting up studies has been greater than that of educational theory.

Training system evaluation can be measured either by trainee performance (that system is effective which graduates skilled students) or by evaluation of the attributes of the training system (that system is effective which has certain desired characteristics). This discussion begins with performance measurement which is the preferred methodology, since the purpose of training is to develop trained personnel. Thus it is a more direct evaluative measure.

The ISD process (Chapter 6) contains evaluation elements: Internal evaluation which is an examination of the documentation built up in the course of creating the training system, and external evaluation which reflects the standards of the operational job and includes interviews with school graduates, supervisors, rating of graduate performance, criterion referenced job performance tests, etc. Supervisor ratings of performance and interviews with graduates are a form of performance measurement, but very indirect and certainly less desirable than direct performance measurement.

The ISD evaluation is performed idependently of the OT, primarily because ISD training is often delayed well beyond acceptance testing of a new system. It is therefore not possible to test the training system in the OT context because the training system is usually not in place at this time. However, one can secure some preliminary information about training adequacy. The tasks performed in OT are routinely checked off as the operator performs them; if the operator cannot, one would suspect a training deficiency (although complete failure to perform is rather unlikely; more common is some evidence of difficulty or a lack of performance quality). It is also possible to question the OT operator to determine if he has been adequately trained for his OT job (this would not apply of course if the OT operator is a contractor-technician already skilled in exercising the system). However, the OT operator may be less than completely honest about his performance deficiencies, to avoid embarrassment, or he may genuinely not know whether his training was adequate. This is an extremely global question, requiring some skill in training matters to answer correctly. Moreover, if the OT involves only a sample of tasks to be performed, it may not provide a sufficient range of experience to enable the operator to make a valid judgment of training adequacy. The OT itself is thus an unsatisfactory setting to evaluate a total training system, even if the training system is fully in place by OT.

Leaving aside OT as a vehicle for training evaluation, what are the various performance ways in which one can evaluate the completed training system?

One must first consider criteria and standards. If a trainee enters a training course without any knowledge of relevant skills, the training system, no matter how poor it may be, will train him to a degree of effectiveness greater than he had when he began. This suggests the traditional pre-test/post-test method of measuring amount trained. Test before training and test after completion of training; the difference is what has been learned. Because of its very simplicity, this method has some built-in dangers (for which see Linn, 1981). For example, the quantity learned (the pre/post-test difference) depends in part on the skills the trainee already had when he began his training. That quantity needs to be subtracted from the pre/post-test difference score, or at least, the latter must be evaluated in terms of the former, though it rarely is. A greater danger is that the evaluator will accept the criterion of the statistical significance of differences between pre- and post-test scores (e.g., "t," analysis of variance) as meaningful. Even a minor difference score can be statistically significant. How much improvement represents an adequate amount of training? Until the evaluator knows this, the statistic is meaningless.

One might also say that if the trainee has passed all his school tests, he has been trained. However, such tests are flawed unless they simulate to a high degree of fidelity the operational tasks for which the student is being trained. Current educational theory emphasizes criterion-referenced tests, but it is difficult in a school environment to simulate the operational job completely. For one thing, the job may involve so many individual tasks that the tests given the student represent only a partial sample of the job. Then, too, the school environment is likely to be simpler and more formal than the job environment, which is often crowded, noisy and time-stressful. Finally, norm-referenced tests are often constructed to allow a certain percentage of the class to pass and the rest to fail. The cut-off score may be administratively rather than job determined.

Even though school tests are supposed to be performance oriented and criterion-referenced—and thus assume a high degree of identity with operational tasks—the pre/post test and internal test evaluations focus on the training system alone, without adequate consideration of the job for which the training has been supplied. Since the training has no utility unless it enables the graduate to perform his operational job, the preceding evaluations cannot be considered valid representations of the worth of the training system because they are confined to the training environment. It is quite common to find graduates who pass school tests but who perform only minimally in the operational situation.

The only truly valid way of evaluating training system effectiveness is to include in the evaluation some measurement of the graduate's performance on the job. This calls for a transfer of training model in which the graduate's performance is measured at the conclusion of his course of study and then, within 30 to 60 days after his introduction to the job, in the operational situation. On-the-job measurement cannot be too soon, because the new graduate may not have had the opportunity to adjust to his new environment, nor too late, because it is possible that the graduate will have learned much of what he needs to do the job from formal or informal OJT, from indoctrination by his peers, or even from simple exposure to the operational situation.

Another qualification of the transfer of training paradigm is that the tests administered at the conclusion of training and then on-the-job must be the same or at least very similar. Otherwise they may tap different skills. The cost and a certain artificiality of special job performance tests in the operational environment make it more desirable to measure the graduate's routine job performance. However, this too creates difficulties, since some operational situations may not be flexible enough to permit the measurement process.

The ideal training evaluation model consists of the pre/post evaluation followed by measurement of ongoing performance in the operational situation. The pre/post test determines that some training has been accomplished. On-the-job measurement indicates that the graduate can perform his job. The operational measurement is most critical. One can dispense with the pre-test and even the post-test and still determine whether personnel can perform the jobs for which they were trained. But without operational measurement the meaning of evaluation statistics is obscure.

To perform the training evaluation and on-the-job measurement the evaluator must have criteria, measures, and methods of measurement just as he does for any other measurement. To develop these he should refer back to the original function/task analysis which should contain the performance criteria on which criterion-referenced school tests were based and which should suggest on-the-job measures.

Measurement of job performance in the operational environment using previously developed job performance tests (the same or much the same as those administered in school) suffers from the fact that the programmed test can be only a simulation of the operational tasks. A carefully constructed job performance test is somewhat artificial just because it is carefully constructed to ignore the extraneous, interfering, delaying inadequacies of the operational environment. Administering the test in the operational environment does not necessarily render the test comparable to the operational task.

The classic transfer of training paradigm as it is applied to the effectiveness evaluation of training devices employs a control group which has received some form of training other than that of the training device—usually on the operational equipment. One can then compare training on the device with training on the operational equipment. To carry this paradigm over to the evaluation of total training system, the evaluator should have a control group which has received its training in an environment other than the school training environment. This environment can only be the operational one, in which personnel learn on-the-job, informally, by observation, tutoring, and hands-on experience. The difference between the two groups' performances following training would indicate the adequacy of the formal training system over the informal one.

It is however difficult to apply the control group in the evaluation of an entire instructional system for two reasons. First, one rarely encounters—in the military at any rate (and one suspects also in industry)—trainees who receive only OJT, because it is expensive to maintain two separate instructional systems. Second, the comparison is rather pointless in any event, because any superiority of formal instruction over OJT would simply indicate superiority over a very weak training methodology. On-the-job training, at least as it is conducted in the military, has little to recommend it. Hence the classic control group is almost never employed in training system evaluations.

In fact, the transfer of training evaluation as it applies to measurement in the operational situation is almost never implemented. There are two reasons for this. The first is *cost*. Tracking the individual school graduate to his operational job and setting up special tests or measuring his routine performance are highly expensive. The second is the *difficulty associated with measurement in the operational environment*. This has been noted several times previously.

There are less formal ways of securing feedback from the operational situation.

1. The graduate may be asked to answer, and return to the school a critique—in questionnaire form—of the training he received in light of his new job responsibilities. However, this does not provide any quantitative evaluation of training effectiveness. Rather, it is diagnostic. The technique leans heavily on the willingness of personnel to volunteer information and their skill in being able to analyze their own performance in training related terms. Results with this technique have not been overly productive.
2. Skilled evaluators and subject matter experts can visit the operational system and observe/rate the school graduate's performance and then interview him and/or his supervisor. How well performance observation substitutes for objective performance measurement is a question the answer to which may depend on the nature of the job. If it is one in which indices of performance quality can be discerned, performance observation can be very useful. However, this method also is only infrequently applied because of the cost involved.
3. Ratings by the graduate's supervisor can be sent back to the school for evaluation but their adequacy depends on the supervisor's evaluational skills. The rating is usually a global one and does not specifically pull out tasks which have been performed well or poorly. This makes it difficult for the training evaluator to relate the rating to specific training needs.

Despite the difficulties these feedback methods encounter, they are worth attempting. Unfortunately, in the military, feedback from the operational environment to the school is usually quite infrequent and cannot be closely related to training systems.

Attribute Evaluation

The other type of training system evaluation is what we have termed *attribute evaluation*. This assumes that an effective training system has certain characteristics. It follows that if the system under examination has these characteristics, it is effective. The assumption is logical, even if it is tautological, but it has two deficiencies. The attributes selected represent an assumption rather than verified fact and, since feedback from the operational system is lacking, there is no empirical evidence that the selected attributes do, in fact, produce an effective training system.

Attribute evaluation is judgmental, molecular, and emphasizes diagnosis rather than a summary quantitative figure of merit. None of the evaluation techniques—even the performance oriented ones—produce such a summary, with the exception of the human reliability metric (see Chapter 5).

The following attribute evaluation technique was developed as a subsystem of, or as the evaluative arm of, the ISD process (Chapter 6). The reason for describing it is that it has aroused considerable interest in the civilian instructional community. Within the military, this system known as IQI or versions of it (Merrill, Riegeluth and Faust, 1979) are now being systematically applied as part of the ISD process.

The *instructional quality inventory* (IQI) is a quality control or evaluation procedure for classifying the three main parts of an instructional program: learning objectives, test items, and instructional materials or presentations. The procedures can be used during the instructional development process or can be used afterwards to evaluate existing instructional programs. Although the IQI was initially designed to parallel and supplement the military's ISD model, it can be applied to any systematically developed program of instruction.

The initial work on the IQI was done under contract to the *U. S. Navy Personnel Research and Development Center* (NPRDC) by Merrill, Wood, Richards, and Schmidt (1977). The initial version was extensively revised and field tested by NPRDC and a final version was published in 1979 (Ellis, Wulfeck, and Fredericks, 1979).

The concept behind the IQI is the necessity of keeping the three parts of the instructional program *in concert*. It is assumed that if they are coordinated, if they all address the same thing, instruction will be effective. The IQI's major areas of interest are cognitive and psychomotor behavior.

Classification of objectives is necessary because it helps make more precise judgments about their adequacy and leads to more precise test item specifications. It also helps make judgments about how consistent objectives and test items are with each other.

Objectives and test items can be classified according to: a. what the student must do, that is, the *task* to be performed, and b. the instructional *content*; that is, the type of information the student must learn.

1. *The Task Dimension.* A student can either remember information, or use the information to do something. This distinction corresponds to the difference between knowledge and application.

Tasks may be performed with or without aid. Without aid the student must remember what must be done and then do it. With aid, the student is provided with a guide to the desired task performance, for instance, instructions.

2. *The Content Dimension.* There are five types of content: facts, categories, procedures, rules, and principles. *Facts* (such as the names of American states) are simple associations between names, objects, symbols, locations, etc. Facts can only be remembered while the other content types can be remembered and used. *Categories* are classifications defined by certain specified characteristics, for example the types of ships or types of stars. *Procedures* (e.g., for running a machine) are ordered sequences of steps or operations performed on a single object or in a specific situation. *Rules* also consist of ordered sequences of operations, but are general enough so that they can be performed on a variety of objects or in various situations. *Principles* involve explanations, predictions or diagnoses based on theoretical or cause–effect relationships.

	FACT- Recall or recognize names, parts, dateś places, etc.	CATEGORY- Remember characteristics or classify objects, events or ideas according to characteristics	Content PROCEDURE- Sequence of steps remembered or used in a single situation or on a single piece of equipment	RULE- Remember or use a sequence of steps, that apply across situations or across equipments	PRINCIPLE- Remember, interpret, or predict why or how things happen, or cause-effect relationships
TASK REMEMBER-Recall or recognize facts, concept definitions; steps, procedures or rules; statements of principle					
USE, UNAIDED- Tasks that require classifying, performing a procedure, using a rule, explaining or predicting with no aids except memory					
USE, AIDED- Same as use, unaided, except job aids are available					

FIGURE 8.2. The content-by-task matrix of the Instructional Quality Inventory.

The interrelationships between the task and content categories are shown in Figure 8.2.

The IQI consists of the following procedures:

1. *Objective adequacy.* Learning objectives are adequate if they satisfy three criteria: a. Content. Is the objective correctly stated? (See Chapter Six). b. Accordance with the task-content matrix shown in Figure 8.2. c. Instructional intent. Is the intent of the objective adequately expressed?

2. *Test item adequacy.* Test items are evaluated against their corresponding objectives to ensure that they are consistent with the objectives (i.e., conditions, standards, and actions for the test items are the same for both). Do test items conform to the rules for proper item construction?

3. *Presentation consistency and adequacy.* Is instructional presentation consistent with the objectives and test items? Does it teach to the task level and content type of the objective/test item as expressed in learning guide lines (see Chapter 6)?

Like all attribute evaluation instruments (e.g., human engineering checklists), IQI is hopelessly subjective. It is, however, a systematic way of ensuring that ISD products are as effective as they can be. Because of the subjectivity of the IQI procedure, it can be employed adequately only by highly skilled instructional technologists.

More detailed information about other systematic approaches to training evaluation can be found in Borich (1979). They all suffer, however, from the subjectivism of IQI, and the latter is the best of the lot.

Training Devices

Training devices, by which we mean any equipment used as an adjunct to training—from static cutaways to highly sophisticated simulators—can also be evaluated using attribute evaluation and performance methods. Among training devices, greatest evaluation attention has been paid to dynamic simulators because these involve very considerable expense (e.g., millions of dollars) and therefore require most justification.

Attribute Approach. The attribute approach to training device evaluation makes greatest use of rating scales because such scales permit the evaluator to quantify his own or others' judgments. When no effort is made to quantify, the evaluator can make use of questionnaire or interview data.

The attribute approach depends on preselected criteria because in effect the evaluator asks himself or subject matter experts, Does this device satisfy these criteria? However, formal training evaluation scales have not been widely published.

A number of criteria have been applied to simulators, of which two are most popular: *fidelity to the operational equipment* and *predicted training effectiveness* (this device should train well or poorly). For many operational personnel who are laymen in regard to training, it appears obvious that the closer the training device is to the operational equipment, the more effectively it should train. Actually, extreme fidelity may not add anything to training effectiveness. Some years back there was an impassioned controversy over the question of whether it was necessary to simulate motion cues in aircraft simulators to achieve maximum training effectiveness. A series of empirical studies on this point (e.g., Gray and Fuller, 1977; Kounce, 1979; Woodruff, Smith, Fuller and Weyer, 1976) concluded that motion cues did not significantly improve pilot training (although see Caro, 1979). A simulator can be a very faithful copy of operational equipment and be either effective or ineffective with respect to a particular training requirement (see McDonald, Waldrop and Reynolds, 1982). Some training equipments deviate markedly and intentionally from the operational system to enhance training.

The fidelity criterion almost always ignores the manner in which the training device will be utilized and the objectives of the training—two considerations that must underlie any determination of training effectiveness.

The rating method of evaluating aircraft simulator adequacy, which is commonly used by industry and buyers, routinely makes use of simulation fidelity as a major evaluation dimension. Pilots rate the simulator in terms of its similarity to the parent aircraft. Adams (1979) has criticized the rating method because of its simplistic assumption that the amount of training transfer is positively related to rated simulator fidelity. He also points out that the accuracy of the rating is a function of individual differences among raters, pilot experience and the interaction of simulator dimensions.

On the other hand, there is some justification for requesting maximum fidelity in training devices. Since we have no data quantifying the amount of fidelity required for training effectiveness, it is a conservative approach to demand as much as possible. Despite the many simulation studies that have been performed over the past 30 years, the question of how much fidelity is still a critical unresolved research area.

Predicted training effectiveness is a global criterion which carries with it a number of unstated subcriteria, so that it is impossible to determine the validity of the judgments made with this criterion. The assumption is made that subject matter experts, operational personnel, and instructors can somehow translate their experience into predictions of training effectiveness. Unfortunately, predicted training effectiveness judgments are often erroneous because they are expressed without regard to how the device will be used or the device's training objectives. Meister, Sullivan, Thompson, and Finley (1971) have shown that estimates of training device effectiveness based upon opinion varied widely among instructors.

As the attribute technique is actually applied, it is little more than formal opinion. If there is nothing better available, it might be of some value to use the technique, for example, in relatively early system development when the training device developer seeks to choose between design alternatives. Once the training device has been developed, however, the evaluation technique selected should be performance oriented.

Performance Approach. A number of performance-oriented designs are available but they all involve some variation of the transfer of training paradigm. Transfer of training is the most appropriate means of evaluating a training device because the paradigm embodies the basic objective of training: the transfer of what has been learned from the training environment to the operational job. The following, which is based in part on Payne (1982), Rolfe and Caro (1982) and Hagin, Osborne, Hockenberger, Smith and Gray (1982), cannot be a completely detailed discussion of the topic and the author recommends that the interested reader refer to these authors for additional details.

In its basic form the transfer of training design for devices requires two groups of trainees: one (experimental) that receives training on the device before proceeding to the operational equipment and another (control) that receives an equivalent amount of training but only on the operational equipment. Both are tested on the operational system and the effectiveness criterion is performance on that system. If the experimental group performs as well as—or, preferably, better than—the control, the device is presumed to be effective. Equal performance for the two groups may also represent success for the training device, since the device is to be preferred when the cost of training with it is much less than that involved in using the operational equipment, such as the cost of gasoline and maintenance in flying aircraft. More complex transfer of training designs may involve more than one experimental group to evaluate particular aspects of the training. Examples are the differential advantage of different amounts of training, the different use-scenarios, etc.

The two groups must be comparable, of course, in terms of relevant prior training, experience, and skill. (Comparability can be established statistically by drawing both groups randomly from the same subject pool and by stratification or matching of subjects.) The control treatment—training on the operational equipment—must not influence that group's subsequent performance in the criterion testing situation. Such an influence could be facilitative—a period of rest for the control group while the experimental group engages in the stressful training—or it could be debilitating—operational missions or extended duty required only of the control group because of their availability for additional assignments. Members of both groups must be prevented from engaging in operational activities likely to influence their performance unequally on criterion tasks and thus to invalidate the experimental/control group comparisons.

The transfer design is particularly advantageous because it is sensitive to both positive and negative transfer effects. Several variations of the transfer design are possible, not all of which are desirable. Indeed, the variations exist as responses to constraints in the testing situation.

THE INTERRUPTION OR PRE/POST TEST DESIGN. This variation might be used when the device is employed at an intermediate stage of training, such as when operational training is interrupted for a period of training in the device. In such a situation the students can serve as their own controls, avoiding the necessity of a separate control group. Their performance on the operational equipment *immediately following simulator training* can be compared with their operational performance *immediately prior to their device training*. The difference in these two sets of operational performance data could be attributed to the intervening device training program.

Rolfe and Caro (1982) point out however that the results of this design might be contaminated because of forgetting, particularly if a significant interval elapses between initial and subsequent performance in the operational system. In addition, performance of some skills that are practiced intensively improves after a brief delay without further practice.

THE PREEXISTING CONTROL TRANSFER DESIGN. In some cases a concurrently trained control group may not be necessary. For example, when device training is added to an existing training program, or when a new device supported training program is substituted for an existing or previous program that did not make use of the device, student data from the previous program can be compared with similar data from the new program to determine the latter's effectiveness. For such a comparison to be valid, however, the preexisting data must have been gathered under conditions which would have been applicable to a control group trained concurrently with the experimental group. A disadvantage of this type of design is that differences in performance between the two sets of data may also result from differences in characteristics of the old and new trainee groups, perhaps also from differences in instructional personnel.

THE DEVICE-TO-DEVICE TRANSFER DESIGN. Some studies of device effectiveness involve transfer of training from one device to another device rather than transfer to the operational equipment. For example, if skills learned to proficiency with Device *A* can be shown to facilitate task performance with Device *B*, some measure of training effectiveness for those skills can be inferred for Device *A*. Ideally, the comparison would be between a control group learning solely on Device *B* as against an experimental group learning first on *A*, then on *B*. Equal training time between the two groups is assumed. If it is known that *B* produces positive transfer to the operational system, and *A* facilitates *B*, then it seems likely that *A* might also produce skills transferrable to the operational system. In other words, if *A* is related to *B* and

B to *C* (the criterion system), then *A* is related to *C* and is assumed to be effective. This is an assumption only, of course, which should be verified if possible using other transfer designs.

In one situation, however, device-to-device transfer is clearly appropriate. This situation exists when Device *B* is actually the criterion system. For example, the effectiveness of training in a part–task trainer (*A*) can be determined by measurement of subsequent performance in a full-mission simulator (*B*) if the objective of the part–task training on *A* is to enhance the use of *B*. Again, the use of a control group training solely on *B* should be compared with an experimental group training first on *A*, then on *B*.

THE BACKWARD TRANSFER DESIGN. In a backward transfer study an operator who has already demonstrated mastery of relevant training objectives in the operational vehicle is "transferred" back to the simulator for that vehicle where he is required to perform tasks corresponding to those he has mastered operationally. If he can perform such tasks to criterion levels immediately (without simulator practice), backward transfer is said to have occurred. From this, one assumes that forward transfer from device to operational system will also ensue.

The backward transfer design should be used with great caution for a number of reasons.

1. The assumption that positive transfer can be inferred from backward transfer may be false.

2. If the device is to be used with novices or relatively inexperienced personnel, the backward transfer design may be inappropriate because experienced personnel already proficient at operational tasks are likely to have general experience and skills (not possessed by novices or recent training program graduates) which enable them to transfer more readily to the device.

3. The device (e.g., a full mission simulator) may be suitable to elicit particular behaviors by skilled performers but may lack the cues necessary to elicit these behaviors from beginners.

THE UNCONTROLLED TRANSFER DESIGN. There are circumstances in which a separate control group cannot be employed and other transfer designs are inappropriate. In the uncontrolled transfer design the single group, trained on a device is then tested immediately upon the students' introduction to the operational system. If their performance on the operational system is satisfactory, the assumption is made that training must have occurred on the device because the trainee had no opportunity to use the operational situation to learn.

Failure to secure a control group may be dictated by a number of considerations either political, administrative, or safety. For example, it might be considered unacceptable to penalize members of a possible control group by requiring that they undergo a different and possibly inferior no-device training program. In some instances a control group is simply not feasible. The effectiveness of lunar landing simulators could not be determined, for example, by employing a no-simulator-training control group of astronauts.

THE DEVICE PERFORMANCE IMPROVEMENT DESIGN. This design is not a transfer design per se. Transfer to the operational system is presumed to occur if improvement occurs in the performance of trainees on a device as a result of the training they received in it. However, there is no measure of performance on the operational system. This design is effective only in a negative sense. If improvement does not occur in the device, there would be little expectation that trainees could function effectively in the operational system as a result of device training. On the other hand, if performance improvement on the device does occur, but there is no test of performance on the operational system, there is no guarantee that graduates will be able to perform effectively on the operational system, when they are exposed to it. Because of this, claims cannot be made validly that improvement in simulator performance proves that simulator training is effective for operational performance. Such claims are often made.

Transfer Effectiveness. In order to employ these designs properly measurements should be made to determine the extent to which training objectives have been met. In using measures such as training time or number of training trials, one needs to determine: (1) The training effort required to learn the task on the job completely without the aid of a simulator (TE − SIM), and (2) The training effort required to learn the task on-the-job when some of the training is undertaken using a simulator (TE + SIM). The difference between (1) and (2) (the anticipation being that (1) is less than (2) provides a measure of the training resources saved by the use of simulator. However, the value of any such savings must be considered in relation to (3), The amount of training effort required to learn the task in the simulator (TE in SIM).

These expressions have been used by Roscoe (1971) to derive what he terms the *transfer effectiveness ratio* (TER). This ratio is obtained by combining the three measures in the following equation:

$$TER = \frac{(\text{TE} - \text{SIM}) - (\text{TE} + \text{SIM})}{(\text{TE in SIM})} \tag{4}$$

Although the equations are phrased in terms of a simulator, they are applicable to any training device.

When the amount of training effort (practice in the operational system) saved is equal to the amount of training effort in the simulator, *TER* = *+1.0*. When the training effort in the simulator is less than the effort saved in the operational situation, *TER is greater than +1.0*. *TERs less than +1.0* arise when the training effort in the simulator is greater than that saved on the job.

A TER greater than *+1.0* indicates that device training is effective and more efficient than training on-the-job, unless simulator costs are much greater than those of the operational system. If a TER is less than *+1.0*, but the simulator's operating costs are significantly less than those of OJT, then training in the simulator may still be desirable.

The methodology for determining training effectiveness must therefore include measures which relate the degree of transfer of training from simulator to job to training costs, and hence utilization. Consequently three additional expressions to complement the TER have been developed by Roscoe (1980). These are:

(i) the training cost ratio (TCR)

$$= \frac{\text{cost of operating the simulator (\$/h)}}{\text{cost of operating the actual equipment (\$/h)}}$$

(ii) the cost-effectiveness ratio (CER) $= \dfrac{\text{TER}}{\text{TCR}}$

CER values greater than 1.0 indicate that cost-effective training can be achieved.

(iii) the simulator utilization ratio (SUR)

$$= \frac{\text{amount of time simulator used for training}}{\text{amount of time simulator available for training}}$$

In the case of aircraft simulators, Rolfe and Caro (1982) suggest that TERs as low as *0.2* may still produce *CERs greater than 1.0*, indicating simulator training is still cost-effective. In Orlansky and String's (1977) examination of flight simulator effectiveness, TERs ranged from *+1.9 to −0.4*. Where the introduction of a simulator increases on-the-job training efforts, a negative TER is possible.

COMMENTARY

Empirical system evaluation methods, viewed as a whole, have certain common characteristics, despite the many differences among them.

1. They are as much or more diagnostic in intent as they are evaluational. It is possible to derive a unitary figure of merit from some of these methods, but in practice this is not often done. This is in line with system engineering/development philosophy which is aimed at discovering and eliminating deficiencies rather than quantifying status.

2. Except for one or two methods like MOAT, the empirical system evaluation methods are fairly simple, even crude, and are not based on theory. Training device evaluation methods can make use of elegant transfer of training designs but it is not clear how often this is actually done.

3. The evaluation methods are both attribute and performance oriented. OT, which is a process, a way of managing a test rather than a specific evaluation method, makes use of many methods of both types. OT as an overall planning methodology is fixed, but the specific methods or processes it employs are contingent upon the nature of the system being evaluated, the specific information one desires to secure from the test and, more important, constraints on the testing process.

One gains the impression that methods for statistically analyzing behavioral data (e.g., analysis of variance) are becoming much more sophisticated and powerful than the methods of data collection which have remained largely unchanged. This is perhaps because behavioral data collection methods are constrained by sensory and cognitive limitations whereas statistical methods of analysis are constrained only by mathematical logic. More powerful assessment methods do squeeze more out of data collected crudely, but there is probably some point at which further statistical sophistication is no longer cost-effective.

One reason why performance-oriented evaluation methods, involving objective measures such as time, measures of task accomplishment and error frequency may be inherently limited is that to make sense of them we need standards of what is normal. And we need to establish what is to be reasonably accepted in the performance of some function. Then whatever deviates from those standards can be viewed as abnormal. What is the largest number of targets a tracker can handle at one time? How many errors of omission should one expect in operating a console consisting of ten meters and five controls? Until we have a quantitative human performance database, most of our objective measures are uninterpretable.

Lacking normative data, we rely in evaluation increasingly on subjective methods of data collection (self-report, rating scales, interviews, checklists) to gather information that will help elucidate the *meaning* of the data we collect. We rely on system personnel, the actors in the performance drama, to tell us not what they did—our objective measures tell us that—but to interpret the meaning of the data. Even in the most highly controlled measurement situation, the laboratory experiment, it would be a foolish researcher who did not debrief his subjects following a test session. Unfortunately, system operators and test personnel are generally not trained to provide the kind of information the evaluator is looking for. They can report what they did and, sometimes, why they did it; on whether the task loaded them, but not how much; on whether they felt fatigued, confident of success, or depressed about anticipated failure. They can relay the special difficulties they experienced in performing a task; what they understood or did not understand about the task; their perceptions and misperceptions; their judgments about whether or not they successfully completed the task—and the errors they made. And they can tell us what they were thinking about—if they remember— their judgment of the good and bad qualities of an equipment, a working situation, and the stimuli presented to them.

All of this is very interesting and informative, but it does not answer the fundamental question: How well did the operator or the team perform? Of course, if performance is errorless or corresponds to some objective requirement, there is no question. But few performances are that clear cut. It is interesting to hear the operator's guess as to how well he did and perhaps to secure a consensus among operators or to secure a subject matter expert's judgment, but again none of this is worth much unless we have hard, objectively gathered, quantitative normative data about how well operators, in general, do when placed in a particular situation. We can leave it to the subject matter expert and, in fact, in many situations we do (for example, an instructor pilot evaluating a student's maneuvers in the air) but we are not very sure how accurate the subject matter expert is.

The need for normative data to serve as a means of comparing any single performance instance against a norm requires a special data gathering effort. Such data are primarily descriptive, rather than experimental, though experimental data can sometimes be helpful. However, all the experiments in all the psychological journals from the time of Wundt to the present have not sufficed to provide us with sufficient, adequate standards for tasks and jobs. Perhaps this is because psychological experiments deal primarily with molecular subtasks. It may be, then, no coincidence that psychological experiments have been most effective in building up a database for very molecular psychophysical functions—visual, for example.

Attribute evaluation—discerning certain dimensions or qualities in performance and scaling these—can expand upon the limitations of performance evaluation, provided, of course, that the attribute evaluation can be consistently applied. If the use of theory enables the evaluator to hypothesize that, for example, effective team performance should have attributes *X, Y* and *Z*, then he can examine that performance to determine if those attributes are present. If they can be applied, the use of attributes can much enrich the evaluation, without relinquishing objective performance evaluation methods. The attribute method is limited only by one's capability to conceptualize relevant attributes and discover ways of determining their presence or absence in performance. Of course, the attributes must actually exist in performance, and must be relevant to the output of the performance being observed.

Although experimental design plays some role in OT and in measurement of operational system effectiveness, major emphasis and ingenuity must be directed at planning how to represent the operational environment correctly.

Operational environment characteristics represent an area that needs investigation so that we can a. simulate those characteristics adequately and introduce them into OT and other types of tests and b. find ways of controlling their effects (extracting them as it were) in field studies of operational systems. The OE may be thought of as consisting of the system, its operational routine, the physical environment and certain *noise* or disturbing qualities: work-irrelevant activities, interruptions to that work, and nontechnical delays (i.e., delays other than those inherent in normal system functioning). That added noise quality may account for the difference in performance between a system under operational test and the same system operating in its assigned environment. If so, to achieve a more valid simulation in our system testing, perhaps we ought to introduce that noise deliberately. But before we could do this we would be compelled to examine the OE in terms of its discordant elements.

In both analysis and evaluation great use is made of subject matter experts as the data source and as data collectors/evaluators. Nevertheless little research has been performed to develop more effective ways of eliciting their judgments and determine to what extent their judgments are valid. This is another research gap that should be filled.

While our evaluation methods are supposed to be directed at the personnel subsystem as a whole, these methods are actually geared more to measurement of individual operator performance. This despite the fact that most of our system processes are now being implemented by teams. None of our methods of evaluation is specifically team oriented, although it can be argued that when we measure the outputs of the team process, we also measure the team itself. There are nonetheless times in a system evaluation when, possibly as a diagnostic function, we wish to determine whether the team process itself is effective.

The special problem of behavioral evaluation is to find ways of relating the personnel subsystem process and output to the total system output. This is the great void in the evaluation of behavioral effectiveness. Because the perception of system managers is that personnel performance has much less impact on the system than hardware/software, it is difficult to persuade them of the importance of behavioral inputs in design. Personnel performance has no significance to anyone beyond the behavior researcher unless he can demonstrate that personnel performance strongly affects the system. Of course, without personnel the man–machine system will not function. Yet, granted that reasonably well trained personnel are at their system stations, do variations in their performance make any real difference to the system? This is not only an important, but for the behavior researcher, an exciting question.

REFERENCES

Adams, J. A. On the evaluation of training devices. *Human Factors,* 1979, *21,* 711–720.

Altman, J. W. Choosing human performance tests and measures. In J. P. Kinkaid and K. W. Potempa (Eds.), *Proceedings of the Human Factors Testing Conference 1-2 October 1968.* Report AFHRL-TR-69-6, Air Force Human Resources Laboratory, Wright-Patterson AFB, OH, October, 1969.

Askren, W. B., and Newton, R. R. *Review and Analysis of Personnel Subsystem Test and Evaluation Literature.* Report AFHRL-TR-68-7, Air Force Human Resources Laboratory, Wright-Patterson AFB, OH, January, 1969.

Baker, J. D., and Johnson, E. M. (Eds.) Special issue: Field testing. *Human Factors,* 1974, *16,* 199–252.

Berk, R. A. (Ed.) *Educational Evaluation Methodology: The State of the Art.* Baltimore: Johns Hopkins University Press, 1981.

Bloom, B. S., Hastings, J. T., and Madaus, G. R. *Handbook on Formative and Summative Evaluation of Student Learning.* New York: McGraw-Hill, 1971.

Bond, N. A., and Towne, D. M. *Troubleshooting Complex Equipment in the Military Services: Research and Prospects.* Technical Report No. 92, Behavioral Technology Laboratories, University of Southern California, Los Angeles, CA, December, 1979.

Borich, G. D. A systems approach to the evaluation of training. In H. O'Neil (Ed.), *Procedures for Instructional Systems Development,* New York: Academic Press, 1979, 205–231.

Briggs, L. D. *Instructional Design: Principles and Applications.* Englewood Cliffs, NJ: Educational Technology Publications, 1977.

Caro, P. W. The relationships between flight simulator motion and training requirements. *Human Factors,* 1979, *21,* 493–501.

Clarkin, J. J. Effects of the operational environment on performance. In L. T. Pope, and D. Meister (Eds.), *Symposium Proceedings: Productivity Enhancement: Personnel Performance Assessment in Navy Systems.* Navy Personnel Research and Development Center, San Diego, CA, October, 1977.

Cohill, A. M., and Ehrich, R. W. Automated tools for the study of human/computer interaction. *Proceedings,* Human Factors Society Annual Meetings, 1983, 897–900.

Coombs, C. H. *A Theory of Data*. New York: Wiley, 1964.

Davies, D. R., and Tune, G. S. *Human Vigilance Performance*. New York: American Elsevier Publishing Company, 1969.

Department of the Army. *Unit Status Reporting*. Army Regulation (AR) 220–1, 1979.

Department of the Army. The Commander's Unit Analysis Profile. U.S. Army: Ft. Hood ARI Field Unit, 1981.

Department of Defense. MIL-H-46855B. *Human Engineering Requirements for Military Systems*. Author: Washington, DC, 31 January 1979.

Department of Defense. Military Standard 1472C. *Human Engineering Design Criteria for Military Systems, Equipment, and Facilities*. Author: Washington, DC, 2 May, 1981.

Department of the Navy. *Operational Test Director Guide,* COMOPTEVFOR Instruction 3960.1B, Operational Test and Evaluation Force, Norfolk, VA, 5 July 1969.

Edwards, W. *How to Use MultiAttribute Utility Measurement for Social Decision Making*. Technical Report 001597-1-T, Social Science Research Institute, University of Southern California, Los Angeles, CA, August, 1976.

Ellis, J. A., Wulfeck, W. H., and Fredericks, P. *The Instructional Quality Inventory: II. User's Manual*. Special Report 79-24, Navy Personnel Research and Development Center, San Diego, CA, August, 1979.

Gagne, R. M. The content analysis of subject matter: The computer as an aid in the design of criterion-referenced tests. *Instructional Science,* 1976, *5,* 1–28.

Geddie, J. C. *Profiling the Characteristics of the Developmental Test Participant*. Technical Memorandum 31–76, U.S. Army Human Engineering Laboratory, Aberdeen Proving Ground, MD, October, 1976.

Geer, C. W. *User's Guide for the Test and Evaluation Sections of MIL-H-46855B*. Report D194-10006-1, Boeing Aerospace Company, Seattle, WA, June 30, 1977 (AD A045 097).

Glaser, R., Damrin, D. E., and Gardner, F. M. *The Tab Item: A Technique for the Measurement of Proficiency in Diagnostic Problemsolving Tasks*. College of Education, University of Illinois, Urbana, IL, 1952.

Goldin, S. E., and Thorndike, P. W. (Eds.) *Improving Team Performance: Proceedings of the Rand Team Performance Workshop*. Report R-2606-ONR, Rand Corporation, Santa Monica, CA, August, 1980.

Gray, T. H., and Fuller, R. R. *Effects of Simulator Training and Platform Motion on Air-to-Surface Weapons Delivery Training*. Report AFHRL-TR-77-29, Flying Training Division, Air Force Human Resources Laboratory, Williams AFB, AZ, July, 1977.

Gropper, G. L. *Diagnosis and Revision in the Development of Instructional Material*. Englewood Cliffs, NJ: Educational Technology Publications, 1975.

Hagin, W. V., Osborne, S. R., Hockenberger, R. L., Smith, J. P., and Gray, T. H. *Operational Test and Evaluation Handbook for Aircrew Training Devices: Operational Effectiveness Evaluation*. Report AFHRL-TR-81-44 (II), Air Force Human Resources Laboratory, Brooks AFB, TX, February, 1982.

Harris, R. N. *Prevention of Boiler Explosions in Aircraft Carrier Main Propulsion Systems: Personnel Factors (AL 2-81)*. Report NPRDC SR 83-25, Navy Personnel Research and Development Center, San Diego, CA, April, 1983.

Harris, R. N., and Williams, H. L. *Seventh Fleet Naval Tactical Data System (NTDS) Detection and Tracking (D&T) Study: Final Report*. Report SR 80-9, Navy Personnel Research and Development Center, San Diego, CA, February, 1980 (Confidential).

Helm, W. R., and Donnell, M. L. *Mission Operability Assessment Technique: A System Evaluation Methodology*. Technical Publication TP-79-31, Pacific Missile Test Center, Point Mugu, CA, 10 October 1979.

Holshouser, E. L. *Guide to Human Factors Engineering General Purpose Test Planning (GPTP) (Airtask A3400000/054C/7W0542-001)*. Technical Publication TP-77-14, Pacific Missile Test Center, Point Mugu, CA, 30 June 1977.

Johnson, C. D., Cory, B. H., Day, R. W., and Oliver, L. W. *Women Content in the Army-REFORGER 77 (REF WAC 77)*. Special Report S-7, Army Research Institute, Alexandria, VA, May, 1978.

Johnson, E. M., and Baker, J. D. Field testing: The delicate compromise. *Human Factors,* 1974, *16,* 203–214.

Keenan, J. J., Parker, T. C., and Lenzycki, H. P. *Concepts and Practices in the Assessment of Human Performance in Air Force Systems*. Report AMRL-TR-65-168, Aerospace Medical Research Laboratories, Wright-Patterson AFB, OH, September, 1965.

Kincaid, J. P., and Potempa, K. W. (Eds.) *Proceedings of the Human Factors Testing Conference 1-2 October, 1968*. Report AFHRL-TR-69-6, Air Force Human Resources Laboratory, Wright-Patterson AFB, OH, October, 1969.

Koonce, J. M. Predictive validity of flight simulators. *Human Factors,* 1979, *21,* 215–223.

Krantz, D. H., and Tversky, A. Conjoint-measurement analysis of composition rules in psychology. *Psychological Review,* 1971, *78,* 151–169.

Linn, R. L. Measuring pretest-posttest performance changes. In R. A. Berk (Ed.) *Educational Evaluation Methodology: The State of the Art*. Baltimore: John Hopkins University Press, 1981, 84–109.

Mackie, R. R., and Christensen, P. R. *Translation and Application of Psychological Research,* Technical Report 716-1, Human Factors Research, Goleta, CA, January, 1967.

McDonald, L. B., Waldrop, G. P., and Reynolds, R. Fidelity of simulation *vs.* transfer of training on a maintenance trainer. *Proceedings,* Human Factors Society Annual Meetings, 1982, 741–745.

Meister, D. *Human Factors in Operational System Testing: A Manual of Procedures*. Report SR 78-8, Navy Personnel Research and Development Center, San Diego, CA, April, 1978.

Meister, D., and Rabideau, G. F. *Human Factors Evaluation in System Development*. New York: Wiley, 1965.

Meister, D., Sullivan, D. J., Thompson, E. A., and Finley, D. L. *Training Effectiveness Evaluation of Naval Training Devices. Part II: A Study of Device 2F55A (S-2E trainer) Effectiveness*. Technical Report NAVTRADEVCEN 69-C-0322-2. Naval Training Device Center, Orlando, FL, January, 1971.

Merrill, M. D., Richards, R. E., Schmidt, R. V., and Wood, N. D. *The Instructional Strategy Diagnostic Profile Training Manual*. Courseware, Inc., San Diego, CA, 1977.

Merrill, M. D., Riegeluth, C. M., and Faust, G. W. The Instructional Quality Profile: A curriculum evaluation and design tool. In H. O'Neil (Ed.), *Procedures for Instructional Systems Development,* New York: Academic Press, 1979, 165–203.

Munger, S. J., Smith, R. W., and Payne, D. *An Index of Electronic Equipment Operability: Data Store*. Report AIR-C43-1/62-RP(1), American Institute for Research, Pittsburgh, PA, January, 1962.

NUREG-0700. Guidelines for control room design reviews. U.S. Nuclear Regulatory Commission, Washington, DC, September, 1981.

Payne, T. A. *Conducting Studies of Transfer of Learning: A Practical Guide*. Report AFHRL-TR-81-25, Air Force Human Resources Laboratory, Brooks AFB, TX, January, 1982.

Rabideau, G. F. Field measurement of human performance in man–machine systems. *Human Factors,* 1964, *6,* 663–672.

Rabideau, G. F. Human factors data gathering in operational systems. In Kinkaid, J. P., and Potempa, K. W. (Eds.), *Proceedings of the Human Factors Testing Conference 1-2 October 1968,* Report AFHRL-TR-69-6, Air Force Human Resources Laboratory, Wright-Patterson AFB, OH, October, 1969, 101–109.

Rolfe, J. M., and Caro, P. W. Determining the training effectiveness of flight simulators: Some basic issues and practical developments. *Applied Ergonomics,* 1982, *13.4,* 243–250.

Rossi, P. H., Freeman, H. E., and Wright, S. R. *Evaluation: A Systematic Approach*. Beverly Hills, CA: Sage Publications, 1979.

Roscoe, S. N. Incremental transfer effectiveness. *Human Factors,* 1971, *13,* 561–567.

Roscoe, S. N. *Aviation Psychology*. Iowa City, IA: Iowa State University Press, 1980.

Seminara, J. L., Gonzalez, W., and Parsons, S. *Human Factors Review of Nuclear Power Plant Control Room Design. Final Report.* Report EPRI NP-309, Lockheed Missiles and Space Company, Palo Alto, CA, for Electric Power Research Institute, March, 1977.

Smode, A. F., Gruber, A., and Ely, J. H. *The Measurement of Advanced Flight Vehicle Crew Proficiency in Synthetic Ground Environments.* Technical Documentary Report No. MRL-TDR-62-2, Behavioral Sciences Laboratory, Wright-Patterson AFB, OH, February, 1962.

Snyder, M. T. Historical development and current trends of human factors testing on Air Force systems. In Kinkaid, J. P., and Potempa, K. W. (Eds.), *Proceedings of the Human Factors Testing Conference 1-2 October 1968,* Report AFHRL-TR-69-6, Air Force Human Resources Laboratory, Wright-Patterson AFB, OH, October, 1969, 7–31.

Stinson, W. J. *Evaluation of LVA Full-Scale Hydrodynamic Vehicle Motion Effects on Personnel Performance*. Report NPRDC TR-79-16, Navy Personnel Research and Development Center, San Diego, CA, April, 1979.

String, J., and Orlansky, J. *Evaluating the Effectiveness of Maintenance Training by Using Currently Available Maintenance Data*. Paper P 1574, Institute for Defense Analysis, Washington, DC, August, 1981.

Struening, E. L., and Guttentag, M. (Eds.) *Handbook of Evaluation Research, Vols. I and II*. Beverly Hills, CA: Sage Publications, 1975.

Vreuls, D., Obermayer, R. W., Goldstein, I., and Lauber, J. W. *Measurement of Trainee Performance in a Captive Rotary-Wing Device*. Report NAVTRAEQUIPCEN 71-C-0194-1, Naval Training Equipment Center, Orlando, FL, July, 1973.

Williams, H. L., Pope, L. T., Pulu, P. S., and Sass, D. H. *Operating the 1200 psi Steam Propulsion Plant: An Investigation*. Report SR 82-25, Navy Personnel Research and Development Center, San Diego, CA, May, 1982.

Woodruff, R. R., Smith, J. F., Fuller, R. R., and Weyer, D. C. *Full Mission Simulation in Undergraduate Pilot Training: An Exploratory Study*. Report AFHRL-TR-76-84, Flying Training Division, Air Force Human Resources Laboratory, Williams AFB, AZ, December, 1976.

CHAPTER NINE

Subjective and Objective Methods

In this chapter I discuss naturalistic or *direct* observation, psychometric *scaling methods*, and *ratings*. All are subjective methods. To these I have added *objective methods* because like the subjective ones they derive ultimately from observation. In subsequent chapters I shall deal with interviews, questionnaires, surveys, and other methodology.

In Chapter One we referred to these measurement methods as generic or fundamental measurement methods because the applied techniques build upon them. More important, the methods we discuss in the remainder of the book can be utilized for many measurement purposes that go beyond system development. They are not design tools—although they can be and are used in design—but methods used in all measurement contexts.

In Chapter One we also indicated that the generic methods began with primitive, observational processes. Figure 9.1 shows how these methods developed out of observation.

One can observe: *oneself* (what I am thinking, doing, feeling?); *others* (what are they doing; what traits and characteristics do they have?); and *things, events* and *phenomena* (what do these objects consist of, what is happening?).

Self-observation can only be reported by oneself (self-report). It can be qualitative, as in an interview, as in completing a questionnaire or as in keeping a diary, etc. These methods are essentially qualitative because one can usually quantify their data only in very limited ways, for example, by content analysis and simple counting of the terms used. Self-report can also be quantitative, when the self-reporter also scales or rates the degree of his behavior, feeling, etc.

Observation of others is more complex. Qualitative observation of others leads only to simple description, because the *observer* (henceforth we shall use the abbreviation *O*) does not scale his observations and hence does not measure. This has limited usefulness. Quantitative observation of others may be performed in two ways. The observer can describe the subject's performance in terms of external indi-

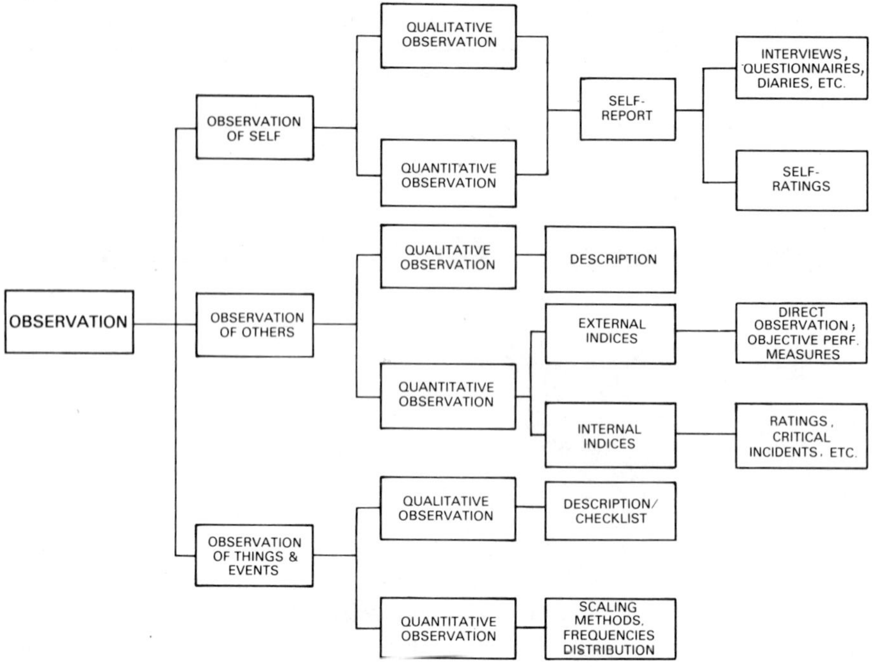

FIGURE 9.1. Hierarchy of observational dimensions and methods.

ces (external to *O* and to the subject) which gives rise to naturalistic or direct observation or by objective performance measures.

Alternatively, if *O* chooses to use himself as a measurement device, he can scale the performance of others on the basis of certain dimensions or attributes (ratings) or can select some performances as particularly distinctive (critical incidents).

Observation of things, events, and phenomena can also be qualitative or quantitative. Elaborate instrumentation exists for measuring such occurrences as meteorologic phenomena, sea states, and the amount of ambient illumination. But when the thing being measured is too complex for instrumentation, we may make use of ourselves as measuring instruments. An example of qualitative observation we have encountered previously is the use of a checklist to count the presence or absence of human engineering characteristics in a console. Quantitative observation of things, like the quantitative observation of self and others, makes use of various scaling methods, frequencies, and distributions of events.

Measurement methods have a philosophical problem: What is reality? What is the standard by which we measure validity? If what we know is conditioned by our sensory apparatus and if perception can provide us with incorrect data, how can we know what is true/real? Dealing with this problem on a philosophical level is beyond our scope. On a pragmatic level that problem is apparently solved by developing a consensus, usually in the form of interobserver agreement. If two or more *O*s agree that something is what they say it is, then it must be. This has, of course, a fatal flaw: one of the *Os* might be incorrect at the time, both might be incorrect at least part of the time, or all *Os* might suffer from the same error. The problem of validity bulks much larger in the generic methods than in the analytic techniques which are simply design tools.

Observation in measurement has several sometimes overlapping uses. These are (1) to record data, as in reading an instrument, or to describe an event; (2) to determine what people do, and how they do it, or what has happened; (3) to determine whether an object or individual possesses certain characteristics; (4) to compare an object with a standard (as in using a human engineering checklist); (5) to determine the status of an object, another individual, or oneself (as in determining whether an equipment has malfunctioned or a person is ill); (6) to evaluate performance, as in judging excellence in sports or music, and to compare performances; (7) to determine how two or more objects or individuals differ (e.g., to determine the differences in attitudes between pre-teens and adolescents). In accomplishing these goals observational techniques are utilized in a variety of work, education, artistic, and sports situations. Examples can be found in medical diagnosis, in job selection, in educational measurement, in psychiatric evaluation, and in system design, as we have seen in previous chapters.

Observation, like any behavioral function, is remarkably sensitive to all sorts of performance shaping factors: the number of *Os*; their training; the complexity of the stimulus situation; immediacy of the observation and its duration; attitudes and biases; viewing workload; the way *O* samples his observation; whether or not *O* participates in the activity being observed; whether or not the subject of the observation is aware of *O*; whether or not O views directly or through a medium like film; the type and number of attributes or stimulus dimensions being observed; whether *O* is constrained by instructions; whether *O* processes his data (quantizes them) during his observation or later; and the format of the data recording instrument. All of these factors make for potential problems in using observational measures (see Weick, 1968, for an analysis of the pros and cons of the observational technique).

Eight of the most common observational errors are: (1) loss of detail through simplification; (2) preference for more familiar and simpler reporting categories; (3) concentrating on the first and last part of a behavior, ignoring the mid-portion; (4) second-guessing the thoughts or motives of the one being observed; (5) allowing behavior immediately prior to the observation to influence the observation; (6) allowing the situational context to distort observations; (7) stereotyping and prejudice; (8) the halo effect (allowing one characteristic of the individual being observed to unduly influence the entire observation).

Each of the factors and errors above has an effect, but often the nature of the effect is unclear. All of them make it remarkably difficult to ascertain the validity (truth) of the observation.

SUBJECTIVE MEASUREMENT TECHNIQUES

The two situations in which subjective measurement methods are applied are: 1. those in which the frequency and duration of performances and behaviors are counted on either a continuous or sampling basis (frequency or direct observation);

and 2. those in which these performances and behaviors are rated, that is, assigned a value representing the magnitude or amount of a performance or behavior the individual possesses or has manifested (rating scales). An example of direct observation is observation of a group of autistic children to determine the frequency of the various behaviors (rocking, drooling, etc.) they manifest. If the same children were observed with a scale which attempted to measure their degree of cooperation with each other, this would be a rating situation.

Within the work environment rating is by far the most frequently employed subjective measurement tool. Comparatively little is done with direct observation. Direct observation is little used in industrial or military work situations because these are often highly structured (e.g., step-by-step procedures). Hence the necessity for determining the nature of the performances or behaviors rarely exists. There are of course exceptions. If the nature (dimensions) of the task and performance are unclear, the starting point of an effort to understand these may be direct observation. An example is team performance; another is troubleshooting behavior.

Direct observation is more often utilized in research, particularly in social psychological, personality, clinical, or child development education situations. The two types of measurement have different purposes. Direct observation determines what behaviors or performances are emitted and ratings determine how much of already specified behaviors or performances there is (e.g., performance quality). Counting is simpler—more fundamental—than rating because it is essentially recognition. Rating requires a somewhat greater amount of cognitive analysis. Of course, rating involves recognition as an initial process.

Subjective measurement methods vary along several dimensions.

1. What is reported may vary in terms of *degree of immediacy*. The observer counts or rates as the object of observation performs or behaves (this is always true of direct observation). Or he may rate some time after the object of observation has performed or behaved (this is never true of direct observation). Although some ratings are made of immediate performances, in many cases *O* rates on the basis of summated, remembered observations.

2. The *content* of what is observed can vary. It can be a performance, a behavior, an attitude, or a trait. We have somewhat arbitrarily defined performance as a job related activity (e.g., analyzing maps, communicating coordinates) which is relatively molar. A behavior is not job related and is usually relatively molecular, such as the rocking behavior of the autistic child. An attitude (such as aggressive contacts with other children) is a combination of behaviors which express (reflect) an emotion or belief. A trait is a combination of performances and behaviors which characterize an individual or group in terms of generalized response patterns. Obviously one can observe and measure work or nonwork activity. The observational data can be reported by oneself or by others.

3. The amount of *detail* in the observation may also vary. Because attitudes and traits involve combinations of behaviors, they are likely to be global—behaviors and performances being more discrete and more detailed. The more global the content of the observation, the more cognitive inferences are involved and the more dif-

ficult to secure a valid and reliable observation. On the other hand, within limits, the more global the observation, the more meaningful it is likely to be. A very simple, discrete action such as throwing a switch on an equipment is likely to be uninterpretable unless it is observed and evaluated as part of a larger task.

4. The *length of the time interval* during which the observation is made can also vary. Again, very brief observation intervals (e.g., 5 seconds) are likely to pick up only simple, discrete responses, since the initiation of the action and its consequence are likely to overlap the limits of the short time interval.

5. Observation also varies as a function of the *amount of inference* it requires. If the activities being observed and measured are simple and discrete, categorization is easily performed. Much direct observation is of this type (e.g., count the number of contacts each child has in a 15 minute period). As the observational content becomes more complex (e.g., rate the degree of team coordination), the proportion of inference increases and the less important the strictly perceptual component of the observation becomes. It is a reasonable hypothesis that the more inference is required in an observation, the greater the decrease in accuracy and reliability.

DIRECT OBSERVATION

The major steps in direct or frequency (for counting) observation are, as paraphrased from Sackett, Ruppenthal and Gluck (1978): (1) deciding to use direct observation methods (in preference to other methods); (2) deciding what to observe (developing a taxonomy of behaviors); (3) deciding on a sampling strategy; (4) determining that the taxonomy and sampling strategy are accurate and reliable; (5) deciding what to do with the data. The following enlarges on these steps.

Direct observation is useful in situations in which subjects are free to vary their responses in many ways with few or no constraints imposed by an investigator. The use of direct observation is necessary when automated measurement techniques are not feasible or the information from experimental or standard situations is inappropriate for the questions asked. Instrumentation for detecting relevant performances may not be available, or, if available, is excessively complex and expensive.

Direct observation is only occasionally employed in work related research, usually only when the performances are fluid. Researchers prefer controlled laboratory experiments. However, much greater use should be made of direct observation in ergonomic studies because surprisingly little is known of how people actually perform in real world work. We assume that the situation/environment in which operational systems routinely perform their operational missions is the only completely "true" research environment for ergonomic research. It follows then that to validate the results of controlled experiments and of standard tests which are somewhat artificial, and to collect the quantitative data bases needed for prediction (Chapter Five), studies of the "real world" should employ direct observation much more than they do. The operational environment is much less structured than the laboratory and the degree of control desired often cannot be achieved. Under these circumstances direct observation becomes the method of choice.

To devise a behavioral taxonomy for direct observation one must consider the molecularity of the measurement categories and their level of abstraction. Observation measurement is based on concrete psychomotor and vocal responses. Taxonomies vary in terms of how close the response categories are to these actual behaviors. A molecular taxonomy defines categories very closely to specific motor responses. Molar taxonomies are more abstract and organize a number of response categories into generic classes defined by the function or outcome of the responses. Examples of such generic classes are function categories such as analysis, coordination, planning and communicating (see Chapter Two for representative taxonomies). Molar taxonomies require detailed definition of terms with lists of the specific responses making up each category.

Observing for molecular responses can be difficult, requiring film or videotape, because molecular responses are quite brief and several can occur simultaneously and change quickly. Scoring of molar observations is easier because the actions that initiate, implement, and end a particular sequence are summarized in a single category which may persist for some time. In ergonomics, tasks (which are a molar category) are emphasized not only conceptually but also in observation. However, there is a significant problem of within and between *O* reliability for molar categories that combine a number of more discrete responses.

It has been impossible, so far, to develop a universal taxonomy because even in a controlled laboratory setting specific research goals and measurement settings change markedly from study to study. Since each change may emphasize different behavioral dimensions, each may require a different taxonomy.

The observer must also decide whether he wishes to observe a live performance or one that has been photographed or videotaped and then replayed. He must also consider continuous observation versus some sampling arrangement. Some of the factors influencing sampling decision include scoring complexity, whether subjects can be continuously observed or may disappear from view, and the number of individuals to be observed simultaneously.

The problem becomes sticky with a group or team. Should *O* observe one individual at a time or groups of subjects? One solution is to observe individuals sequentially for fixed durations. However, if *O* has only a few scoring sessions to collect data, he may not have enough time for all subjects on an individual basis. Moreover, this strategy falls apart when subjects interact. Hence it may be necessary to observe all individuals simultaneously. If, however, there are more than a few observational categories to deal with, the burden on *O* may be excessive. One alternative is to assign a single *O* to watch each subject. Unfortunately this maximizes the need for trained observers who are more difficult to obtain than subjects. If more than a few subjects are to be observed, this solution is impractical.

One solution to the problem of complex taxonomies and many interactive subjects is to film or tape observational sessions and then review them repeatedly until everything of interest has been categorized. Film or tape may be the only practical method if very fine distinctions among molecular behaviors are at issue. However, film and tape are generally feasible only in spatially restricted settings unless one can follow a whole group with a camera. If subjects are dispersed over a wide area, film and tape may not supply more information than direct observation. Sackett et al. (1978) report that live recording catches at least 90 per cent of the information extracted from repeated viewing of 16 mm. film.

Another possible solution to the problem of coding complexity and multiple subjects is time sampling, in which *O* scores some but not all of the behavior.

Sampling Strategy

In most of the published observational research three basic sampling strategies have been used: (1) continuous real-time measurement, (2) measurement at discontinuous probe-time intervals and (3) measurement in successive time intervals with only the first instance of each behavior in the interval being recorded.

Continuous measurement occurs when every onset of, or duration of, a categorizable response is recorded during the session. If the recording maintains the order in which responses occurred, it is possible to perform sequential analyses to identify patterns and cycles.

Frequency and duration measures are comparable when all sessions are the same length. If session lengths vary, adjustments must be made if scores are to be compared, because the responses have different probabilities of being emitted when some sessions are longer than others. Sackett et al. (1978) suggest that an adjustment can be made by calculating rate of occurrence for the frequency measure (rate = frequency/session length) and the percentage of total session time for duration (% duration = duration/session length). Or one could adjust both frequency and duration by the proportion of time the session is in excess of or less than some arbitrary standard time period.

With discontinuous probe-time samples responses are recorded either instantaneously at the end of set time periods (e.g., at the end of each minute of a 30-minute session) or for a short duration at the end of set time intervals.

One problem with the instantaneous probe method is the discriminability of individual responses. Many responses are interpretable only in the context of ongoing behavior. An instantaneous probe measurement which ignores sequence may lead to an incorrect classification. To solve this problem, probe samples can be taken for relatively short duration (fixed or variable) at the end of fixed time intervals. Scores for this method are identical to those using the instantaneous technique.

In modified frequency, time sampling responses are observed in real time. A sampling interval (modified frequency interval) is selected and responses are scored for occurrence once (and only once) per interval regardless of the numbr of actual responses during the interval. The number of occurrences is called the *modified frequency* (MF) score. For example, if a 300-second session is broken into twenty 15-second modified frequency intervals, MF scores for each response would be the number of intervals out of twenty in which the response was seen at least once.

As with probe sampling, when sessions are all equal in length, MF scores are completely redundant with scores reflecting the percentage of total intervals in which the response occurred. It is also necessary to adjust MF scores when sessions have variable lengths resulting in a different number of MF intervals. These adjustments are made following Sackett et al. (1978).

Time sampling has three pragmatic advantages over real-time measurement. Equipment is minimal: one needs only a pencil, a data form, and some method for indicating when to record. Demands on *O* are less. When using MF methods high reliability is almost insured if codes have been well defined. *O* may fail to record a specific response but he can still score that response if it occurs again within the interval. It is therefore possible for two *Os* to generate identical MF scores for a particular response even though they never actually observed the same instances.

There are, however, serious disadvantages in time sampling. Probe sampling is insensitive to infrequent responses because of the low probability of occurrence of such responses at the time the probe is initiated. Similar insensitivity problems can occur with MF using long MF intervals. Responses occurring at moderate frequencies tend to generate MF scores similar to those of responses occurring at much higher frequencies when the average duration of these responses is about the same. This is because only the first instance of the response is scored in any single interval.

Moreover, probe frequency and MF scores may produce uninterpretable data because their scores confound frequency and duration. Observee 1 can emit a response in all 300 seconds of the session broken into twenty 15-second units. Observee 2 emits two responses in each of the twenty intervals but only once per interval. Thus, although the same response was markedly different in the two observees, both receive the same score.

Finally, because data are collected discontinuously, sequential dependencies among successively occurring responses cannot be measured.

Thus, time sampling can provide very inaccurate data (Repp, Roberts, Slack, Repp and Berkler, 1976) and may confound frequency and duration of behavior (Powell, Martindale and Kulp, 1975).

Another factor to be considered is the type of responses to be measured, that is, frequent, infrequent, long and variable duration responses, and momentary ones. Momentary and long duration responses can be emitted either frequently or infrequently. Infrequent momentary responses can be detected only with real-time or interval sampling and long observational sessions. Frequent, brief duration responses may be missed using point sampling. When a large number of responses must be studied, real-time continuous sampling may be the only way to secure representative data.

Observer Reliability

At this point it is necessary to talk about reliability because, as was indicated previously, reliability is critical to the use of observational methods. The discussion here applies equally to the same problem with rating scales. Reliability is a complex measurement issue that involves both accuracy and stability of measures, as well as the conditions under which observations are made. There is, however, no consensus in the terminology used and no agreement about which statistical approaches should be employed.

There is much confusion and misuse of reliability statistics. Susman, Peters and Steward (1976) examined fifteen journals publishing in child development, clinical, and educational areas for reports of observational studies in the previous 16 years. Thirty-two percent of all authors failed to report any estimate of the reliability of their data. The most frequently used statistic, when one was used, was percentage agreement between observers. Very few accuracy and stability coefficients were reported.

Almost all the published observational research measures reliability in terms of percentage agreement among *Os*. This score compares the degree to which two or more *Os* produce the same overall trial summary scores, or actually code the same behaviors at the same time. However, percentage agreement in itself does not indicate reliability unless it includes a correction for chance agreement. This last renders many interobserver reliability scores spurious.

Observer agreement is susceptible to misinterpretation when a relatively high or low number of intervals is scored because of the probability of chance agreements being high. Another difficulty is that the different methods of calculating agreement produce different percentages. Repp, Dietz, Boles, Dietz and Repp (1976) found in a study of two *Os* and five children's behaviors that the agreement percentages measured varied from 64 percent to 94 percent, depending on the method applied. And which one then was the correct one?

Harris and Lahey (1978) suggest that one method of reducing chance agreements is to calculate interobserver agreement for scored intervals only when the observed rate of behavior is low and for unscored intervals only when the observed rate is high. The problem with this solution is that the method may overcompensate by throwing out all the agreement data on unscored or scored intervals, respectively. Moreover, the method is not appropriate for studies in which rates of observed behavior vary.

Another difficulty is that there is no generally accepted level of *O* agreement. Hartmann (1977) and Hopkins and Hermann (1977) suggest that overall percentage agreement might be acceptable if it were compared to the overall agreement expected by chance. They present formulae for calculating chance agreement scores. Yelton, Wildman and Erickson (1977) advanced a probability based formula that gives the exact probability of obtaining at least any given number of overall agreements. Baer (1977) suggested the separate calculation of conventional occurrence and nonoccurrence agreement percentages. However, there are no guidelines as to how much weight to give each coefficient at different rates of observed behavior.

It is possible to achieve perfect reliability with film or tape by using a consensus coding method in which two or more *Os* view and review segments of the record until they agree that a particular response has occurred and the response fits a specific taxonomic category. This method avoids the question of *O*'s reliabiity, since agreement must result, but it does not answer the question of observational validity.

Herbert and Attridge (1975) have pointed out that observer agreement is not a measure of reliability at all, unless it is compared with some previously established standard. Clement (1976) has suggested a formula based on a standard *O*. What a standard *O* is, how he would function, and where one would procure him is not clear. Harris and Leahy (1978) suggest a weighting formula organized around two or more *Os*. Nor does *O* agreement assess stability unless it is measured over repeated trials. As was pointed out in connection with MF sampling, it is possible to obtain high *O* agreement with close to zero reliability as measured by accuracy (or validity, Hollenbeck, 1978) and stability (reliability).

A number of statistical techniques permit the proper determination of observational reliability, although all of them have weaknesses. A very powerful one is *variance analysis*, which can be used to assess error variance contributed both between and within *Os*, as deviation from a standard and from a number of intervening variables unique to a study. For example, Cohen (1968) has suggested a multiple regression model as a general data analytic system. In his approach reliability can be derived from the estimate of the relative contribution of variables. The most comprehensive approach to determining reliability through variance analysis techniques has been developed by Cronbach, Gleser, Nanda and Rajaratnam (1972) in their theory of *generalizability* (G). This theory is based on a multifaceted approach making use of a four-way analysis of variance, in which the relative contribution to variance of each factor can be directly estimated. Reliability coefficients appropriate to any level of data analysis can be determined from a single analysis of variance. Unfortunately not much use is made of G theory, perhaps because of the complexity of the procedures required.

Moreover, these parametric analyses of variance may not be appropriate, since many observational coding schemes do not produce interval scale measures.

Hollenbeck (1978) suggests that interobserver agreement statistics may be used to study *O* scoring on an instrument whose reliability has already been demonstrated. This can be done by comparing the new scores with preestablished standards. Hence agreement statistics can be useful but only after the observational instrument has been demonstrated to be accurate in the first place.

Birkimer and Brown (1979) recommend a graphic technique in which disagreements and chance percentage of disagreements among *O*s would be plotted as a vertical band ("range") about the mean of two *O*s' data points.

Graphing the chance disagreement and agreement ranges allows for easy comparisons between the obtained percentages and those expected by chance. If all goes well, the obtained disagreement percentage will be smaller than that expected by chance and the obtained agreement percentage greater than that expected by chance.

When one samples behavior psychometrically it is assumed that each persons's item response is independent of other item responses. However in observational measures, the responses sampled are usually interrelated.

Yet if one ignores this difficulty, it is possible to apply psychometric theory to the problems of measuring observational reliability. The classic method of determining test reliability is to obtain two scores for test subjects (to determine intra or interscorer reliability) from two parts or two alternative forms of the test (to measure split half or alternative form reliability) or two administrations of the test to the same subjects (test/retest reliability). The correlation between these scores is the reliability of the test.

To use one of these methods it is necessary to make the observations fit the same general pattern as psychological tests. However, instead of one test with many items, intended to measure the same trait characteristic or behavior, the observational researcher has an instrument with a few categories, with each category intended to measure a different trait, characteristic or behavior measured over many time units.

To fit observational data into the psychometric pattern it is necessary to consider each mutually exclusive category or type of behavior as a separate test with its own reliability. Each time unit must be considered as an item, since all time units are intended to measure the same trait, behavior or characteristic. For example, a behavioral code might record a child's proximity to the teacher during each 10-second unit of observation. Each 10-second unit would be an item in a test that measured proximity.

This analogy between test reliability and the reliability of observational data can be extended to apply to each of the traditional ways of obtaining scores: intrascorer or interscorer reliability, split-half, or alternative forms and test/retest reliabiity. Thus one might compare subdivisions of one observation (e.g., odd and even-numbered minutes during a tennis match) or between two very similar observations (first and second halves of the match). Or one might administer the same instrument at two different times. An observer might, for example, visit classrooms on different days to record the teacher's use of a particular instructional technique.

There is little difference between alternative forms and test/retest reliability for observational measures. Since time units serve as items, observations made on different days can be considered either as alternative forms or as test/retest conditions, depending on the situation.

Despite these possibilities, most observational studies fail to make use of them. Interobserver reliability, or agreement, is reported to the virtual exclusion of split-half and test/retest coefficients. Since reliability and observer agreement are not the same, it is possible, as Tinsley and Weiss (1975) illustrated, to have high interobserver agreement and a low reliability correlation coefficient, and vice versa.

It is fairly clear that *O* influences the reliability of his observational data (Johnson and Bolstad, 1973). Several sources of *O* bias have been identified (Rosenthal, 1963). These include errors of omission (failing to score a response that occurred), errors of commission (miscoding a response), and error resulting from *O* expectancy. The latter results when the *O* expects something to happen and he somehow communicates this expectancy to the observee.

Another category of influence problems is the effect of *O* on the subject. There are several potential sources of influence on the subject or resulting from subject characteristics (Johnson and Bolstad, 1973). One is *O*'s conspicuousness. A second is the effect of individual differences in the subjects themselves, such as personality and sex, which may influence *O*'s scoring. Another is the rationale for the observation. The reasons for observing subjects when communicated to the subject may influence his behavior.

Observer drift involves stability across repeated observational measurement times. It implies that the instrument (*O*) becomes less accurate as observations are made. There is some evidence that *Os* who know they are being assessed maintain high levels of agreement. When they are not aware that they are under observation, they agree less often (Johnson and Bolstad, 1973). Another form of *O* error is what is termed consensual drift, in which *Os* appear to drift but they do so systematically and together across trials. Between observer agreement scores remain high, but within observer agreement scores decrease.

Methods of Measuring Observer Agreement

There are at least seven different measures of *O* agreement. The most frequently used statistic is percentage agreement between *Os*. Assuming a modified frequency design, the trial blocks can be coded in three ways: each target response can be scored once within the block, regardless of any further occurrences; a single code can be used to characterize each block; and all responses occurring within a time block can be scored for each time they occur.

The most common way of calculating percentage agreement is:

$$\% \text{ agreement} = \text{agreements/agreements} + \text{disagreements} \times 100 \qquad (9.1)$$

The principal advantages of percent agreement are its ease of computation, its simple interpretation, and its sensitivity to systematic errors. Its greatest weakness is that it gives false information unless chance agreement is taken into account.

Another common method of computing agreement is with the Pearson correlation coefficient. It, too, has inadequacies (Johnson and Bolstad, 1973)—primarily the possibility of overestimating agreement. Robinson (1957) has proposed a method for reducing the problems of correlation as a measure of agreement, but that method in turn has certain disadvantages (Hollenbeck, 1978).

The coefficient of concordance (*W*, Kendall, 1948), which is based on rankings, is suitable to measure *O* agreement when the data are transformed into ranks. The equation is:

$$W = \frac{\Sigma(R_j - R)^2}{(1/12)K^2(N^3 - N)} \qquad (9.2)$$

where R = mean rank = $\Sigma R_j/N$; R_j = the sum of ranks for each response category across responses; N = the number of categories ranked; K = the number of *Os*; denominator = the maximum possible sum of squared deviations. Although *W* also has its weaknesses, it is a valuable descriptive agreement statistic when study results are evaluated using nonparametric statistics for rank order information.

Chi-square can test "goodness of fit" of *O*'s scores compared with a standard of predetermined expected values. The main drawback is that it supplies only an overall index of association for the total distribution of the data. Moreover, when certain data categories are infrequently represented, as often happens in observational research, the use of chi-square is questionable. Scott (1955), making use of a chi-square type of logic, created the first agreement coefficient suitable for nominal score agreement that applies a correction for chance agreement. The equation is

$$\pi = \sum_{c=1}^{k} \frac{P_{oi} - P_{ei}}{1 - P_{ei}} \tag{9.3}$$

where P_o = observed percentage agreement and P_e = expected percentage agreement. Hollenbeck (1978) gives an example.

Again, Scott's method has a limitation, which is the assumption that the distribution of proportions over the data categories is known and equal for both *Os*, which in general is not true in observational research.

Cohen (1960) has developed the *Kappa* statistic that avoids many of the problems already mentioned. It may be computed in many situations where percentage agreement has been used in the past. Kappa is simply the proportion of agreement after chance agreement is removed from consideration, as one sees from the following equation:

$$\text{Kappa} = \frac{(P_o - P_c)}{(1 - P_c} \tag{9.4}$$

where P_o = observed proportion action of agreements and P_c = chance proportion action of agreements. Hollenbeck (1978) provides an example. Unfortunately Kappa has not been widely applied by observational researchers.

Even if one had a foolproof method of determining observational reliability, one would still have to ask: How much reliability is necessary? It has been suggested that any reliability that exceeds chance agreement is adequate, but this merely substitutes statistical for practical significance. Of course, one can take reliability measurement too seriously. When direct observation is used in aid of some applied activity, for example in diagnosis or evaluation, data precision may be only a secondary desideratum. The researcher may be preoccupied by the effort to secure methodologic purity. The practitioner might well care less.

In any event, Hollenbeck (1978) sums up the present situation when he says "few observational scoring systems would meet the measurement standards such as reliability that we use in evaluating other psychological measures" (p. 95).

The outcome of the observer agreement controversy and alternative ways of quantitatively assessing observation and rating accuracy, validity and reliability cannot be written in this chapter—if it ever can. Because of the subjectivity inherent in the observation and other scaling techniques we may never find an optimal external standard of the truth. Researchers will continue the quest for a perfect measure of reliability, but the absence of one is unlikely to disturb practitioner unduly.

The direct observation method described in this section is the most common one. However, there are other observational procedures that should be mentioned, albeit only briefly, Brandt (1972) describes three general types of observational data, narrative, checklist and rating. We shall discuss the rating in detail later, but a few words should be said about narrative (simple description) and the checklist.

The narrative type includes all data that merely reproduce behavioral events in much the same fashion and sequence as in their original form. The material lacks interpretation, although, since everything that happens cannot be recorded, the reporter (or even the cameraman in video recording) exercises some selectivity.

In direct observation checklist data can be organized around specific aspects of behavior on which *O*s can readily agree, such as the sex of the observee, whether it is a child or adult, etc. The checklist used in system design to measure equipment attributes is of course much less structured. The direct observation checklist represents maximal observational structuring and what the checklist format does is to classify. Checklists can be used to record actions in the form of tallies or checks which code the actions into predefined categories. These can provide information about which behaviors occurred or how often during the observation. In the former, the checklist is very similar to direct observation and can be used to provide much the same information.

Activity logs such as those filled out by Navy officers or maintenance personnel are another form of checklist, as are work measurement systems such as methods time measurement, MTM, described in Chapter Two.

Activity Sampling

In the industrial/military system context behavioral observation takes the form of what has been termed *activity sampling* (Chapanis, 1959, from which much of the following is derived). Activity sampling can be performed either by observation of others (as described here) or by a self-report, diary method.

There are many jobs in which the worker does a number of different things in the course of a day. The housewife, for example, cooks, washes, and irons. A librarian types, signs out books, and looks things up in a card catalogue. These jobs differ from most repetitive industrial jobs in that there is no set pattern in which they are, or must be, done. The order in which they are performed and the frequency of their performance may be dependent upon contingent events. What a librarian does depends at least in part on how many people enter the library and the assistance they ask of her.

If one wished to describe these jobs, it would be necessary to determine exactly how much time the worker spends in each of his activities. Activity sampling is the systematic observation of a system through some sort of sampling procedure to describe accurately what the operator does. For example, Christensen and Mills (1967) recorded the operations performed by aerial navigators during 15-hour flights. One might wish to use activity sampling if one were going to analyze the job, to develop a training curriculum for it, or to determine where improvements in job design might be made.

The unit of observation may be either the operator and everything he does in a particular time period or it may be a function (e.g., everything that happens during a particular stage of a job or mission).

The basic technique is simple enough. The observer has a timing mechanism of some sort. At predetermined times he records what the operator/worker is doing at that moment. The similarity to direct observation should be apparent. The recording is usually done on a specially prepared report form but more recently fairly sophisticated instrumentation for recording data in an observational situation has been developed (for which see Chapter Eleven). After the data are recorded, the investigator can then estimate (1) the percentage of the operator's total time spent in various activities, (2) the average length of time spent in each activity, and (3) the sequence in which the worker performs various parts of his job.

The procedure to be followed in conducting an activity analysis has the following steps:

1. It is necessary to secure cooperation of the people being observed, to explain the goals of the observation and that the study will not adversely affect them. Ideally, the observation process would be invisible to the subject of the observation, but this cannot usually be done in an industrial situation, although it is common enough in work with children, when making use of a one-way vision screen in a nursery school.

2. The observer should familiarize himself with the entire job so that he can immediately determine what the subject is doing. This may require study, depending on the complexity of the job and the particular aspects being categorized.

3. He must develop categories of observation, to determine in advance what the units of activity are and how coarse or fine they should be, questions which are in part determined by the purpose of the analysis and what the investigator hopes to find out. Where the activity analysis is part of a research project, the particular categories may be determined by study hypotheses or a theoretic formulation. The categories should exhaust all the activities the operator engages in. Although there must always be a special category of "others," there should be few observations in this class.

Categories should be observable, of course, defined by activities which most observers can agree on and they should not include such covert functions as "thinking," "daydreaming" or "planning." Transitions from one task to another, for example, the time an operator takes to put away old work, or to go from one place to another, must be included. The limits of each activity must be defined. Chapanis (1959) asks . . . "in an activity analysis of a secretary's job, is she 'filing' only when she is literally inserting pieces of paper into a file—or does 'filing' also include 'unlocking the files' and 'opening the file drawers'?" Although it often does not make much difference how narrowly or broadly one defines many of these activities, it is essential to have a clear cut definition of each activity so that there is no ambiguity in the classification. Special problems in this respect may arise if the activity being observed is a group or team activity.

There should not be too many categories for observation, lest *O* find himself getting confused or losing track of the activities being performed. Chapanis (1959) suggests not more than 25 but it is likely that the practical limit is much less.

4. A data recording sheet must be developed. The simplest type lists the categories and provides space for tallies, but more complex ones can be developed which, although more difficult to use, provide more data.

5. A sampling duration must be decided upon. This is the length of time during which observations will be made. That duration can be an entire job cycle or mission (e.g., from energizing a nuclear reactor through a cold shutdown) or some segment of a mission or job activity or simply a convenient unit of time (one day a month, the first two hours of the day, every 10 seconds, etc.).

6. The operator must decide on a sampling interval, the time between successive observations. In the Christensen and Mills (1967) study, for example, the sampling interval was 5 seconds. The initial choice is between a random (i.e., variable) and fixed sampling interval. Random sampling intervals can be used when the investigator is interested only in the distribution of operator activities. Random sampling will not allow the investigator to compute the average length of time spent in various activities or the sequences or activities the operator engages in. Random sampling is generally best suited to operations which continue day after day and which can be observed over long periods of time (e.g., the work of a secretary or stock clerk). Fixed sampling intervals are best suited to jobs which are variable in length and which have a clear cut beginning and end (e.g., the work of a bus driver).

A two-second interval is about as short a period as one can sample. If the interval is shorter than two seconds, *O* is likely to fall behind the sequence of events. Most activity sampling studies are concerned with rather gross units of activity which come in larger time blocks. If one is concerned with very small units of activity and molecular behaviors, he should consider using MTM techniques discussed in Chapter Three. To get a complete description of the operator's activities, the interval between samples should not be longer than the shortest unit of activity. If that interval is longer than certain kinds of activity, these will be missed when they fall between two signals.

The final consideration is that the investigator should end up with a sufficiently large number of observations to get valid and reliable data. Chapanis (1959) recommends 1000 observations as the minimum number of be collected, but this is often contingent on the type of system, the freedom to observe, etc. Since there is an interaction between sampling duration and sampling interval, the product of sampling duration and sampling rate (reciprocal of sampling interval) should be at least 1000. For example, if the sampling interval is 1 minute and the sampling rate is 1 per minute, the sampling duration should be at least 1000 minutes long.

7. A representative sample of subjects, jobs and tasks must be selected. The same job may require different activities depending on individual differences in equipment, weather, size of facility, etc. For example, the librarian in a small rural library has an entirely different kind of job from one in a large urban library and both differ from the librarian's job in a highly specialized research library. It is

therefore necessary to measure across the three types or else confine one's conclusions to the particular variation in libraries studied.

SCALING TECHNIQUES

This section, which deals with scaling techniques, has benefitted extensively from a report by Stillwell, Seaver and Schwartz (1982). They discuss scaling in the context of methods for gathering expert estimates of human error probabilities in nuclear power plant operations. However, the techniques are general enough to be applied to any system or set of occurrences. In any event, of all the judgments one might wish to secure, those of human error and event occurrence probability are probably most relevant to the quantitative study of human performance. To examine the questions involved requires us to consider the literature on probability assessment (Einhorn and Hogarth, 1981; Slovic, Fischoff and Lichtenstein, 1977; Spetzler and Stael von Holstein, 1975) and psychological scaling and measurement theory (Cliff, 1973; Roberts, 1979; Torgerson, 1958). It is necessary to examine the role of subject matter experts in assessing probabilities because it is these people whom one would employ if one is to use the scalar techniques at all. Anyone can provide a scaled judgment of observations, but if he is not what we would consider an expert, we would not have much confidence in his conclusions.

Stillwell et al. (1982) examine the role of expertise in probability judgments in four areas: military intelligence, business, medicine, and weather prediction, which provide conflicting evidence of the quality of those judgments.

Because military intelligence is mostly classified, much of it is inaccessible for research purposes. What is accessible enables us to say that military experts prefer to respond in numerical form when expressing uncertainty, the use of probabilities reduces miscommunication (Kelly and Peterson, 1970) and the reliability intrasubject product moment correlation for repeated judgments has a mean of .79 and a range of .42 to 97, which is good (Johnson, 1977).

The other areas are somewhat in conflict. The business literature presents most of the negative evidence. Bankers and stock analysts (Stael von Holstein, 1972) as well as security analysts (Bartos, 1969, cited by Winkler, 1972) often cannot outperform even a simple strategy in which a uniform distribution (for example, each of n events assigned a probability of $1/n$) is used to predict the performance of some random variable.

Evidence in the medical field is mixed, (Brehmer, 1981) but more positive than negative. Ludke, Stauss, and Gustafson (1977) asked nurses and senior nursing students to estimate distributions of physiological variables (for example, weight of an American baby at birth; systolic blood pressure of American males) using several assessment methods. All proved both reliable (average test/retest correlation across methods = .986) and accurate.

There is, however, some tendency to overestimate the probability of events with severe consequences (Lusted, 1977) which may be explained by a desire to be sure severe consequences are avoided, thus focusing special attention on these events. Nonetheless, medical experts are able to provide subjective estimates of probabilities that agree with relative frequency estimates for the same quantities (DeSmet, Fryback, and Thornbury, 1979).

Weather forecasters are good at providing subjective probability judgments. Average deviations from perfect calibration* for precipitation forecasts ranged from .028 to .044 in two studies (Murphy and Winkler, 1974, 1977b, see also Wallsten and Budescu, 1980 and Murphy and Winkler, 1977a).

Scaling is the process of assigning numbers to objects, events, or properties in such a way that the numbers represent relationships among scaled entities. The purpose of scaling is to allow numbers to substitute for the objects or events in question. Having done so, it is possible to derive additional relationships by performing mathematical operations on those numbers.

Substituting numbers for psychological variables, such as preferences or attitudes, is inherently difficult. Such variables are not directly observable; rather we infer them (a secondary process) from subtle cues that are observable.

Of course, the assignment of numbers to psychological variables must be meaningful. Cliff (1973) gives four conditions under which scaling is meaningful. (1) The scale values are indicative of consistent relationships among the data. (2) There is an underlying measurement theory that assumes knowledge of which scale transformations preserve the data relationships. (3) The scientist has an algorithm for transforming raw data into scale values. (4) It can be demonstrated that the obtained scales have external validity. This last, which is probably the most difficult, requires an additional set of data.

Scaling Methods

Psychologists have studied various scaling methods to enable quantitative manipulation of these variables and the conditions under which number assignment is possible. This latter has been termed measurement theory (Coombs, Dawes, and Tversky, 1970; Roberts, 1979; Suppes and Zinnes, 1963).

The scaling methods are not merely theoretical mathematical instruments; they have been extensively used at one time or another in ergonomic research. Paired comparisons were used by Blanchard et al., 1966 (see Chapter Five), to develop a probabilistic *likelihood of accomplishment scale*. A simple method to determine the attitudes of test personnel to alternative equipment configurations is to ask them to rank the configurations. The author has used a sorting procedure to ask maintenance technicians which of *N* variables had the greatest influence on diagnostic downtime. Rating scales are ubiquitous in research to secure attitudes toward products, in surveys of preferences, etc.

The major scaling methods are:

Scaling by paired comparisons. This method was introduced by Thurstone (1927) as a means of scaling psychological attributes which have no physical basis.

*A calibration curve plots assessed probabilities versus relative frequencies. Perfect calibration results in a curve that is a straight line from (0,0) to (1,1) indicating, for example, that for events assigned a subjective probability of .70, 70 percent occur.

Every possible pair of n stimuli is presented to subjects, whose task is to indicate which member of the pair dominates the other with respect to the attribute to be scaled. If the attribute is subjective probability, for each pair we would ask, "Which event is more likely?" No equality judgments are allowed. The relevant datum for each stimulus pair is the proportion of instances that stimulus j dominates stimulus k. Scale values for each stimulus are derived either according to Thurstone's law of comparative judgment (1927) or the Bradley-Terry-Luce model (Bradley and Terry, 1952; Luce, 1959).

The law of comparative judgment assumes that each stimulus is represented by a distribution of subjective magnitude. In comparing two stimuli, a magnitude is selected randomly from each distribution, which corresponds to selecting a value randomly from the distribution of differences. The proportion of times stimulus j is judged to be greater than stimulus k is taken as an estimate of the area of the distribution of differences where the difference is positive.

The law of comparative judgment further assumes that the distribution of differences is a normal distribution. Scale values are derived by taking the normal deviates associated with the proportions. This is a normal curve transformation of proportions into scale values. The Bradley-Terry-Luce model utilizes a log transformation rather than a normal curve transformation. Scale values derived from both models are closely related (Torgerson, 1958; Yellot, 1977). Methods for controlling bias in the paired comparisons situation have been developed by Ross (1934), Torgerson (1958), and Wherry (1938).

The greatest single criticism that can be levied against the method of paired comparisons is that for a large n, the number of judgments required from each subject is prohibitively large. For example, with 20 stimuli, 190 pairs exist; with 50 stimuli, 1225 pairs; with 100 stimuli, 4950 pairs. Fortunately methods for reducing the number of judgments required are available. Torgerson (1958) suggests some simple practical ways to reduce the required number of judgments. One method is to select a set of standard stimuli from the total stimulus set and compare other stimuli only against the standards. A second method, which requires a rough a priori ranking of stimuli, requires that each stimulus be compared only to others that are similar to it in terms of the characteristic being scaled. Another method divides the stimulus set into overlapping subsets, each of which is scaled separately with the overlapping stimuli used to connect the scales. These produce valid scale values with little loss of information.

Bock and Jones (1968) and David (1963) present more detailed and statistically justifiable designs, as well as designs for use with multiple judges where all judges do not judge the same pairs of stimuli.

Scaling by ranking. Ranking techniques can be considered equivalent to paired comparison techniques, since all paired comparisons can be derived from a rank order of events, and vice versa (Bock and Jones, 1968; Torgerson, 1958). However, a fundamentally different judgmental process may underlie ranking. The general method of rank order (Guilford, 1954) instructs the subject to rank the stimuli in order with respect to the attribute to be scaled. If N subjects each rank order n objects, then there are two basic procedures that can be followed. One approach is to deduce paired comparison proportions from the ranking and to treat them as if they were paired comparisons.

A second method for handling rank order data deals with the problem of intransitivity in the rankings. If intransitive rankings are anticipated, rules can be developed that permit ordering of the objects (Kemeny and Snell, 1962; Luce and Raiffa, 1957). The concept is to derive a group ranking which best (in some sense) summarizes the set, or profile, of individual rankings.

Scaling by sorting. Sorting methods have been developed for situations in which the number of stimuli is large, and there is no clear choice between paired comparisons and ranking (Edwards, 1957). Standard sorting procedures contain elements of both ranking and paired comparisons. A sorting task (involving cards, for example, each of which represents some magnitude of an attitude) requires personnel to place the items being sorted in ordered categories or piles. The endpoints of these piles are labeled according to whatever attribute is being evaluated. For example, the most extreme categories might be labeled "most likely" and "most unlikely." The subject's task is to place each event in the category corresponding to its perceived likelihood.

Scaling by rating. With rating procedures, stimuli are presented one at a time. The task is to rate each stimulus with respect to the attribute in question. The rating may be numerical, adjectival, or graphical. A rating form is basically a set of categories, by means of which a subject partitions the stimuli into mutually exclusive classes.

Rating differs from sorting primarily in the task the subject is required to perform. In the sorting situation, subjects are given all stimuli at once. In rating, only one stimulus is presented at a time. Sorting becomes more difficult as the number of stimuli increases because of the need to consider all stimuli simultaneously. Rating has the practical advantage that for n stimuli only n judgments are required.

Rating will be discussed in greater detail in the next section of this chapter.

Scaling by fractionation. Fractionation methods require that subjects directly report the ratio between two subjective magnitudes. The most common method, magnitude estimation, requires that numbers be directly assigned to objects in accordance with the subjective impressions they elicit (Jones, 1974). Typically one stimulus is considered the standard and assigned an arbitrary value. All other stimuli are judged against the standard. The method is quickly performed and easily yields scale values.

Scaling Comparisons

A few comparisons among the scaling techniques have been made. Arora (1977), studying the sociometric status of 13 to 17-year-old females, found somewhat greater reliability for partial ranking than for paired comparisons, although differences were not statistically significant.

Schriesheim and Schreisheim (1978) compared frequency scale values (e.g., "always," "sometimes") derived from magnitude estimation and rank–order judgments. They found magnitude estimation more closely achieved interval scale measurement than did ranking.

Magnitude estimation also appears to be less subject to fatigue effects than paired comparisions, especially when a large number of stimuli must be judged. It also has high convergent validity (Lodge, Tanenhaus, Cross, Tursky, Foley and Foley, 1976).

Magnitude estimates are also more reliable because there is no need to resort to theory (e.g., distributions of discriminal dispersions) to generate them. Ratio judgments show context effects (Eyman and Kie, 1970; Ross and Di Lollo, 1971; Sjoberg, 1971) and therefore scale values depend upon the set of possible stimuli with which specific stimuli are contrasted.

No simple relationships exist among scale values produced by different methods. However, discrimination scales (e.g., from paired comparisons) are often logarithmically related to magnitude scales (from ratio judgments) and scales from ratings or sorting have a quasilog relation with these other scale types (Cliff, 1973).

If one asks what the best technique is for securing subjective probabilities, there can be no definitive answer because the literature, as usual, is artificial, lacks applied relevance, and is confounded by artificial problems. Some conclusions can, however, be derived. Among direct methods for estimating discrete quantities (i.e., simply asking for the relevant number, usually in terms of probability or in odds), written responses are more consistent over time than are verbal ones, and also tend to be more extreme (Domas, Goodman and Peterson, 1972; Goodman, 1973). Goodman directly compared a number of response modes using data from various types of tasks. He found that correlations between the true probabilities, where they could be calculated, and the subjects' responses were high (range .91–.99) and the intercepts of regressions of judgments on the true values were close to zero. Written responses tend to be more reliable than verbal ones. Average test/retest reliability coefficients were .97, .66, and .96 for verbal estimates and .92, .89 and .97 for written ones.

Factors Affecting Scaling Judgments

Goodman (1973) and Stillwell, Seaver and Edwards (1977) also examined the effects of scale spacing—logarithmic versus linear. Spacing effects were quite strong. In studying responses in probabilities versus odds (Fujii, 1967; Phillips and Edwards, 1966) the responses in odds or likelihood ratios were closer to true values than were responses in probabilities. Where objective probabilities could be determined, the larger responses were also closer to the true values (Domas et al., 1972; Fujii, 1967; Phillips and Edwards, 1966; Stillwell et al., 1977).

Research has also examined the effect of the mode of responding on the judgment of probability distributions. Alpert and Raiffa (1969) found only small differences in the number of true values falling outside the extremes of the requested ranges resulting from techniques which asked for the median, interquartile range, and either the .01 and .99 values, the .001 and .999 values, the "minimum" and "maximum" values, or an "astonishingly low" and "astonishingly high" value.

Seaver, von Winterfeldt, and Edwards (1978) found much the same in examining the proportion of extreme values resulting from the way in which uncertainty was specified (odds, odds on a logarithmic scale, or probability) and the type of response required (uncertainty measures or values of the variable).

A number of authors (Spetzler and Stael von Holstein, 1978; Selvidge, 1973) have recommended procedures for securing probability assessments from subject matter experts.

1. Getting a feeling for the assessor's understanding of probabilities.

2. Explicitly defining the performance, event, or occurrence to be estimated. Selvidge (1973) talks about describing and decomposing the event to the point of identifying assumptions.

3. Multiple procedures (both direct and indirect) should be used to elicit judgments so that results of one technique can be used to check on the other. Responses should be checked for consistency and the SME should be given feedback on his responses.

Group Judgments

Seaver (1976) suggests that multiple experts be used, since their judgments will on the average be more accurate than individual judgments, primarily because of the decrease in the variance around the "true" value. However, this holds true for factual judgments more than value judgments.

A diversity of individual sources of information among group members may lead to more accurate judgments from groups compared with individuals.

Two general approaches using multiple experts to assess probabilities have been extensively explored. In the first, the statisticized group approach, individual estimates are made by multiple judges and mathematically aggregated. A variety of procedures for aggregation have been tried, from a simple arithmetic average of individual estimates to extremely complex procedures, for example, weighting the judgments of different individuals differentially according to their expertise, using either self-ratings, previous performance, or ratings by others as a basis for the weighting (Seaver, 1978; Stael von Holstein, 1971b, 1972; Winkler, 1971). The weighting procedure has however had virtually no effect on the judgments. The more complex aggregation procedures generally rely on some version of Bayes' Theorem to aggregate the individual judgments into a combined group judgment (Dalkey, 1975; Morris, 1974, 1977; Winkler, 1968).

The second approach is to ask the individuals to develop a group estimate by interacting as a group. The constraints put upon their interaction and the instructions they receive before that interaction constitute the major differences among procedures. At one extreme the Delphi procedure (Dalkey, 1969b) requires that the individuals not interact face-to-face at all, but instead, individuals make judgments and are given feedback about what the group as a whole responded. A new set of judgments is then made. If, after some number of iterations, no consensus is reached, mathematic aggregation is often used to provide the final group estimate.

Few differences among the various aggregation methods have been found in the quality of the group product; and subjects prefer the simpler procedures (Gough, 1975; Rowse, Gustafson, and Ludke, 1974; Seaver, 1978; Stael von Holstein, 1972; Winkler, 1971; Winkler and Cummings, 1972). Some of the more theoretically sophisticated techniques have proved difficult or impossible to apply in practice (Dalkey, 1975; Morris, 1971, 1974, 1975). Where differences have been found, a simple weighted additive combination method appears to be at least as good as, or better, than other more complex procedures (Seaver, 1976).

Much attention has focused on two techniques: Delphi, developed by Dalkey and Helmer at the Rand Corporation in the late 60s (e.g., Dalkey, 1969a, 1969b), and the *nominal groups technique* (NGT), developed at the University of Wisconsin (e.g., Delbecq and Van de Ven, 1971). Although other procedures for group interaction appear in the literature, Delphi and, to a lesser degree, NGT, markedly dominate. Delphi will be discussed in more detail in Chapter 11.

In the nominal groups technique the group does not interact in a normal manner: the interaction allowed the group members is tightly controlled. NGT is a four-step procedure: (1) silent judgments by individuals in the presence of the group, (2) presentation to the group of all individual judgments without discussion, (3) group discussion of each judgment for clarification and evaluation, and (4) individual reconsideration of judgments and mathematic combination.

Despite its dominance, evidence is lacking for Delphi effectiveness. Only two studies (Dalkey, 1969a, 1969b) support Delphi as superior to simple face-to-face discussion groups. Other procedures (Brockhoff, 1975; Van de Ven and Delbecq, 1974) apparently produce results as good as Delphi. Studies by Gough (1975) and Seaver (1978) found no significant difference among the various procedures.

Although neither Delphi nor NGT was developed as a probability estimation technique, they have been used for such purposes. Gustafson, Shukla, Delbecq and Walster (1973) compared four procedures (Delphi and NGT, a statisticized group and an interaction group) for determining a group judgment of the likelihood ratio of two hypotheses. NGT produced the best estimates and the Delphi groups produced the worst with the statisticized and interacting groups about the same.

A number of errors (von Winterfeldt, 1980) affect subjective judgment of probabilities. These include rounding errors; internal fluctuations of judgment resulting from fatigue or stress; shifts of judges' emphasis over time; tendency to shift responses to the middle of the response scale and away from extreme values (Lichtenstein et al., 1978); conservatism (failure to revise their probabilities as new information reaches judges, Phillips and Edwards, 1966); the tendency to overestimate the likelihood of events that are easier to recall; neglect of base rates; judges' overconfidence; and contextual influences such as the effect of irrelevant information.

These biases point up the importance of training the SME. Feedback has been found useful by Adams and Adams (1958, 1961), Hoffman, and Peterson (1972) and Schaefer and Borcherding (1973). Studies by Winkler (1967, 1971) and Stael von Holstein (1971a, 1972) suggest that statistical training helps in the estimation of probabilities in situations which are inherently statistical (e.g., estimating the prices of stocks over time).

RATING METHODS

Rating scales are a form of psychometric scaling, the method of successive intervals. Each rating scale has two components: a description of the behaviors to be considered (the continuum) and a set of alternative responses from which the rater must select for each individual being rated.

As Landy and Farr (1980) put it, "the most ubiquitous method of performance appraisal is rating." Guion (1965) reported that 81 percent of the published studies in the *Journal of Applied Psychology* (JAP) and *Personnel Psychology* between 1950 and 1955 used ratings as criteria. Blum and Naylor (1968) found that of those articles in the JAP from 1960 to 1965 that used criterion measurement, 46 percent measured performance using judgmental indices. It is unlikely that the situation has changed much.

There are a number of reasons for this. Almost anything can be rated. No instrumentation except paper and pencil is needed and the rater himself is the means of measurement. Although the development of valid and reliable rating scales requires specialized knowledge and the development process if properly followed is painstaking, anyone with even the slightest knowledge of ratings can develop his own, and quickly too. One cannot of course vouch for the effectiveness of an amateur's scale. In addition, as we shall see later, the rating scale, which can quantify observations of oneself, of peers and of subordinates, is more flexible and versatile than objective performance techniques and indeed than the other psychometric methods described in the previous section.

Ratings are most often employed for a variety of purposes. In the following no distinction is drawn between ratings of others and self-ratings.

1. To evaluate *how well* someone is performing a job (appraisal); or to determine someone's *suitability* to perform that job (selection).

2. To measure some *quality* of performance (e.g., coordination of team members) or an *attitude/trait* of the performer (e.g., degree of cooperation, amount of aggressiveness manifested) or the performer's *feeling* about another person, a condition or event.

3. To quantify the adequacy of some *feature* of a system (e.g., its displays, or job procedures, or the adequacy of parks in the neighborhood).

4. To evaluate the effect of some *condition* (e.g., visibility, crime) which impacts on performance (e.g., target detection, amount of social activity at night).

5. To evaluate the *output* of a performance (e.g., the adequacy of a business decision, the quality of a novel).

The amount of literature written on ratings or which use rating as the vehicle of measurement is so great that no single chapter could attempt to describe it all. We rely to a large extent on previous reviews of the field, in particular the one by Landy and Farr (1980).

Types of Ratings

Great efforts have been made over the years to develop and test new rating formats because each format has been found to be subject to a variety of errors in their use. Changes have been made in the way in which the scale was developed, or the operations required of the rater as he rates, or both. Because there have been so many variations and they have been called by so many names, the literature may appear somewhat confusing.

In general, ratings can vary in the following ways:

1. A continuous or discontinuous line may be used to represent graphically the continuum of the dimension. Alternatively verbal adjectives may represent polar opposites and midpoints of the scale. Still other versions combine both the preceding.
2. The scale can vary in terms of the number of subdivisions or categories representing orders of magnitude of the dimension being rated.
3. The scale can vary in terms of the way in which the orders of magnitude (the subdivision points) are defined and illustrated, for example, merely as trait labels or with critical incidents to illustrate the definition.
4. The operations required of the rater may vary. In the graphic method he may be asked to check a point along the scale representing the amount of the dimension possessed by the object being rated. Or, he may be asked to indicate the frequency with which the ratee displays certain behaviors. Still again, he may have to select among alternative descriptors the one or more that best/least describe the ratee (forced choice method).
5. The way in which the rating scale is developed may vary. The descriptors in the scale may be developed on the basis of the developer's expert judgment or may be based on observed critical incidents. Items included in the final scale may be selected on the basis of item or factor analysis or on the basis of agreement by a group of raters.

Although there are many ways of presenting a rating scale, certain types have been commonly employed. Landy and Farr (1980) divide the types of scales into direct estimation and derived rating systems, with the former including graphic scales (including the most common scale—the Likert-type), *behaviorally anchored rating scales* (BARS), also known as the behavioral expectation scale, and *behavioral observation scales* (BOS). Derived rating systems include forced-choice rating and the mixed standard scale.

The Graphic Rating Scale. This scale, introduced in 1922 by Paterson, consists in most cases simply of an unbroken line with divisions representing points on a continuum, each point being defined by a trait label, definition, and adjectives. (Sometimes a line is absent and the rater checks off discrete categories.) The line can run vertically or horizontally, though it was originally introduced as vertical. The number of divisions and terms can be anything the scale developer wishes (research on these points will be discussed later). This is the type of scale most practi-

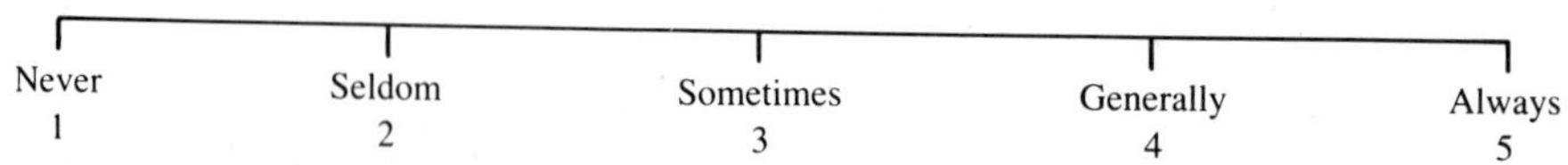

FIGURE 9.2. Graphic rating scale. Characteristic being measured: "Knows the price of competitive products."

tioners are familiar with. An example of a graphic rating scale used to appraise one dimension of salesman capabilities is shown in Figure 9.2. It is more popularly known as the *Likert-type* scale when numbers (1-5, 1-7, 1-9, etc.) denote the scale divisions and the intervals represent supposedly equal orders of magnitude of some measure—always, frequently, sometimes, seldom, never. As commonly used, this is a relatively simple scale usually anchored on the basis of the developer's expert judgment. Later rating scales introduced greater detail and more sophistication in the way in which the scale was developed.

The Behaviorally Anchored Rating Scale. The behaviorally anchored rating scale was introduced by Smith and Kendall (1963). Its major difference from the graphic rating scale is the addition of anchoring illustrations which are to be concrete and specific and located at intervals (to represent low, medium and high amounts) along the vertical scale. The anchors are designed to standardize the rater's observations and to screen out idiosyncracies.

Although there are minor variations in the BARS developmental procedure, it typically includes five steps.

1. *Critical incidents*. Those with knowledge of the job to be investigated (job incumbents and supervisors) are asked to describe specific illustrations of effective and ineffective performance. This step follows Flanagan's (1954) critical incidents technique.

2. *Performance dimensions*. The scale developers then cluster these incidents into a smaller set of performance dimensions (frequently between 5 and 10) which they define.

3. *Retranslation*. Another group of job knowledgeable participants is then instructed to retranslate or reallocate the critical incidents. They are given the definitions of the dimensions and the incidents and asked to assign each incident to the dimension that it best describes. A retranslation criterion is then established as a basis for selecting those incidents that will be retained. Typically an incident is retained if some percentage (e.g., 50 to 80%) of the group assigns it to the same dimension as did the group in step (2).

4. *Scaling incidents*. This second group is also asked to rate (generally on a 7- or 9-point scale) the behavior described in the incident with regard to how effectively or ineffectively it represents performance on the appropriate dimension. The average rating assigned the incident identifies the degree to which the incident describes effective performance on a dimension. The standard deviation of the ratings for each incident represents the amount of agreement among raters about incident effectiveness (the lower the standard deviation, the greater the agreement). A stan-

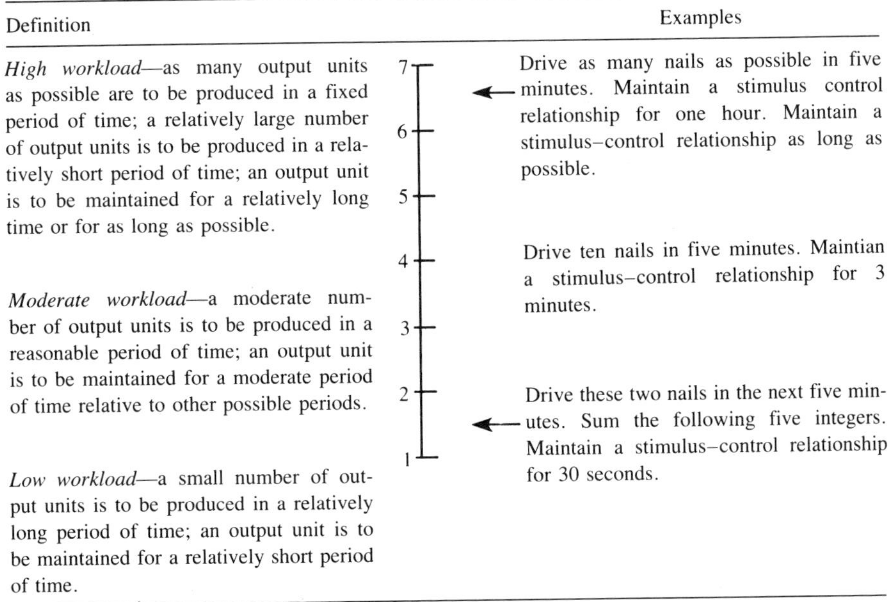

Definition
Examples
High workload—as many output units as possible are to be produced in a fixed period of time; a relatively large number of output units is to be produced in a relatively short period of time; an output unit is to be maintained for a relatively long time or for as long as possible.
Moderate workload—a moderate number of output units is to be produced in a reasonable period of time; an output unit is to be maintained for a moderate period of time relative to other possible periods.
Low workload—a small number of output units is to be produced in a relatively long period of time; an output unit is to be maintained for a relatively short period of time.
7
6
5
4
3
2
1
Drive as many nails as possible in five minutes. Maintain a stimulus control relationship for one hour. Maintain a stimulus–control relationship as long as possible.
Drive ten nails in five minutes. Maintian a stimulus–control relationship for 3 minutes.
Drive these two nails in the next five minutes. Sum the following five integers. Maintain a stimulus–control relationship for 30 seconds.

FIGURE 9.3. BARS scale (modified from Farina and Wheaton, 1973). *WORKLOAD IMPOSED BY TASK GOAL:* Workload is judged in terms of the number of output units to be produced relative to the amount of time allowed for their protection (i.e., output units per time). Rate the present task on the scale below.

dard deviation criterion is then set for deciding which incidents will be retained. Typically these are incidents that have standard deviations of 1.50 or less on a 7-point scale.

5. *The final instrument.* A subset of the incidents (usually 6 or 7 per dimension) that meet both the retranslation and standard deviation criteria are used as behavioral anchors for the performance dimensions. The incident is located along the scale, depending on its rating established in step (4).

An example of a BARS format developed by Farina and Wheaton (1971) to decribe certain task characteristics is shown in Figure 9.3. Note the definition of the task characteristic and the scale values and examples designed to anchor the scale values.

Mixed Standard Scale. Blanz and Ghiselli (1972) proposed this format to minimize halo and leniency errors. Three items are constructed for each rating dimension to reflect low, medium, and high amounts of the dimension. For example, ". . . assume that the trait to be rated is 'initiative' and has on a scale the following three statements, I being the most desirable description, and III the least desirable.

I. He is a real self starter. He always takes the initiative and his superior never has to stimulate him.

II. While generally he shows initiative, occasionally his superior has to prod him to get his work done.

III. He has a bit of a tendency to sit around and wait for directions" (Blanz and Ghiselli, 1972, p. 187).

All items are randomized in their order of presentation and the raters respond to the items without knowledge of the items' dimensionality. The graphic line to be checked does not exist in this format. Raters are required to choose one of the following three responses for each item: the ratee's performance is poorer than the item's description (−); it fits the description (*0*); the performance is better then the item description (+). The three graded statements used in this manner form a 7-point rating scale for each trait.

The developers contend that because the dimensions and their ordinal relationships are concealed, a rater is unable to detect an order of merit and halo and leniency errors are reduced. In contrast to BARS, mixed standard scale items are not constructed of critical incidents and the procedure for selecting scale items is not as rigorous, depending on the expertise of the scale developer. Whether this lack of rigor decreases the scale's validity cannot be determined since comparison tests have not been performed.

Behavioral Observation Scale. The behavioral observation scale is similar to BARS in that (1) both are variations of the critical incident technique; (2) both use rating forms that are worded in the terminology of the user; (3) both are based on relatively observable job behaviors that have been seen by others as critical to job success; and (4) both take into account the multidimensionality or complexity of job performance.

In developing BOS, (1) a large number of incidents/statements related to the dimension in question are collected; (2) a group of individuals are observed and rated on a five point scale as to the frequency with which they engage in the behavior described by each incident/statement; (3) a total score for each individual is determined by summing *O*'s responses to all the behavioral items; and (4) an item analysis (or factor analysis, depending on the size of the sample) is conducted to select the most discriminating items. Those items with the highest correlations with the total score on the scale are retained to form a behavioral criterion. Obviously the scale-item selection procedure is, like that of BARS, fairly rigorous.

The rater's task is to indicate, using a Likert-type scale, the frequency (e.g., always, occasionally, sometimes, usually, never) with which each critical behavior (e.g., "knows the price of competitive products") occurred over a specific period of time. Each critical behavior is listed in questionnaire format. Because the rater assesses the frequency with which certain behaviors have been observed, BOS presumably emphasizes simple observation rather than the more cognitive judgments required by BARS. However, since this frequency rating is based on a memory of what has occurred over some period in the past, say 3 to 6 months, it is subject to memory loss and may actually describe general traits rather than specific instances (Murphy, Martin and Garcia, 1982).

Those who have been advocating BOS (Latham and Wexley, 1977; Latham, Fay and Saari, 1979; and Latham, Saari and Fay, 1980) emphasize its simplicity com-

1 { a. Insists upon his subordinates being precise and exact.
b. Stimulates associates to be interested in their work.

2 { a. Allows himself to become burdened with detail.
b. Does not point out when work is poorly done.

FIGURE 9.4. Sample item from a forced-choice rating scale designed to measure supervisory performance.

pared to BARS. They say that with BARS or graphic rating scales the rater must make complex judgments about expected behaviors whereas with BOS all the rater is required to do is to indicate the frequency with which he has observed the behavior. However, the behaviors being rated for frequency must be adequately described.

A potential problem with BOS is the time needed to complete the form. BARS requires only 4 check marks if the individual is to be evaluated on four criteria. On the BOS if there were four criteria, but each criterion had 8 behaviors, 32 ratings would be required, which may prove a difficult task for the rater.

The Forced-Choice Rating. This rating scale requires the rater to choose from among a set of alternative descriptors (usually four items) some subset that is most characteristic of the ratee. An alternative version requires the rater to choose both the most and least descriptive descriptors. These descriptors function in a manner similar to that of anchors in direct rating. In direct rating schemes, the rater uses anchors to place an individual on a continuum; in a forced choice system the choice of descriptors by the rater allows a rating to be derived, because the descriptors have already been assigned scale values through some prior scaling process. In addition, the descriptors have been equated or balanced for desirability or undesirability. The forced choice method does away with the graphic line which is to be checked and hence eliminates any knowledge of preference and discrimination indices of the various descriptors (see Figure 9.4).

The forced choice methodology has been varied occasionally. Huttner and Katzell (1957) supplemented the conventional forced choice approach by having the rater indicate on a separate scale the extent to which the behavior checked applied to the person being rated. In another variation Kay (1959) used critical incidents as descriptors, but with poor results.

For the sake of completeness we should also include a number of less commonly used performance appraisal techniques. For example, individuals can be ranked (e.g., from best to worst) in terms of dimensions without asking for direct estimation along a scale. These ranks can be treated, if one makes a number of assumptions, to provide more direct estimates of distances between individuals (Guilford, 1954, pp. 178-195). Or one can apply the paired comparison technique by pairing every ratee with every other and the results of the comparisons can be treated to yield psychological distance between ratees (Guilford, 1954, pp. 154-176).

Scale Comparisons

Since the motive force in developing new types of scales is the effort to reduce the common errors found in rating scales and to make the device more valid and reliable, it is important to compare the various scale types in terms of these criteria.

Variations in graphic scale format (changes in the position of the high end of the scale, horizontal vs. vertical orientation, segmented vs. unbroken scale, and numbering of scale levels, *−1* to *9* vs. *−4* to *+4*) have produced statistically significant effects, but practically speaking the effects are unimportant (Madden and Bourdon, 1964). Blumberg, DeSoto and Kuethe (1966) varied the "good" end of the graphic scale (top, bottom, left, right) and found no significant differences. Formatting variations appear to be simply cosmetic.

What one rates depends, of course, on the question one wishes answered, but one common rating dimension is molarity: the rating can be either global or detailed. In the first case one might use a phrase such as "effectiveness" or "cooperation"; in the second case the scale would describe the component behaviors that make up effectiveness or cooperation. The latter are trait names and the components of the trait are more likely to be performance oriented. Several researchers (Campbell et al., 1970; James, 1973; Ronan and Prien, 1966; Smith, 1976) believe that global ratings are more likely to be contaminated by extraneous sources of variance. If this is true, it would suggest that in selecting the content of rating scales (e.g., performance results; observable job behaviors; personal traits) one should emphasize observable performances or behaviors. See Brumback (1972) and Kavanagh (1973) for two opposing opinions.

As far as response categories are concerned, there is apparently no gain in reliability if one increases the number of categories from 5 to 9, but reliability drops with 3 (too gross) or more than 7 (too fine) (Bendig, 1952a, 1952b, 1953, 1954a, 1954b; Finn, 1972). There appears to be little utility in having more than 5 scale categories (Jenkins and Taber, 1977).

There is also a consensus about the utility of the various types of anchors (numerical, adjectival, behavioral). Apparently anchors do improve scale reliability (Bendig, 1952a, 1952b, 1953; Barrett, Taylor, Parker and Martens, 1958; Campbell, Hunt and Lewis, 1958); and behavioral anchors appear to be more effective than numerical or adjectival ones (Barrett et al., 1958; Bendig, 1952a, 1952b; Maas, 1965; Peters and McCormick, 1966; Smith and Kendall, 1963). Finn (1972) did not find this, however.

One of the most difficult aspects of developing a rating scale is the determination of equal scale intervals. In the simplest case the developer might wish to assign 5-scale intervals to a graphic scale in which the dimension being rated is the frequency of occurrence of some phenomenon. The scale might read: always (1); frequently (2); sometimes (3); infrequently (4); never (5). Although these intervals are apparently at equal distances from each other, one can never be sure without some empirical measurement. Does every rater see frequently in the same way; and just how frequently is frequently? (See Chapter Ten for methods of quantizing such intervals.) This problem is exacerbated when the developer introduces behavioral or adjectival anchors.

The most common method for anchoring in BARS is the use of judges to estimate how much of a particular dimension a behavioral anchor represents. The judgment is accomplished using a graphic rating scale for items that have been previously judged for content. Final selection of anchors is based on the resulting mean value of the item and on its standard deviation. However Barnes (1978) has demonstrated that when behavioral anchors are scaled using the paired comparison method, the resultant scale values differ significantly from those produced by the graphic rating method. That the relatively disappointing performance of BARS may be due to a lack of scaling rigor has been suggested by Schwab, Heneman and Cotiis (1975), Bernardin (1977) and Landy and Farr (1980), but it is difficult to see how much more rigor could be applied. Moreover, scaling rigor in the development of rating scales, at least in the practical sphere, is more the exception than the rule.

BARS has been in widespread use the past 10 years or so which may be indicative of utility although not necessarily of validity or reliability. There is a continuing problem with identifying anchors for the central part of the scales (Harari and Zedeck, 1973; Landy and Guion, 1970; Smith and Kendall, 1963). Borman and Vallon (1974) suggest that BARS may be limited to use in the settings in which they were developed, although Goodale and Burke (1975) and Landy, Farr, Saal, and Freytag (1976) did demonstrate generalizability. A central problem of a pragmatic nature is that BARS is expensive and tedious to produce, especially in comparison with the standard Likert-type graphic scale. It requires independent groups of judges performing relatively sophisticated psychometric tasks. One would have to demonstrate added reliability and validity to make its development worthwhile. Campbell, Dunnette, Arvey and Hellervik (1973) compared BARS with summated ratings and concluded that the former yielded less variance, less halo, and less leniency. Borman and Vallon (1974) found BARS to be superior in reliability and rater confidence, but simpler numerical formats produced less leniency and better discrimination among ratees. Burnaska and Hollman (1974) compared BARS with a version of BARS and the traditional graphic scale, finding that BARS reduced leniency and increased variance attributable to rater differences. When BARS and graphic ratings were compared by Keaveny and McGann (1975), neither form could be judged superior. Borman and Dunnette (1975) compared BARS with a BARS version and a graphic scale and found that although BARS was psychometrically superior in terms of halo, leniency, and reliability, these differences accounted for only 5 percent of the variance.

These results and those of Bernardin, Alvares and Cranny (1976), Bernardin (1977), and Friedman and Cornelius (1976) suggest that BARS does not represent a significant advance over graphic ratings, perhaps because so many other factors affect the rating strongly that format is a trivial variable.

A number of studies have compared forced choice ratings with other techniques and suggest that forced choice does produce higher convergent validity (Berkshire and Highland, 1953), shows less leniency bias (Taylor, Schneider and Clay, 1954;

TABLE 9.1 The Effect of *Rater* Characteristics on Rating Performance

Variables	Effect	Citations
Sex	No consistency	Elmore and LaPointe, 1974, 1975; Centra and Linn, 1973; Rosen and Jerdee, 1973; Jacobson and Effertz, 1974; Mischel, 1974; Lee and Alveres, 1977; London and Poplawski, 1976; Hamner, Kim, Baird and Bigones, 1974.
Race	No consistency and unimportant	Crooks, 1972; DeJung and Kaplan, 1962; Cox and Krumholtz, 1958; Hamner et al., 1974; Schmidt and Johnson, 1973.
Age	No effect; younger less lenient	Mandell, 1956; Klores, 1966.
Education	No effect	Cascio and Valenzi, 1977.
Psychological variables	Effects small and uninterpretable	Mandell, 1956; Lewis and Taylor, 1955; Zedeck and Kafry, 1977.
Cognitive complexity	Complex raters are less lenient, have less halo	Schneier, 1977.
Experience	More experienced are more reliable but effect is inconsistent and small	Jurgenson, 1950; Mandell, 1956; Klores, 1966; Cascio and Valenzi, 1977.
High aptitude	More valid ratings	Schneider and Bayroff, 1953; Bayroff, Haggerty and Rundquist, 1954.
Good/poor performers as raters	No great difference but higher peformers rated with greater range	Mandell, 1956; Kirchner and Reisberg, 1962.
Leadership style	Uncorrelated with rating strategies	Zedeck and Kafry, 1977.
Supervisor and peer ratings	Differences found	Borman, 1974.
Supervisor and self ratings	No consistency; self more lenient	Parker, Taylor, Barrett and Martens, 1959; Kirchner, 1965; Lawler, 1967; Klimoski and London, 1974.
Organizational level	Low/moderate agreement between supervisors at different levels; first level supervisors predict job knowledge test scores better than second/third level.	Berry, Nelson and McNally, 1966; Borman and Dunnette, 1975; Campbell et al., 1973; Whitla and Tirrell, 1953; Zedeck and Baker, 1972.

TABLE 9.1 (*Continued*)

Variables	Effect	Citations
Contact between raters and ratees	No consistent effect	Ferguson, 1949; Kleiger and Mosel, 1953; Fisk and Cox, 1960; Gordon and Medland, 1965; Klores, 1966; Hollander, 1957, 1965; Waters and Waters, 1970; Amir et al., 1970; Suci, Vallance and Glickman, 1956; Freeberg, 1969; Landy and Guion, 1970.
Peer ratings compared with observer ratings	Peer ratings more lenient; peer ratings more solid predictors of cognitive skills and future performance.	Freeberg, 1969; Fisk and Cox, 1960; Rothaus, Morton and Hanson, 1965; Kraut, 1975.
Job knowledge requirements	Those who know more predict future performance better	Amir, Kovarsky and Sharan, 1970.

Sharon and Bartlett, 1969), less range restriction and equal reliability with graphic ratings (Lepkowski, 1963). However, Cozan (1959) concluded that improvements in validity resulting from forced-choice did not warrant switching from the graphic rating.

Recently there has been a small controversy between adherents of BARS and those who support BOS (e.g., Latham, Fay and Saari, 1979; Bernardin and Kane, 1980; Latham, Saari and Fay, 1980; Latham and Wexley, 1977), but with no comparative tests, only words.

Factors Affecting Rater Performance

Three factors may influence rating performance: rater and ratee characteristics, and the rating context/process. A number of studies listed in Tables 9.1 and 9.2 have investigated these parameters but unfortunately have derived no clearcut results. The most clearcut effects have been found as a result of rater training, particularly if the training is sustained and includes practice. Since the rater is a measuring instrument, he must be developed (i.e., trained), calibrated and tested like any other instrument. Although some research on the effect of training on accuracy and validity of ratings has been performed, much more needs to be done. One cannot assume that anyone asked to rate—however much technical experience the individual has had with a particular field requiring expertise—can do so validly without extensive prior training.

Types of Errors

As in direct observation raters make errors of omission (failure to note the occurrence of a behavior) or commission (noting the wrong behavior category). Because

TABLE 9.2 The Effect of *Ratee* Characteristics and *Rating Process* on Rating Performance

Variables	Effect	Citations
Sex	Sexual stereotype of job interacts with ratee sex. Females receive less favorable ratings. However, other studies differ.	Schmitt and Hill, 1977; Rosen and Jerdee, 1973; Bartol and Butterfield, 1976; Bigoness, 1976; Hamner et al., 1974; Jacobson and Effertz, 1974.
Race	Ratees receive higher scores from same-race raters. Blacks rated lower than whites. Some studies differ.	Crooks, 1972; Landy and Farr, 1976; DeJung and Kaplan, 1962; Hamner et al., 1974; Schmidt and Johnson, 1973; Huck and Bray, 1976; Schmitt and Hill, 1977; Farr, O'Leary and Bartlett, 1971; Greenhaus and Gavin, 1972; Toole, Gavin, Muddy and Sells, 1972; Fox and Lefkowitz, 1974.
Age	No effect	Klores, 1966; Bass and Turner, 1973.
Favorable/unfavorable behavior	Raters more accurate when rating favorably viewed behavior	Gordon, 1970, 1972.
Actual performance	Actual performance being rated has largest effect on ratings	Bigoness, 1976; Leventhal, Perry and Abrami, 1977; Hamner et al., 1974.
Organizational and job tenure	Very low correlation (.17)	Jay and Copes, 1957; Bass and Turner, 1973; Cascio and Valenzi, 1977; Zedeck and Baker, 1972; Klores, 1966.
Administrative vs. research conditions	Ratings under administrative conditions are more lenient.	Borreson, 1967; Heron, 1956; Taylor and Wherry, 1951; Centra, 1975.
Rater training	Reduces rater errors	Borman, 1975; Wexley, Sanders and Yukl, 1973; Bernardin and Walter, 1977; Gordon, 1970; Friedman and Cornelius, 1976; McIntyre, Smith and Hassett, 1984.
Rating each individual in turn on all traits vs. rating all individuals on trait 1, then trait 2, etc.	No difference	Guilford, 1954; Blumberg et al., 1966; Brown, 1968; Johnson, 1963; Taylor and Hastman, 1956.
Serial effect on ratings (early/late in sequence)	Some effect, nature unclear	Bayroff et al., 1954; Wagner and Hoover, 1974; Willingham, 1958.

rating is more complex than direct observation, raters have the opportunity to make many more errors: leniency and its converse, severity; sequential effects; distribution errors; and intercorrelational errors, of which the most well known is halo (Smith, 1976). The review by Saal, Downey and Lahey (1984) is valuable.

1. In *leniency*, ratings tend to be displaced toward the favorable end of the scale; the average individual is rated as above average. There are many possible reasons for leniency besides the desire to see one's own people in the best possible light. Less common and much more difficult to uncover is the error of severity which involves downgrading everyone.

2. In errors caused by *sequential effects*, the judgment of an item on the rating scale is affected by the items that precede it. Randomization of item order presentation solves the problem.

3. *Distribution errors* cause ratings to pile up in the middle of the response distribution, usually indicating a failure to discriminate among degrees of the dimension being evaluated. More intensive training might aid.

4. The most important *intercorrelational error*, because of its frequency, is the halo effect in which the rating on one characteristic spills over, as it were, to affect ratings on other characteristics which are distinctly different, resulting in high intercorrelations among the various rating dimensions. The rater who discriminates relatively little among dimensions will exhibit little variance, as contrasted with one who regards each dimension separately. This is illustrated in the following example taken from Borman (1975)

	Performance Categories						
Rater	A	B	C	D	E	F	Overall
1	5	6	5	5	6	5	5
2	5	3	6	3	6	7	5

in which the ratings provided by Rater 1 probably contain halo error, whereas those of Rater 2 probably do not.

Accuracy, Validity, Reliabiity

Because the observer is the measuring instrument in subjective techniques, and because he makes errors in observing and rating, it is necessary to determine his *accuracy*, the *validity* of his data and the *reliabiity* of his observations. Much of the previous material dealing with reliability of direct observation is applicable also to ratings, but the significant differences between the techniques require additional comment.

Few issues have generated more controversy in the rating literature than ways of evaluating the adequacy of the rating. The following is only a partial listing of papers written fairly recently on the topic: Harris and Lahey, 1978; Mitchell, 1979; Yelton, 1979; Hopkins, 1979; Hartman and Gardner, 1979; Kratchowill, 1979;

Hawkins and Fabry, 1979; Birkimer and Brown, 1979a, 1979b; Kazdin, 1977; Hartman, 1977; Frick and Semmel, 1978; Cronbach, Gleser, Nanda and Rajaratnam, 1972. The author has listed these studies to permit the interested reader to consult the literature for greater detail, because it is manifestly impossible in one section to discuss the questions that arise in all the detail they deserve.

Let us begin by defining and differentiating between accuracy and validity.

As was indicated previously, there is some confusion about what is meant by accuracy and validity. Hollenbeck (1978) defined accuracy as precision, or whether the measurement is a true representation of what is being observed. Kazdin (1977) defines accuracy as the extent to which observations scored by *O* match those of a predetermined standard for the same data. The standard may be some other known truth about the observations but more often is determined by other *Os*—probably more expert—who reach a consensus about the data; or by constructing observational material, such as videotapes, with predetermined behavioral standards (e.g., Borman, 1978). As we saw with direct observation, accuracy, and interobserver agreement are not the same (Kazdin, 1977). Interobserver agreement reflects the extent to which observers agree on scoring behavior. Unless one develops a standard before test observations are made, there is little basis for concluding that one observer's data are better than another's.

Rating validity is measured by correlations among the variables observed and the methods used to observe (multitrait, multimethod technique, Campbell and Fiske, 1959). Discriminant validity is measured by correlation coefficients derived by a. measuring different variables using the same method, and b. by measuring different variables using different methods. This is a way of testing whether the methods used to observe are responsible for the major part of the variance associated with the data. If they are, the actuality of the variables studied is called into question. Presumably if the difference in the resulting correlation coefficients is small the variance associated with methods is low and the phenomena observed cannot be assigned to methods (and therefore possibly exist). Convergent validity coefficients result when the same variable is measured using different methods. If the coefficients of correlation are significant, this indicates that different methods are picking up the same phenomenon, which suggests again that whatever is out there is genuine.

The demonstration of an acceptable level of interobserver agreement has been thought to be crucial to rating as a measurement technique. Unfortunately, as we saw previously, no current method of calculating interobserver agreement has been widely accepted; all have flaws of one sort of another.

OBJECTIVE MEASURES

In this section we discuss the operations required to secure time, error, and frequency measures. It is possible, as Smode et al. (1962) did, to list many objective measures in fine detail, but these, when considered in terms of their similarity, collapse into the relatively few generic ones just mentioned.

As we have seen, it is quite possible to secure quantitative estimates of performances, behaviors, things, events, and phenomena through purely subjective means. These occurrences can also be measured objectively by timing, counting events, and comparing event occurrences with an external standard such as a procedure. There is, of course, subjectivity in the data recording process. Someone must read a timer or meter or check accuracy, but this subjectivity is visible. Objectivity is defined in terms of the operations needed to report a datum. If I use a clock to time someone's performance, the means of measurement is largely external to me and hence objective. What makes a measurement objective is the absence of my interpretation required in recording the datum. The interpretation (as related to the meaning of the datum) comes later, but it is not a critical part of the measurement process itself.

The advantage of the objective measures is that they lack the extreme subjectivity of observation and judgment which leads to questions of validity and reliability. On the other hand, objective measurements are limited in the dimensions they describe (time, frequency, deviation) and consequently they often provide much less information than do subjective measures.

Everything that was said in previous chapters about the need for a standard to make data meaningful applies to objective as well as to subjective data. For evaluation purposes a time measurement, for example, does not mean anything unless it is related to an explicit or implicit standard. Objectivity does not dispose of this requirement.

The context of the data is also necessary to understand objective data. That context is a task or job. The frequency with which a switch is thrown is uninterpretable unless we know the task of which switch throwing is a subtask. And although it might be possible by means of instrumentation to measure very discrete elements of behavior, those elements would be meaningless unless related to the task/job whole.

Certain contexts do not permit objective measurement. The latter is peculiarly suited to the measurement of task and job performance but not at all for nontask behaviors, attitudes, and traits. Moreover, the task/job performances must be overt. Perceptual and cognitive activities must be self-reported because they are not suitable for instrumentation or observation. When we are concerned about the dimensions of jobs and tasks, such as team coordination, the objective measurement methods may be inadequate because they are not designed to measure attributes.

Timing is easiest to perform because it utilizes instrumentation, it is independent of context (the same dimension across various tasks); and its data are relatively unambiguous since the limits of performance (i.e., start-stop indices) are often, but not always, obvious. However, time as a measure has been criticized on the ground that performance time is influenced by error, task difficulty, and variation in performance conditions. Bradley (1975) indicates that if there are few errors, easy tasks, or ideal conditions, there is little variability among time scores and individual differences are masked. In contrast, where the task produces many errors or is difficult, time distributions tend to be diffuse.

Counting is relatively simple. Errors on the other hand may be difficult to recognize where an external standard, that is, a procedure, is not available or is unclear.

In contrast to time, errors may have varying and complex causes and dimensions which make the topic not only one of practical significance but also interesting on a scientific basis. Timing and counting are relatively independent of the data recorder's internal processes. Yet in covert performances (as in problem solving and diagnosis, for example) the error measure is significantly affected by *O*'s internal processes and thus tends to overlap subjective measures.

Like subjective measures, objective measures have several purposes or uses: to describe, to compare, to evaluate, and to diagnose. The purpose for which one wishes an objective measure should determine which measure is selected. In no case would one utilize a measure unless it were needed to answer an important question.

Reaction Time

Reaction time (RT) is the time between the *occurrence of an event* requiring an action on the part of the operator or team (the initiating stimulus) and the *start of the action* (the RT response) demanded by the event. Since the initiating stimulus must be recognized by an operator, that stimulus is likely to be something observed directly by him or exhibited on a display. The RT response is the operator's action in throwing a switch, making a verbal report, etc.

The major purpose of measuring RT is to determine how quickly the operator/team can react to an initiating stimulus. Before selecting this measure the behavior specialist must ask whether this information is *necessary*.

Reaction time is meaningful only when there is a system or job requirement to react as quickly as possible, for example, an adversary or emergency situation in which failure to respond rapidly could be catastrophic. If the system or job is not time-driven, it would be pointless to measure RT. Military systems are of course the most common example, but in civilian life the fire department, police, and the ambulance are other examples. Reaction time is also measured when a time standard is implicit—for instance, the shortest possible time—even if an explicit standard, a maximum required response time, has not been specified. If a maximum RT is specified, then obviously the evaluator must determine whether the system performs within that time period.

The RT measure is meaningless if applied to anything smaller than a task. Reaction time is measured for a performance, the failure of which could lead to a catastrophic consequences. Part–task actions do not eliminate such possibilities.

If the RT required of an operator is very short, there may be difficulty accomplishing the task. If one examines task requirements in advance of evaluation, and required RT appears to be quite short, then RT measurement may determine if the operator's capabilities are being exceeded. (In general, the shortest time in which an operator can respond to a single, discrete stimulus like the onset of a light is 200 to 300 milliseconds; but as the stimulus event becomes more complex and requires difficult cognitive processes, that minimum period can become a minute or longer.)

If the operator/team is required to react as quickly as possible (even though a fixed RT is not specified), the specialist will wish to determine the shortest RT he can expect of the system. However, this information cannot be used to evaluate the effectiveness of the system unless an RT standard exists or can be inferred from the nature of the system mission.

The recognition of the initiating stimulus for the RT measure is important. Where the stimulus cannot be easily anticipated by *O*, when it is accompanied by irrelevant stimuli from which *O* must distinguish it, or when the initiating stimulus is itself very short, it may be difficult for both the operator and the RT data collector to recognize that stimulus. Before collecting his RT data, the evaluator must decide what the initiating stimulus is.

Another problem is the nature of the RT response. In situations in which the operator's response is covert (i.e., perceptual or analytic), it may be extremely difficult for *O* to pinpoint exactly when the operator has made his response. In surveillance systems, the operator may initially respond to the appearance of a target by continuing to observe until he has classified it. Unless he is required to report verbally or to throw a switch indicating that he has recognized the target, there may be no observable indication that he has in fact recognized the target. It may be necessary for the data collector to wait until the operator activates a control and to consider this activation as the RT response. This is however somewhat less than satisfactory, since the response of interest is the covert activity, not activating a control.

Duration

Duration is the time from the initiating stimulus to the time the task or function is accomplished. It therefore includes the RT measure and extends it. Duration is an extremely common measurement. It is often recorded even when there is no need to verify a duration requirement. However, it is important when the system prescribes a maximum duration for a task or group of tasks. If a task must be performed in no more than 5 minutes, for example, it is important to measure task duration to determine if that requirement is satisfied. On the other hand, even where no maximum duration is specified, if system requirements are such that a duration standard can be inferred—for example, some durations are excessive—the measure becomes important there too. Hence one may wish to record duration simply to ensure that it is within an acceptable bound. Duration in this context would be primarily descriptive. Systems and individuals may be measured against a specified standard. Or, as in sports, they may be compared against each other in terms of duration. Durations may be indicative of a problem. If, for example, a student takes excessively long to complete a task, it may well be because he has not learned requisite skills.

Ordinarily duration measurement does not have to be extremely precise, unless there is some system requirement which necessitates highly precise measurement (e.g., as in timing a foot race). When duration is relatively gross, it is easily recorded, often demanding no more than a stop watch and a single *O*. The problem may become "sticky," however, if one individual performs a number of different tasks which blend into each other and a single data collector must record the duration of each task. Tasks in a series may flow into each other and there may be no clearly defined start and stop point to bound the limits of the measurement. Under such circumstances it will be necessary to decide in advance of measurement what these are and train the data collector to recognize them.

The duration of system operations may not be the same as the duration of tasks performed during those operations. Tasks may be performed prior to the equipment taking over, or the operator may have to wait while the hardware is performing its part of the operation. Measurement of the system operation as a whole will therefore include task duration, but will not necessarily describe it precisely.

Accuracy

Accuracy, or its converse, error, is probably the most common and perhaps the most useful measure of personnel performance. There are systems and tasks in which RT and duration are not important, but accuracy, at least in terms of absence of error, is critical in all. The material in this section may overlap somewhat with error as described in relation to human reliability (see Chapter 5) but error is important in its own right. For example, Deming (1980) has shown that error is intimately related to productivity in a quality control context. When error is reduced, productivity increases.

Some errors will always occur because of the inherent variability of the human. In consequence, error data are usually meaningful only in aggregate, only in terms of how the system is affected by error, and only in relationship to the number of opportunities to make the errors. The single catastrophic error (as in the Three-Mile Island nuclear incident or in automobile and airplane accidents) is important, but it is difficult to understand that error except as one instance of a class of errors.

Some errors have potentially significant or catastrophic effects on task and function accomplishment, others do not. For instance, an error in performing a continuous function such as tracking may be much more significant for performance than one in a discrete task like throwing a switch, where the error is more visible and can more readily be reversed.

In general, errors that have only a minor effect on performance and that are readily corrected need not be counted in the determination of personnel effectiveness, unless there is an excessive number of them.

Determination of the number of opportunities to make an error can be somewhat difficult as the human reliability researchers have discovered (see Chapter 5). If procedures are quite specific and performed only at designated times, the number of opportunities is the number of times the procedures are performed. However, many procedures are performed as considered necessary by personnel and are not reported as occurrences. An example is the opening and closing of valves by maintenance technicians in a plant. To determine the probability of incorrectly opening/closing valves, one must know not only how many valve errors have been made but also how often valves have been opened and closed, a datum not ordinarily reported (Luckas and Hall, 1981).

The problem then becomes one of evaluating the significance of the number and types of errors to system performance. One error is not necessarily equivalent to another. Even if it were, the relationship of a particular number of errors in performance to the system's capability to accomplish its functions depends on a criterion of the maximum number of permissible errors. Suppose that in a new aircraft crewmen made an average of .75 errors in performing a preflight checkout of 38 steps. Does this mean that the checkout procedure for this aircraft was ineffective or that personnel could not perform preflight checkout as required? One cannot answer this question unless the evaluation begins with a standard that *N* errors of a given type are or are not acceptable. The figure of .75 errors is, therefore, just an interesting statistic until its relationship to system success/failure is explored.

In practice, error measurement in the system context is used for diagnostic purposes as much or more than for evaluation. This means that beyond the mere reporting that an error has been made, additional information is required. That is because we endeavor to determine the error cause, so that if possible that cause can be rectified. In building up an error data base, one wishes to know the answers to questions such as a. who made the error; b. when was it made (e.g., in what part of the system mission, on what shift); c. with which equipment (if errors predominate with one equipment or equipment type, it may be because of poor equipment design or training associated with that equipment); d. type of error (psychomotor, motor, perceptual, cognitive); e. error criticality (in terms of safety consequences, incorrect fabrication, etc.); f. where in the plant/system the error was made; g. was the error corrected; h. was the operator aware that he had made an error; i. the nature of error (procedural step omitted; step performed incorrectly; nonrequired action taken; action taken out of sequence, incorrect hypothesis; etc.); j. the apparent cause of error.

It may not be easy to secure all this information, even if the individual who made the error steps forth and reports everything he can. If the error is one of workmanship, one may not even know that an error is made until an equipment is in operation and breaks down. Witness the frequent recalls of new automobiles.

Unless operators are under observation, and in many if not most work situations this is not feasible, our only knowledge of the error will arise from two channels: the error maker who volunteers that he has made an error (most unlikely), or by examination of some system output which makes it apparent that an error has occurred. If a switch is found thrown in the wrong position, someone obviously made an error. Workmanship defects found by quality control often point to continuing error though the error is not necessarily tagged with the name of the perpetrator. Therefore, someone to supply error relevant information may not be available. Where errors accumulate without an immediately apparent cause, it will be necessary to initiate an investigation (see Chapter 8) to determine the general operations that could have led to such errors. In the remote event that the error is tied to a particular individual, he often does not know why he made the error. And since the error is investigated in the *past*, personnel suffer from memory loss and other distortions.

In the operational environment accuracy/error data are important primarily for diagnosis of a problem. An excess of error may be indicative of a design, procedural, training, or workload problem. In the design environment the error is primarily useful as indicating a potential problem which may need fixing. In neither case is the specific individual who made the error particularly important unless he has some special characteristic that made the error more probable.

It is necessary to know not only error frequency but also the type of error made. The nature of the error is potentially diagnostic of a situation that needs modification. It may cast light on what needs to be done.

The evaluator also needs to know the criticality of the error. The evaluator must differentiate between the effect of the error on the individual task and its effect on overall system performance (where more than one task is involved). Some errors impede the performance of the individual task but have little effect on overall system performance, either because the task is not critical to that system performance or because there are compensatory mechanisms in the system which cancel out the error effect.

Errors are usually recorded manually or in the case of control manipulations, by instrumentation. Instrumentation is usually necessary when precise records of frequent control operations are desired.

As in the case of RT, the determination of what constitutes an error presents special problems when the operator's performance is covert. In such cases, the data collector should look for some overt response which is associated with the covert one. If the operator must throw a switch or make a verbal report based on his covert activities, it is throwing the switch or reporting verbally that become the types of data whose accuracy is recorded.

Manual techniques for recording errors include the following:

a. If potential errors can be categorized in advance of observation, one could develop a checklist of these errors and simply check them off as they occur during task performance. This procedure is not recommended because it is difficult to anticipate all errors and simply noting that an error of a given type has occurred does not supply context information (e.g., at what step in task performance the error has been made and what the operator does as a consequence of his making the error).

b. One could attempt to record all of the task actions exhibited by the operator and later sort out those actions that are erroneous. Such complete data recording is difficult for an unaided observer. He would probably have to record the performance with a videotape camera.

c. The most common procedure is to use an operating procedure as a sort of template. As the operator performs his task, the data collector checks off each action on the procedure. A performance deviating from that specified in the procedure would be noted at the appropriate step in the procedure.

With computer controlled systems it is a relatively simple matter to record all operator inputs to the system and even (with some sophistication here, of course) to indicate automatically where errors have been made.

A distinction must be made between an erroneous terminal output of a task/function and an error made in the course of producing that output. Although many errors are inconsequential, an erroneous output is always significant since it directly impacts on the mission of the operator or the team and perhaps the system. An output measure (when available), therefore, should always be gathered.

In addition to error data, the evaluator should be concerned about task accomplishment. The determination of successful task accomplishment is essentially a judgment made by the data collector. That judgment is based on the output of the task performance when it is completed. For example, an air intercept is judged as successful when the interceptor is vectored to a point in space where the pilot can report viewing the aircraft to which he has been vectored.

Task accomplishment is a more molar measure than error, because an error is merely one aspect of task performance. The evaluator's interest is in whether tasks are performed adequately because this determines system success.

Frequency

One may also wish to determine how frequently the operator's responses occur or how frequently certain tasks are performed (when there is no invariant sequence of task occurrence). Frequency, which is occurrence as a function of some time interval, is simply the tabulation of personnel actions (or events/outputs occurring as a result of personnel actions) as a function of time or other events occurring during system operations. One might, for example, record frequency of error in the various stages of an operation. Frequency is easy to secure, provided one can arrange personnel actions on some sort of chronological basis.

Occasionally a standard of personnel performance will specify a required frequency of response. In a factory situation the worker must assemble 6 widgets per hour, in which case it is necessary to verify that personnel do respond with that frequency. More frequently there is no absolute requirement specified, but there is an understanding that certain outputs are too few (an implied standard). In systems that make commercial products frequency of output is important because in part it determines productivity. Frequency is much less important when the system is performing a mission.

Quite apart from what frequency data mean on their own, they may illuminate factors that have affected the operator's performance. The relative frequency of certain types of error, for example, may suggest special difficulties the operator or the technician has in using his equipment or otherwise doing his job. In evaluating team efficiency, the frequency of certain types of verbal reports from one team member to another may indicate the degree of overall team coordination.

Before counting frequencies, some relevant taxonomy of categories to be counted must be developed. Any series of discrete actions can be recorded as a frequency (continuous actions cannot be counted unless the evaluator partitions the event continuum into categories, e.g., the systolic and diastolic components of the heartbeat). Examples of common system/industrial applications in which frequencies are counted are types of: (1) personnel functions/actions performed, (2) errors made in utilizing or fabricating an equipment, (3) verbal reports communicated from one operator station to another, (4) maintenance actions, (5) workmanship defects found in assembly actions and (6) outputs achieved.

As with any other type of objective measure, the actions whose frequency is being tabulated must be observable and distinguishable from other actions. If they are not, the frequency will be incorrect and unreliable.

A special case of frequency is what may be termed logistics measures—amount achieved or amount consumed. Examples of logistics measures can be seen in military aircraft situations where the frequency measurement is number of sorties flown or bomb tonnage dropped, or in an industrial situation, where the situation might be the number of widgets or the amount of scrap produced. We are not dealing with personnel performance as such, but with measures that are related to and reflect personnel performance. The number of rails split by Abraham Lincoln in an hour would have been a measure of his prowess as a rail-splitter.

If we consider the performance of personnel in a logistics situation, the measure indicating personnel performance may be logistical. For example, in one study the performance of simulated taxicab dispatchers was being studied (Moore, 1961). Here personnel efficiency was measured by the number of cabs dispatched in a particular unit of time and how long it took to get them to their destination. The measure itself is not behavioral but since the action being performed results in a physical output, the physical output can be considered a measure descriptive of personnel performance.

COMMENTARY

The objective methods are inherently limited because they measure only relatively simple (although fundamental) dimensions, that is, time, frequency, deviation (error), and amount. Using only these dimensions we secure data that are less subject to error (less invalid?) than subjectively derived data, but which may not satisfy all our desires for information. The operations of gathering objective data involve only single dimensions: timing, counting, comparing. Those of gathering subjective data often involve combinations of dimensions such as interpretation, impressions (of attitudes, for example), qualitative distinctions, and others that cannot be easily verbalized. Despite the fact that these additional dimensions produce greater error and invalidity than one finds in objective methods, subjective methods are employed as widely as they are, simply because of their greater range. It is possible that the human as a measuring instrument is able to integrate simultaneously many molecular behaviors which, even if one could afford to measure them objectively, would be difficult to integrate and understand purely as a combination of discrete behaviors. Without attempting to imply a physiologic explanation, the brain takes a variety of molecular body movements, a frown, etc. and integrates/interprets these as an aggressive attitude. The challenge to the behavior researcher is to control the interpretive process in subjective data gathering and to reduce its error. This requires more training of *O* and more prolonged practice than he ordinarily receives. How much training, is not known. A related question is whether one can reduce error by utilizing rigorous psychometric procedures to develop subjective instruments. The evidence on this point is ambiguous.

It is possible that the ability to observe and to rate is a talent which some have in greater abundance than others. Research is needed to determine if some individuals are better at observation than others.

It may be necessary to accept that there is an irreducible minimum of error in the human as measuring instrument and to *calibrate* the individual just as one does a physical instrument, to determine the amount of error variance one must include in one's evaluations. After all, one calibrates physical instruments—why not human ones?

Theoretically calibration of the human as instrument is possible, but it would be devilishly difficult. It would mean testing hundreds if not thousands of humans under highly controlled conditions (including standardized scaling instruments). Presumably if one tested them after prolonged training and practice, one would secure data on what they could do under ideal circumstances. Calibration would therefore be a critical part of training. Yet to calibrate properly would require a stratified sample of humans functioning under various conditions, making use of different rating scale types, etc. It would be infeasible to select certain individuals as specially qualified for rating and then use them in all rating situations. That is because rating is done by many people (e.g., supervisors, personnel selecting employees, teachers, etc.) who may have few of the characteristics of the ideal rater.

Calibration implies the development of a subjective calibration database which would consist of assigned error values for parameters such as sex, intelligence, amount of training, length of observations, etc. Knowing the characteristics of any individual rater, one could apply a known error factor to the actual rating. If under specified conditions one would expect an observer error of ± 0.455, one would apply this error correction to, for example, the immediate rating of 87.3 to give a true value somewhere between 87.755 and 86.845.

Such calibrated error values would be developed under highly controlled situations (e.g., rating a videotaped scenario) and then verified operationally to the extent that one can verify anything in the real world. Because of the effort required, it is unlikely that this solution will actually be implemented.

REFERENCES

Adams, J. K., and Adams, P. A. Realism of confidence judgments. *Psychological Review*, 1961, *68*, 33–45.

Adams, P. A., and Adams, J. K. Training in confidence judgments. *American Journal of Psychology*, 1958, *71*, 747–751.

Alpert, M. A., and Faiffa, H. *A Progressive Report on the Training of Probability Assessors*. Harvard University, unpublished manuscript, 1969.

Amir, Y., Kovarsky, Y., and Sharan S. Peer nominations as a predictor of multistage promotions in a ramified organization. *Journal of Applied Psychology*, 1970, *54*, 462–469.

Arora, S. A comparative study of two methods of measuring pupils' status in the classroom. *Journal of Psychological Researches*, 1977, *21*, 143-146.

Baer, D. M. Reviewer's comment: just because it's reliable doesn't mean that you can use it. *Journal of Applied Behavior Analysis*, 1977, *10*, 117–119.

Barnes, J. L. *Scaling Assumptions in Behaviorally Anchored Scale Construction*. Paper presented at the meeting of the American Psychological Association, Toronto, Canada, August 1978.

Barrett, R. S., Taylor, E. K., Parker, J. W., and Martens, L. Rating scale content: I. Scale information and supervisory ratings. *Personnel Psychology*, 1958, *11*, 333–346.

Bartol, K. M. and Butterfield, D. A. Sex effects in evaluating leaders. *Journal of Applied Psychology*, 1976, *61*, 446–454.

Bartos, J. A. *The Assessment of Probability Distributions for Future Security Prices*. Indiana University, Ph.D. dissertation, 1969.

Bass, A. R., and Turner, J. N. Ethnic group differences in relationships among criteria of job performance. *Journal of Applied Psychology*, 1973, *57*, 101–109.

Bayroff, A. G., Haggerty, H. R., and Rundquist, E. A. Validity of ratings as related to rating techniques and conditions. *Personnel Psychology*, 1954, *7*, 93–114.

Bendig, A. W. A statistical report on a revision of the Miami instructor rating sheet. *Journal of Educational Psychology*, 1952, *43*, 423–429. (a)

Bendig, A. W. The use of student rating scales in the evaluation of instructors in introductory psychology. *Journal of Educational Psychology*, 1952, *43*, 167–175. (b)

Bendig, A. W. The reliability of self-ratings as a function of the amount of verbal anchoring and of the number of categories on the scale. *Journal of Applied Psychology*, 1953, *37*, 38–41.

Bendig, A. W. Reliability and number of rating scale categories. *Journal of Applied Psychology*, 1954, *38*, 38–40. (a)

Bendig, A. W. Reliability of short rating scales and the heterogeneity of the rated stimuli. *Journal of Applied Psychology*, 1954, *38*, 167–170. (b)

Berkshire, J. R., and Highland, R. W. Forced-choice performance rating—A methodological study. *Personnel Psychology*, 1953, *6*, 355–378.

Bernardin, H. J. Behavioral expectation scales versus summated scales: A fairer comparison. *Journal of Applied Psychology*, 1977, *62*, 422–427.

Bernardin, H. J., Alvares, K. M., and Cranny, C. J. A recomparison of behavioral expectation scales to summated scales. *Journal of Applied Psychology*, 1976, *61*, 564–570.

Bernardin, H. J. and Kane, J. A second look at behavioral observation scales. *Personnel Psychology*, 1980, *33*, 809–814.

Bernardin, H. J. and Walter, C. S. Effects of rater training and diary-keeping on psychometric error in ratings, *Journal of Applied Psychology*, 1977, *62*, 64–69.

Berry, N. H., Nelson, P. D., and McNally, M. S. A note on supervisor ratings. *Personnel Psychology*, 1966, *19*, 423–426.

Bigoness, N. J. Effect of applicant's sex, race, and performance on employers' performance ratings: Some additional findings. *Journal of Applied Psychology*, 1976, *61*, 80–84.

Birkimer, J. C. and Brown, J. H. A graphical judgmental aid which summarizes obtained and chance reliability data and helps assess the believability of experimental effects. *Journal of Applied Behavior Analysis*, 1979, *12*, 523–533. (a)

Birkimer, J. C. and Brown, J. H. Back to basics: Percentage agreement measures are adequate, but there are easier ways. *Journal of Applied Behavior Analysis*, 1979, *12*, 535–543. (b)

Blanz, F., and Ghiselli, E. E. The mixed standard scale: A new rating system. *Personnel Psychology*, 1972, *25*, 185–199.

Blum, M. L., and Naylor, J. C. *Industrial Psychology*. New York: Harper & Row, 1968.

Blumberg, H. H., DeSoto, C. B., and Kuethe, J. L. Evaluations of rating scale formats. *Personnel Psychology*, 1966, 19, 243–259.

Bock, R. D. and Jones, L. U. *The Measurement and Prediction of Judgment and Choice*, San Francisco: Holden-Day, 1968.

Borman, W. C. The rating of individuals in organizations: An alternate approach. *Organizational Beahvior and Human Performance*, 1974, *12*, 105–124.

Borman, W. C. Effects of instructions to avoid halo error on reliability and validity of performance evaluation ratings. *Journal of Applied Psychology*, 1975, *60*, 556–560.

Borman, W. C. Exploring upper limits of reliability and validity in performance ratiangs. *Journal of Applied Psychology*, 1978, *63*, 135–144.

Borman, W. C., and Dunnette, M. D. Behavior-based versus trait-oriented performance ratings: An empirical study. *Journal of Applied Psychology*, 1975, *60*, 561–565.

Borman, W. C., and Vallon, W. R. A view of what can happen when behavioral expectation scales are developed in one setting and used in another. *Journal of Applied Psychology*, 1974, *59*, 197–201.

Borresen, H. A. The effects of instructions and item content on three types of ratings. *Educational and Psychological Measurement*, 1967, *27*, 855–862.

Bradley, J. V. The optimal-pessimal paradox. *Human Factors*, 1975, *17*, 321–327.

Bradley, R. A., and Terry, M. E. The rank analysis of incomplete block designs. I. The method of paired comparisons. *Biometrika*, 1952, *39*, 324–345.

Brandt, R. M. *Studying Behavior in Natural Settings*. New York: Holt, Rinehart and Winston, 1972.

Brehmer, B. Models of diagnostic judgment. In J. Rasmussen and W. Rouse (Eds.), *Human Detection and Diagnosis of System Failures*. New York: Plenum Press, 1981.

Brockhoff, K. The performance of forecasting groups in computer dialogue and face-to-face discussion. In H. Linstone, and M. Turoff, (Eds.), *The Delphi Method: Techniques and Applications*. Reading, MA: Addison-Wesley, 1975.

Brown, E. M. Influence of training, method, and relationship on the halo effect. *Journal of Applied Psychology*, 1968, *52*, 195–199.

Brumback, G. A reply to Kavanagh. *Personnel Psychology*, 1972, *25*, 567–572.

Burnaska, R. F., and Hollmann, T. D. An empirical comparison of the relative effects of rater response biases on three rating scale formats. *Journal of Applied Psychology*, 1974, *59*, 307–312.

Campbell, D. T. and Fiske, D. W. Convergent and discriminant validation by the multitrait-multimethod matrix. *Psychological Bulletin*, 1959, *56*, 81–105.

Campbell, D. T., Hunt, W. A. and Lewis, N. A. The relative susceptability of two rating scales to disturbances resulting from shifts in stimulus context. *Journal of Applied Psychology*, 1958, *42*, 213–217.

Campbell, J. P., Dunnette, M. D., Arvey, R. D. and Hellervik, L. V. The development and evaluation of behaviorally based rating scales. *Journal of Applied Psychology*, 1973, *57*, 15–22.

Campbell, J. P., Dunnette, M. D., Lawler, E. E., III, and Weick, K. E. *Managerial Behavior, Performance, and Effectiveness*. New York: McGraw-Hill, 1970.

Cascio, W. F. and Valenzi, E. R. Behaviorally anchored rating scores: Effects of education and job experience of raters and ratees. *Journal of Applied Psychology*, 1977, *62*, 278–282.

Centra, J. A. *The Influence of Different Directions on Student Ratings of Instructors*. Report ETS RB 75–28, Princeton, NJ: Educational Testing Service, 1975.

Centra, J. A. and Linn, R. L. *Student Points of View in Ratings of College Instruction* (ETS RB 73-60). Princeton, NJ: Educational Testing Service, 1973.

Chapanis, A. *Research Techniques in Human Engineering*. Baltimore: Johns Hopkins Press, 1959.

Christensen, J. M. and Mills, R. G. What does the operator do in complex systems. *Human Factors*, 1967, *9*, 329–340.

Clement, P. G. A formula for computing interobserver agreement. *Psychological Reports*, 1976, *39*, 257–258.

Cliff, N. Scaling. *Annual Review of Psychology*, 1973, 473–505.

Cohen, J. A coefficient of agreement for nominal scales. *Educational and Psychological Measurement*, 1960, *20*, 37–46.

Cohen, J. Weighted Kappa: nominal scale agreement with provision of a scaled disagreement or partial credit. *Psychological Bulletin*, 1968, *70*, 213–220.

Coombs, C. H., Dawes, R. M., Tversky, A. *Mathematical Psychology, an Elementary Introduction*. Englewood Cliffs, NJ: Prentice-Hall, 1970.

Cox, J. A. and Krumboltz, J. D. Racial bias in peer ratings of basic airmen. *Sociometry*, 1958, *21*, 292–299.

Cozan, L. W. Forced choice: Better than other rating methods? *Personnel Psychology*, 1959, *36*, 80–83.

Cronbach, L. J., Gleser, G. C., Nanda, H., and Rajaratnam, N. *The Dependability of Behavioral Measures: Theory of Generalizability for Scores and Profiles*. New York: Wiley, 1972.

Crooks, L. A. (Ed.) *An Investigation of Sources of Bias in the Prediction of Job Performance: A Six-Year Study*. Princeton, NJ: Educational Testing Service, 1972.

Dalkey, N. Analyses from a group opinion study. *Futures*, 1969, *1*, 541–551. (a)

Dalkey, N. An experimental study of group opinion: The Delphi method. *Futures*, 1969, *1*, 408–426. (b)

Dalkey, N. Toward a theory of group estimation. In H. Linstone and M. Turoff (Eds.). *The Delphi Method: Techniques and Applications*. Reading, MA: Addison-Wesley, 1975.

David, H. A. *The Method of Paired Comparisons*. New York: Hafner, 1963.

DeJung, J. E., and Kaplan, H. Some differential effects of race of rater and combat attitude. *Journal of Applied Psychology*, 1962, *46*, 370–374.

Delbecq, A., and Van de Ven, A. A group process model for problem identification and program planning. *Journal of Applied Behavioral Science*, 1971, *7*, 466–492.

Deming, W. E. *Quality, Productivity and Competitive Position*. Cambridge, MA: Massachusetts Institute of Technology, 1980.

DeSmet, A. A., Fryback, D. C., and Thornbury, J. R. A second look at the utility of radiographic skull examination for trauma. *American Journal of Radiology*, 1979, *132*, 95–99.

Domas, P. A., Goodman, B. C., and Peterson, C. R. *Bayes' Theorem: Response Scales and Feedback* (Technical Report No. 037230-5-T). The University of Michigan, Engineering Psychology Laboratory, September, 1972.

Edwards, A. L. *Techniques of Attitude Scale Construction*. New York: Appleton-Century-Crofts, 1957.

Einhorn, H. J., and Hogarth, R. M. Behavioral decision theory: Processes of judgment and choice. *Annual Review of Psychology*, 1981, *32*, 53–88.

Elmore, P. B. and LaPointe, K. Effects of teacher sex and student sex on the evaluation of college instructors. *Journal of Educational Psychology*, 1974, *66*, 386–389.

Elmore, P. B. and LaPointe, K. A. Effect of teacher sex, student sex, and teacher warmth on the evaluation of college instructors. *Journal of Educational Psychology*, 1975, *67*, 368–374.

Eyman, R. K., and Kie, P. J. A model for partitioning judgment error in psychophysics. *Psychological Bulletin*, 1970, *74*, 35–46.

Farina, A. J. and Wheaton, G. R. Development of a taxonomy of human performance; the task characteristics approach to performance prediction. *JSAS Catalog of Selected Documents in Psychology*, 1973, *3*, 26–27 (Ms. No. 323).

Farr, J. L., O'Leary, B. S., and Bartlett, C. J. Ethnic group membership as a moderator of the prediction of job performance. *Personnel Psychology*, 1971, *24*, 609–636.

Ferguson, L. W. The value of acquaintance ratings in criteria research, *Personnel Psychology*, 1949, *2*, 93–102.

Finn, R. H. Effects of some variations in rating scale characteristics on the means and reliabilities of ratings. *Educational and Psychological Measurement*, 1972, *32*, 255–265.

Fiske, D. W. and Cox, J. A., Jr. The consistency of ratings by peers, *Journal of Applied Psychology*, 1960, *44*, 11–17.

Flanagan, J. C. The critical incident technique, *Psychological Bulletin*, 1954, *51*, 327–358.

Fox, H. and Lefkowitz, J. Differential validity: Ethnic group as a moderator in predicting job performance. *Personnel Psychology*, 1974, *27*, 209–223.

Frick, T. and Semmel, J. I. Observer agreement and reliabilities of classroom observational measures. *Review of Educational Research*, 1978, *48*, 157–184.

Freeberg, N. E. Relevance of rater/ratee acquaintance in the validity and reliability of ratings. *Journal of Applied Psychology*, 1969, *53*, 518–524.

Friedman, B. A. and Cornelius, E. T., III. Effect of rater participation in scale construction on the psychometric characteristics of two rating scale formats. *Journal of Applied Psychology*, 1976, *61*, 210–216.

Fujii, T. *Conservatism and Discriminability in Probability Estimation as a Function of Response Mode*. University of Michigan, unpublished manuscript. 1967.

Goodale, J. G. and Burke, R. J. Behaviorally based rating scales need not be job specific. *Journal of Applied Psychology*, 1975, *60*, 389–391.

Goodman, B. C. *Direct estimation procedures for eliciting judgment of uncertain events* (Engineering Psychology Laboratory Technical Report 011313-5-T). University of Michigan, 1973.

Gordon, L. V. and Medland, F. F. The cross-group stability of peer ratings of leadership potential. *Personnel Psychology*, 1965, *18*, 173–177.

Gordon, M. E. The effect of the correctness of the behavior observed on the accuracy of ratings. *Organizational Behavior and Human Performance*, 1970, *5*, 366–377.

Gordon, M. E. An examination of the relationship between the accuracy and favorability of ratings. *Journal of Applied Psychology*, 1972, *56*, 49–53.

Gough, R. The effect of group format on aggregate subjective probability distributions. In D. Wendt, and C. Vlek (Eds.) *Utility, Probability, and Human Decision Making*. Dordrecht-Holland: Reidel, 1975.

Greenhaus, J. H. and Gavin, J. F. The relationship between expectancies and job behavior for white and black employees. *Personnel Psychology*, 1972, *25*, 449–455.

Guilford, J. P. *Psychometric Methods* (2nd ed.). New York: McGraw-Hill, 1954.

Gustafson, D., Shukla, R., Delbecq, A., and Walster, G. A comparative study of differences in subjective likelihood estimates made by individuals, interacting groups, Delphi groups, and nominal groups. *Organizational Behavior and Human Performance*, 1973, *9*, 280–291.

Guion, R. M. *Personnel Testing*. New York: McGraw-Hill, 1965.

Hamner, W. C., Kim, J. S., Baird, L., and Bigoness, N. J. Race and sex as determinants of ratings by potential employers in a simulated work sampling task. *Journal of Applied Psychology*, 1974, *59*, 705–711.

Harari, O., and Zedeck, S. Development of behaviorally anchored scales for the evaluation of faculty teaching. *Journal of Applied Psychology*, 1973, *58*, 261–265.

Harris, F. C. and Lahey, B. B. A method for combining occurrence and nonoccurrence interobserver agreement scores. *J. Applied Behavior Analysis*, 1978, *11*, 523–527.

Hartmann, D. P. Considerations in the choice of interobserver reliabiity estimates. *J. Applied Behavior Analysis*, 1977, *10*, 103–116.

Hartmann, D. P. and Gardner, W. On the not so recent invention of interobserver reliability statistics. *Journal of Applied Behavior Analysis*, 1979, *12*, 559–560.

Hawkins, R. P. and Fabry, B. D. Applied behavior analysis and interobserver reliability: a commentary on two articles by Birkimer and Brown. *Journal of Applied Behavior Analysis*, 1979, *12*, 545–552.

Heneman, H. G., III. Comparisons of self and superior ratings of managerial performance. *Journal of Applied Psychology*, 1974, *59*, 638–642.

Herbert, J. and Attridge, C. A guide for developers and users of observation systems and manuals. *American Education Research Journal*, 1975, *12*, 1–20.

Heron, A. The effects of real life motivation on questionnaire response. *Journal of Applied Psychology*, 1956, *40*, 65–68.

Hoffman, J., and Peterson, C. R. *A Scoring Rule to Train Probability Assessors* (Engineering Psychology Laboratory Technical Report 037230-4-T). Ann Arbor, MI: University of Michigan, 1972.

Hollander, E. P. The reliability of peer nominations under various conditions of administration. *Journal of Applied Psychology*, 1957, *41*, 85–90.

Hollander, E. P. Validity of peer nominations in predicting a distant performance criterion. *Journal of Applied Psychology*, 1965, *49*, 434–438.

Hollenbeck, A. R. Problems of reliability in observational research. In G. P. Sackett (Ed.) *Observing Behavior, Vol. II, Data Collection and Analysis Methods*. Baltimore, MD: University Park Press, 1978.

Hopkins, B. L. Proposed conventions for evaluating observer reliability—a commentary on two articles by Birkimer and Brown. *J. Applied Behavior Analysis*, 1979, *12*, 561–564.

Hopkins, B. L. and Hermann, J. A. Evaluating interobserver reliability of interval data. *Journal of Applied Behavior Analysis*, 1977, *10*, 121–126.

Huck, J. R. and Bray, D. W. Management assessment center evaluations and subsequent job performance of white and black females. *Personnel Psychology*, 1976, *29*, 13–30.

Huttner, L. and Katzell, R. Developing a yardstick of supervisory performance. *Personnel*, 1957, *33*, 371–378.

Jacobson, M. B. and Effertz, J. Sex roles and leadership: Perceptions of the leaders and the led. *Organizational Behavior and Human Performance*, 1974, *12*, 383–396.

James, L. R. Criterion models and construct validity for criteria. *Psychological Bulletin*, 1973, *80*, 75–83.

Jay, R. and Copes, J. Seniority and criterion measures of job proficiency. *Journal of Applied Psychology*, 1957, *41*, 58–60.

Jenkins, G. D., and Taber, T. A Monte Carlo study of factors affecting three indices of composite scale reliability. *Journal of Applied Psychology*, 1977, *62*, 392–398.

Johnson, D. M. Reanalysis of experimental halo effects. *Journal of Applied Psychology*, 1963, *47*, 46–47.

Johnson, E. M. *The Perception of Tactical Intelligence Indications: A Replication* (Technical Paper 282). Alexandria, VA: U. S. Army Research Institute for the Behavioral and Social Sciences, 1977.

Johnson, S. M. and Bolstad, O. D. Methodological issues in naturalistic observation: some problems and solutions for field research. In L. A. Hamerlynck, L. C. Hardy and E. J. Mash (Eds.) *Behavior Change: Methodology, Concepts, and Practice*. Champaign, Illinois: Research Press Company, 1973, 7–67.

Jones, F. N. Overview of psychophysical scaling methods. In E. C. Carterette and M. P. Friedman (Eds.) *Handbook of Perception, Vol. 2*. New York: Academic Press, 1974.

Jurgensen, C. E. Intercorrelations in merit rating traits. *Journal of Applied Psychology*, 1950, *34*, 240–243.

Kavanagh, M. J. Rejoinder to Brumback "The content issue in performance appraisal: A review." *Personnel Psychology*, 1973, *26*, 163–166.

Kay, B. R. the use of critical incidents in a forced-choice scale. *Journal of Applied Psychology*, 1959, *43*, 269–270.

Kazdin, A. E. Artifact, bias and complexity of assessment: the ABCs of reliability. *Journal of Applied Behavior Analysis*, 1977, *10*, 141–150.

Keaveny, T. J. and McGann, A. F. A comparison of behavioral expectation scales and graphic rating scales. *Journal of Applied Psychology*, 1975, *60*, 695–703.

Kelley, C. W., and Peterson, C. R. *Probability Estimates and Probabilistic Procedures in Current Intelligence Analysis* (Report on Phase 1). Gaithersburg, MD: Federal Systems Division, IBM Corporation, 1970.

Kemeny, J. G., and Snell, J. L. *Mathematical Models in the Social Sciences*. New York: Blaisdell, 1962.

Kendall, M. G. *Rank Correlation Methods*. London: Charles Griffin and Co., Ltd., 1948.

Kirchner, W. K. Relationships between supervisory and subordinate ratings for technical personnel. *Journal of Industrial Psychology*, 1965, *3*, 57–60.

Kirchner, W. K. and Reisberg, D. J. Differences between better and less effective supervisors in appraisal of subordinates. *Personnel Psychology*, 1962, *15*, 295–302.

Klieger, W. A. and Mosel, J. N. The effect of opportunity to observe and rater status on the reliability of performance ratings. *Personnel Psychology*, 1953, *6*, 57–64.

Klimoski, R. J. and London, M. Role of the rater in performance appraisal. *Journal of Applied Psychology*, 1974, *59*, 445–451.

Klores, M. S. Rater bias in forced-distribution ratings. *Personnel Psychology*, 1966, *19*, 411–421.

Kratochill, T. R. Just because it's reliable doesn't mean it's believable. *Journal of Applied Behavior Analysis*, 1979, *12*, 553–557.

Kraut, A. J. Prediction of managerial success by peer and training-staff ratings. *Journal of Applied Psychology*, 1975, *60*, 14–19.

Landy, F. J. and Farr, J. L. Performance rating. *Psychological Bulletin*, 1980, *87*, 72–107.

Landy, F. J. and Farr, J. L. Police performance appraisal. *JSAS Catalog of Selected Documents in Psychology*, 1976, *6*, 83. (Ms. No. 1315)

Landy, F. J., Farr, J. L., Saal, F. G., and Freytag, W. R. Behaviorally anchored scales for rating the performance of police officers. *Journal of Applied Psychology*, 1976, *61*, 752–758.

Landy, F. J. and Guion, R. M. Development of scales for the measurement of work motivation. *Organizational Behavior and Human Performance*, 1970, *5*, 93–103.

Latham, G. P. and Wexley, K. N. Behavioral observation scales for performance appraisal purposes. *Personnel Psychology*, 1977, *30*, 255–268.

Latham, G. P., Fay, C. H. and Saari, L. M. The development of behavioral observation scales for appraising the performance of foremen. *Personnel Psychology*, 1979, *32*, 299–311.

Latham, G. P., Saari, L. M. and Fay, C. H. BOS, BES, and Baloney: Raising Kane with Bernardin. *Personnel Psychology*, 1980, *33*, 815–821.

Lawler, E. E., III. The multitrait-multirater approach to measuring managerial job performance. *Journal of Applied Psychology*, 1967, *51*, 369–381.

Lay, C. H., Burron, B. F., and Jackson, D. N. Base rates and informational value in impression formation. *Journal of Personality and Social Psychology*, 1973, *28*, 390–395.

Lee, D., and Alvares, K. Effect of sex on descriptions and evaluations of supervisory behavior in a simulated industrial setting. *Journal of Applied Psychology*, 1977, *62*, 405–410.

Lepkowski, J. R. Development of a forced-choice rating scale for engineer evaluation. *Journal of Applied Psychology*, 1963, *47*, 87–88.

Levanthal, L., Perry, R. P., and Abrami, P. C. Effect of lecturer quality and student perception of lecturer's experience on teacher ratings. *Journal of Educational Psychology*, 1977, *69*, 360–374.

Lewis, N. A. and Taylor, J. A. Anxiety and extreme response preferences. *Educational and Psychological Measurement*, 1955, *15*, 111–116.

Lichtenstein, S., Slovic, P., Fischhoff, B., Layman, M., and Combs, B. Judged frequency of lethal events. *Journal of Experimental Psychology: Human Learning and Memory*, 1978, *4*, 551–578.

Linstone, H., and Turoff, M. (Eds.) *The Delphi Method: Techniques and Applications*. Reading, MA: Addison-Wesley, 1975.

Lodge, M., Tanenhaus, J., Cross, D., Tursky, B., Foley, M. A., and Foley, H. The calibration and cross-model validation of ratio scales of political opinion in survey research. *Social Science Research*, 1976, *5*, 325–347.

London, M., and Poplawski, J. R. Effects of information on stereotype development in performance appraisal and interview context. *Journal of Applied Psychology*, 1976, *61*, 199–205.

Luce, R. D. *Individual Choice Behavior*. New York: Wiley, 1959.

Luce, R. D., and Raiffa, H. *Games and Decisions*. New York: Wiley, 1957.

Luckas, W. J. and Hall, R. E. *Initial Quantification of Human Errors Associated with Reactor Safety System Components in Licensed Nuclear Power Plants.* Report NUREG/CR-1880 and BNL-NUREG-51323, Brookhaven National Laboratory, Upton, NY, January, 1981.

Ludke, R. L., Stauss, F. F., and Gustafson, D. H. Comparison of five methods for estimating subjective probability distributions. *Organizational Behavior and Human Performance*, 1977, *19*, 162–179.

Lusted, L. B. *A Study of the Efficiency of Diagnostic Radiologic Procedures* (Final report on diagnostic efficacy). Chicago, IL: Efficacy Study Committee of the American College of Radiology, 1977.

McIntyre, R.M., Smith, D. E., and Hassett, C. E. Accuracy of performance ratings as affected by rater training and perceived purpose of rating. *Journal of Applied Psychology*, 1984, *69*, 147–156.

Maas, J. B. Patterned scaled expectation interview: Reliability studies on a new technique. *Journal of Applied Psychology*, 1965, *49*, 431–433.

Madden, J. M., and Bourdon, R. D. Effects of variations in rating scale format on judgment. *Journal of Applied Psychology*, 1964, *48*, 147–151.

Mandell, M. M. Supervisory characteristics and ratings: A summary of recent research. *Personnel Psychology*, 1956, *32*, 435–440.

Mischel, H. N. Sex bias in the evaluation of professional achievements. *Journal of Educational Psychology*, 1974, *66*, 157–166.

Mitchell, S. K. Interobserver agreement, reliability, and generalizability of data collected in observational studies. *Psychological Bulletin*, 1979, *86*, 376–390.

Moore, H. G. *The effects of load and accessibility of information upon performance of small teams.* Unpublished dissertation, University of Michigan, Ann Arbor, MI, October 1961. (AD 268 462).

Morris, P. Bayesian expert resolution (Ph.D. Dissertation, University Microfilm No. 72-5959). University of Michigan, Ann Arbor, MI, 1971.

Morris, P. Decision analysis expert use. *Management Science*, 1974, *20*, 1233–1241.

Morris, P. Modeling experts (unpublished manuscript). Xerox Corporation, Palo Alto Research Center, 1975.

Morris, P. Combining expert judgments: A Bayesian approach. *Management Science*, 1977, *23*, 679–693.

Murphy, K. R., Martin, C., and Garcia, M. Do behavioral observation scales measure observation? *Journal of Applied Psychology*, 1982, *67*, 562–567.

Murphy, A. H., and Winkler, R. L. Credible interval temperature forecasting: Some experimental results. *Monthly Weather Review*, 1974, *102*, 784–794.

Murphy, A. H., and Winkler, R. L. The use of credible intervals in temperature forecasting: Some experimental results. In H. Jungermann and G. de Zeeuw (Eds.) *Decision Making and Change in Human Affairs*. Dordrecht-Holland: D. Reidel Publishing Company, 1977. (a)

Murphy, A. H., and Winkler, R. L. Can weather forecasters formulate reliable probability forecasts of precipitation and temperatures? *National Weather Digest*, 1977, *2*, 2–9. (b)

Parker, J. W., Taylor, E. K., Barrett, R. S., and Martens, L. Rating scale content: Relationship between supervisory and self-ratings. *Personnel Psychology*, 1959, *12*, 49–63.

Paterson, D. G. The Scott Company graphic rating scale. *Journal of Personnel Research*, 1922, *1*, 361–376.

Peters, D. L. and McCormick, E. J. Comparative reliability of numerically anchored versus job-task anchored rating scales. *Journal of Applied Psychology*, 1966, *50*, 92–96.

Phillips, L. D., and Edwards, W. Conservatism in a simple probability inference task. *Journal of Experimental Psychology*, 1966, *72*, 346–354.

Pill, J. The Delphi method: substance, context, a critique and an annotated bibliography. *Socio-Economic Planning Sciences*, 1971, *5*, 57–71.

Powell, J., Martindale, A. and Kulp, S. An evaluation of time-sample measures of behavior. *Journal of Applied Behavior Analysis*, 1975, *8*, 463–469.

Repp, A. C., Dietz, D. E. D., Boles, S. M., Dietz, S. M., and Repp, C. F. Differences among 'common' methods for calculating interobserver agreement, *Journal of Applied Behavior Analysis*, 1976, *9*, 109–113.

Repp, A. C., Roberts, D. M., Slack, D. J., Repp, C. F., and Berkler, M. S. A comparison of frequency, interval and time-sampling methods of data collection. *Journal of Applied Behavior Analysis*, 1976, *9*, 501–508.

Roberts, F. S. Measurement theory. *Encyclopedia of Mathematics and Its Applications, Vol. 7*. Addison-Wesley Publishing Co., 1979.

Robinson, W. S. The statistical measurement of agreement. *American Sociological Review*, 1957, *22*, 17–25.

Ronan, W. W., and Prien, E. P. *Toward a Criterion Theory: A Review and Analysis of Research and Opinion*. Greensboro, NC: Creativity Institute of the Richardson Foundation, 1966.

Rosen, B., and Jerdee, T. H. The influence of sex role stereotypes on evaluations of male and female supervisory behavior. *Journal of Applied Psychology*, 1973, *57*, 44–48.

Rosenthal, R. On the social psychology of the psychological experiment: the experimenter's hypotheses as unintended determinant of experimental results. *American Scientist*, 1963, *57*, 1–15.

Ross, R. T. Optimum orders for the presentation of pairs in the method of paired comparisons. *Journal of Educational Psychology*, 1934, *25*, 375–382.

Ross, J., and Di Lollo, V. Judgment and response in magnitude estimation. *Psychological Review*, 1971, *78*, 515–527.

Rothaus, P., Morton, R. B., and Hanson, P. G. Performance appraisal and psychological distance. *Journal of Applied Psychology*, 1965, *49*, 48–54.

Rowse, G., Gustafson, D., and Ludke, R. Comparison of rules for aggregating subjective likelihood ratios. *Organizational Behavior and Human Performance*, 1974, *12*, 274–285.

Saal, F. E., Downey, R. G., and Lahey, M. A. Rating the ratings: assessing the psychometric quality of rating data. *Psychological Bulletin*, 1980, *88*, 413–428.

Sackett, G. P. (Ed.) *Observing Behavior, Vol. II. Data Collection and Analysis Methods*. Baltimore, MD: University Park Press, 1978.

Sackett, G. P., Ruppenthal, G. C. and Gluck, J. Introduction: an overview of methodological and statistical problems in observational research. In G. P. Sackett (Ed.), *Observing Behavior, Vol. II. Data Collection and Analysis Methods*, Baltimore, MD: University Park Press, 1978.

Sackman, H. *Delphi Critique*. Lexington, MA: D. C. Heath and Co., 1975.

Schaefer, R. E., and Borcherding, K. The assessment of subjective probability distributions: A training experiment. *Acta Psychologica*, 1973, *37*, 117–129.

Schmidt, F. L., and Johnson, R. H. Effect of race on peer ratings in an industrial setting. *Journal of Applied Psychology*, 1973, *57*, 237–241.

Schmitt, N. and Hill, T. Sex and race composition of assessment center groups as a determinant of peer and assessor ratings. *Journal of Applied Psychology*, 1977, *62*, 261–264.

Schneider, E. D., and Bayroff, A. G. The relationship between rater characteristics and validity of ratings. *Journal of Applied Psychology*, 1953, *37*, 278–280.

Schneier, C. E. Operational utility and psychometric characteristics of behavioral expectation scales: A cognitive reinterpretation. *Journal of Applied Psychology*, 1977, *62*, 541–548.

Scott, W. A. Reliability of content analysis: the case of nominal scale coding. *Public Opinion Quarterly*, 1955, *19*, 321–325.

Schriesheim, C. A., and Schriesheim, J. F. The invariance of anchor points obtained by magnitude estimation and paired-comparison treatment of complete ranks scaling procedures: An empirical comparison and implications for validity of measurement. *Educational and Psychological Measurement*, 1978, *38*, 977–983.

Schwab, D. P., Heneman, H. G., III, and DeCotiis, T. Behaviorally anchored rating scales: A review of the literature. *Personnel Psychology*, 1975, *28*, 549–562.

Seaver, D. A. *Assessment of Group Preferences and Group Uncertainty for Decision Making* (SSRI Research Report 76-4). Los Angeles: University of Southern California, Social Science Research Institute, 1976.

Seaver, D. A. *Assessing Probability with Multiple Individuals: Group Interaction Versus Mathematical Aggregation* (SSRI Research Report 78-3). Los Angeles: University of Southern California, Social Science Research Institute, December 1978.

Seaver, D. A., von Winterfeldt, D., and Edwards, W. Eliciting subjective probability distributions on continuous variables. *Organizational Behavior and Human Performance*, 1978, *21*, 379–391.

Selvidge, J. E. Assigning probabilities to rare events. In D. Wendt, and C. Vlek (Eds.) *Utility, Probability, and Human Decision Making*. Dordrecht-Holland: Reidel, 1975.

Sharon, A. T., and Bartlett, C. J. Effect of instructional conditions in producing leniency on two types of rating scales. *Personnel Psychology*, 1969, *22*, 251–263.

Sjoberg, L. Three models for the analysis of subjective ratios. *Scandinavian Journal of Psychology*, 1971, 12, 217–240.

Slovic, P., Fischhoff, B., and Lichtenstein, S. Behavioral decision theory. *Annual Review of Psychology*, 1977, *28*, 1–39.

Smith, P. C. Behaviors, results, and organizational effectiveness: The problem of criteria. In M. D. Dunnette (Ed.), *Handbook of Industrial and Organizational Psychology*. Chicago: Rand McNally, 1976.

Smith, P. C., and Kendall, L. M. Retranslation of expectations: An approach to the construction of unambiguous anchors for rating scales. *Journal of Applied Psychology*, 1963, *47*, 149–155.

Smode, A. F., Gruber, A., and Ely, J. H. *The Measurement of Advanced Flight Vehicle Crew Proficiency in Synthetic Ground Environments*. Report MRL-TDR-62-2, Behavioral Sciences Laboratory, Wright-Patterson AFB, OH, February, 1962.

Spetzler, C. S., and Stael von Holstein, C. A. S. Probability encoding in decision analysis. *Management Science*, 1975, *22*, 340–358.

Stael von Holstein, C. A. S. The effect of learning on the assessment of subjective probability distributions. *Organizational Behavior and Human Performance*, 1971, *6*, 304–315. (a)

Stael von Holstein, C. A. S. An experiment in probabilistic weather forecasting. *Journal of Applied Meteorology*, 1971, *10*, 635–645.(b)

Stael von Holstein, C. A. S. Probabilistic forecasting: An experiment related to the stock market. *Organizational Behavior and Human Performance*, 1972, *8*, 139–158.

Stillwell, W. G., Seaver, D. A., and Edwards, W. *The Effects of Response Scales of Likelihood Ratio Judgments* (SSRI Research Report 77-5). Los Angeles: University of Southern California, Social Science Research Institute, August, 1977.

Stillwell, W. G., Seaver, D. A., and Schwartz, J. P. *Expert Estimation of Human Error Probabilities in Nuclear Power Plant Operations: A Review of Probability Assessment and Scaling*. Report NUREG/CR-2255 and SAND81-740, Decision Science Consortium, Falls Church, VA, for the U. S. Nuclear Regulatory Commission, May 1982.

Suci, G. J., Vallance, T. R., and Glickman, A. S. A study of the effects of "likingness" and level of objectivity on peer rating reliabilities. *Educational and Psychological Measurement*, 1956, *16*, 147–152.

Suppes, P., and Zinnes, J. L. Basic measurement theory. In R. D. Luce, R. R. Bush, and E. Galanter (Eds.) *Handbook of Mathematical Psychology, Vol. 1*. New York: Wiley, 1963.

Susman, E. J., Peters, D. J., and Steward, R. B. Naturalistic observational child study, a review. Paper presented at 4th Biennial Southeastern Conference on Human Development, Nashville, Tennessee, 1976. Cited in Hollenbeck, 1978.

Taylor, E. K., and Hastman R. Relation of format and administration to the characteristics of graphic scales. *Personnel Psychology*, 1956, *9*, 181–206.

Taylor, E. K. and Wherry, R. J. A study of leniency in two rating systems. *Personnel Psychology*, 1951, *4*, 39–47.

Taylor, E. K., Schneider, D. E., and Clay, H. C. Short forced-choice ratings work. *Personnel Psychology*, 1954, *7*, 245–252.

Thurstone, L. L. A law of comparative judgment. *Psychological Review*, 1927, *34*, 273–286.

Tinsley, H. E. A. and Weiss, D. J. Interrating reliability and agreement of subjective judgments. *Journal of Consulting Psychology*, 1975, *22*, 358–376.

Toole, D. L., Gavin, J. F., Murdy, L. B., and Sells, S. B. The differential validity of personality, personal history, and aptitude data for minority and nonminority employees. *Personnel Psychology*, 1972, *25*, 661–672.

Torgerson, W. S. *Theory and Methods of Scaling*. New York: Wiley, 1958.

Tversky, A., and Kahneman, D. Causal schemata in judgments under uncertainty. In M. Fishbein (Ed.) *Progress in Social Psychology*. Hillsdale, NJ: Lawrence Erlbaum Associates, 1977.

Van de Ven, A., and Delbecq, A. The effectiveness of nominal, Delphi, and interacting group decision-making processes. *Academy of Management Journal*, 1974, *17*, 605–621.

Wagner, E. E., and Hoover, T. O. The influence of technical knowledge on position error in ranking. *Journal of Applied Psycholoty*, 1974, *59*, 406–407.

Wallsten, T. S., and Budescu, D. V. *Encoding Subjective Probabilities: A Psychological and Psychometric Review* (Draft Report). Research Triangle Park, NC: U. S. Environmental Protection Agency, Office of Air Quality Planning and Standards, April, 1980.

Waters, L. K. and Waters, C. W. Peer nominations as predictors of short-term sales performance. *Journal of Applied Psychology*, 1970, *54*, 42–44.

Weick, K. E., Systematic observational methods. In G. Lindzey and E. Aronson (Eds.), *The Handbook of Social Psychology*, Vol. Two (Second edition). Reading, MA: Addison-Wesley Publishing Company, 1968, 357–451.

Wexley, K. N., Sanders, R. E. and Yukl, G. A. Training interviewers to eliminate contrast effects in employment interviews. *Journal of Applied Psychology*, 1973, *57*, 233–236.

Wherry, R. J. Orders for the presentation of pairs in the method of paired comparisons. *Journal of Experimental Psychology*, 1938, *23*, 651–666.

Whitla, D. K., and Tirrell, J. E. The validity of ratings of several levels of supervisors. *Personnel Psychology*, 1953, *6*, 461–466.

Willingham, W. W. Interdependence of successive absolute judgments. *Journal of Applied Psychology*, 1958, *42*, 416–418.

Winkler, R. L. The assessment of prior distributions in Bayesian analysis. *Journal of the American Statistical Association*, 1967, *62*, 776–800.

Winkler, R. L. The consensus of subjective probability distributions. *Management Science*, 1968, *15*, 61–75.

Winkler, R. L. Probabilistic prediction: Some experimental results. *Journal of the American Statistical Association*, 1971, *66*, 675–685.

Winkler, R. L. The assessment of probability distributions for future security prices. In J. L. Bicksler (Ed.), *Methodology in Finance-Investments*. Lexington, MA: Lexington Books, Heath, 1972, 129–148.

Winkler, R. L., and Cummings, L. On the choice of a consensus distribution in Bayesian analysis. *Organizational Behavior and Human Performance*, 1972, *7*, 63–76.

von Winterfeldt, D. *Some Sources of Incoherent Judgments in Decision Analysis*. Falls Church, VA: Decision Science Consortium, Inc., November, 1980.

Yellot, J. I. The relationship between Luce's choice axiom, Thurstone's theory of comparative judgment, and the double exponential distribution. *Journal of Mathematical Psychology*, 1977, *15*, 109–144.

Yelton, A. R. Reliability in the context of the experiment: a commentary on two articles by Birkimer and Brown. *Journal of Applied Behavior Analysis*, 1979, *12*, 565–569.

Yelton, A. R., Wildman, B. G., and Erickson, M. T. A probability-based formula for calculating observer agreement. *Journal of Applied Behavior Analysis*, 1977, *10*, 127–131.

Zedeck, S., and Baker, H. T. Nursing performance as measured by behavioral expectation scales: A multitrait-multirater analysis. *Organizational Behavior and Human Performance*, 1972, *7*, 457–466.

Zedeck, S., and Kafry, D. Capturing rater policies for processing evaluation data. *Organizational Behavior and Human Performance*, 1977, *18*, 269–294.

CHAPTER TEN

Self-Report Techniques

This chapter discusses two self-report techniques: interviews and questionnaires. There are others—like the diary method—but these two are the ones most commonly used.

The interview and questionnaire are both similar and related to each other. Both ask questions of a respondent; in fact the highly structured survey interview is only a variant of the questionnaire. Both interviews and questionnaires make use of the rating scales described in Chapter 9 because the questionnaire often includes rating scales and the selection interview as we shall see is used primarily as a rating device. The interview is used in a variety of contexts: (1) information gathering in development, test and research situations; (2) selection of job applicants; (3) communication of performance results (performance appraisal); and (4) surveys and job analysis. The questionnaire is, or can be used, in all these situations except perhaps performance appraisal.

Both the interview and questionnaire are a general methodology rather than a more or less fixed procedure. Therefore their content changes with the specific situation in which it is employed. The formless and verbal nature of the interview makes it particularly awkward to describe, because one finds oneself describing the characteristics of the situation in which it is used (e.g., selection and appraisal) rather than the interview itself. Interview relevant research often describes the job function (selection, appraisal) rather than the interview.

The questionnaire is a somewhat different proposition. Because it is written rather than oral and hence more formal than most types of interviews, its salient characteristics (such as the order of item presentation and its verbal descriptors) are more visible. Consequently, it is possible to be more specific about the questionnaire.

The peculiarity of both the interview and questionnaire as measurement instruments is that they are directed at a particular focus—the gathering of information from a respondent. How the subject answers questions is supposedly not at issue, although in the selection and performance appraisal interviews nonverbal characteristics become important. The information is a surrogate for observed performance which is not available. It is supposed to represent how the respondent is thinking and feeling, what he did, what he will do, and why. The ambiguity of language and the fact that that language is only representative of an underlying condition makes the task of interpreting self-report data difficult. Since self-report techniques are the only way of obtaining internal processes, the techniques are indispensable. At the same time they pose particular difficulties in terms of assuring the accuracy and validity of the material elicited via these techniques. There is no external referent for self-report data describing internal processes. Yet we know that because of the human's tendency to distort both consciously and unconsciously we cannot assume that such data are veridical.

THE INTERVIEW

The informational interview and the survey interview seek to determine the respondent's (1) *internal processes,* for instance, his opinion of things and people, how he intends to vote, and what he is doing—as in reporting his diagnostic strategies while troubleshooting; (2) *knowledge of how* a system is operated or how a job is performed, as in the case of a subject matter expert (SME), a stockbroker say, describing how the stock market functions; (3) *perception of external events,* as when he is witness to an accident or reports what has taken place.

The *selection* interview occurs in the context of evaluating an individual and consequently is used much like a rating scale, except that what is rated is what the subject reports and the way he reports it. Information is elicited, but only as part of the process of evaluating the job applicant.

The *performance appraisal* interview communicates to a subject an evaluation of his performance and also serves as a means of examining the individual's response to the evaluation.

The *survey* interview is a verbal form of questionnaire but on a person to person level rather than on the group basis common with the questionnaire.

The common elements among these types of interviews are their structural characteristics: *instructions* to respondents describing the purpose of the interview and the manner in which it will be conducted; the *choice of words* in a question; the way in which a question is *phrased*; the *ordering of* a series of questions; the way in which the response to the question is *recorded*; the *characteristics* of the interviewer and the respondent; the amount of *reinforcement* and motivation inducing phrases provided by the interviewer.

One advantage of the interview is that it is an interpersonal situation. It can be employed, therefore, to influence the subject to respond more adequately by suggesting that his report is considered important, and to work even harder. On the other hand, because it involves person to person contact, the interviewer's characteristics and those of the interview itself influence what the subject reports. This interaction complicates the measurement task and contaminates the resultant data.

The fact that the subject is aware of being measured may result in a distortion of the information—consciously or unconsciously.

A more obvious disadvantage of the interview is that in most cases it is a one on one procedure, which means that it is very costly in time. Since many interviews cannot be very structured or standardized, the analysis of the report is more difficult. The relative freedom of the unstructured interview permits the interviewee to include irrelevant and unimportant responses. Moreover, the respondent is often emotionally tied up in the information he is reporting which may result in biasing his selection of the material he reports.

If one looks at the interview in terms of independent and dependent variables—those factors that can be varied and those aspects of the report resulting from these variations—certain factors must be considered in research on the interview. Among independent variables the following may affect interview data: the length of the interview; the degree of its structure; the sequence in which questions are asked; whether questions are asked by a single interviewer or by a panel of interviewers; the degree to which the interviewer questions the respondent; the amount of interaction between them; the physical, racial, religious or personality characteristics of the interviewer and interviewee.

Among dependent variables one is concerned about the accuracy of the respondent's information; the internal consistency of the single interview and the reliability of successive interviews about the same topic; the amount of information provided and its detail and whether that detail is greater when the subject is questioned than when he reports spontaneously or voluntarily.

Unfortunately only a few of these variables have been investigated empirically and much of what one can say about the interview is based only on logic, common sense, and uncontrolled experience.

The Informational Interview

The informational interview is a technique which is used to gather information during equipment and training system development (as in the use of an SME) or to supplement the data secured in a developmental or operational performance test or laboratory study. In the context of a test or study it follows immediately upon some performance for which the interview is designed to provide additional information. An interview with the subjects of a test or research study should always be held at its completion. The informational interview may also be part of a job analysis to secure information about the characteristics of the job from a worker or supervisor. It plays an important part in problem and accident investigation.

The informational interview is differentiated from the survey interview in several ways. The former has a very narrow focus, whereas the survey interview often has a much wider scope (a national election, a problem area like crime). The informational interview is usually directed at a small number of respondents directly concerned with the topic of interest, whereas the survey interview may be administered to hundreds or thousands. The informational interview may be quite unstructured and informal, whereas the survey interview is almost always highly structured, standardized, and formal.

The following topics are characteristic of the informational interview.

1. What did the subject see while he was observing or do while he was performing? Why did he do what he did? For example, why did the navigator of an aircraft fly 270 degrees rather than 320 degrees?

2. What are the characteristics and procedures of the system? Of a particular job or task?

3. How adequate is the equipment and how easy or difficult to use, does the operator believe the equipment (system, procedure, etc.) to be? How easy were the visual stimuli to perceive?

4. What knowledge does the performer have that should have guided his performance?

5. What test conditions (e.g., night/day) affected him most and why?

6. How well did the operator think he performed in the test situation?

7. With what tasks did the operator experience the most difficulty? Does he know why? What factors does he believe contributed to those difficulties?

8. How would the operator characterize situations *A, B, C . . . ?*

9. In a team operation, how was responsibility divided among the members?

10. In citing a specific factor of interest to the interviewer (e.g., reduced visibility, lack of spares), what effect did that factor have on the operator's performance?

11. Does the subject wish to comment on any aspect of the topic under consideration? This is an openended question, usually asked at the end of the interview and serves as a prelude to closing the interview.

The questions asked must be clear, simple, and precise. They can be made so. Despite the fact that the interview is somewhat informal (answers to questions suggesting other questions), it is possible to pretest the interview, at least the most important questions, to determine the adequacy of the questions, the kinds of responses, and the information they contain.

Because the intent of the informational interview is simply to gather information about job performance, this type of interview is less threatening to the respondent than selection and appraisal interviews. The survey interview is also nonthreatening except when the information requested deals with emotion laden material such as racial and religious attitudes, or sexual practices.

Since the purpose of the informational interview is to provide information, one is naturally interested in whether that information is accurate and to a lesser extent reliable. Accuracy can be measured by determining whether interviewees who say they did or saw something actually did or saw it. Reliability is a function of whether interviewees produce the same information about the same events when questioned on successive occasions. Only a few studies deal with these questions because researchers as a whole are not much interested in the informational interview compared with their interest in the other interview types. Walsh (1967) reviewed 27 studies concerned with the validity of informational interview data. He found that 13 studies reported high validity and 9 low, with the remainder of the studies being ambiguous. He himself tested the validity of biographical information provided by students in three forms: the interview, the questionnaire and the data form. Information bearing on validity was secured by checking against such sources as school records and government archives. In general, the information provided was valid, some questions being answered more accurately than others, and all forms provided essentially the same information. A second study (Walsh, 1968) confirmed the results of the first one.

With regard to worker estimates of job information, test/retest reliabilities for job inventories as reported by McCormick and Ammerman (1960), Cragun and McCormick (1967) and Birt (1968) were 0.61, 0.62, and 0.83, respectively—reasonably good scores but not overwhelming. There is less information about the validity of that information. Burns (1957) used diaries to validate questionnaires—a questionable procedure—and reported that workers tend to overestimate time spent in important activities and to underestimate personal time. Klemmer and Snyder (1972) studied the time workers in a research and development laboratory spent communicating. Questionnaire data reported by workers were evaluated by random activity sampling (observation) of the same communication behaviors. The questionnaire agreed fairly well with observational reports, although time spent in face-to-face conversation was underestimated, time spent reading and writing overestimated.

Hartley, Brecht, Sagerey, Weeks, Chapanis and Hoecker (1977) did a comparative (observation vs. self-report) study to determine the validity of worker self-reports identifying job activities, rank–ordering them in terms of time spent on them, and estimating the time each took.

Spearman rank–order correlations between the observed rank order and estimated rank orders given by subjects and by observers for time devoted to various activities were on the average 0.66 and 0.58 for two organizations. These correlations are slightly higher than validity values commonly cited for job performance predictors in general. The average percent error in estimating activity time was 24.4 percent, a value which the authors feel demonstrates the unsatisfactory nature of the self-report. Self-report accuracy (e.g., in identifying activities) decreased as more highly quantified estimates (of time involved) were required. One would expect this.

Gupta and Beehr (1982) assessed the correlation among self-reports of 650 employees, the company records and observations, relative to pay, fringe benefits, and hazardous plant conditions. In the case of pay, the product-moment correlation was .71 (between 64 and 72 percent for hazardous materials). Correlations for fringe benefits were relatively low (between .15 and .50). There was thus low to moderate agreement.

The self-reports referred to in the preceding studies were simple, yet complex, because very precise quantities were requested. If very precise quantitative data are not requested, self-reports may be quite accurate.

Certainly, if asked to explain the operation of a system, the SME can provide a wealth of detail. If precise quantities were requested (voltages, pressures), however, the SME could have difficulty producing them. Though subject matter experts are often used in behavioral studies, the accuracy of SMEs has rarely been tested. Other factors undoubtedly affect self-report accuracy: whether or not the respondent is reporting about what he did (as contrasted to what others did), and the length of time that has elapsed between the occurring event and the occasion of the self-report.

One can only measure the accuracy of independently observed external events. There is no way of determining the accuracy of reported attitudes and opinions except possibly by the method used in determining convergent validity, that is, the measurement of the same attitudes and opinions by different methods. In the case of the interview varying methods translate into questions asked in a different way. If one were probing attitudes toward mothers, one might ask about these questions directly (e.g., "Did you love your mother?") and indirectly, for example, by asking the respondent to criticize an anecdote involving a mother.

It is well known that witnesses to events are notoriously inaccurate in reporting their observations. The difference between this inaccuracy and the results of the studies cited so far may be between what people say they do or know (fairly accurate) and what they perceive (fairly inaccurate). Moreover, witness situations are almost invariably degraded by poor lighting, brevity of the stimulus situation, and observer emotionality

The interview has degrees of structure. In a structured interview the questioner employs a script of all the inquiries to be asked, in the order in which they are to be asked. The completely structured interview varies little from a questionnaire except that the inquiries are made orally. In the completely unstructured interview the interviewee leads most of the discussion.

Dyer, Matthews, Wright and Yudowitch (1976) believe that the degree of proficiency required of interviewers in conducting an unstructured interview is generally not available during field test evaluations. If the interviewer is a layman, they are probably correct. A structured interview requires the interviewer to have only moderate skill and proficiency, although some training is desirable. The advantages of the semi-structured interview are the opportunity to probe for all the facts when the respondent provides only partial or incomplete responses; an opportunity to ensure that the questions are thoroughly understood by the subject, and an opportunity to pursue other problem areas which may arise during the interview. The semi-structured informational interview is almost always preferable to a questionnaire when the test group is small (10–20) and when time and test conditions permit.

Key questions for which the investigator thinks he needs answers should be developed in advance, although they need not be written out. A key question can be used to initiate the interview. The respondent should be allowed to expand on topics of interest to him but, when he wanders, the interviewer should bring him back to the point by asking another key question. If the subject appears reticent, the interviewer can use his prepared questions to stimulate his response.

The informational interview may take various forms.

1. Individual (one interviewer, one subject). This is the most common form of the interview.

2. Team (one interviewer, several performers being interviewed as a group). This occurs primarily in connection with team operations.

3. The interview may be combined with other subjective methods such as rating scales and with a demonstration of performance by the operator.

When the performance being evaluated is that of a team, the interview should be conducted with the team as a group. If the team consists of many members, it may be unfeasible to interview each one individually. Individual interviews make it more difficult for the evaluator to investigate team interactions.

An interview concerning task performance is commonly held after the task has been performed or at some convenient hiatus in system operations. Where a series of tasks is being performed, the interview should not, if possible, be postponed until every task is completed, because then the subject's memory for events is reduced. It may not be feasible, though, to hold an interview immediately following the performance of each individual task. Obviously, one cannot break in on an ongoing system operation to interview. Consequently, the interviewer should look for natural breaks in the flow of system events to ask his questions.

The subject should be interviewed concerning each task he has not performed previously. If he repeats the same task on several occasions, and task conditions remain the same, it may not be necessary to interview repeatedly. However, it is advisable to secure two interviews (separated by an interval), for each task performed by the operator, to determine the consistency of his interview responses. If test conditions do not change substantially on repeated performances of the same task, the answers the interviewer gets on the first two interviews will probably be repeated in subsequent interviews, and the performers will find the questions boring. Under these circumstances, the scope of the interview can be reduced.

The length of the interview should depend on how much the performer can tell the interviewer, but 20 minutes is a good average length. Beyond 30 minutes, the subject tends to become fatigued.

The conditions under which the interview is conducted are important. Ideally, it should take place away from the test operation (although not too far away lest one has to account for transportation time), in a fairly quiet place, with no interruptions or distractions. A specific room for the interview would be most desirable since this helps to emphasize the importance of the interview to the performer. The fact that an interview will take place should be made known to the subject in advance. He should be reassured at the outset that nothing he says will be held against him, and that he will not be identified in records or reports. He may ask for feedback about his performance since he is understandably concerned about his proficiency in an evaluation. He should be told that the interviewer is not the evaluator but that it appears to the interviewer that the subject's performance was certainly adequate.

The most convenient way of conducting an interview is to tape record it but, if it is a very short one, or the interviewer is highly skilled, it can perhaps be handled by note taking. As far as possible, interview responses should be recorded verbatim without the interviewer making any attempt during the interview to analyze them.

The interviewer's characteristics may affect the interviewee's responses. Differences in status of the two (e.g., rank, position in the organization) may influence the subject's flow of information. For Army field test evaluations Dyer et al. (1976) recommend that the interviewer should be of similar rank or grade to the interviewees. A difference in rank probably introduces a bias in the data which could substantially influence test results. Interviewees tend to give the answer they perceive the higher ranking interviewer favors. If the interviewer is of lower rank than the respondent, the latter may not cooperate.

Differences in response patterns according to the interviewer's sex depend on the interview subject matter as well as on the composition of the respondents. Interviewees often give socially desirable answers to interviewers whose race differs from them, particularly if the subject's social status is lower and the topic of the interview is threatening. With regard to social issues, more valid results can be expected when the interviewer is of the same race as the respondent.

Dyer et al. (1976) report that interviewer experience produces significant differences in interview completion rates. Amount of experience does not however influence the extent to which the interviewer deviates from instructions.

It helps greatly if the interviewee perceives the interviewer as interested in hearing his comments, as supportive, willing to listen and, if the situation requires, able to protect him from recrimination for making adverse evaluations. Such noncomittal comments as "good" or "fine" and actions like smiling and nodding can have a decided effect on the results. Praised respondents normally offer more answers than unpraised ones. Praising the interviewee tends to reduce "don't know" answers.

The interviewer must always be aware of the possibility that he is leading or influencing a respondent's evaluations. Interviewers with marked attitudes toward test subjects, the system being evaluated, or the hypotheses being tested, should be replaced if possible. At the least, they should be sensitized to the potential problems of their bias. Interviewer bias can exist without its being apparent to the interviewer. Some interviewers do not read instructions precisely as written or they change the wording of questions. The intonation given to a question can communicate the interviewer's attitude to the question and thus bias the respondent's answer. Minimal interviewer bias is probably found with questions that can be answered purely factually or with "yes" or "no."

The Selection Interview

Unlike the informational and survey interview, selection and appraisal interviews are not ordinarily aids to the collection of research information but are used to implement certain job functions. Although the selection interview elicits information, that information is used in a projective manner as the interviewer rates the applicant in terms of job criteria. The interview is therefore a stress situation, at least for the applicant. It is also an artificial one with regard to the information supplied by the interviewee. The interviewer has a stereotype (mental model) of idealized successful applicants (Sydiaha, 1959, 1961; Bolster and Springbett, 1960; Hakel, Hollman and Dunnette, 1970). The applicant attempts to understand the interviewer's verbal model of the individual he wants to hire and selects and molds his answers to correspond as closely as possible to that model. If, for example, the interviewer is seeking someone with management experience, the subject will select examples from his past work history that show his management experience in the best light. From the applicant's standpoint, accuracy of information is not a desideratum.

The selection interview does not have a uniform format but it does possess certain common elements. The questions asked will seek to determine from the applicant's work experience whether the subject matches the interviewer's job model. The interviewee may be asked to provide examples of model attributes. A hypothetical situation may be described and the respondent asked to comment. This is, in fact, the foundation for what Latham, Saari, Pursell and Campion (1980) and Latham and Saari (1982) call the "situational" interview, which is based on psychometrically scaled critical incidents transformed into interview questions. Job applicants are asked how they would behave in a given situation. The questions are asked only partially to elicit information. How the interviewee answers the questions is also of great interest and in this respect the questions act almost as a sort of clinical projective test. For example, the question, "Why do you want this job?" is not asked to determine a specific answer but to indicate how the subject reacts to ambiguous stimuli.

The intent of this section, which leans heavily on a number of reviews of the literature, primarily those of Arvey and Campion (1982), Schmitt (1976), Wright (1969) and Ulrich and Trumbo (1965), is to describe guidelines for an effective selection interview process. One should first define what effectiveness in this context is. It is not, as was pointed out above, information accuracy. Rather, from the interviewer's standpoint, it is selection of the most qualified applicant. In effect, the interviewer views the interview and the interviewee's responses as a sort of evaluation scheme or rating scale. In consequence many of the questions raised about the selection interview are the same as were asked about the rating scale in Chapter 9: validity and reliability, the factors that tend to bias the interview data, the effects of interviewer and interviewee characteristics, and the effect of interview format.

All the evidence seems to indicate that the selection interview is less than adequate in achieving what it desires to achieve. Wagner (1949) located 106 articles dealing with the selection interview of which 25 reported quantitative information. Reliability coefficients ranged from .23 to .97 with a median of .57 for ratings of specific traits and a median of .27 for 22 validity coefficients. Intelligence was the only trait consistently rated with high reliability. Wagner (1949) concluded that reliability and validity may be highly specific to situations and interviewers and that reliability could be enhanced if standardized forms were used to elicit and record interview data. Later studies by Schwab and Henneman (1969) and Carlson, Schwab and Henneman (1970) reconfirmed that use of a structured interview guide increases inter-interviewer agreement.

Mayfield (1964) arrived at several general statements which 20 years later are probably still valid.

1. General suitability ratings based on unstructured interviews have low reliability.
2. Material is not covered consistently in unstructured interviews.
3. Interviewers are likely to weight the same information differently.
4. Structured interviews are more reliable.
5. Interview validity is low.
6. The form of the question affects the answers given.
7. In unstructured interviews, interviewers talk more than respondents.
8. Although interviewers may be consistent in their treatment of interviewees, they are inconsistent in their interpretation of the information obtained.
9. Interviewer attitudes bias their judgments.
10. Decisions are made early in the interview.
11. Intelligence is the trait most validly estimated by an interview.

Ulrich and Trumbo (1965) reported reliabilities lower than those usually accepted for individual prediction instruments. More recent research has not been as pessimistic about validity and reliability (so Arvey and Campion, 1982, suggest), but the results are unimpressive. Board or panel interviews seem to increase validity. Anstey (1977) found a validity coefficient of .66 for British civil servant selection. However, Waldron (1974), who used nine psychologists to interview and predict the overall success of 118 Australian Navy candidates, found that the interview did not increase validity beyond that derived from four tests and a life history form. In another panel interview study Reynolds (1979) studied the reliability of an interview used by the Louisiana civil service. Individual reliabilities for 7 rating dimensions varied from .78 to .85. The reliability coefficient for the composite final score across the 67 applicants was .90.

Henneman, Schwab, Huett and Ford (1979) found low validities for predicting the job success of social workers. On the other hand, Latham, Saari, Purcell and Campion (1980), using the situational interview, found interobserver reliability coefficients of .76 and .79 and validity coefficients of .46 and .30 for hourly workers and foremen.

Starting with the work of Webster (1964) the focus of research interest shifted to investigations of molecular elements of the interview that can affect interviewers' decisions. Schmitt (1976), after reviewing 45 studies, concluded that the findings remain inconclusive, ambiguous, and even contradictory.

For example, Springbett (1958) found that the interviewer reached a final decision an average of four minutes after the interview began. Yet Huegli and Tschirigi (1975) found that only 33 percent of their 16 interviewers reported making decisions during the first half of the interview. Hire decisions were made sooner than no-hire decisions. In another study, Tullar, Mullins and Caldwell (1979) found that interviewers took significantly more time to decide on high than low quality applicants. The interview appeared also to be primarily a search for negative information. Just one unfavorable trait rating resulted in a reject decision in 90 percent of the interviews. Hollman (1971) concluded that interviewers could explain why an applicant was unlikely to be a good employee but not why he might be satisfactory. Webster (1964) suggested that interviewers received only negative feedback from employers about past employees and consequently learn to utilize negative information more appropriately. Blakeney and MacNaughton (1971) found that variance due to placement and the content area of negative information were both negligible.

Farr (1973) and Farr and York (1975) found that the order in which positive information was received accounted for most of the variance. Yet Peters and Terborg (1975) found that the sequencing of unfavorable and favorable information had no effect. Anderson (1960) found that interviewers spend more time talking when they came to a favorable decision, either to sell applicants on their company or to gather information to confirm their decision.

Standardized interviews are typically more reliable than open ended ones (Mayfield, 1964; Schwab and Henneman, 1969; Ulrich and Trumbo, 1965; Wagner, 1949; Wright, 1969). Ratings in these evaluations are influenced by many factors, such as contrast, primacy/recency, first impressions, and personal feelings. There were also great individual differences among interviewers in Rowe's (1963) study. Three of the 146 interviewers accepted over 80 percent of the hypothetical applicants, while forty accepted less than 20 percent. More experienced interviewers tended to accept fewer candidates. Valenzi and Andrews (1973) also found wide individual differences in informational cue utilization. Their interviewers made little or no configural use of cues.

Information affects interviewer responses, of course. Stereotypes diminish or are altered by information as the rater continues to evaluate an application (London and Hakel, 1974). With more information interrater reliability increases. No significant differences result from interviewer experience (Langdale and Weitz, 1973). Wiener and Schneiderman (1974) found that interviewers make extensive use of job information. This decreases the effect of irrelevant attributes on decisions but does not eliminate it. They found that as in other studies use of job information was not enhanced by experience.

A whole series of studies indicate that nonverbal sources of information may be as, or even more, important than verbal cues (Amalfitano and Kalt, 1977; Forbes and Jackson, 1980; Imada and Hakel, 1977; McGovern and Tinsley, 1978; Schmitt, 1976; Sigelman, Elias and Danker-Brown, 1980; Sterrett, 1978; Tessler and Sushelsky, 1978; and Young and Beier, 1977). A study by Hollandsworth, Kazelskis, Stevens, and Dressel (1977) indicated the following order of importance in verbal and nonverbal communication dimensions: appropriateness of verbal content, fluency of speech, body posture, eye contact, voice level, and personal appearance.

The similarity of the applicant to the interviewer (e.g., attitude, race, handicap) may be important (Baskett, 1973; Rand and Wexley, 1975; Rose, 1980; Wexley and Nemeroff, 1974). Frank and Herman (1975), cited in Arvey and Campion (1982), found contradictory results. However, the interviewer's race can affect the behavior of the applicant (Ledvinka, 1971, 1973; and Sattler, 1970). There has also been sex discrimination (Cohen and Bunker, 1975; Dipboye, Fromkin and Wilback, 1975; Simas and McCarrey, 1979), but it does not appear that the interview process as such was responsible for this.

The selection interview may be conducted on a one-to-one basis or a group may interview an individual. Since individual differences among interviewers have been found to account for some of the variance in interview judgments (Ulrich and Trumbo, 1965; Wright, 1969), one way of reducing the effect of individual differences is to combine interviewers into groups. Generally most research supports group over individual judgment (Lorge, Fox, Davitz and Brenner, 1957; Maier, 1967; Hall and Williams, 1970), although there are exceptions (Bouchard and Hare, 1970; Campbell, 1968; Dunnette, Campbell and Jaastad, 1963; Moore and Lee, 1974).

Nevertheless, Arvey and Campion (1982) suggest that the use of board or panel interviewers appears a promising means to improve interview validity and reliability.

The effect of interviewer training on evaluations has produced conflicting conclusions. Vance, Kunnert and Farr (1978) found no effect; neither did Henneman (1975). These results conflict with earlier positive findings (Howard and Dailey, 1979; Howard, Dailey and Gulanick, 1979; Latham, Wexley and Purcell, 1975; Mayfield, Brown and Hamstra, 1980; and Wexley, Sanders and Yukl, 1973).

With all its deficiencies, low validity and reliability, its susceptibility to bias and distortion, why is the employment interview still popular? Arvey and Campion (1982) suggest four possible explanations or rationalizations by employers.

1. The interview is really valid because it still yields valid judgments on certain interpersonal dimensions such as sociability, verbal fluency, and work motivation. Thus it acts as a work sample of these behaviors.
2. More elaborate tests may be too costly or time consuming.
3. The interview is not valid but interviewers maintain great faith and confidence in the judgments resulting from the interview.
4. The interview is not valid but it does other things well, such as selling the applicant on the job, answering questions from applicants, and acting as a public relations tool. Utility seems to be more important than validity.

The Performance Appraisal Interview

The performance appraisal interview is designed to communicate feedback to an employess whose performance has been evaluated. In the process the supervisor conducting the interview can supply motivational reinforcement, primarily in a verbal form. Although there is no fixed format for the interview, Leskovec (1967) suggests that there are two approaches which may be used in discussing an appraisal. In the *indirect/direct* approach the manager encourages the employee to appraise his own performance. The interviewer can begin by asking several leading questions, then allowing the employee to develop and analyze to the degree the supervisor feels is justified. However, in this approach the interviewer lacks control over the course of the interview.

The more frequently used method is the *direct approach*: The person conducting the appraisal interview leads the discussion supported with data he has compiled on specific job experiences and criticisms. It is also possible to combine the two methods, using the best aspects of both.

It is best to hold the appraisal interview in a private office. Interruptions tend to minimize the importance of the meeting in the eyes of the employee. The atmosphere should be friendly and positive. The appraisal is discussed before the supervisor shows any written document to the employee. This permits the former to explain the evaluation before the employee examines the document. The employee's strong points are discussed before his weak ones, which helps to build a positive attitude. The employee is asked what he thinks of his rating. He goes away from the meeting understanding the appraisal, even though he may not agree with it.

The procedure described is one in which the interviewee actively participates in the interview as opposed to what might be termed "tell and sell." The advisability of allowing subordinates to participate in their own performance appraisal interviews has been voiced for many years (e.g., Kindall and Gatza, 1963; McGregor, 1957; Likert, 1959). Studies that have experimentally manipulated the amount of participation in appraisal interviews (French, Kay and Meyer, 1966; Wexler, Singh and Yukl, 1973; Greller, 1975) have supported the concept of beneficial effects of participation, such as greater subordinate satisfaction and motivation to improve. On the other hand, Hillery and Wexley (1974) found that nonparticipative interviews brought greater behavior change and interviewee satisfaction than participative interviews. So the question is by no means clearcut (Fletcher and Williams, 1976). A performance appraisal interview may have positive or negative effects but one suspects that this is not because of the interview as a method, but rather because subtle verbal and nonverbal cues conveyed by the manager have significant effects on the interviewee. Burke, Weitzel and Weir (1978) reviewed the literature on six major characteristics of performance appraisal interviews, but only two had anything to do with the structural characteristics of the interview: amount of subordinate participation and the proportion of time in which the subordinate speaks. In the first, the more the employee participates, the more satisfied he is with the process; for the second, data are not available.

The Survey Interview

The survey interview is highly structured, allowing no individual interviewer variations. In form it is the oral (face-to-face or telephone) equivalent of the questionnaire. Its purpose is to collect information—usually about opinions and attitudes. Because of the similarities between the survey interview and the questionnaire, which will be discussed later, guidelines for the latter are applicable to the former.

The following suggestions were not derived from empirical studies. As Cannell and Kahn (1953) put it, "much of the available literature consists of rules of thumb presented as lists of 'do's and dont's' . . . " This statement is as true today as it was 30 years ago. Cannell and Kahn (1953) point out that at best these rules are quite superficial. They do not tell us why a specific interview practice is effective or not.

The design of questions for the survey interview is critical because minor variations in terminology and format can significantly distort the nature of responses. Schuman and Presser (1981) pinpoint the following as key factors in question design; the use of open versus closed questions; a "don't know" response capability; a middle alternative (e.g., "too strict," "too lenient," "about right"); unbalanced versus balanced questions (e.g., stating only the affirmative or negative side of an issue); and agree/disagree items (which may be a special form of imbalance). Even common phrases (e.g., "usually," "weekday") can be misinterpreted by a large percentage of respondents (Belson, 1981).

In the pretest the preliminary interview schedule should be administered on an individual basis to a number of subjects who, after they have responded to the standard questions, are further interviewed intensively with regard to their understanding of the questions. It may be necessary to repeat the pretest process several times before all questions satisfy the objectives of the interview and are quite clearly understood by respondents.

Before selecting an interviewer it is necessary to hypothesize the respondent's perception of the interviewer in terms of sex, age, race, religion, socioeconomic status, etc., in the event that some sensitive topic is being investigated. It is probably inappropriate to send out white male interviewers to ask questions about the impact of illegitimate children on the financial status of black teenage girls. In the military situation it is desirable to use interviewers with roughly the same rank as their subjects.

In interviewer training it is necessary to clarify the goal of the interview and to emphasize the principles of the survey interview: standardization, validity, complete answers from respondents, and no interviewer leading or bias. It is also desirable to motivate the interviewer to genuinely believe in the importance of the data being collected. Practice in interviewing is important. The interviewer trainee watches others, is himself watched, and differences in performance are discussed with him. Videotaping is a very useful training mechanism because it permits the trainee to view his own performance.

During training potential interviewer errors are described. Biases may arise because of interviewer stereotypes and expectations. An example of such a bias might be the interviewer's expecting very brief, incomplete responses from members of ethnic minorities and therefore failing to secure complete information from them.

The interviewer's art consists of putting the respondent at ease so that whatever responses are elicited are as accurate and complete as the respondent can report them. The subject may have a number of *motivations* for responding positively to the request for an interview. If the interview is part of his job, he is coerced. Even so, one cannot expect adequate answers unless the respondent is also positively motivated. It is always possible for him to say as little as possible or to distort the data he provides.

Other motivations are the attraction of having someone of possibly superior status seek the respondent's opinion; or the interviewee may simply be awed by an authority figure. The interview may be therapeutic for the respondent. The expert interviewer tries to shape his introduction to the interview in terms of the subject's goals and motivations, to the extent that these can be discerned. The respondent is first assured that the interview will be interesting and his opinions are important. This builds up the subject's ego and relieves his anxieties, particularly the assurance that his opinions will be anonymous. The interview topic should, if at all possible, be related to the respondent's own interests. The interviewer should also foster the subject's perception of the interviewer as someone who can bring about change, for example, that the interview results can be used to pressure Congress.

The introduction to the interview should be brief, casual and, positive. It should cover (1) explanation of the interview purpose and objectives and its importance; (2) how the respondent was chosen as a subject; (3) the sponsor of the project; and (4) the confidential and anonymous nature of the interview. The first question should be asked as soon as possible to reduce the time available for the subject to build up resistance if he has any. Any legitimate questions the subject may have should, however, be answered. The rationale for the interview should be emphasized (e.g., the information is vitally needed by an agency of the United States government which determines how much income tax you pay).

The interviewer should know his questions well enough so that he need not read them. No surprise should be expressed about any response made by the subject. Irrelevant conversation should be discouraged. Each question must be asked precisely as worded; otherwise comparability of responses secured from different interviewers is impossible. The slightest intonation can change the sense of a question. Questions must be asked in the specified order because their sequence can influence the subject's response. Obviously *all* questions must be asked.

The order in which questions are asked is determined by what Cannell and Kahn (1953) call the "funnel approach." Logic suggests that the first question should be the most general one and each subsequent question will zero in on the details in successively more detailed questions. The funnel sequence helps prevent initial questions from influencing later ones.

Closed-ended questions (those with specified alternatives) are useful in situations in which (1) there is only one frame of reference from which the questions can be answered; (2) there is a known range of possible responses; or (3) within this range, there are clearly defined choice points which accurately represent the respondent's position. For example, the classification of the respondent in terms of marital status (single, married, divorced, separated, widowed) lends itself to a closed-ended question because the range of alternative responses is limited.

Obtaining a specific, complete answer from some respondents may be difficult. Respondents often waffle, answer "don't know," misinterpret the question, or contradict themselves. Part of the development of the interview schedule and the interviewer's training should be a specification of what constitutes incomplete or inadequate responses. The interviewer may have to probe by asking for more information ("please tell me more about that"); this is of course possible only with open-ended questions and the interviewer must avoid leading the subject to a particular response. The Rogerian clinical technique of feeding the respondent's own statement back to him ("you feel that . . .") to check on the accuracy of the recorded response and to elicit more information may be useful.

On precoded questions where the alternative responses are specified, the interviewer need only check a box or circle a code number. With open-ended questions the response must be recorded verbatim. With precoded questions the data recording is simple but subject to error, for example, checking the wrong code or failing to check at all. To avoid such errors the interviewer is advised to review the subject's responses immediately after the last question is asked. For open-ended questions the most desirable means of recording data is to use a tape recorder but this device may inhibit respondents. Ask for permission before using it. When recording by hand, it is perfectly permissable to ask the respondent to wait until the response is written down. Some form of original shorthand (abbreviations) will be useful here.

THE QUESTIONNAIRE

In this section we deal with questionnaires, the outstanding characteristics of which are the fixed order and format in which questions are asked in writing, with the respondent writing his answer. The questionnaire may be given to a group of subjects directly or can be mailed. Experience has shown that the rate of response and the quality of the responses received are lower in the mailed questionnaire than in the directly administered questionnaire. It is much easier to ignore a mailed questionnaire. The administrator's instructions and appeals may increase the number of respondents with positive motivation to complete the questionnaire. This is lacking in mailed questionnaires. In the latter respondents must derive their instructions and motivation from the printed material, with no opportunity to query instructions.

Cost factors often determine whether the researcher will utilize a mailed questionnaire when he would prefer one directly administered. Direct comparison of the mailed questionnaire with directly administered ones is lacking. The studies performed compared the mailed questionnaire with the interview. O'Dell (1962) found that noncommittal responses and the tendency not to answer open-ended questions were more common in mailed questionnaires than in interviews, as might be expected.

As in the case of the survey interview, a distinction must also be made between open-ended questionnaire items and closed-ended ones. Open-ended items are those which permit the respondent to write his answer in his own words and to indicate any qualifications he wishes, whereas closed-ended items utilize already established response alternatives such as multiple-choice or true/false. The results of a series of studies (Ellenbogen and Danley, 1962; England, 1948; Kohen, de Mille and Myers, 1972; Prien, Otis, Campbell and Saleh, 1964; and Scates and Yoeman, 1950) suggest that the open-ended type of questionnaire provides unique information, but the closed-ended type is more reliable.

There are a number of ways in which questionnaire administration can vary but in a field test setting usual practice involves paper and pencil materials, with someone (the developer or a data collector) administering the questionnaire to respondents face-to-face.

Considerable time can be saved by group administration of the questionnaire. Statistical analysis can be initiated with less delay than if one were waiting upon a series of individual administrations. Dyer et al. (1976) point out that if the questionnaire is used to collect information about test performance, group administration minimizes forgetting because no one has to wait on anyone else. Group administration does, however, involve some slight loss. In individual administration one can give the respondent more attention if he needs an item explained to him. This is a minor factor if the questionnaire has been so constructed that item meanings are relatively obvious.

In remote administration the data collector cannot administer the questionnaire himself because subjects are far from him or because of other demands on his time. He must rely on someone unfamiliar with the questionnaire and its intent (e.g., an officer in a remote military unit, the shop steward in a factory) to hand out and retrieve the form and motivate subjects to respond. Remote administration is not as ineffective as mailed questionnaires, but the likelihood of errors and loss of returns is greatly increased.

Structured Interviews and Questionnaires

The choice between structured interviews and directly administered questionnaires is likely to be a matter determined by cost and convenience because there are few differences. Ford (1969) found considerable response consistency between the mailed questionnaire and the interview, as did Bennett, Alpert, and Goldstein (1954) on 26 of 30 questions asked.

Walsh (1967, 1968) compared the interview, questionnaire, and personal data bank for collecting biographical information and found no differences, nor did Boulger (1970). Interviews may inhibit the expression of deviance compared with questionnaires (Knudsen, Pope and Irish, 1967). When questions are potentially threatening, questionnaires are likely to elicit more frank responses than interviews (Ellis, 1948).

If the data collector must choose between questionnaires and structured interviews, a number of pragmatic issues should be considered. Since the structured interview deals with subjects on an individual basis, there must be enough interviewers to process all respondents expeditiously. If only a few personnel must be interviewed, or considerable time is available, only one or two interviewers will be required. In situations in which time is at a premium, one needs a large number of qualified interviewers.

Paper and pencil questionnaires are less expensive, more anonymous, and completed faster than the same number of interviews. The cost of mailed questionnaires is much less than that of the personal interview and, by extension, of the directly administered questionnaire which is given to groups of subjects (Cahalan, 1951; Gibson and Hawkins, 1968; O'Dell, 1962) although others have found no substantive cost differences. Respondents are less likely to report unfavorable events in an interview which is direct and personal than in an anonymous questionnaire. Questionnaires are also more likely to produce self-revealing data. Issues involving socially acceptable or unacceptable attitudes and behaviors will elicit more bias in interviewee responses. During interviews respondents often have a tendency to try to support the norms that they assume the interviewer adheres to. Interviewers with biases on the issues under discussion may reflect them in the content they record as well as in what they fail to record.

Although a structured interview using open-ended questions may produce more complete information than a typical questionnaire containing the same questions, responses to the typical questionnaire tend to be more consistent.

In some situations an interview might be used to aid in designing a questionnaire. Personal or telephone interviews might be used for respondents who do not return questionnaires administered remotely. When respondents are unable to give complete information during an interview, they can be left a copy of a questionnaire to complete and mail in.

Developing the Questionnaire

The general steps in preparing a questionnaire include determining what kinds of information are desired, determining the content of questionnaire items, selecting question forms, wording of questions, formulating the questionnaire, and pretesting. As part of preliminary planning, questions about procedures for administration, sample type and size, location, frequency of administration, experimental design of the field test, and data analysis must be answered. Kidder (1981), basing her discussion on Payne (1951), provides a checklist guide for questionnaire construction. Both sources should be referred to before starting development of the questionnaire.

To gain knowledge about the system or the operations to be queried by the questionnaire, the developer may employ group and/or individual interviews with operational personnel to assist in determining questionaire content. The subject matter of the interview may deal with problems encountered in operating the equipment or the system. Anecdotal and critical incident information (see Chapter Eleven) are solicited as also the most important characteristics of the equipment, system or situation. Particular attention must be paid to the questions for which the data are being collected because of the high frequency of misunderstanding even simple terms.

It is also extremely important to determine the nature of the subject sample and its size, particularly where subjects are highly specialized subpopulations, such as the mentally or physically handicapped and socioeconomically depressed. Where polling on a population-wide basis is involved, there are formulae for determining the sample sizes required to secure reliable data (see following section on surveys), but pragmatic factors such as time, money, population availability, etc. often constrain the sample size. Therefore in many situations we try to get as many subjects as possible.

Types of Questionnaire Items

The questionnaire may include a number of different types of items: open-ended and closed-ended ones; multiple-choice items; rating scales; ranking items; forced-choice and paired-comparison items—even card sorting tasks. The question as to which of these items should be utilized has been explored in a number of studies. We have already discussed research on open-ended and closed-ended items. With regard to the other types, the following can be reported.

Ranking Items. Ranking and rating items are generally comparable (Bartlett, Heerman and Rettig, 1960; Bittner and Rundquist, 1950; Kassarjian and Nakanishi, 1967; Murphy, Bailey and Covell, 1954; Rennick, Grupe, Reich and Sewell, 1954). Studies comparing ranking and paired comparasons produced conflicting evidence (Bernard, 1933; Cohen, 1965; Eng and French, 1948; Kassarjian and Nakanishi, 1967; Paull, 1968; Homant and Rokeach, 1968; Ross, 1955; Slater, 1965; Wilkins, 1950; and Witroyl and Thompson, 1953). The bulk of the evidence suggests that the two techniques produce comparable results. Paired comparisons practically demand personal administration of the questionnaire and much more time of the subjects, of course.

Rating Scale Items. A majority of the studies reviewed found that results obtained from the use of rating scales were comparable to those produced by forced choice or paired comparison techniques (Greenberg, 1963; Greenwald and O'Connell, 1970; Neidt and Merrill, 1951; Newell, 1954; Pilgrim and Wood, 1955; and Scott, 1968). Comparisons of rating scales and card sorts are inconclusive as also comparison of rating scales with checklists (Seashore and Hevner, 1933; Siegel and Siegel, 1962).

Multiple-Choice Items. Comparison of multiple-choice and forced-choice items produced inconsistent results (Dyer et al., 1976).

Open-Ended Items

An example of an open-ended item is: describe any problems you experienced in operating the *XYZ* equipment.

Advantages. The advantages of the open-ended item are that it permits the expression of intermediate opinions that closed-ended items with very limited choices would not permit, as well as the expression of concerns that may not have been identified by the questionnaire developer. They may provide unique information and they are very easy to ask for the questionnaire developer who is a novice and does not know the range of alternative answers. Most important, with an open-ended question it is possible to find out what is important to the respondent.

Disadvantages. The primary disadvantage of open-ended items is that answering them is very time consuming and effortful. Some respondents may say tht they have no problems rather than take the time to describe those problems. Open-ended items often leave the respondent on his own to determine what is relevant in answering the question and he may therefore misinterpret the intent of the question. In consequence, questionnaires making use of closed-ended items are generally more reliable than those using open-ended items. Open-ended questions, if fully answered, are capable of overloading data analysts. They can almost never be handled by machine analysis methods without extensive preliminary coding. And they must be analyzed by someone who has substantial knowledge about the question's content rather than by a clerk. Much of the material obtained may be repetitious or irrelevant.

Open-ended questions should therefore be used only infrequently. The open-ended question can be useful as a pretest to find out what the range of alternative responses is and when there are too many possible responses to be listed or forseen or when it is important to measure the saliency of an issue to the respondent.

Multiple-Choice Items

In a multiple-choice item, the respondent's task is to choose the appropriate or best answer from several options. Multiple-choice items include dichotomous or two-choice items (e.g., true/false) as special cases.

Advantages. There are a number of advantages for multiple-choice methods.

1. The questionnaire developer may select varying numbers of response alternatives, depending upon the amount of detail he wishes to secure and upon his decision to allow or disallow respondents to be noncommital by including a "no preference" alternative.
2. Dichotomous items are relatively easy to develop and permit rapid data analysis.
3. Multiple-choice items are easily scored. Data analysis is inexpensive, requiring no special expertise.
4. Multiple-choice items require considerably less time for respondents to answer and they put all respondents on the same footing when answering.
5. They are easy to administer.

Disadvantages. Multiple-choice items have disadvantages, however.

1. Dichotomous items force the respondent to make a choice even though he may feel there are no differences between the alternatives, or he does not know enough about either to choose one validly. Furthermore, he cannot say how much better one alternative is than the other.
2. Two alternatives might not be enough for some types of questions. The question designer may oversimplify an issue by forcing it into two categories. The response alternatives may overlap.
3. The question maker has to know the full range of significant possible alternatives at the time the multiple-choice question is written.
4. With dichotomous items any slight language difficulty or misunderstanding of even one word can change the answer from one extreme to another. Generally speaking, dichotomous multiple-choice questions should be avoided. If used, they should probably be followed up to determine the reason for a given response. How-

ever, nondichotomous multiple choice items are popular and are considered to have wide utility.

Rating Scale Items

These have been discussed in detail in Chapter Nine. They have certain advantages as part of a questionnaire.

Advantages.

1. When properly constructed they reflect both the direction and degree of the opinion/attitude. The results are amenable to analysis by conventional statistical tests.

2. Graphic rating scales permit as fine discrimination as the respondent is capable of making.

3. They usually take less time to answer than other types of items, can be applied to almost anything, and are generally more reliable than two-way multiple choice items.

Disadvantages. They are, however, more vulnerable to biases and errors than other types of items. Graphic rating scales are harder to score and their results may imply a degree of precision and accuracy which is unwarranted.

Ranking Items

Ranking items call for the respondent to indicate the relative ordering of the members of a presented group of objects on some dimension, such as effectiveness or difficulty. By definition one does not have an interval scale in which the amount of difference between successive members is measured, nor is it implied in rank ordering that successive differences are even approximately equal. As the number of objects to be ranked increases, the difficulty of assigning a different rank to each object increases even more quickly. This means that reliability is reduced. To counter this, one should permit respondents to assign tied rankings to objects when the number of objects exceeds, say, 10 or more.

Advantages. Ranking items have certain advantages. The idea of ranking is familiar to respondents. Ranking takes less time to administer, score, and code than other types of items.

Disadvantages. The disadvantages of ranking items are that:

1. Ranking does not reveal the respondent's judgment as to whether any of the objects are effective or ineffective in an absolute rather than just a relative sense. To learn this, another question must be asked.

2. Ranking does not permit respondents to state the relative amounts of differences between alternatives.

3. Ranking is generally less precise than rating. Generally ratings are preferable to rankings.

Forced-Choice Items

A forced-choice item is one where the respondents must commit himself or herself to one of a pair of choices, two of three, or two of four. A multiple-choice item is also a forced choice item because the respondent is expected to choose one of the response alternatives. If a multiple-choice item includes a "don't know" response alternative, the compulsion to respond is almost totally removed. Likewise, on a rating scale item, the inclusion of a neutral or borderline response category allows the respondent to answer without committing himself.

Advantages. The advantages of forced choice items are that their reliability and validity compare favorably with other methods and forced choice items are more resistant than other items to the effects of bias.

Disadvantages. The disadvantages are that respondents sometimes balk at picking unfavorable statements, or at being forced to make a choice. Forced choice items take more time to develop than do other types of items.

Card-Sorting Tasks

With card-sorting items/tasks, the respondent is given a large number of statements (e.g., 75) each on a slip of paper or card. He is asked to sort them into, say, nine or eleven piles. The piles are in rank order from "most favorable" to "least favorable" or "most descriptive" to "least descriptive", depending upon the dimension to be used. If it is necessary to approximate a normal distribution, each pile has to have a specified number of statements placed into it. However, unless the normal distribution is required, forcing that distribution is not necessary. Each pile is given a score value which is then assigned to the statements placed into it. This makes card-sorting a form of rating.

Advantages. The advantage of the technique is that card-sorts may be capable of counteracting at least some of the biasing effects of response sets. This is in part because the respondent can shift items back and forth if he wishes to do so. The card-sort has greatest value when an individual, equipment, or situation is to be described.

Disadvantages. Card-sorting items may take more time to construct than other types and they generally take more time to administer and score.

Checklists

In checklists, responses are made by checking the appropriate statement or statements in a list of statements. Compared to rating scales, which at least provide a numerical value, check lists are quite crude. They are, however, quite useful when scalar values are unnecessary.

Arrangement Items

With an arrangement item, a number of statements, such as steps in a sequence of events, are presented in random order, and the respondent arranges them in a given way, for example, in order of occurrence, importance, or performance. Since scoring is difficult, the use of such items is extremely limited.

Mode of Questionnaire Presentation

Questionnaire items are usually presented in printed form. However, it is possible to present items or stimuli pictorially. There is some evidence (Blake, 1969; Greenberg, 1959; Jensen, 1930; Rohila, Shanhdhar and Sharing, 1966; and Weitz, 1950) that there are no significant differences in subjects' responses to verbal and pictorial formats. Using a pictorial format may help to elicit responses from respondents with limited verbal comprehension. If pictures are used, they should be pretested for clarity of presentation.

In cases where it is known that respondents have low reading ability, it may be desirable to present the questionnaire by tape recorder (orally). With the introduction of the computer terminal the questionnaire can be administered automatically (with subject control) on a cathode ray tube screen. This may have certain advantages these days since video presentation appears to be inherently more interesting (because it is dynamic?) than a static paper and pencil mode.

Wording of Items

The wording of questionnaire items is a *critical* consideration in obtaining valid and reliable responses. When Payne (1951) administered three questions to three matched groups, questions that differed only in the use of the words "should," "could," or "might," the percent of "yes" replies to the questions were 82, 77, and 63, respectively. The difference of 19 percent between the extremes is probably enough to alter the conclusions of most studies.

A question may be in the form of an incomplete statement, where the statement is completed by checking one of the response alternatives, or in the form of a complete question. For example,

1. Check one of the following. Most industrial supervisors are
   ______Very well qualified for their jobs
   ______Qualified for their jobs
   ______Borderline

Or,

2. How qualified or unqualified for their jobs are most industrial supervisors? (check one)
   ______Very well qualified
   ______Qualified
   ______Borderline

Both formats produce the same effect.

All questionnaire items should, of course, be grammatically and factually correct. They should present the questionm as fully as necessary to allow the subject to answer validly. It should not be necessary for the respondent to infer anything essential. All items should be expressed as neutrally as possible and the subject should be allowed to indicate or select the direction of his preference. If this is not done, the question may influence the distribution of responses. If items cannot be expressed neutrally, then it is necessary to use alternative forms of the questionnaire. In forming questions which depend on respondents' memory, the time period a question covers must be carefully defined.

Questions and response alternatives should be worded so that it is clear what the respondent meant in answering. For example, the questions, "Should this valve be adopted or its alternate?" is ambiguous because if the subject answers "yes," it would still be unclear which valve (this valve, or its alternate) should be adopted.

Positive vs. Negative Wording

Studies comparing positively versus negatively worded statements (Adams, 1956; Blankenship, 1940; Burtt and Gaskill, 1932; Campbell, Siegman and Rees, 1967; Cloud and Vaughn, 1970; Waters, 1966) are generally inconclusive but Dyer et al. (1976) suggest that it is usually undesirable to include negatives in questions unless an alternate form with positives is also used for half the respondents. If it seems necessary to have a particular question in negative form, the negative word (e.g., not, never) should be emphasized and care should be taken to ensure that there are no double negatives.

First-, Second-, and Third-Person Wording

A statement in the first person might be, "Company management understands my needs and problems;" in the second person, "Company management understands your needs and problems;" in the third person, "Company management understands the needs and problems of its personnel." Whatever person is used, it should be used consistently throughout the questionnaire so that responses are comparable. A respondent's opinion of the effects of events affecting his own person is often quite different from his opinions of the effects of the same events on others. Hence questions written in the first and second person may elicit different responses than those to questions written in the third person.

There are occasions when each person is appropriate. For example, the third person might be used when it is desired to elicit information that might be considered too personal for a person to answer about himself. In other cases the first- or second-person form is not applicable, as in, "Capitalism is necessary for the economic growth of the country." The use of the third person permits a larger number of respondents to answer the questions, since some first-person questions that are inapplicable to some individuals are applicable in the third person.

Loaded and Leading Questions

Obviously, these should be avoided. An example of a loaded question is: "Which would you prefer, the fast-acting product ______ or the slow-acting product ______?"

There are many ways that questions can be loaded. One way is to provide the respondent with a reason for selecting one of the alternatives, as with the question, "Should we increase taxes in order to get better schools, or should we keep them about the same?" A question can also be loaded by referring to some prestigious individual or group, as in, "A group of experts has suggested . . . Do you approve of this, or do you disapprove?"

Leading questions are similar to loaded questions. An example is: "Wouldn't any reasonable individual select product ______ rather than product ______?" The difficulty is that most people are reasonably cooperative and would prefer, all other things being equal, to agree with the tenor of the question. The best way to avoid loaded and leading questions is to review them with a disinterested party or pretest the items on someone who has no viewpoint at all.

There are, of course, times when loaded questions probably should be used. This is when, without loading, the question would pose an ego threat to the respondent, so that he might give an untruthful reply. The loading removes the ego threat so that a more valid response can be obtained. An example might be, "Many people are not able to get as much schooling as they would like. What was the last grade you completed in school?"

Other Inappropriate Wording

Subjects should not be asked embarrassing or self-incriminating questions such as, "When was the last time you were drunk?" Compound questions, in which a respondent can agree with one part of the question and disagree with another part, should be avoided. For example, "How complete and accurate was the information provided?" is undesirable, because respondents might want to rate completeness and accuracy differently, since research has shown that they are often negatively correlated. Vague or ambiguous words or questions should, of course, be avoided. For example, the question, "What is your income?" is not sufficiently specific, since the respondent may report monthly or annual income, income before or after taxes, etc.

Formulation of Response Alternatives

When formulating the response alternatives portion of a questionnaire item, the following points should be kept in mind.

1. All response alternatives should follow the question both grammatically and logically, and if possible, be parallel in structure.

2. If it is not known whether or not all respondents have the background or experience necessary to answer an item (or if it is known that some do not), a "don't know" response alternative should be included.

3. When preference questions are being asked (such as, "which do you prefer, the *XYZ* or the *PQR* truck") the "no preference" response alternative should usually be included. The identification of "no preference" responses permits computation of whether or not an actual majority of the total sampled are pro or con.

4. The use of the "none of the above" option or variants of it such as "not enough information" is sometimes useful.

5. For most items, the questionnaire writer desires the respondent to check only one response alternative. Use of the parenthetic "(check one)" should eliminate the selection of more than one alternative. It is important to make it clear to the respondent that he may check more than one alternative in these fairly rare instances where the questionnaire developer does wish to permit this.

Directionality and Intensity in Questions

Directionality (e.g., satisfaction) can be expressed in two ways. In the question itself, for example,

The ______ is a satisfactory automobile

______Agree

______Disagree

or in the response alternatives, e.g.,

The______is

______a satisfactory automobile

______an unsatisfactory automobile

Item Difficulty

One of the general recommendations advanced by almost every source on how to write effective questionnaires is the admonition, "keep it simple." Dyer et al. (1976) report a series of studies dealing with item difficulty but in this matter simple logic and experience supports this recommendation.

Question Length

There is little research in this area to guide the questionnaire developer. It is sometimes desirable to break a question into two or more sentences when the sentence structure would otherwise be overly complex. One sentence can state the situation, one can pose the question. Lengthy questions should be avoided. Longer open-ended questions do not necessarily produce more information nor more accurate information than do shorter ones.

Question Sequence

Two aspects must be considered with regard to sequence. The first has to do with the order of questions within a series of items designed to explore the same topic. The second deals with the order of different groups of questions when each group involves a different topic.

The literature is somewhat inconsistent, some studies showing a marked effect of order (Cohen, 1965; Gross, 1964; Landon, 1971; O'Dell, 1962; Survey Research Center, 1970, 1972) whereas other studies showed no significant effect (Baehr, 1953; Bradburn and Mason, 1964; Blumberg, DeSoto and Kuethe, 1966; Brenner, 1964; Ferber, 1966; Lyman, 1949; Metzner and Mann, 1953; Symonds, 1936). However Dyer et al. (1976) make the following suggestions.

Within a Series of Items. The order of questions on an instrument should be varied or assigned randomly to avoid one question contaminating another. The immediately preceding question or group of questions may place the respondent in a mental set or frame of reference. For example, asking respondents a general question about their feelings regarding automobile exhaust pollution might influence responses to the question, "Do you prefer leaded or nonleaded gasoline?" Although there is little evidence in the literature to support its general existence, this effect may be found in specific settings or with specific questionnaires, so that it is wise to review questions relative to possible contamination.

Sometimes it is recommended that broad questions be asked before specific ones, the rationale being that the subject can more easily and validly answer specific questions after having had a chance to consider the broader context (the funnel approach recommended for the structured interview—Cannell and Kahn, 1953). There are other occasions when it is best to start with the more specific question, especially when the respondent should have experiences or issues in mind when he answers the more general questions. This is also true when the questionnaire deals with a complex issue which the respondent may not have thought too much about.

The order of questions within a series of items will also depend upon whether filter questions are needed. A filter question is used to exclude a respondent from a particular sequence of questions if those questions are irrelevant to him. For example, if a series of items were asked about different kinds of trucks, a "no" response to a question such as, "Have you ever used the ______ truck?" might be used to indicate that the respondent should skip the questions that follow about the truck.

With Different Groups of Questions. It is usually recommended that more difficult or more sensitive questions be asked later in the questionnaire, possibly at the end. One or more easy, nonthreatening and relevant questions should be asked first to build rapport. However, verbal efforts to build rapport with the respondent by the questionnaire administrator are preferable.

Response Alternatives. The number and order of response alternatives must be considered because these two variables may influence the subject's response. Although no firm rules can be established concerning the number of alternatives to use with multiple-choice items, there is some evidence that dichotomous items (with only two alternatives) are statistically inferior to items with more than two. Dichotomous items are easier to score than nondichotomous, but they may not be accepted as well by the subject. On the other hand, many response alternatives may make a questionnaire unduly time consuming. The principle to follow is that the number of choices logically possible should constitute an upper limit to the number of response alternatives.

Order of Response Alternatives

Evidence about the effect of order of presentation of response alternatives on choice of responses is contradictory.

Seven studies (Blumberg, DeSoto and Kuethe, 1966; Campbell and Mohr, 1950; Clark, 1956; Dyer, Klein and Yudovitch, 1974; Feldman, 1969; Kane, 1971; and Symonds, 1936) reported little or no effect with response alternatives. However, Becker (1954) and Madden and Bourdon (1964) found significant effects. Probably care should be taken to alternate the order of response alternatives when this is feasible. Dyer et al. (1976) report that:

1. Respondents have a tendency to select the first response alternative in a set more than the others.

2. With multiple-choice questions there is tendency to choose answers from the middle of the list, if the list consists of numbers, and from either the top or bottom of the list, if the alternatives are fairly lengthy expressions of ideas.

3. Poorly motivated respondents tend to select the center or neutral alternatives with rating scale items.

4. On items about which respondents feel strongly the order of alternatives makes no difference. On items about which the respondent does not feel strongly, most will tend to check the first alternative.

5. Presenting the positive pole of rating scale response alternatives first will improve the reliability of the responses, while decreasing their validity.

Sequence of Multiple-Choice Items

The following suggestions are made by Dyer et al. (1976) regarding the sequencing of multiple-choice items.

1. When the response alternatives have an immediate apparent logical order (e.g., they all relate to time) they should be put in that order.

2. When the response alternatives are numerical values, they should be put in either ascending or decreasing order.

3. When the response alternatives have no immediately apparent logical order, they should generally be put in random order.

4. Alternatives such as "none of the above" or "all of the above" should always be in the last position.

5. Alternative questionnaire forms (e.g., where the order of alternatives is reversed on half of the forms) are often desirable.

Selecting Modifiers for Response Alternatives

It is often necessary to select adjectives, adverbs, or adjective phrases to use as response alternatives. The words must of course be understandable, but beyond that, if the words are to represent equidistant points on a continuum, they must be selected so that to the respondent they do represent equal intervals along the continuum. A number of studies have been conducted to determine the perceived favorableness of commonly used words and phrases. As a result we have scale values and variances for words and phrases which can be used to order the response alternatives. The scale values, standard deviations, and interquartile ranges reported in this section have been taken from the following studies, as cited in Dyer et al. (1976): Altemeyer (1970); Cliff (1959); Dodd and Gerberick (1960); Gividen (1973); Matthews, Wright and Yudowitch (1975); Mosier (1941b); Myers and Warner (1968).

There are several ways of selecting response alternatives, depending on the purpose of the questionnaire and/or on the way the data will be analyzed.

Matching the question. Descriptors can be selected to follow the question. For example, if the question asks for degrees of usefulness, descriptors might be "very useful" and "of significant use." It may be necessary to reword the question so that appropriate response alternatives can be selected.

Mixing descriptors. Descriptors on different continua should not be mixed. For example, "average" should never be used with quantitative terms or qualitative terms such as "excellent" or "good" (since average performance for any single group may well be excellent or good or poor). In fact, the wording of the response alternatives probably should be parallel for balanced scales. For example, if the phrase "strongly agree" is used, then the phrase, "strongly disagree" should also be used. Some pairs of parallel phrases are however not equally distant from a neutral point or from other phrases in terms of their scale values. Hence, parallel wording may not always provide equally distant pro and con response alternatives, although they may be perceived as symmetrical opposites.

Some words, such as, appalling, peerless, and superlative (Mosier, 1941a), are difficult for subjects to use in answering. Some words appear to have two or more distinct meanings. When these words are rated on a continuum of favorableness/unfavorableness, many respondents will check a different place on the scale. Some descriptors are more ambiguous than others, as measured by the variability of responses given to the descriptor (standard deviation or interquartile range). Terms should therefore be selected with small ranges or standard deviations.

When balanced scales with two to five descriptors are sufficient for describing the distribution of respondents' attitudes or evaluations, the questionnaire developer

TABLE 10.1 Response Alternatives Frequently Recommended by the Army Research Institute

( )	Very satisfactory
( )	Satisfactory
( )	Borderline
( )	Unsatisfactory
( )	Very unsatisfactory
( )	Very effective
( )	Effective
( )	Borderline
( )	Ineffective
( )	Very ineffective
( )	Very acceptable
( )	Acceptable
( )	Borderline
( )	Unacceptable
( )	Very unacceptable

can compose them quite satisfactorily by using a term and its literal opposite (e.g., effective vs. ineffective; pleasing vs. unpleasing, etc) for two of the terms. A more extreme pair can be produced by using "very" to modify these two terms.

Once the decision has been made about how extreme the end points of a scale should be, the descriptors should be selected accordingly by selecting those descriptors with the highest and lowest scale values. For a midpoint response alternative the descriptor should actually be neutral in meaning. Some of the commonly used midpoints do not appear as neutral as might be expected.

Some experts argue that, in order to perform analyses on the basis of numerical values or weights, the intervals between rating scale response alternatives should be equal. This would be desirable, but in many cases it is impossible because many words have not been assigned scale values. But when scale values are available, the response alternatives can be selected as equally distant apart.

Table 10.1 lists response alternatives frequently recommended by Dyer et al. (1976).

Response Alternatives for Degree of Frequency

Some questionnaire designers use verbal descriptors to denote degrees of frequency. Table 10.2 is such a list of verbal descriptors. There is great variability in meaning for frequency phrases. Questionnaires should, whenever possible, use response alternatives that include a number designation or percentage of time meant by each word used as a response alternative.

TABLE 10.2 Degrees of Frequency

Phrase	Scale Value	Interquartile Range
Always	8.99	.52
Without fail	8.89	.61
Often	7.23	1.02
Usually	7.17	1.36
Frequently	6.92	.77
Now and then	4.79	1.40
Sometimes	4.78	1.83
Occasionally	4.13	2.06
Seldom	2.45	1.05
Rarely	2.08	.61
Never	1.00	.50

Source: Dyer et al. (1976).

Response Alternatives for Order of Merit

An order of merit list of descriptors (see Tables 10.3 and 10.4) does not provide scale values nor show the variance of each phrase of some continuum. In addition, the list does not represent an equal interval scale. However, such lists are still useful for selecting response alternatives, if the main concern is to select response categories so that each respondent will agree on the relative degree of "goodness" of the terms.

Response Alternatives Using Scale Values

Using scale values and standard deviations to select response alternatives will provide a more refined set of phrases than an order of merit list. In general, response alternatives selected from lists of phrases with scale values should usually have the following characteristics.

1. The scale values of the terms should be as far apart and as equally distant as possible.
2. The terms should have small variability.
3. Other things being equal, the terms should have parallel wording.

Dyer et al. (1976) provide many tables listing phrases which have scale values and when available standard deviations or interquartile ranges.

It is useful to be able to consult lists of response alternatives. The tables in this section give some examples of response alternatives that have been selected on different bases. They do not of course exhaust all possibilities.

The sets of response alternatives shown in Tables 10.5 and 10.6 were selected so that the phrases in each set would be as nearly equidistant (one standard deviation)

TABLE 10.3 Order of Merit of Selected Descriptive Terms

Order of merit	Descriptive Term
1	Very superior
2	Very outstanding
3	Superior
4	Outstanding
5	Excellent
6	Very good
7	Good
8	Very satisfactory
9	Satisfactory
10	Marginal
11	Borderline
12	Poor
13	Unsatisfactory
14	Bad
15	Very poor
16	Very unsatisfactory
17	Very bad
18	Extremely poor
19	Extremely unsatisfactory
20	Extremely bad

Source: Gividen (1973).

from each other as possible without regard to parallel wording. A set would be selected to accord with the subject matter of a question.

Motivational Factors

The results of any study or test will be distorted if those to whom the questionnaire is distributed are not sufficiently motivated to respond adequately. Some of the ways of improving respondent motivation were described in terms of the structured interview. For the questionnaire, the special role of the respondent in the study can be emphasized. Responsibility can be stressed when it is appropriate to do so. The wording of cover letters, if used, affects ego involvement. Help may sometimes be requested on the basis of appealing to the self interests of the respondent.

For mailed questionnaires, return rates may often be significantly improved when a letter is sent in advance notifying the potential respondent that he will receive a questionnaire and his help is needed in filling it out. Stamped and addressed return envelopes must be sent with the questionnaire. This will increase response rate. Although there is contradictory evidence about whether short questionnaires are returned more frequently than longer ones, one would intuitively believe it to be true. Follow-up reminders can be sent to those who do not promptly return their

TABLE 10.4 Order of Merit of Descriptive Terms Using *Use* as a Descriptor

Order of merit	Descriptive Term
1	Extremely useful
2	Very useful
3	Of significant use
4	Of considerable use
5	Of much use
6	Of moderate use
7	Of use
8	Of some use
9	Of little use
10	Not very useful
11	Of slight use
12	Of very little use
13	Of no use

Source: Gividen (1973).

questionnaires. There is some question, however, whether such follow-ups increase response rate greatly.

Evidence is equivocal concerning the extent to which motivation is increased through the use of incentives such as money, time off, and special privileges, although it is generally agreed that such incentives increase response rate with remotely administered questionnaires. Feedback of study results should always be offered to the respondents and they should be praised to the extent that is reasonable and ethical.

Questionnaire administration sessions should not be scheduled when there are conflicts with other activities of greater interest to the respondents. Nor, in general, should they be scheduled very early or very late in the day.

Volunteers are usually more motivated to fill out questionnaires than are nonvolunteers. However, their replies may be biased because they are volunteers.

When respondents are told that they may leave as soon as they have completed the questionnaire they usually do a much more hasty and unsatisfactory job than when they are given a specific time for completion, and are told that they cannot leave until the time period is up.

Administrative Factors

Questionnaire administration time should be determined in advance by pretesting. The sex or race of the administrator appears not to have an effect on the responses received unless the subject matter of the questionnaire is sex or race related. Respondents may at times be influenced by the title of the questionnaire. The word

TABLE 10.5 Sets of Response Alternatives Selected So Phrases Are at Least One Standard Deviation Apart and Have Parallel Wording

Set No.	Response Alternatives	Set No.	Response Alternatives
1.	Completely acceptable Reasonably acceptable Barely acceptable Borderline Barely unacceptable Reasonably unacceptable Completely unacceptable	2.	Wholly acceptable Largely acceptable Borderline Largely unacceptable Wholly unacceptable
3.	Largely acceptable Barely acceptable Borderline Barely unacceptable Largely unacceptable	4.	Reasonably acceptable Slightly acceptable Borderline Slightly unacceptable Reasonably unacceptable
5.	Totally adequate Very adequate Barely adequate Borderline Barely inadequate Very inadequate Totally inadequate	6.	Completely adequate Considerably adequate Borderline Considerably inadequate Completely inadequate
7.	Very adequate Slightly adequate Borderline Slightly inadequate Very inadequate	8.	Highly adequate Mildly adequate Borderline Mildly inadequate Highly inadequate
9.	Decidedly agree Substantially agree Slightly agree Slightly disagree Substantially disagree Decidedly disagree	10.	Moderately agree Perhaps agree Neutral Perhaps disagree Moderately disagree
11.	Undoubtedly best Conspicuously better Moderately better Alike Moderately worse Conspicuously worse Undoubtedly worst	12.	Moderately better Barely better The same Barely worse Moderately worse

TABLE 10.5 (*Continued*)

Set No.	Response Alternatives	Set No.	Response Alternatives
13.	Extremely good Remarkably good Good So-so Poor Remarkably poor Extremely poor	14.	Exceptionally good Reasonably good So-so Reasonably poor Exceptionally poor
15.	Very important Important Not important Very unimportant	16.	Like extremley Like moderately Neutral Dislike moderately Dislike extremely
17.	Strongly like Like Neutral Don't like Strongly dislike	18.	Very much more A good deal more A little more A little less A good deal less Very much less

"test" should not be used in the questionnaire title since it may imply that it is a test of the respondent's knowledge. In some situations it may be necessary to use the supervisors of respondents as questionnaire administrators. When outside administrators are used, they must be carefully instructed to make no comments whatsoever regarding their opinions of the items being evaluated.

Questionnaire pretesting is essential if questionnaire faults are to be discovered and remedied. Pretest respondents who appear to be representative of eventual respondents should be tested one at a time. The questionnaire developer should ask each respondent to read each question and explain its meaning. The latter should also be asked to explain the meaning of the response alternatives and to make his choice, and then to explain why he made that choice.

During pretesting the respondents should be encouraged to make marginal notes on the questionnaire regarding sentence structure, unclear questions, or statements, etc. When attitude questions, especially, are being pretested, individuals who may hold minority views should be included. This will help identify loaded questions. Open-ended questions may, and often should, be included in early pretest versions of a questionnaire in order to identify requirements for additional questions.

Rating scales constructed for use in the questionnaire should be developed on a psychometrically sound basis (see Chapter Nine). If a high proportion of respon-

TABLE 10.6 Sets of Response Alternatives Selected So That Intervals Between Phrases Are as Nearly Equal as Possible

Set No.	Response Alternatives	Set No.	Response Alternatives
1.	Completely acceptable Reasonably acceptable Borderline Moderately unacceptable Extremely unacceptable	9.	Extremely good Quite good So-so Slightly poor Extremely poor
2.	Totally adequate Pretty adequate Borderline Pretty inadequate Extremely inadequate	10.	Remarkably good Moderately good So-so Not very good Unusually poor
3.	Highly adequate Rather adequate Borderline Somewhat inadequate Decidedely inadequate	11.	Without hesitation With little hesitation With some hesitation With great hesitation
4.	Quite agree Moderately agree Perhaps agree Perhaps disagree Moderately disagree Substantially disagree	12.	Strongly like Like quite a bit Like Neutral Mildly dislike Dislike very much Dislike exceedingly
5.	Undoubtedly best Moderately better Borderline Noticeably worse Undoubtedly worse	13.	Like quite a bit Like Like slightly Borderline Dislike slightly Dislike moderately Don't like
6.	Fantastic Delightful Nice Mediocre Unpleasant Horrible	14.	Like quite a bit Like fairly well Borderline Dislike moderately Dislike very much

TABLE 10.6 (*Continued*)

Set No.	Response Alternatives	Set No.	Response Alternatives
7.	Perfect in every respect Very good Good Could use some minor changes Not very good Better than nothing Extremely poor	15.	Very much more A little more Slightly less Very much less
8.	Excellent Good Only fair Poor Terrible		

dents give "no" or a "don't know" response, it should alert the developer that he has problems with his questionnaire. Often more than one pretest is needed. At times questionnaires may have to go through six or more pretests and revisions. After pretesting, each question should be reviewed and its inclusion in the questionnaire justified. Questions that do not add significant information or that largely duplicate other questions can profitably be eliminated.

Response Errors

A number of response sets or errors may compromise the validity of the questionnaire data. The respondent is subject to all the errors described in Chapter Nine (e.g., halo, extreme choices) because a very large part of any questionnaire represents ratings or other scaled response choices.

THE SURVEY

Surveys are conducted either in interview form or by questionnaires. Hence it will not be necessary to describe details of the individual parent techniques.

The survey carries the interview/questionnaire to a representative and hence necessarily large respondent population. It therefore enables us to report opinions and attitudes of large masses of people, as in election polls. Surveys gather data for almost any topic. For example, to determine the relative popularity of presidential candidates, desires for housing and automobiles, preferences in cigarettes, or the incidence of migraine headaches.

In the survey the phenomena studied are naturally occurring and in most cases cannot be manipulated experimentally in a laboratory. We can influence attitudes by experimental manipulations but only artificially. In survey research there are two things we wish to learn—the incidence of attitudes, opinions, and phenomena and the interrelationship of variables producing these attitudes, opinions, and phenomena. It is from these that we can infer causal factors, The first set we can determine directly from survey results. The second set must be inferred by correlation among the variables studied. For example, we can directly measure salaries of men and women at various educational levels performing equivalent work. If we find that at every educational level women earn less than men we can infer that a systematic factor (possibly sex discrimination) is probably responsible.

Although we cannot manipulate naturally occurring phenomena, comparisons can be made among these by selecting a population to be surveyed in which the variables of interest are naturally contrasted. Any phenomenon or condition that can be segmented either naturally or artificially into two or more levels can be contrasted in survey research. Among such variables are: sex, age, race, religion, amount of education, reading habits, income, socioeconomic status, and skill levels. The list goes on.

Surveys can be administered either uniquely or repeatedly. With repeated administration we can develop historical trends or determine the influence of some event or occurrence intervening between administrations (a natural experiment, one might say). For example, the United States government has surveyed job satisfaction among workers in various industries at intervals since the 1930s. Attitudes toward the Soviet Union can be measured before and after the invasion of Afghanistan. Polls are routinely taken during a campaign to assess trends.

Survey Designs

Even though we cannot manipulate survey variables, it is possible to create alternative survey designs based on the questions that we wish to answer and the variables involved.

Incidence Designs. Here we are concerned solely with determining the incidence and distribution of characteristics or relationships among characteristics. Since this type of survey is largely descriptive, our primary concern here is that the study sample is truly representative of the population to which we wish to generalize. So in surveying American attitudes toward the nuclear freeze we would include in the survey population representatives of the various races and religions in America, as well as such criteria as age, educational spectrum and socioeconomic status. Each of these might influence attitudes toward the freeze. Moreover, since these variables are not necessarily distributed equally among the population, the number of respondents we selected to be reprensentative of a subpopulation would be in proportion to the frequency of that group in the overall population (a stratified sample). Results would be reported in terms of each of the variables. The statistical analysis would be comparatively simple, consisting of means (or other "average" scores), measures of variability–together with errors of estimate–and comparison of the subgroup scores.

Group Comparisons. If we wish to know more than the incidence and distribution of phenomena, a research design is required. Such a design can be represented by the example of the independent variable X (education), and dependent variable Y (annual income). The hypothesis is that amount of income is related to amount of education. If one segments X and Y, the relationship between educational level and income can be determined by correlation. This design is illustrated as follows:

X (Education)	Y (Income)
X_1 non high-school graduate	....
X_2 high school graduate	....
X_3 post high-school training	....
X_4 college graduate	....
X_5 post-graduate training	....

Since Y is a dependent variable, the income data are not manipulated (ordered). The levels of X can be determined in advance because they fall into naturally occurring categories. By asking representatives of each of the X levels the income they have, it is possible to develop a distribution of income. The size of the correlation between education and income will suggest a causal relationship between the two variables. Since education and income are correlated with sex and race, it will be necessary to partition the data along these two categories.

Panel designs. We can utilize a panel design to take account of changes over time that may occur with the variable of interest. This incorporates time and changes occurring over time by collecting data at two or more chronological points. Graphically this design can be illustrated as follows:

$$X_{1_1}Y \quad X_{1_2}Y \quad X_{1_3}Y \quad \ldots\ldots\ldots\ldots\ldots\ldots$$
$$X_{2_1}Y \quad X_{2_2}Y \quad X_{2_3}Y \quad \ldots\ldots\ldots\ldots\ldots\ldots$$

where X_{1_1} is for example the first male subject studied on the first survey administration and Y equals income, X_{1_2} is the first male in the second administration, etc. Parallel to this is $X_{2_1}Y$ where X_{2_1} is the first female subject on the first administration and Y is income, etc.

Panel designs would be utilized only where it is known or hypothesized that the variables of interest assume different values over time. The panel design is simply the extrapolation of the group comparison design. If the latter is repeated at different points in time, it becomes a panel design.

In any repeated design the question arises of repeated measurements with the same subjects. Ideally the same subjects would be studied on the several survey administrations. However, where several years elapse between administrations it is quite common for individuals studied to die or otherwise become unavailable to the researcher. We can plan for this in advance by increasing the subject sample to compensate for this shrinkage. If the amount of subject shrinkage is not excessive we will continue with the subject sample as it ultimately emerges.

If shrinkage is excessive we may have to recruit new subjects whose characteristics are similar to those lost. For example, if we are studying the effect of progressive aging on job satisfaction, we might replace one 50-year-old who has died with another 50-year-old whom we have not previously tested. This procedure, while statistically acceptable, is likely to vitiate the validity of our conclusions because the new subjects are not the same as the former ones and the time period at which they are picked up may somehow have affected their attitudes or condition. For example, a college student now and at the time of the Vietnam war might have radically different attitudes toward life. We must be careful, therefore, about the selection of replacement subjects.

It could be said that, since in any longitudinal survey the researcher attempts to determine the characteristics of a group rather than of an individual, any subject with characteristics reasonably similar to the group average could substitute for any other subject. However, this line of reasoning can be carried too far.

Cross-Sectional Designs. The panel design can be complicated by addition of multiple variables, where the variables represent phenomena that occur naturally over a period of time. In the study of American occupational structure by Blau and Duncan (1967), certain variables (e.g., sex, father's occupation) occurred earlier whereas other variables (e.g., respondent's first job) became operative later. This design takes the form A_n, B_n, C_n . . . when A, B, C . . . are sequential variables.

Conducting the Survey

The questionnaire development process for major surveys is simple in concept but actual execution can be complex. These steps are to be followed, generally in the order listed.

1. Identify data requirements.
2. Determine characteristics of the population to be sampled.
3. Develop questionnaires.
4. Pretest and revise questionnaires.
5. Determine required size of sample.
6. Determine procedure for administration.
7. Collect data.
8. Analyze data.
9. Report results.

Since many of these steps have already been discussed, only a few points will be made.

The first step in developing a survey is to determine the variables involved and the questions to be answered. The purpose of the survey determines the nature and number of variables. Questions are developed and pretested as described in the section on questionnaires. The population to which the questionnaire will be administered will also be determined, in part, by the questions that the survey is designed to answer. For example, if the question is Hispanic attitudes, this dictates an Hispanic sample. If the survey attempts to elicit information generalizable to the total population, a stratified sample based on the major characteristics differentiating the population,—age, sex, race, religion, and socioeconomic status—will be required. If the questions asked pertain to special segments of the population, such as attitudes toward education in Hispanic male youths, the sample must be appropriately stratified.

The elements of sampling design are a set of questions that must be answered (see Kidder, 1981).

1. What is to be the sampling unit and how is it defined?
2. How are the units to be selected?
3. Should the population be stratified and, if so, what types and number of stratifications should be selected?
4. Should the sample be selected by some area restriction design, in groups or clusters, or singly?
5. Should the sample be replicated?
6. How large should the sample be?

This last question (size of sample) is determined ultimately by the amount of sampling error accepted by the researcher. In mathematic language, we are interested in obtaining an estimator p of the population proportion P by sampling n persons out of the total population of N persons. The usual model for a solution is to allow a margin for error in the estimator d, and a probability α of exceeding that margin for error with the estimator. The sample size is then established so that the probability that the estimated value p differs from the population value P more than d is less than

$$\text{Prob} \quad [|p - P| > d] \quad \leq \alpha \tag{10.2}$$

From statistics we know that

$$\frac{P - p}{\sqrt{\dfrac{N - n}{N - 1} \cdot \dfrac{P(1 - P)}{n}}} \tag{10.3}$$

is a normal variable on Z score. This gives us

$$d = Z\alpha/2 \quad \sqrt{\frac{N - n}{N - 1}} \quad \sqrt{\frac{P(1 - P)}{n}} \tag{10.4}$$

TABLE 10.7 Effect of d and α on Sample Size

d	.10	.05	.02	.01
.10	68	96	135	166
.05	270	384	543	666
.02	1691	2401	3399	4160
.01	6765	9604	13572	16641

where $Z\alpha/2$ is the abscissa of the normal curve which has probability $\alpha/2$ in each tail.

Solving the above expression for n, we get

$$n = \frac{N}{1 + \dfrac{d^2}{(Z_{\alpha/2})^2} \cdot \dfrac{N-1}{P(1-P)}} \tag{10.5}$$

Since P is unknown, this expression is not very helpful in determining the sample size n. Noting however that $P(1 - P)$ is always less than or equal to $^1/_4$ for all $0<P<1$, we obtain the conservative solution

$$n = \frac{N}{1 + \dfrac{d^2}{(Z_{\alpha/2})^2} \cdot \dfrac{N-1}{^1/_4}} \tag{10.6}$$

which is larger than any solution for known P. If we sample

$$\frac{N}{1 + \dfrac{d^2}{(Z_{\alpha/2})^2} \cdot \dfrac{N-1}{^1/_4}} = n \text{ of the population,} \tag{10.7}$$

then we can determine that the probability of the estimated proportion differing from the true proportion by more than d is less than $\propto$.

Equation (10.7) is very unwieldy; but there is a useful approximation to it, if N is large. In this case, we assume that $\dfrac{N-n}{N}$ *equals 1*, which however will involve a certain error in the determination of n. If N is *10 times n*, the error in the solved sample size will be approximately one percent; but since our initial sample size was conservative, this error is usually unimportant. The approximate equation is

$$n \leq \frac{(Z_{\alpha/2})^2}{4d^2} \tag{10.8}$$

Using this approximation and some usual values for d and α Table 10-7 illustrates their effect on sample size.

As the requirements for accuracy of the estimated proportion and the probability of making an error become more stringent, the sample size quickly becomes excessive. A compromise must be made between the useful accuracy of the estimators and the cost of sampling to obtain these estimators. The most common choice is to allow a five percent possibility of making an error (d) in excess of five percent (∝). This choice requires a sample size of 384. Because of the statistical sophistication involved, the investigator should check his sample size estimates with a mathematician or better yet, have the latter develop those estimates for him.

Since not everyone returns a questionnaire, the response rate is always less than 100 percent. Based on response rate data from previous surveys it is possible to estimate the number of "no-shows" in the new survey and add that number to the sample size to produce the necessary N.

The goal of statistically analyzing survey data, beyond the mere reporting of incidence, is to determine causal relationships. The most common method of inferring causal relationships is by determining that the variables surveyed co-vary. For example, to say that education and income co-vary, or are correlated, is to say that there is some tendency for lower levels of income to occur with lower levels of education. And, as would follow, for higher income levels to be associated with higher educational levels.

Correlation does not of course demonstrate causation. To do so we must be able to eliminate alternative explanations of the association between the variables. Kidder (1981) provides an example of a correlation between the number of fire trucks called to a fire and amount of damage in dollars resulting from the fire. This correlation would not suggest that the trucks caused the damage, because other explanations (such as the severity of the fire determining how many fire trucks are called to a fire) are much more convincing.

It is beyond the scope of this chapter to discuss the various types of correlational statistics available: parametric, nonparametric, product-moment, rank–order, etc. These are fully described in readily available textbooks.

In addition, it is possible to apply tests of significance of difference when measures of various categories or levels are contrasted. Let us assume that the following hypothetical frequencies are developed relating age and sex (independent variables) with incidence of jogging (dependent variable).

Sex/Age	Number Jogging
Males below 40	320
Males above 40	170
Females below 40	205
Females above 40	30

The hypotheses to be tested are that (1) males jog significantly more than do females; and (2) younger males and females jog more than do older males and females. Although these hypotheses seem reasonable by inspection of the table above, we have much more confidence if we apply a statistical technique such as chi-square to these frequencies to verify that they are not merely the product of random association.

COMMENTARY

Although it may appear as if the outstanding research question to be answered about the self-report techniques is their accuracy, this is true only to the extent that the object of the self-report is the collection of factual data. In the informational interview accuracy equals validity, although the information elicited in such interviews has usually been discrete facts, such as amount of income. One wonders what would happen if the information requested were more complex (this might affect the adequacy of what is reported). In the survey interview and the questionnaire we have a slightly different situation because these two instruments pick up not only facts but also attitudes and opinions, which have no accuracy measure except insofar as these attitudes and opinions are manifested in some action. For example, the accuracy of a reported intent to vote for a candidate in an election would be verified if it could be determined that the reporter actually voted for that candidate. This kind of verification is rarely achieved, although "exit-poll" questioning of voters provides a measure of polling validity.

The selection/appraisal interview cannot be viewed in accuracy/validity terms because it is used essentially as a rating scale. The researcher's concern for accuracy/validity is not the interview but the total selection/appraisal process of which the interview is only a part. If the selection process selects candidates later found to be effective employees, this validates the process, not the interview.

With all these qualifications having been pointed out, the question of the error in self-report requires much more investigation than it has received. We know that the self-report techniques, like other subjective methods such as ratings, are sensitive to even minor factors such as the order in which questions are asked. However, aside from determining that this sensitivity exists, we do not know the extent of the error they induce.

More fundamentally, we must ask, what are the criteria for error in self-report techniques? The error criterion for discrete, factual material can be developed fairly easily. For anything more complex there is an extensive gray area. If an experience or performance consists of *X* amount of material or detail, and the subject reports less than that, how much error is involved? If a witness reports seeing an automobile at the scene of a shooting but can report only its color—black—but not its license plate or the people in the car, how many errors are being made? An experience or a performance consists of many attributes, only a few of which are reported by the typical subject. Is what is left unreported errors of omission? The answer is not obvious. A systematic attack on the problem is required. One way might be to develop a taxonomic classification of the various ways in which an observed performance can vary and match this template against what the subject can and does report when questioned. Perhaps it would be possible eventually to do the same thing for the dimensions of an internal process (attitude, opinion). This is a far off possibility, if it exists at all.

Research on the interview is sparse and mostly in the context of the job function (selection, appraisal) in which the interview occurs. We know little of the interview as a generic method and this may be in part because it is difficult for the researcher to extract the kernel of the interview from the situational shell in which it resides. In consequence the ground rules for developing and conducting the interview are so general as not to be particularly helpful.

Research on the interview qua interview will require development of controlled but realistic scenarios as events to be observed by and participated in by the subject. Carefully varied interview formats could be applied afterward. Even in this controlled simulation it will be difficult to divorce the interview from the respondent's perception and memory of events.

The situation is much better with the questionnaire because of its fixed and relatively obvious verbal structure. The research paradigm here is comparative: to try alternative formats to determine if they produce dissimilar responses. It is essential moreover that the amount of variance accounted for by each variation be determined, because unless the contribution of a variation is large, its importance is minimal, no matter how statistically significant the differences are.

REFERENCES

Adams, J. S. An experiment on question and response bias. *Public Opinion Quarterly,* 1956, *20,* 593–598.

Altemeyer, R. A. Adverbs and intervals: a study of Likert scales. *Proceedings,* American Psychological Association Annual Convention, 1970, *5* (pt 1), 397–398.

Amalfitano, J. G. and Kalt, N. C. Effects of eye contact on the evaluation of job applicants. *Journal of Employment Counseling,* 1977, *14*, 46–48.

Anderson, C. W. The relation between speaking times and decision in the employment interview. *Journal of Applied Psychology*, 1960, *44*, 267–268.

Anstey, E. A 30-year follow-up of the CSSB procedure, with lessons for the future. *Journal of Occupational Psychology,* 1977, *50,* 149–159.

Arvey, R. D. and Campion, J. E. The employment interview: a summary and review of recent research. *Personnel Psychology*, 1982, *35,* 281–322.

Baehr, M. E. A simplified procedure for the measurement of employee attitudes. *Journal of Applied Psychology*, 1953, *37*, 163–167.

Bartlett, C. J., Heermann, E., and Rettig, S. A comparison of six different scaling techniques. *Journal of Social Psychology,* 1960, *51,* 343–348.

Baskett, C. S. Interview decisions as determined by competency and attitude similarity. *Journal of Applied Psychology,* 1973, *57,* 343–345.

Becker, S. L. Why an order effect? *Public Opinion Quarterly,* 1954, *18,* 271–278.

Belson, W. A. *The Design and Understanding of Survey Questions.* Aldershor, England: Gower, 1981.

Bennett, E. M., Alpert, R., and Goldstein, A. C. Communications through limited-response questioning. *Public Opinion Quarterly,* 1954, *18,* 303–308.

Bernard, J. An experimental comparison of ranking and paired comparisons as methods of evaluating of questionnaire items. *Papers of the American Sociological Society*, 1933, *28*, 81–84.

Birt, J. A. *The Effect of the Consistency of Job Inventory Information upon Simulated Airmen Reassignment*. Unpublished Ph.D. dissertation, Purdue University, Lafayette, IN, 1968.

Bittner, R. H., and Rundquist, E. A. The rank–comparison rating method.. *Journal of Applied Psychology* , 1950, *34*, 171–177.

Blake, R. Comparative reliability of picture form and verbal form interest inventories. *Journal of Applied Psychology*, 1969, *53*(1), 42–44.

Blakeney, R. N. and MacNaughton, J. F. Effects of temporal placement of unfavorable information on decision making during the selection interview. *Journal of Applied Psychology*, 1971, *55*, 138–142.

Blankenship, A. B. Does the question form influence public opinion poll results? *Journal of Applied Psychology*, 1940, *24*, 27–30.

Blau, P. M. and Duncan, O. D. *The American Occupational Structure*. New York: Wiley, 1967.

Blumberg, H. H., De Soto, C. B., and Kuethe, J. L. Evaluation of rating scale formats. *Personnel Psychology*, 1966, *19*(3), 243–259.

Bolster, B. I. and Springbett, D. M. The reaction of interviewers to favorable and unfavorable information. *Journal of Applied Psychology,* 1961, *45,* 97–103.

Bouchard, T. J. and Hare, M. Size, performance and potential in brainstorming groups. *Journal of Applied Psychology,* 1970, *54,* 51–55.

Boulger, J. G. Comparison of two methods of obtaining life history data: structured interview versus questionnaire. *Proceedings of the Annual Convention of the American Psychological Association,* 1970, *6*(Pt. 2), 557–558.

Bradburn, N. M., and Mason, W. M. The effect of question order on responses. *Journal of Marketing Research,* 1964, 57–61.

Brenner, M. H. Test difficulty, reliability, and discrimination as functions of item difficulty order. *Journal of Applied Psychology,* 1964, *48,* 98–100.

Burke, R. J., Weitzel, W., and Weir, T. Characteristics of effective employee performance review and development interviews: Replication and extension. *Personnel Psychology,* 1978, *31*(4) 903–919.

Burns, T. Management in action. *Operational Research Quarterly,* 1957, *8,* 45–60.

Burtt, H. E. and Gaskill, H. V. Suggestibility and the form of the question. *Journal of Applied Psychology,* 1932, *16,* 358–373.

Cahalan, D. Effectiveness of a mail questionnaire technique in the army. *Public Opinion Quarterly,* 1951, *15,* 575–578.

Campbell, J. Individual versus group problem solving in an industrial sample. *Journal of Applied Psychology,* 1968, *52,* 205–210.

Campbell, D. T., Siegman, C. R. and Rees, M. B. Direction-of-wording effects in the relationship between scales. *Psychological Bulletin,* 1967, *68,* 293–303.

Campbell, D. T., and Mohr, P. J. The effect of ordinal position upon responses to items in a check list. *Journal of Applied Psychology,* 1950, *34,* 62–67.

Cannell, C. F. and Kahn, R. L. The collection of data by interviewing, In L. Festinger and D. Katz (Eds.), *Research Methods in the Behavioral Sciences,* New York: Dryden Press, 1953.

Carlson, R. E., Schwab, D. P., and Henneman, H. G. Agreement among selection interview styles. *Journal of Applied Psychology,* 1970, *5,* 8–17.

Clark, E. L. General response patterns to five-choice items. *Journal of Educational Psychology,* 1956, *47,* 110–117.

Cliff, N. Adverbs as multipliers. *Psychological Review,* 1959, *66,* 27–44.

Cloud, J. and Vaughn, G. M. Using balanced scales to control acquiescence. *Sociometry,* 1970, *33,* 193–202.

Cohen, R. The position effects problem. *Public Opinion Quarterly,* 1965, *29,* 456.

Cohen, S. L. and Bunker, K. A. Subtle effects of sex role stereotypes on recruiters' hiring decisions. *Journal of Applied Psychology,* 1975, *60,* 566–572.

Cragun, J. R. and McCormick, E. J. *Job Inventory Information: Task and Scale Reliabilities and Scale Interrelationships.* Report PRL-TR-67-15, Personnel Research Laboratory, Aerospace Medical Division, Lackland Air Force Base, TX, 1967.

Dipboye, R. L., Fromkin, H. L., and Wiback K. Relative importance of applicant sex, attractiveness, and scholastic standing in evaluation of job applicant resumes. *Journal of Applied Psychology,* 1975, *60,* 39–43.

Dodd, S. C., and Gerberick, T. R. Word scales for degrees for opinion. *Language and Speech,* 1960, *3,* 18–31.

Dunnette, M. D., Campbell, J. and Jaastad, K. The effect of group participation on brainstorming effectiveness for two industrial samples. *Journal of Applied Psychology,* 1963, *47,* 30–37.

Dyer, R. F., Klein, R. D., and Yudowitch, K. L. *Analysis of Alternative Forms of a VOLAR/MVA Questionnaire.* Palo Alto: Operations Research Associates, 1974 (Prepared for the Army Research Institute for the Behavioral and Social Sciences, Fort Hood, Texas under Contract DAHC19-74-C-0032).

Dyer, R. F., Matthews, J. J., Wright, C. E. and Yudowitch, K. L. *Questionnaire Construction Manual,* Report P-77-1, Army Research Institute Field Unit, Fort Hood, TX, July 1976.

Ellenbogen, B. L., and Danley, R. A. Comparability of responses to a socially concordant question: "Open-end" and "closed." *Journal of Health and Human Behavior,* 1962, *3*(2), 136–140.

Ellis, A. Questionnaire versus interview methods in the study of human love relationships. II. Uncategorized responses. *American Sociological Review,* 1948, *13,* 61–65.

Eng, E., and French, R. L. The determination of sociometric status. *Sociometry,* 1948, *11,* 368–371.

England, L. R. Capital punishment and open-end questions. *Public Opinion Quarterly,* 1948, *12,* 412–416.

Farr, J. L. Response requirements and primacy recency effects in a simulated selection interview. *Journal of Applied Psychology,* 1973, *57,* 228–233.

Farr, J. L. and York, C. M. Amount of information and primacy recency effects in recruitment decisions. *Personnel Psychology,* 1975, *28,* 233–238.

Feldman, S. Evaluative ratings of adjective-adjective combinations, predicted from ratings of their components. *Dissertation Abstracts International,* 1969, *30*(2-B), 864.

Ferber, R. Item nonresponse in a consumer survey. *Public Opinion Quarterly,* 1966, *30,* 399–415.

Fletcher, C. A., and Williams, R. The influence of performance feedback in appraisal interviews. *Journal of Occupational Psychology,* 1976, *49*(2), 75–83.

Ford, N. M. Consistency of responses in a mail survey. *Journal of Advertising Research,* 1969, *9*(4), 31–33.

Forbes, R. J. and Jackson, P. R. Nonverbal behavior and the outcome of selection interviews. *Journal of Occupational Psychology,* 1980, *53,* 65–72.

French, J. R. P., Jr., Kay, E., and Meyer, H. H. Participation and the appraisal system. *Human Relations,* 1966, *19,* 3–20.

Gibson, F. K., and Hawkins, B. W. Interviews versus questionnaires. *American Behavioral Scientist,* 1968, *12,* 9–16.

Gividen, G. M. *Order of Merit-Descriptive Phrases for Questionnaires.* Army Research Institute Field Unit, Fort Hood, TX, 22 February, 1973.

Greenberg, A. Pictorial stereotypes in a projective test. *Journal of Marketing,* 1959, *23,* 72–74.

Greenberg, A. Paired comparisons vs. monadic tests. *Journal of Advertising Research,* 1963, *3*(4), 44–47.

Greenwald, H. J., and O'Connell, S. M. Comparison of dichotomous and Likert formats. *Psychological Reports,* 1970, *27*(2), 481–482.

Greller, M. M. Subordinate participation and reactions to the appraisal interview. *Journal of Applied Psychology,* 1975, *60*(5), 544–549.

Gross, E. J. The effect of question sequence on measures of buying interest. *Journal of Advertising Research,* 1964, *4,* 41.

Gupta, N. and Beehr, T. A. A test of the correspondence between self-reports and alternative data sources about work organization. *Journal of Vocational Behavior,* 1982, *20,* 1–13.

Hakel, M. D., Hollman, T. D., and Dunnette, M. D. Accuracy of interviewers, certified public accountants, and students in identifying the interests of accountants. *Journal of Applied Psychology,* 1970, *54,* 115–119.

Hall, J., and Williams, M. S. Group dynamics training and improved decision making. *Journal of Applied Behavioral Science,* 1970, *6,* 39–68.

Hartley, C., Brecht, M., Pagerey, P., Weeks, G., Chapanis, A., and Hoecker, D. Subjective time estimates of work tasks by office workers. *Journal of Occupational Psychology,* 1977, *50,* 23–26.

Henneman, H. G., III. The impact of interviewer training and interview structure on the reliability and validity of the selection interview. *Proceedings of Academy of Management,* 1975, 231–233.

Henneman, H. G., Schwab, D. P., Huett, D. L., and Ford, J. L. Interviewer validity as a function of interview structure, biographical data, and interview order. *Journal of Applied Psychology,* 1979, *64,* 748–753.

Hillery, J. M., and Wexley, K. N. Participation effects in appraisal interviews conducted in a training situation. *Journal of Applied Psychology,* 1974, *59,* 168–171.

Hollandsworth, J. G., Jr., Kazelskis, A., Stevens, J., and Dressel, M. E. Relative contributions of verbal, articulative, and nonverbal communication to employment decisions in the job interview setting. *Personnel Psychology,* 1977, *24,* 503–509.

Hollman, T. D. Employment interviewers' errors in processing positive and negative information. *Journal of Applied Psychology,* 1971, *54,* 45–52.

Howard, G. S. and Daily, P. R. Response-shift bias: A source of contamination of self-report measures. *Journal of Applied Psychology,* 1979, *64,* 144–150.

Howard, G. S., Dailey, P. R., and Gulanick, N. A. The feasibility of informed pretests in attenuating response-shift bias. *Applied Psychological Measurement,* 1979, *3,* 481–494.

Huegli, J. M. and Tschirgi, H. An investigation of the relationship of time to recruitment interview decision making. *Proceedings of Academy of Management,* 1975, 234–236.

Imada, A. S. and Hakel, M. D. Influence of nonverbal communications and rater proximity on impressions and decisions in simulated employment interviews. *Journal of Applied Psychology,* 1977, *62,* 295–300.

Jensen, M. B. An evaluation of three methods of presenting true false examinations. *School and Society,* 1930, *32,* 675–677.

Kane, R. D. Minimizing order effects in the semantic differential. *Educational and Psychological Measurement,* 1971, *31*(1), 137–144.

Kassarjian, H. H., and Nakanishi, M. Study of selected opinion measurement techniques. *Journal of Marketing Research,* 1967, *4,* 148–153.

Kidder, L. H. *Selltiz, Wrightsman and Cook's Research Methods in Social Relations* (4th Ed.). New York: Holt, Rinehart and Winston, 1981.

Kindall, A. F., and Gatza, J. Positive program for performance appraisal. *Harvard Business Review,* 1963, *41,* 153–166.

Klemmer, E. T. and Snyder, F. W. Measurement of time spent communicating. *Journal of Communication,* 1972, *22,* 142–158.

Knudsen, D. D., Pope, H., and Irish, D. P. Response differences to questions on sexual standards: An interview questionnaire comparison. *Public Opinion Quarterly,* 1967, *31,* 290–297.

Kohan, S., deMille, R., and Myers, J. Two comparisons of attitude measures. *Journal of Advertising Research,* 1972, *12,* 29–34.

Landon, E. L., Jr. Order bias, the ideal rating, and the semantic differential. *Journal of Marketing Research,* 1971, *8,* 375–378.

Langdale, J. A. and Weitz, J. Estimating the influence of job information on interviewer agreement. *Journal of Applied Psychology,* 1973, *57,* 23–27.

Latham, G. P. and Saari, L. M. *The Situational Interview: Examining What People Say Versus What They Do Versus What They Have Done.* Report GS-16, Graduate School of Business Administration, University of Washington, Seattle, WA, June 1982.

Latham, G. P., Saari, L. M., Pursell, E. D., and Campion, M. A. The situational interview. *Journal of Applied Psychology,* 1980, *65,* 422–427.

Latham, G. P., Wexley, K. M., and Purcell, E. D. Training managers to minimize rating errors in the observation of behavior. *Journal of Applied Psychology,* 1975, *60,* 550–555.

Ledvinka, J. Race of interviewer and the language elaboration of black interviewees. *Journal of Social Issues,* 1971, *27,* 185–197.

Ledvinka, J. Race of employment interviewer and reasons given by job seekers for leaving their jobs. *Journal of Applied Psychology,* 1973, *58,* 362–364.

Leskovec, E. W. A guide for discussing performance appraisal. *Personnel Journal,* 1967, *46,* 150–152.

Likert, R. Motivational approach to management development. *Harvard Business Review,* 1959, *37,* 75–82.

London, M. and Hakel, M. D. Effects of applicant stereotypes, order, and information on interview impressions. *Journal of Applied Psychology,* 1974, *59,* 157–162.

Lorge, I., Fox, D., Davitz, J., and Brenner, M. A. A survey of studies contrasting the quality of group performance and individual performance, 1920–1957. *Psychological Bulletin,* 1958, *55,* 337–372.

Lyman, H. B. A comparison of the use of scrambled and blocked items in a multi-scale school attitude inventory. *Journal of Educational Research,* 1949, *43*(4), 287–298.

Madden, J. M., and Bourdon, R. D. Effects of variations in rating scale format on judgment. *Journal of Applied Psychology,* 1964, *48,* 147–151.

Maier, N. R. F. Assets and liabilities in group problem solving: the need for an integrator's function. *Psychological Review,* 1967, *74,* 239–249.

Matthews, J. J., Wright, C. E. and Yudowitch, K. L. *Analyses of the Results of the Administration of Three Sets of Descriptive Adjective Phrases.* Operations Research Associates, Palo Alto, CA, 1975.

Mayfield, E. C. The selection interview: A reevaluation of published research. *Personnel Psychology,* 1964, *17,* 239–260.

Mayfield, E. C., Brown, S. H., and Hamstra, B. W. Selective interviewing in the life insurance industry: An update of research and practice. *Personnel Psychology,* 1980, *33,* 725–739.

McCormick, E. J. and Ammerman, H. L. *Development of Worker Activity Checklists for Use in Occupational Analysis.* Report WADD-TR-60-77, Personnel Laboratory, Wright Air Development Division, 1960.

McGregor, D. An uneasy look at performance appraisal. *Harvard Business Review,* 1957, *35,* 89–94.

McCovern, T. V. and Tinsley, H. E. Interviewer evaluations of interviewee nonverbal behavior. *Journal of Vocational Behavior,* 1978, *13,* 163–171.

Metzner, H., and Mann, F. Effects of grouping related questions in questionnaires. *Public Opinion Quarterly,* 1953, *17,* 136–141.

Moore, L. G. and Lee, A. J. Comparability of interviewer, group and individual interview ratings. *Journal of Applied Psychology,* 1974, *59,* 163–167.

Mosier, C. I. A psychometric study of meaning. *Journal of Social Psychology,* 1941, *13,* 123–140(a).

Mosier, C. I. Tables from a quantitative study of meaning. Unpublished manuscript, 1941 (b).

Murphy, E. F., Bailey, R. M., and Covell, M. R. Observations on methods to determine food palatability and comparative freezing quality of certain new strawberry varieties. *Food Technology,* 1954, *8,* 113–116.

Myers, J. H. and Warner, W. G. Semantic properties of selected evaluation adjectives. *Journal of Marketing Research,* 1968, *5,* 409–412.

Neidt, C. O., and Merrill, W. R. Relative effectiveness of two types of response to items of a scale on attitudes toward education. *Journal of Educational Psychology,* 1951, *42,* 432–436.

Newhall, S. M. Comparability of the single stimuli and the method of paired comparisons. *American Journal of Psychology,* 1954, *67,* 96–103.

O'Dell R. Personal interviews or mail panels? *Journal of Marketing,* 1962, *26*(4), 34–39.

Paull, D. Reliability of ordinal scales derived by ego-involved judges. *Journal of Social Psychology,* 1968, *76,* 143–144.

Payne, S. L. *The Art of Asking Questions.* Princeton University Press, Princeton, NJ: 1951 (Revised Ed., 1963).

Penner, L., Homant, R., and Rokeach, M. Comparison of rank–order and paired-comparison methods for measuring value systems. *Perceptual and Motor Skills,* 1968, *27*(2), 417–418.

Peters, L. H. and Terborg, J. R. The effects of temporal placement on unfavorable information and of attitude similarity on personnel selection decisions. *Organizational Behavior and Human Performance,* 1975, *13,* 279–293.

Pilgrim, F. J., and Wood, K. R. Comparative sensitivity of rating scale and paired comparison methods for measuring consumer perference. *Food Technology,* 1955, *9,* 385–387.

Prien, E. P., Otis, J. L., Campbell, J. R., and Saleh, S. Comparison of methods of measurement of job attitudes. *Journal of Industrial Psychology,* 1964, *2*(4), 87–97.

Rand, T. M. and Wexley, K. N. Demonstration of the effect, "similar to me," in simulated employment interviews. *Psychological Reports,* 1975, *36,* 535–544.

Rennick, V. G., Grupe, J. E., Reich, E. L., and Sewell, M. R. Exploratory study of rating procedures used to analyze material received on parents' reports. *Union College Studies of Character Research,* 1954, 101–124.

Reynolds, A. H. The reliability of a scored oral interview for police officers. *Public Personnel Management,* 1979, *8,* 324–328.

Rohila, P., Shanhdhar, S. C., and Sharma, V. Comparison of a nonverbal interest inventory with its verbal equivalent. *Journal of Psychological Researches,* 1966, *10*(1), 32–36.

Rose, G. L. *Employment Decisions Regarding the Handicapped: Experimental Evidence.* Presentation at American Psychological Association, Montreal, Canada, September 1, 1980.

Ross, R. T. A linear relationship between paired comparisons and rank order. *Journal of Experimental Psychology,* 1955, *50,* 352–354.

Rowe, P. M. Individual differences in selection decisions. *Journal of Applied Psychology,* 1963, *47,* 304–307.

Sattler, J. M. Racial "experimenter effects" in experimentation, testing, interviewing, and psychotherapy. *Psychological Bulletin,* 1970, *73,* 137–160.

Scates, D. E., and Yoemans, A. V. *Developing an Objective Item Questionnaire to Assess the Market for Further Education Among Employed Adults.* Washington, DC: American Council on Education, 1950.

Schmitt, N. Social and situational determinants of interview decisions: Implications for the employment interview. *Personnel Psychology,* 1976, *29,* 79–101.

Schuman, H. and Presser, S. *Questions and Answers in Attitude Surveys.* New York: Academic Press, 1981.

Schwab, D. P. and Henneman, H. G. Relationship between interview structure and interinterviewer reliability in an employment situation. *Journal of Applied Psychology,* 1969, *53,* 214–217.

Scott, W. A. Comparative validities of forced-choice and single stimulus tests. *Psychological Bulletin*, 1968, *70*(4), 231–244.

Seashore, R. H., and Hevner, K. A time-saving device for the construction of attitude scales. *Journal of Social Psychology*, 1933, *4*, 366–372.

Siegel, L. C., and Siegel, L. Item sorts versus graphic procedure for obtaining Thurstone Scale judgments. *Journal of Applied Psychology*, 1962, *46*, 57–61.

Sigelman, C. K., Elias, S. F., and Danker-Brown, P. Interview behaviors of mentally retarded adults as predictors of employability. *Journal of Applied Psychology*, 1980, *65*, 67–73.

Simas, K. and McCarrey, M. Impact of recruiter authoritarianism and applicant sex on evaluation and selection decisions in a recruitment interview analogue study. *Journal of Applied Psychology*, 1979, *64*, 483–491.

Slater, P. The test retest reliability of some methods of multiple comparison. *British Journal of Mathematical and Statistical Psychology*, 1965, *18*(2), 227–242.

Springbett, B. M. Factors affecting the final decision in the employment interview. *Canadian Journal of Psychology*, 1958, *12*, 13–22.

Sterrett, J. H. The job interview: Body language and perceptions of potential effectiveness. *Journal of Applied Psychology*, 1978, *63*, 388–390.

Survey Research Centre. *A Comparison of the Vertical and Horizontal Systems of Presenting Differential Rating Scales*. London: Reprint Series, Survey Research Centre, London School of Economics and Political Science, 1970.

Survey Research Centre. *The Extent and the Nature of Order Effects in Using the Semantic Differential Scaling Technique*. London: Reprint Series, Servey Research Centre, London School of Economics and Political Science, 1972.

Sydiaha, D. On the equivalence of clinical and statistical methods. *Journal of Applied Psychology*, 1959, *43*, 395–401.

Sydiaha, D. Bales' interaction process analysis of personnel selection interviews. *Journal of Applied Psychology*, 1961, *45*, 393–401.

Symonds, P. M. Influence of order of presentation of items in ranking. *Journal of Educational Psychology*, 1936, *27*, 445–449.

Tessler, R. and Sushelsky, L. Effects of eye contact and social status on the perception of a job applicant in an employment interviewing situation. *Journal of Vocational Behavior*, 1978, *13*, 338–347.

Tullar, W. L., Mullins, T. W., and Caldwell, S. A. Effects of interview length and applicant quality on interview decision time. *Journal of Applied Psychology*, 1979, *64*, 669–674.

Ulrich, L. and Trumbo, D. The selection interview since 1949. *Psychological Bulletin*, 1965, *63*, 100–116.

Valenzi, E. and Andrews, I. R. Individual differences in the decision process of employment interviewers. *Journal of Applied Psychology*, 1973, *58*, 49–53.

Vance, R. J., Kuhnert, K. W., and Farr, J. L. Interview judgments: Using external criteria to compare behavioral and graphic scale ratings. *Organizational Behavior and Human Performance*, 1978, *22*, 279–294.

Wagner, R. The employment interview: A critical summary. *Personnel Psychology*, 1949, *2*, 17–46.

Waldron, L. A. The validity of an employment interview independent of psychometric variables. *Australian Psychologist*, 1974, *9*, 68–77.

Walsh, W. B. Validity of self-report. *Journal of Counseling Psychology*, 1967, *14*, 18–23.

Walsh, W. B. Validity of self-report: Another look. *Journal of Counseling Psychology*, 1968, *15*, 180–186.

Waters, L. K. Effects of instructions and item tone to forced-choice pairs. *Personnel Psychology*, 1966, *19*, 45–53.

Webster, E. C. *Decision making in the Employment Interview*. Montreal: Eagle, 1964.

Weitz, J. Verbal and pictorial questionnaires in market research. *Journal of Applied Psychology,* 1950, *34,* 363–366.

Wexley, K. N. and Nemeroff, W. F. Effects of racial prejudice, race of applicant, and biographical similarity on interviewer evaluations of job applicants. *Journal of Social and Behavioral Sciences,* 1974, *20,* 66–78.

Wexley, K. N., Sanders, R. E., and Yukl, G. A. Training interviewers to eliminate contrast effects in employment interviews. *Journal of Applied Psychology,* 1973, *57,* 233–236.

Wexley, K. N., Singh, J. P., and Yukl, G. A. Subordinate personality as a moderator of the effects of participation in three types of appraisal interviews. *Journal of Applied Psychology,* 1973, *58,* 54–59.

Wiener, Y. and Schneiderman, M. L. Use of job information as a criterion in employment decisions of interviewers. *Journal of Applied Psychology,* 1974, *59,* 699–704.

Wilkins, L. T. Incentives and the young male worker in England: with some notes on ranking methodology. *International Journal of Opinion and Attitude Research,* 1950, *4,* 541–562.

Witroyl, S. L., and Thompson, G. C. An experimental comparison of the stability of social acceptability scores obtained with the partial rank–order and the paired-comparison scales. *Journal of Educational Psychology,* 1953, *44,* 20–30.

Wright, O. R., Jr. Summary of research on the selection interviews since 1964. *Personnel Psychology,* 1969, *22,* 341–413.

Young, D. M. and Beier, E. G. The role of applicant nonverbal communication in the employment interview. *Journal of Employment Counseling,* 1977, *14,* 154–165.

CHAPTER ELEVEN

Application Techniques

The techniques described in this chapter are applications of the measurement methods previously described: critical incidents (based on observation); job analysis (observation and self-report); Delphi (self-report); policy-capturing (ratings); accident investigation (interviews, self-report); work sample tests (observation); and behavioral instrumentation. All of these techniques overlap each other; although instrumentation may appear anomalous in the company of the others, it too is ultimately based on observation.

Because these techniques have the characteristics, the advantages, and the disadvantages of the measurement methods from which they derive, there is not much more one can say about them that was not said about their parents earlier. Although these are applications of more fundamental methods, they generalize broadly because they can be applied to almost any job, system, or topic. Thus, any job can be analyzed; policy can be captured from any rating, and instrumentation is, of course, quite neutral and hence can be utilized everywhere.

CRITICAL INCIDENTS

We first met the *critical incident* (CI) in Chapter 5 where it was the basis for one method of calculating human reliability. We met it again in Chapter 9 as an inherent element in the development of the behavioral observation scale and other rating techniques. One element of job analysis is the CI. The essential goal of the CI technique is to determine the critical requirements of the job, that is, those that make a difference between success and failure in performing the job. Because of this, the technique has a large number of applications. It can be used in the development of criteria and measures of proficiency; selection, classification and training of personnel; job design; operating procedures; equipment design; and motivation and leadership. CI can be used most particularly as the basis for inferring the qualities or attributes relevant to successful performance.

The critical incident procedure is a more or less formal way of collecting observations of human behavior. Whereas direct observation as described in Chapter 9 emphasized very molecular behaviors, those collected by CI are relatively molar. The critical incident is defined as an incident which has special significance and meets systematically defined criteria. To be critical, an incident must occur where the intent of the act and its consequences are reasonably clear to the observer. The CI procedure has been best described by Flanagan, who, during World War II and afterwards, developed the technique and whose 1954 paper (Flanagan, 1954) forms the basis for the following description. All further references to Flanagan are from that paper.

CI PROCEDURAL STEPS

The CI technique does not consist of a single set of procedural rules but rather of principles which are modified to meet the needs of the specific situation. The following are the major procedural steps.

1. Determine the *general aims* of the activity whose effective/ineffective behaviors are to be described. We cannot determine whether an individual's behavior was effective or ineffective unless we know what that individual is expected to accomplish. Flanagan suggests that for all except the most specific of work activities there is probably no one general aim which is the correct one. The manager of a production facility may have a somewhat different viewpoint about the goal of his activity than the first level supervisor or the worker. This is, however, less true of the proceduralized activities found in MMS.

The CI methodology is likely to be more successful when the activities to which it relates are relatively concrete and contain quantitative work standards. This does not, of course, prevent the researcher from utilizing CI in less well defined activities but the effort must be made to define these as precisely as possible.

2. *Specify the criteria* of the effective/ineffective behaviors to be observed. These criteria, which must be highly specific, relate to a. the situations to be observed (the place, the persons, the conditions and the activities); b. the relationship of the behaviors to the general aim of the activity; c. the importance of the behavior to that aim; and d. who should observe. The first and last of these are relatively easy to specify but not the others. If the activity goal is general, it may not be easy to describe the component behaviors that lead to accomplishment of that goal. If we are attempting to measure the effectiveness of a supervisor's behaviors that lead to a goal such as "maintain a high degree of motivation in subordinates," it may not be easy to specify and to recognize those behaviors, nor to determine how significant those behaviors are. Data can be secured from job incumbents, from their supervisors, from observers of their performance, and from interviewers of these observers.

Obviously those most qualified to make such an observation are the individuals performing the activity. This does not mean that job incumbents and their supervisors are automatically qualified to observe without receiving specific training in observation. Despite their technical expertise there is some doubt about whether subject matter experts can perform without some training in observation and reporting procedures.

3. *Collect the data*. The event should be described while it is still fresh in the observer's mind. Ideally the observer (*O*) should note his observations as he perceives them. In practice however there may be some delay between the observation and data recording. Since, as part of his training to report CI, *O* will have been told the behaviors to look for, this should stimulate his memory. Flanagan reports that provided the incidents reported are fairly recent, the memory effect is not serious, but evidence for this is not available.

Data can be secured in several ways—the personal interview, group interviews, questionnaires, and checklist or recording on forms. Each has advantages and disadvantages.

The most satisfactory procedure is the personal interview, which can be conducted in two ways. Ideally, after having been briefed individually about what to look for and the criteria of effective/ineffective behaviors, *O* goes to the operational area, makes and records his observations, then returns to be personally reinterviewed (debriefed). An alternative is the same, except that the initial briefing of *O*s is a group interview. Flanagan describes a personal interview in which *O*s are briefed (trained) as above, but then they do not leave to make observations but immediately report their observations orally, based on what they had observed some time before they had been briefed. Manifestly in this situation, they are reporting about what they had observed before they had any inkling of the CI effort.

Since the personal interview is extremely time consuming, a group interview procedure may be used. In this respondents are briefed about what is expected of them. Then each respondent is asked to write descriptions of incidents in answer to specific questions contained on a specially prepared form. An example of the kinds of questions asked (also suitable for the personal, oral interview) is: "Think of something a person (a subordinate for example) did that was extremely helpful in meeting a production schedule. What were the general circumstances leading up to this incident? Exactly what did the person do that was so helpful? Why was this helpful (what was so significant about it)? When did the incident occur? What was the person's job? How long has he been on the job?"

Flanagan reports that the amount of interviewer time per CI is significantly reduced by this procedure and that the quality of the incidents appears to be the same as that secured in the personal interview.

If the group is reporting CIs in writing on a standardized form, manifestly they are using a sort of questionnaire. As we saw in Chapter Ten, alternative questionnaire versions are possible, one of which, the mailed questionnaire, Flanagan explicitly discusses. He suggests that where observers are motivated to read the instructions carefully and answer questions conscientiously "this technique seems to give results which are not essentially different from those obtained by the (group) interview method." In fact, the forms are identical except for introductory remarks.

In view of the poor track record mailed questionnaires have, one must keep an open mind about the quality of the results achieved in this manner.

Another method of eliciting CIs is by means of written records. One type of written record is produced by having an observer make notes on incident details as they occur, presumably after having been trained about what to observe and record. This is as we indicated previously the ideal way in which to record CIs, since there is presumably little fabrication and loss because of memory defects. A variation of this is to record incidents on checklist forms, in which the checklist contains detailed descriptions of the general types of incidents to be noted. The checklist technique is not recommended unless great care has been taken to derive the incident descriptions. It is necessary to do a preliminary study of the typical kinds of CIs that one would expect to encounter, and such a study, if performed adequately, would itself involve extensive collection of CI data.

In general, the most desirable technique for collecting these data can be summarized in the following steps.

1. Train observers either individually or in a group. The information transmitted in such an interview consists of a. who has sponsored/authorized the study; b. the purpose of the study, including its value to the observer; c. why the individual has been selected specifically as an observer; d. the anonymity of the data, the individual's right to refuse to participate (mandated by regulation if the government is conducting the study); e. the criteria of what constitutes a CI; that is, effectiveness/ineffectiveness, importance of the item to performance of a required job, and the aim of the activity whose effectiveness/ineffectiveness is being studied.

2. The operator then proceeds to the work station and looks for CIs of the type desired over some specified time period (day, week, month), depending on the size of the sample that is desired and arrangements that have been made with management.

3. The operator reports back to analyst for debriefing. This involves a. reviewing each incident reported in detail to secure additional information. The operator is questioned by the analyst, b. each incident is rated by *O* on a scale of effectiveness/ineffectiveness and on a scale of significance to the job.

There does not appear to be a simple answer to the question of the desired sample size (i.e., number of CIs to be reported). Flanagan suggests that if the activity or job being defined is relatively simple, 50 or 100 incidents may be satisfactory. If the activity is highly complex, several thousand incidents may be needed. The size of the sample also depends on the precision of the definition desired. If a relatively precise definition of each critical behavior or category is needed, it may be necessary to get at least three or four examples of each critical behavior. The general rule is the more precise the definition, the more incidents are needed.

It is suggested that the analyst keep a running account of the number of new critical behaviors added to the classification system with each additional 100 incidents. Flanagan considers that adequate coverage has been achieved when the addition of 100 CIs to the sample adds only two or three critical behaviors.

Considering the limitations ordinarily imposed on researchers working in industry or in a military environment, it is a wise procedure simply to try to get as much as one can during the observer time made available and with the personnel supplied.

Critical incident data must of course be analyzed. The purpose of the data analysis is to summarize the data and abstract certain categories which represent significant job attributes such as "communicates information precisely to customer." There are three major problems in data analysis.

1. Selection of a frame of reference (taxonomy) for describing the incidents. This is highly subjective. The principal consideration here is the use to be made of the data, for example, for selection, training, measurement, etc. If the incidents are to be used for selection, the most appropriate taxonomy might be types of psychological traits used in selection. For training uses, the taxonomy might be categories that describe stages of training or training principles.

2. Inductive development of a set of major area and subarea categories. This too is subjective, lacking simple rules. The usual procedure is to sort a relatively small sample of incidents into piles of file cards, each pile representing the categories in the selected frame of reference. After tentative categories have been established (e.g., communications incidents, strong leadership, weak leadership), brief definitions of these are written and additional incidents are classified into the categories. This permits redefinition of categories if some incidents do not fit into the initial classification scheme. Broader categories are subdivided into smaller ones, and incidents that describe very nearly the same type of behavior are placed together.

3. Determining the most appropriate level of specificity or generality to use in reporting the data, a matter of tradeoff between the advantages of specificity in categories and the advantages of a relatively small number of classes. The more specific the categories, the greater the researcher's burden of sorting on the basis of fine differences. The smaller the number of categories, the more gross his data analysis becomes.

There seems little question about the utility of the technique, since the technique has been used in many applications in the last 30 years. McCormick (1979) specifically cites its value for performance appraisal and personnel selection, less so for job analysis. However, there seems to be very little information about the validity and reliability of the CI. The studies that investigated these and other parameters were performed by Flanagan and his students in the early 1950s and were reported by him in his 1954 article. To our knowledge there were only two other studies applying the technique reported in the literature, one positive (Kirchner and Dunnette, 1957) and the other somewhat negative (Kay, 1959). The technique appears to have entered the methodologic inventory almost on a face validity basis, because the respondent is simply reporting what he observed. However, this is true only if the respondent has been properly instructed and trained and if he observes correctly after that training rather than, as is implied in Flanagan's description, some time before. Some of the ways in which CI data can be collected appear to be excessively anecdotal and uncontrolled.

Despite these caveats, the technique can be quite useful, but only if precautions are taken to increase the amount of control over the technique. One limitation of CI that is inherent in its fundamental assumptions is that it describes the extremes of the job and thus may be relatively insensitive to its more routine aspects.

JOB ANALYSIS

In the previous CI section it was possible to provide a relatively complete description of the method. It is not possible to do so with *job analysis* (JA) because of its greater scope and space restrictions in this book. Those interested in greater detail should read McCormick (1979).

Our emphasis in this chapter is on JA methods. These have been applied for various purposes, such as the prediction of wage scales, but we shall expend relatively little effort on such specific applications.

Job analysis makes use of the more generic measurement methods in its special applications. These methods—taxonomic classification, observation, interviews, questionnaires, etc.—have been considered previously and our concern in this chapter is not with these methods, per se, but how they are utilized in JA.

Job analysis is nothing new. Rohmert and Landau (1983) suggest that work analysis methods can be traced back several centuries and that since 1970 many variations of the basic methodology have been published.

Definition and Differentiation

JA is the collection of information which describes the job; it is a relatively molar *process* rather than a specific step-by-step technique, although parts of the process include specific procedures. In terms of the extensive front-end analysis performed in developing the system, one would have thought that the fundamental question asked by JA (how is the job performed?) would already have been answered. However, many jobs are developed without analysis. The specific purpose of the JA may require data not already available, the nature of the job may have changed over time, and certain consquences of the job such as fatigue or stress might not have been anticipated.

Job information is a requirment in system and equipment design, workplace layout, safety analysis, training, personnel selection and performance assessment. McCormick (1979) also talks about vocational guidance, manpower planning, job design and evaluation, recruiting, management-union relationships, and population analysis.

Job and task analysis shade into each other. The difference is one of scale. JA deals with the job as a whole, task analysis with the individual tasks comprising that job. The general JA methodology may include a task analysis as a subsection. JA inventories the specific tasks that comprise a job and describes the skills, abilities, and responsibilities required of the employee for that job. Within JA task analysis does much the same thing for individual tasks and subtasks in terms of the stimuli and required responses, accuracy, and coordination requirements. Logically the first step in the examination of work content is JA because one wishes to analyze the basic nature and content of the work process. Siegel, Bartter and Kopstein (1981) supply a nice analogy: "The gross features and their relationships must be established first, much as the anatomist first establishes gross structures before proceeding to the micro-anatomy of each."

Collection of Job Information

Certain questions must be answered before a JA can be performed. These questions are very similar to those that must be answered in collecting critical incidents. What types of information are to be obtained? What method will be used to collect the information and present it? How will the information be analyzed? Who or what will collect the data?

Types of JA Information Collected. Types of job analysis information collected include: a. work activities/processes or functions describing what is accomplished—repairing, cleaning, adjusting, etc.— and how, why or when activity is accomplished; b. the procedures used in performing the activity; c. behaviors—decision making, discriminating, communicating—used in performing the job; d. machines and tools used; e. physical products or outputs associated with the job such as materials processed, products created, services rendered or knowledge applied; f. work performance measurement—the time taken to perform the job or errors made; g. the job context, such as physical working conditions, schedule, organizational context, incentives; h. personnel requirements such as required knowledge or skills, experience, aptitude, and personality.

Methods of Collecting Job Information. Job information may be either qualitative or quantitative. Qualitative material is typically verbal, narrative, or descriptive, usually describing job content. Examples of quantitative job information are error rates, frequencies of objects handled, and size of work group.

Among the methods available for collectng job information one finds all the old reliables described in previous pages: observation; individual and group interview; technical conference (a form of group interview with subject matter experts (SMEs)); questionnaires; diary; critical incidents; equipment design information such as blueprints, and the recording of job activities. The more important of these methods will be described in somewhat more detail later.

The Agent of Job Data Collection. The source of the data collected is usually the job incumbent himself or his supervisor, because they know most about the job. The agent or the one who collected the data is usually someone other than the job incumbent. He may be an industrial psychologist or industrial engineer, someone working in personnel, safety, or the work study department. In some circumstances equipment may be used. For instance, the activities performed may be videotaped or physiological measurement apparatus may be attached to the worker.

Gathering Data by Observation

Job analytic data may be collected by an analyst who directly observes performance by job incumbents. This technique appears optimal because it affords the opportunity to question the job incumbent at any stage of the work. It allows photographs and physical and time measures to be taken and it may permit the analyst to perform some or all of the job. Data collected in this way are likely to be relatively objective and accurate, since the method does not rely on the job incumbent's memory or ability to verbalize. However, if all portions of a job are to be analyzed, the method is very costly in terms of analyst and worker time. The presence of the analyst may also influence the behavior of the worker, reducing the validity of collected data, and the data secured can be influenced by the analyst's skill. It is highly desirable that the analyst have some job knowledge, although he need not be as skilled as an employee; if he is not knowledgeable, he is likely to misinterpret what he sees. Observation can, of course, be applied only to analysis of a job currently being performed.

Finally, the technique is suitable for the overt, observable aspects of job performance, but may not be as effective for analysis of less observable, that is cognitive, aspects.

Interview Methods

Job analytic data are often collected through interviews with job incumbents or supervisors. Interview data are generally collected away from the job site. The analyst will usually follow a structured or semistructured interview form. The goal of the interview may be to collect data descriptive of the job itself, or to collect data concerning some underlying job performance dimensions, such as required aptitude, skill, or training requirements. Interviews are relatively inexpensive, they yield a variety of data, and group interviews allow immediate review of data accuracy by the entire group. On the negative side, accuracy and completeness of collected data are affected by the capability of the interviewees to communicate. [If one asks subject matter experts to describe the knowledges, skills or abilities required for successful job performance, the former may be somewhat baffled because these are often abstract concepts which they do not fully understand (Tenopyr and Oeltjen, 1982).]

Data collected concerning time spent on tasks, levels of difficulty, and skills required, may be affected by incumbents' imperfect memory and bias, tending to reflect their expectations and the image they wish to present, rather than actual experience or behavior. Moreover, such data are likely to be colored by the range of skills and experiences held by the responding expert.

The interview allows the acquisition of respondent insights beyond the simple categorical reply characteristic of questionnaires and task lists. It allows respondents to elaborate more fully on their responses, and to supply their own points of view. It also allows the interviewer to probe and to follow up on areas of doubt, concern, or ambiguity. However, interviews are time consuming, and open-ended responses are subject to interpretive vagaries. The qualitative data emerging from interviews are often more difficult to analyze.

Questionnaires and Task Lists

Collection of job analytic data by means of questionnaires is appealing for reasons of economy. Very little time is required of the analyst for data collection. However, the questionnaire must first be developed, which is a task involving some small effort if the instrument is to be effective. Moreover, the analyst has no control over and little idea of the respondents' attention or understanding in completing the questionnaire. The results may be biased by the wording of the questions employed or by their form.The response rate may be low and problems may arise in analyzing obtained data.

The task list approach is a variant of the questionnaire approach. A list of the tasks performed on the job is presented to the job incumbents or their supervisors. They are asked to complete a structured set of ratings relative to each task. The ratings may describe how frequently each task is performed, how hard it is to learn to perform, how serious the consequences of inadequate performance of each task are, how complex each task is, the length of time between training and performance, how long it takes to perform each task, how important the task is, or whether or not that task is performed in an emergency.

The task list method assumes that the person completing the form is knowledgeable about the job, can accurately report that knowledge, and is free from bias; that the list is comprehensive and that the job has not changed during the interval between initial list development and its application; and that the sequential ordering of tasks is not a significant factor. Validity coefficients relative to reporting accuracy are reasonably adequate. Test/retest reliability of these lists, even when administered by mail, range around .70.

The method has been employed most often by the Air Force to survey a number of task characteristics such as frequency of task performance, amount of supervision required or exercised, task complexity, training or knowledge requirements, and task difficulty (Morsh, 1964). Christal (1974) found the task list approach to be economical and quantifiable, yielding data that can be manipulated by computer and amenable to standard statistical methods.

Diary

In the daily diary approach to job analysis workers are asked to keep detailed records of their daily activities. This method is inexpensive and may provide accurate data, but primarily for the determination of the tasks composing a job and the time spent performing those tasks. The obtained data are, however, usually in a form which is not readily amenable to statistical analysis. Moreover, unless workers complete the diaries during the course of their work, they are apt to forget details. Completing such a diary during the course of the work may interfere with the work itself. Many blue collar workers do not feel at ease with this method because they are unaccustomed to any task requiring writing.

Critical Incidents

This technique has been previously described. It is less useful than the others described in this section for developing a detailed description of a job or the factors and abilities underlying that job, because it emphasizes the extremes of the behaviors required by the job. However the technique may provide a basis for recommendations for job modification or redesign.

It is difficult to compare the methods in terms of effectiveness. They supplement rather than compete with each other. Ideally workers would be observed on the job and either interviewed or handed a questionnaire/task list to complete. If for some reason it were impossible to observe or interview personnel, the job analyst would probably rely on the questionnaire/task list. He would resort to the diary and CI techniques much less frequently.

Specific Job Analysis Techniques

These center around structured questionnaires or taxonomies.

Conventional Job Analysis. McCormick (1979) cites the practices of the *United States Training and Employment Service* (USTES) as an example of conventional JA procedures. The information collected includes job summaries, work performed ratings, worker trait ratings, and task descriptions. The description of work activities presents most difficulty because it depends on the analyst's skill in verbal description to reproduce the physical job on paper. The description is supposed to indicate what the worker does, how and why he does it.

Functional Occupational Classification Approach. This approach is also utilized by USTES. It consists in part of amplification and organization of the data gathered during conventional JA activity, together with new types of information. These last require classification of the job in terms of taxonomies (standard categories) describing a. worker functions, b. work fields, c. machine, tools, equipment, and work aids, d. materials, products, subject matter and services, and e. worker traits rated on scales involving training time, aptitudes, interests, physical demands and working conditions.

Task Description and Analysis. This has been described in Chapter 2.

Job Inventories or Task List. This was described previously (see Christal, 1969; Morsh, 1969; Morsh and Archer, 1967). In its simplest form the job incumbent completes an inventory as it describes his own position by indicating whether or not he performs a particular task. Usually, however, further responses are asked of him (primary and secondary task rating factors). The primary task rating factors describe the task in terms of its importance to the overall job, with reference to time required by the task or the frequency with which the task is performed. An example of how time is used to describe the task is the Relative Time Spent Scale used by the Air Force (Morsh and Archer, 1967):

> Compared with other tasks you do in your job, the time you spend on the task you are rating is:
>
> 1. Very much below average
> 2. Below average
> 3. Slightly below average
> 4. About average
> 5. Slightly above average
> 6. Above average
> 7. Very much above average

Another scale developed by Hemphill (1959) has been found to be usable by Air Force officers (Cragun and McCormick, 1967).

> Part-of-Job Task Rating Scale
>
> 0. Definitely not part of the position
> 1. Under unusual circumstances is a minor part of position
> 2.
> 3.
> 4. A substantial part of the position
> 5.
> 6.
> 7. A most significant part of the position

Secondary task factors may be continuous or categorical. Continuous factors include task complexity, task criticality, difficulty of learning the task and of performing it, experience needed for task performance, training required, satisfaction in performing the task, and supervision requirements.

Categorical task rating factors include method of learning the task, amount of special training needed, and task performance.

Development of Job Inventories

The development of a job inventory is very time consuming, demanding significant efforts of the job analyst and SMEs.

Determination of Task List Scope and Dimensions. The first step in the process is selection of the job classifications to be surveyed. The following questions must be answered to define the scope of the survey and to establish its dimensions. Will the survey be wide (e.g., all plants) or local (e.g., individual regions)? Will it cover a series of jobs (e.g., maintenance mechanics, ground vehicle operators, etc.)? Will it cover all levels of each job (entry to senior)? How many facilities must be surveyed (sampling)?

Development of the Task Set. Once the jobs to be analyzed are defined, a complete set of the tasks performed on the job is required. To secure such a list, any of the methods discussed previously may be employed. Review of available documents (e.g., training manuals) and interviews with job incumbents and their supervisors are frequently used.

Developing the task set is not necessarily easy. The actual tasks performed, such as by a maintenance mechanic, may differ depending on where the maintenance is being performed. The same job title may require different tasks or the same job may have different job titles in different locations.

Archer and Fruchter (1963) describe two alternative approaches to the development of the task set. One can develop a large pool of task statements from the source materials and then organize them into larger groupings called duties (functions); or one can start with a set of hypothesized duties and try to fit the task statements within the framework of each duty or subduty.

Preliminary inventories can be developed by first asking job incumbents or technical experts to list the activities they perform, or know are performed. These statements can then be consolidated, eliminating duplications, and ending up with a single list of tasks. The statements are edited into a reasonably consistent form. Task statements should (1) describe actual job activities, of course, and not qualifications, skills, etc.; (2) be brief, clear, and unambiguous so they are easily understood; (3) be so worded that the task rating scales (such as "time spent") make sense when applied to them.

The preliminary form of the inventory is then reviewed by several SMEs who add tasks that have been omitted and indicate whether tasks should be consolidated or broken down further. Also, whether task statements are understandable.

The task attributes to be rated by job incumbents have been listed previously—task importance, time required, task difficulty, etc. Most often the incumbent is asked to respond (provide an answer about each task relative to an attribute) by checking a rating scale, usually one with seven categories. As with any questionnaire, the instrument can be given to respondents directly or mailed; respondents can be gathered together to complete the inventories (this is preferred), or they can complete them on their own time.

Data Reduction and Analysis. The types of analyses applied to the data are, of course, determined by the purposes for which the survey was initiated and the job information was sought.

TABLE 11.1 Job Inventory Data Reliability

Response or Rating scale	(a)	(b)	(c)
Task occurrence	.70 & .73	.87	.63, .64 & .65
Time spent on task	.61	.83	.62
Part-of-position (of task)		.83	.63
Importance (of task)			.56
Difficulty (of task)	.47		.35

Reprinted, by permission of the publisher, from *Job Analysis: Methods and Applications*, by Ernest J. McCormick, p. 132 © Amacom, a division of American Management Associations, New York. All rights reserved.

For many purposes the results obtained from a JA conducted at the task level can be applied directly. One wishes to know, for example, which are the most important tasks, which ones are most difficult, and which demand the most experience.

Reliability of Job Inventory Information

Job inventory reliability can be determined on the basis of two administrations to the same sample of respondents, preferably a week or two apart (not much longer, since the job content may change over time). Data on job inventory reliability have been reported by (a) McCormick and Ammerman (1960), (b) Birt (1968) and (c) Cragun and McCormick (1967), as shown in Table 11.1. These coefficients reflect individual reliability, the reliability of those who respond to individual task statements on two separate occasions. One can also view the reliability question in terms of whether a second sample of respondents would give the same results (Christal, 1969). When the questions dealt with percent performing the tasks and the time spent on them, the correlations were .978 and .957 respectively, which is very good indeed. These reliability correlations say nothing about validity, but in self-report validity often has to be inferred from reliability.

Standardized JA Formats

All JA is individual to the particular job being analyzed. There have been, however, attempts to develop standardized formats which can be tailored to fit the individual situation.

Position Analysis Questionnaire. The best known standard format is McCormick's *position analysis questionnaire* (PAQ) (McCormick, Jeanneret and Mecham, 1972). The PAQ questionnaire analyzes jobs in terms of 187 job elements that presumably characterize or imply the behavior involved in jobs. Hence the PAQ can be used in a wide variety of situations.

The following material is derived from McCormick (1979). The job elements in the PAQ are organized in six divisions as follows:

1. *Information input*. (Where and how does the worker get the information he uses in performing his job?) Examples are the use of written materials and near-visual differentiation.

2. *Mental processes*. (What reasoning, decision making, planning, and information-processing activities are involved in performing the job?) Examples are the level of reasoning in problem solving and coding/decoding.

3. *Work output*. (What physical activities does the worker perform and what tools or devices does he use?) Examples are the use of keyboard devices and assembling/disassembling.

4. *Relationships with other persons*. (What relationships with other people are required in performing the job?) Examples are instructing and contacts with public and customers.

5. *Job context*. (In what physical or social contexts is the work performed?) Examples are high temperature and interpersonal conflict situations.

6. *Other job characteristics*. (What activities, conditions, or characteristics other than those described above are relevant to the job?) Examples are specified work pace, and the amount of job structure.

Each job is rated on each job element, using six types of rating scales: extent of use, importance to the job, amount of time, possibility of occurrence, applicability, and special code (used in the case of a few specific job elements).

A specific rating scale is designated to be used with each job element, in particular the scale considered most appropriate to the content of the element. All but the applicability scale are 6-point scales.

Rating	Importance to the Job
N	Does not apply
1	Very minor (importance)
2	Low
3	Average
4	High
5	Extreme

The applicability scale is dichotomous, that is, "Applies" or "Does not apply" are the criteria used. The scale is used only in the case of some of the job context job elements, such as regular work hours.

Job analysis with the PAQ is typically carried out by job analysts, methods analysts, personnel officers, or supervisors. In some instances job incumbents—managerial, professional, and other white collar workers—are asked to analyze their own jobs.

The evaluation of PAQ reliability is based on analyses of 62 jobs, each having been analyzed by two analysts independently. The coefficient of reliability was .79, which is rather respectable.

Occupation Analysis Inventory. The *occupation analysis inventory* (OAI) was developed by Cunningham and his associates (Cunningham, Tuttle, Floyd, and Bates, 1974; Cunningham, Boese, Neeb and Pass, 1983) as a step toward the description and classification of occupations for educational purposes.

The OAI represents a job analysis approach similar to that of the PAQ with two important differences, to be discussed later. It consists of 622 work elements grouped into five categories. These are listed here along with a couple of illustrative work elements from each.

Category	No.	Examples of Work Elements
Information received	125	Tables and graphs Mechanical drawings
Mental activities	41	Numerical computation Verbal comprehension
Work behavior	267	Cutting by sawing (nonpowered) Copying/recording
Work goals	112	Mechanical devices installed or assembled Verbal material transcribed
Work context	77	Electrical hazards Dirty environment

The work elements are generally rated on three standard scales:

Significance to the job	(6-point scale)
Extent of occurrence	(6-point scale)
Applicability	Does apply and does not apply

Certain work elements have special rating scales. Many of the work elements are identical or similar to PAQ job elements. The organization of the two forms is also similar in that both include elements dealing with information input, mental processes, and work output (paralleling the *S-O-R* paradigm referred to in Chapter Two). One feature that differentiates the two questionnaires is that the OAI incorporates many elements that have technological associations. Thus, it includes work elements that are associated with medical/veterinary activities (such as applying medicines), with mechanical and electrical maintenance and repair activities (such as adjusting/tuning), and with certain specific processes (such as stitching, knitting, and weaving). The second differentiating characteristic is that the OAI incorporates work elements which deal with work goals.

Job Information Matrix System. Another approach to providing standardized job information is the *job information matrix system,* JIMS (Stone and Yoder, 1970). It provides a standardized basis for gathering and recording job information of the following categories: a. what the worker *does* on the job; b. what the worker *uses*; c. what *knowledge* the worker must have; d. the *responsibilities* of the worker; e. the *working conditions* of the job.

For each of these categories of information JIMS provides standardized terms.

WHAT THE WORKER DOES ON HIS JOB. The analysis of what the worker does is carried out with a standardized listing of job activities, tasks such as those found in task inventories. Such task listings are developed for individual occupational areas such as the metal machining area, for example, interpret engineering drawings and drill center holes.

Such tasks would be rated by job analysts in terms of the relative frequency with which they are performed. There is also provision for describing those major tasks that occupy most of the worker's time. The analyst is asked to describe these tasks in narrative fashion, using, however, verbs related to the three hierarchies of the functional job analysis approach (data, people and things). An example for data and people (it does not work as well for things) would contain terms like investigate and scrutinize for the function of analyzing. Each verb is defined in order to standardize its use.

WHAT THE WORKER USES AND WHAT HE HAS TO KNOW. The analyst has available for the individual occupational area a previously prepared listing of terms for machines, tools, equipment, work aids, etc.

The entries to be made are related to the individual tasks, as in the following example.

Task: Scribe reference lines and points on work piece

Uses: gauges, blueprints, dividers, scribers, templets, straight edge

Must know: trigonometry, set-up procedures, blueprint reading

JOB RESPONSIBILITY. The job responsibilities are those which are relevant to the occupational area. In the case of the machine occupations, for example, there is provision for indicating both the dollar value of the product and the responsibility for equipment such as preventive maintenance, minor repairing, and so forth.

WORKING CONDITIONS. The working-conditions phase of the JIMS essentially parallels the procedures used by the USES in characterizing working conditions, hazards, and so forth.

The Job Element Method. Primoff (1975) has developed a procedure for job analysis in terms of job elements. He considers as job elements knowledges, abilities and skills, and personal characteristics which may affect job success. Primoff's method provides for developing, for any given job, a set of (tentative) job elements that presumably would be relevant to the job in question. Some of these may be developed specifically for the job, and some may be drawn from prepared lists of job elements for two categories of jobs—trades and labor occupations and clerical positions. Some examples of job elements from these lists are given here.

1. *Job elements for trades and labor occupations.* These include the operation of motor vehicles, the knowledge of welding, the ability to use electrical drawings, and troubleshooting (mechanical).

2. *Job elements for office positions.* These include the ability to proofread by oneself, the ability to help people find things in files, accurate and rapid typing, and memory for the names and faces of people.

Job analysis in terms of these elements typically is performed by several supervisors and expert employees, using a 3-point scale.

0 (0) The element is not present in the job.

✓(1) The element is present in the job but not of extreme importance.

+(2) The element is present and of extreme importance to the job.

The value of a given element is the sum of the ratings of several raters. These values are then used as the basis for deriving an estimate of the validity, called a *J-Coefficient,* of one or more standardized tests for use in personnel selection.

The second application of the job element method is to serve as the basis for developing job relevant tests. The same job elements are used, as discussed previously, except that the raters use four 3-point ratings, instead of one. The rating factors and the rating scale appear below.

Barely acceptable workers now on the job: (B)
+ (2) All have
✓ (1) Some have
0 (O) Almost none have

To pick out acceptable workers the element is: (S)
+ (2) Very important
✓ (1) Valuable
0 (O) Does not differentiate

Trouble likely if the element is not considered: (T)
+ (2) Much trouble
✓ (1) Some trouble
0 (O) Safe to ignore

Practicality. Demanding this element we can fill: (P)
+ (2) All openings
✓ (1) Some openings
0 (O) Almost no openings

Using the numerical values assigned to the three rating categories (2, 1, and 0), an item index is derived, $SP + T$ as well as others ($S \times P$), which are used as the basis for developing the job content of tailor-made tests to be used for the job.

AET (Ergonomic Job Analysis Procedure). The AET method described by Rohmert and Landau (1983) was developed after 1975 in Germany, primarily to determine the workload and stress in the system. It is a questionnaire in three parts. In part A (work system analysis) types and properties of work objects, the equipment to be used, and the physical, social and organizational working environment are documented on a scale of duration (proportion of time spent in a given activity). Part B is called task analysis, but is actually the identification of the major functions involved in three types of tasks, material work, abstract work, and work related to others. The analyst selects from a list of categories (e.g., operating/controlling, arranging/classifying) the one(s) most descriptive of the work performed. McCormick's PAQ (McCormick, et al., 1969) was the starting point for many of the items. Part C is a job demand analysis, in which the extent, duration, and frequency of stress are rated, usually on a 5-point scale. Analysis of the AET ratings produces not a single overall score but a graphic profile which can be derived either by inspection of the individual scores per questionnaire item or by factor analysis. In general, the methodology is much the same as in American job analytic procedures previously reviewed, with the possible exception of the emphasis on stress.

Job Components Inventory. The British contribution to JA techniques is the *job components inventory* (Banks, Jackson, Stafford and Warr, 1983). It is a questionnaire with five principal sections: tools and equipment; perceptual and physical requirements; mathematic requirements; communications requirements; decision making and responsibility. There appears to be nothing extraordinary about the technique except that it was developed by the British for British jobs.

Measures of Perceived Task Characteristics. The techniques previously described have emphasized the identification of job components.The Job Diagnostic Survey (Hackman and Oldham, 1975) and the Job Characteristic Inventory (Sims, Szilagyi and Keller, 1976) were developed to measure employees' perception of task characteristics and thus to assist in job redesign. The two instruments consist of 7 and 5 point (respectively) rating scales to tap job incumbents' feelings about such dimensions as task identity, autonomy, variety, significance and feedback. These dimensions have been associated to some degree with job satisfaction, job performance, absenteeism and stress. Unfortunately, there are serious questions about the validity and reliability of these scales (Aldag, Barr and Brief, 1981).

DISCUSSION

An essential aspect of all the standard JA formats is a set of taxonomies and rating scales for particular jobs and tasks and their characteristics. Everything depends on how adequately the taxonomies and scales describe the job. Given the adequacy of these classification schemes, the self-report of the job incumbent or supervisor is apparently quite simple, conceptually. The rating scales applied to these taxonomies are relatively simple compared to the rating scales described in Chapter Nine.

Nevertheless there is some question about the adequacy of the JA methodology. The central problem as always is how to describe physical work activities with verbal descriptors (Cowan, 1969). In addition there is the major problem of differentiating job units, such as tasks and duties. Tenopyr and Oeltjen (1982) indicate that "a duty will more likely appear as a separate dimension if the analyst has broken it down and has written several task statements representing it; a duty is less likely to appear as a performance dimension if only one statement has been written for it (or none at all)" (p. 583).

Some JA methods are more difficult to use than others. For example, the job elements method, most commonly used in public service, is considered by analysts as more difficult to use than task analysis, PAQ or critical incidents (Levine et al., 1981).

As always there is a continuing need to determine the validity and reliability of responses from informants; the relationship between job function components and person characteristics; the relation between job functions and performance style; and the relation between function characteristics (such as time requirements and difficulty level) and person characteristics (Prien and Ronan, 1971).

One cannot quarrel with utility, and the various JA methods do perform a service. Nevertheless, one wonders how adequately these methods do represent the reality of actual jobs. It is significant that validity data are scarce. There is an implicit assumption almost that reliability equals validity.

DELPHI

Delphi (Dalkey, 1969) is a self-report technique for analysis of complex problems, in which decision making, predicting, and communicating are important functions. . . . "a process whereby subjective judgements or the implicit decision-making processes of experts can be made more objective and explicit" (Sander, 1975).

To accomplish the "structured communication" characteristic of Delphi the following elements must exist: feedback of individual information to the entire group, assessment of the group judgment, an opportunity to modify individual views as a function of the feedback, and anonymity for the individual responses.

The technique is a way of directing a group to focus their individual opinions and thus reduce group variability. The opinions may derive from previous observations but because of the rather abstract and abstruse nature of the problems for which Delphi is used, the observation is often material read or learned.

Delphi has been under development for some thirty years. It is a spinoff from an Air Force sponsored Rand Corporation project studying expert opinion. Over the years some hundreds of Delphi studies have been performed. Nevertheless, the methodology is by no means fixed but, if we believe Linstone and Turoff (1975), is still evolving and still being researched.

The uses to which Delphi have been put are various. Linstone and Turoff (1975) list these among others: gathering current and historical data; examining the significance of historical events; evaluating possible budget allocations; exploring urban and regional planning options; and putting together the structure of a model. Although it may appear as if these particular applications are not particularly work oriented if one may use such a term, the general methodology appears applicable to a wide variety of work situations in which external referents are not available, or where one has to extrapolate to, or predict, a future situation. For example, one might use a quasi-Delphi procedure to develop human performance criteria (where these do not exist in sufficiently precise, quantitative form) as part of the process of establishing a personnel performance test plan.

These problem areas suggest that Delphi (which emphasizes structured expert opinion) is applied because more exact methods will not suffice. Since the problem attacked does not lend itself to more precise empirical or analytic techniques, subjective judgments have value. In a situation in which no exact analysis or measurement is possible, it is comforting and perhaps more effective to have the wisdom of several "old heads," rather than only one.

Turoff (1972) has identified other conditions in which Delphi may be useful: (1) when a group cannot meet often enough because of time or distance constraints; (2) when anonymity of committee members must be preserved; (3) when the group is too large for telephone calls or committee exchanges; (4) when disagreements among group members are too great for face-to-face meetings; and (5) to avoid domination by strength of personality (Gustafson, Shukla, Delbecq and Walster, 1973).

Delphi has two forms. The more common is the paper and pencil version which is ordinarily called a *Delphi exercise*. In this version a small monitor team designs a questionnaire which is sent to a larger respondent group. After the questionnaire is returned, the monitor team summarizes the results, and based upon these results, develops a new questionnaire for the respondent group. Typically the exercise consists of four or five iterations over a period of six or more months. Each iteration consists of 1. providing each participant with a new response form and a summary of the previous round's responses; and 2. formulation and return of the participant responses to the Delphi monitoring group. To a certain extent this form of Delphi is a combination of a polling and a conference procedure which shifts the communication effort from the larger respondent group to the smaller monitor team.

The second version sometimes called a *Delphi Conference* replaces the monitor team to a certain extent by a computer which compiles the group results. This has the advantage of eliminating at least part of the delay involved in summarizing each Delphi round. However, computerization requires that communication characteristics be well defined before Delphi is undertaken. In a paper and pencil Delphi, the monitor group can readily adjust these characteristics as a funtion of the group responses.

Delphi in either version has four phases. Phase 1 explores the topic under discussion; each group member contributes additional information to the issue. Since this is a mailed communication process, the effectiveness of the first phase depends very significantly on how well the monitor team has defined the problem under discussion, the rules of engagement, and how communication is to be achieved. Phase 1 requires reaching an understanding of how the group views the issue (i.e., where members agree or disagree and what they mean by relative terms such as importance or feasibility). Each group member independently expresses his opinion either qualitatively or quantitatively. There is no interaction among group members at this point. The information developed by group members is sent to the monitor team which analyzes the information, summarizes it, and returns to the group members the group consensus. If there is significant disagreement among group members, that disagreement is explored in the third phase to bring out the underlying reasons for the differences and possibly to evaluate them. One assumes that the monitor team provides this evidence to the group members because the latter have no means of communicating among themselves.

The last phase, the final evaluation, occurs when all previously gathered information has been analyzed and the evaluations have been fed back for consideration.

The four phases described are general ones. More specifically the tasks required of the monitor group can be summarized as follows:

Phase 1

1. *Selection of the topic to be investigated.* Here one must be certain that the topic is appropriate for the use of Delphi. What is the probability that Delphi will be successful? The answer to this question is not only a technical one but one of financial, logistical, and scheduling dimensions. For example, does an appropriate respondent group exist? Will they cooperate? Is there time enough to perform a satisfactory Delphi?

2. *Selection of the respondent group.* This requires personal, mail, or telephone contacts. What selection criteria should be applied? How much expertise is needed? Does a prospective member of the group have crippling biases or personality constraints?

In this connection, Salancik et al. (1971) suggest that one means of establishing a group of experts is to ask the participants what questions they felt qualified to answer, and determine their familiarity with the information required to make a response. Results demonstrated that experts showed greater consensus than nonexperts and provided more valid information. Helmer (1965, 1967a and b) showed that an improved forecast was made by utilizing only those responses that were made by individuals who ranked themselves highly competent with regard to the questions.

3. *Development of Delphi instructions.* The analyst must examine the dimensions of the problem to determine what information should be given to respondents. How shall the Delphi game be played: rigidly, flexibly? It will be necessary to write very specific instructions for players to follow because it is impossible for players to ask questions of the moderator. It will also be necessary to pretest these instructions by exposing them to subjects similar in background to the respondent group.

The selection of question format is an important consideration (Cyphert and Gant, 1970). They found that unstructured questions resulted in a significant decrease in Delphi participation.

4. *Determination of data analysis methodology.* How shall the responses be analyzed? With what statistics? Will a computer be available?

Phase 2

1. *Transmission by mail (usually) of instructions to respondent group.* Participants respond and mail responses back to monitor group.

2. *Analysis of the information provided, summarization and development of the second round materials.* In phase 1 a plan was adopted for analysis (mean, median, standard deviation) of the first round data. Delphi scales for qualitative data allow respondents to rate the importance of information, confidence in judgment, desirability of potential solution, probability of event occurrence, and feasibility of solution.

Questions to be answered are: Are the statistics originally conceptualized satisfactory for the data as received? Can they be improved? Does the heterogeneity of the group response indicate a possible failure to understand the instructions, a systematic bias in one direction or another, or a polarization? Will new instructions be required?

Phase 3

1. *Transmission to respondents of first round summary and further instructions.* (Respondent group performs and transmits in turn its second round responses.)

2. Further analysis and documentation in accordance with step 2 of phase 2.

Phase 4

1. *Transmission of second round summary and further instructions to respondents.* (Respondent group performs and transmits its responses.)

2. Repeat step 2 phase 2.

There are no fixed number of Delphi iterations or rounds. It all depends on the amount of respondent variability and how quickly it can be reduced. Also there is the question of how much the respondents will stand for, because the process is infinitely tedious and most respondents cannot stand up under many rounds.

Superficially Delphi is a simple concept that can easily be implemented, but it is easy enough to fail. Linstone and Turoff (1979) suggest that there are perhaps as many who have had disappointing experiences with Delphi as those who have been pleased. Among the possible reasons for nonsuccess are: failure to select an appropriate respondent group; overspecifying and constraining the structure of Delphi; inadequate instructions and summarization of responses so that a common interpretation of the evaluation scales used in the exercise is not achieved; ignoring disagreements so that dissenters become discouraged and drop out; failing to compensate respondents for their efforts, or otherwise failing to recognize the demands imposed on respondents by Delphi.

Data Intergration

When the response data are quantifiable, the range and median of the response values are computed and then provided to each participant in every round. Considering this information, the participants are requested to revise their previous responses if they choose.

Special Problems

Some disadvantages are inherent in the Delphi. Time and costs, for example, can become prohibitive, as noted by Craver (1972). He reported that it took seven months to select participants and to prepare, process, and edit the Delphi materials. Communication among Delphi participants concerning the issues under study may affect the resultant consensus. A participant may not express his true opinion when he knows that others may disapprove. The objective of Delphi may change as the rounds progress. A participant with sufficient expertise during the initial stages may not be qualified as an expert in the concluding rounds, when the content area has changed. This possibility emphasizes the need for continued assessment of participants' expertise through succeeding Delphi rounds.

Additional guidelines for carrying out Delphi are:

1. There should be at least two monitors on the team so that one can check the other.
2. A month or more is needed to develop the first round questionnaire. A factual summary of background material is also usually supplied and in some cases single or multiple sets of scenarios, for example future economic conditions such as the inflation rate.
3. Each questionnaire should be pretested on coworkers who were not involved in the design. This will help identify confusing items.
4. Compound statements to be voted upon should be avoided or broken into two separate items.
5. Since the participants, if new to Delphi, will probably respond with compound, lengthy comments, a sample of a desired response format should be sent them along with the questionnaire (e.g., short, specific, singular).
6. The respondents should be allowed to suggest changes in the wording of items which should then be introduced as new items. Voting on an item is very sensitive to wording.

When asking for further votes on an item, the individual respondent should be shown his original vote. He should also be provided two copies of the questionnaire so that he can use one for rough work or retain it for later reference.

Since the respondents must be convinced that they are participating in an exercise which involves a peer group, it is usually necessary in the letter of invitation to indicate the types of backgrounds reflected in the participant group. In some cases a list of participants should be provided if there is no other effective way of convincing the group of the significance of the exercise.

With regard to the validity of this technique, the reader will recall from Chapter 9 that a comparison of Delphi with other group consensus methods did not prove particularly advantageous to Delphi. Delphi validity is in any case difficult to measure because the product of the technique is usually a forecast or an extremely complex analysis. Empirical measurement of the forecasted or analyzed events may be impossible. An exception is a study by Gray and Niles (1983) which reported very accurate forecasts of development in the personal computer field. Those who are proponents of Delphi (Helmer, 1967a, b; Turoff, 1970; Dalkey, Brown and Cochran, 1969; Brown and Helmer, 1964; and Salancik, Wenger and Helfer, 1971) naturally interpret it favorably. Others (Sackman, 1975; Rohrbaugh, 1979) are less complimentary. It may be that the traditional concept of validity has no significance in Delphi, that its value exists only in its being a tool to sharpen decision making.

POLICY CAPTURING

Rating is an extremely common means of selecting candidates, setting policy, or evaluating personnel or alternative strategies. Where multiple cues are used to make these assessments, we often wish to know the basis on which these judgments have been made. Suppose, for example, we wish to know what factors in the opinion of maintenance technicians are most important in determining maintenance efficiency? We ask them to rate some hypothesized factors and relate their ratings to some overall judgment they make of maintenance efficiency.

The policy of a rater has been defined as "what raters do" when they respond to a series of stimuli (Naylor and Wherry, 1965). The rater's policy can be captured to the extent that one can predict the actions of a rater from the known characteristics of the stimuli to be evaluated. For example, suppose we ask judges to rank 10 salesmen in terms of overall competence, and four factors enter into that judgment; knowledge of the product, motivation, ability to communicate information, and energy. If we could predict the overall ranking by a particular judge, using his judgments on these four factors, we would have captured that judge's policy in terms of the factors he considered most important.

A number of policy capturing methods (e.g., Christal, 1963, 1968; Madden, 1963; Naylor and Wherry, 1965; Bottenberg and Christal, 1968) have been developed to represent the way people weight information or cues in making global judgments about some set of stimuli. Since this is not a textbook on mathematic statistics we will not go into the mathematics of these models. The interested reader should consult the sources.

The general methodology for generating a rater's policy is by performing a multiple regression analysis with cues as independent variables and the rater's global judgments as the dependent variable. The vector of regression weights represents the rater's policy. Each of these weights may be thought of as an index of importance. A relatively high regression weight for a particular cue implies that the cue is important to the rater for making judgments about dependent variable stimuli.

Smaller regression weights indicate cues of lesser importance to the rater. Thus a rater's policy or the way he uses cue information to form global impressions can be captured in the form of a multiple regression equation which describes his use of cues in making these overall judgments.

It is, naturally, not quite so simple. The usefulness of policy capturing has been thought to be limited to the case in which the evaluative cues are uncorrelated. Otherwise the various indices of cue importance often do not agree. Lane, Murphy and Marques (1982) argue that an orthogonal cue structure is not an assumption necessary for inferring importance from regression weights, and that the rater's use of a linear model does not prevent the method from providing a reasonably accurate description of human decisions.

The size of the multiple correlation between cues and the overall judgments indicates the degree to which the rater's evaluations are predictable by linear regression. Two factors may cause this multiple R to be less than 1.00—a configural or nonlinear rating strategy, or an inconsistent policy. Although many judgments are related to each other in a nonlinear manner, Goldberg (1970) and Slovic and Lichtenstein (1971) among others have concluded that raters very seldom configure their rating strategies. That is, a linear model accounts for almost all of the variance in judgments across a variety of rating tasks. Consequently, the major part of the difference between obtained R and 1.00 can be expected to be related to inconsistency in rater policy. This result can be used to assess the consistency of a rater group's composite policy. A relatively low R for a group of raters indicates that the group's composite policy is inconsistent. This in turn implies that different raters in the group are using different policies. Conversely, a relatively high R for a rater group suggests that the raters in the group have similar policies.

Policy capturing is validated by making a prediction of new ratings based on regression analysis of previous ratings. For example, if 200 judgments were made by the same raters, they could be split into two sets of 100. The policy used in the initial sample of 100 would be determined and verified (validated) by determining how well the resulting equation predicted the actual judgments made in the second sample of 100. From that standpoint, there is little new about policy capturing as a technique. Ratings are made as they would be ordinarily, after which they are treated mathematically.

The important question is whether the technique has been applied and has been useful. Christal (1968) reports that many studies were performed in the Air Force's Personnel Research Laboratory. The resultant equations have held up on cross-application. For example, equations developed to simulate officer promotion boards predict with great accuracy the ratings a board will give to officers under consideration (Christal, 1965). Equations were developed to simulate the actions of career counselors in making initial assignment of airmen graduating from basic training (Naylor and Wherry, 1964). These equations were then used in an operational computer aided assignment system. Dunnette and Borman (1974) utilized policy capturing to develop an index of naval personnel status.

Although the policy capturing methodology was developed under military auspices, it can be used just as effectively in civilian applications—in studying police promotion procedures, for example, the effectiveness of workers or the quality of beefsteaks.

Before one begins a policy capturing study, however, one must first develop valid and reliable rating scales for the factors to be captured. This may be more difficult than performing the mechanics of policy capturing.

ACCIDENT INVESTIGATIONS

An accident is an unanticipated event which damages the system and/or the individual or affects the accomplishment of the system mission or the individual's task. Accidents are a major social/industrial/economic problem. Figures given by Pimble and O'Toole (1982) suggest that the cost to British industry in one year (April 1978-April 1979) was around 585 million pounds. It cannot be much less for the United States and other industrialized countries. Precise criteria of what constitutes an accident for reporting purposes are a matter of some controversy. Suchman (1961a, b, cited in Hale and Hale, 1972) refers to

1. low degree of expectedness, avoidability, and intention;
2. the production of injury; and
3. the duration of occurrence as criteria. The more indicators are present, the more likely it is that an event will be called an accident.

Many accident investigations are mandated by law. For example, the Federal Aviation Administration (FAA) performs an investigation of every aircraft accident to determine its cause. Local law enforcement agencies investigate automobile accidents. The purpose of the investigation is not only to assess blame but to determine the causal factors and thus to redesign the system or modify procedures to avoid further accidents.

Accident or safety research is performed to determine the causal factors of accidents in general. In the course of that research statistics are collected of accidents in industry, on the highway, and the home.

In this chapter we are concerned primarily with the behavioral aspects of accident investigation. Unfortunately, the ergonomic contribution to accident research has been slight. Indeed the involvement of industrial psychologists and ergonomists in industrial safety is low. Adams and Hartwell (1977) point out that of the 355 references in a comprehensive review of the literature (Hale and Hale, 1972) only 126 references are taken from psychological or ergonomic sources. There is very little ergonomic information provided in the typical accident reporting form, and indeed accident reporting systems as a whole provide very little information to management and few improvements are based upon them (Adams and Hartwell, 1977).

The methods used in accident investigation are familiar to the reader: interviews, questionnaires, checklists, and data recording forms. Since the accident is always unexpected, it can be observed only by a participant or observer—and all the information that can be supplied is post facto. In most accidents there is no possibility of securing many objective measures (with the possible exception of aircraft instrument recorders), so the participant or witness acts as a reporter of the events that occurred.

The effort in accident research is to get a sufficiently large, valid, and reliable database so that acceptable conclusions can be derived from it. Often this is difficult to do because those with the responsibility of gathering these data do so only in a half-hearted way. Adams and Hartwell (1977) point out that "the statistics typically prepared by a plant or industry . . . provide very little information that is of direct use to management . . . the current accident-reporting systems do not generate as much information as they might" (p. 285–6).

The initial problem in accident investigation research is to determine what questions to ask of participants and witnesses and then how best to ask these questions. There have been efforts to develop standard forms but the idiosyncratic nature of most accidents makes this difficult. A completely satisfactory method of investigating the human factors aspects of accidents has not yet been developed (Fegetter, 1982).

Traditional accident investigation techniques, for aircraft, at any rate, have concentrated on the search for a technical or mechanical failure together with routine examination of pilot statements to confirm that regulations have been obeyed. If these are violated, the report is made of pilot error. Of course this does not tell us what we really want to know—why the pilot erred.

Because there are both advantages and disadvantages to interviews and questionnaires, Fegetter (1982) emphasizes a checklist which would be utilized along with an interview. Indeed this checklist is essentially a series of headings around which an interview is organized: sensors, perception, attention, memory, etc.; visual illusions resulting from fog, refraction, ground texture; false hypotheses; habits; motivation; experience and skills; personality factors; fear, social pressure, role conflict, physical, psychological and environmental stress; and ergonomics (cockpit arrangement, etc.).

The checklist is designed as an interview aid. The interview takes place privately and begins with an explanation about its purpose. The interviewee is told that the human factors report is confidential and that the interview is not concerned with blame but with accident prevention. The interviewee is asked to describe in his own words the events leading up to the accident. Once the investigator has recorded the event history, he asks for clarifications of meanings of words or phrases and notes any apparent gaps in the account, any special emphasis, or any distortion. These are followed up. It may be necessary to ask about events several years prior to the accident, reasons why the individual took up flying and his attitude toward it. Fegetter (1982) indicates that during the interview the investigator assesses the personality of the subject, but this may be expecting more of the investigator than he can reasonably do.

Another ergonomic accident investigation technique is a bit more theoretical, focusing specifically on task analysis and task demands (Drury and Brill, 1983). They conclude that task analysis is applicable to accidents because all accidents involve goal directed activity. The operator is conceptualized as being composed of a number of subsystems, for example, anthropometric, metabolic, or environmental, that may limit human performance. The need is to match task demands (those required to operate/maintain an equipment) against these limiting subsystems. Where there is a significant mismatch, an accident is more likely.

It should be noted that theories of accident causation have had only slight influence on accident investigation. Many of the causal mechanisms hypothesized are covert and difficult to unearth. The following have been advanced as predisposing to accidents: operator accident proneness, poor work behavior and motivation, operator stress, human error, inadequacies in system design that lead to unsafe conditions, inadequate training, undesirable social conditions, even an unconscious desire to be hurt. Task analysis is not the only methodology available. An alternative technique (Saari, 1976) uses a checklist like Fegetter's to focus the analyst's attention on potential man–machine interface problems.

A distinction must be made between accident investigations and accident reporting. The report should be the output or the product of the investigation but often —usually—is not. In many if not most industrial accidents there is no investigation and an accident report, based on the worker's or supervisor's statement, is issued only to comply with legal or insurance requirements. The investigation is always more intensive and probing than the report. Hence one finds it in use primarily in situations in which there has been loss of life.

Accident reporting begins of course with the accident report form and considerable attention has been paid to the information categories on that form and how it is to be reported. If the form is too complex or time consuming, it will be incorrectly filled in or not returned at all because no one will spare the time to do it properly. Beaumont (1980) estimates that accidents in manufacturing are probably underreported by 15 to 20 percent.

On the other hand, the report must be exhaustive if it is to be useful for formulation of accident prevention policies. Contrast the requirement for a short reporting form with the large number of categories recommended by Fegetter (1982) for human factors investigations of aircraft accidents.

Few researchers are satisfied with the report forms in current use. The design of the report form probably contributes significantly to the poor quality of the information provided. There have been many attempts to arrive at a more acceptable and comprehensive report form (Hartwell, 1973; Hale, 1974) but no general agreement on such a standardized form has been achieved.

Adams et al. (1981) and Edwards (1981) have suggested that report forms should satisfy the criteria of a good questionnaire because the report writing skills of users may not be very high. Many people are incapable of writing a narrative type description of the accident and the factors that influence it. For that reason some suggest the use of checklists. Adams et al. (1981) would use checklists to emphasize causes rather than effects. On the other hand, long checklists, required if the report is to be exhaustive, may be incorrectly completed by personnel in a hurry. Moreover, the use of a checklist or report form suggests that the information will be provided without the guidance of an accident specialist.

It is important to emphasize in all accident reports the circumstances leading up to an accident; to discover the failure rates of machinery, equipment, and operators and to take these into account when work processes are analyzed and priorities set (Kletz, 1976; Lagerlof, 1980; Strandberg, 1980). Considerable detail is required. On the other hand, the accident form must be completed quickly by witnesses to the accident because memory loss occurs quickly.

It is important to include in the accident report any deviation from the norm (near misses and "trivial" events) (Kjellan, 1980; Carlsson, 1980; Adams, 1974).

The items of information the accident investigator wishes to collect in any accident report include:

1. Did the accident occur on the job or off? To whom did the accident occur? The person's age? Experience? Was the person performing under supervision or independently? Was the person working to a written procedure or on the basis of a learned skill? Was the procedure consulted during the work or was it merely remembered?
2. What piece of equipment was involved? What job function was being performed?
3. When did the accident occur? Were there any abnormal environmental occurrences (e.g., rain, fog, etc.) at the time of the accident?
4. What were the activities performed by the equipment and by the operator immediately preceding the accident?
5. What was the nature of the accident? What took place?
6. What were the effects of the accident?
7. Did the operator or anyone else notice any deviant conditions (e.g., meter readings beyond normal) in the equipment at the time the accident occurred?
8. What does the operator think is the immediate cause of the accident?
9. What does the operator think is the long-term underlying cause of the accident?

These questions are based on a system model such as that of Edwards (1982) in which the accident is viewed as a failure for which the system as a whole is responsible, and any system element or element interaction may be the accident cause. The operator's performance is influenced by performance shaping factors (Chapter 5). The operator's performance may be affected by the stimulus inputs to the operator at the time of the accident and the person's cognitive and emotional responses to those inputs.

Accident investigation has much in common with problem investigation (described in Chapter 8). Indeed, the two may coincide, as in the study performed by Harris (1983) of the behavioral causes of a series of boiler near-explosions on U. S. Navy ships. In this situation Harris was not investigating a particular explosion which had occurred in the past but rather the potential for explosions (based on near-accidents). His data were obtained from interviews, observations of how the boiler lighting-off and monitoring operations occurred aboard ships, and reference to operating manuals. The investigation began with development of a list of conditions that could be forerunners of explosion. Respondents were asked: If this condition were present, what indications would you notice during job performance? Interviewees were asked to describe visual, auditory, vibratory, and thermal indications of potential explosions. As suggested by Fegetter (1982), the interviews ranged far afield to deal with issues such as training, morale, workload, etc. Personnel were observed to see whether they followed standard operating procedures. The guidance documents they received were examined for clarity of expression. Their training was reviewed to determine if it provided the information needed to follow standard procedures. The adequacy of boilermen's knowledge was evaluated by their direct responses to questions about knowledge and their scores on qualification tests. The data gathered were only in few instances quantitative. In accident investigations as in problem investigations the solutions usually derive from qualitative rather than quantitative conclusions.

One of the major foci of accident research is the effort to predict accident frequency, using probabilistic statistics. The difficulty in this situation is entirely analogous to the prediction of human error (Chapter 5) in that it is necessary to determine the opportunities for error or accidents. This is often difficult to do in making cross-occupational comparisons because occupational classifications vary depending on the particular use made of them (Pimble and O'Toole, 1980). Thus the classification used for salary calculations is not necessarily related to that used for accident records. Industries sometimes change their job classifications, combining some occupations under common headings, or they create new jobs.

Taxonomies are therefore important in accident research because of the need to make cross-industry comparisons. Pimble and O'Toole (1980) found that few job descriptions were available in British industry and so it was difficult to ensure that jobs with the same title were comparable across different industries. Moreover, it is likely that accident reporting rates of different firms vary considerably. Those industries with the highest recorded accident rates may be those with the most efficient safety practices and reporting procedures.

Because of such problems, comparisons between industries are probably meaningless at present. Still, figures from within a particular industry, if treated in an identical manner each year, can be extremely useful in highlighting areas requiring further investigation, such as age groups most at risk.

Within most industries the coding of accident data is carried out by someone other than the one who reported the accident. This means that errors of omission and commission are compounded.

Adams and Harwell (1977) raise the question of how much reliance can be placed on current accident statistics, given the unknown amount of underreporting, biased reporting, and inaccurate categorizations. There is also a lack of sufficient research on accident reporting and inadequate effort in the development of more effective accident reporting systems. One can establish, as Senneck (1974) does, criteria of how an accident reporting system should function, but these criteria are molar and idealistic and there appears to be no very clear way of moving from these goals to a specific reporting system.

WORK SAMPLE TESTS

There are, in general, two ways in which one can measure job performance: *on-the-job measurement* (OJM) and measurement of performance in some situation that deviates from the job condition. OJM represents the only completely valid work measurement situation and is therefore to be preferred to any other variety. There are situations in which it is not feasible to measure on the job. Then again, there are certain advantages to off-job measurement, one of which is greater control from an experimental standpoint. Chapter 8 pointed out that OJM may be contaminated by interferences from extraneous sources, inability to control the measurement situation sufficiently, and lack of cooperation by management.

Where OJM is not feasible, it is common to develop what can be termed *work sample tests* to represent or simulate OJM. A work sample test can be defined as an artificially created situation in which individuals are asked to perform tasks that are considered to be representative of the actual job, either because they contain tasks identical with those performed on the job, or because the work sample tasks contain qualities or impose requirements which the actual job presumably possesses or requires. There is always some artificiality about the work sample test because even when it includes actual tasks performed on the job these tests are abstracted from the job environment and are performed outside the job routine.

Work sample tests are utilized in a variety of situations.

1. For selection of an applicant for a job. If the work sample test accurately represents job requirements, and if the applicant does well on the test, it is hypothesized that he will do well on the job (see Siegel, 1978).

2. For measurement of training effectiveness. Before being graduated to the actual job, the trainee may be asked to perform one or more of the tasks he will encounter later. A trainee for the radioman's position may for example be given a simple radio with a fault inserted and required to find the fault. A physical simulator is a sort of work sample test, particularly if it presents only a part–task situation.

3. For measurement of job proficiency. While it may be preferable to measure a worker's proficiency through OJM, the number of tasks performed on the job may be so great that an inordinate length of time would be consumed measuring performance on all of them. Alternatively, there may be some tasks that are so rarely performed, or performed only in an emergency, that a synthetic task is the only practical substitute (this is particularly the case for emergency tasks).

4. For research to discover certain general responses to various job dimensions. The need to control conditions of administration for research purposes might require some sort of work sample test because tests can be more readily controlled than can OJM. The synthetic test situations described in Chapter 3 to study the effects of stress (Chiles, Alluisi, and Adams, 1968) are an example of generalized work sample tasks for research purposes.

The work sample test has certain implications:

1. Where it is impossible to measure the individual's performance on the job, the researcher selects from the actual job certain tasks supposed to be representative of that job or which are modeled on the skills the job requires. The relationship of the tasks selected to the actual job is critical because, for example, preemployment tests which are not clearly and directly job-related are illegal in the United States. The basis for selecting work sample tasks from the job are criteria such as criticality, frequency of performance, complexity or the demand these tasks presumably impose on the performer. A prior function/task/job analysis will help determine job required capabilities.

2. Since what the researcher presents to the applicant, the trainee, the job incumbent, or the research subject is not the actual job itself, he is presenting a simulation. The question of simulation fidelity, or the degree to which certain characteristics of the actual job must be included in the work sample test, becomes important. It will therefore be necessary for us to say a few words about simulation fidelity, although the topic is so broad and has so long a history that we cannot present a comprehensive discussion of this topic. The paper by Hays (1980) is useful.

3. Since the work sample test is an abstraction of OJM, not actual OJM, the question naturally arises: How well does the sample test predict performance on the job or training effectiveness? This is a question of validity.

Work sample tests are expensive to develop and to administer. In consequence, in the military at any rate, there has been much greater reliance on job information/knowledge tests (Vineberg and Joyner, 1982). Policies related to civil rights in employment have led to greater interest in work sample testing.

Work Sample Tests for Selection

Work sample tests for selection are practically mandated by government regulations which require selection tests to be directly related to job requirements. In fact, the interest in work sample tests for selection purposes has stemmed largely from that requirement. Adverse impact on minorities and women is illegal, and according to the Uniform Guidelines on Employee Selection Procedures (1978), adverse impact exists whenever the selection rate for any race, sex or ethnic group is less than 80 percent of the rate for the group with the highest rate.

The procedure used to develop selection work sample tests has been described in detail by Plumlee (1975) and here we shall simply outline that procedure.

1. One starts, as always, with a comprehensive job/task analysis and all that that implies: what the worker does, the procedures performed, equipment and tools used, end product, the knowledges, skills, and abilities required (including entry level requirements).

2. The tasks to be tested are selected on the basis of criteria of criticality, error consequences, difficulty level, frequency, and average performance time (in that order of priority). Practical considerations enter here. Some tasks may be too difficult or too lengthy to test without, in some fashion, abstracting their major dimensions.

3. A decision is made whether to test for a developed skill or the aptitude for developing the skill. The consideration here is whether the job is sufficiently specialized that special training must be given (e.g., as in the case of police training), whether one can draw from an already experienced pool of applicants (e.g., welders), or whether one is throwing the job open to the nonskilled because of governmental requirement (e.g., affirmative action decrees, etc.).

If the objective of the performance test is to assess developed skills, then actual work samples can be presented to the applicants. If the objective is to assess aptitude for developing a skill, the work samples can be simulated or synthetic. Here too, one has a choice. One can abstract part–tasks that are considered most representative of total task requirements and have the applicant perform these. For example, Cascio and Phillips (1979) report testing for a concession attendant's position in which the applicant had to count cash, make change from a register, fill out a revenue report, etc.

Alternatively, one might develop or utilize a test of the abilities required to perform a job, assuming one can determine the essence of those abilities. For example, if a task required great manual dexterity, one might use one of the standard tests of manual dexterity like the Purdue Pegboard. This procedure presents difficulties, however. Fleishman (1953, 1954) concluded that simple motor skills tests have shown insignificant validities and indeed Asher and Sciarino (1974) found that validity coefficients (as determined by relationship of test scores to job proficiency measures) were usually lower for special aptitude tests.

4. Quantitative standards for acceptable performance and the relative weight to be assigned to other relevant criteria such as quality, speed, or safety are determined, again on the basis of information derived from the job/task analysis.

5. If observers who are performance raters are involved, instructions for these personnel must be developed and they must be trained. Nugent, Laabs and Panell (1982) found that the degree of structure imposed on the rating situation significantly affected rating performance. Professionals in the various work areas should be used as raters (see Cascio and Phillips, 1979, for a description of how such raters are trained to perform). Rater training is particularly important because skill in a particular work area does not necessarily translate to more accurate, reliable rating (Nugent et al., 1982).

6. Scoring or rating procedures are developed.

7. And most important, a preliminary tryout of each test, with revisions as required, is necessary.

The proof of the pudding for work sample tests is in the validities they achieve when measured against one or more job performance criteria. Asher and Sciarino (1974) divided the studies they reviewed into two categories: motor and verbal. Most of the validities reported were significant at beyond the .01 statistical level.

Robertson and Kandola (1982), carrying on the work of Asher and Sciarrino, reviewed data from over 60 different validation studies, some with multiple validity criteria. They categorized the types of tests as psychomotor, situational decision making, job related information and group discussion. Only coefficients based on sample sizes of 20 or more were considered. Psychomotor and job related information tests had the highest validity coefficients (median of .39 and .40 respectively, although the range is very great). Situational decision making was the weakest of the four categories and had the lowest median, the greatest proportion of coefficients below 0.30 and the smallest proportion above 0.50.

These studies used various measures of criterion performance. Some of the studies concentrated on job related criteria such as supervisors' ratings or production data, others measured performance at the end of training, and so on. The different types of criteria used may be grouped into four categories:

1. Job performance criteria (mostly supervisors' ratings, but occasionally including production data);
2. Job progress criteria (usually measures of job level or salary);
3. Training criteria (exam performance or instructor ratings) and;
4. Work sample criteria, that is, performance on another work sample test (usually longer than the predictor test).

Referring again to the Robertson and Kandola (1982) study, psychomotor and group discussion tests had the highest median validities (.44 and .35 respectively) when job performance criteria are used. This suggests that the comparatively good validities obtained for job related information tests are enhanced by the use of training criteria. Job related information tests do not seem to produce such good validities (.21) when job performance criteria are employed.

As Cascio and Phillips (1979) found, excluding biographical data, psychomotor work sample tests produce better validities than any of the more conventional tests.

Siegel (1983) has described the validities he has found in using a minature job training and evaluation situation as a personnel selection device. He and his collaborators (Siegel and Wiesen, 1977) developed a battery of nine miniature job training level exercises and administered them to 140 Navy recruits who had been determined on the basis of paper and pencil tests to be ineligible for assignment to a Navy school. Multiple correlation coefficients between test results and assessor estimates of probability of success on the job were .68, .81 and .65, compared to correlations with paper and pencil tests of .12, .41 and .23. Unfortunately, validation scores gathered after subjects were in the Navy 9 and 18 months were only .37 and .30 (based on supervisor ratings).

The relatively low correlations found in work sample tests for selection have been emphasized by Vineberg and Joyner (1982). They found in their review of military studies of job performance predictions that correlations between job sample tests of proficiency and paper and pencil tests of job knowledge were generally low, between .00 and .30. This may be because knowledge tests and job sample tests measure different components of performance. Knowledge tests are developed by instructional personnel and the material is often derived from general descriptions of procedures or information based on theory, not on the way in which the actual job is performed. The problem of determining validity is complicated by the fact that the major validation criterion used, supervisor ratings, is quite weak.

Work Sample Training Tests

Where there are many tasks to be performed under many conditions, as in equipment maintenance, it may not be feasible to provide training on, or test all, of them. The training specialist could then select some smaller number of tasks and situations from the total job, those most critical or frequently required. Or he could perhaps combine parts of all the tasks into a new (but supposedly representative) set of tasks. In either case, what he is doing is creating a work sample. In developing tests to be given during or following training on these tasks, he also constructs a work sample test. Such a test should be as similar to the operational job as possible, because what one hopes to measure is anticipated proficiency on the job. However, many training establishments, paraticularly those of the military, fail to satisfy this criterion because it is more difficult to construct operationally similar work samples and work sample tests than to simplify them artificially.

Unfortunately, in the training situation complete test fidelity to the characteristics of the operational job may be quite expensive. A single aircraft simulator, for example, may cost millions of dollars to develop and fabricate. Moreover, it is not quite clear just how much increased training/testing effectiveness one receives for a given degree of operational fidelity (see discussion in Chapter 8). The two primary questions that need to be answered in developing training work sample tasks and tests are: How much simulation fidelity is required? Which aspects of the job and the equipment require simulation and which do not? Unfortunately the answers to these questions, despite an extensive search for general principles of simulation fidelity, may depend on the characteristics of the individual job and its equipment. In general, military and industrial training establishments do very well in reproducing the physical aspects of the job, but less well with the behavioral aspects. Stimuli are often correct but artificially simplified, lacking the complexity of the operational environment and thus adequate only for novice training. For example, in teaching students to interpret radar stimuli (and needless to say, in testing them) the many characteristics such as fog, rain, and beam inversion that complicate the actual stimuli are often lacking.

Apart from fidelity, criteria for selecting training/test work sample tasks are the same as those for personnel selection, e.g., criticality, frequency of usage, etc. The validity of training and of tests to measure training effectiveness is largely unknown because very few transfer studies to the job environment are ever performed (but see Siegel, 1978).

Work Sample Tests for Measurement of Proficiency

The optimal environment for measurement of operator proficiency is, as we said, the job environment itself. Often there are compelling reasons why this is not feasible. If the population to be measured is large and the intent is to determine population norms rather than individual effectiveness, it may be more practical to develop special tests which represent the range of activities to be sampled and to administer these to a sample of the total population.

Such work sample tests containing a number of tasks can be dealt with psychometrically just like any other test material. Two tasks testing the capability to perform the same function can presumably be treated as equivalent tests for test/retest or split-half reliability purposes.

It is necessary to validate these measurement tasks or tests by some other criterion measurement of actual job proficiency. Unfortunately, the most commonly used external measure of job proficiency is the supervisor's global rating which has been found to be quite inadequate (e.g., Vineberg and Joyner, 1978; Dunnette and Borman, 1979). One could of course attempt to collect on-the-job proficiency measures to validate the work sample test results, but to secure a satisfactory sample of on-the-job performance would be almost as much trouble as the on-the-job data collection one attempts to avoid by developing work sample tests. In this situation most researchers probably resort to supervisor ratings, peer ratings or ranking or some other technique that is relatiely easy to administer.

Work Sample Tests for Research

One can also use work sample tests as a tool to perform research and to test hypothesized variables and their interrelationships. The general methodology is to examine the characteristics of the real world job one wishes to simulate. The researcher then creates one or more tasks which incorporate the underlying behavioral processes of those tasks and thus makes it unnecessary to measure actual job performance. Having developed what one might call a generic task(s), results secured with this task can be generalized to apply to many individual task situations. This also avoids the constraint of being tied too closely to a specific real world situation, which would reduce the generalizability of findings.

Examples of this procedure abound. A prime example are the tasks developed by various researchers to study vigilance or alertness phenomena. Mackworth (1950) developed his famous Clock Test by first noting the conditions under which radar operators worked: the monitoring task was prolonged; often the task was a matter of waiting for nothing to happen. False alarms were not unusual, for example, target and nontarget stimuli were often indistinguishable. The operator worked in relative isolation and the object of the operator's search was difficult to discriminate, being a small spot of light on a screen covered in noise. The visual signal, when it appeared, was brief and the time limit for action short (Mackworth, 1950).

The Clock Test simulated the essentials of the radar operator's task while permitting strict experimental controls to be applied. Subjects watched a rotating black pointer six inches in length which described a circle on a blank white background in discrete steps. Each jump of the pointer took 1 second, and 100 of these completed a circle. Subjects were instructed that at irregular intervals the point would move through twice its usual distance. This double jump was the signal to which subjects were required to respond by pressing a key. A response made within 8 seconds after signal occurrence was a correct detection. Twelve signals were presented in each half hour of the two hour task at various intervals. The last 10 minutes of each half hour contained no signals; the temporal sequence of signals was repeated in each 30 minutes of the task. Subjects were not allowed to wear watches and had difficulty in estimating how long they had been at the task.

There are other examples. Chiles, Alluisi and Adams (1968) developed a special equipment to study work schedules and performance during confinement using not a single function but several in a workload context (see Chapter 3).

The measures taken had to be meaningfully related to critical operational tasks but also had to maximize the generalizability of the results. This led to a rejection of the exact simulation approach (essentially duplication of an operational equipment and procedures), which in addition to constraining generalizability, also presented problems of equipment complexity, unreliability, and expense. On the other hand, to have developed an equipment that simulated a class of system functions without relevance to real world tasks would also be of little use since all systems require much the same range of behaviors.

The identification of the performance functions to be included in the test equipment was based on rational analysis of the tasks required in the kind of systems to which generalization was desired. This was difficult because no useful catalogue of operator tasks existed then nor does even now.

Selection of the performance tasks to be measured was based on the following criteria.

1. The tasks must measure functions performed by operators in advanced systems.

2. The tasks must appear to the subject to give the appearance of measuring something valid and important (if the subject did not think so, variations in his performance might simply reflect changes in his motivation).

3. Test retest and equipment reliability of the tasks must be satisfactory.

4. If the tasks were independent processes, the task measures must be orthogonal.

5. The task must be sensitive to performance impairment, but not so sensitive that it responded to too many operationally unimportant factors.

6. Asymptotic levels of performance had to be achievable within a reasonable training time.

7. Functions would have to be time-shared because this is characteristic of many operational systems and measurement of each function separately (as in traditional laboratory studies) would be quite artificial. These criteria can be applied to the development of any set of synthetic tasks.

The functions Chiles et al. selected for development were monitoring of system status, discrimination among stimuli, operation or storage of information, control manipulation, and communication. For each of these functions a task was developed. Monitoring of static processes was represented by warning lights and an auditory vigilance task. Monitoring of dynamic processes involved meters which fluctuated apparently randomly about an average reading at the 12 o'clock position. Stimulus discrimination (target identification) involved a 6 × 6 array of lights. Information processing was represented by arithmetic computations; procedural performance by a code-lock task in which information from different sources had to be analyzed to determine the key that would "unlock" the code. The whole was performed in a two-hour schedule.

More recently a battery of synthetic tasks is under development by Kennedy and his co-workers at the Naval Biodynamics Laboratory (Carter, Kennedy and Bittner, 1980). However, their tasks which are much more molecular than those of Chiles et al. must be shown to be diagnostic of brain damage, sensitive to environmental stressors, or measure some aspects of information processing. Nevertheless, their selection process began as did Chiles et al., with the determination of criteria for selection. Criteria for development of the Navy tests are primarily statistical. They must be statistically suitable for repeated measurements before, during, and after experiencing an unusual environment. And they must be statistically stable and possess constant standard deviations and cross-session reliabilities.

Since this application of work sample tests is to a research program, the usual way of establishing validity or representativeness can be applied but only with difficulty, since there is no specific, single, actual job which the work sample tests are supposed to represent. One could of course compare conclusions reached from the research studies with the performance of actual personnel on jobs which the synthetic tasks simulated. More often researchers have preferred to rely on construct validity, the apparent correspondence between the operational characteristics of a work situation and the characteristics incorporated into the synthetic work sample tests.

The use of work sample tests is a convenience to overcome certain practical constraints. The trick of developing these tasks is to determine the significant operational characteristics of real tasks and to incorporate these dimensions into the synthetic task or test. To the extent that the developer or researcher achieves this, his task or test can be considered behaviorally valid. He has to do this by logical analysis and to a large extent by intuition, without having a very clear idea of what dimensions are necessary to the synthetic simulation or how much validity he has added by including one or the other characteristic.

BEHAVIORAL INSTRUMENTATION

An adequate description of instrumentation for behavioral purposes demands at least a short book but unfortunately the available literature fails to provide one. Sidowski's handbook (Sidowski, 1966) describes experimental methods more than instrumentation and it is oriented toward academic psychology rather than work related performance. His two reviews in the *American Psychologist* (Sidowski and Ross, 1969; Sidowski, 1975) cover only fragments of the available instrumentation and the major journal devoted to this topic, *Behavioral Research Methods and instrumentation,* concentrates most of its attention on specially developed devices, rather than general purpose instrumentation which can be commercially secured.

There are certain questions that require instrumentation for measurement.

1. What is the frequency of occurrence of certain behavioral events? Instrumentation in support of direct observation will be discussed later.

2. What did the human do in a specific situation? To answer this question the behavioral scientist can record what the subject did, using videotape (Crites, 1969; Potempa, Talcott, Loy and Swartz, 1970) or a tape recorder for recording communications or interviews; remote biotelemetry (Miklich, Purcell and Weiss, 1974) can be used to record personnel movement over large areas; the subject can use radio communication to report his behaviors in remote locations (Askren, Schwartz, Bower and Schmid, 1969); in more controlled situations, as when the subject is operating an experimental equipment, the equipment can be developed to record the subject's responses automatically. When measurement equipment is built into the equipment being operated, it is likely to be special purpose instrumentation and not available commercially.

3. What is the physiological state of the operator and how much effort does he exert? If the heart is of interest, one uses an electrocardiogram; if it is the brain, the electroencephalogram; if it is respiration, the recording spirometer; if blood pressure, the sphygmomanometer; and so on. The various physiological devices are described in great detail in Cromwell, Weibell, Pfeiffer and Usselman (1973). (See also Chapter Three.)

4. What is the status of the environment and its effect on personnel? Here we are concerned with light (photometer), heat (thermometer), noise (sound level meter), vibration and acceleration (accelerometer), and humidity (hygrometer). (For additional details, see Eastman Kodak, 1983.)

5. What is the physical capability of the operator? Here we consider such categories as: visual acuity (e.g., Bausch and Lomb ortho-rater); peripheral vision (perimeter); auditory acuity (hearing tester); and hand strength (dynamometer).

With the exception of special purpose instrumentation (which is often necessary), all the devices noted above are commercially available. What one selects depends on the particular question to be answered. There would be very little point, for example, in procuring physiologic instrumentation unless one had to answer questions about the operator's physiologic status. On the other hand, if the human factors specialist has a laboratory, it would be useful to have on hand light-, sound-, and (possibly) vibration-measuring equipment. For most behavioral research purposes videotaping and tape recording equipment are very useful. Those who anticipate making field observations would find it most useful to have computer aided data collection equipment.

Behavioral measurement equipment is fairly expensive. For many uses, such as describing what the operator has done, the investigator may find that cheaper, if less elegant, techniques may work almost as well and still be within his financial constraints.

The Computer in Performance Measurement

The most significant single advance in instrumentation has been the continuing refinement of the computer. The computer can be used to program and run experiments, to present questionnaires and psychometric tests to subjects and to record their responses, to conduct interactive dialogues with patients, to act as a teaching tool (computer assisted and computer managed instruction), and to aid field observation. If an equipment functions using computer processes, special software can be developed to record operator responses automatically.

Our concern in this discussion, which is based largely on Bailey, Hennessy and Wylie (1978), is the use of a computer in experimental measurement of subject performance. We disclaim any attempt to describe how computers function in an experimental mode (for this see Finkel, 1975). We will examine only those factors the researcher should consider in making the computer an element—perhaps the central element—in the experimental situation.

We presuppose a particular situation: the development of a manned system research laboratory (MSRL) which studies performance of personnel in a man-machine context, for example, operators in nuclear power plant control rooms or the combat information center of a Navy ship. Such a laboratory simulates the operational characteristics of a variety of systems without exactly reproducing the characteristics of any single one [the same rationale is involved here as those that impelled Chiles et al. (1968) to develop their synthetic task equipment; as discussed previously]. The laboratory will therefore include a number of operator consoles with discrete indicators, alphanumeric readouts, CRT displays, voice communication to interface team members, and input devices such as trackballs, buttons, lightpens, etc. In a physical space to accommodate at least three fairly large consoles and eight people, both individual operator and team studies will be performed. A major characteristic of a computer controlled laboratory is that the stimulus sequence of a simulated scenario must be programmed to be contingent upon subject actions. The computer system will control, synchronize, coordinate, and interface all aspects of that scenario.

Before beginning development of the computer controlled laboratory, it is necessary to ask and answer a number of questions.

1. For what type of research will the MSRL be used? This will largely determine the kind of behavioral instrumentation needed.
2. To what extent is simulation display fidelity important? The computer is the primary mechanism for achieving that fidelity and the greater the demand for fidelity, the more expensive the computer system will be.
3. Automatic performance monitoring will be part of MSRL. All subject inputs to the equipment controls will be recorded automatically. Are there, however, any special or additional data acquisition needs that do not come from subject inputs, for example, physiological measures, observational data, video, or audio recording?
4. Will the experimenter wish to intervene or control the scenario manually?

A critical guideline directing the development of the computer system is the need to be flexible. It must be relatively easy to change the application software and operator consoles to satisfy different research goals. Flexibility implies that the computer system software and consoles should have a high degree of modularity. If additional software routines or equipments need to be added or deleted for particular research purposes, it should be easy to do so.

An important consideration for flexible design is the amount of computer processing power required to support the anticipated research. If a computer system utilized a single *central processing unit* (CPU), it would have to have sufficient power to support the most complex experiment anticipated. It might be necessary to upgrade the computer system later as research needs increased. A better approach would be to use a distributed processing system. That is, rather than a single large computer, the use of several small computers, linked together, would allow the processing load to be distributed among the various CPUs. Additional processing power would be added in a modular fashion.

Another guideline is something called software intensiveness. This means that all aspects of the simulated system and requirements such as data gathering are under control of the computer system and all functions of the display and input devices are routed through the computer system. Under this approach, use of devices with built in functions is minimized. Information to or from the operator consoles can be routed throughout the entire system under software control. Rewiring should never be necessary to reroute information or change the function of any device. In a few cases, patch panels might be used for this purpose.

Software should be modular in the sense that each component should perform a definite function with as much generality of application as possible. By specifying algorithms for communications between modules, systems and applications programs can be synthesized in a building block fashion with only sufficient additional software required for specific details of a particular application. Applications programs should be written in as general form as possible so that they have potential use in future applications.

In determining the specifications of a computer system for extensive simulation of system operations, a number of questions arise. The first is, how much computing power is required? This is extremely difficult to quantify because the power requirements of unspecified research studies cannot be determined. While it is possible to estimate computing power on a theoretical basis, the results leave much to be desired. The general procedure is to list the times required to execute each member of a machine's instruction set and then to multiply each such time by the anticipated frequency of execution in a typical program. Although the individual execution times may be determined with great accuracy, gross misconceptions of power often result from the inherent inaccuracy of frequency estimates. Anyone who claims to have numbers that reflect the overall relative power of any computer has most likely oversimplified the problem.

Another question is: How much storage capacity will be needed? A considerable quantity of on-line storage must be provided for any set of studies. Disk storage is the best medium for interim storage of data collected during an experiment. The use of magnetic tape for this purpose has provided disappointing in terms of both reliability and attainable data rates. Where one anticipates lengthy experiments involving complex scenarios, disk storage is also indicated.

To define the state of the system being simulated large data bases are required. These must be updated or referenced at a sufficiently high frequency that their storage on disk is infeasible. Further, the size of the algorithms necessary to drive such simulations is often large. Bailey et al. (1978) recommended a core memory of 196 kilobytes for their laboratory. Without assuming some specific simulation it is impossible to justify exact sizes.

The software intensive approach suggested implies a great deal of intimate contact between the computer system and things happening in the external world (which in the case of a simulation are the operator consoles). This intimate contact may be dealt with in terms of a dimension that can be called surface area. The surface area of any computer system depends principally on its peripheral interfacing scheme. One of the greatest problems in using a large computer in an application demanding high surface area is the extreme overhead that can result from these external interfaces.

If the central computer were to deal directly with all external interfaces, it would be connected by a large cable to each console. Every time a subject pressed a button or adjusted a control, the central computer would need to stop whatever it was doing. It would need to determine and execute the appropriate reaction to the operator input and to make any necessary alternations to the state of the simulation, and possibly to log the transaction or extract from it some data element for later analysis.

A reasonable alternative would be to place a microcomputer in each console. The microcomputers would have responsibility for implementation of all console functions, in the sense of closing all feedback loops with the operators that logically happen within the consoles. This approach would reduce a considerable portion of the work load of the central computer, permitting it to assume a supervisor role in the conduct of experiments. A typical task of the supervisory computer would be to simulate the system under study, by receiving ony those inputs from the console computers that affect the system as a whole and disseminating to the consoles only those transactions that affect their operation. Naturally, all information transfer between consoles—and all data collected from the equipment—would be channeled through the supervisory computer, but at a much reduced rate.

Thus far we have confined our discussion of the computer system to processors, memory, and mass storage devices, since these are the most important dimensions in which sufficient raw capability must be assured. Several additional elements are necessary.

At least one large (9-track, 800 cpi) tape drive should be attached to the central computer. A storage medium must be available so that data collected can be communicated to another computer for further processing (assuming that the MSRL computer system is not going to do extensive data processing).

The MSRL would be inconvenient to use if it lacked capability for producing hard copy output directly. It is necessary to obtain listing of programs, memory dumps, or diagnostic output in a form that can be marked up. It may be very desirable also that summary or logging data for an experiment be produced directly.

The researcher will need a console enabling him to communicate with the computer system. A single CRT terminal can satisfy any such communication needs, provided that the terminal chosen is sufficiently flexible, something capable of displaying around 24 lines of 80 characters with full cursor control, and a full ASCII key-board with some reasonable complement of special function keys.

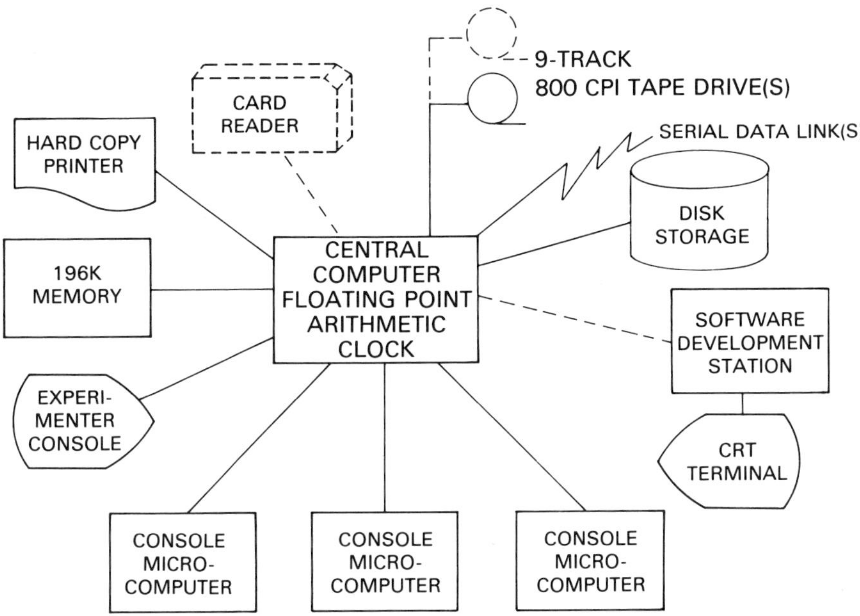

FIGURE 11.1. Block diagram of the supervisory computer system.

Although the researcher console constitutes an adequate terminal device for interactive programming of the computer system, such usage would prevent the development of software during the conduct of experiments. This suggests a separate CRT terminal for programmers to use.

A critical element in the distributed processing philosophy is the communication links between the supervisory computer and each console. In distributed systems freedom in allocating functions among processors increases as a function of the bandwith of the communications system. The laboratory should implement links capable of transferring data between processors at disk speeds (e.g., 10 to 50 microseconds per word). To minimize communications overhead in the processors, the links should employ direct memory access techniques.

Figure 11.1 is a block diagram of the supervisory computer system.

The importance of software in the success of behavioral instrumentation is obvious. MSRL derives its flexibility by assigning total responsibility for its behavior to computer programming. For each experiment to be conducted in MSRL, there will exist a corresponding body of software responsible for controlling the experiment, defining and implementing the behavior of the system under study, and collecting data of interest to the researcher. The demands placed on these bodies of software will vary widely from experiment to experiment. While simple experiments, dealing with simple systems, can be dealt with by trivial programs, there will undoubtedly be experiments requiring extreme complexity or speed, or both. All of this emphasizes the need to include as part of MSRL a programming capability at a highly professional level and requires us to consider the various types of languages it will work with. It is impossible to specify a particular software language because that will depend on the individual research requirement. However it is possible to list a set of requirements for programming language processors:

1. *Assembler.* A processor enabling the programmer to work in machine language should have a good macro capability and should enable the programmer to generate coding that exercises any part of the hardware.

2. *High-level Language.* Some sort of high-level programming language should be available. The language should be one that is especially useful in writing heavily procedural programs and should not penalize the user unduly in space or time for invoking subroutines or subprocedures.

All programming languages should support interactive programming and check-out. This implies interactive, symbolic debugging capabilities from consoles, and a viable text editor. The languages should enable programs to be written concisely since lengthy programs are not easy to work on interactively. Batch-type programming is definitely not recommended for MSRL.

The object code for the high-level language should be inherently compact, and it should be possible for the programmer to produce a code representing the extremes in any tradeoff between space and speed, as he sees fit. It is of paramount importance that compactness be achieveable: "overlay" programs are seldom desirable for real-time use, so complex programs must be compactible to fit into available memory in their entirety.

3. *Problem Oriented Language Metacompiler.* There must be a tool enabling the application programmer to create languages for use by personnel (e.g., researchers) who are not experienced programmers. These languages would be used for overall control of experiments and for the definition of data extraction procedures. While requirements in this area will be highly variable, the tools should result in languages that are easy to use.

MSRL should incorporate at least three distinct operating environments.

1. *Hardware Management.* Each peripheral device in the system should be studied carefully to determine the requirements for interfacing with it. Efficient device drivers should be written that solve this interfacing problem without presupposing the structure of data interchanged with the devices. Error recovery should be taken to lengths appropriate to the probability and consequences of an error.

2. *Data Management.* MSRL operations, while not oriented toward data processing as such, will still require tools aiding in the management of data. On-line storage will be used as a repository for programs and for data files representing the input to and output from experiments. Tools must be provided for managing the allocation of mass storage for these files, and others must exist for describing their contents to programs using them. While various file structures, such as sequential and indexed, are useful at times, their presence in the software support is not absolutely essential so long as a good, efficient scheme for direct access is implemented.

3. *Program Management.* Basically, this implies a mechanism to load and execute programs (and dispose of them afterward). However, since MSRL will cer-

tainly require multiprogramming, the problem becomes one of loading and executing many programs in several computers. The need for dynamic storage allocation exists and should permit concurrent execution of many programs, intercommunication between these programs, and their sharing of resources with provision for temporary exclusive use.

Attention should be given to intercommunication between programs in separate processors, which includes the ability for programs in one processor to use peripherals attached to another. The system should make special efforts to support the use of reentrant coding.

Each operating system design implies a set of routine maintenance or administrative chores. Often, these have to do with manipulating or backing up mass storage files. Whatever routine work the operating system might demand of the user should be supported by appropriate, easily used utility programs.

Certain modular pieces of software should be quite useful.

1. *Mathematical Routines*. For example, functions such as square root, logs, exponentials, trigonometric functions, and vector arithmetic will be required for many applications. Random number generators and various statistical functions are often used as stimuli for simulations.

2. *Graphics*. A comprehensive graphics package should be prepared, capable of exercising all the features of the primary display.

3. *Terminal Modules*. Specialized, skeletal software should be developed for interfacing to each of the input or output devices that may be configured into a console.

In addition, at least two levels of documentation will be required:

1. *Internal System Documentation*. This should contain sufficient information to enable those who study it to alter or maintain any part of the system software. Flowcharts are not required, but glossaries of symbolic names, diagrams of databases, and thorough functional descriptions are of vital importance.

2. *Programmer's Reference Manual*. This should describe the use of all system software.

Observational Instrumentation

Observation of behavior requires the observer to recognize and classify behaviors into specified categories, to note the occurrence of that behavior, and to record its frequency and sometimes its duration. When behavior changes frequently and is of short duration, the observer is stressed in making his measurements. Further, the sheer volume of material may make the process of data reduction difficult. At this point instrumentation enters the picture.

A number of computerized devices have been developed to assist the observer. These are described by: Crossman, Williams and Chambers, 1978; Sykes, 1977; Sanson-Fisher, Poole, Small and Fleming, 1979; Torgerson, 1977; Fitzpatrick,

1977; Celhoffer, Boukydis and Minde, 1977; Stephenson and Roberts, 1977; Scott and Masi, 1977; Sawin, Langlois and Leitner, 1977; Conger and McLeod, 1977; Miklich, Purcell and Weiss, 1974; Long, 1974; Smith and Begeman, 1980; Magyar and Fitzsimmons, 1979; Flowers and Leger, 1982; Bernstein and Livingston, 1982; Flowers, 1982. Most of these devices have been developed specifically for a particular project. A few are commercial devices.

The Datamyte is probably the most popular computerized observational recording device available commercially and is described here because its characteristics are typical of other data recorders. Its history began in 1967 and has proceeded through several versions to its present state (this description is based on a paper by Torgerson, 1977; it may therefore be somewhat out of data). The Datamyte 900 is a hand-held, solid-state data collector using microprocessor technology. The device is $12 \times 10 \times 2$ inches and weighs 4 pounds. It has an integrated circuit memory that stores from 16,000 to 32,000 characters. Data are recorded in computer code, ready for immediate transmission. The system transmits ASCII, a code compatible with most computer terminals. Depressing *XMIT* transmits the stored data to the terminal for printout or for recording on cassette tape or paper tape, or to a computer for storage on file.

The Datamyte 900 has 14 character keys, 10 numerical (0–9) and 4 alpha (C, F, H, *), that permit a large number of code combinations.

An internal clock reads in hundredths of minutes. A built-in rechargeable battery permits 8 hours of use between charges.

Most Datamyte users design and write their own computer programs. However, there are a number of commercial software systems. Two input modes permit rapidly changing behaviors of one or two subjects to be tracked. Time records automatically to the nearest .01 minute along with a one- or two-digit behavior code.

Multiple subject interactive behavior can be studied by multiple passes of videotaped or filmed scenes, selecting a different focal subject for each pass or using multiple observers each with a Datamyte. The data are merged by the computer.

Complex behavioral codes (subject, activity, recipient, location, etc.) can be entered by using mode 1. Time is recorded automatically each time the ENTER button is pressed. Up to 12 characters can be displayed at one time.

Data can be recorded on a sampling basis (e.g., every 30 seconds). A built-in interval timer signals in an earphone at switch-selectable intervals of .5, 1, 1.5, 2, 3, 4, 5, 10, 16 or 32 minutes to signal sampling periods.

Remote entries from observers or from subjects can be recorded via an accessory remote input module. This permits switch closures, such as microswitches, relay contacts, transistors, gates, or photocells to operate the Datamyte.

Extensive training of observers in the use of the device is necessary. Practice in using the keyboard is required because it is relatively easy to make keying errors. Observers must memorize a code number for each behavioral event to be sampled. Thus, a disadvantage of the Datamyte is that, for large coding systems, the training of observers takes longer than would be necessary with paper and pencil techniques where observers can use acronyms or symbols that have inherent meaning. The translation of behavioral events into less meaningful code numbers, pressing the correct Datamyte keys in the correct order and doing this rapidly require highly skilled and thoroughly trained personnel. As much as four to six weeks training may be required to achieve acceptable levels of interobserver reliability if the coding system is complex. Even with highly skilled and highly trained observers, errors from pressing the wrong keys occur occasionally and must be subsequently searched for and identified by an error program and by review of the printout of behavior records. The errors must be corrected on the computer magnetic tape files by subsequent editing of the behavior records. This process is quite time consuming. Of course, errors that are incorrect because one legal code number has been substituted for another cannot usually be detected by the error program, or by visual inspection, and can only be ascertained by reliability checks.

The types of data to be analyzed consist of a coded record of behaviors, one or more schedules filled out by the observer and possibly narrative comments of the observer about special problems experienced during the observation period. Coordination of these different forms of data is no small task.

Coded protocols are different from written protocols. They are much more complex than the average written protocol because much more can be coded than is possible under manual writing conditions. Each code within a particular case may be quite complex. Since the behavior of humans in natural settings is often subject to contingencies, such as interruption by some overriding event, the computer must be able to recognize such an interruption. Because data from the coded record go directly into computer memory, cleaning and editing of the record must take place afterward, not before as with punched cards. These conditions require that very carefully written records of the data be maintained, that is through an observation record, an edit record, an equipment record, and data inventory. The observation record is the master list of observations that have been made. These data come from the identification information the observer enters in the Datamyte—who observed, what was observed, when and what equipment was used. This information enables the computerized data to be checked at a later time.

The edit record keeps track of the program of the data from entry into computer memory to final form. As many as 37 individual steps (Sykes, 1977) may be involved in recording a single observational session.

More recently the personal computer (e.g., Apple II) has been applied to the measurement of observational behavior (Flowers and Leger, 1982; Bernstein and Livingston, 1982; Flowers, 1982). Other data recording systems are developed by users for their own purposes and are not commercially available (e.g., the DART 1 system, Sanson-Fisher, Poole, Small and Fleming, 1979).

COMMENTARY

The methods described in this chapter are quite disparate and yet they depend ultimately on a relatively few generic methods described in previous chapters: observation and classification of events, interviews, self-reports, and ratings. One may ask, are there not new methods that represent breakthroughs, that depend on some function other than observation and classification? It appears not.

Nevertheless, one must be impressed by the very great amount of research that needs to be done in order to make these methods truly valid, reliable, and useful. Although these methods have spawned a vast amount of literature, only the first steps have been taken to make them more effective. Validity coefficients, for example, of work sample tests are much too low (averaging about.30). The difficulties of utilizing these methods practically are very great (e.g., accident data discrepancies). About all one can say confidently about these methods is that they are useful, which is a criterion not to be blithely ignored as irrelevant.

REFERENCES

Adams, N. L. Using injury statistics to set safety goals. *Personnel Practice Bulletin,* 1974, *3*, 244–256.

Adams, N. L. and Hartwell, N. M. Accident reporting systems: A basic problem area in industrial society, *Journal of Occupational Psychology,* 1977, *50,* 285–298.

Adams, N. L., Barlow, A., and Hiddlestine, J. Obtaining ergonomics information about industrial injuries: A five-year analysis. *Applied Ergonomics,* 1981, *12*, 71–81.

Aldag, R. J., Barr, S. H., and Brief, A. P. Measurement of perceived task characteristics. *Psychological Bulletin,* 1981, *90*, 415–431.

Archer, W. B. and Fruchter, D. A. *The Construction, Review, and Administration of Air Force Job Inventories*. Report PRL-TDR-63-21, Personnel Research Laboratory, Aerospace Medical Division, Lackland AFB, TX, August, 1963 (AD 426 755).

Archer, J. J. and Sciarrino, J. A. Realistic work sample tests: A review. *Personnel Psychology,* 1974, *27,* 519–533.

Askren, W. B., Schwartz, N. F., Bower, S. M., and Schmid, M. D. *A Voice-Radio Method for Collecting Human Factors Data*. Report AFHRL-TR-68-10, Air Force Human Resources Laboratory, Wright-Patterson AFB, OH, January 1969.

Bailey, G. V., Hennessy, R. T., Wylie, C. D. *Functional Requirements and Other Design Features of a Manned System Research Facility*. Technical Note 78-4, Navy Personnel Research and Development Center, San Diego, CA, January 1978.

Banks, M. H., Jackson, P. R., Stafford, E. M. and Warr, P. B. The Job Components Inventory and the analysis of jobs requiring limited skill. *Personnel Psychology,* 1983, *36,* 57–66.

Beaumont, P. B. Analysis of the problem of industrial accidents in Britain. *International Journal of Manpower,* 1980, *1,* 28–32.

Bernstein, J. L. and Twery, R. J. Forecasting techniques in R & D planning. *Chemical Engineering Process,* 1970, *66,* 15–19.

Bernstein, D. and Livingston, C. An interactive program for observation and analysis of human behavior in a long term continuous laboratory. *Behavioral Research Methods and Instrumentation,* 1982, *14,* 231–235.

Birt, J. A. *The Effect of the Consistency of Job Inventory Information upon Simulated Airmen Reassignment*. Ph.D. Dissertation, Purdue University, West Lafayette, IN, 1968.

Borman, W. C. and Dunnette, M. D. *Selection of Components to Comprise a Naval Personnel Status Index (NPSI) and a Strategy for Investigating Their Relative Importance*. Report NPSI-02, Personnel Decisions, Inc., Minneapolis, MN, March, 1974.

Bottenberg, C. A. and Christal, R. E. Grouping criteria—a method which retains maximum predictive efficiency. *Journal of Experimental Education,* 1968, *36,* 28–34.

Brown, B. B. and Helmer, O. *Improving the Reliability of Estimates Obtained from a Consensus of Experts*. Rand Corporation, Santa Monica, CA, September, 1964.

Campbell, J. P., Dunnette, M. D., Lawler, E. E. III, and Weick, K. E., Jr. *Managerial Behavior, Performance, and Effectiveness*. New York: McGraw-Hill, 1970.

Carlsson, J. Accident prevention planning: II. Suggestions for improvements. *Elmia-Arbetsmiljo,* 1980, September, 17–25.

Carter, R. C., Kennedy, R. S. and Bittner, A. C. Jr. Selection of performance evaluation tests for environmental research. *Proceedings,* Human Factors Society Annual Meeting, Los Angeles, CA, 1980, 320–324.

Cascio, W. F. and Phillips, N. F. Performance testing: a rose among thorns? *Personnel Psychology,* 1979, *32,* 751–766.

Celhoffer, L., Boukydis, C., and Minde, K. The DCR-II event recorder: a portable high speed digital cassette system with direct computer access. *Behavioral Research Methods and Instrumentation,* 1977, *9,* 442–446.

Chiles, W. D., Alluisi, E. A. and Adams, O. S. Work schedules and performance during confinement. *Human Factors,* 1968, *10,* 143–195.

Christal, R. E. *JAN; A Technique for Analyzing Individual and Group Judgment.* Report PRL-TDR-63-3, Personnel Research Laboratory, Aerospace Medical Division, Lackland AFB, TX, February, 1963 (AD 403 813).

Christal, R. E. *Officer Grade Requirements Project. 1. Overview.* Report PRL-TDR-65–15, Personnel Research Laboratory, Aerospace Medical Division, Lackland AFB, TX, September 1965 (AD 622 806).

Christal, R. E. Selecting a harem—and other applications of the policy capturing model. *Journal of Experimental Education,* 1968, *36,* 35–41.

Christal, R. E. Comments by the Chairman. *Proceedings,* Division of Military Psychology Symposium, 77th Annual Convention of the American Psychological Association, 1969.

Christal, R. E. *The United States Air Force Occupational Research Project.* Report AFHRL-TR-73-75, Air Force Human Resources Laboratory, Lackland, AFB, TX, January, 1974 (AD 774 574).

Conger, R. D. and McLeod, D. Describing behavior in small groups with the Datamyte event recorder, *Behavioral Research Methods and Instrumentation,* 1977, *9,* 418–424.

Cowan, J. Discussion. *Proceedings,* Division 19 Military Psychology Symposium: Collecting, analyzing and reporting information describing jobs and occupations (77th Annual Convention of American Psychological Association). Personnel Research Division, Air Force Human Resources Laboratory, Lackland AFB, TX, September, 1969, 71–72.

Craver, J. K. *The Effect of the Future on Today's Decisions.* Paper presented to AICHE 72nd National Convention, St. Louis, MO, May 1972.

Cromwell, L., Weibull, F. J., Pfeiffer, E. A. and Usselman, L. B. *Biomedical Instrumentation and Measurements.* Englewood Cliffs, NJ: Prentice-Hall, Inc., 1973.

Crossman, E. K., Williams, J. G. and Chambers, J. H. Microcomputers in observational and field research: Using the PET microcomputer for collecting and analyzing observational data in the classroom. *Behavioral Research Methods and Instrumentation,* 1978, *10,* 563–566.

Cragun, J. R. and McCormick, E. J. *Job Inventory Information: Task Reliabilities and Scale Interrelationships.* Report PRL-TR-67-15, Personnel Research Laboratory, Aerospace Medical Division, Lackland AFB, TX, 1967.

Crites, C. D. *Videotape Recording as a Technique for Personnel Subsystem Test and Evaluation.* Report AFHRL-TR-69-18, Air Force Human Resources Laboratory, Wright-Patterson AFB, OH, September 1969.

Cunningham, J. W., Tuttle, T. C., Floyd, J. R. and Bates, J. A. *The Development of the Occupation Analysis Inventory: An "Ergometric" Approach to an Educational Problem. JSAS Catalog of Selected Documents in Psychology,* 1974, *4,* 144 (Ms. No. 803).

Cunningham, J. W., Boese, R. R., Neeb, R. W. and Pass, J. J. Systematically derived work dimensions: Factor analyses of the Occupational Analysis Inventory. *Journal of Applied Psychology,* 1983, *68,* 232–252.

Cyphert, F. R. and Gant, W. L. The Delphi technique: A tool for collecting opinions in teacher education. *Journal of Teacher Education,* 1970, *21,* 419–420.

Dalkey, N. C. *The Delphi Method: An Experimental Study of Group Opinion*. Rand Corporation, Santa Monica, CA, June 1969.

Dalkey, N. C., Brown, B. B. and Cochran, S. *The Delphi Method. III. Use of Self-ratings to Improve Group Estimates*. Rand Corporation, Santa Monica, CA, November, 1969.

Drury, G. G. and Brill, M. Human factors in consumer product accident investigation, *Human Factors*, 1983, *25*, 329–342.

Eastman Kodak Co., Human Factors Section. *Ergonomic Design for People at Work. Vol. I. Workplace, Equipment and Environmental Design*. Belmont, CA: Wadsworth, 1983.

Edwards, A. L. *Statistical Methods*. (Second edition). New York: Holt, Rinehart and Winston, 1967.

Edwards, M. The design of accident investigation procedure. *Applied Ergonomics*, 1982, *12*, 111–115.

Fegetter, A. J. A method for investigating human factor aspects of aircraft accidents and incidents. *Ergonomics*, 1982, *25*, 1065–1075.

Finkel, J. *Computer Aided Experimentation: Interfaces to Minicomputers*. New York: Wiley/Interscience, 1975.

Flanagan, J. C. The critical incident technique. *Psychological Bulletin*, 1954, *51*, 327–358.

Fleishman, E. A. *An Evaluation of Two Psychomotor Tests for the Prediction of Success in Primary Flying Training*. Research Bulletin 53-9, Human Resources Research Center, Lackland AFB, TX, May 1953.

Fleishman, E. A. *Evaluations of Psychomotor Tests for Pilot Selection: The Direction Control and Compensatory Balance Tests*. Report AFPTRC-TR-54-131, Air Force Personnel and Training Research Center, Lackland AFB, TX, December 1954.

Flowers, J. H. Some simple Apple II software for the collection and analysis of observational data. *Behavioral Research Methods and Instrumentation*. 1982, *14*, 241–249.

Flowers, J. H. and Leger, D. W. Personal computers and behavioral observation: an introduction. *Behavioral Research Methods and Instrumentation*, 1982, *14*, 227–230.

Goldberg, L. R. Man versus model of man: a rationale, plus some evidence, for a method of improving on clinical inferences. *Psychological Bulletin*, 1970, *73*, 422–433.

Gordon, M. E. and Kleiman, L. S. The prediction of trainability using a work sample test and an aptitude test: A direct comparison. *Personnel Psychology*, 1976, *29*, 243–253.

Gray, P. and Niles, J. M. Evaluating a Delphi forecast on personal computers. *IEEE Transactions on Systems, Man and Cybernatics*. 1983, vol. SMC-13, 222–224.

Gustafson, D. H., Shukla, R. K., Delbecq, A. and Walster, G. W. A comparative study of differences in subjective likelihood estimates made by individuals, interacting groups, and nominal groups. *Organizational Behavior and Human Performance*, 1973, *9*, 280–291.

Hackman, J. R. and Oldham, G. R. Development of the Job Diagnostic Survey. *Journal of Applied Psychology*, 1975, *60*, 159–170.

Hale, A. R. and Hale, M. *A Review of the Industrial Accident Research Literature*. Research paper, Committee on Safety and Health at Work, Her Majesty's Stationery Office, London, England, 1972.

Harris, R. N. *Prevention of Boiler Explosions in Aircraft Carrier Main Propulsion Systems: Personnel Factors (AL 2-81)*. Report NPRDC SR 83-25, Navy Personnel Research and Development Center, San Diego, CA, April, 1983.

Hartwell, N. M. *Report on Efficient Operations—Safety Objectives and Accident Causation Fault Categories*. British Steel Corporation Report, Asborne Hill College, BSC, 1973.

Hays, R. T. *Simulator Fidelity: A Concept Paper*. Technical Report 490, Army Research Institute, Alexandria, VA, November, 1980.

Helmer, O. *Social Technology*. Rand Corporation, Santa Monica, CA, February 1965.

Helmer, O. *Analyses of the Future: The Delphi Method*. Rand Corporation, Santa Monica, CA, March 1967a.

Helmer, O. *Systematic Use of Expert Opinions*. Rand Corporation, Santa Monica, CA, March 1967b.

Hemphill, J. K. Job descriptions for executives. *Harvard Business Review*, 1959, *37*, 55–67.

Jeanneret, P. R. and McCormick, J. A. *The Job Dimensions of "Worker Oriented" Job Variables and of Their Attribute Profiles as Based on Data from the Position Analysis Questionnaire*. Report 2, Occupational Research Center, Dept. of Psychological Sciences, Purdue University, West Lafayette, IN, 1969.

Kay, B. R. The use of critical incidents in a forced-choice scale. *Journal of Applied Psychology*, 1959, *43*, 269–270.

Kirchner, W. K. and Dunnette, M. D. Using critical incidents to measure job proficiency factors. *Personnel*, 1957, *34*, 54–59.

Kjellen, V. Accident prevention planning. I. Results of an analysis of accident prevention in six companies. *Elmia-Arbetsmiljo*, 1980, September, 5–16.

Kletz, T. Z. Accident data—the need for a new look at the sort of data that are collected and analyzed. *Journal of Occupational Accidents*, 1976 *1*, 95–105.

Lagerlof, E. Opportunities provided by the new accident statistics, *Elmia-Arbetsmiljo*, 1980, September, 41–51.

Lane, D. M., Murphy, K. R. and Marques, T. E. Measuring the importance of cues in policy capturing. *Organizational Behavior and Human Performance*, 1982, *30*, 231–240.

Levine, E. L., Ash, R. A. and Bennett, N. Exploratory comparative study of four job analysis methods. *Journal of Applied Psychology*, 1980, *65*, 524–535.

Linstone, H. A. and Turoff, M. (Eds.) *The Delphi Method: Techniques and Applications*. Reading, MA: Addison-Wesley Publishing Co., 1975.

Linstone, H. A. and Turoff, M. Introduction. In H. A. Linstone and M. Turoff (Eds.) *The Delphi Method: Techniques and Applications*. Reading, MA: Addison-Wesley Publishing Co., 1975, 1–12.

Long, J. L. A stereotape recorder technique for observational data. *Human Factors*, 1974, *16*, 154–160.

Mackworth, N. H. *Researches on the Measurement of Human Performance*. Special Report 268, Medical Research Council, London, England: Her Majesty's Stationery Office, 1950.

Madden, J. M. *An Application to Job Evaluation of a Policy Capturing Model for Analyzing Individual and Group Judgments*. Report PRL-TDR-63-15, Personnel Research Laboratory, Aerospace Medical Division, Lackland AFB, TX, May 1963.

Magyar, R. L. and Fitzsimmons, J. R. A multichannel, portable "real time" event encoder–decoder for laboratory and field experiments. *Behavioral Research Methods and Instrumentation*, 1979, *11*, 47–50.

McCormick, E. J. Job and task analysis. In M. D. Dunnette (Ed.) *Handbook of Industrial and Organizational Psychology*, Chicago, IL: Rand McNally College Publishing Co., 1976, 651–696.

McCormick, E. J. *Job Analysis: Methods and Applications*. New York: AMACOM, 1979.

McCormick, J. A. and Ammerman, H. L. *Development of Worker Activity Checklists for Use in Occupational Analysis*. Report WADD-TR-60-77, Personnel Laboratory, Wright Air Development Division, Lackland AFB. TX, 1960.

McCormick, J. A., Jeanneret, P. R. and Mecham, R. C. *The Development and Background of the Position Analysis Questionnaire*. Occupational Research Center, Purdue University, West Lafayette, IN, 1969.

McCormick, J. A., Jeanneret, P. R. and Mecham, R. C. A study of job characteristics and job dimensions as based on the Position Analysis Questionnaire (PAQ). *Journal of Applied Psychology*, 1972, *56*, 347–368.

Miklich, D. R., Purcell, K. and Weiss, J. H. Practical aspects of the use of radio telemetry in the behavioral sciences. *Behavioral Research Methods and Instrumentation*, 1974, *6*, 461–466.

Morsh, J. E. Job Analysis in the United States Air Force. *Personnel Psychology*, 1964, *17*, 7–18.

Morsh, J. E. *Computer Analysis of Occupational Survey Data,* Personnel Research Division, Air Force Human Resources Laboratory, Lackland AFB, TX, 1969.

Morsh, J. E. and Archer, W. B. *Procedural Guide to Conducting Occupational Surveys in the United States Air Force.* Report PRL-TR-67-11, Personnel Research Laboratory, Aerospace Medical Division, Lackland AFB, TX, 1967 (AD 664 036).

Naylor, J. C. and Wherry, R. J., Sr. *Feasibility of Distinguishing Supervisor's Policies in Evaluation of Subordinates by Using Ratings of Simulated Job Incumbents.* Report PRL-TR-64-25, Personnel Research Laboratory, Aerospace Medical Division, Lackland AFB, TX, October 1964 (AD 610 812).

Naylor, J. C. and Wherry, R. J. The use of simulated stimuli and the "JAN" technique to capture and cluster the policies of raters. *Educational and Psychological Measurement,* 1965, *25,* 969–986.

Nugent, W. A., Laabs, G. J. and Panell, R. C. *Performance Test Objectivity: A Comparison of Rater Accuracy and Reliability Using Three Observational Forms.* Report NPRDC-TR-82–30, Navy Personnel Research and Development Center, San Diego, CA, February 1982.

Pimble, J. and O'Toole, S. Analysis of accident reports. *Ergonomics,* 1982, *25,* 967–979.

Plumlee, L. B. *A Short Guide to the Development of Performance Tests.* U. S. Civil Service Commission, Professional Series 75-1, Washington, DC, January 1975.

Potempa, K. W., Talcott, D. R., Loy, S. S., and Schwartz, N. F. *Videotape as a Tool for Improving Human Factors Test and Evaluation Activities.* Report AFHRL-TR-70-6, Air Force Human Resources Laboratory, Wright-Patterson AFB, OH, May 1970.

Prien, E. P. and Ronan, W. W. Job analysis: A review of research findings. *Personnel Psychology,* 1971, *24,* 371–396.

Primoff, E. S. *How to Prepare and Conduct Job-Element Examinations.* Technical Study 75-1, U. S. Civil Service Commission, U. S. Government Printing Office, Washington, DC, 1975.

Robertson, I. T. and Kandola, R. S. Work sample tests: Validity, adverse impact, and applicant reaction. *Journal of Occupational Psychology,* 1982, *55,* 171–183.

Rohmer, W. and Landau, K. *A New Technique for Job Analysis.* New York: International Publications Service, Taylor and Francis, Inc., 1983.

Rohrbaugh, J. Improving the quality of group judgment: Social judgment analysis and the Delphi technique. *Organizational Behavior and Human Performance,* 1979, *24,* 73–92.

Saari, J. Typical features of tasks in which accidents occur. *Proceedings,* International Ergonomics Association meeting, 1976.

Sackman, H. *Delphi Critique.* Lexington, MA: Lexington Books, 1975.

Salancik, J. R., Wenger, W. and Helfer, E. The construction of Delphi event statements. *Technological Forecasting and Social Change,* 1971, *3,* 65–73.

Sanso-Fisher, R. W., Poole, A. D., Small, G. A. and Fleming, I. R. Data acquisition in real time—an improved system for naturalistic observations. *Behavior Therapy,* 1979, *10,* 543–554.

Sawin, D. B., Langlois, J. H. and Leitner, E. F. What do you do after you say hello? Observing, coding and analyzing parent-infant interactions. *Behavioral Research Methods and Instrumentation,* 1979, *9,* 425–428.

Scott, K. G. and Masi, W. S. Use of the Datamyte in analyzing duration of infant visual behaviors. *Behavioral Research Methods and Instrumentation,* 1977, *9,* 429–433.

Senneck, C. R. *The need for accident data: What, Why?* Technical paper 9, Safety in Mines Research Establishment, London: Department of Energy, 1974.

Sidowski, J. B. (Ed.) *Experimental Methods and Instrumentation in Psychology,* New York: McGraw-Hill, 1966.

Sidowski, J. B. Instrumentation and computer technology: Applications and influences in modern psychology. *American Psychologist,* 1975, *30,* 191–468.

Sidowski, J. B. and Ross, S. Instrumentation in psychology. Special Issue, *American Psychologist,* 1969, *24,* 187–384.

Siegel, A. I. The miniature job training and evaluation approach: additional findings. *Personnel Psychology,* 1983, *36,* 41–56.

Siegel, A. I. and Musetti, L. L. *Analysis of Electromechanical Switching Jobs.* Applied Psychological Services, Wayne, PA, September 1978.

Siegel, A. I. and Wiesen, J. P. *Experimental Procedures for the Classification of Navy Personnel.* Report NPRDC TR-77-3, Navy Personnel Research and Development Center, San Diego, CA, August 1977.

Siegel, A. I., Bartter, W. D. and Kopstein, F. F. *Job Analysis of Maintenance Mechanic Position for the Nuclear Power Plant Maintenance Personnel Reliability Model.* NUREG/CR-2670, ORNL/TM-8301, Oak Ridge National Laboratory, Oak Ridge, TN, June 1982.

Siegel, A. I., Federman, P. J. and Welsand, E. H. *Perceptual/Psychomotor Requirements Basic to Performance in 35 Air Force Specialities.* Applied Psychological Services, Wayne, PA, December 1980.

Sims, H. P., Szilagyi, A. D., and Keller, R. T. The measurement of job characteristics. *Academy of Management Journal,* 1976, *19,* 195–212.

Slovic, P. and Lichtenstein, S. Comparison of Bayesian and regression approaches to the study of information processing in judgment. *Organizational Behavior and Human Performance,* 1971, *6,* 649–744.

Stephenson, G. R. and Roberts, T. W. The SSR system 7: A general encoding system with computerized transcription. *Behavioral Research Methods and Instrumentation,* 1977, *9,* 434–441.

Stone, C. H. and Yoder, D. *Job Analysis, 1970.* California State College, Long Beach, CA, 1970.

Strandberg, L. *The Mechanics of Slipping Accidents.* Investigation Report 1980: 29E, National Board of Occupational Safety and Health Accident Research Section, 1980.

Suchman, E. A. On accident behavior. In, *Behavioral Approaches to Accident Research.* Association for the Aid of Crippled Children, New York, 1961a.

Suchman, E. A. A conceptual analysis of the accident phenomena. *Social Problems,* 1961, *8,* 241 (b).

Sykes, R. E. Techniques of data collection and reduction in systematic field observation. *Behavioral Research Methods and Instrumentation,* 1977, *9,* 407–417.

Tenopy, M. O. and Oeltjen, P. D. Personnel selection and classification. *Annual Review of Psychology,* 1982, *33,* 581–618.

Torgerson, L. Datamyte 900. *Behavioral Research Methods and Instrumentation,* 1977, *9,* 405–406.

Turoff, M. The design of a policy Delhi. *Technological Forecasting and Social Change,* 1970, *2,* 149–171.

Uniform Guidelines on Employee Selection Procedures, 43 FR 38289–038309, August 25, 1978.

Vineberg, R. and Joyner, J. N. *Prediction of Job Performance: Review of Military Studies.* NPRDC TR-82-37, Navy Personnel Research and Development Center, San Diego, CA, March 1982.

CHAPTER TWELVE

Statistical Techniques

Statistical techniques are like the analytic techniques reviewed in Chapters Two through 6—decision aids to help decide whether research hypotheses are probably the result of a systematic condition that produced effects reflected in the data (in which case one accepts the hypothesis as being reasonably true); or the results of random effects, in which case the data effects were probably produced by chance. Hypotheses are phrased in terms of lack of significant differences—the null hypothesis—so one accepts the null hypothesis when one actually rejects the presumption of a systematic effect.

It is obviously impossible to describe all the statistical methods or experiment designs available for particular contingencies, since this would require a book of its own. It is assumed that the reader has at least a nodding acquaintance with the common experimental designs such as *analysis of variance* (ANOVA) and correlational techniques.

This chapter emphasizes advanced techniques, in particular central-composite design and response surface methodology. These techniques have been brilliantly adapted to behavioral problems by Williges and his colleagues, e.g., Williges, 1981, and Williges and Mills, 1982. Much of this chapter is based on their work. The orientation of this discussion is toward the special problems faced by those who measure human performance in complex systems. In discussing these problems, which are listed in Table 12.1, we will suggest sources of solution but without going into the detailed mathematics involved, which would make this chapter impossibly long.

These problems arise in large part from some of the characteristics of man–machine systems.

1. The system functions at multiple levels: the individual operator, the team, the subsystem (which may or may not be coordinate with the team), and the overall system. There may be a number of subsystems and several hierarchical levels of

TABLE 12.1 Potential Experimental Difficulties in System Research

1. It may not be possible to collect all data using a factorial design.
2. The number of data observations required may be excessive. How can these be reduced?
3. It may not be possible to manipulate all the treatment conditions.
4. It may be necessary to collect data in stages and/or a series of studies, rather than simultaneously and within a single study.
5. Too much replication may be required.
6. It may be difficult to determine in advance which independent/dependent variables are important and should be emphasized, and which are trivial.
7. It may not be possible to assign subjects to treatment conditions randomly.
8. It is necessary to measure team as well as individual performance and methods of measuring team performance are not well articulated.
9. Certain data values may be missing.
10. System performance almost certainly will vary over time.
11. It will be necessary to estimate optimal system performance.
12. It will be necessary to decide at which system level(s) to measure.

subsystems. The fact that there are multiple levels raises the question of the level at which to measure. If one measures at more than one level, how is performance at the various levels correlated?

2. During its functioning and because of its various levels, the system produces intermediate products as well as terminal outputs. How does one describe the relationship between the intermediate subsystem outputs and terminal outputs?

3. Any complex system is usually multidimensional, which means that it can be described by more than one measure. For example, the performance of an aircraft can be measured in terms of its speed, range, fuel consumption, maximum altitude, and the amount of space available to passengers. Given that measures of various dimensions exist, how does one select the one or several dimensions to measure? how does one relate the various measures? and how does one combine them into a summary measure?

4. System performance varies over time: How can one reflect this quantitatively?

5. Some of the measures that describe the system are qualitative as well as quantitative. How does one deal with the qualitative measures?

The tendency of those unaccustomed to thinking in terms of systems is to feel that these problems exist only with MMS, such as weapon systems or transportation vehicles, as they function in the uncontrolled real world environment. Presumably this is not true if one studies, for example, learning problems, consumer decision making or child behavior under the controlled conditions of the laboratory. This is quite untrue. System considerations (and all of these problems arise because performance occurs in a system context) are important even when individuals are tested in the laboratory. It is simply that traditional experimentalists ignore the system context, probably because their rather molecular training makes them unaware of that context. Williges and Mills (1982) point out that "all systems experimentation dealing with human performance must be concerned with human factors implications. *These considerations are often quite different from those of basic psychological laboratory investigations, because the behavior of the individual or individuals must be considered in a systems context.*" (p. 4, emphasis in the original) Only if one considers the individual as divorced from any context at all (unfortunately characteristic of much psychological research) can one ignore the system aspects of human performance.

In the MMS, a system created by humans, the many variables involved are laid bare to inspection during the system's development and therefore must be dealt with in analyzing/measuring the system. In real world situations as many or more variables also exist and must be dealt with, but these are often obscured by behavioral noise—extraneous events and irrelevancies. Because they are obscure the researcher feels safe to ignore them or at least to deal with them by attempting to hold them constant while varying only a few selected variables. Nonetheless, the variables are still there, exerting an effect, even if ignored.

Human performance research conducted in systems therefore poses important methodological challenges. Because of system complexity, the researcher must consider simultaneously a number of interactive factors that affect multidimensional aspects of individual and group performance.

GENERAL APPROACHES TO SYSTEM RESEARCH

Three general approaches can be used in conducting system-oriented human performance research. One approach is observational: to examine system parameters through direct observational measurement of the operational system. This is difficult when one lacks control over other interacting factors. Direct measurement will nonetheless permit one to indicate where the system is malfunctioning, even if it does not isolate the source of the problem.

Another approach is that of computer simulation/mathematical modeling. As we saw in Chapter 4, these methods can be useful in the conceptual design stages of new development when a number of configurations are under consideration. However, these methods are limited primarily by the inadequacy of the human performance database needed to exercise the models.

A third approach is to use real-time (i.e., human-in-the-loop) simulation and manipulate various systems parameters as part of that simulation. Here traditional experimental design methods become critical. This laboratory approach provides the control missing in operational measurement and can also be used to build up the human performance database needed for mathematical modeling. If the simulation is sufficiently realistic, it avoids the artificiality of the usual laboratory study. This type of research has traditionally focused on the performance of a single operator and a single control-display interface; to be useful for system considerations it must include several factors simultaneously ("multifactor studies"). Although a variety of experimental design procedures exist, unfortunately only a limited number of them have been used in system research. The amount of methodologic research addressing complex behavioral experimentation issues is quite small.

DESIGN ALTERNATIVES

System research problems may have other constraints that must be considered in the experimental design. For example, some factors cannot be crossed in the real world and are "nested" within other factors. Many behavioral problems require the simultaneous investigation of several factors, thereby making a completely crossed factorial design unwieldy. This is because of the large number of treatment combinations, since all levels of one independent variable must appear at all levels of another variable. Because of the large number of potentially relevant system variables, pretesting is required to reduce these variables to a feasible number. Apparently irrelevant variables such as equipment variations, experimenter differences, and time limitations on an experimental session must be taken into account.

A number of design alternatives in addition to the standard analysis of variance and quasi experimental designs, and including fractional factorial, hierarchical, and central-composite designs can satisfy system research constraints. However, these more advanced methods are not used extensively in behavioral research. They are discussed to a limited extent in texts such as Box, Hunter and Hunter, 1978; Cochran and Cox, 1957; Hicks, 1973; Keppel, 1978; Kirk, 1969; Myers, 1972; and Winer, 1971.

Development of an appropriate research design also requires the assignment of subjects to treatment conditions as a means of controlling intersubject variability through randomization, blocking or using each subject as his own control. In randomization each subject is equally likely to be assigned to any treatment condition defined by the independent variables. Although this strategy is fundamental to experimental design, it is often difficult to accomplish in actual practice because it requires equal sample size and is affected by subject attrition. The researcher also has the option to match subjects or block variables that affect individual differences. Finally he can control the subject variables by having each subject serve as his own control through repeated observations on the same subjects. All these approaches have implications for choosing *between-subjects, within-subject,* or *mixed-factor* designs.

Strategies for collecting data in stages are usually necessary in any complex system research problem. Such a strategy requires that after a sequential design is chosen, the data are collected and analyzed with the resulting feedback being used in choosing the next design. In developing a sequential design strategy the researcher must evaluate a number of alternatives dealing with response surface exploration, behavioral research strategies and augmented screening designs. The remainder of this chapter describes some of the procedures designed to solve the problems listed in Table 12-1.

Reducing the Number of Data Observations (Single-Observation Factorials)

A simple approach to reducing the number of data observations is to eliminate replication across complex, crossed factorial designs. The complete set of treatment combinations in the factorial design is used but only one observation is made in each cell of the design. For example, a complete factorial design having six factors each at two levels would result in 64 treatment combinations. If only one subject rather than five, for example, were observed, the data collection effort would be reduced by one-fifth. Statistical pooling procedures are used in single-observation factorial designs to obtain error terms for lower-order effects from nonsignificant higher-order effects. Such a design is particularly useful in organizing pretesting procedures, but even then the resulting number of treatment combinations can still become too large when many factors are included.

Inability to Manipulate All Treatment Conditions (Hierarchical Designs)

In many behavioral situations environmental constraints do not allow all the variables into which the system can be classified or subdivided to be crossed with the independent variables. For example, in an experimental evaluation of various aids provided to inspectors on the production line of one plant, it may not be possible to manipulate all the treatment conditions because set-up costs on the inspection line are prohibitive. It may be necessary to set up each of the two aids separately in individual plants. However, the special characteristics of the plants, now nested within the inspection aids treatment conditions, may affect research results.

Whenever factors other than subjects are nested (i.e., the levels of one factor appear only at one level of another factor) within other factors, the design is called a *hierarchical design* because of the hierarchical or pyramidal shape of the treatment conditions. This experimental design reduces the number of treatment conditions as compared to a completely crossed factorial design. Hierarchical designs, however, do not permit evaluation of the interaction among nested variables. Care must be taken in defining these nesting relationships if hierarchical design is used solely for data reduction.

The Necessity for Collecting Data in Stages (Blocking Designs)

It may not be possible to obtain data from the entire factorial design at one time. The researcher may be forced to collect data in stages, or blocks. These blocks may involve different testing times or different experimenters collecting subsets of data. There can be a great variation among blocks, and certain aspects of the factorial design may be confounded with these block differences. The researcher can systematically confound certain components of the design with block differences, at the same time balancing the remaining aspects of the design within each block. One need only sacrifice all or part of a higher-order interaction while keeping the rest of the design balanced.

Williges (1981) provides an example in which the researcher is evaluating two

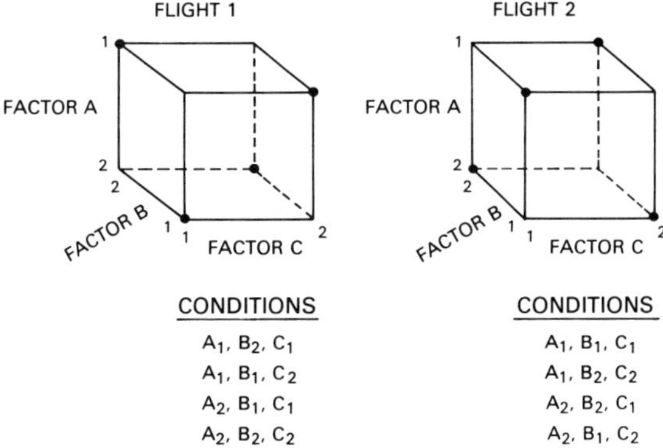

CONDITIONS
A_1, B_2, C_1
A_1, B_1, C_2
A_2, B_1, C_1
A_2, B_2, C_2

CONDITIONS
A_1, B_1, C_1
A_1, B_2, C_2
A_2, B_2, C_1
A_2, B_1, C_2

FIGURE 12.1. Blocked 2 × 2 × 2 factorial design. (From Williges, 1981.)

data entry procedures (Factor A) under two levels of pilot workload (Factor B) in two different area navigation displays (Factor C). The tests are being conducted in an aircraft simulator. It is impossible to collect the data on all eight treatment conditions in one flight. Only four conditions can be evaluated in each flight. Figure 12.1 shows how the design can be blocked into two flights of four treatment conditions each so that the main effects and two-way interactions of the three variables will not be confounded with possible flight differences. Only the three-way interaction is completely confounded with the two flight effects.

At times the researcher will wish to make all comparisons with equal precision without sacrificing entire effects to blocking (as the three-way interaction does in Figure 12.1). Alternative procedures (balanced and partially balanced incomplete block designs) have been developed for this purpose when one factor consisting of several levels is under study. Designs of this type include a number of treatment levels and block sizes. The number of treatment levels must exceed the block size.

Inability to Collect All Data from a Higher-Order Factorial Design (Fractional-Factorial Designs)

If the researcher cannot for whatever reason collect all his data from a higher-order factorial design, some information will be lost and certain effects will be confounded. Fractional-factorial designs enable the researcher to determine the nature and extent of the confounding by specifying for data collection a subset of treatment combinations from the complete factorial design. Considerable useful information can still be obtained from that subset. The number of levels of each variable must be restricted and the designs are usually limited to two-, three-, and five-level factorial combinations.

For example, if, in the previous example there were only enough time on the simulator to collect data on four of the eight treatment combinations, the researcher could choose to collect data in either flight 1 or flight 2. Each flight represents a one-half replicate of the complete factorial design; either half evaluates the three main unconfounded effects. Only the three-way interaction is completely lost.

EMPIRICAL MODEL BUILDING

For each of these design strategies it was assumed that the design would be used to collect data for hypothesis testing, that is, the experimenter wishes to determine whether or not a particular variable (or variable level) had a statistically significant effect on the operator's performance. Quite often, the researcher's aim is to determine a quantitative relationship between operator performance and several system parameters. Such a relationship allows predictions of operator performance to be made as a function of alternative system configurations.

The general expression for such a relationsip is

$$\eta = f(\Theta_i, X_i) \tag{12.1}$$

where η is the dependent variable, Θ_i is a set of system parameters and X_i is the set of independent variables. Because of the complexity of most systems, this theoretical model must be transformed into an empirical model based on polynomial expressions, most often a second-order approximation.

The general form of the second-order polynomial model is

$$Y = \beta_0 + \sum_{i=1}^{k} \beta_i X_i + \sum_{i=1}^{k} \beta_{k+i} X_i^2 + \sum_{i=1}^{k} \sum_{j=i+1}^{k} \beta_{2k+i} X_i X_j + \varepsilon, \tag{12.2}$$

where human performance, Y, is expressed in terms of an intercept value, β_0 and the weighted linear combinations of first-order terms, X_i, pure quadratic second-order terms, X_i^2, and linear interaction, second-order terms, $X_i X_j$, of the k system (independent) variables stated in terms of X's. The value ε is the estimate of error in prediction.

Polynomial regression is a powerful data analysis procedure for estimating the empirical model used in specifying functional relationships (Box, Hunter, and Hunter, 1978) and central-composite designs provide an efficient means of collecting the data to solve these polynomial regressions (Box and Wilson, 1951). The graduated polynomial can be used to estimate higher-order effects (e.g., quadratic and cubic effects) as well as linear effects. Additionally, a subsequent analysis of variance can be calculated on the regression analysis to test the goodness of fit of the empirical model. Polynomial regression models of this type assume that the factors being manipulated are continuous and quantitative in nature. The number of independent variables should be restricted to 7 or less in the final polynomial model.

The polynomial may be either orthogonal or nonorthogonal. When the polynomial is orthogonal, its partial regression weights are not correlated. This facilitates the interpretation of the resulting model. In order to have an orthogonal solution, however, the appropriate experimental design must be selected. In cases where the solution is not orthogonal, ridge regression procedures may improve the fit (Hoerl and Kennard, 1970a, 1970b).

A separate functional relationship can be determined for each dependent variable. In most systems research studies the set of dependent variables is quite large and, if this procedure is used, will result in an unwieldy number of prediction equations. Williges and Williges (1982) recommend the use of principal component analysis to collapse the dependent variables into multivariate clusters. Subsequent polynomial regressions can be calculated on these multivariate clusters to provide more parsimonious prediction equations.

Various designs have been developed to collect data for generating first- and second-order polynomial regression models. The most flexible and most widely used is central-composite design (Clark and Williges, 1973; Myers, 1971).

CENTRAL-COMPOSITE DESIGNS

Box and Wilson (1951) developed a method (central-composite design) for determining the optimal combinations of various factors present in chemical processes to maximize yield. The interesting feature of this method is its ability to predict performance levels corresponding to various levels of system variables, together with the ability to determine the system variable levels needed to maintain a given performance level.

Box and Wilson used polynomial regression models to define chemical yield relationships and developed second order central-composite designs as the data collection methodology. Response surface methodology is a special case of the Box/Wilson approach. Unlike traditional factorial ANOVA designs which merely determine the significance of a relationship between factors, response surface methodology determines the function relationship (i.e., the response surface) between the response and continuous quantitative variables, using a derived polynomial equation.

The following discussion of central-composite designs has been abbreviated from Williges (1981). He uses as an example the need to assess an operator's driving error (Y) in an automobile simulator as a function of frequency (X_1), velocity (X_2), and direction (X_3) of wind gusts. A three-factor, central-composite design as shown in Figure 12.2 could be used to collect the data necessary to solve the second-order polynomial regression equation which predicts driving error as a function of the three wind gust conditions. The design itself is a composite of a 2^3 factorial design, augmented by a center point and two to three additional points (star). These additional points radiate from the center, from which comes the term central-composite design. In general any second order, central-composite design can be specified as having unique data points, T,

$$T = F + 2K + 1, \tag{12.3}$$

where F equals the number of data points in the 2^k factorial design and K equals the number of k factors.

The 15 treatment combinations for the three-factor driving simulator example are

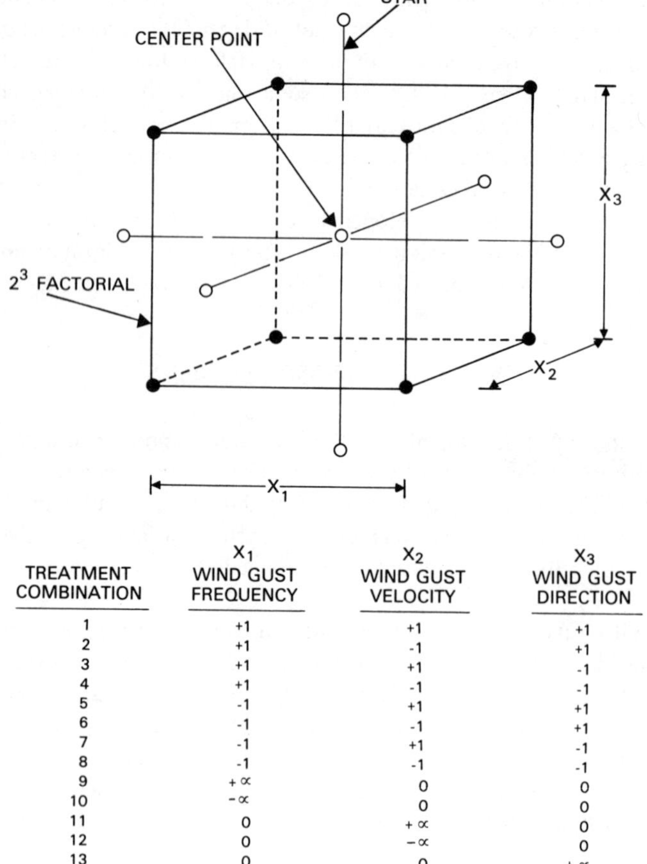

TREATMENT COMBINATION	X_1 WIND GUST FREQUENCY	X_2 WIND GUST VELOCITY	X_3 WIND GUST DIRECTION
1	+1	+1	+1
2	+1	-1	+1
3	+1	+1	-1
4	+1	-1	-1
5	-1	+1	+1
6	-1	-1	+1
7	-1	+1	-1
8	-1	-1	-1
9	$+\propto$	0	0
10	$-\propto$	0	0
11	0	$+\propto$	0
12	0	$-\propto$	0
13	0	0	$+\propto$
14	0	0	$-\propto$
15	0	0	0

FIGURE 12.2. Example of a three-factor, second-order, central-composite design used to evaluate automobile driving performance (Y) as a function of wind gust characteristics (X_1, X_2, X_3). (From Williges, 1981.)

listed below the geometric representation of the data points in Figure 12.2. The levels of these data points are listed in coded form (i.e., in an actual study they would be transformed into specific system levels of the wind gust parameters). Treatment combinations 1 to 8 represent the 2^3 factorial portion of the design; combinations 9 to 14 represent the $2 \cdot 3$ star portion; and treatment combination 15 is the center point. Each of the three wind gust factors appears at five distinct levels ($+\propto$, $+1$, 0, -1, $-\propto$). If these 15 treatment combinations are compared with the 125 combinations of a corresponding 5^3 factorial design, the efficiency of central-composite designs becomes quite apparent.

The three-factor design shown in Figure 12.2 can be extended to any number of k factors. As the number of variables increases, a 2^{k-p} fractional-factorial design is usually substituted for the 2^k factorial portion of the design and for the value of F in equation 12.3. Care must be taken to choose a fractional replicate so that all first- and second-order components are present. (Cochran and Cox, 1957, describe several examples of central-composite designs using fractional replicates.)

Ordinarily replication in a central-composite design is conducted only at the center point for data collection economy. The number of central point replications depends upon certain mathematical criteria, such as uniform precision and orthogonality of regression weights. Uniform precision insures that the accuracy of the predicted response is approximately equal for all points from the center out to a distance of (usually) ± 1 coded units. Orthogonality of regression weights eliminates any correlation among the coded values of parameters in the second-order polynomial regression. Myers (1971) provides a detailed explanation.

Replication is often conducted across the entire design to obtain a stable estimate of error. Equal replication across the entire design is an important design alternative for behavioral research (Clark and Williges, 1973). For example, if a different subject is observed at each treatment condition (i.e., a between-subjects design) more degrees of freedom for replications may be needed to obtain a stable estimate of error. On the other hand, if each subject receives every treatment combination (i.e., a within-subject design), then equal replications across the design would be appropriate when collecting data on more than one subject.

Figure 12.2 lists the coded value of the star components of the central-composite design as $\pm \propto$. Obviously, these $\propto$'s must be translated into specific values for the individual study. Choice of an $\propto$ value depends upon considerations of design rotatability, orthogonal regression weights, and blocking (Box and Hunter, 1957, and Myers, 1971).

Rotatability exists when the variance of the predicted response is the same for all points equidistant from the center regardless of direction. This is convenient when the researcher is unaware of the underlying response function relative to the orientation of the factor axes. For central-composite designs to be rotatable, the value of $\propto$ must be,

$$\propto = F^{1/4} \tag{12.4}$$

(Box and Hunter, 1957).

One difficulty in using second-order polynomial regression procedures for predicting human performance is that the higher-order effects (i.e., pure quadratic effects in Equation 12.2) may be intercorrelated. Orthogonal, second-order, central-composite, designs in coded form, can be described according to the following relationship (Myers, 1971):

$$\propto = \left(\frac{QF}{4}\right)^{1/4}, \tag{12.5}$$

where $Q = [(F + 2K + C)^{1/2} - F^{1/2}]^2.$

In this equation, the term C represents the total number of center points. If equal replication is used, the value of C reduces to 1 and the terms in parenthesis equal the unique data points, T, in a central-composite design as specified in Equation 12.3.

An additional feature of central-composite designs which affords the researcher greater efficiency and flexibility is blocking. Under blocking conditions subsets of the complete set of data collection points are studied together. If the blocking is orthogonal, any differences in mean performance among blocks are independent of any main effects due to the independent variable manipulations. Hence they do not affect the underlying quantitative relationship between factors and performance. Blocking can be used either to control unwanted effects (e.g., differences resulting from different experimenters or testing days) or to collect data in stages. The block mean effect must however be orthogonal to any first- and second-order effects resulting from the variables being manipulated. Orthogonal blocking of central-composite designs requires that (Box and Hunter, 1957),

$$\propto = \left[\frac{F\,(2K + C_S)}{2\,(F + C_F)}\right]^{1/2}, \tag{12.6}$$

where C_S equals the number of replicated center points in the star portion and C_F equals the number of center points in the factorial portion so that $C = C_S + C_F$.

In central-composite designs, the blocking is accomplished by separating the design into the K factorial and the set of $2K$ points comprising the star portion. If additional blocks are required, the factorial portion can be further divided by fractional replicates as in Figure 12.1. When replications occur only at the center point, they must appear in both the star and factorial portions of the design as in Equation 12.6 by C_S and C_F. If replications are equal across the design, then the center point only appears in the block using the star portion. C_S reduces to 1 and C_F reduces to 0 in Equation 12.6.

CENTRAL-COMPOSITE DESIGNS IN BEHAVIORAL RESEARCH

Williges and Simon, 1971, and Clark and Williges, 1973, present a general discussion of how central-composite designs can be used in behavioral research. These applications can be divided into three types, depending upon the manner in which subjects are assigned to treatment conditions. These three classes are between-subjects, within-subject, and mixed-factors design applications.

Between-Subjects Design

If a different subject is assigned randomly to each of the 15 different treatment conditions of the central-composite design shown in Figure 12.2, the design is called between-subjects. This design can be replicated across either the entire design or at the center point only with the restriction that each subject is observed only once. This assignment is least sensitive from a statistical viewpoint because between-subject variability is included in each set of observations. Moreover, between-subjects assignment requires more subjects in order to complete data collection. Randomized blocking (Keppel, 1978) can be used to make between-subjects designs more sensitive.

In certain situations the nature of the independent variables will permit only one treatment condition to be administered to each subject. For example, if the experimental variables represent alternative training conditions, the effects of one training condition would influence subsequent performance in another training condition. Therefore each subject can legitimately receive only a single training procedure.

Williges and Baron (1973) used such a between-subjects design to evaluate transfer of training in a tracking task as a function of three independent variables: time between trials, number of practice trials, and difficulty of training task. Their study replicated both at the center point only and across the entire design. Although the resulting first-order polynomial prediction equation of transfer performance did not change, the statistical reliability of the partial regression weights did change as a function of method of replication. The regression weights were not statistically significant with replication at the center point only, but were significant when replication occurred across the entire design. The latter added degrees of freedom to the error term, producing a more sensitive test of significance. The researcher must therefore be cognizant of the increased intersubject variability present in between-subject designs and choose the number of required replications accordingly.

Within-Subject Design

It is often possible to cross subjects with treatment conditions so that every subject receives every treatment combination in the central-composite design. This procedure yields a within-subject design in which the main effect of subjects can be separated from experimental error. Within-subject designs usually provide more sensitive error terms as well as require fewer subjects because of repeated observations. Usually it is more convenient to replicate equally across the central-composite design when it is a within-subject version. In this way, the experimenter can generalize the data over more than one subject and avoid the situation of having repeated observations on the same subject at the center point.

Constraints such as subject availability restrict the use of these designs. Moreover, the order of presentation of treatment conditions must be counterbalanced (e.g., balanced Latin square procedures) and there may be a problem of differential transfer (Poulton, 1969). For more details, see Williges and North (1973) and Williges (1981)

Mixed-Factor Design

Often it is not possible to manipulate all the factors in an experiment as either within-subject or between-subjects factors and the resulting design (called a mixed-factor design) is a combination of both types of factors (Clark, Scanlon, and Williges, 1973). The mixed-factor design is the most common in system studies.

TABLE 12.2 Design Matrix for a Mixed Factors Central-Composite Design Involving Three Within-Subject Factors (X_1, X_2, X_3) and One Between-Subjects Factor (X_4).

Subjects	X_1	X_2	X_3	X_4
S_1 and S_2	+1	+1	+1	+1
	−1	+1	+1	+1
	+1	−1	+1	+1
	−1	−1	+1	+1
	+1	+1	−1	+1
	−1	+1	−1	+1
	+1	−1	−1	+1
	−1	−1	−1	+1
S_3 and S_4	+1	+1	+1	−1
	−1	+1	+1	−1
	+1	−1	+1	−1
	−1	−1	+1	−1
	+1	+1	−1	−1
	−1	+1	−1	−1
	+1	−1	−1	−1
	−1	−1	−1	−1
S_5 and S_6	$-\alpha$	0	0	0
	$+\alpha$	0	0	0
	0	$-\alpha$	0	0
	0	$+\alpha$	0	0
	0	0	$-\alpha$	0
	0	0	$+\alpha$	0
	0	0	0	0
S_7 and S_8	0	0	0	$-\alpha$
S_9 and S_{10}	0	0	0	$+\alpha$

Source: Williges (1981).

Clark (1976) proposed a mixed-factor design alternative which is constructed by initially disregarding the within-subject or between-subjects status of all factors and by determining the data points solely in accordance with central-composite design procedures. Once the unique data points are specified, subjects are assigned to the various treatment combinations in such a way that no subject experiences more than one level of the between-subject factors(s). An example of this version of a mixed-factor design is given in Table 12.2 which includes three within-subject factors and one between-subjects factor.

Williges and Mills (1982) make the following recommendations: (1) Use within-subject assignment whenever possible to increase the sensitivity of the design and reduce the number of required subjects; (2) Counterbalance the order of presentation when within-subject assignment is used and check for the presence of differential transfer effects; (3) Use randomized blocking procedures when possible with between-subject assignment to increase the precision of estimate; (4) Use pretesting to determine the number of subjects required. Usually a sample size of 6 is sufficient for most simulation studies.

SEQUENTIAL DESIGN PROCEDURES

In many cases system research questions cannot be answered in a single study and it is necessary to conduct a series of studies. It would be incorrect for the reader to infer that all the design alternatives described so far imply a single study. That is because all system studies require some pretesting in order to choose appropriate variables and their levels. If the researcher commits a great amount of time and effort in one large study without careful pretesting, the results could be wasteful. Box, Hunter and Hunter (1978) suggested that no more than one quarter of the experimental effort should be invested in the first experimental design.

Most of the strategies suggested in conducting sequential research have been developed within the orientation of response surface methodology. What the researcher is attempting to do in using this technique is to determine the point of maximum performance (or minimum error) for all significant variables. Cochran and Cox (1957) discuss three general approaches.

One procedure is merely to use a random and independent selection of experimental data points (Anderson, 1953). After a specified number of trials including random treatment combinations, the combination yielding the highest overall response is regarded as the optimum. Although this approach lacks sophistication, it may be the researcher's only choice when the system problem involves so many factors that the use of ordered designs becomes impossible.

Random selection can be supplemented either by using the randomly chosen treatment combinations in polynomial regression to specify an empirical model, or by using sequential design procedures to search systematically the region of optimality defined by the random selection method.

A second approach, proposed by Friedman and Savage (1947), is called the single-factor method, because it is characterized by a series of small experiments in which one factor at a time is optimized. The researcher estimates an optimal combination of factors based on background and/or pretest knowledge. The variable assumed to have the greatest effect on performance is optimized first in a three-level design while the other factors are held constant. Subsequently, all the other factors are optimized one at a time until an optimal configuration of all factors is achieved. Variations in this procedure can include simultaneous changes in all factors and/or the dropping of some factors in subsequent experimental rounds. The emphasis is on first-order effects, not on higher-order ones.

The third approach to sequential design and probably the most widely used, is the method of steepest ascent proposed by Box and Wilson (1951). The three general steps followed in this approach include: (1) the use of first-order designs to determine a local slope; (2) the use of the method of steepest ascent to approach an optimum; and (3) the use of second-order designs to characterize the local region around an optimum.

A series of small 2^k (or 2^{k-p}) factorial designs is used as the first-order design procedure. Following each 2^k factorial study, the researcher adjusts the ranges of each factor by the method of steepest ascent. This method changes the levels proportional to the first-order partial regression weights. This procedure is repeated until the investigator approaches an optimum point on the response surface. Second order, central-composite designs have been developed by Box and his colleagues to specify the region around an optimum. By using blocking procedures the factorial portion of the design is used iteratively with the method of steepest ascent. Then only the star portion need be added to complete the second-order model around the optimum.

Two types of statistical analysis may be performed on the data from a response surface design.

1. A least squares multiple regression analysis can be performed to determine the functional relationship between performance (Y) and system variables (X). Multiple regression simply extends linear regression by including more than one predictor. A matrix algebra solution using correlation matrices rather than raw score matrices enables the researcher to deal with a number of possible regression equations within the same computer program. A correlation matrix solution produces a standard regression equation which can be converted into a nonstandard or raw score regression equation.

2. A second analysis is an ANOVA performed on the regression analysis. The ANOVA partitions the sum of squares into variation due to regression and a residual. The regression sum of squares is further subdivided into the variation of the partial regression weights resulting from the previous multiple regression analysis. The residual sum of squares can also be further subdivided into block effects, subject effects, lack of fit, and error. The ANOVA is used to test the significance of the partial regression weights and any significant lack of fit. This last might indicate that additional parameters are needed for the regression equation. All the sums of squares are converted to mean squares by dividing by the appropriate degrees of freedom. The resulting F ratios are created by using the error mean square as the denominator.

A PARADIGM FOR MULTIFACTOR STUDIES

Most of the response surface methodology procedures were designed primarily for research applications other than human performance, in, for example, the chemical industry. Along with Williges, the one researcher who has attempted to integrate response surface methodology along with other techniques into a research paradigm for multifactor designs is Simon (1971; 1973; 1974; 1975; 1977a; 1977b). The basic principles of his paradigm are: avoid replicating basic experimental designs unnecessarily; avoid collecting data on higher-order effects until evidence for their existence is found; collect and evaluate data in a sequence of progressive iterations; substitute experimenter's knowledge and analytical skills for data collection; and minimize bias effects on each inidividual measurement (Simon, 1973). The following is a brief description of Simon's approach. It is impossible in a single chapter to do justice to all the details of his procedures; for those details the reader is referred to the original reports.

The start of his work is an analysis he performed of experiments published in *Human Factors* between 1958 and 1972 (described in Simon, 1973). The effectiveness of the 239 studies in accounting for variability in operator performance was determined by reanalyzing their ANOVA tables. Since the median number of factors studied was only two, the chance that their data would predict performance in an operational situation was extremely slim. The more equipment factors included in a study, Simon found, the greater the proportion of performance variability accounted for by those factors. With less than four independent variables in an experiment the factors purposefully varied accounted for less of the variability in performance on the average than the other conditions (not studied or controlled) in the study. The point that Simon noted was that the quality of the data improves as the number of independent variables increased. Quality he defined as the ratio of the proportion of variance associated with independent variables to the proportion of variance associated with irrelevant variance sources. Simon believed that the results of his analyses forecasted the characteristics that future human factors studies must have if the goal of predicting operational performance from laboratory data is to be achieved. Hence the emphasis on multifactor studies. Specifically, experiments must contain many more independent variables than are currently included in a single study and the number of observations must be held to a minimum to make multifactor experiments economically feasible. Simon suggests on the basis of his analyses that 10 factors per study would be optimal.

The General Strategy

Traditional experimentalists build a body of information through a series of small experiments. They make the assumption that by conducting enough small experiments—a few variables at a time—they can eventually combine the results to form a more complex, multivariate space reflecting the effects of variables. In practice, Simon suggests, there are never enough small experiments, results are never quantitatively combined, and no "big picture" ever emerges.

Simon's paradigm begins by examining the overall structure of the operational space in order to obtain the big picture first. Additional data are collected to improve the information, to approximate the operational space better. This assumes that by first obtaining an overview, however sparse, considerable economy in the data collection process is achieved since it will be easier to determine in what parts of the experimental space further refinement is needed. By including all variables, presumed to be of some importance to the task, in the initial empirical examination, it is possible to eliminate the trivial ones before a more detailed examination is made. Where the function fails to reflect reality the most, more data are obtained to correct the model.

The success of this strategy is predicated on certain principles.

1. *Experimental/operational equivalence.* The more closely the experimental world approximates the real world, the more likely experimental data will predict operational behavior. Therefore, the more critical variables within operations ranges that are included in the study, the more precise the prediction.

2. *Variable criticality.* Although a large number of variables could conceivably affect results, in fact, only a relatively few will be critical and many will be trivial.

3. *Behavioral simplicity.* Human behavior can generally be approximated by a second- or third-order equation. Higher-order effects are tentatively assumed to be trivial when proper scaling is employed.

4. *Error variance triviality.* By accounting for most of the performance variance in a complex task, little error variance will remain in the residual.

5. *Minimal replication.* In general, collecting data more than once under the same conditions is to be avoided.

The paradigm is divided into five phases: a. Define the problem; b. Identify the critical variables; c. Develop an appropriate response surface; d. Refine the equation; and e. Verify experimental results.

We will discuss only the first three phases since these are sufficient to explore the paradigm. The relationships among phases, goals, and methodology are shown in Table 12.3.

Phase 1. To define the problem, the researcher must place limits on the multivariate space in which the system performs. The general question to answer is: What precisely is the task and under what conditions of the equipment, environment, personnel, and time considerations is it performed? This must be done in two steps. First, the researcher must dimensionalize the problem as it exists under operational conditions.

A fundamental principle in the design of any experiment is that the definition of the task and the conditions under which performance will be measured must be based on real world considerations. Decisions to include or exclude, duplicate, or approximate in the experiment should be made on the basis of their anticipated impact were the same thing to occur under operational conditions. Only after an operational (i.e., task) analysis of the real world situation is made should the researcher begin to translate the problem into questions and conditions that can be dealt with experimentally.

In the second step of the problem definition phase, the reality of the operational situation will often clash with the reality of the experimental situation. This is the time when the requirements for the experiment must be balanced against the practical limits imposed by money, time, and availability.

Phase 2. Whereas the objective of the traditional experiment has been to identify statistically significant effects, the objective in Phase 2 of the paradigm is to dis-

TABLE 12.3 Relationship among Phases, Goals, and Methodology as the Experiment Progresses

<table>
<tr><td>PHASE:</td><td>1
Defining the problem</td><td colspan="2">2
Identifying critical variables</td><td colspan="2">3
Approximating response surfaces</td><td colspan="3">4
Equation refinement</td><td colspan="2">5
Verification</td></tr>
<tr><td>GOAL:</td><td colspan="2">Exploring and limiting the problem</td><td colspan="4">Building a quantitative database</td><td colspan="4">Evaluating</td></tr>
<tr><td>LOCATION:</td><td>Field*</td><td colspan="5">Laboratory or Field</td><td colspan="4">Field</td></tr>
<tr><td>APPROACH:</td><td>Undesigned (No control; measure)</td><td colspan="6">Systematic (manipulation, control; measure)</td><td colspan="3">Systematic or undesigned</td></tr>
<tr><td>METHOD:</td><td>Literature search
Interview
Observe
Experience
Measurement</td><td colspan="3">Fractional factorials screening—group, individual measure</td><td colspan="2">Central-composite designs; refinement points</td><td colspan="3">Replication; interation</td><td>Test-residual analysis</td></tr>
<tr><td>ANALYSIS:</td><td>Correlational:
factor analysis
ridge regression
cluster analysis
etc.</td><td colspan="3">Analysis of Variance:
mean differences
eta squared
ordered graphics
etc.</td><td colspan="4">Correlational:
ridge canonical regression</td><td colspan="2">Correlation;
significance</td></tr>
</table>

Source: Simon (1977b).
* May not be possible if system doesn't exist; simulator may serve instead.

cover empirically which of the long list of candidate variables selected rationally in Phase 1 are really important in the performance of the task.

The term screening refers to the need to, and the procedures to, reduce a large set of independent variables (dependent variables as well) to a small, more manageable number. In most system research the investigator is faced with the problem of isolating a small subset of independent variables which are critical to system performance from the large set of potential independent variables that *might* be important. All the variables that could be manipulated in simulating the system are potentially important. If we cannot reduce their number, the research design will either be so large as to be unfeasible or irrelevant variables will be tested, forcing us to make expensive and useless observations. Both analytic and experimental design procedures can be used for screening.

Simon assumes that the magnitude of the effects of the very large number of variables associated with a particular task will approximate an exponential distribution. This means that for any one task, the effects of a relatively few variables will account for most of the observed variance.

By eliminating the smaller, noncritical variables from all subsequent studies, valuable data collection time will be saved. Since the response surface will be built upon data collected only for the more important variables, the derived equation of the response surface should predict performance well under operational conditions.

The first step in planning the screening phase is to divide the candidate list of predictor variables into two groups—those that can be controlled by the researcher and those that cannot. Only the first can be dealt with by the screening design.

Economy in data collection is achieved with screening designs because a sequential approach is used. A block of data is collected and analyzed to determine whether or not more is needed to identify the important variables. Since each block is only a small fraction of the total factorial, this iterative process keeps data collection to a minimum.

The following are screening principles.

1. Collect only enough data in each block to estimate the magnitude of all main effects independently of one another, but confounded with all higher-order effects.
2. Collect enough additional data, which, when combined with the data from the first block, will isolate all main effects from all two-factor interactions.
3. Collect enough additional data, if necessary, to isolate and estimate the effects of specific disordinal two-factor interactions or three-factor interactions that might affect the ordering of the main effects.
4. Keep replication to a minimum, if at all.

This sequential strategy is basic to the new experimental paradigm, that is, the procedure of collecting as little data as possible until examination of the data shows that more is actually needed. The traditional approach of immediately collecting enough data to estimate higher-order effects is wasteful. According to Simon, seldom, if ever, are there reliable fourth-order interaction effects and when these do occur, their effects are likely to be trivial. Even nontrivial third-order effects occur infrequently. If under unusual circumstances they turn out to be critical, they can be isolated after the fact has been established, not before.

A researcher can choose among several forms of screening designs. Analytical methods for screening involve both expert judgment and logical structuring. Expert judgment is based on experience with similar systems, previous system research and knowledge of the research literature. Logical structuring involves partitioning the variables into subsets of parameters, constants and independent variables (System Development Corporation, 1979). Later the variables are manipulated systematically across several studies.

The strategy utilized by Geiselman and Samet (1982) was to conduct a preliminary study in which all task-related variables were free to be set at any level that the subject desired. After the subjects completed their tasks, the researcher selected the levels chosen by those subjects who performed best on the task. If one level is consistently chosen, this variable becomes a constant. If varying levels are chosen by the best subjects, these levels are systematically compared in subsequent studies.

A number of experimental design procedures are also available. All these designs (including fractional-factorial and hierarchic designs) are based on the premise that higher-order interactions among variables can be sacrificed. For maximum efficiency in screening a large number of variables, the techniques should be used sequentially.

Williges and Mills (1982) make the following recommendations. Use fractional-factorial designs for the screening exercise. Use 2^k designs in all initial screening studies and 3^k designs in final screening studies (k is the number of independent variables). Use 2^k designs in the fractional replicates whenever curvilinear effects are not expected, 3^k designs when they are.

A similar screening problem exists with dependent variables, such as system performance measures, metrics, and figures of merit. In systems of any size the potential set of performance measures may be quite large. The expert judgment of those familiar with the type of system under study, as well as analytical procedures, can be used.

Where the system under study is a MMS, purely physical (engineering) characteristics may constrain the choice of dependent variables.

Optimization procedures based on operations research techniques can also be used to screen dependent variables if there are few of these. Otherwise this approach becomes unwieldy as the number of variables increases. Optimization techniques are moreover inappropriate when convexity or concavity of the data does not exist (Gillio, 1978). Multivariate clustering procedures, especially principal components analysis with orthogonal rotations, are useful in collapsing large sets of dependent variables into meaningful subsets (Harris, 1975; Tatsuoka, 1971). Component scores can then be determined from the resulting principal components analysis to represent the multivariate dependent variables.

Simon (1977) divides his screening methods into those for very large numbers of variables (100) and those for screening only large (e.g., 30) numbers of variables. Designs for screening a very large number of variables include supersaturated designs which may be either random balance or systematic. Group screening designs may be either two-stage or multistage. Designs for screening large numbers of individual variables include Box and Hunter designs, Plackett and Burman designs and those of Simon himself.

SCREENING 100 OR SO VARIABLES. *Supersaturated designs* are factorial designs in which there are more variables than there are observations. Mathematically, in this case, it is not possible to isolate every main effect from every other main effect. Those who propose this method assume that out of the total number of variables only a few will have a critical effect. Thus there will be more observations than there are critical variables, and the critical effects can be isolated. Two approaches in designing these experimental plans have been proposed.

Random balance designs (Satterthwaite, 1959; Budne, 1959a, 1959b, 1959c) are created by choosing the levels of each variable for each experimental condition at random. As many variables as desired would be included in the description of each condition, a desirable feature when one wishes to locate the condition in the coordinate space. For each condition, the level—generally one of two alternatives—at which each variable is set is selected at random. Ordinarily approximately 50 or so observations are all that would be required in these designs. Budne (1959b) suggests that restricted randomization might be desirable, such as having the levels of each factor represented an equal number of times. He also describes a grouping technique with combinations among groups randomized. Scatter diagrams are used to analyze the data and a computer is useful for plotting these diagrams. The largest effects are discovered by simple examination of the data. After these are removed, the data are replotted so that lesser effects of some magnitude can be identified. Two-factor interactions can be examined in the same way. The technique is like a graphic stepwise regression and may have all of its inherent dangers. Random balance designs have been used by some and criticized by others.

Booth and Cox (1962) propose a supersaturated design in which the levels are systematically selected. They assume no interaction effects and only a few critical main effects. They provide designs for up to 36 variables and 18 observations. Some, such as Kleijnen (1975) consider the Booth/Cox method unfeasible and recommend group screening designs instead.

Group screening designs, like the supersaturated designs, are intended to provide a rough, first cut at a large number of variables to reduce their number to thirty or so. Group screening designs (Watson, 1961; Patel, 1962; Li, 1962) handle a large number of factors by combining them into groups and then treating each group as if it were a single factor. The assumption is made that if a group factor is found to have a trivial effect (insignificant), then all factors within the group will be insignificant. Those factors in groups found to be significant would be studied further. Those in groups with trivial effects would be dropped. Both size and content of the groups are important, natural groupings being preferred.

Watson (1961) proposed a two-stage group screening plan in which factors are tested in groups in the first stage and individually in the second stage. If the number of factors is quite large, however, multistage group screening might be necessary. Patel (1962) and Li (1962) both proposed plans that allow for more than two stages. Groups that survive after the first stage are partitioned into smaller groups for the second and subsequent stages until the number of individual variables remaining is small enough to be handled by individual screening designs.

A number of assumptions hold in all of these plans, the most important and restricting being that there are no interactions, and that the direction of possible effects is known. These are needed to make certain that several effects within a group do not cancel one another out. In behavioral studies the second assumption is tenable, but the first may not be. Disordinal interactions rather than the ordinal ones are the most important, and the least likely to exist. Unequal group sizes in these designs are possible and may be used to avoid cancellations by putting questionable effects in different groups.

SCREENING 30 OR SO VARIABLES. With *Box and Hunter's designs* (see Simon, 1973, pp. 89–101; 105–114) the main effects of each variable can be estimated independently of one another, but are completely "aliased" with specific sets of higher-order interaction effects, including two-factor interactions. The minimum number of experimental conditions for these designs is equal to the first power to two greater than the number of variables to be studied.

With *Plackett and Burman's designs* (see Simon, 1973a, pp. 102–103) the main effects of each variable can be estimated independently of one another, but are partially confounded with two-factor and higher interaction effects. The minimum number of experimental conditions for these designs is equal to the first multiple of four greater than the number of variables to be studied.

With Simon's designs (see Simon, 1977a, pp. 8–24) the main effects are independent of one another and of all two-factor interactions, the latter being aliased in sets of independent strings. Designs are robust to linear, quadratic, and cubic trends, and can be adjusted to minimize factor level change counts. These designs require a minimum number of observations equal to twice the first power of two greater than the number of variables to be studied.

If any string of interaction effects appear to be nontrivial, or if the investigator suspects certain two-factor interactions to be of the disordinal type, he will want to collect enough additional data to isolate the critical ones. The purpose of this is not to improve the equation resulting from the screening data, although this would happen, but to be assured that the order of main effects (i.e., the independent variables) is not disarranged. Techniques for doing this may be found in Daniel (1976, pp. 246–247), John (1966) and Simon (1973a, pp. 115–125).

Replication can be accomplished by testing the same subject several times on the same condition(s) or by testing several subjects on each condition, or both.

Two principles apply to replication:

1. The general principle is do not replicate unless the gain in information is cost-effective.

2. The principle specific to screening designs is: As long as the factorial design has not been completed—which is usually the case with screening studies—it is better to run a different fraction of the factorial to isolate additional effects than it is to repeat the same fraction.

For screening purposes, the researcher will rank the independent variables in order of their magnitude, but he will also need additional data to help him decide how to categorize them as crucial, marginal, and trivial. Several criteria can be applied.

1. Is the mean difference between low and high conditions of each effect one of practical importance?

2. Does each variable account for a nontrivial amount of the total variance (eta squared) in the experiment?

3. Is the cumulative proportion of variance in the experiment accounted for by all variables designated trivial still a trivial amount?

4. Which variables appear to be significant when plotted on a half-normal grid?

Calculating the data needed to apply these criteria (Simon, 1977a, Section V) is relatively simple and straightforward when the performance measure is a single, dependent value. Nonetheless, the classification of variables as crucial, marginal, and trivial is a highly subjective process without precise rules.

Phase 3. The third phase of the multifactor study is to develop a response surface, using the response surface methodology described previously.

As we have seen, the data from the initial screening design enable one to write the relationship between predictor and response variables in the form of a first order polynomial equation. Simon's version (1977, p. 71) is:

$$\bar{Y} = b_0x_0 + b_1x_1\ b_2x_2 + \ldots + b_Nx_N \tag{12.7}$$

where:

$\bar{Y}$ = estimated performance
b_i = coefficients
x_i = terms or variables

With an unreplicated, saturated screening design of N observations and $(N - 1)$ variables, there is no estimate of error. The term, b_0x_0 is the mean. Each main effect in these designs is confounded with higher-order interactions which are tentatively assumed to be negligible. Until more data are gathered, main effects cannot be isolated from two-factor interactions.

For the basic screening design, data are collected at selected corners of a 2^k factorial space. Since each variable is measured at two levels, no nonlinear representation of the experimental space is possible. When human performance is involved, a nonlinear relationship between predictor and response variables might give a more unbiased approximation of the response surface. The next step in the paradigm is to determine whether or not a first-order model adequately approximates the experimental space.

To test this, more data must be collected. Expanding the screening design provides data regarding two-factor, linear-by-linear interactions, but nothing about the curvature of the space. To get this information economically, it is necessary to collect data at the center of the experimental space as defined by the critical variables in the screening study. The coordinates of the center point are (0, 0, 0 . . . 0) when the coordinates of the screening design are combinations of the coordinates (± 1, ± 1, ± 1, . . . ± 1). Thus each variable will be measured at three levels (− 1, 0, + 1) but not factorially. This additional information, when combined with the original screening data, is enough to test for the presence of quadratic effects in the data. Individual quadratic effects cannot be isolated. However, that estimate can provide the investigator with the necessary information to decide whether or not he should collect still more data to isolate quadratic terms of the critical variables.

Unreplicated screening designs have no provision for estimating the error variance unless untenable assumptions about higher-order interactions are made. Replicating the complete design to obtain an estimate is uneconomical and actually unwarranted as long as data for the full factorial have not been gathered. A rough estimate of error can be obtained by taking repeated measures at the center point. This measure of error combined in an *F-test* with the composite measure of quadratic effects has been used to test the fit of the model (Simon, 1970b, pp. 32–33; 1977a, Section IX).

Still there are usually so few degrees of freedom involved that this F-test of statistical significance has little power and to use it as a basis of judging the adequacy of fit is unwise (Simon, 1971, pp. 30–33, 44–46; 1977a, pp. 14–18). The proportion of total variance accounted for by the lack of fit is preferable.

If, on the basis of the test, the investigator believes that no quadratic model is required, he may consider the equation derived from the screening design as an adequate approximation of the experimental space.

If there is evidence of considerable lack of fit due to curvature, the investigator must be prepared to collect additional data making use of the central-composite (response surface) designs described previously.

ADDITIONAL PROBLEMS

Team Performance Criteria

Special problems arise when systems are composed of teams or groups. Hence, special consideration must be given during pretesting to team performance criteria. Factors to be considered include the training of subjects, the specification of team structure, and the possibility that some team members may compensate for the performance of other team members.

To evaluate team behavior in an operational system context the subjects must achieve some specified level of proficiency before beginning the experiment. The researcher must specify both the measures of team performance to be considered and the acceptable levels of these measures.

In designing a new system team member roles, team structure and task allocation may not be very clear. Before conducting the study team structure must be specified, that is the dimensions of teamwork, critical team tasks and critical member skills. Dimensions of teamwork may include team composition, communication constraints, degree of coordination required, and level of authority structure (who directs whom and what). Team members must be grouped and matched in terms of critical skills used in teamwork. Matching can be accomplished either by allowing roles of each team member to emerge naturally during the course of training and pretesting or by using analytical methods. System studies may be confounded by compensatory team performance so that the effects of certain independent variables are masked or eliminated. In consequence, in totally new systems, it is necessary to conduct extensive pretesting to allow for the emergence of team roles and structures.

Treatment of Missing Data

Even though one generally designs a study to include equal sample sizes, the researcher may find some of his data missing. Where simulation is involved, for example, equipment malfunctions can result in loss of data which is discovered only after data collection is completed. If the study is being performed in the operational environment, subjects who are operational personnel may be required to return to other duty assignments before completing the study. The amount of data collection required by the experimental strategy may be too large for any feasible time frame. Or missing data may result from inadequate pretesting to determine the precise amount of data to collect and the time needed to collect those data.

Missing data can bias the statistical analysis. For example, ANOVA is robust to violations of assumptions of normality and homogeneity of variance when sample sizes are equal (Norton, 1953), but not when data are lacking. The variance in prediction using central-composite designs will be affected by the number of observations at the center point of the design (Box and Wilson, 1957).

What is the researcher to do? The experimenter may be in a position to collect additional data to complete the original design. If, however, only a few data points are missing within a treatment level, the researcher may consider estimating each data point. One method would be to use the means of the other scores and weight them by the bias of the individual subject as measured in other observations within the design.

Special analysis procedures are available in some statistical techniques whereby unequal sample sizes are considered directly. Winer (1971) and Keppel (1978) discuss both weighted means and unweighted means analyses for unequal sample sizes in ANOVA.

Time Series Investigations

Many experiments examine human performance in complex systems that are characterized by event-based or steady-state behavior. In real systems, the operator's performance is often time varying and the system itself may operate on a time base.

Data from studies in which system performance varies over time require special analysis procedures in order to evaluate the time-dependent characteristics of the data. Most of these analyses are special cases of regression analysis which incorporate autocorrelations and partial autocorrelations. Little behavioral research has been conducted in which time-dependent aspects of operator performance are considered in specifying functional relationships. In fact, methodology for dealing with this problem is presently very limited. The few methods available consist of:

1. *Theil's inequality coefficient,* which is a ratio allowing the researcher to compare actual and/or predicted singular or multiple time series data at various discrete points (Kheir and Holmes, 1978).

2. Box and Jenkins (1976) provide the most comprehensive data analysis methodology for evaluating interrupted time series design. Their family of models is called *ARIMA* (autoregressive integrated moving average) and each model is characterized by an autoregressive term, stationarity differencing and a moving average. Because of the complexity of the resultant computations, computerized analysis procedures are advisable. Examples are provided by Cook and Campbell (1979).

3. Box, Hunter and Hunter (1978) describe the use of time series models for forecasting, feedback control, and intervention analysis, all of which may be useful in system studies. Forecasting models can be used to predict time varying operator performance. Feedback control applications enable the researcher to input system

research results to computer analytical modeling data bases. Intervention analysis can be used to evaluate the effect of time varying operator/team workload on system performance.

When time series designs are appropriate, the researcher must decide when in the mission required measures should be taken. Often this requires careful pretesting to determine critical periods in the mission profile. Task characteristics, such as changes in peak workload, onset of team activities, major stages in the mission, may suggest measurement periods for time series analysis.

4. Cook and Campbell (1979) describe quasi experimental designs that incorporate intervention analysis. These are called *interrupted time series* designs because a treatment effect (e.g., introduction of a target in an aerial surveillance mission) occurs at a specific point to interrupt the time series. Cook and Campbell (1979) discuss various designs for data collection: a. simple interrupted time series; b. nonequivalent, no-treatment control group interrupted time series; c. nonequivalent dependent variable, interrupted time series; d. removed treatments, interrupted time series designs; e. multiple replications, interrupted time series; and f. switching replications, interrupted time series designs. The researcher must of course find the design that fits his particular problem.

Estimating Optimal System Performance

Most system research studies involve a number of dependent variables, and each one can be used to evaluate the functional relationship among the independent variables manipulated in the study. Often the researcher is faced with the task of determining the optimum for a set of equations which describe performance of a system. Finding the optimum for one equation will not necessarily yield optimal values across all equations.

Partial derivatives can be used to determine the optimal values for the composite set of equations. This approach often leads however to negative values or values which are not possible in real-world terms.

Linear programming for first-order equations and nonlinear programming methods for higher-order equations can also be considered, providing certain mathematic constraints are satisfied. The resulting functions are often not convex (or concave), thereby making nonlinear programming procedures inappropriate.

Brute force iteration can be used to yield approximate optimal values by simply choosing the best possible (maximum or minimum) performance values based on all predictors, with subsequent iterations to remove at each iteration the one term which accounted for the least variation. This continues until only a single term remains in the equation. This procedure can quickly become unwieldy as the number of predictors and/or dependent measures increases. However, brute force iteration is currently the most feasible approach for obtaining an estimate of the best response.

Selection of Quasi Experimental Designs

In planning a system experiment one must of course give careful consideration to the choice of experimental design. A critical factor determining the choice of design is the researcher's ability to assign subjects randomly to treatment conditions. If random assignment is possible, then true experimental designs like ANOVA can be considered. If random assignment is not possible the researcher's best bet may be quasi experimental procedures. These designs, which allow the researcher to control sources of contamination, are divided into those that deal with nonequivalent control groups and alternatives that deal with interrupted time series (see Campbell and Stanley, 1966, and Cook and Campbell, 1979).

Additional detail about these special problems can be found in Williges and Mills (1982)

COMMENTARY

One cannot help but be impressed by the sophistication of the techniques described in this chapter and the bold attempt of mathematical psychologists to apply methodology developed originally for chemistry and agriculture to the crudities of behavior research. It should be noted that much of the emphasis in the response surface and central-composite techniques is as much on the selection of variables for measurement as it is on the analysis of data after measurement. This is singularly different—and refreshing—from much traditional behavioral research in which the selection of variables is a purely intellectual, idiosyncratic and informal exercise. These techniques are in part forced upon us by the need to consider so many variables that they cannot be juggled mentally with ease. Nevertheless, nagging questions persist.

Simon's point—that most behavioral research has so far dealt only with a few variables and these generally one at a time—is quite valid. Certainly the system orientation demands that to the extent possible all variables inherent in the system be examined simultaneously. I must confess that I have difficulty conceptualizing situations in which one hundred or so variables exist. If they do, most of them must be so trivial that some slight thought should be enough to eliminate them. For example, in a task performance measurement situation the lighting of the space in which the performance is measured is certainly a variable, but unless that lighting is quite poor—so that subjects have difficulty seeing what they are supposed to be doing—the effect is trivial and the researcher will probably ignore the variable. Undoubtedly such a variable would be eliminated formally and statistically by the procedures described previously. Still the end result is the same. It may be that a little thought will be sufficient to eliminate most trivial variables, after which the subtle techniques Williges and Simon recommend should be applied.

The outstanding incongruity is the discrepancy between the sophistication of these analytic techniques and the comparative primitiveness of the methods, such as observation and interview, that collect the data on which they operate. Using an analogy from chemistry, it is possible by using more sophisticated assay methods to extract more information from the same data, but is there not a point at which even the most sophisticated technique will yield no further information increment? The discrepancy between the statistical analysis and data collection techniques suggests that without ceasing our efforts in statistics, more attention must be paid to upgrading data collection methodology.

Another doubt is the extent to which the researcher can apply these statistical techniques to research situations other than those that make use of objective measures like wind speed. To use these methods the researcher has to be able to control these situations very closely. On the other hand, Williges and Mills (1982) point out that statistical techniques are available when we cannot partition factors or when uncertainty is such that that researcher has to assign subjects at random. And there are always the quasi experimental methods of Cook and Campbell (1979).

Ten years have passed since the *Human Factors* journal presented a special issue dealing with response surface methodology (Williges, 1973). It would be interesting to determine what percentage of the studies published in the journal since 1973 in fact utilized the techniques recommended by Williges, Simon, and their colleagues. One suspects very few, if any, have done so. One must of course expect technological "lag" in conceptual matters as well as in industry, but it remains to be seen whether these specialized techniques, demanding as they do a certain mathematical expertise, will catch on with the bulk of behavior specialists. Perhaps a new generation of such specialists inured to computers and advanced statistics will adopt a more receptive attitude than my generation which was raised largely on ANOVA and nonparametric techniques.

REFERENCES

Anderson, R. L. Recent advances in finding best operating conditions. *Journal of American Statistical Association*. 1953, *48*, 789–798.

Booth, K. H. V., and D. R. Cox. Some systematic supersaturated designs. *Technometrics*, 1962, *4*, 489–495.

Box, G. E. P. and Hunter, J. S. Multifactor experimental designs for exploring response surfaces. *Annals of Mathematical Statistics*, 1957, *28*, 195–241.

Box, G. E. P., Hunter, W. G., and Hunter, J. S. *Statistics for Experimenters: An Introduction to Design, Data Analysis, and Model Building*. New York: Wiley, 1978.

Box, G. E. P. and Jenkins, G. M. *Time Series Analysis: Forecasting and Control*. San Francisco: Holden-Day, 1976.

Box, G. E. P. and Wilson, K. B. On the experimental attainment of optimum conditions. *Journal of the Royal Statistical Society, Series B (Methodological)*, 1951, *13*, 1–45.

Budne, T. A. Application of random balance designs. *Technometrics*, 1959, *1*, 139–155. (a)

Budne, T. A. Random balance: Part I—the missing statistical link in fact finding techniques. *Industrial Quality Control*, 1959, *15*, 5–10. (b)

Budne, T. A. Random balance: Part II—techniques of analysis. *Industrial Quality Control*, 1959, *15*, 11–16. (c)

Campbell, D. T. and Stanley, J. C. *Experimental and Quasi Experimental Designs for Research*, Chicago: Rand McNally, 1966.

Clark, C. Mixed-factors central-composite designs: A theoretical and empirical comparison. Technical Report ARL-76-13/AFOSR-76-6, University of Illinois, Aviation Research Laboratory, August, 1976.

Clark, C., Scanlon, L. A., and Williges, R. C. Mixed-factor response surface methodology central-composite design considerations. *Proceedings,* Annual meeting of the Human Factors Society. October 1973, 281–288.

Clark, C. and Williges, R. C. Response surface methodology central-composite design modifications for human performance research. *Human Factors,* 1973, *15,* 295–310.

Cochran, W. G. and Cox, G. M. *Experimental Designs.* New York: Wiley, 1957.

Cook, T. D. and Campbell, D. T. *Quasi Experimentation.* Chicago: Rand-McNally, 1979.

Daniel, C. *Applications of Statistics to Industrial Experimentation.* New York: Wiley, 1976.

Friedman, M. and Savage, L. J. Planning experiments seeking maxima, in *Techniques of Statistical Analysis.* New York: McGraw Hill, 1947.

Geiselman, R. E. and Samet, M. G. Notetaking and comprehension for computer-displayed messages: personalized versus fixed formats. *Proceedings of the ACM Conference on Human Factors in Computer Systems.* Gaithersburg, MD, March, 1982, 45–50.

Gillio, A. A. *Computer Analysis and Optimization of Remotely Piloted Vehicles and System Simulation Data.* Technical Report UDR-TR-78-15, University of Dayton Research Institute, Dayton, OH, January, 1978.

Harris, R. J. *A Primer of Multivariate Statistics.* New York: Academic Press, 1975.

Hicks, C. R. *Fundamental Concepts in the Design of Experiments.* New York: Holt, Rinehart, and Winston, 1973.

Hoerl, A. E. and Kennard, R. W. Ridge regression: Biased estimation of nonorthogonal problems. *Technometrics,* 1970, *12,* 55–56. (a)

Hoerl, A. E. and Kennard, R. W. Ridge regression: Applications to nonorthogonal problems. *Technometrics,* 1970, *12,* 69–82. (b)

John, P. W. M. Augmenting 2^{n-1} designs. *Technometrics,* 1966, *8,* 469–480.

Keppel, G. *Design and Analysis: A Researcher's Handbook.* New York: Wiley, 1978.

Kheir, N. A. and Holmes, W. M. On validating simulation models of missile systems. *Simulation,* 1978, 117–128.

Kirk, R. E. *Experimental Design: Procedures for the Behavioral Sciences.* Belmont: Brooks/Cole, 1969.

Kleijnen, J. P. C. Screening designs for polyfactor experimentation. *Technometrics,* 1975, *17,* 487–493.

Li, C. H. A sequential method for screening experimental variables. *Journal of the American Statistical Association.* 1962, *57,* 455–477.

Myers, J. L. *Fundamentals of Experimental Design.* Boston: Allyn and Bacon, 1972.

Myers, R. M. *Response Surface Methodology.* Boston: Allyn and Bacon, 1971.

Norton, D. W. An empirical investigation of some effects of non-normality and heterogeneity on the F-distribution. In E. F. Lindquist (Ed.) *Design and Analysis of Experiments in Psychology and Education.* Boston: Houghton Mifflin, 1953, 78–86.

Patel, M. S. Group screening with more than two stages. *Technometrics,* 1962, *4,* 209–217.

Poulton, E. C. Bias in experimental comparisons between equipments due to the order of testing. *Ergonomics,* 1969, *12,* 675–687.

Satterthwaite, F. E. Random balance experimentation. *Technometrics,* 1959, *1,* 111–137.

Simon, C. W. *Considerations for the Proper Design and Interpretation of Human Factors Engineering Experiments.* Technical report No. P73-325, Hughes Aircraft Company, Culver City, CA, December, 1971.

Simon, C. W. *Economical Multifactor Designs for Human Factors Engineering Experiments.* Technical Report No. P73-326A, Hughes Aircraft Company, Culver City, CA, June, 1973.

Simon, C. W. *Methods for Handling Sequence Effects in Human Factors Engineering Experiments.* Technical Report No. P74-415 A, Hughes Aircraft Company, Culver City, CA, December, 1974.

Simon, C. W. *Methods for Improving Information from "Undesigned" Human Factors Experiments.* Technical Report No. P75-287, Hughes Aircraft Company, Culver City, CA, July, 1975.

Simon, C. W. *Design, Analysis and Interpretation of Screening Studies for Human Factors Engineering Research.* Technical Report CWS-03-77, Canyon Research Group, Westlake Village, CA, September, 1977. (a)

Simon, C. W. *New Research Paradigm for Applied Experimental Psychology: A System Approach.* Technical Report (CWS-04-77, Canyon Research Group, Westlake Village, CA, October, 1977. (b)

System Development Corporation. *Some Experimental Protocol Considerations for the MISVAL Program's MIL Experiments.* Technical Report TM-HU-535/000/01, System Development Corporation, Santa Monica, CA, November, 1979.

Tatsuoka, M. M. *Multivariate Analysis: Techniques for Educational and Psychological Research.* New York: Wiley, 1971.

Watson, G. S. A study of the group screening method. *Technometrics,* 1961, *3,* 371–388.

Williges, R. C. Development and use of research methodologies for complex system/simulation experimentation. In J. Moraal and K. F. Kraiss (Eds.) *Manned System Design Methods, Equipment, and Applications.* New York: Plenum Press, 1981, 59–87.

Williges, R. C. Preface. *Human Factors,* 1973, *15*, 293.

Williges, R. C. and Baaron, M. L. Transfer assessment using a between subjects central-composite design. *Human Factors,* 1973, *15,* 311–319.

Williges, R. C. and North, R. A. Prediction and cross-validation of video cartographic symbol location performance. *Human Factors,* 1973, *15*, 321–336.

Williges, R. C. and Mills, R. G. *Catalog of Methodological Considerations for Systems Experimentation.* Final Report, Contract F33615-78-D-0629-0032, for AFSC Aeronautical Systems Division and AF Aerospace Medical Research Laboratories (AFAMRL), Wright-Patterson AFB, OH, June 1982.

Williges, R. C. and Simon, C. W. Applying response surface methodology to problems of target acquisition. *Human Factors,* 1971, *13,* 511–519.

Williges, R. C. and Williges, B. H. Modeling the human operator in computer based data entry. *Human Factors,* 1982, *24,* 285–299.

Winer, B. J. *Statistical Principles in Experimental Design.* New York: McGraw-Hill, 1971.

CHAPTER THIRTEEN

Methodological Practices and Research Recommendations

We end as we began, with the analytic techniques and with the statement made in Chapter One that the methods as actually applied are not necessarily the same as their description in books such as these. What is methodological practice in actual system development? We do not know because there have been only a handful of studies of that process and those were done under controlled conditions (Meister et al., 1968, 1969).

In reviewing the literature that serves as the foundation of a book such as this, one finds a significant, disquieting gap. There are in fact *two* gaps. The first is the discrepancy between the needs of those working in system development for refined methods and supporting data, and what behavioral research provides them. In the absence of relevant quantitative data and principles to which they can refer, practitioner recommendations are (must be) based largely on experience, common sense, and intuition; adequate perhaps, but not good enough. The second gap is the lack of feedback from the behavioral user about the adequacy of our analytic techniques.

RESEARCH SUPPORT

When the author surveyed practitioners a few years ago (Meister, 1979), 78% felt that human factors research did not adequately support their efforts. There is no reason to believe that the situation has changed substantially. Moreover, when one reviews the papers published in journals like *Human Factors* or *Ergonomics* and sorts these (on the basis of relationship to system characteristics) into three categories—directly relevant, indirectly relevant and irrelevant to development questions or problems—most papers are only indirectly relevant. The problem is that most studies focus on the operator's performance without attempting to relate that performance directly to some set of system characteristics. This does not mean that stimulus conditions are ignored; it is simply that system characteristics are usually not among those examined. From the practitioner's viewpoint, such studies miss the point just slightly; but that slight miss renders the study results of little use to him.

What is the cause of this? The topic calls for much more detailed treatment than is possible here (but see Meister, 1974, 1977, 1978 and 1980). In brief, the psychological orientation which is what most behavioral researchers have been trained in places far more emphasis on the individual than on the system, which is of course what the practitioner is primarily concerned about.

LACK OF FEEDBACK

The second gap is that we lack information about how these methods are employed, how useful they are, whether they do what they are supposed to do, or how easy it is to use them. Feedback information is important for the generic methods, too. There are some (but not much) validation and reliability data for them because behavior specialists have been concerned about their validity and reliability. There is apparently no corresponding concern for the analytic techniques. There is no feedback from the users of these methods. For behavior specialists, who preach the importance of feedback, this is quite astonishing.

User feedback is critical for the analytic techniques because these, with few exceptions, do not produce quantitative data which are the means of assessing validity. Reliability is a different matter. The reliability of analytic methods (which in many cases is actually the reliability of the specialists who apply them) is relatively easy to determine, but requires controlled studies, which are almost never performed.

Instead of validity as a criterion, which is inappropriate for the analytic techniques, (since they are only design tools, to assist in arriving at a design configuration), we can apply the utility criterion, where utility is a composite of effectiveness, ease of application, low cost, flexibility and range (see Chapters 1 and 3 for definitions and examples of these criteria).

We could simply assume that methods are actually used as they are described in various texts. System development, however, presents serious problems (e.g., the relative speed with which design decisions are made; the inadequacy of behavioral resources of money and personnel; the resistance of engineers) that make this unlikely. Since the system development process is a highly degraded one, it is possible that the analytic techniques (and perhaps even the measurement methods when used in development) are modified to fit these conditions, simplified, condensed, and stripped of subtlety. For all we know (and we do not know) behavioral methods do not work as well as they should, or they work in ways that the original developers of the methods did not think of. Certainly no one has reason to be satisfied with behavioral methods. Witness the continuing efforts to improve rating scales, performance appraisal methods, and other behavioral tools.

An hypothesis cries out to be tested. Only the cheapest, easiest to use, and least demanding of methods are employed frequently in system development because that process is hostile to sophisticated, expensive, or data-hungry ones. That may be why we find manual methods used much more frequently than their computerized versions (Williges and Topmiller, 1980).

Certain methods, despite their potential promise, are only infrequently employed in system development. An outstanding example is the mathematical model which is a powerful tool that is only rarely used for system development purposes. Why is this? Is it too powerful, too complex or too clumsy to use in system development? It would be highly desirable to find out.

The point is that in system development utility is often more important than any other criterion by which we judge the value of our methods. A simple, easy to use but less precise tool may be more useful than one that is complex, highly precise, but data-hungry—when you don't have the data. A method that can be applied in hours, or a day or two, is more effective than one that requires weeks—even if the latter is much more sophisticated. Of course the easy method cannot be too imprecise, but if the easy method gives reasonable answers (within the ball park, as it were), it is likely to be preferred.

Outside the academic community (and perhaps even there too) the researcher who selects a particular method for use in a specific situtiion usually does so not so much on the basis that one method has greater validity than another but on the basis of other qualities possessed by the method. These include relative cost in terms of time to administer the method and/or personnel resources required, complexity of administration, ease of application, speed with which data are secured, and amount of detailed data secured.

Although utility is often at the heart of method selection, we know little about it because information about application of a method cannot be derived through the usual experimental means (since the experiment is inherently artificial). Utility feedback requires observation of the uses to which methods are put, and the self-report of behavior specialists.

ONE EMPIRICAL STUDY

Although there are no studies from the actual using environment, there are some suggestive data from a recent study by Williges and Topmiller (1980). A six-person study team was commissioned by the Air Force to conduct a one-year examination of human factors methods. Over 135 methods were reviewed including all the analytic techniques described in this book as well as some of the measurement methods we have described. In addition, the following were considered: traditional experimental methods used in statistical analysis; databases; human performance metrics; models; simulation; and manual and computerized design procedures. The assessment of these methods was accomplished by means of a two-day workshop attended by 26 academic, industry, and government representatives—obvious establishment figures. What is reported here are their opinions which are obviously not the best evidence, since they were not based on discrete events but on the synthesis of many overlapping experiences. One hundred and sixty-six industrial and government human factors managers were also polled to determine the use made of these methods.

The following summary of current behavioral technology from Williges and Topmiller (1980) is worth quoting in full:

> The development of HFE* technology has generally moved from simple manual procedures toward more sophisticated, automated procedures which attempt to represent the complexities of human–machine integration in modern weapon systems and subsystems. This trend can be seen in terms of an approach toward integrated databases, tailored design guides, systems-related research methodology, detailed modeling of operator performance, complex simulations, and the existence of computer aided design procedures and computer analytic models for manpower planning in maintenance and logistics support. Several significant shortfalls, however, appear in current HFE technology. These shortfalls include an emphasis on the use of manual procedures as opposed to computer based procedures, a recognized importance but under utilization of engineering design simulation, a lag in the HFE technology transfer of computerized design procedures, a requirement for updating and packaging of the HFE data base, sparse consideration of advanced human–macine interface concepts, and limited application of HFE technology throughout the RDTE&O** cycle. (pp. 2–3)

The study also found that improvements were required in the utilization of existing methods. Direct management support is needed to foster increased development and to insure increased use of behavioral technology (i.e., to get designers to use behavioral design inputs). Moreover, current use of behavioral methods emphasizes manual procedures even though computer based procedures (see Chapter 4) are supposedly available.

It might appear that computer based techniques should be inherently simpler to apply than manual ones, but the behavior specialist may not have access to a computer. The older generation may lack the specialist skills needed to use the computerized technique. And the technique may require more input data than the manual ones do. In short, there may be disadvantages that cancel out computer advantages.

The emphasis on management attention is entirely warranted. Within the military/industrial defense establishment both contractors and government monitors are entirely too willing to ignore behavioral inputs and methods. With their proverbial bias toward physicalistic factors and against behavioral factors, contractors would rather not be bothered to conform to government requirements for behavioral inputs, as long as government monitors are prepared to wink at the requirements. Enough. This is not a book on how government should manage its behavioral needs, although a great deal could be said about this (see Meister, 1981).

In addition, industry and government respondents in the Williges/Topmiller study listed the average use percentages of 19 methodological categories. The results indicated that, as suggested previously, manual methods are used much more often than computerized procedures—the ratio approaching 5 to 10 times more fre-

*See Glossary of Abbreviations

**See Glossary of Abbreviations

quently. The most regularly employed technologies are reference sources such as textbooks, MIL STD 1472C (Department of Defense, 1981), static mockups, task analysis, anthropometric measures, and questionnaires, though not necessarily in that order.

Behavior specialists working in laboratories tend to use statistical methods more frequently, industrial specialists (practitioners) tend to use them very infrequently. That is because statistical methods are of value primarily in experiments which are rarely performed during system development.

Evaluative comments about the various methods include

1. *Reference data sources.* Handbooks, design guides and specifications are used heavily. Design guides are usable only by behavior specialists. Databases need to be updated, maintained and expanded.

2. *Experimental design methods.* Often money and time are not available in system development to employ controlled research designs.

3. *Performance metrics.* Anthropometric measures are often used. Subjective opinions are also used frequently in test and evaluation phases of design.

4. *Models.* Databases are still somewhat limited.

5 *Engineering design simulation.* This is especially useful when analytic techniques are not appropriate and/or (which is much more likely) when the appropriate performance data base is not available.

6. *Procedures.* Manual procedures such as task description and task analysis are often used, but the time required to complete detailed task analysis often precludes its usefulness in early design. The adequacy of the human factors database limits the utility and validity of computer analytic procedures, the maintenance of which is, in any case, costly.

The study team considered that design guides must be tailored to specific behavioral considerations. Multivariate procedures need to be used more often and experimental designs pertaining to complex system-related research need further development. There is a need for multivariate scaling procedures and automated performance measurement. Reliable measures and models of W/L are needed, as is further consideration of how much fidelity is required in simulations. Integration of task analysis procedures for design and training purposes should be considered and databases for computer analytic procedures need refinement.

Why is available methodology not being used? The study team's responses were that they are often not required by contract and there is no time to apply them. The customer does not monitor the application of these methods closely. With regard to the suitability of current methods, information is often not specific enough for system application. There is a need for more databanks, industry is often not required by the customer to use behavioral technology, early behavioral participation in the design process is more important than the specific methods used. In many cases, the effectiveness of the behavioral design input is not as much limited by the methods available, as by the designer's refusal to accept the input. Some practitioners are not qualified to use more advanced (e.g., computerized) methods.

The results of the Williges and Topmiller (1980) study, unique and subjective as it is, tend to support some of the points made earlier in this book. However the researchers exhibit a somewhat simplistic confidence that computerization in various forms—in particular, simulation—will solve these problems. I am not so certain of this. The emphasis on computerization as a solution is hope rather than knowledge. As yet, little is known about the relation between system development and methodology.

RESEARCH RECOMMENDATIONS

It is traditional to complete a paper or book by making recommendations for further research. Since I am not an iconoclast, here are my suggestions. I am not sanguine enough to believe that all or even most will be implemented.

Research Relevancy

This problem may be intractible, involving as it does long established academic attitudes toward research and science. What we need to do is to discuss the problem realistically; at any rate, this would be a first step.

Feedback

The greatest immediate need is to conduct studies to determine how the various methods are actually used. Without empirical feedback it is hard to see what we can do to improve these methods.

I proposed (Meister, 1983) the gathering of information about utility by having behavior specialists report (voluntarily and anonymously, either by survey, critical incident, or historic documentation methods) about the effectiveness, ease, and frequency of use of the methods they employ.

Validity/Reliability

Although it may be difficult to do so, it is necessary to examine the validity of those measurement methods for which validity data can be secured. The reliability with which specialists apply their methods can be determined with much greater ease by requiring a number of specialists to apply the same method to a number of different problems or different methods to the same problem. However, such studies have to be performed in a relatively controlled situation which rules out actual (although not simulated) system development and operational environments. Before we can do anything it may be necessary to attempt to define what the concept of validity means when applied to methods in general and particularly for the analytic techniques which are design aids only.

Utility

A great deal has already been said about this. I need only point out that it would be highly desirable to determine whether it is reasonable to apply a utility criterion to the various methods. We must, of course, decide in advance what this criterion comprises.

Sensitivity

It would be highly desirable to test the sensitivity (responsiveness) of the analytic techniques and measurement methods to variations in task (stimulus) situations. Extremes of sensitivity are undesirable: A method that is too sensitive increases variance unduly, one that is relatively insensitive will fail to pick up critical data. No studies of this have as yet been done with the analytic methods and relatively few with the generic ones. Some may feel that any research involving a particular method, in a sense, tests its sensitivity. As yet, controlled comparisons of this factor have not been performed.

Individual Differences

We cannot divorce methods from those who employ them. In some methods such as observation and rating, or in techniques such as function allocation, human skills play a larger role than in more proceduralized techniques such as OSDs. Human skills, though, are important in all techniques and methods. More research remains to be done to examine the effect of individual differences in skill (and perhaps even talent) on the effectiveness of the method. This, too, is a form of sensitivity testing.

Empirical Comparisons

A few comparisons between methods addressing the same problem have been performed. For instance, different job analysis techniques and the rate of return for mailed surveys vs. the rate of return for direct interview. Much more of this needs to be done, particularly with reference to computerized vs. manual versions of the same methods (e.g., computerized vs. manual workload analyses), to settle the question of relative value.

Operational Environment

A great deal has been made in this book about the operational environment. For behavioral science disciplines it is the only reference situation (one that provides ground truth) that matters. To determine the characteristics of the OE it is necessary to investigate it systematically, not merely to rely on anecdotal evidence. If we could determine the most important OE characteristics, it might be desirable to introduce whatever the results suggested into controlled experimental research.

It is possible that the reason experimental data often do not correspond to data we collect (or would collect) if the OE was added in is that the OE includes some very special characteristics. Kane (1981) for example reported on the conditions he found facing maintenance personnel at three air bases: noise, poor weather, and inadequate lighting, of course; failure to have the crew chief present when the technician arrived at an aircraft to be maintained; the aircraft was often too crowded with other technicians; the technician often had the wrong technical data or no data at all; a part was needed from supply; a malfunction was recognized which was not part of the original discrepancy . . . the list goes on. All of these influence task performance in some way. If we had performed a study of aircraft troubleshooting that did not include at least some of these OE characteristics, the resulting data would almost certainly deviate from reality (how much is not known). To include OE characteristics in our studies we must investigate the OE and learn what these characteristics are and whether they cut across systems.

The researcher who reports a study in the journals should be required to state what OE his measurement situation was supposed to simulate and the conditions to be included in his study. This would enable the reader to compare the subject responses with those of the operational personnel. (For a completely different point of view, see Mook, 1983). I believe it is unlikely that this recommendation will be implemented, except when the study gathers data specifically about performance in a MMS (e.g., an aircraft simulator). In that situation one simulates OE conditions as closely as possible. For studies in which a particular system is not the focus and the effort is to discover fundamental truths, there is almost never any attempt by the researcher to model the measurement situation on a special or even a general OE.

Quantitative Databases

The critical need to have a quantitative human performance database was noted in Chapter 5. Many methods cannot be utilized effectively without such a database, the most prominent example being mathematical models and predictive techniques like workload analysis. The development of such a database (or several) is a research effort of some magnitude. But it is the lack of such a database that is perhaps the one most critical problem in behavioral science.

Development of New Methods

Before a systematic effort is mounted to improve old methods and develop new ones, it is necessary to examine the question of what is meant by improvement and what improvements are possible. I am somewhat skeptical about the possibility of developing radical new methods, even with the aid of computers, but this too should be talked about. To discuss potential improvements it is necessary first to perform the empirical feedback studies referred to previously. It is impossible to talk meaningfully about improvement before we know what needs improving.

The methods described in this book are the foundations of behavioral science, particularly as that science attempts to investigate and describe human work performance. It is necessary to learn more about these methods, to experiment with them, and to test them thoroughly if the discipline is to retain its vitality, its utility, and its importance.

REFERENCES

Department of Defense. Military Standard 1472C. *Human Engineering Design Criteria for Military Systems, Equipment, and Facilities*. Washington, DC, 2 May 1981.

Kane, W. D. *Task Accomplishment in an Air Force Maintenance Environment*. Report AFOSR-TR-81-0478, Western Carolina University, February 1981 (AD A101108).

Meister, D. Where is the system in the man-machine system? *Proceedings,* Human Factors Annual Meeting, 1974, 287–292.

Meister, D. Implications of the system concept for Human Factors research methodology. *Proceedings*, Human Factors Society Annual Meeting, 1977, 453–456.

Meister, D. A theoretical structure for personnel subsystem measurement. *Proceedings,* Human Factors Society Annual Meeting, 1978, 475–478.

Meister, D. The influence of government on Human Factors research and development. *Proceedings,* Human Factors Society Annual Meeting, 1979, 5–13.

Meister, D. The concept of macro-basic research in Human Factors. *Proceedings,* Human Factors Society Annual Meeting, 1980, 458–461.

Meister, D. Are our methods any good? A way to find out. *Proceedings,* Human Factors Society Annual Meeting, October 1983, pp. 75–79.

Meister, D. *Behavioral Research and Government Policy: Civilian and Military R&D*. New York: Pergamon Press, 1981.

Meister, D., Sullivan, D. J., Finley, D. L. and Askren, W. B. *The Effect of Amount and Timing of Human Resources Data on Subsystem Design*. Report AFHRL-TR-69-22, Air Force Human Resources Laboratory, Wright-Patterson AFB, OH, October 1969.

Meister, D., Sullivan, D. J. and Askren, W. B. *The Impact of Manpower Requirements and Personnel Resources Data on System Design*. Report AMRL-TR-68-44, Aerospace Medical Research Laboratories, Wright-Patterson AFB, OH, September 1968.

Mook, D. G. In defence of external invalidity. *American Psychologist,* 1983, 38, 379–387.

Williges, R. C. and Topmiller, D. A. *Task III. Final Report. Technology Assessment of Human Factors Engineering in the Air Force*. 30 April, 1980.

Glossary of Abbreviations

APS	Analytic profile system
BARS	Behaviorally Anchored Rating Scale
BOS	Behavioral Observation Scale
CAD	Computer aided crewstation design model
CAFES	Computer aided function allocation evaluation system
CGE	Crewstation geometry evaluation model
CM	Corrective maintenance
CRT	Cathode ray tube
D/A	Decision/action (Diagram)
DEI	Display Evaluative Index
DODT	Design option decision tree
DT&E	Developmental testing and evaluation
ECP	Evoked cortical potentials
EEG	Electroencephalogram
EMG	Electromyography
FA	Function allocation
FAM	Function allocation model
FFD	Function flow diagram
G	Generalizability (theory)
GSR	Galvanic skin response
HECAD	Human engineering computer aided design
HEP	Human error probability
HF	Human factors
HFE	Human factors engineering

HIF	Human-initiated failure
HOS	Human operator simulator
HR	Human reliability
HRA	Human reliability analysis
IQI	Instructional quality inventory
ISD	Instructional system development
JA	Job analysis
JPA	Job performance aid
JPM	Job performance measure
L/A	Link analysis
LO	Learning objective
LS	Learning step
MF	Modified frequency
MMI	Man–machine interface
MMS	Man–machine system
MOAT	Mission operability assessment technique
MTM	Motion time measurement
MTTR	Mean time to repair
O	Observer
OE	Operational environment
OJM	On-the-job measurement
OJT	On-the-job training
OSD	Operational sequence diagram
OT	Operational test(ing)
OT&E	Operational testing and evaluation
PSF	Performance shaping factor
RDTE&O	Research, Development, Test, Evaluation, and Operations
RT	Reaction time
SAINT	Systems analysis for integrated network of tasks
SAT	System approach to training
SK	Skill analysis
SME	Subject matter expert
S/W	Siegel/Wolf
TA	Task analysis
TD	Task description
TD/I	Task description/identification
TEMP	Test and evaluation master plan
TEPPS	Technique for establishing personnel performance standards

TER	Transfer effectiveness ratio
THERP	Technique for human error rate prediction
TI	Task identification
T/L	Time line (analysis)
TLO	Terminal learning objective
T/M	Time and motion (method)
W	Coefficient of concordance
WAM	Workload assessment model
W/L	Workload

Index